5/2017

LIBRARY

P9-AFZ-793

WITHDRAWN

The Future of Financial Regulation

A number of changes have been made to the supervision and regulation of banks as a result of the recent financial meltdown. Some are for the better, such as the Basel III rules for increasing the quality and quantity of capital in banks, but legal changes on both sides of the Atlantic now make it much more difficult to resolve failing banks by means of taxpayer funded bail-outs and could hinder bank resolution in future financial crises. In this book, Johan A. Lybeck uses case studies from Europe and the United States to examine and grade a number of bank resolutions in the last financial crisis and establish which were successful, which failed, and why. Using in-depth analysis of recent legislation, he explains how a bank resolution can be successful, and emphasizes the need for taxpayer-funded bail-outs to create a viable banking system that will promote economic and financial stability.

JOHAN A. LYBECK is CEO of Finanskonsult AB. As an academic, he has been, inter alia, a Chaired Professor of Economics, an Associate Research Professor of Econometrics and an Adjunct Professor of Finance. His banking career includes positions as Senior Vice President of Swedbank (Stockholm) in charge of financial strategy and Chief Economist at Matteus Bank. He is the author of *A Global History of the Financial Crash of 2007–2010* (Cambridge University Press, 2011).

The Future of Financial Regulation

Who Should Pay for the Failure of American and European Banks?

JOHAN A. LYBECK

CAMBRIDGE
UNIVERSITY PRESS

CAMBRIDGE
UNIVERSITY PRESS

University Printing House, Cambridge CB2 8BS, United Kingdom

Cambridge University Press is part of the University of Cambridge.

It furthers the University's mission by disseminating knowledge in the pursuit of education, learning and research at the highest international levels of excellence.

www.cambridge.org
Information on this title: www.cambridge.org/9781107106857

© Johan A. Lybeck 2016

This publication is in copyright. Subject to statutory exception and to the provisions of relevant collective licensing agreements, no reproduction of any part may take place without the written permission of Cambridge University Press.

First published 2016
Printed in the United States of America by Sheridan Books, Inc.

A catalogue record for this publication is available from the British Library

Library of Congress Cataloguing in Publication data

Lybeck, Johan A., 1944-
The future of financial regulation : who should pay for the failure of American and European banks? / Johan A. Lybeck. — First Edition.
    pages cm
Includes bibliographical references and index.
ISBN 978-1-107-10685-7 (hardback) — ISBN 978-1-107-51450-8 (paperback)
1. Financial services industry—United States.   2. Financial services industry—Great Britain.   3. Financial services industry—Law and legislation—United States.   4. Financial services industry—Law and legislation—Great Britain.   5. Banks and banking—United States.   6. Banks and banking—Great Britain.   I. Title.
HG181.L93   2015
332.1094—dc23
                                                            2015029105

ISBN   978-1-107-10685-7 Hardback

ISBN   978-1-107-51450-8 Paperback

Cambridge University Press has no responsibility for the persistence or accuracy of URLs for external or third-party internet websites referred to in this publication, and does not guarantee that any content on such websites is, or will remain, accurate or appropriate.

I wish to dedicate this book to Sheila Bair, chair of the Federal Deposit Insurance Corporation, 2006–11, who more than anybody else is to be thanked for the successful solution to the past crisis in the US, though we do not agree on the role of taxpayers in the next one

Contents

List of figures   x

List of tables   xii

List of boxes   xiv

Preface   xv

Acknowledgements   xix

List of abbreviations   xx

Introduction   xxv

**Part I A chronological presentation of crisis
events January 2007 – December 2014**   1

**Part II Bail-out and/or bail-in of banks in Europe:
a country-by-country event study on those
European countries which did not receive outside support**   143

1 United Kingdom: *Northern Rock, Royal Bank of
Scotland (RBS), Lloyds Banking Group*   149

2 Germany: *IKB, Hypo Real Estate, Commerzbank,
Landesbanken*   175

3 Belgium, France, Luxembourg: *Dexia*   191

4 Benelux: *Fortis, ING, SNS Reaal*   199

5 Italy: *Monte dei Paschi di Siena*   209

6 Denmark: *Roskilde Bank, Fionia Bank and the others vs.
Amagerbanken and Fjordbank Mors*   216

Part III   Bail-out and/or bail-in of banks
in Europe: a country-by-country event study
on those European countries which received
IMF/EU support   225

7   Iceland: *Landsbanki, Glitnir and Kaupthing*   227

8   Ireland: *Anglo Irish Bank, Bank of Ireland,*
    Allied Irish Banks   237

9   Greece: *Emporiki, Eurobank, Agricultural Bank*   259

10 Portugal: *Caixa Geral, Banco Espirito Santo,*
    Millennium Bank   267

11 Spain: *Bankia and the other ex*-cajas   270

12 Cyprus: *Bank of Cyprus, Popular Bank (Laiki)*   278

Part IV   The TARP program and the bailing out
(and bailing in) of US banks   285

13 The roles of the FDIC, the Treasury and the
    Fed in the crisis   287

14 USA: *Bear Stearns, Merrill Lynch and Lehman Brothers*   303

15 USA: *Countrywide, IndyMac, Washington Mutual and*
    Wachovia   334

16 USA: *AIG, Citibank and Bank of America:*
    zombies too big to fail?   358

Part V   Summary of the micro studies   389

Part VI   Political and regulatory responses to
the crisis: to bail out or to bail in, that's the question   395

17 Future bail-outs in the United States under
    Dodd–Frank and OLA   397

18   Future bail-outs in the European Union under
     the Single Resolution Mechanism and the Bank
     Recovery and Resolution Directive   437

     Conclusion: *toward host-country supervision
     and resolution?*   479

Addendum   487
Bibliography   489
Index   538

List of figures

1. Public sector interventions in selected countries during the financial crisis, 2007–9, percentage of GDP — xxxi
2. Amount of state aid in the European Union actually used — xxxiii
3. The nucleus of the banking crisis — 144
4. Leverage of UK banks, 2000–8 — 150
5. UK household savings ratio, percentage of disposable income — 151
6. Composition of Northern Rock's liabilities before and after the run — 154
7. The share price of major UK banks June 2007 – December 2008 — 163
8. Value of shares in RBS held by UKFI and amount spent, billion pounds — 167
9. Government capital support and value of shares held in Lloyds Banking Group — 172
10. Concentration ratio (market share of top five banks in total assets) — 176
11. Banking in different EU countries, percentage of national GDP — 177
12. Share price of IKB (euro), 2003–13 — 180
13. Share price of Commerzbank, 1997–2014 — 186
14. The operative structure of Fortis — 201
15. Share price of ING on the Amsterdam stock exchange — 207
16. Ratio of gross government debt to GDP, percentage, first quarter 2014 — 210
17. Government debt ratio to GDP and domestic financial sector holdings — 211
18. Percentage of banking assets held in domestic government bonds, July 2013 — 211

19. Ten-year yield spread between Italy and Germany   213
20. House price developments in the Nordic countries, 1995–2010   218
21a. Yield spread of selected Nordic bank bonds, 2010–12   220
21b. CDS spread on senior unsecured debt in some Nordic banks, 2009–13   221
22. Total assets of recovered and disposed activities, 2008–12   223
23a. Iceland GDP growth rate, 2000–14   228
23b. Iceland current account as a percentage of GDP, 2004–13   229
23c. Iceland government debt to GDP ratio, 2004–13, percentage   229
24a. Irish GDP growth rate, 2004–13   239
24b. Current account in Ireland as a percentage of GDP, 2004–13   240
24c. The budget balance and government debt in Ireland, 2004–13, both expressed as a ratio to GDP   241
25. Irish stock market index, 1998–2014   243
26. Ten-year bond yields in the euro area, 2010–14   261
27. Forecast Cyprus debt-to-GDP levels, 2012–20   279
28. Output loss of the financial crisis   289
29. Spreads between three-month interbank money market rates and official rates, percentage   328
30. VIX volatility on the Chicago Board Options Exchange (implied volatility of the S&P 500 futures option, standard deviation of annualized daily percentage changes, monthly averages)   330
31. Share price of AIG, January 1985 – July 2014   367
32. Ratio of the Deposit Insurance Fund to insured deposits, March 2006 – September 2009   419
33. Bank equity issues in the US and Europe, 2004–2013, percentage of total assets   440
34a–d. Aspects of European banks, 2007–12   441
35. CET1/RWA ratios for the major European banks at the end of 2013   483

List of tables

1. Financial sector support, selected economies, percentage of GDP — xxx
2. State aid to the banks in the European Union, 2008–11 — xxxii
3. Financial support from the EU and IMF to some European countries, 2010–13 — xxxiv
4. Salaries and bonuses given to major bank CEOs in 2009 and 2010 — 80
5. "Too big to fail" international banking groups (as defined by FSB and BCBS) — 87
6. Capital required for EU banks to fulfill core Tier 1 capital adequacy ratio of 9 percent (EBA) — 90
7. Selected data from Royal Bank of Scotland, 2006–10 — 161
8. The carving up of ABN AMRO — 164
9. A comparison of Lloyds TSB and HBOS, 2007–8 — 169
10. Return on equity and capital–asset ratios of the major Landesbanken, percentage — 190
11. Bank restructuring plans and associated reductions in balance sheets — 197
12. Some data for Irish banks, 2007, 2008 and 2009 — 245
13. Increasing recapitalization requirements for Irish banks, 2009–11, billion euro — 249
14. Loan acquisitions from participating institutions at end 2011, billion euro — 255
15. Estimated and actual capital demand by Greek banks — 263
16. Estimated and actual capital demand by Portuguese banks — 268
17. Ratio of non-performing loans (NPL) to total loans for Cyprus banks — 280

18. Potential and actual amounts in the various US financial
    support programs at the peak by September 2009,
    billion dollars   290
19. US regulatory authorities and those they supervise   296
20. Number of supervised institutions and their assets by
    major US regulator   298
21. Leverage ratio (total assets/Tier 1 equity) in some
    universal and investment banks   304
22. Payments to AIG counterparties, billion dollars   371
23. The 10 major US banks by assets 2007 and 2013   383
24. Capital received under TARP/CPP and implicit subsidy
    (billion dollars)   384
25. Track record of the regulatory authorities in 15 countries   390

List of boxes

1. Criticisms of Dodd–Frank legislation   399
2. The Dodd–Frank Act: Federal Reserve System Provisions   423
3. The Dodd–Frank Act: Orderly Liquidation Authority   426
4. The Dodd–Frank Act: Orderly Liquidation Fund   430
5. A chronology of major events in the sovereign debt crisis, 2010–14   444
6. Remarks by EU internal-markets Commissioner Michel Barnier, 27 June 2013   450
7. Directive on the recovery and resolution of credit institutions (BRRD)   463

Preface

As a result of the financial crisis which began in 2007 and was still continuing in 2014, albeit at lower intensity, in countries such as Portugal and Italy, a number of measures have been undertaken to make a repeat of a crisis of a similar magnitude less likely but also to facilitate the recovery and resolution of failing banks should a (systemic) financial crisis nevertheless occur again.

Foremost among measures to increase the resistance of banks to financial stress are the Basel III rules for increasing the quality and quantity of capital as well as the introduction of liquidity coverage ratios, implemented by the Dodd–Frank legislation in the United States and by the CRD IV package in the European Union. Additional measures to improve stability are enhanced supervision, in particular of the too-big-to-fail (TBTF) banks, and a focus on stringent stress testing of banks. Countries such as Sweden and Switzerland have gone further than the required minima in setting higher capital requirements, especially for their TBTF banks. Other important measures include increasing the transparency and stability of the OTC derivatives market, forcing most trades to pass through clearing houses and increasing the capital requirements on those that don't. The Dodd–Frank Act places restrictions on the ability by US banks to own hedge and equity funds and forbids banks' proprietary trading, a half step back to the Glass–Steagall division into banks and investment banks. In Europe, countries such as the UK and France are forcing banks to ring-fence their core activities, especially insured deposit-taking, from riskier investment-bank activities.

Whether the measures taken will be sufficient is hotly debated. Some see the failure to break up the TBTF banks as an indication that the next crisis may be similar to the last one. Others think that the curtailment of banks' activities will instead lead to a crisis beginning in some part of the less-supervised so-called shadow banking system.

Be that as it may, measures have also been undertaken to change and hopefully improve the manner in which a banking crisis is resolved. In the United States, the Orderly Liquidation Authority (OLA) under Title II of the Dodd–Frank Act enhances the powers of the Federal Deposit Insurance Corporation (FDIC) to seize not only banks but also bank holding companies and other systemically important financial institutions, as well as its powers to impose losses on holders of unsecured debt on top of those of shareholders. Prepaid government-guaranteed deposit insurance funds are introduced in Europe in those countries that still lack them and increased in size in the United States. Under the Single Resolution Mechanism (SRM), an EU-wide single resolution authority is created and a gradually communalized single bank resolution fund is established for the euro area countries; some member states such as Sweden and Germany have already established industry-financed stabilization funds of their own. The United States has, however, rejected the use of prefunded resolution funds, preferring a pay-as-you-go financing of bank liquidation.

A trait common to OLA and the European Bank Recovery and Resolution Directive (BRRD) is to severely restrict – their respective authors would claim, making impossible – the possibility to bail out banks with taxpayers' money. The new US rules also severely curtail the ability of the Federal Reserve to utilize its powers under section 13(3) of the Federal Reserve Act to lend to individual non-bank institutions (such as Bear Stearns and AIG during the last crisis), invoking 'unusual and exigent circumstances'. In the future, such facilities must be broad-based and directed at providing liquidity to a group of financial institutions rather than individual firms.

To my mind, the restrictions imposed on the regulatory authorities' tool-kit may severely curtail their ability to resolve the next financial crisis, implying unnecessary costs not only to financial firms and the financial sector but unnecessary output losses and unemployment in the real economy. It seems that the last crisis has not been adequately researched to try to see which bank resolutions were successes, which were failures, and why. Can we distill from these case studies common traits which have contributed to successful interventions and resolutions and see whether these arrangements could be utilized in creating an improved system of resolution?

We will find, in particular, that the use of taxpayers' money is an inevitable feature of successful interventions. A credible resolution authority, irrespective of whether financing means are prefunded or not, depends on having the Treasury (i.e. the taxpayer) as a last resort. This implies that instead of curtailing bail-outs, we should try to deduce how to use taxpayers' money in an effective and equitable way, simultaneously guaranteeing its eventual return to the investors with a decent profit. Similarly, we will find that the bailing-in of unsecured bondholders and uninsured deposits was a significant factor behind creating additional uncertainty and financial instability, which points to the fact that bailing-in should only be undertaken using instruments such as subordinated debt and CoCo (Contingent Convertible) bonds, where the possibility of losses and/or forced conversion into equity was part of the contract and hence part of investors' perception of the risk/reward trade-off. Even better, an adequate capital cushion will be the best safety net against a repeat of the disaster of 2007–13.

In deducing which resolutions in the last crisis were successes, which were not and why, 29 case studies have been undertaken of the major interventions in the United States and Europe. The actions by the regulatory authorities have been graded on a standard academic scale of A–F where an 'F' means fail. Many readers will most certainly disagree with my evaluations but that is the way to start a debate, in this case a very important debate on the resolution of the next crisis.

One of the main findings of the book is that the United States, after Dodd–Frank, presents a consistent framework of resolution where some minor things need to be changed, as indicated in the body of the book. Europe, on the other hand, is in a total mess. Whereas in the United States, the three "legs" of a banking union (supervision, resolution, and deposit insurance) are in place, the European Union has introduced a Single Supervisory Mechanism (SSM) housed in the European Central Bank but without communalizing the other two "legs." A Single Resolution Board has been created but without adequate (common) resources and without the vital taxpayer-funded backstop. Common rules for deposit insurance have been enacted but without the necessary common Deposit Insurance Fund.

Either the European Union decides, within a very short period of time, to implement a true European Banking Union or it would be preferable to reintroduce supervision and resolution at the national level. In that case, it would also be preferable to move from home country control to host country control, where cross-border banking would have to be undertaken by subsidiaries rather than branches.

This kind of "ring-fence" will not only increase average levels of capital in the banking system but also facilitate the resolution of cross-border banks. In demanding that large international banks operate as separately capitalized US subsidiary bank holding companies under the supervision of the Federal Reserve, the United States may actually have shown a credible way forward also for the European Union, a road that the United Kingdom also appears ready to take.

Acknowledgements

A number of people have been kind enough to read and comment on the manuscript in earlier versions or helped in other ways. I wish to thank them all, especially Professor David Mayes from the University of Auckland, Professor Anat Admati from Stanford University, Daniel Ker from the British Office of National Statistics, Dr. George Tavlas from the Monetary Policy Council of the Central Bank of Greece, David Green, member of the Independent Commission on the Future of Banking at the Central Bank of Cyprus, Thorsteinn Thorgeirsson, senior advisor to the governor of the Central Bank of Iceland, Johanna Lybeck Lilja, state secretary at the Swedish Finance Ministry, Daniel Barr and Hans Lindblad, director and director general, respectively, at the Swedish National Debt Office and Jens Lundager, assistant governor at Danmarks Nationalbank.

All remaining errors and misconceptions as well as the responsibility for opinions stated are mine and mine alone.

List of abbreviations

ABCP	asset-backed commercial paper
AIB	Allied Irish Banks
AIG	American International Group
AIGFP	American International Group Financial Products division
AMF	Autorité des Marchés Financiers
ARM	adjustable-rate mortgage
BaFin	Bundesanstalt für Finanzdienstleistungsaufsicht
BAMC	Bank Asset Management Company
BBVA	Banco Bilbao Vizcaya Argentaria
BCCI	Bank of Credit and Commerce International
BofA	Bank of America
BIL	Banque Internationale de Luxembourg
BIS	Bank of International Settlements
BOI	Bank of Ireland
BRRD	(European) Bank Recovery and Resolution Directive
BSAM	Bear Stearns Asset Management
CAM	Caja de Ahorros de Mediterráneo
CAMELS	Capital Adequacy, Assets, Management Capability, Earnings, Liquidity, Sensitivity
CBO	Congressional Budget Office
CCP	Central Counterparty (Clearing)
CDC	Caisse des Depôts et Consignations
CDO	collateralized debt obligation
CDS	credit default swap
CEPS	Centre for European Policy Studies
CET1	Core Equity Tier 1 Capital
CFTC	Commodity Futures Trading Commission
CGER	Caisse Générale d'Épargne et de Retraite (ASLK in Flemish)
CoCos	contingent convertible bonds

COP	Congressional Oversight Panel
CPDO	constant proportion debt obligation
CPFF	Commercial Paper Funding Facility
CPP	Capital Purchase Program
CRD	Capital Requirements Directive
CRR	Capital Requirements Regulation
DeKa	Deutsche Kapitalanlage
DNB	Den Norske Bank
Depfa	Deutsche Pfandbriefanstalt
DIF	Deposit Insurance Fund
DINB	Deposit Insurance National Bank
DGP	Debt Guarantee Program
DMA	Dexia Municipal Agency
DTA	deferred tax assets
EAA	Erste Abwicklungsanstalt
EBA	European Banking Authority
EBS	Educational Building Society (Ireland)
ECB	European Central Bank
ECJ	European Court of Justice
ECN	Enhanced Capital Notes
ECOFIN	Economic and Financial Affairs Council
EFSF	European Financial Stability Facility
EFTA	European Free Trade Association
EIOPA	European Insurance and Occupational Pension Authority
ELA	Emergency Liquidity Assistance (Bank of England and ECB)
EMIR	European Market Infrastructure Regulation
ESMA	European Securities and Markets Authority
ESRC	European Systemic Risk Council
ETF	exchange-traded funds
EU MS	European Union Member States
FASB	Financial Accounting Standards Board
FCIC	Financial Crisis Inquiry Commission
FDIC	Federal Deposit Insurance Corporation
FDICIA	Federal Deposit Insurance Corporation Improvement Act
FHFA	Federal Housing Finance Agency

FIRREA	Financial Institutions Reform, Recovery, and Enforcement Act (1989)
FME	Fjármálaeftirlitsins (Financial Services Authority, Iceland)
FMS-WM	FMS Wertmanagement AöR
FOMC	Federal Open Market Committee
FPC	Financial Policy Committee (Bank of England)
FR	Financial Regulator (Ireland)
FRBNY	Federal Reserve Bank of New York
FRN	floating rate note
FROB	Fondo de Reestructuración Ordenada Bancaria
FSA	Financial Services Authority
FSB	Financial Stability Board
FSCS	Financial Services Compensation Scheme
FSOC	Financial Stability Oversight Council
FTT	Financial Transaction Tax ("Tobin tax")
GAAP	Generally Accepted Accounting Principles
GM	General Motors
GMAC	General Motors Acceptance Corporation
GSE	government-sponsored enterprise
G-SIFI	globally systemically important financial institution
HBOS	Halifax Bank of Scotland
HFSF	Hellenic Financial Stability Fund
HGA	A Hypo Group Alpe Adria
HMT	Her Majesty's Treasury
HRE	Hypo Real Estate group
IASB	International Accounting Standards Board
ICE	InterContinental Exchange
IFRS	International Financial Reporting Standards
IKB	Deutsche IndustrieBank
IL&P	Irish Life & Permanent
IMF	International Monetary Fund
INBS	Irish Nationwide Building Society
ING	Internationale Nederlanden Groep
IPO	Initial Public Offering
IRR	interest rate risk
IRS	Internal Revenue Service
ISDA	International Swaps and Derivatives Association
KDB	Korea Development Bank

KfW	Kreditanstalt für Wiederaufbau
LB	Landesbank Bayern
LBBW	Landesbank Baden-Württemberg
LCR	liquidity coverage ratio
LIBOR	London Inter-Bank Offered Rate
LTRO	long-term refinancing operation
MAC	material adverse change
MBIA	Municipal Bond Insurance Association
MBS	mortgage-backed security
MPS	Monte dei Paschi di Siena
NAMA	National Asset Management Agency (Ireland)
NBER	National Bureau for Economic Research
NBI	Nyí Landsbanki
NCG	Nova Caixa Galicia
NPL	non-performing loans
NYSE	New York Stock Exchange
OECD	Organisation for Economic Co-operation and Development
OCC	Office of the Comptroller of the Currency (US Treasury)
OFT	Office of Fair Trading
OLA	Orderly Liquidation Authority
ORA	Orderly Resolution Authority
ORF	Orderly Resolution Fund
OTC	over the counter
OTS	Office of Thrift Supervision
PCA	Prompt Corrective Action
PDCF	Primary Dealer Credit Facility
PIIGS	Portugal, Ireland, Italy, Greece, Spain
PRA	Prudential Regulatory Authority (Bank of England)
RBC	Royal Bank of Canada
RBS	Royal Bank of Scotland
RMBS	residential mortgage-backed security
RWA	risk-weighted assets
SAREB	Sociedad de Gestión de Activos Procedentes de la Reestructuración Bancaria
SCAP	Supervisory Capital Assessment Program
SEB	Skandinaviska Enskilda Banken
SEC	Securities and Exchange Commission
SEF	swap execution facility

SFIL	Société de Financement Local
SIFI	systemically important financial institution
SIGTARP	Special Inspector General for the Troubled Asset Relief Program
SIV	structured investment vehicle
SNB	Swiss National Bank
SNCI	Société National de Crédit à l'Industrie
SoFFin	Sonderfonds Finanzmarkt-stabilisierung
SPV	special purpose vehicle
SRB	Single Resolution Board
SRF	Single Resolution Fund
SRM	Single Resolution Mechanism
SSM	Single Supervisory Mechanism
SWF	Sovereign Wealth Fund
TAF	Term Auction Facility (Federal Reserve)
TALF	Term Asset-Backed Securities Loan Facility
TARP	Troubled Assets Relief Program
TBTF	too-big-to-fail
TCE	True Core Equity
TCE	Tangible Common Equity
TLGP	Temporary Liquidity Guarantee Program
TSB	Trustee Savings Bank
TSLF	Term Securities Lending Facility
UKAR	UK Asset Resolution
UKFI	UK Financial Investments
WaMu	Washington Mutual savings bank

Introduction

Because of this reform, the American people will never again be asked to foot the bill for Wall Street's mistakes. There will be no more taxpayer-funded bailouts – period.

President Barack Obama, 21 July 2010[1]

(a) Liquidation required
   All financial companies put into receivership under this subchapter shall be liquidated. No taxpayer funds shall be used to prevent the liquidation of any financial company under this subchapter.
(b) Recovery of funds
   All funds expended in the liquidation of a financial company under this subchapter shall be recovered from the disposition of assets of such financial company, or shall be the responsibility of the financial sector, through assessments.
(c) No losses to taxpayers
   Taxpayers shall bear no losses from the exercise of any authority under this subchapter.

Dodd–Frank Wall Street Reform and Consumer Protection Act of 2010, H.R. 4173, Title 1, chapter 53, subchapter II, § 5394[2]

We worked hard to make sure taxpayer bailouts are completely prohibited. I think the language is very tight on that. One of the things that frustrate me with critics of Title II is that they perpetuate the myth of Too Big To Fail by insisting that the government is still going to do bailouts, notwithstanding clear language in Dodd–Frank to the contrary. And that just continues the moral hazard by reinforcing market perceptions that the big institutions won't be allowed to fail.

Sheila Bair, former chairman of the FDIC,
interview in the Washington Post, 18 May 2013[3]

---

[1] www.youtube.com/watch?v=MBEY24qyBIM
[2] www.gpo.gov/fdsys/pkg/BILLS-111hr4173eh/pdf/BILLS-111hr4173eh.pdf
[3] www.washingtonpost.com/blogs/wonkblog/wp/2013/05/18/sheila-bair-dodd-frank-really-did-end-taxpayer-bailouts/

The capital requirements on banks must be set to ensure that the need for the exceptional support of Governments is never again required.

Ireland's former Taoiseach (prime minister)
Brian Cowen in a speech on 21 March
2012 at Georgetown University[4]

The financial crisis highlighted that public authorities are ill-equipped to deal with ailing banks operating in today's global markets. In order to maintain essential financial services for citizens and businesses, governments have had to inject public money into banks and issue guarantees on an unprecedented scale: between October 2008 and October 2011, the European Commission approved €4.5 trillion (equivalent to 37% of EU GDP) of state aid measures to financial institutions. This averted massive banking failure and economic disruption, but has burdened taxpayers with deteriorating public finances and failed to settle the question of how to deal with large cross-border banks in trouble.

The proposals adopted today by the European Commission for EU-wide rules for *bank recovery and resolution* will change this. They ensure that in the future authorities will have the means to intervene decisively both before problems occur and early on in the process if they do. Furthermore, if the financial situation of a bank deteriorates beyond repair, the proposal ensures that a bank's critical functions can be rescued while the costs of restructuring and resolving failing banks fall upon the bank's owners and creditors and not on taxpayers.

EU Commission, press release, "New crisis
management measures to avoid future
bank bail-outs," 6 June 2012[5]

Resolution: The objective of resolution is to minimise the extent to which the cost of a bank failure is borne by the State and its taxpayers.

EU Commission, "EU Bank Recovery and Resolution Directive
(BRRD): frequently asked questions," 15 April 2014[6]

---

[4] www.corkeconomics.com/wp-content/uploads/2012/03/3.21.12-Cowen-Speech.pdf
[5] http://europa.eu/rapid/press-release_IP-12-570_en.htm
[6] http://europa.eu/rapid/press-release_MEMO-14-297_en.htm

In reading the above statements from policy makers and regulators from both sides of the Atlantic, one is struck by their sincerity and their absolute conviction: taxpayer-funded bail-outs of banks will in the future not only be forbidden but made impossible by the new legislation. This raises two questions:

- Is that really so? There will be no more taxpayer-funded bail-outs for sure? As we will come back to in Part VI of the book, opinions on this issue are in reality more varied than the above-quoted statements indicate, especially among academics. Many would say that the too-big-to-fail (TBTF) banks are still alive and kicking and will be bailed out next time also, even though the procedures for fiscally financed bail-outs may have been made more difficult. According to a survey of finance professionals in November 2013, 97 percent of the interviewed did not think that the actions taken to improve banking supervision would prevent another market crash in the future.[7]
- If it were true, is it a good thing that the financial sector will be left to deal with its own recurrent crises? After all, we know from Reinhard and Rogoff that there have been 138 financial crises since World War II, 23 of them occurring in the Anglo-Saxon and West European countries on which this book focuses.[8,9] Have really all bail-outs been failures? Haven't taxpayers sometimes, perhaps even most of the time, got their money back with a return, sooner or later? Shouldn't we focus on the *conditions* to enhance this possibility rather than ruling out bail-outs *a priori*? Haven't there also been failed bail-ins of creditors (e.g. Cyprus)? What happens to the real

---

[7] *Financial Times Fund Management,* 25 November 2013.

[8] Carmen M. Reinhart and Kenneth S. Rogoff, *This Time is Different: Eight Centuries of Financial Folly* (Princeton University Press, 2009), table A.3.1, pp. 344 ff.

[9] This gives one country one observation each until the authors' cut-off date of 2008. Should we add another five years (–2013), we would add at least seven countries/crises for a total of 30 crises. Should we go by years of crises, irrespective of the number of countries involved, we would find eight periods of crises in a 40-year period. This numbering presumes that the financial crisis of 2007 onwards is treated as one crisis rather than several. This in turn raises the question of whether the European sovereign debt crisis is a crisis in itself or "only" the continuation of the banking crisis that began in 2007. We will come back to this question in Parts II and III.

sector (growth and unemployment) if a financial crisis is worsened as a result of the non-involvement of the taxpayer?

It's hardly surprising that the reaction from the general public, and, hence, from their elected representatives, to the recent financial crisis should have been so harsh. After all, banks worldwide wrote down over 2,000 billion dollars in credit losses. Loss ratios varied from a high in the United States at 7 percent of total lending and 5 percent in the UK, 3 percent in the euro area to just over 1 percent in Asia.[10] To these numbers should be added (as we do below) losses from 2011 onwards from the interacting sovereign debt crisis and a banking crisis in countries such as Portugal, Italy, Ireland, Greece and Spain (the so-called PIIGS countries[11]) as well as Cyprus. Other countries with banks in financial trouble will most certainly be added as this book goes into production; Slovenia and Malta are frequently mentioned candidates.[12]

To a large extent, the lost capital had to be replaced by taxpayer-funded capital injections into the banking system. The International Monetary Fund (IMF) has recently provided the calculations in Table 1. Note that they come from two different sources and cover slightly different periods and data. Nevertheless, a few clear conclusions appear:

- A large part of the new equity capital raised, over 1,700 billion dollars, has come from governments/taxpayers rather than from the market. Only in a very few cases (Barclays and Lloyds in the UK, BNP Paribas in France, Deutsche Bank in Germany, *cajas* in Spain, Monte dei Paschi in Italy, large US banks, to mention the most visible) have banks been ordered by their regulatory authorities to raise more capital from private investors. Otherwise improvements in equity and hence increase in capital ratios, in particular in the United States, have been made possible by the return of the banking sector to profitability as well as by the suppression of dividends.

---

[10] International Monetary Fund, *Global Financial Stability Report*, October 2010, figure 1.12, p. 13.

[11] Although, for the purpose of this book, PIIGS should rather refer to Portugal, Iceland, Ireland, Greece and Spain, since Iceland but not Italy has sought and received IMF aid.

[12] *Financial Times*, 21 November 2013, "Slovenia battles to avoid bailout over banks' huge black hole."

- Of the taxpayer-funded bail-outs, just over half had been repaid by the end of 2013 worldwide. The United States gives an even more positive picture. Under the TARP program, a total of 707 banks received 205 billion dollars in capital injections (Capital Purchase Program, CPP). Of these, 196 billion had been repaid by December 2013, 2 billion had been written off and hence 7 billion dollars remained outstanding. During the lifetime of the program, taxpayers had also received dividends and other income of 47 billion dollars from the entire TARP program (of which 10 billion from the CPP and the Systemically Failing Financial Institutions (SFFI) program).[13]
- Whereas the first column in Table 1 represents direct capital injections into banks, the second encompasses other financial firms. For the United States, the 1.5 percent corresponds to the Capital Purchase Program (CPP) while the higher figure in column 2 includes also capital support to AIG, Freddie Mac and Fannie Mae and the auto industry finance companies GMAC (now Ally Financial) and Chrysler Financial. For Germany, the left-hand column includes only federal capital injections (Commerzbank, Hypo Real Estate, IKB, WestLB) whereas column 2 includes also asset purchases. For Ireland, the data do not include the asset purchases by NAMA (the National Asset Management Agency) since it is funded independently outside the government budget. For Luxembourg, the sums stem from the Luxembourg parts of nationalized Fortis and Dexia. For the Netherlands, the higher figure in the second column includes asset guarantees to ABN AMRO/Fortis and ING.
- For most of the countries, taxpayer support is in single-digit numbers, making this crisis comparable to the savings and loan crash in the United States in the 1980s or the Nordic financial crises in the 1990s.[14] Three countries stand out, however: (a) Iceland, where bank assets were ten times GDP, and which saw a budget impact of 44 percent of GDP (original IMF estimates were even at 80 percent of GDP); (b) Ireland at a similar cost of 40 percent of GDP and assets at eight times GDP; and (c) Greece, where the banking crisis is

---

[13] SIGTARP, Office of the Special Inspector General for the Troubled Asset Relief Program, *Quarterly Report to Congress*, 29 January 2014, www.sigtarp.gov/ Quarterly%20Reports/January_29_2014_Report_to_Congress.pdf

[14] Johan A. Lybeck, *A Global History of the Financial Crash of 2007–2010* (Cambridge University Press, 2011), table 8.1, p. 281.

Table 1. *Financial sector support, selected economies, percentage of GDP*

Country	Gross injection	Impact on gross public debt	Recovery to date	Impact after recovery
Austria	2.9	4.9		
Belgium	6.0	7.4	1.5	5.9
Cyprus		10.0	–	10.0
Denmark	2.8	3.1		
France	0.5	1.3		
Germany	1.8	12.8	2.0	10.8
Greece	25.4	19.7	4.3	15.4
Iceland	34.1	44.2	23.7	20.5
Ireland	40.7	40.5	4.4	36.1
Italy	0.3			
Luxembourg	7.7			
Netherlands	6.6	14.6	10.0	4.6
Spain	2.0	7.3	2.9	4.4
United Kingdom	5.0	6.7	1.5	5.2
United States	1.5	4.8	4.2	0.6
Average		7.0	3.7	3.3
SUM (US dollar billion)		1,729	914	815

Sources: International Monetary Fund (Luc Laeven and Fabian Valencia), "Systemic banking crises: a new database," IMF Working Paper 2008/224, updated June 2012, IMF Working Paper 2012/163, www.imf.org/external/pubs/ft/wp/2012/wp12163. pdf; International Monetary Fund, *Fiscal Monitor,* "Fiscal adjustment in an uncertain world," April 2013, table 5, p. 14. Note: data are through February 2013.

mostly a reflection of the sovereign crisis and the decision to write down the value of privately held Greek debt, largely held by Greek (and Cyprus) banks.

Much higher figures for the state aid provided to banks result from adding also guarantees for deposits and other debt and the myriads of liquidity support extended by the central banks under a variety of

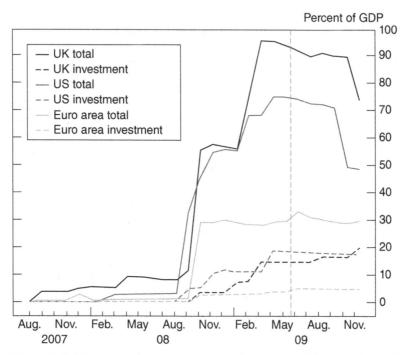

Figure 1. Public sector interventions in selected countries during the financial crisis 2007–9, percentage of GDP
Source: Bank of England Financial Stability Report, December 2009, chart 1.1.

schemes. As shown in Figure 1, the total attained almost 100 percent of GDP in the UK and 75 percent of GDP in the United States as contrasted to "only" 30 percent of GDP in the euro area.[15]

Table 2 specifies in greater detail the 4.5 trillion euro (36.7 percent of GDP) potential support in the European Union. For the purpose of this book on "bail out or bail in," the major interest is in the column "Recapitalizations."

Amounts actually used were, however, only one-third of these potentials or 1.6 trillion euro (corresponding to 13 percent of EU GDP).

---

[15] My own calculations for the United States came out with a figure even higher than GDP by including also the guarantee extended by the FDIC to insured deposits. Lybeck, *Global History*, table A7.2, pp. 270 ff. Other calculations have been even higher.

Table 2. *State aid to the banks in the European Union, 2008–11*

Years	Guarantees	Liquidity	Recapitalizations	Impaired assets	Total
2008	3,097	85	270	5	3,457
2009	88	5	110	339	542
2010	55	67	184	78	384
2011	49	40	34	0	123
TOTAL	3,290	198	598	421	4,506

Source: European Commission, "'High level expert group on reforming the structure of the EU banking sector" (Liikanen report), October 2012, p. 21 (billion euro).

However, the differences between the individual countries were substantial as seen in Figure 2 (the indeterminate columns for Ireland and Denmark are due to their unlimited deposit insurance).

However, it should be noted that the figure on government interventions stops before the European sovereign debt crisis exploded. Since then, a total of 519 billion euro has been made available to five euro area countries (Ireland, Portugal, Spain, Greece and Cyprus) by the various EU support funds and the International Monetary Fund. This sum corresponds to over 3 percent of the GDP of the euro area. Perhaps more relevant is to relate it to the GDP in the recipient countries, in which case we arrive at 20 percent of GDP but with the wide differences shown in Table 3.

This book takes a micro perspective to the financial crisis and the proposed changes in bank supervision and regulation, resolution and possible resurrection. It takes, if you like, a case-by-case approach to banks in distress to try to deduce from these cases some general principles, as well as evaluating what was done well and what was done less well.[16]

In Part I, this micro aspect is emphasized by a detailed chronology (timeline) of the evolving financial crisis from the beginning of 2007.

---

[16] For a contrasting and complementary view from the macro side, see Martin Wolf, *The Shifts and the Shocks: What We Have Learned – and Have Still to Learn – from the Financial Crisis* (London and New York: Allen Lane and Penguin, 2014).

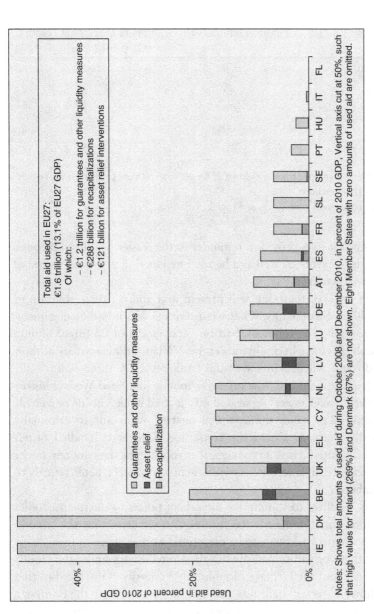

Figure 2. Amount of state aid in the European Union actually used

Source: Same as Table 2, which builds on European Commission Competition, "The effect of temporary State aid rules adopted in the context of the financial and economic crisis," Staff Working Paper, 5 October 2011, p. 11.

Table 3. *Financial support from the EU and IMF to some European countries, 2010–13*[a]

Country	Support in billion euro	Share of recipient country GDP 2012 (%)
Portugal	78	28
Ireland	85	31
Greece	246	76
Spain	100	6
Cyprus	10	33

[a]This does not include the write-down of Greek sovereign debt which cost investors some 110 billion euro.
Source: European Commission and own calculations.

This timeline may provide a reminder to the reader who lived through the crisis of events, as well as a handy introduction to the discussion of individual banks in Part II.

Parts II–IV of the book will present and analyze the resolution of some 30 problem banks. What went wrong? Was it bad management, bad economic environment, bad business model or all three? Should the problems have been obvious earlier? What did supervisory authorities do and when? How was the bank resolved: resurrection, sale/ merger or liquidation? Was taxpayer money involved? Were creditors hit? Were "toxic assets" separated into a "bad bank," inside or outside the bank? Was senior management ousted? Were culprits criminally or civilly charged? Could the resolution have been handled faster/ more efficiently? Have taxpayers, if involved, got their money back? How was the upside for taxpayers achieved once a bank returns to profitability?

Parts V–VI try to summarize the salient points of the micro studies and draw conclusions for the future. Can we generalize the circumstances when a bail-out is to be preferred to other forms of resolution? Could there be future bail-outs in the United States under the Dodd–Frank Act and the Orderly Liquidation Authority (OLA) and in that case how? How will bail-outs and bail-ins be handled in the European Union under the Single Resolution Mechanism (SRM) and the Bank Resolution and Recovery Directive (BRRD)? How wide should the safety net of deposit insurance be? Should the insurance fund ever be used for resolution purposes? Should unsecured senior debt investors ever be bailed in? What about uninsured depositors? Under what circumstances should the banking industry pay for the mistakes of its own "rotten apples," *ex ante* or *ex post*?

The book concludes that the promise not to involve taxpayers' money next time is neither credible nor desirable. Despite such coordinating bodies as the Financial Stability Oversight Council in the United States (chaired by the secretary of the Treasury) and the European Systemic Risk Board (chaired by the president of the ECB), the response mechanisms focus on the resolution of individual banks rather than the financial system. Threats to bail in unsecured bondholders and, even worse, uninsured depositors, are hardly likely to be credible in the midst of a full-blown financial crisis, as in 2008, with hundreds of banks failing, nor is the promise to claw back any government money spent by an *ex post* levy on the remaining still viable banks.

Capital ratios have been raised, especially for the TBTF (too-big-to-fail) banks, and should be raised even higher, as in Sweden, Denmark or Switzerland. The focus in the denominator of the capital–asset ratio has been shifted from risk-weighted assets to total assets in order to minimize the possibility that banks will "game" the rules by their own internal risk-evaluation models. The emphasis in the numerator is now on Core Equity Tier 1 capital (CET1), mainly common stock and retained earnings, rather than on other types of capital like preferred shares, hybrids and subordinated debt. Liquidity coverage ratios have been introduced.

All this is fine but we have seen in the latest crisis that much more money will be needed to create confidence in the system than what is presently proposed. With capital–asset ratios set low at 3 percent in Europe and 6 percent in the United States (for its TBTF banks), with prepaid resolution funds lacking in the United States and set at ridiculously low levels in the EU (55 billion euro), credibility requires a taxpayer-funded backstop, a safety net politicians insist is no longer available.

Rather than ignoring the problem, with politicians repeating unanimously in ostrich-fashion that there will be no more bail-outs, legislators should focus on *how* a taxpayer bail-out should be organized. On both sides of the Atlantic, this involves changing legislation to allow for the injection of public funds into an existing bank, being placed in conservatorship under the FDIC in the United States and run by the national or European resolution authorities in the EU (European Resolution Board for eurozone members, Swedish National Debt Office, UK Financial Investments, Danish Finansiel Stabilitet, etc. for the others).

Decision making on resolving a failing bank must be made much simpler than what is presently legislated in the United States and in the European Union; there is no time for complex colleges involving a number of bodies and, worse, a number of countries. From closing on Friday afternoon until the opening of the Asian markets early in the morning on Monday is only some 55 hours and it must suffice to have a transfer of assets or a bridge bank or a capital infusion into an existing bank in place in that space of time. While the Treasury secretary in the United States has received wide-ranging powers to act in consort with the FDIC and the Federal Reserve, involving the 28 members of the ECOFIN Council in EU decisions on top of the national and European resolution authorities and the EU Commission is simply impossible, not to say ridiculous.

In the United States, the FDIC must be given much more leeway on how to use the funds borrowed from the Orderly Liquidation Fund (which, moreover, should be renamed the Orderly Resolution Fund). Preferably, despite resistance from Congress, the Fund should at least partly consist of a prepaid, industry-financed fund rather than the pay-as-you-go set up introduced by Dodd–Frank. Fortunately, the Deposit Insurance Fund is a true fund and its aim to attain 2 percent of insured deposits ambitious but necessary, even though it is presently far from its goal.

In the European Union, the prepaid industry-funded Resolution Fund must either be sharply increased in size from its present 55 billion euro and its communalization speeded up or, if that is politically impossible given resistance from some member states to burden-sharing, complemented by national funds amounting to at least 2 percent of GDP. These funds are additional to the Deposit Insurance Funds which should only be used to pay off depositors in liquidated banks and where one also needs to build prepaid, industry-financed funds in those countries where they are still lacking, such as the UK.

The alternative, if the will to create a true European banking union is lacking, will be spelled out in the Conclusion to the book.

PART I

A *chronological presentation* of crisis events January 2007 – December 2014

There exist already some 300 books and even more articles on the financial crisis, its causes and remedies; there is no need to add one more.[1] Many of them are quoted in the list of literature at the end of the book. Especially recommended is the comparison and evaluation of some of the better ones by MIT Professor Andy Lo.[2] Hence this part of the book makes no pretence at explanations; it gives a hopefully neutral and chronological description of events.

The Liikanen report[3] contains a very useful summary of the "waves" following one after the other (p. 18):

- Wave 1: "Subprime crisis phase" (mid 2007 to September 2008): investment portfolios collapse (especially in MBSs and CDOs linked to subprime loans);
- Wave 2: "Systemic crisis phase" (from September 2008): unprecedented state aid to the banking sector is required as liquidity evaporates;
- Wave 3: "Economic crisis phase" (from 2009): automatic stabilizers kick in following the recession, and fiscal sustainability is imperiled through fiscal stimulus and state aid;
- Wave 4: "Sovereign crisis phase" (from 2010): bank–sovereign feedback loops raise significant challenges given the existing institutional EU framework;
- Wave 5: "Crisis of confidence in Europe phase" (from 2011 and present): EU at a crossroads.

---

[1] See http://businesslibrary.uflib.ufl.edu/financialcrisesbooks and www.investorhome.com/crisisbooks.htm

[2] Andrew W. Lo, "'Reading about the financial crisis: a 21-book review," *Journal of Economic Literature*, 50:1 (March 2012), pp. 151–78.

[3] European Commission, 'High level expert group on reforming the structure of the EU banking sector' (Liikanen report), October 2012.

These "waves" should be borne in mind while reading the timeline below.

5 February 2007: The mortgage bank Mortgage Lenders Network, the fifteenth largest subprime lender in the United States, becomes the first victim of the subprime crisis when it files for Chapter 11 protection.

7 February 2007: The British megabank HSBC announces a new reservation of 1.8 billion dollars for potential losses in its portfolio of US subprime loans; its head of US mortgage banking is fired.

27 February 2007: The semi-government owned mortgage bank Freddie Mac announces that it will no longer purchase (and securitize) subprime mortgages.

28 March 2007: Treasury Secretary Hank Paulson appears before a committee of the House of Representatives, saying that "From the standpoint of the overall economy, my bottom line is we're watching it closely but it appears to be contained."

2 April 2007: New Century Financial, the second largest subprime lender in the US, files for protection under Chapter 11. The value of its stock has fallen from 1.75 billion dollars at the beginning of the year to basically zero. Accused of "significant improper and imprudent practices related to its loan originations, operations, accounting and financial reporting processes," it settles with the Securities and Exchange Commission (SEC) for an unknown sum, its CEO and two other officers being barred from holding directorships in public companies for five years. Since it had not taken deposits, it had not been supervised by any state or federal superviser.

17 April 2007: The Supreme Court of the United States ends a four-year quarrel between state banking regulators and the federal banking regulator OCC (Office of the Comptroller of the Currency within the Treasury Department). North-Carolina-based Wachovia Bank had refused to abide by state laws concerning restrictions on mortgage lending on account of its being a nationally chartered bank under OCC supervision. The Supreme Court ruled five to three in Wachovia's favor, leaving the OCC as its sole regulator. In deep trouble and on the brink of bankruptcy, Wachovia was later acquired by Wells Fargo (see below, 9 November 2007, 29 and 30 September 2008 and 3 October 2008).

23 April 2007: Bank of America agrees to take over LaSalle Bank for 21 billion dollars in cash. The Chicago-based bank with assets of 116 billion dollars was a subsidiary of Dutch bank ABN AMRO which wanted to get its American subsidiary out of the way as it was fighting against a hostile takeover by Fortis, RBS and Santander (see below, 17 October 2007).

3 May 2007: Swiss bank UBS closes its internal hedge fund Dillon Read Capital Management, taking the positions onto its own books but continuing the investment in securities linked to subprime mortgages.

7 June 2007: The American investment bank Bear Stearns disallows withdrawals from two of its hedge funds which have invested in American CDOs whose value has fallen sharply. The two funds, High-Grade Fund and Enhanced Leverage Fund, are basically worthless. The head of Bear Stearns Asset Management, BSAM, Ralph Cioffi, administered both 11 CDOs (collateralized debt obligations) as well as the two hedge funds. Since he picked the CDOs that the hedge funds would invest in, he was sitting on both sides of the transaction in a clear conflict of interest between his CDO investors and his hedge fund investors. Cioffi and an associate were later arrested and charged with misleading investors. They were, however, acquitted in November 2009, the jury finding them not guilty of "conspiracy, and securities and wire fraud" in the first criminal trial after the collapse of the subprime mortgage market. In February 2012, they settled a civil suit with the SEC, Cioffi paying a fine of 800,000 dollars and accepting a three-year ban from the industry.

6 July 2007: The CEO of Swiss bank UBS, Peter Wuffli, is fired by the board.

10 July 2007: Standard & Poor's and Moody's begin a dramatic downgrading of AAA/Aaa rated residential mortgage-backed securities (RMBS) and corresponding CDOs. On this one day, Standard & Poor's downgraded 498 subprime-related issues with a nominal value of around 6 billion dollars, Moody's 399 issues worth 5.2 billion. During the second half of 2007, Standard & Poor's downgraded more than 9,000 RMBS ratings. Over 90 percent of RMBS originally rated AAA/Aaa in 2006 and 2007 would by 2010 have been downgraded to junk status. Among the worst performers was

Washington Mutual savings bank (WaMu) and its subsidiary Long Beach Mortgage Company, being responsible for 6 percent of securities issued in 2006 but 14 percent of the downgrades. All of the 75 RMBS issues by Long Beach would be downgraded to junk status. WaMu would later fail in the largest American bank bankruptcy ever.

19 July 2007: The Dow Jones stock market index exceeds 14,000 for the first time.

30 July 2007: The German investment bank IKB Deutsche Industriebank AG, majority owned by the German federal state via Kreditanstalt für Wiederaufbau (KfW), unable to roll (refinance) its liabilities in the form of asset-backed commercial paper (ABCP), is rescued by a loan of 3.5 billion euro by Commerzbank, Deutsche Bank and the KfW, later increased to 5 billion euro. In its Dublin-based Rhinebridge subsidiary (an SIV, structured investment vehicle), it had borrowed on ABCP to finance, mainly, investments in US mortgage-related CDOs as well as synthetic CDOs, such as Goldman Sachs' Abacus 2007-AC1 (see below). Its total assets were 15 billion euro. Since the ABCP had been sold with put options, the investors were able to sell the securities back to KfW which took the loss onto its own books.

5 August 2007: The co-president of Bear Stearns, Warren Spector, is forced to resign over the two failed funds he oversaw.

6 August 2007: American Home Mortgage, the tenth largest mortgage bank in the US, files for protection under the bankruptcy laws, not having been able to roll over its funding on ABCP. From a peak of 1.2 trillion dollars in mid 2007, the total US ABCP market outstanding would halve by the end of 2008.

9 August 2007: The largest French bank BNP Paribas freezes three of its funds for withdrawals after the market for CDOs based on US subprime mortgages has fallen by 20 percent.

9–10 August 2007: To alleviate the resulting lack of liquidity in the frozen interbank market, the major central banks inject money into the system: the Federal Reserve 43 billion dollars, ECB 95 billion euro (with an additional 300 billion added by December) and the Bank of Japan 8 billion dollars (equivalent). Bank of England does, for the moment, nothing.

16 August 2007:   Countrywide Financial, the largest US mortgage bank, narrowly avoids bankruptcy by receiving emergency loans of 11 billion dollars from a consortium of banks. The news, however, triggers a bank run, where 8 billion dollars in deposits are withdrawn on a single day.

22 August 2007:   ECB announces 40 billion euro liquidity support through the three-month scheme Longer-Term Refinancing Operation (LTRO).

26 August 2007:   The regional German savings bank Landesbank Baden-Württemberg (LBBW) takes over Landesbank Sachsen which would otherwise have gone bankrupt. Through two Dublin-based SIVs, Ormond Quay and Georges Quay, it had invested heavily in American mortgage-related CDOs. The 'toxic assets' cost the taxpayers of the state of Sachsen 2.8 billion euro, assets which LBBW refused to take over. The affair cost the Ministerpräsident (minister-president) of Sachsen his job.

31 August 2007:   Ameriquest, the largest remaining subprime lender, goes bankrupt. Citigroup takes over its mortgage-servicing unit for an undisclosed sum. Despite widespread allegations of mortgage fraud, having led to a 325 million dollar settlement in 2005, with financial regulators in 49 states and Washington, DC, accusing Ameriquest of misrepresenting and failing to disclose loan terms, charging excessive loan origination fees and inflating appraisals to qualify borrowers for loans, the former CEO of Ameriquest, Roland Arnall, is appointed by President George W. Bush as US ambassador to the Netherlands.

1–3 September 2007: At the annual central bank conference in Jackson Hole, Wyoming, Yale economics professor Robert J. Shiller predicts that house prices in the United States may fall by 50 percent over the next couple of years. The actual figure turned out to be 25 percent (according to the 20-city Case–Shiller index) for the two-year period and 35 percent from peak to trough.

3 September 2007: The German investment bank IKB, majority owned by the German federal state via Kreditanstalt für Wiederaufbau, reports a loss of over one billion dollars on account of American mortgage-related bonds (see also above for Rhinebridge SIV, 31 July 2007, and below for Abacus, 16 April 2010).

6 September 2007: ECB adds another 75 billion euro to its LTRO lending.

10 September 2007: Victoria Mortgage Funding in the UK becomes the first European victim of the global financial crisis. While not a bank, it had originated high-risk mortgages, repackaged and resold to banks.

13 September 2007: BBC reports that the Bank of England has secretly given the mortgage bank Northern Rock liquidity support to the tune of 21 billion pounds (later extended to over 55 billion). The news leads to a run on the bank the next day, the first major bank run in Britain since 1866 (which was aimed at Overend, Gurney and Company, a discount house).

17 September 2007: The chancellor of the exchequer, Alistair Darling, extends a government guarantee to all deposits in Northern Rock and, implicitly, in any other UK bank with problems (confirmed on 9 October but applicable only to deposits made after 19 September).

18 September 2007: The Federal Reserve continues its decreases of the Fed Funds rate which brings the rate from 5.25 to 1 percent in a year.

28 September 2007: Netbank, one of the largest internet banks in the United States, is closed by its supervisor, the Office of Thrift Supervision (OTS). It becomes the largest savings bank failure since the 1980s. Its deposits are taken over by Dutch bank ING Direct.

1 October 2007: Dublin-based Depfa (Deutsche Pfandbriefanstalt) is taken over by Hypo Real Estate in Munich.

2 October 2007: The Swiss bank UBS reports credit write-downs of 3.6 billion dollars on account of losses on American mortgage-related bonds.

9 October 2007: The Dow Jones share index tops at index level 14,165. The low point of 6,627 is reached in March 2009 for a fall of 53 percent in 17 months. The old peak would be breached first on 13 March 2013.

11–19 October 2007: Standard & Poor's and Moody's downgrade more than 2,500 bond issues linked to subprime mortgages, worth some 80 billion dollars in original nominal value.

15 October 2007: Citigroup, the largest bank in the United States, reports a write-down of 8.5 billion dollars for the third quarter.

15 October 2007: A consortium of American banks and investment banks plan to create a government-supported "super fund" of 100 billion dollars in order to buy mortgage bonds, thereby supporting their prices. The plan collapses on 24 December on account of the falling prices on these bonds and the impossibility of assessing what the reasonable price would be.

17 October 2007: The Dutch bank ABN AMRO is bought for 71 billion euro (the largest takeover in banking history) by a consortium consisting of the Benelux bank Fortis, the Spanish Grupo Santander and the Royal Bank of Scotland (RBS) which divide up the bank among them. Fortis pays 24 billion euro for its share, mainly the Dutch parts of the bank. Santander gets the South American and Italian operations, the latter (Banca Antonveneta) being immediately sold to Monte dei Paschi di Siena for 9 billion euros, a profit of 36 percent for two months' holding. RBS receives the global banking business and wholesale clients. RBS will, on account of the purchase, post a record loss before tax of 40.7 billion pounds for 2008, of which 30.1 billion was write-down of goodwill largely (22 billion) related to the purchase of ABN AMRO. Losses on credit trading were 17.7 billion pounds, also mostly related to the CDS and CDO portfolio taken over from ABN AMRO.

24 October 2007: The largest American investment bank, Merrill Lynch, makes reservations for credit losses of 7.9 billion dollars for the third quarter alone (later increased to 8.4 billion), leading to a net loss of 2.3 billion dollars. The losses occurred despite the fact that the bank had warehoused mainly the super senior tranches in the CDOs they had constructed, selling the lower-rated tranches. At the end of September, it held a gross position of 55 billion dollars in CDO-related paper. The chairman and CEO, Stanley O'Neill, is forced to resign three weeks later. Despite the company's write-downs, he receives a severance payment (a "golden parachute") of 161 million dollars, on top of his normal annual salary of 48 million dollars.

31 October 2007: Deutsche Bank makes reservations for credit write-downs of 3 billion dollars (equivalent).

1 November 2007: Credit Suisse reports a write-down of 1 billion dollars (equivalent).

1 November 2007: The Federal Reserve injects 41 billion dollars in liquidity, the largest operation since 9/11 in 2001.

5 November 2007: Citigroup is forced to make a new reservation of 11 billion dollars on top of the 5.9 billion taken one month earlier. Its total subprime exposure was stated at 55 billion dollars. The CEO and chairman Charles "Chuck" Prince resigns. His severance payment is "only" 12 million dollars in cash, the rest, 24 million, being paid in stock which would eventually become virtually worthless as the price per share falls from 36 dollars on the day of his resignation to below 1 dollar at the lowest.

7 November 2007: The small monoline (i.e. an insurance company for credit products only) insurer ACA reports a loss of 1 billion dollars on Credit Default Swaps which wipes out its entire equity.

8 November 2007: The investment bank Morgan Stanley reports losses related to subprime loans of 3.7 billion dollars.

8 November 2007: ECB adds two tranches of 80 billion euro each to its LTRO.

9 November 2007: Wachovia, the fourth largest bank in the US, reports write-downs of 1.7 billion dollars.

13 November 2007: Bank of America, the largest bank in the United States by deposits, writes down 3 billion dollars in credit losses.

14 November 2007: The credit crisis reaches Europe whose largest bank (by capital), HSBC (Hong Kong and Shanghai Banking Corp), makes a credit write-down of 3.4 billion dollars (equivalent). Most of it referred to its American subsidiary.

15 November 2007: Barclays, the second largest bank in the UK by assets and number three by capital, makes write-downs of 2.6 billion dollars (equivalent).

15 November 2007: The Federal Reserve adds over 47 billion dollars in liquidity to mitigate rising interbank rates.

20 November 2007: The American mortgage bank "Freddie Mac," Federal Home Loan Mortgage Corporation, a government-sponsored enterprise (GSE), is forced to take a credit write-down of 1.2 billion dollars. It issues new stock worth 6 billion dollars to private investors.

26 November 2007: HSBC reports having given its investment fund for structured products ("SIV") a support loan of 45 billion dollars to cover write-downs on its investments in CDOs and CDSs.

27 November 2007: The sovereign wealth fund of Abu Dhabi buys shares in Citigroup for 7.5 billion dollars, thereby becoming the bank's largest shareholder.

4 December 2007: The American mortgage bank "Fannie Mae," Federal National Mortgage Association, also a GSE, issues new stock worth 7 billion dollars.

6 December 2007: Royal Bank of Scotland, RBS, the biggest bank in the United Kingdom and the world by assets, writes down 2.5 billion dollars (equivalent) in credit losses.

10 December 2007: Swiss bank UBS is forced to reserve another 10 billion dollars (equivalent) for credit losses but receives a capital injection of 10 billion Swiss francs from Middle East investors.

12 December 2007: The Federal Reserve starts to lend to banks under the program TAF, Term Auction Facility, with maturities of between 28 and 84 days. Banks borrowed a total of 40 billion dollars within two weeks. The Fed also initiates a swap program with some major foreign central banks, allowing them to swap their national currencies for dollars. It initially involves the Bank of Canada, the Bank of England, the European Central Bank (ECB) and the Swiss National Bank (SNB). The total potential swap volume of 24 billion dollars would later swell to a maximum of 580 billion dollars.

16 December 2007: The CEO of failed Northern Rock, Adam Applegarth, leaves the company with full salary and pension rights though without any severance payment.

19 December 2007: Morgan Stanley reports another 9.4 billion dollars in credit write-downs and receives 5 billion dollars in new capital from the Chinese sovereign wealth fund CIC (China Investment Corporation), corresponding to approximately 10 percent of its share capital.

24 December 2007: The largest American investment bank Merrill Lynch receives a capital injection of 6.2 billion dollars from Davis Advisors and Temasek Holdings, Singapore's sovereign wealth fund, later increased by another 3.4 billion.

9 January 2008: The investment bank Bear Stearns reports write-downs related to subprime loans of 1.9 billion dollars. Its chairman and CEO, James Cayne, resigns, selling his shares in the company for 61 million dollars. A year earlier, they had been worth over a billion dollars.

11 January 2008: Countrywide, the largest mortgage bank in the United States, is purchased by Bank of America for 4.1 billion dollars. In 2006, Countrywide had had a market share of 20 percent of all outstanding residential mortgage loans in the United States. Its CEO, Angelo Mozilo, is later charged by the SEC with insider trading and securities fraud (having sold some 300 million dollars' worth of shares knowing of the bank's problems). The bank had recently shifted regulator from the Federal Reserve and OCC (Office of the Comptroller of the Currency) to the more lenient OTS (Office of Thrift Supervision).

15 January 2008: Citigroup writes down credits for 18 billion dollars for the fourth quarter of 2007.

17 January 2008: Merrill Lynch writes down an additional 14.1 billion dollars, leading to a net loss for 2007 of 8.6 billion dollars, but receives 6.6 billion dollars in fresh capital from the sovereign wealth funds of Kuwait and South Korea as well as Japanese bank Mizuho.

18 January 2008: The second largest bond insurer in the United States, Ambac, loses its AAA rating from Fitch and is placed on credit watch by Standard & Poor's after having canceled a planned sale of equity of 1 billion dollars.

24 January 2008: The National Association of Realtors in the US reports the first fall in house prices to have occurred since the Depression.

25 January 2008: Douglass National Bank in Missouri becomes the first bank to become insolvent in the New Year. Another 24 banks would follow later that year.

30 January 2008: Standard & Poor's downgrades or puts on credit watch over 8,200 RMBS and CDO securities, most with a AAA rating, worth a total nominal sum of 534 billion dollars, warning that investors may lose up to 265 billion dollars on their investments.

31 January 2008: The insurance company MBIA whose main business is credit insurance (it is a so-called monoline) reserves 2.3 billion dollars for expected losses.

8 February 2008: Deutsche Bank makes further write-downs of 3.2 billion dollars (equivalent).

13 February 2008: Deutsche IndustrieBank (IKB) reports further losses on its Rhinebridge Irish subsidiary and receives a capital injection of 1.5 billion euro from the federal state.

14 February 2014: UBS reports a loss of 18.4 billion dollars on US subprime investments.

19 February 2008: The French bank Société Générale issues new stock worth 5.5 billion euro in order to cover losses of 4.9 billion euro made by one single trader, Jérome Kerviel. The larger part of the loss was incurred when the bank decided to close unauthorized positions in stock index futures amounting to 50 billion euro in three days, thereby creating a huge impact on prices. Mr. Kerviel was later sentenced to five years in prison and obligated to pay the bank's loss. The bank also wrote down 3.2 billion dollars (equivalent) for credit losses related to American mortgage products.

19 February 2008: Credit Suisse reports an additional write-down of 2.85 billion dollars (equivalent) on account of erroneous prices used to value its portfolio of CDOs.

22 February 2008: The British mortgage lender Northern Rock is nationalized, meaning that its 100 billion pounds in liabilities are added to the British national debt, which thereby increases from 37 to 45 percent of GDP. A holding company, UK Financial Investments (UKFI), is created for the purpose of being the formal owner of the state's long-term holdings of bank shares. Later the state holdings in Bradford & Bingley, Lloyds Banking Group and Royal Bank of Scotland (RBS) would be added (see below). UK Asset Resolution (UKAR) will later be created as a "bad bank" for the remaining "toxic" mortgage assets of Northern Rock; Bradford & Bingley to be divested after the good assets (retail operations and branch offices) are sold to Virgin Money and Abbey National (Santander), respectively. See below, 17 November 2011 and 18 May 2012 (for Northern Rock) and 29 September 2008 (for Bradford & Bingley).

25–26 February 2008: Monoline insurer MBIA completes a 1.1 billion dollar stock sale, prompting Standard & Poor's and Moody's to confirm its AAA/Aaa rating (however, with a negative outlook).

28 February 2008: The world's largest insurance company by market value, AIG, one of only six AAA-rated US companies, reports a 11.1 billion dollar write-down on subprime mortgages for the fourth quarter of 2007, leading to a loss of over 5 billion. It also reveals a book of CDS (Credit Default Swaps) written for a nominal 441 billion dollars in its London-based AIG Financial products. It did not reveal that, until January, it had had no model for evaluating

the market value of these swaps. Nor did it reveal that because of the loss of market value of the underlying CDOs, its counterparties, mainly Goldman Sachs, had demanded over 3 billion dollars in collateral, demands that would be sharply raised as AIG was downgraded by both major rating agencies. The share price dipped by 12 percent for the day to 45 dollars; at the peak in 2002, it had been close to 2,000. It would not return and exceed 45 dollars until May 2013. Its president and CEO, Martin J. Sullivan, was later ousted (15 June).

1 March 2008: Landesbank Bayern receives a capital injection of 10 billion euro from the state of Bavaria after having made losses on US subprime-related bonds. A loan of 4.8 billion euro would later be granted to Bavaria from the German SoFFin (Sonderfonds Finanzmarkt-stabilisierung) when the federal bank rescue package was announced in October 2008.

3 March 2008: HSBC adds 13.8 billion dollars (equivalent) to its reserves.

5 March 2008: First Franklin Financial Corp., the fifth largest subprime lender bought by Merrill Lynch in December 2006 for 1.3 billion dollars, halts loan originations.

7 March 2008: The Federal Reserve allows its member banks to borrow against mortgage bonds issued by the GSE's Fannie Mae and Freddie Mac as collateral.

11 March 2008: The Federal Reserve introduces the program Term Securities Lending Facility (TSLF), whereby all primary dealers (the counterparties to the Fed in open market operations, banks as well as broker-dealers) can exchange less liquid bonds for government bonds. In order to lend to institutions other than banks, the Fed had had to invoke the emergency section 13(3) of the Federal Reserve Act, specifying "unusual and exigent circumstances." The program did not begin until 27 March and hence could not help Bear Stearns survive (see below).

17 March 2008: The American bank JPMorgan Chase buys the investment bank Bear Stearns. The initially agreed price of 236 million dollars or 2 dollars per share was, due to angry shareholders, raised to 10 dollars per share a few days later. Still, the price had been at a level of 133 dollars per share during the year before. The Federal

Reserve issues a non-recourse loan to JPMorgan Chase of up to 29 billion dollars to guarantee potential future losses of the bank's holdings of subprime-backed securities, JPMorgan taking only the first billion dollars in loss. Maiden Lane is created by the Fed to park "toxic" securities.

18 March 2008: Federal Reserve begins its Primary Dealer Credit Facility, PDCF, by which all their primary dealers can borrow from the Fed, whether commercial banks, investment banks or broker/dealers.

26 March 2008: The Federal Deposit Insurance Corporation (FDIC) orders the company owning Fremont Investment & Loan to either recapitalize or sell the bank. It was at the time the fifth largest subprime lender. It was later sold to CapitalSource Inc.

28 March 2008: The ECB begins refinancing operations with longer maturities.

1 April 2008: UBS makes further write-downs of 19 billion dollars, making its total losses on US mortgages 37 billion dollars. It announces a right issue of stock of 15 billion Swiss francs. Its chairman, Marcel Ospel, steps down three weeks later on 23 April.

1 April 2008: Deutsche Bank writes down 3.9 billion dollars (equivalent).

1 April 2008: Lloyd Blankfein, CEO of Goldman Sachs, says that "we're closer to the end than the beginning" of the global credit crisis.

7 April 2008: Washington Mutual (WaMu), the largest savings bank in the United States, receives a capital injection of 7.2 billion dollars from private-equity investors led by TPG Capital. It would all be lost half a year later (see 25 September 2008). This corresponded to 8.75 dollars per share, to be compared with a full purchase of the bank by JPMorgan Chase, simultaneously offering 8 dollars per share, an offer WaMu rejected.

17 April 2008: Merrill Lynch writes down a further 4.5 billion dollars for a first-quarter loss of 2 billion dollars.

18 April 2008: Citigroup follows with write-downs of 12 billion dollars and a 5.1 billion dollar loss for the first quarter.

21 April 2008: The Bank of England announces a Special Liquidity Scheme, offering to swap mortgage-backed and other securities (around 50 billion pounds) for UK Treasury bills.

21 April 2008: The Royal Bank of Scotland (RBS) writes down 5.9 billion pounds (9.4 billion dollars) and issues new stock worth 12 billion pounds (19 billion dollars).

22 April 2008: The Bank of England presents a scheme for banks to swap their (illiquid) mortgage assets for government bonds.

2 May 2008: The Federal Reserve includes AAA-rated asset-backed bonds (ABS) in allowable collateral.

2 May 2008: The new CEO of Merrill Lynch, John Thain, ex-NYSE and ex-Goldman Sachs, hires two friends from Goldman, who over their base salary of 600,000 dollars are guaranteed bonuses of 39.4 and 29.4 million dollars for 2008, irrespective of their actual performance.

12 May 2008: HSBC writes down 3.2 billion dollars (equivalent) for the first quarter, mostly related to its US subsidiary.

15 May 2008: Barclays follows suit with 2 billion dollars (equivalent).

2 June 2008: As the first CEO of a major bank to be ousted in the crisis, Kennedy "Ken" Thompson leaves Wachovia, the fourth largest bank in the United States. The main reason was his purchase in 2006 of Golden West Financial (with its thrift subsidiary World Savings Bank) for 26 billion dollars at the height of the housing boom. Ailing Wachovia was later sold to Wells Fargo (see 29 September 2008 and 3 October 2008).

6 June 2008: The investment bank Lehman Brothers gives notice that it needs 6 billion dollars in additional capital.

6 June 2008: Standard & Poor's downgrades the two monoline insurers Ambac and MBIA from AAA to AA; bonds insured by them and affected amount to 1 trillion dollars.

10 June 2008: Bank of America sells its prime brokerage operations, serving basically hedge and private equity funds, to BNP Paribas.

16 June 2008: The investment bank Lehman Brothers reports a quarterly loss of 2.8 billion dollars.

27 June 2008: Senator Chuck Schumer (D-NY) sends a surprising open letter to the FDIC and other regulatory authorities expressing concern over IndyMac savings bank (see 11 July) whose "financial deterioration poses significant risks to both tax payers and borrowers... and that the regulatory community may not be prepared to

take measures that would help prevent the collapse of IndyMac or minimize the damage should a failure occur." IndyMac collapses two weeks later after a run on its deposits. Its share price had fallen from a peak of 50 dollars to 0.31 dollars and it had been downgraded by Standard & Poor's to CCC.

1 July 2008: Ailing Landesbank Rheinland-Pfalz is integrated into Landesbank Baden-Württemberg (LBBW).

11 July 2008: IndyMac, the largest savings bank in the Los Angeles area and the seventh largest mortgage bank in the United States, is seized by its supervisor, the FDIC. The name of the bank stands for the Independent National Mortgage Corporation and tries to mimic the semi-public Freddie Mac with which it has no connections. It becomes the fourth largest banking collapse in US history. The bank had total assets of 32 billion dollars and the cost to the FDIC to bail out insured depositors exceeded 10 billion dollars, uninsured depositors (those with deposits above 100,000 dollars) losing some 270 million dollars. It had specialized in so-called Alt-A mortgages ("liar loans") as well as jumbo mortgages, loans too big to sell to Fannie Mae or Freddie Mac. The nationalized bank was later sold in January 2009 to a private equity consortium. The leading officers of IndyMac would be charged by the SEC in February 2011 for securities fraud for not informing investors about the declining financial condition of the bank. The CEO, Michael W. Perry, was, with 16 million dollars in total compensation, one of the highest-paid CEOs in 2006 (see 11 February 2011 and 14 December 2012).

13 July 2008: The Treasury and the Federal Reserve save the Government Sponsored Enterprises (GSE) Fannie Mae and Freddie Mac by guaranteeing their liabilities and giving them temporary borrowing facilities.

15 July 2008: The SEC issues an emergency order forbidding naked short sales of shares in 19 American financial institutions, among them Fannie Mae and Freddie Mac.

17 July 2008: Merrill Lynch reports a quarterly loss of 4.7 billion dollars. However, it also sells its share in the Bloomberg news agency and other assets for almost 8 billion, more than making up for the loss.

22 July 2008: Wachovia bank reports an 8.9 billion dollar loss for the second quarter. Its CEO, Ken Thompson, had been fired in early

June. Most of the losses stemmed from the purchase of Golden West, where credit losses on its option ARM (where the borrower can choose whether to amortize at all or even accumulate the interest due to the capital balance) were expected to rise to 22 percent of the balance outstanding.

22 July 2008: Washington Mutual (WaMu), the largest savings bank in the United States with assets over 300 billion dollars and also the sixth largest bank in the country, reports a loss of 4.4 billion dollars for the first half of 2008 due mainly to credit losses of 9.4 billion. Over the next weeks, depositors withdraw over 17 billion dollars (almost 10 percent) of deposits.

23/26 July 2008: The Housing and Economic Recovery Act is adopted by Congress to help Fannie Mae and Freddie Mac by loans and/ or capital. The new Federal Housing Finance Agency (FHFA) is appointed their regulator.

28 July 2008: Private equity firm Lone Star buys a nominal worth of 30.6 billion dollars of CDOs with subprime underlying from Merrill Lynch, implying a write-down in the third quarter of 4.4 billion dollars. Merrill also announces a planned issue of 8.5 billion in common stock.

31 July 2008: Deutsche Bank sees write-downs of 8 billion dollars (equivalent) for the first half of 2008.

26 August 2008: The Danish central bank (Nationalbanken) takes over Roskilde Bank, the tenth largest bank in Denmark, in the first Danish nationalization since 1928. Ownership is later transferred to the newly created agency Finansiel Stabilitet. Shareholders and holders of subordinated debt (Tier 2 capital) lose their investments while senior unsecured bondholders are protected.

31 August 2008: The German insurance company Allianz sells its subsidiary Dresdner Bank to Commerzbank for 9.8 billion euro, Dresdner writes down 1.3 billion dollars (equivalent) in bad loans.

6 September 2008: The CEO of Freddie Mac, Richard F. Syron, is dismissed with immediate effect. In 2007, his total compensation had been 19 million dollars. Together with the CEO of Fannie Mae, Daniel Mudd, and other senior executives of the two GSEs, he is charged in December 2011 by the SEC for securities fraud, in that they "knew and approved of misleading statements claiming the

companies had minimal exposure to subprime loans at the height of the home mortgage bubble."

7 September 2008: The US government seizes Freddie Mac and Fannie Mae, which are placed in public conservatorship under the Federal Housing Finance Agency. They get a capital injection of a maximum of 100 billion dollars each (later increased to 200 billion each). The US government will ultimately control up to 79.9 percent of the share capital in both organizations (above 80 percent ownership, they would have had to be integrated into the federal accounts). Under conservatorship, their liabilities are guaranteed by the US government. Senior management is replaced.

7 September 2008: Silver State Bank in Nevada becomes the eleventh victim in 2008 of the banking crisis.

8 September 2008: The long-term CEO and president of Washington Mutual (WaMu), Kerry Killinger, is fired by the board of directors, though leaving with a 15 million dollar severance payment. Its stock price had fallen from a peak of 45 dollars per share in 2006 to under 2 dollars (and would shortly become worthless). Simultaneously, WaMu signs a memorandum of understanding with its regulators, the OTC and the FDIC, on improving risk management.

9 September 2008: The news that a deal between the investment bank Lehman Brothers and the Korea Development Bank has fallen through leads to a 55 percent fall over the day in Lehman Brothers' share price. It also announces next day an estimated quarterly loss of 3.9 billion dollars, the worst in the company's history.

11 September 2008: Moody's downgrades the debt of Washington Mutual to "junk" status, leading to a run on the bank, 17 billion dollars' worth of deposits (12 percent of total deposits) being withdrawn in two weeks.

14 September 2008: The largest US investment bank, Merrill Lynch, is bought by Bank of America for 50 billion dollars or 29 dollars per share, a 70 percent premium over the latest closing price of 17 dollars per share. At year end 2006, the share price had been 256 dollars.

15 September 2008: The (now) smallest investment bank, Lehman Brothers seeks protection under Chapter 11. With 639 billion dollars in total assets, it is easily the biggest bankruptcy ever worldwide.

Its American "good" assets will later be purchased by Barclays for 1.75 billion dollars and its Asian operations by Nomura Securities. Since assets in London-based Lehman Brothers International are automatically frozen under British bankruptcy laws, own funds as well as customer funds, Lehman customers face severe liquidity problems.

15 September 2008: The Federal Reserve extends markedly the range of securities acceptable as collateral.

16 September 2008: The Reserve Primary Fund, a 62 billion dollar money market fund, severely hit by its investments in Lehman commercial paper, faces a run that causes it to "break the buck," its shares being priced under 1 dollar.

16 September 2008: The Federal Reserve extends a bridge loan of up to 85 billion dollars to the world's largest insurance company, AIG (American International Group), and takes the majority of its stock as collateral. Its share price had fallen by 61 percent in one single day of trading the day before to under 5 dollars (compared with an all-time high of almost 2,000 dollars). The interest rate charged is a hefty LIBOR plus 8.50 percentage points or, at the time, 11.50 percent. Support from the Fed and the Treasury in the form of capital and loans would ultimately reach 182 billion dollars. However, with a book of OTC derivatives of 2.7 trillion dollars, AIG was "too big to fail." Given its AAA rating, AIG had not had to post collateral – until it was downgraded. Its downgrading on September 15 (by 2–3 notches) had triggered demands for additional collateral on CDS contracts of 13 billion dollars to a total of 35 billion dollars. Nor had it set aside any reserves for the CDSs since it did not anticipate any losses.

17 September 2008: Lloyds TSB agrees to purchase the mortgage bank HBOS (Halifax Bank of Scotland) for 12 billion pounds, which would turn out to be a disastrous decision.

18 September 2008: The Federal Reserve extends its swap arrangements with other central banks (Bank of England, ECB, SNB and Bank of Sweden) by 180 billion dollars to 247 billion dollars.

18 September 2008: The British Financial Services Authority (FSA) forbids the short-selling of shares (both naked and covered) in 32 UK financial corporations. Ireland follows suit the day after. The US Securities and Exchange Commission (SEC) extends its earlier

ban from 15 July to cover both naked and covered short-selling of stocks in almost 800 US financial institutions.

18 September 2008: FDIC downgrades Washington Mutual's CAMELS rating from 3 to 4, thus putting it on the problem bank list. Although banks are not named on the list, the addition of a 300-billion-dollar-asset institution pinpoints WaMu and will almost certainly bring down the bank when the list is published at the end of September. The leniency of its main supervisor, OTS, up to this point may be explained by the fact that WaMu alone stood for 15 percent of the total revenue of its regulator.

19 September 2008: US Secretary of the Treasury Hank Paulson outlines a program of support for the banking system labeled TARP, "Troubled Assets Relief Program": 700 billion dollars will be spent to recapitalize banks or purchase mortgage-related assets. At the same time, short-selling of banking shares is temporarily outlawed. The amount covered by deposit insurance is temporarily raised from 100,000 to 250,000 dollars (an increase made permanent in July 2010).

19 September 2008: The Federal Reserve starts purchasing ABCP, Asset-Backed Commercial Paper. Financial as well as non-financial paper qualifies, provided it has a rating of not lower than A1 (Standard & Poor's), F1 (Fitch), P-1 (Moody's). By 19 November, 272 billion dollars' worth of paper had already been bought.

20 September 2008: Ireland unilaterally raises deposit insurance coverage from 20,000 to 100,000 euro. While stemming a public bank run, it did little to stem the outflow of wholesale deposits from Irish banks.

21 September 2008: The two remaining large investment banks Morgan Stanley and Goldman Sachs are accepted as bank holding companies by the Federal Reserve. This implies that the Fed rather than the SEC will be their main supervisor in the future and gives them the borrowing rights of commercial banks. Also, they can participate in the TARP program.

22 September 2008: The largest bank in Japan, Mitsubishi UFG, buys stock in Morgan Stanley for 9 billion dollars, corresponding to 21 percent of the share capital. Later on, the investment is converted to preference shares.

24 September 2008: The billionaire Warren Buffet's Berkshire Hathaway buys 9 percent of the stock in Goldman Sachs, preferred stock with a dividend of 10 percent, with an option for a further

5 percent. At the same time, Goldman issues new stock for an additional 5 percent of its capital.

25–6 September 2008: The Office of Thrift Supervision (OTS) seizes Washington Mutual (WaMu), placing it in receivership under the FDIC. With assets of more than 300 billion dollars, it is easily the largest bank failure in American history and the second largest bankruptcy ever (after Lehman brothers). Next day, JPMorgan Chase purchases the banking activities for 1.9 billion dollars while the holding company seeks protection under Chapter 11. In sharp contrast to the handling of creditors of AIG and Bear Stearns, unsecured and subordinated creditors in WaMu were not bailed out, even senior creditors receiving only 55 percent of the nominal value of the bonds, 2 billion dollars in preferred shares and over 20 billion dollars of bonds being wiped out. The CEO of Washington Mutual, Alan Fishman, resigns after only 17 days in his post with salary and signing bonus of 7.5 million dollars, amounting to half a million dollars in salary per working day. He abstains, however, from the severance pay to which he was formally entitled.

26 September 2008: The sale of Washington Mutual and the loss enforced upon unsecured creditors leads to a run on Wachovia, the fourth largest American bank at end 2007. In one day, it lost almost 7 billion dollars of deposits and commercial paper and faced demands from creditors for immediate repayment of 50–60 billion dollars. The value of its 10-year bonds fell from 73 to 29 percent of nominal value and its share price by 27 percent.

26 September 2008: The Federal Reserves's swap lines with other central banks are increased to 290 billion dollars.

26 September 2008: Newspaper reports of problems lead to a run on Fortis Bank, losing 20 billion euro in deposits that day.

28 September 2008: The Benelux authorities partly nationalize Fortis Bank for a sum of 11.2 billion euro paid to the existing shareholders (Belgium 4.7 billion, the Netherlands 4.0 and Luxembourg 2.5), representing 49.9 percent of total equity.

28 September 2008: The Swedish central bank grants a credit of 2.4 billion SEK to troubled Carnegie Investment Bank. The bank was later nationalized on 10 November.

29 September 2008: The Federal Reserve increases to 620 billion dollars the amounts placed at the disposal of some foreign central

banks by means of swap arrangements: Bank of Canada, Bank of Japan, Bank of England, Bank of Denmark, Bank of Norway, Bank of Sweden, Schweizerische Nationalbank (SNB) and the ECB.

29 September 2008: The US House of Representatives rejects the government's TARP plan, which leads to a collapse in share prices: Dow Jones −7.0 percent, NASDAQ −9.1 percent and S&P 500 −8.8 percent in one single day. For Dow, the fall by 778 points was the largest fall ever in points (though vastly overshadowed in percentage terms by the 22.6 percent fall on "Black Monday," 19 October 1987).

29 September 2008: Great Britain nationalizes the mortgage lender Bradford & Bingley after a run on the bank had cost it tens of millions of pounds. The bank gets a bridge loan from the Bank of England of 17.9 billion pounds. The 197 branch offices and 20 billion pounds worth of deposits are sold to Abbey National (owned by the Spanish bank Grupo Santander) for 612 million pounds while the troubled mortgage book is taken over by the state.

29 September 2008: Wachovia agrees to be taken over by Citigroup for 2.2 billion dollars in cash, 1 dollar per share. Citi will take the first 42 billion dollars in losses and FDIC only losses above that amount, receiving preferred stock of 12 billion dollars in Citi in return. On 2 October, however, Wells Fargo bids 15.4 billion dollars (in stock), a bid which moreover does not require the support by the FDIC (see below, 30 September). Wells Fargo wins, despite a court challenge by Citigroup. The failure by Citi to conclude the merger and expand its deposit base led to an immediate fall in its share price by 18 percent, and 43 percent within the week.

29 September 2008: The Icelandic Glitnir bank receives support funding of 864 million dollars (equivalent) from the government, which thereby takes a 75 percent stake in the bank.

29 September 2008: The major mortgage bank in Germany, Hypo Real Estate, gets financial support of 35 billion euro by a consortium consisting of the ECB, the Bundesbank and some commercial banks. A week later, the loan volume is raised to 50 billion, of which 20 are from the Bundesbank.

29 September 2008: Bloomberg reports that since mid 2007, banks worldwide have written down 591 billion dollars in assets but

raised 434 billion dollars in common stock, preferred shares, subordinated and hybrid debt that count as Tier 1 or Tier 2 capital.

30 September 2008: The reason for the renewed interest by Wells Fargo in Wachovia is a new ruling by the Internal Revenue Service (IRS) that an acquiring bank can offset its operating profits by losses sustained by the acquired bank even prior to the acquisition. Under the old rule, Wells Fargo would have had the possibility of deducting only 18.6 billion of Wachovia's losses but spread out over 20 years. With the new rule, it could utilize all of Wachovia's 74 billion dollar loss for an immediate tax saving of 19.4 billion (to be compared with the 15.4 billion it paid for Wachovia).

30 September 2008: The French-Belgian bank Dexia (ex-Crédit Local and Crédit Communal) gets an injection of new capital of 6.4 billion euro (9.2 billion dollars) by the French (3 billion), Luxembourg (0.4 billion) and Belgian (3 billion) states. It also receives guarantees for its liabilities of up to 150 billion euro (on 9 October). In return, it has to sell assets in Spain, Italy and Slovakia, wind down its operations in the United States (FSA) and shrink its balance sheet by 35 percent, decrees the EU Commission. The chairman, Pierre Richard, and CEO, Alex Miller, are both dismissed, the former being replaced by the respected former prime minister of Belgium, Jean-Luc Dehaene. In a short period of time, 15 billion euro, almost 10 percent of deposits, have been withdrawn in a silent bank run.

30 September 2008: As the first country in the European Union, Ireland extends its deposit insurance to cover an unlimited amount, including not only deposits but also bank bonds and dated subordinated debt (thus excluding perpetual floating rate notes (FRNs) used as upper Tier 2 capital). Liabilities worth 440 billion euro are guaranteed for two years in the six major domestic banks and building societies, a sum corresponding to 287 percent of Ireland's then GDP. Greece follows suit. The European Commission claims that this action is in violation of the free movement of capital but cannot act when a few days later some other countries, including Austria, Germany, Belgium and Denmark, follow the example. Ireland is, however, forced after pressure to include also foreign-owned Irish subsidiaries in the scheme, not only Irish-owned banks.

30 September 2008: "The National Debt Clock" on Times Square in New York registers 10 trillion dollars, 10,000,000,000,000.

1 October 2008: The Senate of the United States votes 74-25 in favor of a revised version of the TARP program, the House of Representatives follows suit on 3 October (263-171).

3 October 2008: President Bush signs the Emergency Economic Stabilization Act, authorizing the spending of 700 billion dollars under TARP.

3 October 2008: The Netherlands buys the Dutch part of Fortis Bank for 16.8 billion euro, 12.8 billion for the bank, i.e. the Dutch remainder of ABN AMRO, and 4 billion to Fortis Holding for the Dutch insurance business, in violation of the agreement of 28 September, angering Belgium.

3 October 2008: Wachovia and Wells Fargo announce their merger (see above, 29 September).

5 October 2008: BNP Paribas purchases most of the nationalized Belgian (75 percent) and Luxembourg (66 percent) parts of Fortis for 11 billion euro in new stock, making the state of Belgium the largest shareholder of BNP with 12 percent and making BNP Paribas the biggest bank by deposits in the euro area. The deal is blocked, however, by a court order on initiative of angry shareholders and not approved until April 2009.

6–10 October 2008: The largest fall in stock prices over a week since the Depression occurs. Dow Jones falls –22.1 percent and Standard & Poor's –18.2 percent during the week. In London, FTSE 100 falls by –21.1 percent, in Frankfurt DAX falls by –21.6 percent and in Tokyo, Nikkei 225 falls by –24.3 percent.

6 October 2008: The Federal Reserve raises the amount of credit granted to member banks to 900 billion dollars. It also starts paying interest on the banks' reserves in the central bank.

6 October 2008: Bank of America makes some changes in the terms of condition for loans to 400,000 customers taken over from Countrywide Financial, thus avoiding being sued for predatory pricing.

6 October 2008: The Danish government guarantees all domestic bank deposits. Banks must, however, themselves build up a fund of 6.5 billion dollars (equivalent) to save banks in trouble.

6 October 2008: The Icelandic government announces measures to combat its exploding financial crisis and the falling krona. Strict

capital controls on outflows are instituted by the central bank. The Financial Supervisory Authority (FME) is given the right to nationalize banks or put them into receivership without nationalization. All deposits of Icelandic branches of Icelandic banks are guaranteed fully, thus excluding Landsbanki's "Icesave" accounts as well as Kauphing Edge accounts, held by British, Dutch and German nationals. Trading in all bank shares is suspended.

6 October 2008: The German government and a consortium of banks increase guarantees in Hypo Real Estate to 50 billion euro. Its CEO resigns.

7 October 2008: Lending by the Federal Reserve to its member banks rises to 1.3 trillion dollars.

7 October 2008: Royal Bank of Scotland (RBS), finding normal supplies of liquidity insufficient, receives support from the Bank of England under the Emergency Liquidity Assistance (ELA) program. On that day alone, it lost 6 billion pounds in customer deposits.

7 October 2008: The Federal Reserve allows commercial paper to be used as collateral for borrowings from the Fed. Potentially, this means that the Fed is guaranteeing a market of 2,400 billion dollars.

7 October 2008: The Financial Supervisory Authority of Iceland (FME) takes over the banks Landsbanki and Glitnir; the Swedish subsidiary of the latter is later sold to HQ Bank and its Norwegian subsidiary to the Sparebank1-group. British, German and Dutch depositors lose an estimated 6.7 billion euro on their Landsbanki "Icesave" internet accounts, a sum repaid by the respective governments, setting up a dispute on accountability between Iceland and the three governments. Iceland would later be found to have acted correctly by the EFTA Court of Justice (see 28 January 2013).

7 October 2008: The European Union raises the minimum coverage in the deposit guarantee scheme from 20,000 to 50,000 euro.

7 October 2008: Merrill Lynch succeeds in raising 10 billion dollars in fresh equity.

8 October 2008: Moody's lowers the rating of Ireland two steps, from Aa2 to A1.

8 October 2008: A number of central banks lower their interest rates in a concerted action: the Federal Reserve, the Bank of England,

the Reserve Bank of Canada, the Bank of Sweden, Schweizerische Nationalbank, the ECB and the People's Bank of China.

8 October 2008: The UK government promises a 500 billion pound rescue package for the financial sector: loans 200 billion, guarantees 250 billion and recapitalization 50 billion, of which 25 billion in common stock and 5 billion in preference shares.

8 October 2008: The Icelandic Financial Supervisory Authority nationalizes the largest bank, Kaupthing. Its British subsidiary Singer & Friedlander is nationalized by Britain. All British assets of the three Icelandic banks as well as those of the government and central bank of Iceland are frozen under the Anti-Terrorism, Crime and Security Act of 2001. Singer & Friedlander is placed under administration. Deposits in Kauthing Edge, a subsidiary of Singer & Friedlander, were later sold to the internet bank ING Direct. Kaupthing's Swedish subsidiary receives a loan of 5 billion Swedish kronor from the Swedish central bank. Heritable Bank, a subsidiary of Landsbanki, is seized and its deposits later sold to ING Direct.

9 October 2008: The government of Italy announces that no Italian bank will be allowed to fail, no depositor will lose money.

11 October 2008: The leaders of the seven major countries in the world (G-7) meet in Washington but no concrete decisions are taken.

11 October 2008: The CEO of Royal Bank of Scotland, Sir Fred Goodwin, announces his intention to step down at year end. This statement came two days before the bank was effectively nationalized.

12 October 2008: The prime minister of Australia extends the deposit-guarantee scheme with a fee-based guarantee for Australian wholesale debt securities.

13 October 2008: Meeting with the Treasury's Hank Paulson, the CEOs of nine major US banks accept to receive a combined 125 billion dollars in new capital under the TARP program: Jamie Dimon, JPMorgan Chase (25 billion), Richard Kovacevich, Wells Fargo (25 billion), Vikram Pandit, Citigroup (25 billion), Kenneth Lewis, Bank of America (15 billion), John Thain, Merrill Lynch (10 billion), Lloyd Blankfein, Goldman Sachs (10 billion), John Mack, Morgan Stanley (10 billion), Robert Kelly, Bank of New York Mellon (3 billion), Ronald Logue, State Street Bank (2 billion). All

banks had been forced to participate to avoid stigmatizing those who really needed the injection, especially Citi. The Treasury will hold preferred non-voting stock yielding 5 percent interest (rising to 9 percent after five years) plus warrants to purchase common stock. By December 2010, all the nine banks had repaid the TARP money with a good return to the taxpayer. Of the nine participating CEOs, four will be gone within the year and only two remain in power five years later, Jamie Dimon of JPMorgan Chase and Lloyd Blankfein of Goldman Sachs. The Treasury would invest a total of 205 billion dollars in 707 participating banks under the TARP program to which should be added 40 billion to AIG and 81 billion to GM and Chrysler and their respective finance companies.

13 October 2008: The French president Sarkozy promises to guarantee French banks' borrowing up to 320 billion euro and sets aside 40 billion euro for recapitalizing the banking system.

13 October 2008: The Spanish prime minister Zapatero promises to guarantee banks' borrowing up to 100 billion euro.

13 October 2008: The Netherlands will guarantee bank borrowing for 200 billion euro and set up a fund for recapitalization of banks of 20 billion euro.

13 October 2008: Germany follows up with 400 billion euro in guaranteed bank borrowing and 70 billion euro for the recapitalization of banks. SoFFin (Sonderfonds Finanzmarkt-stabilisierung) is set up by the Bundestag.

13 October 2008: The British government announces injections of capital into Royal Bank of Scotland (RBS), Lloyds TSB and Halifax Bank of Scotland (HBOS) totaling 37 billion pounds, of which 20 billion in RBS (later raised to 25.5 billion) and 17 billion in the merged Lloyds TSB-HBOS (renamed the Lloyds Banking Group). The state will thereby become a majority owner of RBS with 58 percent of the share capital, later rising to 82 percent, and 43 percent of Lloyds. The chairman of RBS, Sir Tom McKillop, announces his early retirement.

13 October 2008: Denmark establishes a state-owned institution for failed and nationalized banks, Finansiel stabilitet. Two years later, it owned, inter alia, Roskilde Bank, Fionia Bank, EBH Bank and some small savings banks; in all, 12 banks had been taken over (and 12 others merged with stronger partners).

13 October 2008: The ECB announces that it will lend an indefinite amount (sic) at the refi rate of interest.

13 October 2008: The Federal Reserve extends the swap arrangements with the above-mentioned central banks (Bank of England, ECB, SNB) to the amounts demanded without limitations. This means that these central banks can lend an infinite amount also in dollars.

13 October 2008: The Japanese bank Mitsubishi UFJ purchases 21 percent of Morgan Stanley, an investment of 9 billion dollars, of which 7.8 billion in preferred but convertible stock at a dividend of 10 percent and 1.2 billion in preferred non-convertible shares. Since both the US and Japan were closed for Columbus Day, payment was made by the largest check ever written, for 9 billion dollars.

14 October 2008: Under the Temporary Liquidity Guarantee program (TLGP), FDIC extends guarantees of up to 1,400 billion dollars against a fee of between 0.5 and 1.0 percent, depending on the bank's capital strength. TLGP has two components: the Debt Guarantee Program, by which the FDIC will guarantee the payment of certain newly issued senior unsecured debt, and the Transaction Account Guarantee Program, by which the FDIC will guarantee certain non-interest-bearing deposits.

16 October 2008: The Swiss bank UBS reaches an agreement with its central bank SNB whereby 60 billion dollars in illiquid US mortgage bonds are shifted to a "bad bank" ("Stabfund") capitalized by the SNB but run by UBS.

19 October 2008: The Dutch state injects 10 billion euro of new capital into ING Groep on condition that the group divest its insurance and asset management arms. By 2013, most of the aid had been repaid.

20 October 2008: The Swedish government proposes a plan for "safeguarding the stability of the financial system." New bank borrowing is guaranteed up to 1,500 billion SEK (190 billion dollars) against a fee. Only Swedbank joins the program initially, SEB joins in April 2009.

20 October 2008: France wants to give its banks capital support of 10.5 billion euro: Crédit Agricole (3 billion), BNP Paribas (2.5 billion), Société Générale (1.7 billion), Crédit Mutuel (1.2 billion), Caisses d'épargne (savings banks, 1.1 billion) and Banque Populaire

(950 million). The program is, however, initially stopped by the EU Commission on ground of distorted competition but is later accepted (8 December).

21 October 2008: The Federal Reserve sets up the facility MMIFF, Money Market Investor Funding Facility, whereby money-market funds may separate out their "toxic assets" to a special Structured Investment Vehicle, guaranteed by the Federal Reserve Bank of New York.

9–22 October 2008: The domestic parts of Iceland's three major banks are restarted with government money: NBI (Nýí Landsbanki) was set up with 200 billion kronúr in equity and 2,300 billion in assets, Nýí Glitnir with 110 billion kronúr in equity and 1,200 billion in assets, Nýja Kaupthing with 75 billion in equity and 700 billion in assets. Assets in foreign currency were left out and regarded as totally inadequate to repay foreign depositors. The combined assets of the three new banks, 4,200 billion kronúr or 35 billion dollars at the ruling exchange rate (the kronúr having depreciated by 50 percent), may be compared to the 184 billion dollars the three banks held at year end 2007 (according to *The Banker*, July 2008), over 10 times Iceland's GDP.

24 October 2008: The volatility index VIX on the Standard & Poor 500 index reaches 90 percent, its highest value ever.

24 October 2008: Iceland receives a loan from the IMF of 2.1 billion dollars. It is the first developed nation to borrow from the IMF since Britain did so in 1976. The other Nordic countries and Poland add another 3 billion dollars.

24 October 2008: PNC Financial Services buys National City Bank of Cleveland, Ohio, which otherwise would have gone bankrupt, in a deal worth 5.6 billion dollars. The bank was one of the major lenders in the subprime market.

26 October 2008: The IMF gives Ukraine a loan amounting to 16.5 billion dollars.

27 October 2008: 21 intermediate-size American banks share 38 billion dollars in capital support under the TARP program: PNC Financial Services (7.7 billion), Capital One (3.55 billion), Fifth Third (3.45 billion), Regions Financial (3.5 billion), Suntrust (3.5 billion), BB&T

(3.1 billion), Key Corp (2.5 billion), Comerica (2.25 billion), Marchhall & Ilsley Corp (1.7 billion), Northern Trust Corp (1.5 billion), Huntington Bancshares (1.4 billion), Zions Bancorp (1.4 billion), First Horizon National (866 million), City National Corp (395 million), Valley National Bancorp (330 million), UCBH Holdings Inc (298 million), Umpqua Holdings Corp (214 million), Washington Federal (200 million), First Niagara Financial (186 million), HF Financial Corp (25 million) and Bank of Commerce (17 million).

28 October 2008: The IMF, the EU and the World Bank lend a total of 24.8 billion dollars to Hungary.

29 October 2008: The ECB announces that its lending operations have risen to 773.7 billion euro, or an equivalent of exactly 1 trillion (1,000,000,000,000) dollars, excluding the lending in dollars under the swap arrangement with the Federal Reserve.

31 October 2008: Barclays Bank avoids using the government support program by issuing 7 billion pounds (11.8 billion dollars) in preference shares (at an interest rate of 14 percent) to investors in Abu Dhabi and Qatar. Protests from shareholders make it doubtful if the issue will be accepted.

1 November 2008: Freedom Bank in Florida becomes the seventeenth bankrupt bank in 2008 and is placed under conservatorship, its deposits being taken over by Fifth Third Bank in Michigan.

3 November 2008: Germany's largest bank, Commerzbank, which had recently bought Dresdner Bank, gets a capital injection of 8.2 billion euro by the German state. Deutsche Bank avoids government support by switching accounting principles, thereby avoiding marking some assets to market.

3 November 2008: UK Financial Investments (UKFI) is set up to handle the government's shares in RBS and Lloyds Banking Group.

7 November 2008: The Federal Housing Finance Agency decides to temporarily raise the limit for mortgage loans underlying the CDOs or MBSs that Fannie Mae and Freddie Mac can purchase or guarantee from 417,000 to 625,500 dollars. Other loans are "jumbos" and disallowed for investment.

8 November 2008: Security Pacific Bank in Los Angeles becomes the year's nineteenth victim of the banking crisis.

8 November 2008: The Latvian government nationalizes the country's largest bank, Parex Bank, paying a symbolic 2 lats (4 dollars) for 51 percent of the stock.

10 November 2008: The support to AIG is extended and changed after losses of 24.5 billion dollars for the third quarter have been reported. The insurance company gets a capital injection of 40 billion dollars under TARP and the credit line is increased to 112.5 billion dollars. The interest rate is lowered from LIBOR + 8.5 percent to LIBOR + 3 percent.

10 November 2008: The credit card company American Express becomes a bank and can henceforth get access to TARP money.

10 November 2008: HSBC announces credit write-downs for the third quarter of 4.3 billion dollars and altogether, since the start of the crisis 38 billion dollars, most of it related to its US subsidiary.

10 November 2008: Fannie Mae takes losses of 21.4 billion dollars for the third quarter, the bank forecasts becoming insolvent by the end of the year, forcing capital injections under the 100 billion dollars available for capital support.

10 November 2008: The Federal Reserve refuses to say which banks are the borrowers of its lending programs now totaling almost 2 trillion dollars. The decision is charged in court by the news agency Bloomberg.

10 November 2008: The Swedish bank resolution agency, the National Debt Office, seizes control of Carnegie Investment Bank on account of its bad risk management and lack of control of major credits. The bank is sold in January 2009 to private equity firms Altor and Bure Equity.

11 November 2008: The EU Commission establishes a working party to harmonize financial supervision among the member countries.

11 November 2008: Fannie Mae eases terms for hard-hit borrowers. They may get a reduction of the rate of interest or the amount borrowed, provided they are more than 90 days delinquent and the sum of interest and amortization exceeds 38 percent of their disposable income.

12 November 2008: The Treasury department makes a U-turn concerning how the 700 billion dollars of TARP money is to be spent. Purchases of mortgage-related securities are no longer contemplated

but the entire sum is to be used to recapitalize financial institutions and help homeowners directly.

12 November 2008: GE Capital is allowed to join the FDIC's Temporary Liquidity Guarantee Program despite not being a bank. It would ultimately issue 70 billion dollars under the government guarantee, its parent company GE, one of the few remaining AAA-rated companies, promising to indemnify the FDIC against any losses.

13 November 2008: Dexia Credit Local sells its US subsidiary Financial Security Assurance (FSA), one of the four big monoline insurers, to Assured Guaranty for 1 billion dollars but the deal specifically excludes the financial products division. During 2008, Dexia has already recapitalized its American subsidiary by 800 million dollars.

14 November 2008: Freddie Mac writes down 20 billion dollars for the third quarter and seeks an injection of 13.8 billion dollars out of the 100 billion dollars granted by the government.

15 November 2008: By buying the small bank Federal Trust in Florida for 10 million dollars, the insurance company Hartford Financial Services, one of the largest in the United States, transforms itself into a banking conglomerate, thereby being able to access money from the Federal Reserve's TAF (Term Auction Facility). It also calculates on receiving 1–3 billion dollars in new capital under TARP.

15 November 2008: The leaders of G-20 gather in Washington to discuss the economic and financial crisis but take no decisions.

16 November 2008: The top executives of Goldman Sachs, including CEO Lloyd Blankfein and CFO David Viniar, announce that they will not accept any bonus for 2008.

19 November 2008 – 31 December 2008: The Fed allows AIG to repay its counterparties in securities lending and Credit Default Swaps in full: 71 billion dollars plus the 35 billion that the institutions already held in collateral for a total of 106 billion dollars. A public outcry ensued, in particular since some of the major receivers were foreign banks such as Société Générale (receiving 17.4 billion), Deutsche Bank (14.0 billion), Barclays (8.5 billion), BNP Paribas (4.9 billion) or investment banks, recently converted to banks, such as Goldman Sachs (18.8 billion).

19 November 2008: Iceland receives a support package of 5.1 billion dollars, of which 2.1 billion is from the IMF and 3 billion in bilateral

aid from the other Nordic countries. Iceland becomes the first West European country to receive IMF aid since Britain in 1976. The Icelandic inflation rate after the depreciation reaches over 17 percent.

19 November 2008: Citibank transfers CDOs worth over 17 billion dollars from its SIV onto its own books. Its share price drops by 23 percent the next day and by 60 percent for the week. The market for Credit Default Swaps indicates a 25 percent probability that Citigroup will become bankrupt within five years.

21 November 2008: The Treasury announces that a total of 36.5 billion dollars in TARP money has been paid to 44 medium-sized banks.

23 November 2008: The FDIC, the Federal Reserve and the Treasury save Citigroup by giving it a further 20 billion dollars in capital on top of the earlier 25 billion under the TARP program. During the five quarters from 2007: IV to 2008: IV, the bank had run up 29 billion dollars in losses. The three supervisors will also guarantee 306 billion dollars of "toxic assets." Citi will take the first 37 billion dollars of losses, thereafter the FDIC will bear 90 percent of further losses, maximized at 10 billion dollars, with the Federal Reserve taking any further losses. The authorities are paid by receiving 7 billion dollars' worth of preference shares, yielding 8 percent interest, plus warrants corresponding to over 4 percent of common stock. The share price of Citigroup rises 62 percent on the news (but it had fallen from 60 dollars per share to under 4 dollars at this time).

25 November 2008: The Federal Reserve agrees to take on 800 billion dollars in risk by purchasing bonds. It will buy up to 100 billion dollars in bonds issued by Fannie Mae or Freddie Mac and up to 600 billion dollars in MBSs guaranteed by Fannie Mae or Freddie Mac. Moreover, under its new program, Term Asset-Backed Securities Loan Facility (TALF), the Fed will buy up to 200 billion dollars of AAA-rated bonds or paper guaranteed by the Small Business Administration and containing loans to education, car loans and credit card loans. The result was a marked decrease in the 30-year mortgage rate of interest from 6.38 percent to 5.70 percent.

27 November 2008: Three former top executives of the Swiss bank UBS voluntarily repay bonuses received to the tune of 58 million dollars (equivalent).

28 November 2008: Bayern LB receives 7 billion euro in capital support from its major owner, the state of Bavaria, the federal stability

fund SoFFin ("Sonderfonds Finanzmarktstabilisierung") adding 15 billion euro in guarantees.

1 December 2008: The London Scottish bank is seized by the British government and placed in administration.

9 December 2008: The chairman of the Federal Reserve, Ben Bernanke, writes a letter to Congress stating that the Federal Reserve Act will not allow it to act as "lender of last resort" to the auto industry.

12 December 2008: Sanderson state bank in Texas becomes the twenty-eighth victim of the crisis, the twenty-fifth and final for the year 2008.

12 December 2008: A court in Belgium stops the purchase by BNP Paribas of Fortis, awaiting shareholders' approval.

12 December 2008: The European Commission accepts the French proposal for the recapitalization of the six major banking groups.

15 December 2008: Great Britain lowers the fees for banks using its 250 billion pound guarantee program, also extending the guarantee to five years from three years.

15 December 2008: Ireland proposes to use up 10 billion euro to recapitalize its six biggest banks: 3.5 billion (later lowered to 2 billion) each for Bank of Ireland and Allied Irish Banks (AIB) and 1.5 billion for Anglo Irish Bank. The first two banks claim they don't need it.

18 December 2008: Credit Suisse takes the innovative step of paying this year's bonuses in illiquid American CDOs of doubtful value.

19 December 2008: The Belgian government is forced to resign on account of the "Fortis affair."

19–20 December 2008: The chairman and CEO of Anglo Irish Bank both resign on account of the "loans to directors" affair.

19 December 2008: Two of America's biggest car companies are bailed out with TARP money. GM receives a loan of 13.4 billion dollars and Chrysler 4 billion.

22 December 2008: Darrel Dochow, the OTS (Office of Thrift Supervision) director responsible for supervision of savings banks in 10 western states, among them California, is removed from office after the failures of IndyMac and Washington Mutual. He is, however, allowed to retire and is never charged by the (now defunct) OTS or the Treasury with any misdemeanor or regulatory offense.

24 December 2008: GMAC, General Motors Acceptance Corporation, is transformed into a bank and gets an immediate capital injection from TARP of 5 billion dollars. Chrysler Financial follows suit on 16 January 2009 and receives 1.5 billion.

28 December 2008: The Bank of England estimates the losses to the world's banks for the crisis at 1.8 trillion pounds, which would turn out to be very close to the mark.

29 December 2008: Merrill Lynch, which was to become a part of Bank of America by the end of the year, pays out 4 billion dollars in bonuses, one month earlier than normal.

29 December 2008: GMAC receives 5 billion dollars of TARP money.

31 December 2008: The Austrian authorities seize control of Bank Medici, which had invested its own and client money in the bankrupt US investment firm owned by Bernard Madoff.

2 January 2009: The bankrupt IndyMac bank is sold by its conservator, the FDIC, to a private equity group led by Dune Capital Management and J. C. Flowers.

8 January 2009: Commerzbank receives another 8.2 billion euro in loans and 1.8 billion euro in new equity from SoFFin to ensure that its solvency ratio does not fall short of 10 percent even after the purchase of Dresdner Bank from the insurance company Allianz. The state thereby becomes the largest shareholder of the bank with a 25 percent stake.

9 January 2009: The chairman of the Irish Financial Services Regulatory Authority, Patrick Neary, is forced to retire ahead of time.

15 January 2009: The Senate votes to release the second half of the 700 billion dollars allocated under TARP.

15 January 2009: Bank of America (BofA), which has already received 25 billion dollars of TARP money, gets a further injection of 20 billion dollars in preferred stock plus a guarantee for 118 billion in "toxic assets," on and off balance, mainly the heritage of Merrill Lynch. BofA will take the first 10 billion in losses and 10 percent above that, the FDIC and the Treasury will take the next 20 billion. The guarantee quickly turned out to be unnecessary but the government insisted on its fee (425 million dollars) anyway. The same day, BoA releases its earnings for the fourth quarter of 2008; of the total loss of some 24 billion dollars, 22 billion were attributed to

Merrill Lynch. The injection of the 20 billion was a verbal promise from Treasury Secretary Hank Paulson and Fed chairman Ben Bernanke in December 2008 to prevent BofA from backing out of the purchase of Merrill Lynch, citing materially changed conditions.

16 January 2009: The Irish government nationalizes the Anglo Irish Bank instead of simply recapitalizing it, finding the proposed 1.5 billion euro far too little.

16 January 2009: Merrill Lynch repays 550 million dollars to investors in its stock. Thus the company avoids being sued for "issuing false and misleading statements about collateralized debt obligations and other assets backed by subprime mortgages, artificially inflating Merrill Lynch's shares."

16 January 2009: National Bank of Commerce in Illinois and Bank of Clark County in Washington are closed by the FDIC, the first victims of the New Year. This year 138 more banks will follow them into bankruptcy.

19 January 2009: The British government extends its ownership of the Royal Bank of Scotland by exchanging preference shares for common stock. The stake owned by the government increases from 58 to almost 70 percent. Simultaneously, a new program ("Asset Protection Scheme") is set up under which the government takes 90 percent of losses on the portfolios of "toxic assets," provided banks promise to increase their lending.

20 January 2009: The French government injects a further 10.5 billion euro into the six largest banks, provided their top managers abstain from bonuses.

20 January 2009: The Icelandic government foresees a negative growth of almost −10 percent for 2010. The actual growth turned out to be −6.6 percent with another −4.1 percent in 2010.

21 January 2009: German Hypo Real Estate gets another 12 billion euro in guarantees from SoFFin.

22 January 2009: John Thain, the former CEO of Merrill Lynch, is fired by Bank of America as it turns out that he has (a) purposely underestimated the losses for the fourth quarter in order to complete the merger, these losses turning out to be 15.4 billion dollars, almost 22 billion dollars before tax; (b) given the top managers of Merrill Lynch bonuses worth 4 billion dollars one month earlier

than usual, three days before the completion of the merger; (c) redecorated his personal Merrill Lynch office for 1.2 million dollars while losses exploded. John Thain would later be hired as chairman and CEO of the CIT group bank. Bank of America would pay a fine of 33 million dollars to the SEC for not properly informing investors about the ability of Merrill Lynch to pay bonuses under the merger agreement.

27 January 2009: New York's district attorney Andrew Cuomo issues a subpoena to John Thain and Kenneth Lewis, CEO of Bank of America, in order to discover the circumstances surrounding the bonus payments.

29 January 2009: President Obama criticizes Wall Street bonus payments for 2008 of a total of 17.4 billion dollars, to be compared with 34.3 billion and 33 billion dollars, respectively, for the two preceding years.

2 February 2009: The Bank of England commences to purchase corporate bonds, syndicated loans and commercial paper with top rating, for a maximum of 50 billion pounds.

3 February 2009: Sweden announces a plan to use up to 50 billion SEK (6.3 billion dollars) to recapitalize banks. The participants are placed under restrictions not to raise salaries or give bonuses to top management.

4 February 2009: President Obama decides that banks receiving support from the government must limit the top management's salary to a maximum of 500,000 dollars. Amounts above may be given in the form of shares to be sold only when all government support has been repaid.

10 February 2009: The new Treasury secretary of the United States, Tim Geithner, presents a plan for how the residual TARP money is to be spent. A combination of private and public initiatives will purchase delinquent loans of up to 1,000 billion dollars from the banking system. The proposal is considered too vague in not answering the question whether undercapitalized banks will be nationalized or closed. US stock markets fell by −5 percent on the proposal.

11 February 2009: Ireland injects 1.5 billion euro in new capital into each of Bank of Ireland and Allied Irish Banks (AIB).

12 February 2009: The director of the Office of Thrift Supervision (OTS), John Reich, steps down after the failures of OTS-supervised AIG, Countrywide, IndyMac and Washington Mutual. OTS itself is later folded into the OCC.

20 February 2009: Nationalized Anglo Irish Bank reveals that it lent 451 million euro to ten customers to buy shares in the bank.

23 February 2009: Prime Minister Gordon Brown proposes that in future mortgage loans are to be restricted to 95 percent of the value of the property, i.e. buyers must pay at least 5 percent down in cash.

23 February 2009: In a joint statement by the US Treasury, the Federal Reserve, the FDIC, the OCC and the OTS, the pledge is made to capitalize the major US financial institutions with government capital (TARP) to attain the desired level and keep them well-capitalized should they fail to raise sufficient capital privately. No limit is mentioned on the potential capital or liquidity support from the Treasury and the Federal Reserve, respectively.

24 February 2009: Share prices of Bank of America and Citigroup rise by over 20 percent after the statement by the Fed chairman, Ben Bernanke, that the supervisory authorities do not plan to nationalize banks in crisis but continue to support them by purchases of preference shares.

24 February 2009: The authorities seize the ninth largest bank in Denmark, Fionia Bank in Odense, which gets a capital support of 1 billion DKK. It is the third Danish bank to be nationalized during the crisis.

24 February 2009: HSH Nordbank, the Landesbank of Hamburg and Schleswig-Holsten, receives 3 billion euro in capital and 10 billion in guarantees from its owners as well as 17 billion euro in federal guarantees (under a total potential of 30 billion decided in December 2008). Its CEO was dismissed in October 2008.

25 February 2009: The US begins an investigation of the 19 largest banks, those with assets above 100 billion dollars, in order to ascertain by means of stress tests (so-called "Supervisory Capital Assessment Programs," SCAP) whether they will need to hold more capital.

26 February 2009: The Royal Bank of Scotland (RBS) reports a loss of 24 billion pounds for 2008, the biggest loss ever reported by a British company.

26 February 2009: RBS, already 70 percent owned by the government, utilizes the state guarantee to insure 325 billion pounds of assets. RBS will take the first 19.5 billion pounds in losses plus 10 percent of the residual. The fee to the government of 6.5 billion pounds in stock and a recapitalization of 13 billion pounds will lead to the state owning 84 percent of the bank when/if the preference shares are converted to common stock. Moreover, a "bad bank" is set up to handle assets worth a nominal 540 billion pounds.

26 February 2009: The partly nationalized American mortgage bank Fannie Mae reports a loss for the fourth quarter of 25.2 billion dollars, bringing the loss for the full year to 58.7 billion. The bank needs 15.2 billion dollars in new capital from the state to avoid equity from becoming negative.

27 February 2009: The US government and Citigroup agree that up to 25 billion dollars of preference shares held by the government be converted to common stock, raising the stake of the government in the bank to 36 percent. Citi's share price falls by an identical proportion on the news.

27 February 2009: The third-largest Austrian Bank, Erste Bank, gets a capital injection of 1.9 billion euro from the federal state in the form of preferred shares yielding 8 percent interest.

2 March 2009: The insurance company AIG which has already received 152.5 billion dollars in support (capital and loans) gets another 30 billion dollars from the Fed. At the same time, the state converts its 70 billion dollars' worth of preference shares to common stock in order to strengthen its control over the company. The loss for the year 2008 is reported at almost 100 billion dollars, the largest loss ever reported by any company in the world. The person most responsible, Joseph Cassano, head of the (basically unregulated) AIG Financial Products Division in London, had been forced out in March 2008, having earned 315 million dollars in salary and bonuses during his 20 years with the company.

6 March 2009: The ECB prolongs for an unspecified period of time the possibility of borrowing infinite amounts at the refi rate of interest.

6 March 2009: BNP Paribas and the Belgian state reach a new agreement concerning Fortis. BNP will purchase 75 percent of the nationalized bank. Non-performing assets worth 11.4 billion euro

are to be shifted to a "bad bank" capitalized by the Belgian state. The Fortis holding company will become in essence an insurance company with the rest of the Fortis assets. The deal is approved at a general meeting of shareholders on 28 April, despite shoes being thrown at the members of the management present.

6 March 2009: Lloyds TSB signs an agreement with the British government, similar to the earlier RBS deal. Assets worth 260 billion pounds will be guaranteed by the state. Lloyds will take the first 25 billion pounds in losses and 10 percent of the rest. The fee to the government in the form of preference shares will lead to a government stake of 77 percent of the bank once the preference shares are converted into common stock; until then the state's share is 43 percent.

7 March 2009: HSH Nordbank receives a further 30 billion euro in guarantees from SoFFin.

8 March 2009: Fannie Mae reports a quarterly loss of 23.2 billion dollars.

9 March 2009: The fourth remaining major bank in Iceland, Straumur-Burdaras, is seized by the supervisory authority.

10 March 2009: Italy's fourth largest bank, Banco Populare, becomes the first to apply for government support. The bank issues 1.45 billion euro in bonds to the state which may be converted into non-voting preference shares.

11 March 2009: The European Council and the Parliament adopt Directive 2009/14/EC which raises the amount covered by deposit insurance to 50,000 euro (and to 100,000 euro in December 2010).

12 March 2009: The other American GSE mortgage bank Freddie Mac reports a loss for the fourth quarter of 23.9 billion dollars, the loss for the entire year of 2008 being a staggering 50.1 billion dollars. The bank gets a further capital injection of 30.8 billion dollars under the "Senior Preferred Stock Purchase Agreement" set up to recapitalize Fannie and Freddie.

11 March 2009: The Swiss bank UBS reports the largest loss in Swiss corporate history, over 27 billion Swiss francs for 2008. Total writedown on US subprime mortgage securities amounted to over 50 billion dollars, 11,000 jobs worldwide having been cut since 2007.

18 March 2009: The Federal Reserve announces a doubling of its purchases of mortgage bonds and other securities issued by Freddie Mac, Fannie Mae and other "agencies" to a maximum of 1.45 trillion dollars. The Fed will also throughout the year purchase 300 billion worth of long-term government bonds. The 10-year bond yield fell by 50 basis points on the news.

20 March 2009: The German parliament (Bundestag) adopts legislation enabling the nationalization of banks even when opposed by a minority of shareholders. The concrete bank in question concerns the mortgage bank Hypo Real Estate. This would be the first time since 1931 that the German state nationalizes a bank. A week later, the government buys a first stake, 60 million euro for 9 percent of the bank. The government already owned a majority stake, 50 percent of the capital plus one share.

23 March 2009: Tim Geithner, US Treasury secretary, makes a more concrete proposal on how banks are to be rid of their "toxic assets," the Public Private Investment Program, PPIP. A number of competing funds are to be set up, financed by both private and public capital. These will buy up to 1,000 billion dollars' worth of assets. The government will make an initial capital injection of 100 billion dollars from the TARP program, to which will be added guarantees to private investors' borrowing by the FDIC.

26 March 2009: Tim Geithner proposes new legislation that would place hitherto unsupervised hedge funds, private equity funds and OTC derivatives under supervision. The FDIC and the Fed are also to get the authority to close down financial companies, even if they are not banks, provided they are judged to be of systematic importance.

27 March 2009: Omni National Bank of Georgia is closed by its supervisor, bringing to 49 the number of banks closed since the beginning of 2007.

29 March 2009: Spain's central bank is forced to carry out its first bank support operation, giving a loan of 9 billion euro to the savings bank Caja de Ahorros Castilla La Mancha (later absorbed into Cajastur).

30 March 2009: SoFFin in Germany purchases 8.7 percent of Hypo Real Estate for 600 million euro.

30 March 2009: Ireland is downgraded from AAA to AA+ by Standard & Poor's.

2 April 2009: The American FASB (Financial Accounting Standards Board) suspends the principle of mark-to-market and gives the banks the opportunity to use their own judgment and their own models in valuing assets for which there are no established market prices. This is deemed to reduce by at least 20 percent the necessary write-downs for the first quarter.

2 April 2009: The leaders of the G-20 countries, meeting in London, agree on measures to combat the economic and financial crisis. Included are new regulations concerning hedge funds, private equity funds and OTC derivatives such as Credit Default Swaps. The European Commission proposes that funds with assets above 100 million euro be put under supervision. The G-20 also agrees on "principles for sound compensation practices" to avoid "perverse incentives" that contributed to the financial crisis. The principles include adjusting compensation to better take into account risks, deferring a portion of bonus payouts, and linking the size of the bonus pool to the firm's overall performance.

3 April 2009: Nordea becomes the first bank in Sweden to be recapitalized by the government. It was not intended by the bank, however. The Swedish state, through the National Debt Office, decided to invest in the new issue of shares by using the Stabilization Fund rather than through the budget. The state's stake in the bank will remain at 20 percent.

22 April 2009: The International Monetary Fund forecasts that the total write-downs in banks and insurance companies may reach over 4 trillion dollars, of which only some 1,500 billion dollars have been realized so far. Of these, two-thirds involve the United States and one-third Europe, Asian countries having minimal exposures.

29 April 2009: Kenneth Lewis of Bank of America is stripped of his role as chairman but remains CEO – for the time being.

30 April 2009: Chrysler Corporation, the third largest auto manufacturer in the US, files for protection under Chapter 11, having been unable to strike a deal with its bondholders.

30 April 2009: Efforts to stabilize the financial system could cost the US taxpayer up to 1,900 billion dollars or over 13 percent of GDP,

the IMF estimates. This is over three times as much as the cost of the thrift crisis of the 1980s. Of these costs, the direct support through TARP would cost 450 billion, FDIC guarantees 800 billion and Fed operations 600 billion dollars.

30 April 2009: The chairman, CEO and finance director of Allied Irish Banks (AIB) quit.

6 May 2009: Standard & Poor's downgrades the ratings of five of Germany's seven "Landesbanken." They have been reported to hold 816 billion euro's worth of "toxic assets."

7 May 2009: The European Central Bank joins the Federal Reserve and the Bank of England in purchasing bonds. Sixty billion euro will be devoted to buying mainly covered mortgage bonds, in Germany called *Pfandbriefe*. The Bank of England raises the volume of its bond purchases to 125 billion pounds. The ECB also extends maturities of loans to one year.

7 May 2009: Results of the stress test of 19 US banks conducted by the Federal Reserve and the FDIC reveal that they need an additional 74.6 billion dollars in capital. Bank of America alone needs 33.9 billion dollars (a result of overpaying for Merrill Lynch), Wells Fargo 13.7 billion, GMAC 11.5 billion and Citigroup 5.5 billion. Nine of the banks, among them Goldman Sachs and JPMorgan Chase, were judged to already have sufficient capital.

7 May 2009: American Express Bank, one of the 19 banks deemed to be sufficiently capitalized, becomes the first bank to apply for permission to repay the TARP funds received.

19 May 2009: The FDIC's borrowing limit from the Treasury is raised to a temporary 500 billion dollars as the insurance fund dwindles to 13 billion dollars.

19 May 2009: The chairman of Bank of Ireland "resigns."

21 May 2009: Standard & Poor's gives Great Britain a "negative outlook" in its rating, the result of a government debt predicted to attain 100 percent of GDP and a total support to the financial sector of 1,400 billion pounds in capital support, guarantees and loans.

22 May 2009: While 17 small American banks have so far repaid the TARP money, Old National Bancorp in Indiana becomes the first to repurchase the warrants given to the Treasury to give the taxpayers some upside when banks recover.

27 May 2009: The US government's Aaa credit rating is stable "even with a significant deterioration" in the nation's debt, Moody's Investors Service said, signaling confidence in a rebound from the recession. Standard & Poor's added that its recent negative outlook for the British AAA rating should not be construed as a warning to the United States.

29 May 2009: Ireland is forced to inject 4 billion euro into nationalized Anglo Irish Bank, corresponding to its losses over the first half-year.

3 June 2009: With a 3 billion euro capital injection the German state takes full control over Hypo Real Estate.

8 June 2009: Ten big banks are authorized to repay 68 billion dollars of TARP funds, being judged sufficiently stable without government support. JPMorgan Chase repaid 25 billion dollars to TARP, while Goldman Sachs Group Inc and Morgan Stanley repaid 10 billion each.

Among other banks, US Bancorp repaid 6.6 billion, Capital One Financial Corp 3.6 billion, American Express 3.4 billion, BB&T Corp 3.1 billion, Bank of New York Mellon 3 billion, State Street 2 billion and Northern Trust 1.57 billion. They will also have to buy back some 5 billion dollars' worth of warrants at "fair value" to repay the taxpayers' risk in TARP.

10 June 2009: Spain sets up a 9 billion euro rescue fund for the banking sector, in particular aimed at the ailing savings banks, *cajas de ahorro*. The fund may leverage itself tenfold and hence inject up to 90 billion euro in capital into the banks.

10 June 2009: Germany extends its "bad bank" to encompass also the regionally owned Landesbanken, which, however, have shown little interest in the scheme, having in the main been bailed out by their owners, the regional government and savings banks.

17 June 2009: The Obama administration announces proposals for changing financial oversight in the United States. Among them is the merger of the OTS and the OCC, creating a single supervisor for all nationally chartered banks as well as the creation of a Consumer Financial Protection Agency.

18 June 2009: The Swiss National Bank threatens to limit the size of Swiss banks, which would affect, in particular, Credit Suisse and UBS.

1 July 2009: Freddie Mac and Fannie Mae receive permission to refinance residential mortgages up to a limit of 125 percent loan-to-value, in an effort to stem the rising wave of foreclosures.

6 July 2009: The European Central Bank begins the first of its promised purchases in the market, buying 60 billion euro of covered bonds.

8 July 2009: The British Secretary of the Treasury unveils proposals following the Turner review for making banks more stable, including capital provisioning during the business cycle and increasing resources for macro-prudential supervision.

9 July 2009: The International Swaps and Derivatives Association (ISDA) rules that the non-payment of interest by the British mortgage bank Bradford & Bingley is a "credit event," triggering payment on credit default swaps worth 416 million dollars. The nationalized lender had refused to pay interest.

9 July 2009: The Irish state injects another 4 billion euro into Anglo Irish Bank.

13 July 2009: The European Commission and the Basel Committee on Banking Supervision propose to double the capital charge that banks face on their proprietary trading. They also toughen capital charges on re-securitization, proposing a risk weight of 1,250 percent (i.e. 100 percent of the asset since the normal risk weight is 8 percent) for repackaged securities unless banks can show that the risk has really been shifted.

14 July 2009: The International Accounting Standards Board (IASB) proposes new rules for the reporting of fair value. If an instrument such as a government bond has a predictable flow of revenues, it may be carried on the books by a mechanism that smoothes out market fluctuations in value. Items with unpredictable cash flows like derivatives will still be carried at current market value.

15 July 2009: The FDIC and the Federal Reserve push for tougher measures to curb the size and risk-taking of the largest financial firms in the US. The FDIC will propose slapping fees on the biggest bank holding companies to the extent that they carry on activities, such as proprietary trading, outside traditional lending.

21 July 2009: Neil Barofsky, special inspector general for the Treasury's Troubled Asset Relief Program (SIGTARP), claims in a report that,

potentially, the US government may have to spend 23.7 trillion dollars (almost twice the level of GDP) if all existing programs were to be used to the maximum. Barofsky's estimates include 2.3 trillion dollars in programs offered by the FDIC, 7.4 trillion dollars in TARP and other aid from the Treasury and 7.2 trillion dollars in federal money for Fannie Mae, Freddie Mac, credit unions, Veterans Affairs and other federal programs. Total money actually spent is less than 2 trillion dollars.

22 July 2009: Goldman Sachs becomes the first bank to free itself from all TARP limitations as it repurchases warrants for 1.1 billion dollars on top of having repaid the 10 billion dollar preferential share infusion.

23 July 2009: Sheila Bair, chair of the FDIC, suggests that Congress should create a "Financial Company Resolution Fund," funded by the banks themselves just like deposit insurance, to provide working capital and cover unanticipated losses when government steps in to unwind a failed firm. It would impose charges on large or complex institutions that create potential risks to the financial system, thereby providing an economic incentive for an institution not to grow too large.

6 August 2009: Morgan Stanley, having repaid its TARP funds of 10 billion dollars in June, joins Goldman Sachs in also repurchasing the warrants held by the US government, thereby freeing it from all obligations connected with the program. Including dividends, it has paid the government 1.26 billion dollars; a 20 percent annualized return on the government's investment last fall.

6 August 2009: The Bank of England decides to increase its asset purchases from 125 to 175 billion pounds.

7 August 2009: The closure of Community First Bank of Oregon brings to exactly 100 the number of American banks or savings banks closed since the beginning of the financial crisis in early 2007.

9 August 2009: The IMF calculates the total "cost" of the global banking crisis at 11.9 trillion dollars, over 20 percent of world GDP, 10.2 trillion of which will hit developed nations and only 1.7 trillion developing nations. The cost includes capital injections as well as loans and guarantees and liquidity support by central banks.

12 August 2009: With the financial crisis abating, the Federal Reserve decides to end its purchases of open-market paper by October. Or

to cite the FOMC statement: "to provide support to mortgage lending and housing markets and to improve overall conditions in private credit markets, the Federal Reserve will purchase a total of up to 1.25 trillion dollars of agency mortgage-backed securities and up to 200 billion dollars of agency debt by the end of the year (2009). In addition, the Federal Reserve is in the process of buying 300 billion dollars of Treasury securities. To promote a smooth transition in markets as these purchases of Treasury securities are completed, the Committee has decided to gradually slow the pace of these transactions and anticipates that the full amount will be purchased by the end of October."

14 August 2009: Colonial Bank in Alabama with assets of 26 billion dollars is seized by its regulator and placed in receivership with the FDIC, having been swindled by the purchase of fake mortgages to the tune of 1.5 billion dollars (see 19 April 2011). Its branches, loans and deposits are later sold to South-Carolina-based BB&T Bank, which could afford the purchase after having received over 3 billion dollars in TARP money. The acquisition made BB&T the tenth largest bank in the US.

17 August 2009: The Federal Reserve extends in time the Term Asset-Backed Securities Loan Facility (TALF) program, with a capacity of as much as 1 trillion dollars. It will expire on 30 June 2010, for newly issued commercial mortgage-backed securities instead of on 31 December 2009.

20 August 2009: UBS became the first major European bank having received aid to free itself from government control as the Swiss government sold all its shares in the bank, reaping a profit of over 1 billion Swiss francs in the process.

24 August 2009: A US District court judge orders the Federal Reserve to release the names of all counterparties in the 11 liquidity-support programs it runs, totaling some 2,000 billion dollars. The Federal Reserve claims that releasing the names of individual banks having received support may subject them to runs by nervous depositors.

25 August 2009: French banks and the government agree on principles for bonus payments, to be suggested also to the G-20 meeting. Only one-third of bonus payments due may be paid for the first year, the rest saved until the next two years and clawed back if losses occur,

one-third of the deferred payments to be made in stock rather than cash. A "pay general" is appointed to supervise the system, Michel Camdessus, a former governor of Banque de France and managing director of the IMF.

4 September 2009: The US Treasury Department says that 70 billion dollars of TARP money has already been repaid by receiving banks.

7 September 2009: The Basel Committee proposes changes to the Basel II framework to be implemented by 2011. Tier 1 capital should in principle include only common stock and retained earnings, goodwill, hybrids etc. being deducted. At least half of Tier 1 capital should be "True Core Equity," TCE or CET1, the Tier 1 ratio raised to 8 percent from 4 percent. A maximum leverage ratio of 25 (later changed to 33), defined as unweighted assets over capital, should be introduced as a complement to the Basel II risk-based assessments. Countercyclical capital requirements ("dynamic provisioning") should be added to existing Pillar 1 requirements. Systemically important banks may be subjected to extra capital charges. The whole is obviously named "Basel III."

8 September 2009: The rating company Moody's reassures the Aaa-rated large countries (USA, France, Germany, UK and Spain) that they do not risk being downgraded, despite rising budget deficits and debt levels. In June 2010, Moody's changed its mind and warned Spain of being down-rated (which it also was, to Aa1).

17 September 2009: Ireland becomes the first country to actually implement a "bad bank" which will acquire the toxic assets of the main commercial banks. The National Asset Management Agency (NAMA) will pay 54 billion euro to take over a nominal 77 billion of toxic assets with a market value of 47 billion euro. Critics say that the 35 percent discount amounts to an actual subsidy of the banks involved. *Ex post* it was found that the 74 billion transferred had been bought for 32 billion, or on average at 43 percent, implying a 57 percent discount ("haircut").

29 September 2009: BNP Paribas will become the first European bank to repay the government's infusion of capital after having raised 4.3 billion euro in a new issue of common stock.

29 September 2009: The Federal Deposit Insurance Corporation (FDIC) asks its member banks to prepay 45 billion dollars of future

assessments until 2012 in order to bolster its reserve ratio. Among the biggest payers would be Bank of America (3.5 billion dollars), Wells Fargo (3.2 billion), JPMorgan Chase (2.4 billion) and Citigroup (1.2 billion).

30 September 2009: Bank of America announces that its CEO and president Kenneth Lewis, who orchestrated the expensive purchases of Countrywide and Merrill Lynch, will be leaving the bank by the end of the year, to be replaced by Brian Moynihan.

2 October 2009: The European Union reports results from stress-testing the 22 largest banks in the area. Even under adverse conditions, no bank's Tier 1 ratio will fall below 6 percent and the average will be 8–9 percent, depending on assumptions. New stress tests were conducted in July 2010 (see below).

5 October 2009: The German government buys the residual shares in Hypo Real Estate for 1.30 euro, thereby completing the nationalization. The private equity firm J. C. Flowers had a year earlier taken a 25 percent stake at 22.50 euro per share. The bank had already received 102 billion euro in loans and capital from the federal government (via SoFFin), Bundesbank and a consortium of banks. The "toxic assets," at 210 billion euro half of the balance sheet, are taken over by "bad bank" FMS Wertmanagement AöR (FMS-WM).

9 October 2009: The new German Conservative–Liberal government proposes to strip the financial supervisory authority Bundesanstalt für Finanzdienstleistungsaufsicht (BaFin) of its banking supervisory powers and combine them with the Bundesbank's macro prudential supervision. The Conservatives in Britain similarly promise to abolish the FSA and give its powers to the Bank of England, should they win the next election in May 2010. See below.

13 October 2009: The Landesbank HSH Nordbank is revealed to have improved its capital ratios by means of a derivative transaction ("Omega 55") in late 2007 with BNP Paribas, shifting holdings of American CDOs to a "bad bank." It was not reported to its supervisor, BaFin. The transaction ultimately cost HSH 160 million euros. On 24 July 2013, the CEO responsible for the deal, Dr. Jens Nonnenmacher, and five other executives were finally charged with "breach of trust" and "false accounting."

19 October 2009: After months of political haggling, Iceland agrees to borrow 2.35 billion pounds from the UK and 1.2 billion euro from

the Netherlands to cover its deposit-insurance liabilities to depositors in the failed Landsbanki "Icesave."

21 October 2009: Bank of England governor Mervyn King breaks ranks with the government in suggesting that big banks be broken up along commercial bank–investment bank lines, a proposal already aired by the former chairman of the Federal Reserve Board Paul Volcker (and to be made a part of the Dodd–Frank Act as the "Volcker rule").

26 October 2009: The European Commission requires that Dutch bank ING, which has received 15 billion euro in state support, divest itself of its insurance and investment management units as well as its American arm, ING Direct USA. Fears that similar requirements will be placed on other recipients of state aid such as Lloyds and RBS lead to a fall in European bank shares.

30 October 2009: Nine banks are seized by the authorities in the United States in the largest one-day sweep during this crisis, bringing the total since the start of 2007 to 143 failed banks.

1 November 2009: The American commercial lender CIT, a major lender to small and medium-sized enterprises, files for bankruptcy. With assets of 60 billion dollars, it is one of the biggest bankruptcies in US history. Taxpayers stand to lose 2.3 billion dollars in TARP money, CIT being the largest bank to go bankrupt after having been bailed out by the Treasury.

3 November 2009: Royal Bank of Scotland (RBS) is forced to sell off its insurance division and some bank branches after decisions taken by the European Commission's competition commissioner and the UK Treasury. The bank will sell some branches in England and Wales, as well as its NatWest branches in Scotland. RBS also agrees to put 282 billion pounds of assets into the government's Asset Protection Scheme and take an additional 25.5 billion pounds of investment from the Treasury. As a result, the government will increase its stake in RBS to 84.4 percent. RBS will increase the first loss on the assets protected under the government insurance program to about 60 billion pounds, from the 42.2 billion pounds initially agreed.

3 November 2009: Lloyds Banking Group says it plans to raise 22 billion pounds in Britain's biggest rights issue ever and deny the government majority control of the country's largest mortgage lender (after the purchase of Halifax Bank of Scotland, HBOS). Lloyds

will not take part in the government's asset protection scheme, which would have increased the UK's stake to about 62 percent from today's 43.5 percent. Lloyds will sell a retail banking unit with a 4.6 percent share of the current account market and 19 percent of the group's mortgage balances to gain Commission approval for last year's 17 billion pound bail-out. The government will invest an additional 5.8 billion pounds by taking up its rights in the Lloyds share sale. Seven billion pounds will be issued in the form of ECNs (enhanced capital notes), also known as contingent convertible Core Tier 1 securities ("CoCo bonds"). These bonds will be automatically converted to equity should Lloyd's Core Tier 1 ratio fall below 6 percent. Both RBS and Lloyds have also agreed to sell its units only to smaller or new competitors.

9 November 2009: The Federal Reserve announces that of the ten banks ordered in May to raise new capital after stress tests had shown them to be undercapitalized, only GMAC Financial Services had failed to comply with its target and might be recapitalized by returned TARP funds. The other nine banks raised a total of 71 billion dollars in fresh capital.

13 November 2009: Sheila Bair, chair of the Federal Deposit Insurance Corporation (FDIC), says that, in retrospect, injecting government money into the largest US banks was not a good thing.

20 November 2009: The American Mortgage Bankers Association reports a record number of mortgage delinquencies and foreclosures. The percentage of borrowers with at least one payment overdue more than 90 days rose to 14.4 percent in the third quarter. Also, 23 percent of all house owners, 10.7 million households, live in houses where the mortgage exceeds the value of the property.

20 November 2009: The Dutch government announces plans to inject a further 4.4 billion euro into the merging banks Fortis Bank Nederland and ABN AMRO, both of which are nationalized. The total injection of capital will then amount to 24 billion euro.

23 November 2009: The Chinese regulatory authority tells the country's five major banks to raise their capital adequacy ratio to 13 percent as compared to around 11 percent at present and the regulatory minimum of 8 percent.

24 November 2009: The German federal government agrees to inject 4 billion euro in new capital into the ailing ex-savings bank

Westdeutsche Landesbank (WestLB). If converted to common stock, it will give Germany a 49 percent ownership in the bank. WestLB also agrees to offload some 85 billion euro in toxic assets to a "bad bank," EAA (Erste Abwicklungsanstalt), with losses underwritten by the bank's owners, the state of Nordrhein Westfalen and the local savings banks.

24 November 2009: Lloyds Banking Group (Lloyds TSB – HBOS) issues the world's largest-ever rights issue at 13.5 billion pounds, thereby avoiding having to pay 15 billion pounds to the state for the insurance of toxic assets. The government's stake in the bank will remain at 43.5 percent. On top of shares, the bank also issues 7.5 billion pounds of "CoCo bonds," contingent convertible securities that will automatically convert to equity should Lloyds' Core Tier 1 ratio fall below 6 percent.

30 November 2009: The Financial Stability Board (FSB) identifies 30 financial groups worldwide that are considered to create systemic risk and should be supervised cross-border:

5 US banks Goldman Sachs, JPMorgan Chase, Morgan Stanley, Bank of America Merrill Lynch, Citigroup
1 Canadian bank Royal Bank of Canada (RBC)
4 British banks HSBC, Barclays, Royal Bank of Scotland (RBS), Standard Chartered (Lloyds banking group incl HBOS is missing having been downsized and being mostly domestic)
2 Swiss banks UBS and Credit Suisse
2 French banks Société Générale and BNP Paribas (the largest bank by capital, Crédit Agricole, has mainly domestic operations)
2 Spanish banks Santander and BBVA
2 Italian banks UniCredit, Banca Intesa San Paolo
1 German bank Deutsche Bank
1 Dutch bank ING
4 Japanese banks Mizuho, Sumitomo Mitsui, Nomura, Mitsubishi UFJ
6 insurance groups AXA (France), Aegon (Netherlands), Allianz (Germany), Aviva (United Kingdom), Zurich Financial Services (Switzerland) and Swiss Re (Switzerland)

30 November 2009: Bank of Ireland and Allied Irish Banks sell a combined value of 28 billion euro of "toxic securities" to the country's newly started bad bank, National Asset Management Agency (NAMA).

2 December 2009: The European Union finance ministers agree to set up three coordinating agencies for micro prudential supervision. Under a compromise, countries acting through the auspices of the ECOFIN Council can set aside decisions of the three bodies by a simple majority of countries. There will also be a European Systemic Risk Board, comprising the central banks, the three supervisory bodies and the EU Commission.

3 December 2009: Bank of America repays the 45 billion dollars for itself and for Merrill Lynch received from the TARP program, thereby freeing the bank from hampering pay restrictions. Of these, 19.3 billion dollars came from a record issue of preferred shares.

4 December 2009: The UK secretary of the Treasury sharply cuts the amount expected to be lost in the financial support to the banking system from 20–50 billion pounds estimated earlier to 10 billion pounds. The major reason is the decision by Lloyds Banking Group not to participate in the government's guarantee scheme for "toxic securities," the government's share of Lloyds thereby remaining at 43 percent. The major participant in the scheme, RBS, owned 84 percent by the Government, has reduced its participation in the scheme by 43 billion pounds to 282 billion pounds.

8 December 2009: An independent evaluation finds that the correct value of compensation to former shareholders in the nationalized British bank Northern Rock is nil.

9 December 2009: The British chancellor of the exchequer, Alistair Darling, imposes a one-time tax on bankers' bonuses for 2009 above 25,000 pounds. The tax is to be paid by the banks as a surcharge on income. Coming on top of the increase in the British top marginal tax rate from 40 to 50 percent on incomes over 150,000 pounds, the measure threatens an exodus of bankers from London. France, however, decides to follow on the bonus tax on incomes over 7,500 euro. In the United States, the government's "pay czar" Kenneth Feinberg has set a limit of 500,000 dollars for executives in the companies still receiving support from the TARP program: Bank of America, Citigroup, AIG, GM and GMAC. Chrysler and its finance company have no employees reaching the limit. Two senators proposed a 50 percent tax on 2009 bonuses above 400,000 dollars at firms that have received more than 5 billion dollars in government assistance but the measure does not win a majority in the Senate.

9 December 2009: Bank of America repays in full its 45 billion dollar TARP support in order to escape from government-imposed pay limitations.

10 December 2009: Anticipating new rules from BIS and the EU, Britain's Financial Services Authority (FSA) proposes more stringent rules for banks' proprietary trading. The new rules are estimated to cost British banks an additional 29 billion pounds in core Tier 1 capital.

11 December 2009: The Dutch bank ING repays 5.6 billion euro of the total support received of 10 billion in capital support and 21.6 billion in guarantees on US mortgage-related assets.

11 December 2009: In its first auction of warrants received by the Treasury under the TARP program, warrants on stock in JPMorgan Chase generate a profit of 936 million dollars to the Treasury.

11 December 2009: The US House of Representatives votes a comprehensive package of financial reform, including the creation of a new supervisory authority for consumer credits. The narrow vote of 223 for and 202 against makes it probable that it would fail to gain a majority in the Senate in the present form.

14 December 2009: Citigroup repays 20 billion dollars of support given under the TARP program in order to escape from the imposed pay limits. It also terminates the guarantee given on 301 billion dollars' worth of "toxic assets."

14 December 2009: Austria nationalizes the country's sixth largest bank, HGAA (Hypo Group Alpe Adria), majority owned by Landesbank Bayern (LB) which will receive 1 euro (sic) for its 67 percent ownership. LB had invested a total of 3.7 billion euro in the bank. HGAA also receives a capital injection of 900 million euro from the Austrian state. The affair cost both the CEO of the bank and its chairman, the finance minister of Bavaria, their jobs.

15 December 2009: Wells Fargo also repays its 25 billion dollars in TARP support, becoming the last of the big US banks to exit the TARP program.

18 December 2009: The Basel Committee publishes a proposed set of regulations for banks. Among the changes is the phase-out of hybrid capital in Tier 1, focusing on True Core Tier 1 (common equity and retained earnings). Other proposals involve liquidity ratios, a global leverage ratio and countercyclical capital buffers.

29 December 2009: GMAC receives an additional 3.8 billion dollars from the TARP program on top of the 12.5 billion already received. The US government owns 56 percent of the lender, the rest being owned by Cerberus, a private equity firm.

1 January 2010: John Mack retires as CEO of Morgan Stanley, succeeded by James Gorman. Ken Lewis retires from the position as CEO of Bank of America, succeeded by Brian Moynihan. Dick Kovacevich retires as chairman of Wells Fargo, succeeded by John Stumpf as chairman and CEO. All this happens in one day.

5 January 2010: The Icelandic saga continues as the president unexpectedly vetoes the payment of 3.8 billion euro to 320,000 Landsbanki Icesave investors in Britain and the Netherlands, forcing the issue to a referendum.

7 January 2010: The regulatory authorities in the United States release an advisory to depository institutions on sound practices in managing interest rate risk (IRR).

14 January 2010: The US administration proposes a fee on all financial institutions (banks and insurance companies) with assets over 50 billion dollars. It would encompass around 35 banks and 15 insurance groups. The fee would be set at 0.15 percent on assets minus Core Tier 1 capital and insured deposits. Over 10 years, the fee is estimated to collect 90 billion dollars. The stated purpose is to recover losses on the TARP program. An objection is that most banks have already repaid their TARP contributions with profit to the Treasury, the remaining losses being capital injected into AIG, the two auto firms and their finance companies and the Affordable Housing Program. Hence banks are essentially being asked to pay twice. The US initiative is said to copy a Swedish scheme to build a "stability fund" of 2.5 percent of GDP. The Swedish fee is levied on all banks and set at 0.036 percent of liabilities.

21 January 2010: President Obama takes the financial sector by surprise in proposing restrictions on banks' proprietary trading, ownership of hedge and equity funds as well as absolute size (the "Volcker rule").

1 February 2010: The Federal Reserve closes the Asset-Backed Commercial Paper Money Market Mutual Fund Liquidity Facility, the Commercial Paper Funding Facility, the Primary Dealer Credit

Facility and the Term Securities Lending Facility, as well as the temporary liquidity swap arrangements between the Federal Reserve and other central banks. The Federal Reserve is also in the process of winding down its Term Auction Facility: 50 billion dollars in 28-day credit will be offered on 8 February and 25 billion in 28-day credit will be offered at the final auction on 8 March. The anticipated expiration date for the Term Asset-Backed Securities Loan Facility remains set at 30 June for loans backed by new-issue commercial mortgage-backed securities and 31 March for loans backed by all other types of collateral.

19 February 2010: The Irish state becomes the owner of 16 percent of the Bank of Ireland.

23 February 2010: Austria decides to follow Sweden in imposing a levy on banks, set at 0.07 percent of total assets, in order to finance the cost of the financial aid given to banks, including the nationalization of Hypo Group Alpe Adria and Kommunalkredit. The levy is planned to raise 500 million euro.

27 January 2010: The Fed and ECB end their mutual swap facilities.

1 March 2010: State Street CEO Ronald Logue retires and is replaced by Joseph Hooley.

2 March 2010: The insurance company AIG, which has received support from the Treasury and the Federal Reserve totaling 182 billion dollars, agrees to sell its Asian subsidiary AIA to Prudential for 35 billion dollars, 25 billion of which will be used to repay the Fed. As a result, AIG's shares rose over the day by over 4 percent while those of "Pru" fell by 11 percent the first day and another 8 percent the day after. Later the shareholders of "Pru" rejected the deal, which fell through, AIG refusing to renegotiate the deal at a lower price. A few days later, AIG agrees to sell its foreign life insurance unit to MetLife Inc. for about 15 billion dollars in cash and stock, 9 billion of which will be used to repay the government.

2 March 2010: London-based investment banks ignore the government's efforts to hold down bonus payments, preferring to pay the 50 percent surcharge tax rather than losing qualified staff. Barclays increases its payments of salary and bonuses in 2009 by 93 percent vis-à-vis 2008, Royal Bank of Scotland by 73 percent, despite the latter being majority-owned by the British state. The tax is now

expected to bring in four times as much revenue as the government originally planned.

3 March 2010: President Obama sends to Congress a formalized proposal of the so-called "Volcker rule." In an addition, banks would be forbidden to acquire other banks if the new entity has more than 10 percent of total US bank liabilities. An exception is made if the acquired bank is in default. It should be pointed out that both JPMorgan Chase and Bank of America already exceed a similar restriction, based on the relative size of deposits, with no reaction from the authorities.

3 March 2010: Bank of America sells the bail-out warrants connected with the TARP program at a total of over 1.5 billion dollars, the biggest such sale yet. This dwarfs the 1.1 billion raised from a similar warrant sale by Goldman Sachs and 950 million by JPMorgan Chase.

6 March 2010: In a referendum, Icelandic voters overwhelmingly (93-2) reject the deal negotiated by the government regarding repayment to the Netherlands and Britain for their payment of deposit insurance to Icesave depositors.

17 March 2010: Regulatory authorities in the United States issue new guidelines on the management of liquidity risk. The authorities are the Federal Reserve, the FDIC, the Office of Thrift Supervision (OTS), the National Credit Union Administration and the Conference of State Bank Supervisors.

24 March 2010: Denmark abolishes the unlimited guarantee for deposits but raises the former limit to 100,000 euro, double the minimum requirement of the EU. The government also underscores that in Denmark, it is the financial sector itself and not the state that bears the primary responsibility for saving banks in trouble.

24 March 2010: The remaining "toxic assets" in nationalized Northern Rock and Bradford & Bingley are transferred to the newly started UK Asset Resolution Ltd.

29 March 2010: The French arm of the clearing house LCH Clearnet starts the clearing of euro-denominated corporate credit default swaps (CDS) contracts in competition with the London subsidiary of the InterContinental Exchange (ICE Europe).

30 March 2010: The NAMA (National Asset Management Agency), the Irish "bad bank," starts buying toxic assets from banks. In all,

it plans to buy loans for 81 billion euro (107 billion dollars), apply-ing an average "haircut" of 47 percent, i.e. loans will be purchased for just about half their nominal value. In combination with raised capital adequacy requirements ahead of changes enforced by BIS (minimum core Tier 1 ratio of 8 percent, minimum equity core Tier 1 ratio of 7 percent) this leads to banks having to raise more capital: Allied Irish Banks 7.4 billion euro, Bank of Ireland 2.7 billion euro, Irish Nationwide 2.6 billion euro, the Educational Building Society (EBS) 0.9 billion euro and the nationalized Anglo Irish Bank Corp may need 18.3 billion euro, of which 8.3 are injected immediately. Share prices in the first two banks fall sharply, by 20 percent in Allied Irish Banks (AIB) and by 10 percent in the Bank of Ireland. AIB could risk having to have a government ownership of 70 per-cent, Bank of Ireland 40 percent. Nationwide and EBS are to be nationalized completely. Bank of Scotland and Fortis have already left their Irish market joint ventures.

31 March 2010: The Federal Reserve ends its program for support of the mortgage market, under which it has purchased 1.43 trillion (sic) dollars' worth of mortgage and agency bonds.

31 March 2010: Nationalized Anglo Irish Bank reports the worst loss ever in any Irish company, 12.7 billion euro.

1 April 2010: Westdeutsche Landesbank becomes the first German bank to announce that it will be selling "toxic assets" to the fed-eral "bad bank" scheme, in total loans worth a nominal 85 billion euro. WestLB is also the only one of the Landesbanken in trouble (the others are HSH Nordbank, BayernLB and Landesbank Baden-Württemberg) to have accepted a federal bail-out, the others having been recapitalized by the respective states, their owners, the role of the federal government being limited to guarantees.

13 April 2010: Two former executives of failed Northern Rock are fined by the Financial Services Authority for misrepresenting mort-gage arrears data and banned from ever working in a regulated financial firm.

16 April 2010: The SEC (Securities and Exchange Commission) takes the market by surprise in charging the Goldman Sachs Group Inc. and one of its employees, Fabrice Tourre, with fraud in connection with repackaging and selling CDOs (Collateralized Debt Obliga-tions) linked to subprime mortgages. In its lawsuit, the SEC alleged

that Goldman structured and marketed a synthetic collateralized debt obligation (Abacus 2007-AC1) that hinged on the performance of subprime residential mortgage-backed securities. It alleges that Goldman did not tell investors "vital information" about Abacus, including that the fact that a hedge fund by the name of Paulson & Co was involved in choosing which securities would be part of the portfolio. It also alleges that Paulson took a short position against the CDO in a bet that its value would fall. According to the SEC, the marketing materials for the CDO showed that a third party, ACA Management LLC, chose the securities underlying the CDO. Paulson & Co paid Goldman 15 million dollars to structure and market the CDO, which closed on 26 April 2007, the SEC said. Little more than nine months later, 99 percent of the portfolio had been downgraded. Paulson reputedly netted 1 billion dollars on Abacus, investors such as ACA and IKB losing a similar amount. The Goldman Sachs stock fell by over 12 percent during the day, Citigroup by 7 percent and Bank of America Merrill Lynch by 5 percent.

17 April 2010: The Central Bank of China increases to 50 percent the minimum down payment in purchasing a new home, up from 40 percent.

21 April 2010: General Motors announces that GM has repaid the remaining 5.8 billion dollars in loans from the US and Canada. The US government still owns a 61 percent stake in the company (and Canada 11 percent) after GM received over 61 billion dollars in aid after its 2009 bankruptcy.

22 April 2010: The EU statistical agency Eurostat rules that capital injections into nationalized Anglo Irish Bank must be treated as government expenditure, hence raising both the budget deficit and public debt. The projected Irish budget deficit for 2010 then becomes an unheard-of 32 percent of GDP (the actual deficit would turn out to be 30.8 percent, falling to 13.4 percent in 2011).

26 April 2010: The countries in the G-20 group meet without being able to agree other than in general terms on the need to improve both the quantity and quality of capital. In particular, the countries disagree on the need for a US-type overall leverage ratio of maximum 25 times (opposed by, in particular, Germany where Deutsche Bank was leveraged 71 times) as well as a bank bail-out

tax (opposed by, in particular, Canada and Australia where bank bail-outs were not necessary).

27 April 2010: Standard & Poor's lowers the rating of Greece from BBB- to BB+, i.e. "junk," the first time this happens to a Eurozone country. Portugal is simultaneously lowered two notches from A+ to A-. Standard & Poor's would also lower Portugal to junk in January 2012.

30 April 2010: The European Commission issues a set of recommendations for remuneration in the financial sector.

1 May 2010: China raises the cash reserve requirement for large banks to 16.5 percent to combat excessive house price inflation.

2 May 2010: The European Union's eurozone members, the ECB and the IMF, agree a 110 billion euro support package for Greece, conditioned on austerity measures in the budget and the sale of 50 billion euro state assets.

3 May 2010: Greece sets aside 10 billion euro to support its banking system as the austerity plan forces it to cut government expenditure by 13 percentage points of GDP in three years.

3 May 2010: The ECB breaks its own rules by deciding that Greek banks may use Greek sovereign debt as collateral for borrowing even though the bonds have been downgraded to "junk."

5 May 2010: The Swedish Financial Supervisory Authority (Finansinspektionen) decides that new mortgages as well as increases in existing mortgages must not exceed 85 percent of the market value of the property. This makes Sweden the first country to introduce explicit ceilings on loan-to-value after the crisis. Germany, France and Denmark already have such limits.

9 May 2010: The Federal Reserve restarts its emergency currency-swap tool by providing as many dollars as needed to the ECB, the Bank of England and Schweizerische Nationalbank (SNB), allowing them to provide the "full allotment" of US dollars as needed. The swaps are authorized through January 2011.

9 May 2010: The 27 finance ministers in the EU ECOFIN Council decide to set up the European Financial Stability Facility (EFSF).

13 May 2010: The US Senate adopts the Collins amendment to the Dodd–Frank Act, requiring that capital levels for the major banks

shifting to Basel II (or Basel III) cannot be lower than the Basel I rules applicable for smaller banks.

13 May 2010: The Irish government takes an 18 percent equity stake in Allied Irish Banks (AIB) after the European Commission forbids the payment of interest on its preferred stock.

17 May 2010: The European Central Bank (ECB) reveals that it has bought 16 billion euro of eurozone bonds in the first such attempt to create liquidity, a move that was heavily criticized by the two German members of the Governing Council. By early June, the volume had risen to 40 billion euro.

19 May 2010: Germany decides to go it alone and ban the selling of naked default swaps, i.e. the situation of buying insurance without having the underlying risk. The ban encompasses EU government bonds as well as the shares in certain German banks. Germany's euro partners, not having been informed of the move, are deeply offended.

20 May 2010: The US Senate votes to overhaul financial regulation, a bill that must now be reconciled with that taken by the House of Representatives.

23 May 2010: The Bank of Spain seizes control over the ailing Cajasur de Andalusía, run by the Catholic Church. The initial cost is calculated at 500 million euro.

26 May 2010: The European Commission proposes a levy on banks to be paid upfront into a stability fund to insure against future financial failures. Germany calculates that its banks would pay around 1 billion euro per year. The UK and France oppose that plan, arguing that the existence of a fund will create moral hazard, encouraging higher risk levels. The UK also argues that the proposal must be agreed by unanimity in the ECOFIN Council since it is a matter of taxation. This would guarantee that the plan fails.

26 May 2010: The US Financial Accounting Standards Board (FASB) proposes that a much larger proportion of bank assets in the future be carried at "fair," i.e. market values. This would apply not only to derivatives but also many loan categories such as credit card debts, corporate lending, unsecured loans, and some mortgage debt. Banks would report on a separate line, the smoother "amortized cost."

2 June 2010: The European Commission proposes that rating companies operating in the EU countries be supervised by the new

EU-wide regulatory body the European Securities and Markets Authority (ESMA).

5 June 2010: Finance ministers from the G-20 countries fail to agree on a global bank tax to finance future interventions, leaving each country to go it alone. In particular Japan, Australia and Canada, which have not had to support their banks in the financial crisis, as well as Brazil and India among the developing nations, are against the idea. Sweden, the United Kingdom, Germany and Austria have already introduced various forms of bank taxes.

7 June 2010: Finance ministers agree on a common stabilization fund for the euro countries (plus Sweden and Poland), encompassing 750 billion euro in potential support to countries in difficulty, the European Financial Stability Facility (EFSF). Each country will share proportionately into a Special Purpose Vehicle (SPV), located in Luxembourg. Sharper sanctions will be applied to countries which repeatedly break the budgetary rules. The fund should be compared with claims on Portugal, Spain and Greece held by European financial institutions amounting to some 2,000 billion euro.

9 June 2010: The Irish government's stake in Bank of Ireland rises to 36 percent after a capital injection of 3.5 billion euro.

13 June 2010: Greece is downgraded by Standard & Poor's to CCC, the lowest rating in the world.

16 June 2010: The newly elected Conservative–Liberal British government proposes a complete overhaul of financial regulation and supervision. The Financial Services Authority (FSA) is to be abolished. Its personnel and its functions will reappear as the Prudential Regulatory Authority, an independent division of the Bank of England. As in the United States, a Consumer Protection and Markets Authority is to be set up, outside the Bank of England. Executive power will lie in the Financial Policy Committee, a body parallel to the present Monetary Policy Committee. Both committees will be chaired by the governor of the Bank of England.

16 June 2010: The partly nationalized mortgage banks Fannie Mae and Freddie Mac are delisted from the New York Stock Exchange since their shares have long traded at prices below one dollar.

22 June 2010: The new British government proposes a levy on banks which would tax their balance sheets starting in January 2011,

generating 2 billion pounds of revenue per year. The tax will be set at 0.04 percent in 2011, before increasing to 0.07 percent. The levy will apply to British banks as well as the subsidiaries and branches of overseas banks. Firms will only be liable for the levy when their relevant aggregate liabilities exceed 20 billion pounds. The proposal may be compared with the already existing Swedish "stability fund" into which all banks pay 0.036 percent of their liabilities, with the exclusion of such subordinated liabilities that count as Tier 2 capital. The difference is, however, that the British levy will go directly into the budget, not to build up a fund. The levels may be compared with the 0.15 percent that the US proposes to levy on its 50 biggest banks (but on the other hand, the American tax is levied on liabilities minus equity and minus all FDIC-insured deposits). The British tax will be levied at total liabilities minus core capital and insured deposits. Liabilities with more than one year maturity would be taxed at half rate.

25 June 2010: A committee with members from both the US Senate and the House of Representatives succeeds in compromising the two bills passed by the respective houses in the form of the Dodd–Frank Bill, which needs to be taken by the two chambers.

27 June 2010: The leaders of the G-20 countries meeting in Toronto make very little headway toward financial reform. Higher standards for capital and liquidity ("Basel III") are agreed in principle but their introduction postponed. There will be no global bank tax, some countries going their own way (Britain, Germany, Austria, France and Sweden). Also achieving a common set of global accounting principles appears to fail as the International Accounting Standards Board (IASB) and the US Financial Accounting Standards Board (FASB) fail to agree.

30 June 2010: The US House of Representatives passes by 237 to 192 the bill HR 4173, Restoring American Financial Stability Act of 2010, also called the Dodd–Frank Bill. See below for Senate passing the bill.

30 June 2010: The European Union agrees on new rules for remuneration in banks as well as hedge funds. At least 40 percent (or 60 percent for large bonuses) of the bonus must be postponed for three to five years and the payment upfront must be limited to half the amount, the rest being paid in stock. The cash portion is thus

reduced to 20–30 percent of the total. Some EU countries already have similar rules, following the previous recommendation by the EU Commission K (2009) 3159.

1 July 2010: The US Treasury department announces that it has sold in the market part of its holdings in Citigroup, bringing down its stake from at most 36 to 18 percent of equity. The price per share, 4.03 dollars, gives the taxpayer a handsome profit, since at the bottom of the crisis the shares were worth one dollar.

1 July 2010: The name Fortis in the Netherlands disappears as the residual of the bank is integrated into also-nationalized ABN AMRO.

5 July 2010: An independent evaluation of nationalized British mortgage bank Bradford & Bingley finds that the correct value of compensation to previous shareholders in the bank is nil.

9 July 2010: Spain's troubled savings banks (*cajas*) will be allowed to sell half their equity to private investors in the future to recapitalize their losses.

12 July 2010: On behalf of Fannie Mae and Freddie Mac, their new regulator, the Federal Housing Finance Agency, issues 64 subpoenas for details on underlying loans in transactions where the two GSEs lost money.

13 July 2010: Moody's lowers the sovereign rating of Portugal from Aa2 to A1.

15 July 2010: Goldman Sachs pays a record 550 million dollar fine to the SEC, without admitting guilt, for its role in the Abacus affair (see 16 April 2010). The only individual charged is Fabrice Tourre (see below, 11 June 2011 and 1 August 2013).

15 July 2010: The US Senate adopts the Dodd–Frank bill for the reform of financial regulation (The Wall Street Reform and Consumer Protection Act) by 60-39, passed by the House of Representatives on 30 June. Its main points are:

- The power of the Federal Reserve is strengthened. It keeps its supervisory role over banks, big as well as small. The Federal Reserve Board will include a new vice chairman responsible for financial stability, reporting to Congress twice a year. It gets responsibility for supervising financial holding companies deemed to pose systemic

risk even if they do not include any banks. Large financial companies that pose a systemic risk will also be subject to more stringent capital and liquidity requirements, set by the Fed. The new
Consumer Financial Protection Bureau will be an independent part
of the Fed, to police the financial industry and protect the consumers, especially as regards credit card fees and mortgage loans. The
Fed also succeeded in eliminating the requirement that they reveal
the names of banks having borrowed from the Fed; this will now be
required with a two-year lag to prevent "runs."

- Emergency lending by the Fed is restricted in that it must be
  approved by the Secretary of the Treasury and adequate collateral
  collected (vide AIG).
- Large bank-holding companies that have received TARP money will
  not escape supervision from the Federal Reserve by dropping their
  banking subsidiaries ("the hotel California provision").
- "Living wills": large, complex financial companies are required to
  periodically submit plans for their rapid and orderly shutdown and
  sale of assets should the company risk going bankrupt.
- The "Volcker rule" would have prohibited proprietary trading
  (trading for their own accounts and profit) by firms being able to
  access Fed liquidity, i.e. banks. In the adopted version, banks may
  continue to trade derivatives for customers as well as for their own
  hedging operations and mostly also for their own profit (see below).
- The Federal Deposit Insurance Corporation (FDIC) already has the
  power to liquidate failed commercial banks, this power now being
  extended to failing financial firms even though they may not be banks.
- Banks may continue to invest their own money in hedge funds and
  private equity funds, though they are limited to no more than 3 percent of the fund's capital and no more than 3 percent of their own
  Tier 1 capital.
- Hedge funds and private equity funds large enough to pose a sys-
  temic risk are required to register with the Securities and Exchange
  Commission.
- Mortgage banks and originators of Mortgage-Backed Securities and
  Collateralized Debt Obligations will be required to retain at least 5
  percent of the loan in their own book.
- As a result of the SEC charging Goldman Sachs with acting against
  investors' interest, the bill prevents a firm acting as underwriter

in an asset-backed security from undertaking actions resulting in a conflict of interest, such as shorting (selling) the security in question.

- Banks may continue to trade interest and foreign currency swaps for customers as well as for their own books. Credit default swaps, however, must either be centrally cleared or traded by a separately capitalized subsidiary. End users such as non-financial companies are exempted from the legislation.
- A new Financial Stability Oversight Council is created to coordinate the various agencies as regards the macro-prudential supervision and systemic risks. It consists of 10 members from the Fed, the Consumer Protection Bureau, the Federal Deposit Insurance Corporation, the Federal Housing Finance Agency, the National Credit Union Agency, the Commodity Futures Trading Commission, the Securities and Exchange Commission, the Comptroller of the Currency, one independent member, all chaired by the Secretary of the Treasury. With 2/3 vote it may require a financial company deemed to pose systemic threats to divest assets. It will be aided by a new Office of Financial Research within the Treasury.
- The Office of Thrift Supervision (OTS) is abolished and its powers transferred to the Office of the Comptroller of the Currency (OCC). Both are departments within the Treasury.
- A new Federal Insurance Office is set up within the Treasury to provide for the first time for nationwide monitoring of the insurance industry, hitherto regulated solely by the individual states.
- The protection offered by the FDIC is raised permanently to 250,000 dollars per person, the fee for the insurance is to be based on a bank's total liabilities, not just their deposits, which shifts the burden from small deposit-taking institutions to the major banks and in particular the former investment banks Morgan Stanley and Goldman Sachs with only minimal deposits.
- Minimum underwriting standards are created for home mortgages. In future the lender is required to assess whether the borrower can repay interest and amortizations by verifying income and credit history and job status. This does away with so-called Alt-A loans ("liar loans").
- Thrifts (savings and loan associations and mutual savings banks) will continue as before but supervised by an overall banking regulator.

Several aspects of the original proposal by President Obama have been dropped or modified along the road:

- The proposed tax on banks to repay the TARP funds has been dropped. The only requirement is that bail-outs must never cost the taxpayer anything; all expenditures during a crisis must be recovered.
- Proposals to change the way in which rating companies such as Moody's or Standard & Poor's operate have been postponed for further study.
- The bill does not attack the "too big to fail" syndrome. Banks may continue to grow organically even though they have more than 10 percent of a particular business area, but they may not acquire or merge with another firm if that should cause them to exceed the limit.
- The bill places no new restrictions on compensation structures. Shareholders' meeting may have a non-binding vote on the company's compensation practices.
- The future of Fannie Mae and Freddie Mac is not included in the bill.

18 July 2010: On account of the 85 billion euro planned support to Ireland and its banking system, Moody's downgrades its sovereign rating from Aa1 to Aa2 (see 21 November 2010).

21 July 2010: President Obama signs into law the Dodd–Frank Act, stating "Because of this reform, the American people will never again be asked to foot the bill for Wall Street's mistakes. There will be no more taxpayer-funded bailouts – period."

22 July 2010: The Congressional Budget Office (CBO) calculates that the two mortgage giants Fannie Mae and Freddie Mac, placed in conservatorship under the government, having already cost 145 billion dollars in new capital, might cost the taxpayer a total of 389 billion dollars by 2019.

23 July 2010: The stress-testing of 91 European banks is published. All but seven banks pass the test, implying that their Tier 1 capital ratio will exceed 6 percent even in a stressed situation.

26 July 2010: The Basel Committee on Banking Supervision agrees rules for a new leverage ratio (Tier 1 capital over total asset including off-balance-sheet items) of 3 percent, meaning a maximum gearing of 33 (rather than the 25 originally proposed).

28 July 2010: The former finance director of failed mortgage bank Northern Rock, David Jones, is fined by the FSA and forbidden from ever working in the City.

23 August 2010: Ireland's NAMA reveals that it is paying just 39 percent of the nominal value of assets acquired from Anglo Irish Bank instead of the planned 47 percent, implying a 61 percent mark-down ("haircut"). A total of 34 billion euro in assets has been transferred from Anglo Irish.

24 August 2010: Arguing that bank bail-outs will cost 50 billion euro instead of official estimates of 35 billion, Standard & Poor's downgrades Ireland from AA to AA-.

30 August 2010: The Irish government estimates the cost of Anglo Irish Bank at 29–34 billion euro.

30 August 2010: The chairman and CEO of Allied Irish Banks (AIB) are both ousted.

2 September 2010: HSBC warns that it might relocate to Hong Kong if an attempt is made to break up the bank. Its chief executive is already Hong Kong-based since January 2010.

12 September 2010: The new higher capital requirements under Basel III were revealed by the Basel Committee, to be decided upon by the G-20 group of countries. Focusing on core Tier 1 capital, basically equity and reserves, the new rules demand an increase of the absolute minimum from 2 to 4.5 percent. In order to guarantee this minimum, a conservation buffer of 2.5 percent is added, making the effective rate 7 percent. Banks below this level will face restrictions on dividend and bonus payments. Other buffers under discussion are a countercyclical buffer of up to 2.5 percent (as used already in Spain) and an additional buffer of 1–2 percent placed on banks deemed to be systemically important ("too big to fail"). The total Tier 1 ratio is raised from 4 to 6 percent, while the total capital ratio is maintained at 8 percent (excluding the conservation buffer). The new rules will be phased in gradually. The 4.5 percent minimum must be attained by 1 January 2015, while the buffer capital has until 2019. The new liquidity standard also has to be fulfilled by 2015. The use of hybrid capital in Tier 1 capital will be phased out with an adjustment period stretching until 2023.

15 September 2010: The European Commission proposes new rules for trading. First, rules on short-selling of shares and government

bonds require dealers to reveal to the authorities any short position above 0.2 percent of issued capital and to the market if the position is larger than 0.5 percent. A new authority also provides the legal means of banning short-selling altogether in certain securities at times of market unrest. Second, in order to push trades in OTC derivatives such as Credit Default Swaps to exchanges or at least to central clearing after the trade, new capital requirements will require far higher capital demands for trades cleared bilaterally.

22 September 2010: The EU Parliament votes in favor of the new system of financial regulation and supervision in the European Union, making possible the start on 1 January 2011 of the European Banking Authority (EBA, London), the European Securities and Markets Authority (ESMA, Paris) and the European Insurance and Occupational Pension Authority (EIOPA, Frankfurt) as well as the European Systemic Risk Council (ESRC, Frankfurt).

22 September 2010: The Securities and Exchange Commission (SEC) and the Commodity Futures Trading Commission (CFTC) start revealing how derivatives trading will look like after the implementation of the Dodd–Frank bill. Twenty to 30 exchanges called "swap execution facilities" (SEFs) are envisioned with centralized clearing facilities.

30 September 2010: The government of Ireland gives notice that it might have to inject more capital into Allied Irish Banks (AIB), increasing the state's share from 18.7 percent to possible majority control. The government has already spent 33 billion euro to prop up its banking system, of which 22 billion euro went into Anglo Irish Bank, which is already majority owned. The total might rise to 50 billion euro, warns the finance minister. The actual figure by 2013 is 64 billion euro (40 percent of Ireland's GDP this year), of which 30 billion in promissory notes came from the nationalized Anglo Irish Bank

30 September 2010: The bailed-out insurance company AIG and the US government agree that the government's holding of preferred stock (49.1 billion dollars) be converted to common shares, to be sold on the open market over an 18–24-month period. This will reduce the share of stock held by present private shareholders from 20 to 7.9 percent.

1 October 2010: The US Treasury notifies that it has reduced its stake in Citigroup to 12 percent by selling 1.5 billion ordinary shares at a profit of just over 1 billion dollars.

1 October 2010: Denmark introduces new laws regarding the resolution of failed banks, avoiding any government bail-out after this date. While banks are taken over by the Finansiel Stabilitet and their viable assets and deposits sold, even senior unsecured creditors may face losses, as were to occur with Amagerbanken and Fjordbank Mors. See below.

4 October 2010: Switzerland proposes a sharp increase in the capital requirements for their two largest, systemically important, banks, UBS and Credit Suisse. By 2019, they would have to hold at least 10 percent True Core Equity, TCE (as compared with the 7 percent proposed by the Basel group) and 19 percent total capital (as compared with 8 percent today and 10.5 percent proposed by Basel). Of the TCE, at least 5.5 percent has to be in common equity, while the residual may be CoCo bonds (contingent convertible bonds). The government will not, however, recommend the break-up of banks nor limit the size of operations such as proprietary trading.

5 October 2010: Landesbank Baden-Württemberg sues Goldman Sachs for 37 million dollars lost in a CDO investment built on subprime loans. The CDO ("Davis Square Funding VI") was characterized as "safe, secure and nearly risk free," while Goldman itself bought protection through credit default swaps linked to the failure of the Davis securities.

15 October 2010: The former CEO of failed Countrywide Bank, Angelo Mozillo, charged by the SEC with insider trading and securities fraud, having received a total compensation of close to 500 million dollars, reaches an agreement with the SEC to avoid criminal charges. He pays a fine of 67.5 million dollars and accepts a lifetime ban on serving as an officer or director of any publicly owned company. The former Chief Operating Officer of Countrywide paid a fine of 5.5 million dollars and the Chief Financial Officer 130,000 dollars.

15 October 2010: The French supervisory authority AMF (Autorité des Marchés Financiers) in its Position 2010-05 prohibits the marketing and selling of "complex debt securities" to retail investors.

21 October 2010: The eight funds created under the "Public Private Investment Program" to buy toxic assets from banks report a 36 percent return on the Treasury's money, showing the increased stability in the economy and tighter credit spreads. Unfortunately, the total sum involved is a meager 7 billion dollars.

21 October 2010: The British Treasury calculates that the levy on banks in the UK will yield an estimated 2.5 billion pounds by 2012. For all banks, liabilities of up to 20 billion pounds will be untaxed, meaning large institutions get hit harder. Since international banks with a UK presence will be taxed on their UK operations, there is a risk of double taxation on banks from other countries which have adopted a bank levy such as Germany, France, Austria and Sweden.

22 October 2010: The Federal Housing Finance Agency (FHFA) calculates that the two Government-Sponsored Enterprises (GSEs) Fannie Mae and Freddy Mac may need a total of 363 billion dollars in taxpayer aid. Of this amount, 148 billion has already been drawn. The calculation may be compared with the more pessimistic figure of 390 billion dollars emanating from the Congressional Budget Office (CBO) and the more optimistic figure of 160 billion dollars from the White House Office of Management and Budget.

26 October 2010: The European Union agrees on new rules for hedge funds and private equity funds. Capital and disclosure requirements will be placed on "alternative investment funds," while a common EU passport for EU as well as outside providers will be created, but only from 2018.

1 November 2010: The US Treasury Department announces that the troubled insurance company AIG will draw 22 billion dollars in unspent TARP funds, which allows it to repay in full credits extended by the Federal Reserve. In this way the taxpayer rather than the Fed will reap the profits.

2 November 2010: In US elections, the Republican Party gains control of the House of Representatives and picks up sufficient seats in the Senate to block Democratic proposals. It will enable them to influence the more than 240 rules necessary to fully implement the Dodd–Frank financial legislation. Hence the outcome for such rules as capital standards, especially as concerns big banks, derivatives trading and clearing, and banks' proprietary trading is unclear.

3 November 2010: The Federal Open Market Committee decided that as a further monetary stimulus was needed, the Fed will until summer 2011 purchase another 600 billion dollars in marketable securities, having already bought 1,700 billion from September 2008 when the liquidity problems became acute. The move has been criticized by several well-known economists such as Alan Greenspan (former chairman of the Federal Reserve) and Martin Feldstein (former head of the NBER).

3 November 2010: General Motors, 61 percent owned by the US government, plans an issue of common stock that will lower the government's share to 33 percent. The issue, finalized on 17 November, became, at 23 billion dollars, the largest IPO (Initial Public Offering) ever, beating the 22 billion IPO by the Agricultural Bank of China.

5 November 2010: China starts a market for Credit Default Swaps, CDSs, called "credit risk mitigation." However, protection can only be bought if one has the underlying asset. Central clearing will be compulsory.

8 November 2010: Monoline insurer Ambac files for bankruptcy under Chapter 11.

9 November 2010: The FDIC proposes two changes to the way fees for deposit insurance are calculated. Firstly, fees will be charged on a much larger base, assets minus tangible capital, but the rates lowered correspondingly. Secondly, fees will be risk-based by means of forward-looking scorecards rather than capital adequacy. The change will impact the largest banks most and, in particular, the ex-investment banks Morgan Stanley and Goldman Sachs with few deposits.

16 November 2010: Despite its budget deficit of over 10 percent of GDP, Moody's confirms that the US Aaa rating is not in danger this year or the next but could be in the longer run.

21 November 2010: Ireland officially seeks financial support from the EU and the IMF.

28 November 2010: Ireland, the IMF and the European Union agree on a loan to shore up the Irish banking system. Out of a total sum of 85 billion euro, 35 billion will be used to recapitalize banks, aiming for a core Tier 1 ratio of 12 percent, and 50 billion to restore the consequences for the budget of the blanket guarantee of banks'

deposits. As a consequence, Allied Irish Banks (AIB) will join Anglo Irish Bank in being totally nationalized, while the government will become majority owner of the Bank of Ireland. The interest rate charged is, at 5.8 percent, some 3 percentage points above German levels. The European Financial Stability Mechanism (EFSM), the European Financial Stability Facility (EFSF) and the International Monetary Fund (IMF) will each contribute 22.5 billion. The rest is bilateral support from the United Kingdom, Denmark and Sweden. The Irish government will seek in the years to come to refinance this expensive loan by a loan from the future EU European Stability Mechanism (ESM) but has problems since the ESM will not finance "legacy assets," that is, loans extended to failing banks before the ESM was created.

6 December 2010: The US government sold off its remaining shares in Citigroup Inc. for 4.35 dollars each, marking an exit from ownership in the bailed-out banking giant with a 12 billion dollar gross profit for taxpayers.

9 December 2010: Iceland strikes a new deal with the Netherlands and the UK concerning the Icesave accounts. While acknowledging the debt of 4 billion euro, the rate of interest to be paid is lowered to 3.3 rather than 5.55 percent in the previous agreement. This deal still has to be approved by parliament and the president, and probably by a referendum.

15 December 2010: The Basel Committee calculates that 263 European banks would have needed an additional 602 billion euro in equity capital had the new Basel III 7 percent rule on True Core Equity been in force in 2009. They also calculated that the world's major banks needed to have an additional 1,730 billion dollars in liquid assets to fulfill the new liquidity ratio due by 2015.

16 December 2010: The European Systemic Risk Board (ESRB) begins operations following approval of the EU Regulation 1092/2010.

17 December 2010: Moody's downgrades the rating of Ireland by a full five notches, from Aa2 to Baa1.

20 December 2010: The Irish government estimates the cumulative bank losses of the banking crisis at 41 billion euro.

23 December 2010: The Irish government injects 3.7 billion euro into Allied Irish Banks (AIB), raising the government's stake from

18.7 to 93 percent. The result was a sharp drop in its share price, –23 percent, which has thereby declined almost 99 percent from the peak.

1 January 2011: The three new EU financial watchdogs (the European Banking Authority, EBA in London, the European Insurance and Occupational Pensions Authority, EIOPA in Frankfurt, and the European Securities and Markets Authority, ESMA in Paris) begin operations following the adoption of the EU Regulations 1093/2010, 1094/2010 and 1095/2010, respectively. Regulation 1096/2010 charges the European Central Bank with providing analytical, statistical, administrative and logistical support to the newly created European Systemic Risk Board, ESRB, where the president of the ECB is chairman ex officio.

1 January 2011: The German bank restructuring Act (Gesetz zur Restrukturierung und geordneten Abwicklung von Kreditinstituten) enters into force. Apart from specifying resolution principles, it also sets up a restructuring fund financed by the banks through levies to aid in future resolutions. The bank aims to have a capital of 70 billion euro on top of which it may borrow 100 billion euro for guarantees and 20 billion euro for capital injections.

4 January 2011: Bank of America agrees to pay 2.6 billion dollars to Freddie Mac and Fannie Mae as compensation for faulty information on loans sold by Countrywide, the lender that BofA acquired in 2008.

4 January 2011: Bloomberg reports that banks worldwide have since mid 2007 lost 1,554 billion dollars in write-downs but added 1,333 billion dollars in capital (common and preferred stock as well as hybrids and subordinated debt).

7 January 2011: The German Landesbanken agree to sell their investment banking unit DeKaBank to their part-owners, the local savings banks, for 2.3 billion euro. The savings banks already own half of DeKa (Deutsche Kapitalanlage) and will now acquire the rest.

10 January 2011: The Basel Committee on Banking Supervision agrees on countercyclical capital buffers. A country may require its banks to hold up to 2.5 percent extra core Tier 1 capital (i.e. 9.5 instead of 7 percent) if the ratio of credit to GDP is deemed excessive. Other countries are required to follow suit. If the UK applies the

full 2.5 percent and a US bank has 20 percent of its operations in Britain, the US would be required to raise its capital demand on this bank by 0.5 percentage points.

12 January 2011: The Congressional Oversight Panel for the Troubled Asset Relief Program (COP) estimates that the TARP program will end up costing the taxpayer only 15 billion dollars, compared with initial estimates as high as 350 billion. Auto industry bail-out costs are lowered from 40 to 19 billion dollars. Citigroup which received 45 billion in capital and a guarantee for 301 billion of impaired assets has exited both programs with a gain to the taxpayer of 12 billion dollars.

13 January 2011: The bailed-out insurance company AIG retired its Federal Reserve credit line and converted the Treasury's preferred stock to common stock. The 79.9 percent public stake in AIG will be sold on the market gradually.

20 January 2011: Investors of over 5 billion euro of subordinated debt in the almost-fully nationalized Allied Irish Banks (AIB) are offered 30 percent of face value in a buy-back.

21 January 2011: Spain announces plans for the ailing savings-bank sector (*cajas*). Problem savings banks are to be converted into commercial banks and, if needed, recapitalized by the state bank resolution fund (Fondo de Reestructuración Ordenada Bancaria, FROB). Estimates of the capital necessary lie in the range between 25 and 50 billion euro, 3–5 percent of GDP. First out is the Barcelona-based Caixa which transformed into a commercial bank would have a core Tier 1 ratio of 10.9 percent and becoming the tenth largest bank in Europe by capital. All Spanish banks have to have a core ratio of 8 percent as contrasted with a minimum of 7 percent under Basel III.

28 January 2011: The Bank of England releases a research paper under which the optimal capital ratio of banks is set at 50 percent of risk-weighted assets and 17 percent of total assets rather than 7–9.5 and 3 percent respectively under Basel III.

6 February 2011: The Danish Amagerbanken, the fifth-largest bank, goes bankrupt and is taken over by the government's agency Finansiel Stabilitet. The blanket guarantee of deposits and bonds having been abolished in September 2010, unsecured bondholders

lose 41 percent of their holdings, the first "bail-in" of senior creditors in the recent crisis. Shareholders and holders of subordinated debt are wiped out. This leads to an immediate market reaction in the pricing of Danish bank debt vis-à-vis other Scandinavian banks, Danske Bank, DNB (Norway), Nordea (Sweden), SEB (Sweden), Handelsbanken (Sweden) and Swedbank (Sweden). See also 21 July 2014.

8 February 2011: The British government increases temporarily the charge on banks to 0.1 percent on short-term liabilities and 0.05 percent for long-term liabilities for March and April, after which months the rate will return to the previously set 0.075 percent rate for short-term and 0.0375 percent for long-term liabilities. The temporary increase is expected to yield an additional 800 million pounds for an annual total of 2.5 billion pounds.

11 February 2011: The Securities and Exchange Commission (SEC) charges three former executives at failed savings bank IndyMac with securities fraud for misleading investors about the mortgage lender's deteriorating financial condition.

16 February 2011: Westdeutsche Landesbank (WestLB), having received unacceptable support from the German Federal government in setting up a "bad bank," as decreed by the EU Commission, is proposed to be split into several parts and put up for sale or wound down.

16 February 2011: Financial companies in the US with more than 50 billion dollars in assets, where at least 85 percent of their revenue stems from financial transactions, are to be regarded as systemically important financial institutions and hence subject to decisions by the Financial Stability Oversight Council.

17 February 2011: German banks' subordinated debt of a total of 24 billion euro were downgraded by the rating firm Moody's Investors Services after a change in German legislation allowed authorities to impose losses on investors in these securities even without bankrupting the bank. Deutsche Bank and Commerzbank were among the banks involved.

18 February 2011: The FDIC reports that so far this year 22 banks have been closed; this is to be compared with 140 failures in 2009 and 157 in 2010.

18 February 2011: The new Financial Policy Committee (FPC) in the Bank of England is created by the interim naming of 11 members, headed by the Bank of England governor Mervyn King as chairman. The FPC has the authority to order an increase in banks' capital-adequacy requirements, limit bank lending, increase collateral requirements or place more restrictive loan-to-value demands on mortgages.

18 February 2011: Investors rush to purchase the proposed 2 billion dollars' worth of CoCo bonds (contingent convertible bonds) issued by Credit Suisse. The issue was oversubscribed 11 times. The issue was the first in Switzerland after the authorities set the required core Tier 1 capital ratio at 19 percent. Only Rabobank in the Netherlands and Lloyds Banking Group in Britain have so far issued CoCos.

23 February 2011: Thomas Hoenig, president of the Federal Reserve Bank of Kansas City, said in a speech that the largest financial institutions, those being "too big to fail," should be broken up.

10 March 2011: The Bank of Spain estimates that its banks may need an additional capital of 15 billion euro, concentrated in the major savings banks such as Bankia (formed by Caja Madrid and six smaller savings banks), Novacaixagalicia and Catalunya Caixa. Moody's has set the shortfall at 40–50 billion euro. Spain has also decreed that its banks must attain a core Tier 1 ratio of 8 percent for listed banks and 10 percent for unlisted banks by September 2011.

10 March 2011: The new stress test by the EBA of 88 European banks appears to be just as irrelevant as last year's exercise. Firstly, the assumed economic downturn is very mild (a –0.5 percent GDP fall, a –15 percent fall in equity markets). Secondly, the floor of failure/pass is set at a low 5 percent core Tier 1 capital. Thirdly, only effects of sovereign holdings on trading-book assets are included (–20 percent haircut on Portuguese bonds, –15 percent on Spanish bonds), no effects on banking-book assets are assumed. Hence the test does not include credit risk, only market risks. Commodity prices and commercial real estate shocks are not included.

11 March 2011: Sweden's Financial Supervisory Authority aims at directing the country's banks to hold 12 percent core Tier 1 capital,

the four banks of systemic importance 14.5 percent, rather than the 7 percent plus a countercyclical buffer of 2.5 percent agreed under the Basel III arrangements.

16 March 2011: The US Federal Deposit Insurance Corporation (FDIC) sues the former chief executive and other top executives of the failed Washington Mutual, accusing the leaders of the then largest savings bank in the United States of reckless lending.

19 March 2011: Goldman Sachs is given permission to repurchase the 5 billion dollars' worth of preferred shares bought by Warren Buffet's company Berkshire Hathaway during the crisis.

22 March 2011: Sweden, Luxembourg and Italy criticize the proposed ban on naked short-selling of EU government bonds, arguing that it will diminish liquidity and thus raise volatility and interest costs.

23 March 2011: The Basel Committee on Banking Supervision is considering requiring banks "too big to fail" to hold an additional 3 percentage points' core Tier 1 capital. The proposed rule has been sharply criticized by the banking community, especially the Institute of International Finance and its chairman Josef Ackermann from Deutsche Bank.

29 March 2011: US regulators propose that when banks securitize mortgage credits, they have to retain at least 5 percent "skin in the game," unless the underlying house purchase has been made with at least a 20 percent cash down-payment.

31 March 2011: After concluding stress tests, Irish banks have been told to raise an additional 24 billion euro in capital, bringing the total rescue cost to 70 billion euro (almost 50 percent of GDP), to be compared with the 35 billion envisaged in the EU rescue plan for Ireland. Allied Irish Banks must raise an additional 13 billion, Bank of Ireland 5 billion. It appears likely that they will, like Anglo Irish Bank, find themselves nationalized.

1 April 2011: The US Treasury calculates a 24 billion dollar profit on the aid that it and the Federal Reserve have extended to the banking system. The Fed's mortgage bond investments are expected to bring a 110 billion dollar profit, offset by losses of 73 billion on guarantees to Fannie Mae and Freddie Mac.

5 April 2011: Moody's sharply lowers the sovereign rating of Portugal from A1 to Baa1.

7 April 2011: The EBA spells out the details of the forthcoming stress test of 90 European banks. The macro environment envisages a mild recession rather than a deep downturn. Banks are expected to show a minimum 5 percent core Tier 1 capital ratio after the shock. Only effects on the trading book are to be included despite the fact that most sovereign debt is held in the banks' banking book. Since the results are going to be published, it is certain from the start that some banks will fail but most will pass.

9 April 2011: In a referendum, the population of Iceland again rejects the agreement with Britain and the Netherlands concerning Icesave, despite milder payment conditions.

11 April 2011: The Independent Commission on Banking (the Vickers Commission) in Britain proposes that the biggest banks should hold 10 percent core Tier 1 equity capital.

15 April 2011: Moody's downgrades Ireland from Baa1 to Baa3, just above "junk" status.

5 May 2011: Twelve billion out of the 78 billion euro granted in aid from the EU and the IMF will be used to capitalize Portuguese banks, according to the agreement. Banks will have to attain a 9 percent core Tier 1 ratio by the end of 2011 and 10 percent by the end of 2012.

9 May 2011: In the first quarter of 2011, 28 percent of US homeowners had negative equity, i.e. the value of the house was less than the amount of the mortgage. In Las Vegas, the corresponding ratio was 85 percent.

9 May 2011: Standard & Poor's lowers the sovereign rating of Greece two notches to B, warning that any write-down of debt would be treated as a default.

9 May 2011: Dexia reveals a loss for 2010 of 3.6 billion euro, in large part due to interest-rate swaps taken to hedge against increases in interest rates when actually they fell.

16 May 2011: The eurozone ministers, ECB and the IMF approve a loan package of 78 billion euro for Portugal.

26 May 2011: The EU Commission proposes to ease some of the ingredients of Basel III for the benefit of EU banks. They can continue to issue hybrid capital longer than previously agreed, and make use of

more than the agreed maximum of 10 percent (of the total capital base) in their insurance subsidiaries.

1 June 2011: The European Union proposes to harmonize capital requirements, thereby preventing member states from imposing higher True Core Equity ratios than 10 percent.

3 June 2011: The US Treasury Department sells its remaining shares in Chrysler to Fiat. After this transaction, Chrysler has repaid all but 1.3 billion of the 12.5 billion dollars received in support from the American government.

6 June 2011: The German financial supervisory authority BaFin criticizes the forthcoming EU-wide stress tests of banks in that they exclude the Tier 1 hybrid capital that the German Landesbanken have in the form of guarantees from their owners, the German states.

6 June 2011: Seven EU member states (the UK, Spain, Sweden, Slovakia, Estonia, Lithuania and Bulgaria) protest the proposal from the EU Commission that True Core Tier 1 ratios be maximized at 7 percent for banks (and at 9.5 percent for systemically important institutions) in contrast with the normal EU way of setting minimum standards while allowing higher levels.

11 June 2011: A federal judge in the US rules that Goldman Sachs' executive director Fabrice Tourre must face a lawsuit brought by the SEC for violating securities legislation in that he misled investors in the Abacus case. See 10 April and 15 July 2010 as well as 1 August 2013.

15 June 2011: In Ireland, the state owns 93 percent of Allied Irish Banks after the injection of 7.2 billion euro in capital. The Bank of Ireland, 36 percent owned by the state after having received 3.5 billion euro, will become majority-owned by the state unless its share offer can raise its core Tier 1 ratio to the required 10.5 percent.

15 June 2011: Ireland, which has injected a combined 34.7 billion euro into the nationalized banks Anglo Irish Bank and Irish Nationwide, is merging both lenders. It also proposes to let even senior bondholders share in the losses, while guaranteeing that no similar actions will be taken against creditors of Bank of Ireland and Allied Irish Banks.

15 June 2011: The *Financial Times* publishes the "pay-back" salaries and bonuses given to major bank CEOs in 2010 in comparison with the "meager" year 2009 (salary and bonus, million dollars). The average rose to 10 million dollars, an increase of 36 percent. This is shown in Table 4.

16 June 2011: The Bank for International Settlements' Basel Committee proposes that the world's 30 largest banking groups face an additional Core Tier 1 capital charge of up to 2.5 percent, depending on size and interconnectedness. The Federal Reserve is contemplating 3 percent for the biggest banks in the USA.

28 June 2011: In Denmark, the failed regional bank Fjordbank Mors is taken over by the Finansiel Stabilitet and later sold to Jyske Bank. Like Amagerbanken, investors of senior unsecured bonds will take a haircut, here estimated at 26 percent.

Table 4. *Salaries and bonuses given to major bank CEOs in 2009 and 2010*

Name	Bank	2009	2010
Jamie Dimon	JPMorgan Chase	1.3	20.8
John Stumpf	Wells Fargo	18.8	17.6
James P Gorman	Morgan Stanley	n a	14.8
Lloyd Blankfein	Goldman Sachs	0.9	14.4
Brady Dougan	Credit Suisse	17.6	11.8
Stephen Hester	RBS	10.0	11.5
Michael Geoghegan	HSBC	8.9	9.0
Josef Ackermann	Deutsche Bank	10.6	8.5
Eric Daniels	Lloyds Banking Gr	5.0	8.4
Francisco Gonzales	BBVA	9.0	8.0
John Varley	Barclays	1.8	5.9
Corrado Passera	Intesa Sanpaolo	5.3	5.0
Baudouin Prot	BNP Paribas	3.4	3.5
Frédéric Oudéa	Société Générale	1.6	2.3
Brian Moynihan	Bank of America	n.a.	1.2

30 June 2011: The Swedish government allows its twin program for bank guarantees and recapitalization of its banks to lapse.

30 June 2011: In one of the few convictions following the financial crisis, Lee B. Farkas, chairman of mortgage lender Taylor, Bean & Whittaker, is sentenced to a jail term of 30 years and a payment of 38.5 million dollars for 14 counts of "securities, bank, and wire fraud and conspiracy to commit fraud." Other executives in the company received prison sentences ranging from three months to eight years. They had sold Colonial Bank of Arkansas 1 billion dollars' worth of non-existing mortgages by means of which the bank was able to access 550 million of TARP money. The bank failed on 14 August 2009, having assets of 26 billion dollars and 346 branches, the largest bank bankruptcy in 2009 in the United States, costing the FDIC 2.8 billion dollars.

1 July 2011: The two nationalized Irish banks Anglo Irish Bank and Irish Nationwide Building Society are merged into the Irish Bank Resolution Corp., charged with the task of unwinding the assets.

5 July 2011: The Dutch government introduces a bank tax à la Germany, Austria and Sweden, aiming at collecting 300 million euro annually.

5 July 2011: First out among the rating agencies, Moody's cuts Portugal's sovereign debt by four notches, from Baa1 to Ba2, i.e. "junk." Standard & Poor's follows suit in January 2012.

11 July 2011: The European Stability Mechanism (ESM), with a lending capacity of 500 billion euro, is created.

13 July 2011: Ireland becomes the third eurozone country after Greece and Portugal whose debt is classified as "junk," as Moody's lowers its rating from Baa3 to Ba1.

14 July 2011: The day before European stress tests are to be published, the Landesbank Hessen Thüringen (Helaba) explicitly forbids the EBA to publish results for the bank, citing the decision by the EBA to exclude owner states' "silent participation" as core Tier 1 capital. Without it, the bank would fail the stress test.

15 July 2011: Results of stress testing 91 European banks are published by EBA. Banks were tested in a mild recession 2011–12. Haircuts in the trading book were foreseen for Greek, Irish and Portuguese bonds though much less than current market conditions. Sovereign

defaults were not included and hence no banking-book effects were included. The results were treated as laughable. Eight small banks failed to maintain a 5 percent core Tier 1 ratio in the stressed conditions, requiring capital additions of 2.5 billion euro. An additional 16 banks came in at ratios between 5 and 6 percent. The capital need may be contrasted with the view by Standard & Poor's that European banks need an additional 250 billion euro in capital. The reason is not least capital needs by Europe's major banks, as shown by the stress tests where Deutsche Bank found itself with a core Tier 1 ratio of only 6.5 percent, Royal Bank of Scotland 6.3 percent, Société Générale 6.6 percent and UniCredit 6.7 percent.

The good news is, however, that the banks were forced to publish detailed information about their sovereign bond holdings, by country and by maturity, enabling outsiders to conduct their own stress tests of individual banks. The 91 banks held a total of 98 billion euro of Greek bonds, which, valued at the going market rate of 48 percent (of par), would lead to a combined capital need of 50 billion euro just for the Greek exposure. Adding haircuts in the banking book also for Portuguese and Irish bonds would lead to a total capital need of 75 billion euro for these three sovereigns. Europe's banks held a total of 736 billion euro in sovereign bonds issued by the "PIIGS" countries. The National Bank of Greece, for instance, passed the test with a core Tier 1 capital ratio of 11 percent. But the bank held 12.9 billion euro of Greek sovereign bonds, which, if marked-to-market, would almost wipe out the entire core Tier 1 capital of the bank. Euroland's largest bank, BNP Paribas, came in with a stressed core Tier 1 ratio of 7.9 percent but held vast amounts of sovereign bonds: 24 billion euro in Italy, 5 billion in Greece, 4 billion in Spain and 2 billion in Portugal.

18 July 2011: The EU Commission accepts the German aid to mortgage bank Hypo Real Estate, having received capital injections of 10 billion euro, guarantees of 145 billion euro and a transfer to "bad bank" FMS-WM of 210 billion euro, half its 2008 balance sheet, with an aid element of 20 billion euro.

22 July 2011: The new proposed solution to the EU debt crisis foresees bondholders taking a 21 percent hit on their holdings of Greek sovereign bonds as they are rolled over into longer-term maturities but with an EU guarantee. The haircut will cost Europe's major

banks around 20 billion euro, of which BNP Paribas alone will lose 1 billion and Société Générale 500 million euro.

25 July 2011: The Irish government sells a large part of the partly nationalized Bank of Ireland to a consortium of foreign investors which will own at least 68 percent of the bank, leaving the state with only some 30 percent.

5 August 2011: Standard & Poor's downgrades the United States sovereign rating from AAA to AA+, the first downgrade for the American economy in the 70-year history of ratings.

31 August 2011: Bank of New York Mellon announces that its CEO Robert Kelly is stepping down with immediate effect, replaced by Gerald L. Hassel.

31 August 2011: Iceland emerges officially from the IMF-led bail-out.

2 September 2011: The government of Iceland declares that the residual assets of failed Landsbanki are sufficient to repay Britain and the Netherlands 11.4 billion dollars' worth of deposit guarantees paid by these countries to depositors in the Icesave scheme. This ends a two-year-long quarrel. Simultaneously, the IMF declared that Iceland has met all the Fund's requirements. Growth has been restored, the fiscal balance improved by 10 percentage points of GDP and the banking sector restored to profitability, albeit at a much smaller size, total assets of some 200 percent of GDP being less than one-fifth of the amount before the crisis. The CDS swap spread indicates a lower default risk for Iceland than average for the European Union as a whole. The total gross fiscal cost of bank recapitalization and restructuring over the years 2008–11 amounted to 44 percent of GDP (as against initial IMF estimates of 80 percent), the net cost has fallen to 20 percent. Simultaneously the legal process against former premier Geir Haarde starts, making him the first politician to be charged with negligence over the financial crisis.

2 September 2011: The Federal Housing Finance Agency (FHFA) sues 17 major banks for misrepresenting the quality of underlying assets of residential mortgage-backed securities sold to Fannie Mae and Freddie Mac. Among the "culprits" are JPMorgan Chase (33 billion dollars' worth of securities sold), Bank of America Merrill Lynch (30.8 billion), Deutsche Bank (14.2 billion),

Credit Suisse (14.1 billion), Goldman Sachs (11.1 billion), HSBC (6.2 billion) Barclays (4.9 billion), UBS (4.5 billion) and Citibank (3.5 billion). The FHFA claims the two mortgage banks, earlier government sponsored enterprises (GSEs), now under government conservatorship, lost over 30 billion dollars on these transactions.

12 September 2011: The Independent Commission on Banking, also named the Vickers Commission after its chairman, releases its final report. Its main recommendation is that British banks "ring-fence" their core retail operations from the rest. This means independent capitalization and an independent board of directors. However, banks have some latitude in where to place the fence regarding, for instance, corporate deposits. Banks should hold 10 percent of their risk-weighted assets in the form of Tangible Common Equity (TCE) rather than the 7 percent prescribed by Basel III on top of which may come 7–10 percent CoCo (contingent convertible) bonds.

18 September 2011: UBS reveals a loss of 2.3 billion dollars from unauthorized trades in stock index futures by Kweku Adoboli, a director of the bank's London-based Global Synthetic Equities Trading team. The CEO of UBS, Oswald Grübel, resigns a few days later together with other leading management figures. On 13 December 2013, US court dismissed charges on UBS from investors of fraud, stating that "mismanagement" was not a crime.

21 September 2011: Fears arise that the restrictions on proprietary trading by banks under the Dodd–Frank legislation may be made less binding by exemptions concerning repo transactions, securities lending, and trading in foreign currency and commodities. Fears also arise concerning the difficulty of separating (forbidden) proprietary trading from legitimate trading on behalf of customers and market making.

28 September 2011: The European Commission proposes a tax on financial transactions ("Tobin tax") where at least one party is a European financial institution (including insurance companies and funds). Stock and bond spot transactions are to be taxed at 0.1 percent and derivatives at 0.01 percent. Spot foreign exchange transactions are excluded. The tax is claimed to yield an annual income of 30–50 billion euro. Eleven of the (then) 27 EU states agreed to join the scheme. Due to its construction, a tax would be levied even if both contracting parties are from non-participating countries if the security/derivative traded

is issued by a participating country. This aspect has led Britain to refer the matter to the European Court of Justice. The court, however, dismissed the appeal on 30 April 2014, regarding the case as premature since the details of the tax had not yet been presented.

30 September 2011: The Spanish government's Fund for Orderly Bank Restructuring (FROB) spends almost 5 billion euro in recapitalizing and nationalizing three savings banks: Nova Caixa Galicia, Catalunya Caixa and Unnim, these banks having failed in time to reach the desired 10 percent True Core Equity (CET1/RWA) ratio.

7 October 2011: The rating agency Moody's lowers the credit rating of 12 UK banks (including RBS, Lloyds Banking Group and Santander) on account of the acceptance by the Treasury and the Bank of England of the recommendations by the Vickers Commission that banks should in the future be capitalized so strongly that government support won't become necessary.

10 October 2011: The Belgian-French-Luxembourg bank Dexia has to be saved again by the involved governments. The bank had already received a capital injection of 6.4 billion euro in 2008. Now the Belgian retail bank is nationalized at a price of 4 billion euro, leading to a down-rating warning of the Belgian state by the rating agency Moody's. A "bad bank" is to be set up, guaranteed up to 90 billion euro by the three governments. The French municipal-finance arm Dexma (ex-Crédit Local) is to be integrated into state-owned Banque Postale and Caisse des Depôts et Consignations (CDC).

14 October 2011: The EBA (European Banking Authority) proposes new stringent rules for stress-testing Europe's banks. A minimum 9 percent core Tier 1 ratio after write-downs is set rather than the 5 percent used in the tests conducted in the summer of 2011. Also in contrast to those tests, haircuts will be used on holdings of sovereign bonds also in the banking (investment) book. The result is an additional capital requirement of 275 billion euro according to some calculations, 66 banks failing the test, which may be contrasted with eight banks failing the earlier stress test and needing a combined 2.5 billion euro. The EBA itself calculates the need at 106 billion euro, however.

18 October 2011: Moody's downgrades the sovereign debt of Spain from Aa2 to A1.

31 October 2011: MF Global, one of the leading US derivatives bro-ker-dealer as well as a primary dealer, files for bankruptcy. The firm had speculated heavily in European sovereign debt and used money in customer accounts to cover deficits in its proprietary trading. According to the trustee overseeing the liquidation, the final amount missing in customer accounts could reach 1.6 billion dollars. The CEO, Jon Corzine, a former CEO of Goldman Sachs as well as gov-ernor of New Jersey and US senator, is later sued by the supervisor CFTC and banned from the industry. The firm itself paid a 100 mil-lion dollar penalty to the CFTC.

1 November 2011: Mario Draghi replaces Jean-Claude Trichet as president of the European Central Bank.

4 November 2011: The Financial Stability Board (FSB) and the Basel Committee on Banking Supervision (BCBS) set out a list of 29 inter-national banking groups, which because of their size, complexity and interconnectedness are judged to be "too big to fail" and will be required to hold an extra 1.0–2.5 percent equity capital (with total assets at year end 2010). This list is shown in Table 5. Of these banks, eight are located in the United States, four in the UK, four in France, three in Japan, two in Germany, two in Switzerland and one each in Belgium, the People's Republic of China, Italy, the Netherlands, Spain and Sweden.[4]

8 November 2011: Rather than cutting dividends or raising new equity, some of Europe's major banks plan to increase capital ratios to the required 9 percent (see 14 October) by reclassifying risk weights, allowed under both Basel II and Basel III subject to regula-tory approval. The major two Spanish banks Santander and BBVA calculate that this procedure will go half-way towards the required increase in the ratio. Other banks planning to reclassify risk weights

---

[4] It should be noted that the valuations of total assets are dependent on account-ing regime. Should US banks report according to the international IFRS rules rather than GAAP, their total assets would rise by 50–100 percent for trading-active banks like Bank of America, Goldman Sachs, JPMorgan Chase or Morgan Stanley but only marginally for banks such as Bank of New York Mellon, State Street and Wells Fargo. See www.fdic.gov/about/learn/board/hoenig/capitalizationratios.pdf. The presence of Bank of New York Mellon and State Street Bank with relatively small balance sheet assets is explained by their dominating position as international custodial banks.

Table 5. *"Too big to fail" international banking groups (as defined by FSB and BCBS)*

	Billion dollars
Bank of America (USA)	2,264
Bank of China (PRC)	1,723
Bank of New York Mellon (USA)	237
Banque Populaire CdE (France)	1,404
Barclays (UK)	2,600
BNP Paribas (France)	2,677
Citigroup (USA)	1,914
Commerzbank (Germany)	1,010
Credit Suisse (Switzerland)	960
Deutsche Bank (Germany)	2,554
Dexia (Belgium)	760
Goldman Sachs (USA)	911
Group Crédit Agricole (France)	2,320
HSBC (UK)	2,454
ING Bank (Netherlands)	1,671
JPMorgan Chase (USA)	2,289
Lloyds Banking Group (UK)	1,548
Mitsubishi UFJ FG (Japan)	2,400
Mizuho FG (Japan)	1,985
Morgan Stanley (USA)	808
Nordea (Sweden)	779
Royal Bank of Scotland (UK)	2,267
Santander (Spain)	1,632
Société Générale (France)	1,517
State Street (USA)	161
Sumitomo Mitsui FG (Japan)	1,701
UBS (Switzerland)	1,302
UniCredit Group (Italy)	1,245
Wells Fargo (USA)	1,258

are Commerzbank, Lloyds Banking Group and HSBC. US banks complain since, firstly, they are still on Basel I with fixed risk weights and, secondly, they are subject to a leverage ratio restricting total (unweighted) assets over capital. In Europe, the ratio of risk-weighted assets to total assets is 32 percent in the UK, 31 percent in France, 35 percent in Germany, roughly half US values.[5]

15 November 2011: Federal Reserve Bank of Dallas president Richard Fisher says that regulators should break up banks that are too big to fail, just adding extra capital requirements of 1–2.5 percent is not enough.

16 November 2011: The EU Commission's Michel Barnier, responsible for the internal market, abandons attempts to prevent rating firms from publishing sovereign rating announcements under special troubled circumstances, as defined by the ESMA, the EU securities markets regulator.

16 November 2011: Bloomberg reports that the financial services industry worldwide seems set to lose 200,000 jobs in 2011 after having increased employment slightly in 2010. Among the major banks, BNP Paribas is cutting 1,400 jobs and Citigroup around 3,000. In 2008, 130,000 financial jobs were lost and another 174,000 in 2009.

17 November 2011: The good parts of the bankrupt and nationalized UK bank Northern Rock, including 75 branch offices, are sold to Sir Richard Branson's Virgin Money for an initial sum of 747 million pounds. This means an immediate 400 million pound loss to the owner, UK Financial Investments (UKFI), i.e. the British taxpayer. The residual toxic (mortgage) assets remain with UK Asset Resolution to be sold.

21 November 2011: The Spanish government nationalizes ailing Banco de Valencia, injecting 1 billion euro in capital from FROB. The bank is sold in November 2012 to CaixaBank.

25 November 2011: The Swedish government officially proposes sharply raised core Tier 1 capital (CET1) ratios for the country's four major banks, deemed to be of systemic importance. From

---

[5] But note the previous footnote!

2013, the minimum ratio will be 10 percent of risk-weighted assets (RWA), rising to 12 percent in 2015. This is 5 percentage points higher than demanded under Basel III, except for Nordea which has been included on the Financial Stability Board's list of internationally systemic banks G-SIFIs (see 4 November 2011). On top of this may come a countercyclical buffer of 0–2.5 percent, bringing the potential total CET1/RWA to 14.5 percent.

5 December 2011: Questions have arisen concerning the possibility of implementing the so-called "Liquidity Coverage Ratio" as planned in 2015. The downgrading of several European countries has left banks with fewer highly rated sovereign bonds to be included in the numerator. JPMorgan Chase has estimated that few of the largest European banks would comply with the ratio as of end 2011, leaving an aggregate shortfall of over 500 billion euro.

8 December 2011: The European Banking Authority (EBA) publishes the amount of capital required for the EU banks in order to fulfill a core Tier 1 capital adequacy ratio of 9 percent with regard taken to "haircuts" on sovereign bonds in the banking book. This is shown in Table 6.

9 December 2011: The Thompson Reuters governance, risk and compliance unit reports that financial firms worldwide are hit by 60 new regulatory changes each working day (sic!), a total of 14,215 changes from November 2010 to November 2011. This includes the passage of laws and short-selling bans as well as policy announcements in speeches or consultation papers. Of these, 57 percent pertain to the United States, indicative of the changes wrought by the Dodd–Frank legislation.

15 December 2011: The Boston Consulting Group estimates that the major banks worldwide would have to raise 350 billion euro in new capital to comply with Basel III requirements or cut assets by 5,000 billion euro, 17 percent. Banks in Asia and America face a capital shortfall of 70 billion each implying that the major problem is undercapitalized European banks having to raise almost 200 billion euro in fresh capital, to be contrasted with the 115 billion euro required by the EBA (see above).

16 December 2011: In a settlement with the FDIC, three executives (former CEO Kerry Killinger, former president Steve Rotella

Table 6. *Capital required for EU banks to fulfill core Tier 1 capital adequacy ratio of 9 percent (EBA)*

	Billion euro
Austria (AT)	3.9
Reiffeisen Zentralbank	2.1
Volksbanken	1.1
Erste Bank group	0.7
Belgium (BE)	6.3
Dexia	6.3
Cyprus (CY)	3.6
Marfin Popular (Laiki)	2.0
Bank of Cyprus	1.6
Germany (DE)	13.1
Commerzbank	5.3
Deutsche Bank	3.2
Hypo Real Estate	2.4
Denmark (DK)	–
Spain (ES)	26.2
Santander	15.3
BBVA	6.3
Banco Popular	2.6
Finland (FI)	–
France (FR)	7.3
Banque Populaire et Caisse d'Ep.	3.7
Société Générale	2.1
BNP Paribas	1.5
Crédit Agricole	–
Great Britain (GB)	–
Greece (GR)	30.0
Not distinguished	
Hungary (HU)	–
Ireland (IE)	–
Italy (IT)	15.4

Table 6. **Capital required for EU banks to fulfill core Tier 1 capital adequacy ratio of 9 percent (EBA)** *(cont.)*

	Billion euro
UniCredit	8.0
Banca Monte dei Paschi	3.3
Banco Populare	2.7
UBI Banca	1.4
Intesa Sanpaolo	–
Luxembourg (LU)	–
Malta (MT)	–
Netherlands (NL)	0.2
SNS Bank	0.2
Norway (NO)	1.5
DNB NOR	1.5
Poland (PL)	–
Portugal (PT)	7.0
BCP	2.1
Caixa geral	1.8
Espirito Santo	1.6
Sweden (SE)	–
Slovenia (SI)	0.3
NLB	0.3
TOTAL	114,685 million euro

and the former president of home loans David Schneider) from the failed bank Washington Mutual agree to forgo payments of 65 million dollars from the bank. Neither has been criminally charged by any supervisory authority.

19 December 2011: With the charges by the Securities and Exchange Commission (SEC) against six leading executives in Fannie Mae and Freddie Mac, 45 individuals and 42 companies have been charged in connection with the financial crisis, mostly for fraud or misleading information in connection with the sale of subprime

mortgages or derivatives on these. Among the sued individuals are the former CEOs of failed mortgage lenders New Century, IndyMac and Countrywide. While banks most often settle without admitting guilt (Goldman Sachs paying a record 550 million dollar fine), individuals fight the allegations. See 14 December 2012.

29 December 2011: After the issuing of equity required by the EBA stress tests, Allied Irish Banks and Irish Life & Permanent are wholly owned by the Irish government, while boasting core Tier 1 ratios well above 20 percent. The Bank of Ireland, successful in issuing equity to private investors, has seen the government's share fall to 15.1 percent. The perceived cost of the bail-out of the Irish banking system is set at over 70 billion euro (the actual figure is 63 billion by 2013).

16 January 2012: The world's first international tribunal for complex financial transactions opens in The Hague, giving parties an alternative to litigation in London or the US.

1 February 2012: In a unique action, former Royal Bank of Scotland CEO Sir Fred Goodwin's knighthood is "cancelled and annulled" by the Honours' Forfeiture Committee.

9 February 2012: Bank of America pays the Justice Department a fine of 1 billion dollars for 'false mortgage claims' originating in its Countrywide division.

9 February 2012: The Federal Reserve fines five of the largest banks in America a total of 26 billion dollars to compensate borrowers subjected to hasty and erroneous foreclosure proceedings: JPMorgan Chase, Wells Fargo, Citigroup, Ally Financial (ex-GMAC) and Bank of America.

13 February 2012: JPMorgan Chase is fined 275 million dollars by the Federal Reserve for "unsafe and unsound" practices in residential loan servicing and processing, mainly the result of its purchase of Washington Mutual.

15 February 2012: Citigroup pays the Justice Department a fine of 158 million dollars for false mortgage claims originating in its CityMortgage division.

21 February 2012: The "troika" (EU Commission, the IMF and the ECB) agrees to a second bail-out of Greece worth 130 billion euro for a total of 240 billion for the two packages.

23 February 2012: A number of executives of the crashed Icelandic bank Kaupthing, among them the chairman and the CEO, as well as the CEO of Glitnir, are charged with fraud and market manipulation.

24 February 2012: The FDIC reports losses of almost 87 billion dollars over the period 2008–11 on account of the financial crisis. These losses occurred in around 400 federally insured banks. The FDIC has, however, only recovered a few hundred million dollars in damages from negligent bank executives, a sum to be contrasted with the 1.3 billion dollars recovered after the savings and loan crisis in the 1980s.

1 March 2012: Out of 398 Dodd–Frank rule-making requirements, only 67 (29.8 percent) have been met with finalized rules.

1 March 2012: The ECB allocates 530 billion euro in loans to 800 banks in a three-year lending operation.

8 March 2012: Private holders of Greek government bonds, mainly banks, are asked to take a "haircut" of 53.5 percent of the face value on their holdings, corresponding to a write-down of 75 percent of actual values or 107 billion dollars. About one-third of this will hit Greek banks, which also need additional capital on account of the agreement that they reach a core Tier 1 ratio of 10 percent by mid 2013. The operation will lower the Greek debt/GDP ratio by 30 percentage points.

13 March 2012: Moody's downgrades the sovereign debt of Cyprus to "junk." Cyprus demands an emergency loan from the European Union.

19 March 2012: On account of the "haircut" and of the retroactive introduction of collective action clauses forcing more investors to participate in the debt restructuring, the International Swaps and Derivatives Dealers' Association (ISDA) declares a "credit event" leading to net payments of 3.5 billion euro for those who bought credit default swap protection for Greek sovereign bonds.

19 March 2012: The Federal Reserve follows up on its earlier judgment against the five biggest banks by fining a number of second-tier banks for hasty and erroneous foreclosure proceedings: EverBank, Goldman Sachs, HSBC Financial Holdings, PNC Financial Services, MetLife, OneWestBank, Sun Trust Banks and US Bancorp.

29 March 2012: The European Parliament adopts the European Market Infrastructure Regulation (EMIR) which demands reporting of all OTC derivatives trades and central counterparty clearing (CCP) of all standardized OTC derivatives contracts as well as interoperability between clearing houses.

13 April 2012: The Group of 30 proposes that international banks should split the role of chairman and CEO, which of course is the traditional situation in US banks such as JPMorgan (Jamie Dimon), Morgan Stanley (James Gorman), Goldman Sachs (Lloyd Blankfein) and Wells Fargo (John Stumpf) even though some banks such as Bank of America and Citigroup have already separated the roles.

14 April 2012: The US Treasury estimates the long-run net cost of the TARP program at 60 billion dollars.

24 April 2012: Geir Haarde, former prime minister of Iceland, is found guilty of negligence in the (so far) only legal procedure against a politician in the global financial crisis. However, no punishment will be imposed and the government will pay his legal costs. He was found innocent of the charge that he failed to attack the too-big-to-fail problem and two other charges.

6 May 2012: Royal Bank of Scotland (RBS) repays the last 5.7 billion pounds of a liquidity support that at its peak amounted to 75 billion (special liquidity and credit guarantee schemes). The state remains, at 82 percent, its main shareholder, however.

9 May 2012: The Spanish state bank support agency (FROB) becomes majority owner of Bankia after an injection of 4.4 billion euro. The bank, Spain's fourth largest, was formed by the merger of Caja Madrid and six other savings banks. Its chairman, former minister of the economy and IMF managing director Rodrigo Rato, steps down.

11 May 2012: Deutsche Bank agrees to pay the US Justice Department 202 million dollars under the False Claims Act for having misrepresented the quality of mortgages in its US Mortgage IT division.

18 May 2012: The British National Audit Office finalizes the cost to the taxpayer of the nationalization of failed mortgage lender Northern Rock, the viable parts of which were sold to Virgin Money in November 2011. Out of a total investment of 37 billion in the two parts of the bank (the sold parts and the retained "bad bank") the government almost broke even, losing less than 0.5 billion pounds.

25 May 2012: The capital need of partly nationalized Spanish Bankia is raised to 23.5 billion euro after the bank lost over 19 billion euro for the year 2012.

8 June 2012: Dexia succeeds in finally selling its Turkish subsidiary Denizbank to Russian Sberbank for 3 billion euro.

9 June 2012: The eurozone finance ministers agree in principle to a loan to recapitalize Spain's ailing banks of up to 100 billion euro.

14 June 2012: Moody's downgrades the sovereign debt of Spain to Baa3, just a notch above "junk."

14 June 2012: Jerry Williams, former CEO of failed Florida-based Orion Bank, is sentenced to six years in prison on charges of "conspiracy and lying to regulators." He had orchestrated a scheme whereby the bank lent money to a customer who bought shares in the bank, making it seem better capitalized than it was. The bank was put into receivership under the FDIC in November 2009.

27 June 2012: Barclays Bank pays fines for its role in the rigging of LIBOR interest rates: 200 million dollars to the US CFTC, 160 million dollars to the US Department of the Treasury and 60 million pounds to the British Financial Services Authority, for a total of 450 million dollars. The chairman of the bank, Marcus Agius, and its CEO, Bob Diamond, both resign.

30 June 2012: The brand Westdeutsche Landesbank (WestLB) disappears as the viable parts of the bank are taken over by the Landesbank Hessen-Thüringen (Helaba).

12 July 2012: Ireland, having lost its Aaa rating as late as in March 2009, is downgraded to Ba1 (i.e. "junk") by Moody's.

13 July 2012: JPMorgan Chase reveals a loss of 6.2 billion dollars, mostly in CDS contracts, in its London investment office, occasioned by trader Bruno Iksil, named the "London whale" on account of the size of his transactions (his derivatives book when closed was 157 billion dollars). Ina Drew, the bank's head of investment and risk management, resigns, together with the head of international CIO, Achilles Macris, along with chief financial officer Douglas Braunstein and Jes Staley, CEO of the investment bank. JPMorgan clawed back more than 100 million dollars in pay from Drew and the other managers. See also 14 August 2013 and 17 September 2013.

24 July 2012: In the first European criminal case outside Iceland, three former executives of failed Anglo Irish Bank, among them the former chairman Sean FitzPatrick, are charged with financial irregularities in connection with the crisis, in particular having lent money to individuals to buy shares in the bank in order to prop up the share price. FitzPatrick was also charged with hiding loans of 155 million euro to himself from Anglo Irish by transferring them to Irish Life & Permanent over the day of reporting.

25 July 2012: The former CEO of Citigroup, Sandi Weill, joins the widening group of people saying that big banks should be broken up, perhaps along the lines of commercial banks – investment banks (re-establishing Glass–Steagall), perhaps simply because they are too big.

27 July 2012: The viable parts of Greek Agricultural Bank are bought by Piraeus Bank.

9 August 2012: Mark O'Connor, former CEO and chairman of First City Bank of Georgia, is sentenced to 12 years in prison and repayment of 7 million dollars. His main crime was letting the bank lend money to himself, through straw borrowers/house buyers, money used to buy foreclosed properties, then resold at a profit.

6 September 2012: The ECB begins its Outright Monetary Transactions (OMT) to maintain bond yields low.

10 September 2012: The US Treasury sells 18 billion dollars' worth of shares in the bailed-out insurance company AIG, which will diminish the state's share to 21.5 percent from 53.4 percent and from an original 79.9 percent. Taxpayers have already gained 12 billion dollars on the rescue. With the state now owning less than 50 percent, the Federal Reserve will become AIG's main regulator in its capacity as a financial holding company.

12 September 2012: In one of the very few punishments for mismanagement during the financial crisis, the British Financial Services Authority (FSA) fined the former head of commercial lending at HBOS (Halifax Bank of Scotland, taken over by Lloyds TSB in 2008) 500,000 pounds and barred him for life from working in the financial sector.

28 September 2012: Bank of America agrees to pay 2.43 billion dollars to investors claiming that the bank did not adequately inform

them about the spiralling losses in Merrill Lynch before stockholders voted in January 2009 to agree to the purchase.

9 October 2012: In its ongoing rationalization plan to repay 10 billion euro state support, ING Groep sells ING Direct to Barclays. By end 2012, 7.8 billion euro of the 10 billion received by ING has been repaid plus 2.4 billion in interest.

11 October 2012: The Congressional Budget Office (CBO) calculates the end cost to taxpayers of the TARP program at 24 billion dollars, down from the initial estimate of 356 billion in March 2009. Most of this figure resulted from the Housing Support Programs, regarded as a subsidy. Through the TARP's Capital Purchase Program (CPP), the US Treasury invested 204.9 billion dollars in 707 institutions. As of 31 December 2012, 258 of those institutions remained in TARP; in 46 of them, the Treasury holds only warrants to purchase stock. CBO estimated a gain of 18 billion to taxpayers from the CPP itself. Of the total 182 billion invested in AIG, the net loss was estimated by CBO to be 14 billion as of October 2012. See also 11 December 2012.

16 October, 2012: Vikram Pandit resigns as CEO of Citigroup, replaced by Michael Corbat.

17 October 2012: Royal Bank of Scotland (RBS) exits from the Asset Protection Scheme agreed to in 2009, after having paid in to the Treasury some 2.5 billion pounds in fees on covered assets of 282 billion pounds of loans and derivatives with no payments whatsoever from the Treasury.

19 October 2012: Morgan Stanley gets regulatory approval to use a revised VaR model showing dramatically lower risk, especially in the credit portfolio, and hence higher capital-adequacy ratios.[6]

17 October 2012: The Federal Reserve Bank of New York has exited all holdings of the so-called Maiden Lane securities, which gave a loan to the insurance giant AIG. After repayments, taxpayers have gained 9.4 billion dollars. The ownership by the US Treasury of the company is down to 16 percent after four share sales during 2012.

---

[6] It should be noted that Morgan Stanley, being an ex-investment bank, is on Basel II in contrast to other US banks which have remained on Basel I.

26 October 2012: Andy Haldane, director of financial stability at the Bank of England, calculates that the subsidy given to 29 too-big-to-fail banks worldwide is a stunning 70 billion dollars annually.

1 November 2012: The Financial Stability Board (FSB) updates the list of extra capital charges to be held by the Globally Systemically Important Financial Institutions (G-SIFIs). Lloyds Banking Group, Commerzbank and Dexia are dropped from the list on account of their downsizing or break-up, Standard Chartered and BBVA are added. This is the new list:

Surcharges of 3.5 percent: presently empty

Surcharges of 2.5 percent: Citibank, Deutsche Bank, HSBC, JPMorgan Chase (4)

Surcharges of 2.0 percent: Barclays, BNP Paribas (2)

Surcharges of 1.5 percent: Bank of America, Bank of New York Mellon, Credit Suisse, Goldman Sachs, Mitsubishi UFJ FG, Morgan Stanley, RBS, UBS (8)

Surcharge of 1.0 percent: Bank of China, BBVA, Groupe BPCE, Crédit Agricole, ING, Mizohu FG, Nordea, Santander, Société Générale, Standard Chartered, State Street, Sumitomo Mitsui FG, UniCredit, Wells Fargo (14)

Nationally, we find of the SIFIs: 8 from the US, 4 from France, 4 from the UK, 3 from Japan, 2 from Switzerland, 2 from Spain, 1 from China, 1 from Germany, 1 from Italy, 1 from Sweden and 1 from the Netherlands.

5 November 2012: An Australian court finds both the investment bank involved, ABN AMRO, and Standard & Poor's liable for the losses of an AAA-rated product called "Constant proportion debt obligations" (CPDOs).

9 November 2012: Nationalized French-Belgian bank Dexia, earlier the leading municipal lender in the world, received another injection of 5.5 billion euro in preferred shares from its owners.

27 November 2012: Nationalized Spanish bank Banco de Valencia is sold to CaixaBank for one euro.

3 December 2012: Finance ministers of the euro area agree to pay from the financial salvation funds 39.5 billion euro to recapitalize the Spanish banking system, in particular the four nationalized

banks Bankia, Catalunya Banc, NCG Banco and Banco de Valencia. In principle, support of 100 billion euro has been granted. The first three banks are to be down-sized; the fourth is to be sold. A "bad bank" is to be created to handle up to 50 billion euro of failed loans.

5 December 2012: Standard & Poor's cuts the rating of Greece to "selective default" on account of the write-down of debt.

10 December 2012: The FDIC wins a 168 million dollar settlement against former executives of failed IndyMac Bank for "breach of fiduciary duty." The defendants – Scott Van Dellen, Richard Koon and Kenneth Shellem – ran IndyMac's Homebuilder Division, a sideline to the thrift's main business of residential mortgage lending. See 14 December 2012.

11 December 2012: The US Treasury sells off its last shares in the insurance giant AIG. At the peak, the government owned 79.9 percent of the company. The rescue operation was paid back in full, netting the government 22.7 billion dollars in profit (although the TARP program itself lost 13 billion on AIG). AIG has during the four years shrunk from 1 trillion dollars in totals assets to 550 billion and its headcount from 116,000 to 57,000.

11 December 2012: HSBC agrees to pay the Office of the Comptroller of the Currency (OCC) 500 million dollars in fines for violating the Bank Secrecy Act, for Trading with the Enemy Act and other money laundering laws.

12 December 2012: The finance ministers of the European Union (the ECOFIN Council) agree on the concepts of a banking union, with the ECB made directly responsible from March 2014 for the supervision of the area's major banks (200 banks with assets above 200 billion euro or over 20 percent of the home country's GDP). Smaller banks (around 6,000) will continue to be supervised nationally but the ECB may intervene at the request of the European Stability Mechanism. Common rules for deposit insurance funds and bank resolution will come later.

13 December 2012: In approving the second aid package to Greece, the two totaling 240 billion euro, 50 billion euro is set aside to recapitalize Greek banks. This sum may be compared with the 30 billion deemed necessary by the EBA just a year earlier (see 9 December 2011).

13 December 2012: Ninety percent of the shares in Dexia Banque Internationale in Luxembourg are sold to Precision Capital, owned by Qatar's royal family, for 730 million euro, the residual being held by the state of Luxembourg. Precision also buys KBL, the Luxembourg subsidiary of Belgian KBC, for 1.05 billion euro.

14 December 2012: Lenders with more than 50 billion dollars of global assets and/or more than 10 billion dollars in the United States will be required by the Federal Reserve to house their US businesses, including securities trading, within regulated holding companies. The 10 billion threshold excludes the domestic assets that are connected to a US branch of a bank. About 25 institutions would fall under this requirement. This means separately capitalizing their US operations, passing annual stress tests and holding liquid dollar assets sufficient for 30 days. Before Dodd–Frank, foreign banks needed only to be well capitalized overall, not specifically in the US.

14 December 2012: In one of the few cases brought to court after the financial crisis, the FDIC as receiver of failed mortgage lender IndyMac settled with ex-CEO Michael W. Perry in an agreement that will bar him from banking and that recovers 1 million dollars in personal assets and up to 11 million of insurance policy money without acceptance of liability on his part.

17 December 2012: The Spanish government starts a "bad bank" SAREB (Sociedad de Gestión de Activos Procedentes de la Reestructuración Bancaria) with capital of 4.8 billion euro. The state bank restructuring fund FROB has contributed 45 percent of the capital and private interests 55 percent, among them Santander, Ibercaja, Bankinter, Unicaja, Cajamar, Caja Laboral, Banca March, Cecabank, Caixabank, Banco Sabadell, Banco Popular, Kutxabank and Banco Caminos as well as foreign banks Deutsche Bank and Barclays and a number of insurance companies such as Generali, Zurich and AXA.

19 December 2012: GM will repurchase 200 million of its own shares at 27:50 dollars from the Treasury, corresponding to 5.5 billion dollars or 40 percent of the Treasury's remaining 26 percent of the company. GM received a total support of 51 billion dollars; taxpayers have already recouped 24 billion to which is now added 5 billion more.

19 December 2012: France follows Britain in proposing ring-fencing of banking activities. However, the French proposal is weaker than the British in that proprietary trading but not market making is to be undertaken in a specially capitalized subsidiary. The ring-fenced unit is banned from high-frequency trading and commodity derivatives trading. Banks will also have to pay into a bank resolution fund aimed at reaching 10 billion euro in 2020 to fund future potential bank failures.

19 December 2012: Swiss bank UBS reaches an agreement with the Swiss supervisory authority, the UK Financial Services Authority and the US Department of Justice and the Commodity Futures Trading Commission, paying a fine of 1.5 billion dollars for its role in manipulating the setting of LIBOR interest rates. The US Department of Justice also announced that it would seek extradition of the two traders involved.

28 December 2012: Two senior managers, the CEO Lárus Welding and the head of corporate finance, Gudmundur Hjaltason, of failed Icelandic bank Glitnir are sentenced to nine months in prison for their role in the credit bubble.

6 January 2013: The Basel Committee on Banking Supervision decides on changes to the proposed Liquidity Coverage Ratios (LCR). The committee's oversight body agreed to phase in the rule from 2015 over four years and widen the range of assets banks can put into the buffer to include shares and retail mortgage-backed securities (RMBS), as well as lower-rated corporate bonds, though with a hefty haircut. However, the rule excludes MBSs based on "walk-away mortgages" (where the borrower has no further liability than his house), which is the dominant feature of all US residential mortgages.

Similarly, the lowering of the required liquidity coverage of deposits, while lowered from 5 to 3 percent of insured retail deposits, applies only to banks operating in countries where the deposit-insurance system is pre-funded, thereby excluding banks in the UK, Australia and Italy, among other countries.

7 January 2013: In two separate settlements, a number of major US banks agree to pay out over 20 billion dollars on home loans. Bank of America (mainly on account of its Countrywide purchase) agrees

to pay Fannie Mae 11.6 billion dollars for misstating the quality of mortgage loans sold and securitized. In a separate settlement, ten mortgage lenders (Bank of America, Wells Fargo, JPMorgan Chase, Citigroup, etc.) agree to pay over 8 billion dollars to settle allegations that they systematically abused the foreclosure system that allowed banks to seize homes from borrowers in default.

28 January 2013: The EFTA Court of Justice supports entirely the claim by Iceland that it is not obligated to pay Britain and the Netherlands for payments made to investors in the failed Landsbanki online Icesave scheme, deposits booked in Iceland. The stated reason is firstly the lack of clarity in international deposit-insurance cooperation and secondly the dire straits of the Icelandic economy after the crisis.

29 January 2013: The EU Commissioner responsible for banking and regulatory questions, Michel Barnier, makes it clear that the Commission proposal, due later in 2013, will not follow the Liikanen report in proposing ring-fencing the investment bank activities of universal banks. This follows proposals by Germany and France that are much more limited in scope. The question then remains whether the UK, having national proposals on these lines, following the Vickers Commission, will go it alone.

1 February 2013: As an indication of lingering bank problems linked to the mortgage markets, the Dutch government nationalizes the fourth-largest bank and insurer SNS Reaal Bank at a cost of 3.7 billion euro in capital and 1.6 billion in guarantees. The bank had lost heavily in the Spanish mortgage market. Not only shareholders lost their investments but also junior bond investors were totally wiped out, a first in euro area bank salvation (but seen before in e.g. Denmark). See also 11 July 2013.

1 February 2013: Greek Emporiki Bank is sold by French Crédit Agricole to Alpha Bank.

3 February 2013: The UK chancellor warns banks that unless they follow the proposed ring fence separating commercial and investment banking activities, they will be broken apart completely.

4 February 2013: The ratings agency Standard & Poor's (owned by McGraw-Hill) is being sued by the United States Justice Department over claims that it knowingly understated the credit risks of the

instruments that it rated. The charge is "mail fraud, wire fraud and financial institutions fraud" under the Financial Institutions Reform, Recovery and Enforcement Act of 1989. S&P issued credit ratings on more than 2.8 trillion dollars' worth of residential mortgage-backed securities (RMBS) and about 1.2 trillion worth of collateralized-debt obligations (CDOs) from September 2004 through October 2007, according to the complaint. S&P downplayed the risks on highly rated portions of these securities to gain more business from the investment banks that issued them; the US attorney general said, "its desire for increased revenue and market share in the RMBS and CDO ratings markets led S&P to downplay and disregard the true extent of the credit risks."

6 February 2013: The German government proposes the division ("ring-fencing") of banks into a commercial-bank unit and an investment-bank unit, provided that investment-bank activities, such as proprietary trading and market making, encompass more than 20 percent of total assets or more than 100 billion euro. This means that only Deutsche Bank, Commerzbank and Landesbank Baden-Württemberg (LBBW) will be affected. Lending and guarantees to hedge and private equity funds will also have to take place in the investment bank part of the bank.

6 February 2013: The Irish Parliament (Dail) votes to liquidate the nationalized Anglo Irish Bank (renamed the Irish Bank Resolution Corporation), thereby giving up hopes that it could become viable again. Remaining assets are transferred to the "bad bank" NAMA. Its former president Sean FitzPatrick and two other executives face judicial charges for fraud. The Irish government also persuades the ECB to exchange the promissory notes (10-year notes at 8 percent interest) issued at the time of rescue for longer-term debt at 3 percent. The swap is said to save Irish taxpayers 20 billion euro over the next decade. At the same time, Irish banks (especially the biggest, Bank of Ireland, still 15 percent state-owned) are ordered to cut payroll costs by 6–10 percent, by reducing the number of employees, pension benefits or salaries/bonuses.

6 February 2013: British bank RBS, majority-owned by the government, is fined 390 million pounds (615 million dollars) in payment to the British and US supervisory authorities for its role in the rigging of LIBOR interest rates.

12 February 2013: Switzerland becomes the first major country to apply countercyclical capital buffers in order to cool the booming housing market. From 30 September, banks will have to hold an additional 1 percent in capital to risk-weighted assets (out of a potential buffer of 2.5 percent). This is tantamount to raising some 3 billion Swiss francs in new capital.

12 February 2013: Ailing Banco de Valencia, merging with Caixabank, writes down 90 percent of its subordinated debt in one of the few bail-ins in the banking crisis (Danish Amagerbanken, Dutch SNS Reaal, Anglo Irish Bank).

13 February 2013: Ireland is raised to BBB+ by Standard & Poor's.

21 February 2013: Partly nationalized French-Belgian municipal bank Dexia reports losses for 2012 of 2.9 billion, down from 11.6 billion in 2011. It has received around 11 billion euro in state aid as well as state guarantees for 90 billion euro in assets. Its share price has fallen from 22.56 euro in May 2007 to 5 cents (!) in February 2013.

22 February 2013: Like Sweden, the Hong Kong Monetary Authority sets a floor of 15 percent under the risk weight for residential mortgages.

22 February 2013: Moody's downgrades the sovereign credit of the United Kingdom from Aaa to Aa1.

28 February 2013: Ailing Spanish savings bank Bankia, nationalized to 45 percent, reveals losses for 2012 of 19 billion euro, the largest loss ever for a Spanish corporation. It has received 24 billion euro in state aid (out of a total for Spanish banks of 98 billion) and transferred a nominal 22 billion in assets to the Spanish "bad bank" SAREB (Sociedad de Gestión de Activos Procedentes de la Reestructuración Bancaria), started at the end of 2012 (see 17 December 2012), at an average 46 percent discount. SAREB has also bought assets worth a nominal 6.7 billion from nationalized Catalunya Banc as well as 5.7 billion from NCG Banco-Banco Gallego and 2 billion from Banco de Valencia. Altogether, SAREB's portfolio is just over 50 billion euro, consisting at present of 76,000 empty homes, 6,300 rented homes, 14,900 unbuilt plots of land and 84,300 individual loans.

28 February 2013: The world's oldest bank and Italy's third largest, Banca Monte dei Paschi di Siena, receives a bail-out of

4.1 billion euro from the Italian state via Banca d'Italia to maintain the required capital-adequacy ratio. The bank also sues its former chairman and its former CEO for their role in the loss of 730 million euro on derivative trades in 2008–9. On 16 July, the EU Competition Commissioner, however, rejects the proposed changes by the bank, demanding more cost-cutting and lower risk profile. Should the Commission ultimately reject the plan, the money has to be returned. On 8 September, a revised plan is accepted. Monte dei Paschi has to raise at least 2.5 billion euro in new equity, or else the loan from the state ("Monti bonds") will be converted to equity, and sell 400 branch offices.

1 March 2013: As of this date, only 148 (37.2 percent) of the 398 total required rulemakings under the Dodd–Frank legislation have been finalized, 121 (30.4 percent) are at some stage underway while 129 (32.4 percent) rulemaking requirements have not yet even been proposed.

3 March 2013: Swiss voters in a referendum enforce strict limits on executive (incl. banking) pay. Golden handshakes as well as golden parachutes are explicitly forbidden, the annual meeting of shareholders must decide on the pay structure of the Board of Directors and the Management Board.

5 March 2013: In a meeting of EU finance ministers (ECOFIN Council), Britain loses its bid to change the strict bonus rules that the EU Parliament tacked onto the Capital Adequacy Directive (CRD IV). In future, bonus payments may not exceed fixed pay or, with a qualified majority of the members of the annual meeting of shareholders, twice the fixed portion. The rule applies to all EU banks worldwide, even to subsidiaries and branches located outside Europe.

7 March 2013: The Federal Reserve releases the results from the annual stress tests required under the Dodd–Frank legislation for the largest US banks. Seventeen of the 18 largest banks would weather a deep recession, maintaining regulatory capital above the required minimum of 5 percent. Under the most adverse scenario studied, US GDP was assumed stagnant or falling for six consecutive quarters. Unemployment peaked at 12.1 percent, while real disposable household income fell for five consecutive quarters. Stock prices tumbled 52 percent, and house prices fall 21 percent.

Under this scenario, only Ally Financial (ex-GMAC), still majority-owned by the American taxpayers, fell below the required 5 percent Tier 1 equity (CET1) common ratio. Morgan Stanley showed a minimum CET1 of 5.7 percent and Goldman Sachs a ratio of 5.8 percent. Projected losses for the 18 banks would total 462 billion dollars over nine quarters, the aggregate Tier 1 common capital ratio falling from an actual 11.1 percent in the third quarter of 2012 to 7.7 percent in the fourth quarter of 2014.

The 18 firms represent more than 70 percent of the assets in the US banking system. In the scenario, the 18 lenders would lose a total of 316.6 billion dollars on souring debts, led by Bank of America (57.5 billion dollars), and followed by Citigroup (54.6 billion). JPMorgan Chase and Wells Fargo would both lose almost 54 billion. Home loans were the largest source of bad debt in the Fed's tests with 60.1 billion in projected losses on first mortgages and 37.2 billion on junior lien and home equity loans.

The Fed said in November 2012 that the largest banking groups had nearly doubled their Tier 1 common capital to 803 billion dollars in the second quarter of last year from 420 billion in the first quarter of 2009.

7 March 2013: Standard & Poor's raises the rating of Portugal to BB, still together with Greece in "junk" territory (whereas Ireland has been raised to investment grade).

11 March 2013: The part of the Dodd–Frank Act dealing with OTC derivatives enters into force, making clearing through a central counterparty compulsory for the majority of derivatives which are sufficiently standardized.

11 March 2013: The Parliamentary Commission on Banking Standards, scrutinizing a bill designed to make Britain's banks safer, demands for a second time that the chancellor of the exchequer toughen the legislation, threatening to break up the entire banking industry if it doesn't comply with ring-fence rules to protect retail operations from investment bank operations. The Commission also demands higher leverage ratios than the 3 percent proposed by Basel III. All banks should rather follow at least the 4 percent ratio proposed in the Banking Act for the major banks only.

12 March 2013: The Spanish bank support agency FROB injects capital into three banks: 730 million euro in ordinary stock into Banco

Mare Nostrum, 124 million euro in CoCos into Liberbank and 407 million euro in CoCos into Banco Grupo Caja 3.

14 March 2013: Commerzbank, which received total state aid of 18.2 billion euro during the crisis, seeks to issue 2.5 billion euro in new shares. This would have the double advantage of lowering the German federal state's ownership from 25 percent, a blocking minority, to less than 20 percent (17 to be exact), while simultaneously raising its capital ratio under Basel III rules from 7.6 to 8.6 percent.

15 March 2013: The European Union's Regulation 648/2012 on OTC derivatives, central counterparties and trade repositories (European Market Infrastructure Regulation, EMIR) enters into force.

16 March 2013: The European Union's euro area finance ministers agree to aid Cyprus with aid worth 10 billion euro. However, in an unprecedented move, uninsured depositors will lose 9.9 percent of their balances, insured depositors 6.75 percent, to provide for another 6 billion euro to recapitalize its banks. The plan is rejected by the Cypriot parliament on 19 March with not a single legislator voting for the package.

19 March 2013: National governments and the EU parliament agree on the first step of the planned banking union, the Single Supervisory Mechanism (SSM), parliament gaining the right to approve the heads of supervision within the ECB, the ECB to be the overall supervisor of 6,000 banks and the EBA gaining powers to request information from national supervisory authorities. The "price" exacted by the EU parliament for agreeing to the union was a limit on bonuses in financial firms, these being no more than the fixed salary. Exceptionally, with agreement by a qualified majority of shareholders, bonuses may be twice the fixed portion.

19 March 2013: The European Banking Authority (EBA) and the Financial Stability Board (FSB) report that banks worldwide halved their capital needs (to attain a minimum of 7 percent CTE1/RWA) to fulfill the Basel III requirements. 180 billion dollars were raised in 2012 as a result of new capital and asset sales, "only" 208 billion remained. The ratio calculated according to Basel III rules had been raised from 7.7 percent to 8.5. The 28 G-SIFI groups will be required to hold at least 8.5–9.5 percent capital. The 44 major European banks studied had ratios of, on average, a ratio

of 7.7 percent compared with the 11.1 percent they enjoy under current Basel 2.5 rules.

22 March 2013: Norway follows Sweden, Switzerland and Britain in proposing higher capital requirements than Basel III. From 2016, its biggest bank, DnB NOR, must have at least 12 percent TCE1/RWA.

22 March 2013: The French Senate adopts a French version of ring-fencing whereby "speculative activities" (defined to specifically include trading in commodities and high-frequency trading) above a certain size have to be conducted through separately financed subsidiaries. The two major banks, BNP Paribas and Société Générale, calculate that less than 1 percent of revenue will be affected. The other two major banks, Banque Populaire and Crédit Agricole, have already separated their trading activities into subsidiaries, Natixis and Cacib, respectively.

25 March 2013: In a total turnaround of principles, the final agreement between Cyprus and the international lenders (ECB, IMF and European Union), a bail-in of bank uninsured depositors is demanded as a precondition for a loan of 10 billion euro to the state of Cyprus. The second largest bank, Laiki bank (Cyprus Popular Bank), majority owned by the government, is to be wound down. Its good assets, together with deposits under 100,000 euro (the maximum amount guaranteed under EU deposit insurance), is to be transferred to the biggest bank, Bank of Cyprus. Bonds and higher-denomination deposits are converted into stock and, together with remaining assets, transferred to a "bad bank." In the Bank of Cyprus, deposits above 100,000 will be frozen until it can be established how much will have to be used to reach the sum necessary to capitalize the bank to 9 percent TCE1/RWA. An estimated 60 percent of these deposits will be compulsorily swapped into equity. The two banks' Greek operations are sold to Piraeus Bank, which acquired net assets valued at 2.8 billion euro for a price of 524 million euro.

26 March 2013: In an effort to revive competition in a banking market dominated by four big banks, the British FSA proposes that newly started banks should be allowed to operate with the minimum 4.5 percent TCE1/RWA capital adequacy ratio demanded by Basel III and the corresponding EU regulation. They will be prevented from paying dividends until they reach the 7 percent

capital adequacy ratio that includes a capital conservation buffer. This contrasts with the 10 percent ratio to be required of the big four (Barclays, Lloyds Banking Group, Royal Bank of Scotland and HSBC), which have 75–85 percent market shares in most segments.

26 March 2013: Iceland charges a number of former executives in failed Kaupthing and Landsbanki, among them the two CEOs, with market manipulation in that the bank lent money to be used to buy shares in the banks, in particular to members of their boards. Top executives from the third crashed bank, Glitnir, already serve nine-month sentences for fraud.

27 March 2013: The Bank of England states that UK banks lack 25 billion pounds in capital to reach Basel III targets. That is sharply down from 60 billion in November 2012.

1 April 2013: The new Prudential Regulatory Authority (PRA) within the Bank of England takes over banking supervision from the FSA. Arthur Bailey assumes the role of deputy governor for Prudential Regulation and CEO of the Prudential Regulation Authority as well as ex officio member of the Financial Policy Committee (FPC).

2 April 2013: Fannie Mae reports a record profit of 17.2 billion dollars for 2012, an indication of the turnaround in the housing market. The two government-owned giants Fannie Mae and Freddie Mac have returned 50 of the 187.5 billion dollars they received in support from the Treasury.

5 April 2013: Senators Sherrod Brown (D, Ohio) and David Vitter (R, Louisiana) propose higher capital requirements for US banks. While all banks would have to hold 10 percent capital in relation to total assets, including derivatives, banks with assets above 400 billion dollars would have to hold an additional 5 percent. This compares with the proposed 3 percent leverage ratio under Basel III (and 4 percent for the major UK banks). US regulatory authorities would be prevented from implementing Basel III in the United States. Financial aid from the US Treasury would only be made available to insured banks.

9 April 2013: Sir James Crosby, the former CEO of Halifax Bank of Scotland (HBOS), asks for his knighthood to be revoked after a scathing report by parliament found that he sowed the "seeds of destruction" at one of Britain's biggest banks. Thereby he probably

avoided the fate of Fred Goodwin, former CEO of RBS, who was stripped of his knighthood.

12 April 2013: In one of the few criminal convictions after the financial crisis, the head of Credit Suisse's London-based structured credit trading division, Kareem Serageldin, having been extradited to the US, pleads guilty to charges of conspiracy and fraud. He had deliberately mispriced mortgage bonds based on subprime mortgages, hiding a loss of 351 million pounds, in order to keep his bonus.

15 April 2013: The European Parliament adopts the parallel Capital Requirements Regulation (CRR) and the Capital Requirements Directive (CRD), which will enter into force on 1 January 2014.

27 April 2013: Credit Suisse together with the American private equity firm Lone Star agree to buy the "bad bank" resulting from the failure of Belgian Fortis Bank, Royal Park Investments SA, for 6.7 billion euro, 1 of which goes to repay the Belgian state.

9 May 2013: After return to profitability, the two quasi-nationalized mortgage lenders Fannie Mae and Freddie Mac have started to pay back the money received from the government during the crisis. In May 2013, Fannie Mae paid the Treasury 59 billion dollars and will thus have repaid 95 billion of the 117 billion capital infusion received. Freddie Mac will have repaid 36 billion out of drawn 72 billion.

9 May 2013: Monoline insurer MBIA (see 31 January 2008) receives a 1.7 billion dollar settlement from Bank of America (owner of the Countrywide brand) for misrepresentation of mortgages included in MBSs insured by MBIA.

9 May 2013: The new Icelandic government says foreign creditors in the failed banks Kaupthing, Landsbanki and Glitnir will lose their 3.8 billion dollar investments. These losses come on top of the refusal of Iceland to repay the United Kingdom and the Netherlands the amounts these countries paid out for deposit insurance in the failed banks, in particular the Icesave accounts in Landsbanki.

17 May 2013: In an indication that Spain is following Iceland, Ireland and Germany in prosecuting leading figures behind the financial crisis, Miguel Blesa, the former chairman of Caja Madrid (now a part of nationalized Bankia), is jailed for his role in the acquisition of City National Bank of Florida in 2008. His successor at Caja

Madrid and later Bankia, former IMF managing director Rodrigo Rato, is also under investigation but so far not charged.

21 May 2013: The Economic and Monetary Affairs Committee of the European Parliament adopt plans for bank resolution. Under the draft rules, a struggling bank's own assets and liabilities would be used first to resolve a crisis or wind it down (the "bailing-in" system). The recent Cyprus mess clearly demonstrated the need for clear procedures to ensure that shareholders, bondholders and only then uninsured depositors foot the bill. The approved position broadly retains the Commission's proposed order of bank creditors to take a hit. However, it also inserts clauses stipulating that insured deposits of below 100,000 euro can never be used, and that uninsured ones, i.e. those above 100,000 euro, may only be used as a last resort. The text also deletes the possibility, suggested by the Commission, of diverting funds from deposit guarantee schemes to help pay for bank resolution measures. Simultaneous plans from the Commission require approval by the Commission for all restructuring before any taxpayer money is committed. In Spain and the Netherlands (SNS Real) as well as in Denmark, junior and even senior claims have already been bailed-in in restructurings.

23 May 2013: The new Prudential Regulation Authority (PRA) under the Bank of England estimates that UK banks still need to raise an additional 25 billion pounds of capital or sell off assets correspondingly. This is down from the 50 billion estimated by the Bank of England's Financial Policy Committee (FPC) in November 2012. The largest shortfalls stem from the Royal Bank of Scotland (nationalized to 82 percent) and Lloyds Banking Group (nationalized to 39 percent).

29 May 2013: The German bank supervisor, BaFin, estimates that the major German banks were still short of 14 billion euro in capital according to Basel III rules by end of 2012, down from 32 billion at mid-year. Unfortunately, most of the improvement has come from twiddling with the risk weights in the internal risk models rather than raising new equity.

3 June 2013: Denmark's FSA, following Sweden in requiring its systemically important banks to hold higher capital buffers than the 1–2.5 percent required under Basel III, decides that the six Danish banks identified as SIFIs must hold a 1–3.5 percent extra ratio of

core capital to RWA, a ratio which may be raised in times of crisis, and secondly that they must also hold 5 percent of RWA in core capital or CoCos or similar instruments which convert to equity or are written off in a situation where the bank is in resolution.

3 June 2013: The Financial Stability Oversight Council (FSOC) designates non-bank holding companies AIG, Prudential and GE Capital as being of sufficient size to have systemic financial impact, warranting increased supervision by the Federal Reserve and the possibility of resolution by the FDIC.

5 June 2013: The US Treasury, which invested a total of 49.5 billion dollars into auto maker GM as part of the TARP program, is selling a further 30 million shares, lowering its ownership from the present ownership at 16.4 percent of total stock outstanding.

14 June 2013: Greek banks have by this date to come up with plans for capital adequacy. Of the aid received from the EU and the IMF (240 billion euro), 50 billion are aimed at recapitalization of the banking system, hit by toxic loans as well as by the "haircut" on privately held Greek government bonds. Of these 50 billion, 17 have been used for losses in defunct banks and 7 billion is being held in reserve. The remainder, 28 billion, is used to recapitalize the four major banks. Of these, Eurobank Ergasias has been nationalized and recapitalized by the Hellenic Financial Stability Fund (HFSF). The situation for the other three is uncertain. Provided a bank can raise at least 10 percent of its capital requirement, it can remain under private control and avoid complete nationalization.

17 June 2013: Denmark's Finanstilsynet (FSA) orders Danske Bank to add 100 billion kroner (18 billion dollars) to its risk-weighted assets after finding flaws in its internal ratings model for corporate exposures. This will raise capital requirements under Pillar 1 by 8 billion. Denmark's biggest bank with assets equivalent to 182 percent of the economy appealed the order a month later.

19 June 2013: The Swedish government reduces further its stake in Nordea, the bank nationalized in the financial crisis of 1992, from 13.4 to 7.8 percent.

20 June 2013: The new Prudential Regulatory Authority (PRA) within the Bank of England decides that UK banks must raise an additional total of 13.4 billion pounds to overcome a capital shortfall by the

end of the year in order to attain a ratio of 7 percent of equity to risk-weighted assets. Barclays, the UK's second-largest bank by assets, must raise 3 billion pounds in fresh capital, while Lloyds Banking Group must boost capital by 8.6 billion pounds. Standard Chartered, HSBC and Banco Santander's UK unit already comply. The PRA simultaneously enforces a 3 percent leverage ratio, noting that Barclays is at 2.5 percent and Nationwide Building Society at just 2 percent.

20 June 2013: The Swiss National Bank orders its two main banks, UBS and Credit Suisse, to conform to a 3 percent leverage ratio. Both stand at 2.3 percent.

20 June 2013: The finance ministers of the euro group decide rules for future bail-outs of banks from the European Stability Mechanism (ESM) fund. If the bank's ratio of core equity to risk-weighted assets is less than the minimum 4.5 percent, the bank's home country must first contribute the difference. For banks fulfilling the requirement, the home country must provide 20 percent of the necessary additional capital for two years and 10 percent thereafter. The maximum of the ESM fund to be allocated to direct bank support is set at 60 billion euro. Whether banks in bailed-out countries like Ireland and Greece may be given support retroactively will be decided when the bail-out mechanism becomes available in 2015 since the role of the ECB as bank supervisor for euro area banks must first be put in place.

20 June 2013: The US Federal Reserve and the FDIC propose informally to increase the leverage ratio (CET1 divided by total assets) demanded by the biggest banks from 4 to 6 percent. Of the major banks, only Wells Fargo would at this date comply. The figure may be compared with the 3 percent proposed under the Basel III arrangement and implemented under CRD IV in the EU.

24 June 2013: Reflecting regulatory and investor pressure, total pay in 2012 for the CEOs of the world's major banks fell by some 10 percent to just under 1 million dollars per month. Among the best paid (in annual terms) were John Stumpf (Wells Fargo) at 19.3 million dollars, Jamie Dimon (JPMorgan Chase) 18.7 million, Lloyd Blankfein (Goldman Sachs) 13.3 million, Stuart Gulliver (HSBC) 12.9 million, Mike Corbat (Citigroup) 12.4 million and António Horta-Osório (Lloyds Banking Group) 10.7 million.

24 June 2013: Erste Bank of Austria, having received 1.2 billion euro in state capital injection, plans to raise 660 million in fresh equity in a first pay-back.

25 June 2013: Senators Bob Corker (R) and Mark Warner (D) introduce a Bill in the US Senate to abolish the mortgage institutions Fannie Mae and Freddie Mac over a five-year period.

27 June 2013: Meeting in Brussels, finance ministers of the entire EU area reach an agreement on resolution rules for failed banks. France, Great Britain and Sweden want to retain the possibility for a taxpayer bail-out, nationally decided and financed, whereas Germany, the Netherlands and Finland want to exclude a priori any future taxpayer involvement. In a compromise that needs the approval of the EU Parliament, bank equity and creditors must first lose 8 percent of total liabilities before a taxpayer-financed bail-out is allowed. The order of bail-in is also established, with uninsured deposits ranking higher than other subordinated unsecured bank debt.

1 July 2013: Citigroup agrees to pay Fannie Mae 968 million dollars for misstating the quality of mortgage loans sold and securitized.

1 July 2013: Mark Carney replaces Sir Mervyn King as governor of the Bank of England. He remains chairman of the Financial Stability Board.

2 July 2013: The Federal Reserve establishes Basel III minima as the new US standards for capital adequacy, that is, a minimum of 7 percent True Core Equity (CET1) to risk-weighted assets, including changes in the measurement of derivatives positions. Internationally active banks will have to hold an additional 1–2.5 percent. It also proposes that the eight largest institutions apply a minimum leverage ratio of CET1 to total assets of perhaps as high as 6 percent rather than the standard 3 percent. Nearly 95 percent of banks with more than 10 billion dollars in total assets and 90 percent of smaller banks already meet the Fed's minimum requirement of 7 percent common equity Tier 1 capital.

9 July 2013: The FDIC and the Office of the Comptroller of the Currency (OCC) follow the Fed in proposing higher leverage ratios for the eight largest US banking groups, those identified as "SIFIs" by the Financial Standards Board. The holding company has to have a leverage ratio of 5 percent and their banking subsidiary 6 percent from the beginning of 2018. It is calculated that presently only Wells Fargo and Bank of America fulfill these ratios, the combined eight having a capital shortfall of 63 billion dollars and an additional 89 billion at the banking level, according to FDIC calculations.

10 July 2013: The European Commission proposes that the ultimate resolution decision to wind down failing European banks be given to the EU Commission itself rather than the ECB or the new supervisory body or to a board of national supervisors. Under the Commission's plan, a bank resolution board, involving national regulators as well as the ECB and the Commission, would assess whether a bank's finances have deteriorated to the point where intervention is needed, and if so, make a recommendation to the Commission to initiate resolution. The newly created Single Bank Resolution Mechanism (SRM) would then wind down/reconstruct the bank, aided by a Single Resolution Fund of 55–60 billion euro, comprising presently national stabilization funds such as in Germany. The fund would amount to 1 percent of insured deposits of all banks in the participating countries. The German government rejects the proposal which it deems requires treaty changes. As part of the proposal on state aid to failing banks, top staff of banks receiving state funds could earn a maximum of 10 times the salary of the average bank employee. In nationalized RBS, the departing CEO has a basic salary of 35 times the earnings of an average employee, to say nothing of bonuses, cost compensations and pension benefits.

11 July 2013: A Dutch Court of Appeal orders the Dutch government to compensate stockholders and investors in subordinated debt in nationalized SNS Reaal Bank, though without giving an indication of level.

12 July 2013: Senators Elizabeth Warren and John McCain and some others introduce a bill to restore the Glass–Steagall Act, requiring total separation from deposit-taking institutions and investment-banking activities, hence going far further than the Dodd–Frank Act currently being implemented.

15 July 2013: Following demands for privatization from the "troika" (the ECB, EU Commission and IMF), the Greek Hellenic Financial Stability Fund (HFSF) sold the state-owned New Proton Bank to

the fourth largest bank, Eurobank. Having been recapitalized by 6 billion euro, Eurobank is 93.6 percent owned by the HFSF.

16 July 2013: The German bank holding fund Sonderfonds Finanzmarktstabilisierung (SoFFin) seeks to sell its 17 percent share in Commerzbank to UBS.

18 July 2013: France becomes the first European country to vote for a separation of commercial and investment banking activities in a scaled-down version of the Liikanen proposals, proprietary trading (with less than 1 percent of bank revenues) being removed to a separate subsidiary. As part of the reform, the Prudential Supervisory Authority will be renamed the Prudential Supervisory and Resolution Authority (Autorité de contrôle prudentiel et de resolution, ACPR) and will be given the additional task of undertaking winding-up measures.

19 July 2013: The French Cour des Comptes estimates that the nationalized French-Belgian bank Dexia, which has received around 11 billion euro in state aid as well as state guarantees for 90 billion euro in assets, may cost France alone 6.6 billion euro, to which should be added the risk of a further capital injection. It made a loss of almost 1 billion euro for the first half-year.

20 July 2013: The six major US banks by assets (JPMorgan Chase, Wells Fargo, Citigroup, Bank of America, Goldman Sachs and Morgan Stanley) report net profits of 23.1 billion dollars for the second quarter of 2013, for the first time returning to pre-crisis levels. Given higher levels of capital, the return on equity is however 'only' 10 percent, as compared with above 20 percent before the crisis.

25 July 2013: UBS comes to an agreement with the Federal Housing Finance Agency (FHFA) to repay 885 million dollars to Fannie Mae and Freddie Mac for overstating the quality of the underlying mortgages in MBSs worth 6.3 billion dollars sold to the two GSEs. UBS is one of 18 banks sued by the FHFA.

30 July 2013: Barclays, under orders to raise its leverage ratio from presently 2.2 percent under full Basel III rules to 3 percent, decides on a rights issue worth 5.8 billion pounds to counter a capital shortfall of 12.8 billion pounds. It will also sell assets for 80 billion pounds, shrinking its balance sheet to 1.5 trillion pounds. It will also sell 2 billion pounds convertible "CoCo" bonds. The actions

undertaken are supposed to raise Barclays' CET1/RWA ratio under Basel III to 10.5 percent by 2015.

1 August 2013: In a victory for the SEC, former Goldman Sachs vice president Fabrice Tourre is convicted of "intention to defraud" and "negligence" (see 16 April 2010 and 11 June 2011) in one of the very few criminal convictions following the mortgage crisis.

5 August 2013: The Cyprus financial authorities rule on the final bail-in of uninsured deposits in the Bank of Cyprus: 47.5 percent will be forcibly converted into stock, leaving the bank with a 9 percent CET1/RWA ratio. However, even most of the rest will be inaccessible to their owners for up to two more years.

6 August 2013: UK Asset Resolution (UKAR), the government-owned "zombie bank," the owner of the residual mortgage assets from Northern Rock and Bradford & Bingley, has returned 6.6 billion pounds to the government. It originally owed 48.7 billion pounds when it was created in October 2010.

7–8 August 2013: Freddie Mac pays dividends of 4.4 billion dollars to the US government. It will then have repaid 41 of the 71 billion dollars received in bail-out funds from the government. Fannie Mae will similarly repay the government 10.2 billion dollars of its second-quarter profits, having then repaid 105 billion out of a total of 117 billion received. The two GSEs together will then have repaid 146 billion (78 percent) out of 188 billion received.

8 August 2013: Despite the promise of the new chairman of the Securities and Exchange Commission, Mary Jo White, to bring more fraudsters from the financial crisis to justice, Ebrahim Shabudin, former chief operating officer and chief credit officer of the failed United Commercial Bank in San Francisco, is allowed to pay a fine of 175,000 dollars without admitting guilt. He was charged with covering up the extent of delinquent loans in the bank both to its supervisor and its auditor, KPMG. The bank had received 300 million dollars in TARP money, which was lost in the 2009 bankruptcy, also costing the FDIC 1.2 billion dollars in settling guaranteed deposits.

14 August 2013: The SEC decides not to charge Bruno Iksil, who lost 6.2 billion dollars on CDS contracts for JPMorgan Chase's London-based Chief Investment Office but who is cooperating with the authorities. However, his immediate superior and his book-runner

are criminally charged with conspiracy to commit fraud, falsifying records and making false statements to the SEC. In particular, Javier Martin-Artajo is accused of ordering his team to modify registered prices in order to cover up losses. Iksil made 6.76 million dollars in 2011, Martin-Artajo made 10.98 million dollars (see 13 July 2012). JPMorgan's CEO, Jamie Dimon, labeled the affair "the stupidest and most-embarrassing situation I have ever been a part of."

19 August 2013: Delinquent loans in Spanish banks reached a record 11.6 percent of total loans in June, reports the central bank, Banca d'España.

20 August 2013: A report shows that the majority of London-based financial services companies have dramatically (20 percent or more) increased the fixed salary part of their best-paid employees, those earning more than 500,000 euro per year, anticipating the introduction of the bonus restrictions under CRD IV (see 5 March 2013).

22 August 2013: Because of lower probability of a government bailout after the introduction of the Dodd–Frank Act, Moody's warns of downgrades of one or two notches for some of America's largest banks: JPMorgan Chase and Wells Fargo (presently rated A2), Goldman Sachs (A3), Morgan Stanley (Baa1), Citigroup and Bank of America (Baa2). JPMorgan may have to post 1 billion dollars more in collateral if downgraded one notch and 3.4 billion if two notches, Goldman Sachs 1.3 billion for one notch downgrade and 2.2 billion for two notches.

23 August 2013: The Netherlands proposes a 4 percent leverage ratio for its major banks, higher than the 3 percent required under Basel III, in addition to risk-weighted capital requirements, if there can be no agreement within the euro area to go beyond Basel.

26 August 2013: In a prejudicial ruling, the Supreme Court of New York State orders JPMorgan Chase to pay Ukrainian-American investor Len Blavatnik 50 million dollars for losses in mortgage-related securities, originally rated AAA, underwritten and recommended by the bank.

26 August 2013: Nationalized German mortgage bank Hypo Real Estate puts its subsidiary Depfa up for sale (see above).

26 August 2013: The Swedish government proposes the Financial Supervisory Authority as the lead regulator for Swedish banks,

including giving the FSA the right to impose countercyclical capital buffers. A Financial Stability Council will have a coordinating function between the FSA, the central bank (the Riksbank), the National Debt Office (which is responsible for deposit insurance as well as bank resolution) and the Finance Ministry, under the chairmanship of the minister for financial markets.

27 August 2013: Bloomberg's news agency calculates that the six major US banks have spent over 100 billion dollars since the financial crisis up to June 2013, approximately equally divided between legal and litigation costs, and costs for compensating mortgage investors for substandard loans and homeowners for faulty foreclosures. Two banks are due 75 percent of the amount, JPMorgan Chase (largely on account of its purchases of Bear Stearns and Washington Mutual) and Bank of America (ditto Merrill Lynch and Countrywide).[7]

6 September 2013: The judicial services of the European Council find that the proposed Financial Transaction Tax, FTT ("Tobin tax") violates EU treaties both as regards the limitation of the free movement of capital and as discrimination of non-participating countries.

9 September 2013: The FDIC sells to the public 2.4 billion dollars' worth of subordinated notes in Citigroup, originally used as payment for the federal guarantee of 301 billion dollars' worth of assets, thereby ending all public support for the banking group from the FDIC, the Treasury and the Federal Reserve.

9 September 2013: Ordered by the EU competition authorities to downsize, partly nationalized Lloyds Banking Group resuscitates the TSB (Trustee Savings Banks) brand name in creating a separate subsidiary with 631 branch offices in preparation for a sell-off. Interest in buying is declared by, among others, the private equity group J. C. Flowers.

---

[7] In this chronology, only legal costs connected with the financial crisis are enumerated. Legal costs to settle claims for aiding American citizens to avoid tax (e.g. Credit Suisse's 1.8 billion dollar payment in May 2014), fines for money laundering with forbidden countries such as Iran, Cuba or Sudan (e.g. BNP Paribas's 8.9 billion dollar settlement in July 2014) or fines for rigging LIBOR and other interest rates (e.g. Barclays' 450 million dollar fine in June 2012) are excluded. See, however, "Capital punishment," *The Economist*, 5 July 2014.

11 September 2013: The law firm handling the bankruptcy of Lehman Brothers estimates that creditors in the 639-billion-dollar-asset crash will ultimately receive 18–22 cents on the dollar of their investments. Estimates from the estate indicate even a repayment of over 80 billion dollars, 26 cents on the dollar, to the 70,000 creditors. Creditors of the Lehman US brokerage as well as its London-based international operations may even receive their money back with interest.

12 September 2013: The EU Banking Union takes a step forward as the European Parliament meeting in Strasbourg gives the go-ahead to the ECB becoming the overall supervisor of the 6,000 banks and in particular the 150 major banks in the eurozone from mid 2014, the "Single Supervisory Mechanism." Quarrels on a single resolution mechanism for winding down failing banks and a single and funded deposit insurance system, the other two "legs" of the banking union, remain to be resolved.

12 September 2013: In attempting to give its ailing banks aid while circumventing new BIS and EU rules on capital adequacy, Spain decides to allow banks to reclassify "deferred tax assets" (DTA) as tax credits. The former are disallowed from core Tier 1 capital under the new Basel III rules. DTA amounts to some 50 billion euro for the Spanish banking system, corresponding to no less than 83 percent of the total CET1 of partly nationalized Bankia, 64 percent for Sabadell, 40 percent of Santander and Banco Popular, and 20–25 percent of BBVA and Caixabank.

12 September 2013: The advocate general to the European Court of Justice proposes stripping the Paris-based European securities regulator ESMA of the power to forbid the short-selling of stock in emergencies. ESMA also lost its bid to have the sole responsibility for setting LIBOR; it was given instead to a group of national regulators including the UK Financial Conduct Authority, but with ESMA as moderator.

16 September 2013: UK Financial Investments reduces its share of Lloyds Banking Group from 38.7 to 32.7 percent in a partial payback of the rescue. The price received in the marketplace slightly exceeds what the government paid, leading to a profit of 60 million pounds for taxpayers.

16 September 2013: Former Barclays CEO Bob Diamond writes in the FT that "too big to fail" is still a threat to the financial system.

16 September 2013: Denmark's largest bank Danske Bank fires its CEO Eivind Kolding with immediate effect, replacing him with Thomas E. Borgen. The bank fell foul of the regulatory authorities because it had been using poorly calculated risk weights in its internal models, leading to risk-weighted assets being 100 billion DKK too low.

19 September 2013: JPMorgan Chase agrees with the SEC, the Justice Department, Federal Reserve, OCC and the British Financial Conduct Authority to pay a fine of 920 million dollars (the second largest fine ever) for bad risk management in the "London Whale" affair, having already cost the bank 6.2 billion dollars. The CFTC is investigating whether the market for credit default swaps was manipulated by the bank and the US District Attorney of Manhattan has filed criminal charges against those involved (see above). In a first of such cases, JPMorgan Chase is also forced to acknowledge wrongdoing in the form of bad risk controls.

24 September 2013: The Swedish government announces the sale of its residual ownership of 7 percent in Nordea, a souvenir of the nationalization of its predecessor Nordbanken in the 1992 financial crisis. Taking account of the sale of assets in the two bad banks created after the nationalization of Nordbanken and GOTA Bank, dividends and share sales, taxpayers gained some 15 billion SEK on 65 billion spent.

27 September 2013: The RBS Group confirms it has agreed to sell 308 RBS branches in England and Wales and six NatWest branches in Scotland to the Corsair consortium. The branches will be separated from the group by 2015 as a standalone business operating under the dormant Williams & Glyn's brand.

30 September 2013: The CEO of Italy's second largest bank, Intesa Sanpaolo, Enrico Tommaso Cucchiani, is forced out after only 21 months in the job on account of a three-quarter decline in net revenue; he is replaced by Carlo Messina, an ex-professor and long-time head of the retail division.

1 October 2013: Wells Fargo comes to an agreement with the Federal Housing Finance Agency (FHFA) to repay 869 million dollars to

Freddie Mac for overstating the quality of the underlying mortgages in MBSs. Citigroup had already reached a similar agreement for 395 million dollars the week before.

3 October 2013: Barclays raises 5.6 billion pounds in fresh share capital, thereby attaining and exceeding the 3 percent leverage ratio decreed by the PRA.

9 October 2013: The Danish parliament proposes strict rules for seven Danish SIFIs, enumerated as Danske Bank, Nykredit Realkredit, Jyske Bank, Sydbank, Nordea Bank Danmark, BRF Kredit and DLR Kredit. They will face SIFI charges of 1–3 percent of risk-weighted assets on top of a standard charge of 10.5 percent, implying a capital charge of 11.5–13.5 percent (to be compared with the 14.5 percent demanded by Sweden for its four SIFIs).

11 October 2013: JPMorgan Chase takes the markets by surprise by reporting a small loss for the third quarter, occasioned by a one-off charge of 9.2 billion dollars before tax for litigation and regulatory settlements (see below, 18 October 2013).

14 October 2013: The Norwegian FSA (Finanstilsynet) decides that banks using the Advanced IRB model to measure risk and capital must place a floor of 20 percent on the loss-given-default (LGD) parameter of residential mortgages.

16 October 2013: JPMorgan Chase agrees to pay a 100 million dollar fine to the Commodity Futures Trading Commission (CFTC) over and above the 920 million dollars already paid in fines, while also accepting wrongdoing in the "London whale" affair.

16 October 2013: Spanish banks tell their supervisor that they need to set aside only an extra 5 billion euro on account of more stringent requirements for reporting risky loans, much less than feared.

18 October 2013: JPMorgan Chase comes to a tentative agreement to pay 13 billion dollars for mortgage business stemming from the purchase of Bear Stearns and Washington Mutual. The deal would resolve civil probes by three US attorneys, two state attorneys general and three federal regulators. It includes 4 billion dollars in relief for consumers and 9 billion dollars in fines and other payments. The payouts would cover a 4 billion accord with the Federal Housing Finance Agency over the bank's sale of mortgage-backed securities to Fannie Mae and Freddie Mac. In anticipation of a deal,

JPMorgan took a 7.2 billion dollar charge after tax for expenses tied to regulatory matters and litigation in the third quarter, leading the bank to announce a 380 million dollar loss on 11 October. It is still unclear whether JPMorgan will also face criminal charges in relation to the mortgages and mortgage-backed securities sold. It had to admit having sold substandard mortgages without sufficient due diligence in the final deal signed on 19 November.

Reuters has calculated that US and European banks have paid 43 billion dollars in fines and penalties in 2013 to date.

18 October 2013: The Spanish bank BBVA raises 1 billion euro by reducing its holdings in the Chinese Citic Bank from 15 to under 10 percent. While the sale is at a loss, it still increases the core capital of the bank under Basel III by 2.4 billion euro to above 9 percent of risk-weighted assets.

18 October 2013: In order to avoid the compulsory use of swap execution facilities (SEFs) as decreed by the Dodd–Frank Act, US asset managers, hedge funds and banks are moving trades off shore as well as to London, thereby avoiding centralized clearing and the compulsory paying of collateral.

23 October 2013: The ECB states the conditions for the stress test to be conducted for those banks falling under ECB supervision in late 2014. It has tentatively identified 124 banks of the required minimum size, total assets above 30 billion euro. The requirement will be a core Tier 1 ratio of 8 percent under stressed conditions, corresponding to a minimum 4.5 percent, a 2.5 percent conservation buffer and a 1 percent addition since all the banks involved are of systemic importance.

23 October 2013: Dutch Rabobank settles with regulators in the Netherlands, the UK and the US on a 1 billion dollar fine for its participation in rigging LIBOR rates, the second largest fine after UBS at 1.5 billion dollars. Its CEO, Piet Moerland, resigns a week later.

24 October 2013: The Bank of England widens the allowed collateral for borrowing as well as lengthening the maturities.

24 October 2013: The Federal Reserve proposes implementing the Basel Liquidity Coverage Ratio (LCR) excluding covered bonds and private-sector MBSs. The rule will also come fully into force one year earlier than the BIS proposal.

25 October 2013: As part of the 13 billion dollar settlement (see above), the Federal Housing Finance Agency settles with JPMorgan for 5.1 billion dollars claims for loans with misrepresented quality sold to Fannie Mae and Freddie Mac, a legacy of the purchase of Washington Mutual.

28 October 2013: The governor of Banque de France, Christian Noyer, hits out at the EU Commission's proposal for a financial transactions tax (FTT), saying that it "would trigger the destruction of entire sections of the French financial industry, trigger a massive offshoring of jobs and so damage the economy as a whole…" as well as posing "an enormous risk in terms of reduction of output in the FTT jurisdiction; increased cost of capital for governments and corporations; a significant relocation of trading activities and decreased liquidity in the markets…" "The most important concern for the central banks is the risk of the total drying-up of repo markets. This means the transmission of our monetary policy would be seriously impaired and the risk in terms of financial stability would not be negligible."

29 October 2013: In her quarterly review to congress, the SIGTARP Christy L Romero finds that only 7 billion dollars remain to be repaid to the government from the CPP bank finance program but 32.5 billion from the aid to the auto industry. However, American taxpayers lost 9.7 billion dollars on GM and 2.9 billion dollars on Chrysler. While the government has recovered 35 billion from the investment in GM, reducing its stake to 7 percent of the company, to sell remaining shares at a profit would require a share price of 148 dollars per share as compared to the present price of 36 dollars.

31 October 2013: The ECB makes permanent its bilateral swap agreements with the Federal Reserve, the Bank of Canada, the Bank of England, the Bank of Japan and the Swiss National Bank in order to allow euro area banks borrowing facilities in these currencies as well as in euro.

1 November 2013: Sir Jon Cunliffe replaces Paul Tucker as deputy governor of the Bank of England in charge of financial stability and an ex officio member of the Financial Policy Committee (FPC).

1 November 2013: The UK Treasury decides that the Royal Bank of Scotland, 82 percent owned by the government, is to set up an

internal "bad bank" encompassing 38.3 billion pounds of assets. It is expected that the transfer will cause a write-down of 4.5 billion pounds for the fourth quarter.

1 November 2013: In preparing for the stress test of the major bank holding companies, the Federal Reserve said that the 18 bank holding companies tested previously have increased their aggregate Tier 1 common capital to 836 billion dollars in the second quarter of 2013 from 392 billion in the first quarter of 2009. Their Tier 1 common ratio, which compares capital to risk-weighted assets, has more than doubled to a weighted average of 11.1 percent from 5.3 percent.

6 November 2013: A Spanish court orders the arrest of five leading managers of failed Caja de Ahorros de Mediterráneo (CAM) in Alicante, sold in December 2011 to Banco Sabadell for 1 euro.

8 November 2013: UBS buys back the "bad bank" ("Stabfund") set up in 2008 to handle toxic assets. The fund which was run by UBS but funded by the Swiss National Bank is bought back for 3.8 billion dollars. During the five years, UBS has paid SNB 1.6 billion dollars in interest (see 16 October 2008).

8 November 2013: In response to the proposal by the EU Commission on 10 July 2013 (above) that the Commission be given the ultimate power to wind down failing banks, Germany proposes that this power be given to the Council of Ministers or the European Council.

8 November 2013: RBS becomes the latest bank to come to terms with the SEC, paying 150 million dollars to settle claims of 2.2 billion dollars' worth of substandard MBSs, sold through its Greenwich Capital Markets (as it was then called).

8 November 2013: Fannie Mae and Freddie Mac, having received 188 billion dollars in capital support, will by the fourth quarter of 2013 have paid in dividends 114 billion (Fannie) and 71 billion (Freddie) to the government.

11 November 2013: The FSB updates its list of G-SIFIs, changing the additions applied to various banks as below, adding one bank, ICBC, making for a total of 29:

Surcharges of 3.5 percent: presently empty
Surcharges of 2.5 percent: HSBC, JPMorgan Chase (2)

Surcharges of 2.0 percent: Barclays, BNP Paribas, Citibank, Deutsche Bank, (4)

Surcharges of 1.5 percent: Bank of America, Credit Suisse, Goldman Sachs, Mitsubishi UFJ FG, Morgan Stanley, RBS, UBS, Crédit Agricole (7)

Surcharge of 1.0 percent: Bank of China, BBVA, Bank of New York Mellon, Groupe BPCE, Industrial and Commercial Bank of China (added), ING, Mizohu FG, Nordea, Santander, Société Générale, Standard Chartered, State Street, Sumitomo Mitsui FG, UniCredit, Wells Fargo (16).

14 November 2013: Stating that the US government is less likely to support its too-big-to-fail banks, Moody's lowers the rating of four major banks one notch. Bank of New York Mellon was cut to A1 from Aa3, Goldman Sachs was lowered to Baa1 from A3. JPMorgan Chase was cut to A3 from A2, and Morgan Stanley was downgraded to Baa2 from Baa1.

14 November 2013: Belgium sells its remaining 25 percent stake in BNP Paribas Fortis for 3.25 billion euro, making a capital gain of 900 million euro.

14 November 2013: The group of euro finance ministers decides that Ireland as well as Spain may exit the support programs, being able to resume borrowing on their own. The Spanish support was exclusively to recapitalize its banking system.

21 November 2013: The US Treasury announces that it has sold another 70 million shares in GM, bringing its remaining holdings to 2.2 percent of the company. These will be sold during the rest of the year, finalizing the loss to taxpayers to around 10 billion dollars.

28 November 2013: The board of Monte dei Paschi di Siena approves an IPO of 3 billion euro to (partly) repay the loan from the state, thereby exceeding the demands from the EU Commission which was 2.5 billion. In April 2014, it was raised to 5 billion euro.

4 December 2013: The EU Commission makes public the fines which some major banks face for having rigged the Euribor and Euroyen markets during 2005–8: Barclays and UBS nil (since they were the whistleblowers), Deutsche Bank 725 million euro (986 million dollars), Société Générale 446 million euro (606 million dollars), RBS

391 million euro (531 million dollars), Citigroup 70 million euro (95 million dollars); other banks' cases (Crédit Agricole, JPMorgan Chase, HSBS) are still pending since the banks have refused settlement, not wanting to agree to having committed a legal infraction which may open them to further litigation.

5 December 2013: Having bought the Belgian and Luxembourg parts of Fortis, BNP Paribas continues its expansion by buying Rabobank's Polish subsidiary, Bank Gospodarki Zywnosciowej, for 1 billion euro.

9 December 2013: The US Treasury department sells the last of its shares in General Motors. In contrast to most of the capital injected into banks under TARP, taxpayers will lose 11 billion dollars on the 50 billion dollars spent. The bail-out of GM and Chrysler has, however, been estimated to have saved 1.5 million jobs.

10 December 2013: The five US regulatory authorities (Fed, FDIC, OCC, SEC, CFTC) approve the details of the part of the Dodd–Frank Act called the "Volcker rule," limiting the ability of insured banks to conduct proprietary trading. While market making is still allowed, strict supervision will be placed on banks' hedging activities to ensure that the trade really was undertaken to hedge another position. Banks have until July 2015 to comply.

11 December 2013: A compromise is reached between the Council of Ministers, the EU Commission and the European parliament on the new Bank Recovery and Resolution Directive (BRRD) to enter into force on 1 January 2015. National stabilization funds will be built up in all the 28 countries, gradually reaching 1 percent of insured deposits (around 70 billion euro) and also gradually (but only for the euro members) transferred to a common Single Resolution Fund. Rules are also specified for how and when a member country may support or nationalize a failing bank. Before support may be given, 8 percent of the liabilities of the bank must be bailed-in from shareholders and investors in unsecured debt (CoCo bonds, subordinated debt, bank bonds, uninsured deposits). After this bail-in, the state may inject up to 5 percent of assets into ailing but viable banks or nationalize them, but only with permission from the EU Commission and only if threatened by a financial instability crisis. Stress tests specified by the European Banking Authority will establish that a bank to be supported is long-run viable.

12 December 2013: Four former executives of failed Icelandic bank Kaupthing, among them the chairman Sigurdur Einarsson and the CEO Hreidar Mar Sigurdsson, are sentenced to prison for between three and five and a half years for fraud and manipulation in connection with an IPO where the capital injected into the bank was in fact financed by a loan from the bank.

17 December 2013: The European Banking Authority (EBA) reports that banks in the European Union have shed more than 817 billion euro of assets since the end of 2011 in a shift away from risky investments such as asset-backed debt and trading positions. Banks' core Tier 1 capital ratios rose to 11.7 percent from 10 percent over the time period. Holdings of sovereign debt issued by EU countries remained steady at a total of 1.7 trillion euro. But the home-country bias has been strengthened. The proportion of sovereigns owned by home-country banks increased from 64 to 66 percent but to 99 percent in Greece, to 89 percent in Spain, to 84 percent in Ireland and to 76 percent in Italy (10 percent of total assets of Italian banks and 9.5 percent in Spain).

17 December 2013: The EU parliament and EU finance ministers agree on common rules concerning deposit insurance. The covered sum remains at 100,000 euro but within 10 years, member states must build up a fund corresponding to at least 0.8 percent of covered deposits. Today, a large number of countries lack such funds altogether: United Kingdom, Austria, France, Italy, Luxembourg, the Netherlands, Slovenia. The period for payment to depositors when a bank capsizes is also lowered to seven days.

18 December 2013: Finance ministers of the ECOFIN Council agree on further steps along the road to a European banking union in the form of a Single Resolution Mechanism and a Single Resolution Board (SRB) of five members. The single supervisor, the ECB, will suggest to the SRB that a bank needs to be resolved. The SRB will make a detailed proposal with comments from the EU Commission. In case of disputes, the ECOFIN Council as well as the national regulatory authorities need to become involved. However, financing a bail-out during the 10-year phasing in of the Single Resolution Fund is unclear. Also the procedure for resolution is cumbersome and in conflict with the version adopted by the EU parliament.

18 December 2013: The British Banking Reform Act is signed into law, encompassing, inter alia, the ring-fencing of banking activities as proposed by the Independent Commission.

19 December 2013: Having committed 9 billion euro to save nationalized Nova Caixa Galicia (NCG), the Spanish banking authority FROB, committed by EU rules to sell it within five years, gives notice that the bids received are nowhere near the 200 million lower limit set. Perhaps it will finally have to accept what it received for the failed *caja* CAM, sold for 1 euro to Banco Sabadell.

20 December 2013: Standard & Poor's downgrades the European Union to AA+, citing "diminishing cohesion" among the member states.

20 December 2013: Deutsche Bank agrees to pay a fine of 1.9 billion dollars to the Federal Housing Finance Agency for misrepresentation of mortgages sold to Fannie Mae and Freddie Mac. It has already paid 725 million euro to the European Commission for its part in rigging interest rates linked to the London interbank offered rate (LIBOR). It has also reached a settlement to forfeit a claim of 221 million euro to end a derivatives contract (Santorini) with Monte dei Paschi di Siena (see below, Chapter 6).

27 December 2013: Instead of breaking the link between banks and sovereigns, the European debt crisis has reinforced it since banks have been pressured to buy their "home sovereign's" bonds. In this way, the share of total assets invested in its own sovereign bonds has in two years risen from 5 to 9.4 percent in Spain, from 6.4 to 10.3 percent in Italy, from 4.6 to 7.8 percent in Portugal and from 7.8 to 10 percent in Slovenia.

27 December 2013: The newly started government-run "bad bank" of Slovenia, BAMC, purchases its first toxic loans from the banking system.

28 December 2013: Shareholders of Monte dei Paschi di Siena postpone until May an urgently needed issue of 3 billion euro in new stock, thereby raising the possibility of a forced return of a state grant received and the bank's nationalization.

29 December 2013: Wells Fargo agrees to pay Fannie Mae 591 million dollars for losses occasioned by low-quality mortgages. It had already in September settled similar claims from Freddie Mac by paying 869 million dollars.

1 January 2014: The Basel III rules are introduced into the European Union by the Directive and Regulation under the CRD IV package. Banks will phase in gradually and have until 2019 to comply fully. British banks are, however, expected to fully comply with the Basel III targets five years ahead of time, including a 3 percent leverage ratio.

7 January 2014: JPMorgan Chase agrees to pay 1.7 billion dollars to resolve claims that it facilitated Bernard Madoff's Ponzi scheme, the largest in US history. The bank entered into an agreement with Manhattan US attorney Preet Bharara, acknowledging oversight lapses related to an account Madoff used to fund his multibillion-dollar fraud.

8 January 2014: Ireland, freed from the restrictions of the EU/ECB/IMF program, sells 3.75 billion euro of 10-year bonds. The extra yield investors receive for holding the securities instead of benchmark German bunds narrowed to 1.35 percentage points from a high of more than 11.5 percentage points in July 2011.

17 January 2014: The US Treasury sells an additional 410,000 shares in Ally Financial (ex-GMAC), reducing to 37 percent its remaining stake of the original 16 billion dollar investment, 15.3 billion of which have been repaid including dividends.

17 January 2014: Moody's restores the credit rating of Ireland to investment grade, Baa3. Standard & Poor's never lowered Ireland to lower than BBB+.

23 January 2014: In a first active use of the countercyclical buffers introduced by Basel III, Switzerland raises its buffer capital demand from 1 to 2 percent of risk-weighted assets to cool the property market.

29 January 2014: The finance commissioner of the European Union, Michel Barnier, surprisingly proposes a "Volcker rule" Regulation for EU banks following the Liikanen group proposals, going much further than the US rule and far beyond present ring-fencing in countries like France. All proprietary trading in SIFI (defined as banks with total assets more than 30 billion euro or important trading activities) will be relegated to separately run and capitalized subsidiaries of the holding company, even market making, unless there is an immediate customer demand. All instruments are

included except EU countries' sovereign bonds, thus including also mortgage and covered bonds. Countries which have already introduced similar ring-fencing (the UK) may receive derogation. The proposal will, however, be taken up only by the new EU parliament and a new Commission.

30 January 2014: Nationalized Austrian Hypo Group Alpe Adria which has already received 1.75 billion euro in state aid in 2013 is set to receive a further 1 billion euro. Its toxic assets will be wound down after having been placed in a bad bank jointly run by the government and the other major banks, Erste Bank (a subsidiary of Italian UniCredit) and Raiffeisen Bank International.

31 January 2014: Bank of America agrees to pay 8.5 billion dollars in compensation to mortgage-bond investors such as BlackRock to compensate for misleading or erroneous information as to their quality. The suit is mainly a result of BofA's purchase of Countrywide Financial. On top of this payment, the US government is asking for 2.1 billion dollars in penalties for bad mortgages sold to Fannie Mae and Freddie Mac.

10 January 2014: The Dutch central bank and the British Financial Services Compensation Scheme sue the Icelandic deposit guarantee fund for some 6.7 billion dollars resulting from insurance claims on the failed Icesave deposits of Landsbanki.

12 February 2014: EMIR (European Market Infrastructure Regulation) enters into force, making banks as well as non-financial counterparties report OTC derivatives trades to so-called trade repositories.

18 February 2014: Foreign-owned lenders with more than 50 billion dollars of assets in the United States will be required by the Federal Reserve under section 165 of the Dodd–Frank Act to house their US businesses, including securities trading, within US regulated holding companies. The 50 billion threshold excludes the domestic assets that are connected to a US branch of a bank. About 17 institutions would fall under this requirement. This means separately capitalizing their US operations, passing annual stress tests and holding liquid dollar assets sufficient for 30 days. Before Dodd–Frank, foreign banks needed only to be well capitalized worldwide, not specifically in the US (see 14 December 2012).

21–26 February 2014: Royal Bank of Scotland (RBS), 81 percent owned by the UK government, intends to cut staff in the investment bank division by 30,000. It has already shed 40,000 employees from 230,000 at the peak in 2008. For the year 2013, its loss amounted to 9 billion pounds, of which 4.8 billion were caused by the setting up of an internal "bad bank." The loss in 2012 was 5 billion pounds.

24 February 2014: In the continuing consolidation of the overbanked Danish financial industry, the second-largest bank, Jyske Bank, purchases the fourth-largest mortgage lender BRF Kredit for 7.4 billion DKK (1.4 billion dollars).

27 February 2014: The 7.3 billion pound UK loan portfolio of Anglo Irish Bank (under liquidation) is sold to a group of private equity investors, among them the US Lone Star.

28 February 2014: The Spanish government began the re-privatization of nationalized Bankia by selling 7.5 percent of the bank for 1.5 billion euro.

6 March 2014: Preparing for the ECB's stress test later in 2014, the Central Bank of Greece orders the four major Greek banks to raise an additional 6 billion euro in capital: nationalized Eurobank 2.9 billion, National Bank of Greece 2.2 billion, Pireaus Bank 425 million and Alpha Bank 262 million. "Troika" members would prefer to see 8–9 billion euro.

11 March 2014: Austria's central bank warns that winding down nationalized Hypo Alpe-Adria could cost an additional 3.6 billion euro loss to the government budget, in particular caused by the setting up of a "bad bank" of 17.8 billion euro in toxic mortgage assets. The bank has already received 4.8 billion euro in state aid (see 14 December 2009, 30 January and 13 June 2014).

12 March 2014: In anticipation of the ECB Asset Quality Review, Italy's largest bank UniCredit writes down losses to create an annual loss of 14 billion euro for 2013, wiping out 10 years of profits. It is also setting up an internal "bad bank" encompassing 87 billion euro of toxic assets.

20 March 2014: The European Council and the EU parliament agree on the principles of the Single Resolution Mechanism (SRM) and its financing. The SRM would apply to all banks supervised by the

Single Supervisory Mechanism (SSM). The Single Resolution Board (SRB) would prepare resolution plans and directly resolve all banks directly supervised by the ECB and cross-border banks. National resolution authorities would prepare resolution plans and resolve banks which only operate nationally and are not subject to full ECB direct supervision, provided that this would not involve any use of the Single Resolution Fund (SRF).

Centralized decision-making would be built around a strong SRB and would involve permanent members as well as the Commission, the Council, the ECB and the national resolution authorities. In most cases, the ECB would notify that a bank is failing to the Board, the Commission, and the relevant national resolution authorities. The Board would then assess whether there is a systemic threat and any available private-sector solution. If not, it would adopt a resolution scheme including the relevant resolution tools and any use of the fund. The EU Commission is responsible for assessing the discretionary aspects of the Board's decision and endorsing or objecting to the resolution scheme. If resolution entails state aid, the Commission would have to approve the aid prior to the adoption by the Board of the resolution scheme.

A Single Resolution Fund is to be constituted to which all the banks in the participating member states would contribute. The fund has a target level of 55 billion euro. The fund would be owned and administered by the Board. The SRF would reach a target level of at least 1 percent of covered deposits over an eight-year period.

20 March 2014: In stress tests of the 30 largest US banks, only one, Zions Bancorp, failed. Five additional banks, among them Citigroup, will however continue to face restrictions on dividends and share buybacks. Citi's share price fell 6 percent on the news. Requirements involved a minimum core Tier 1 equity ratio to risk-weighted assets under stressed conditions of 5 percent and a minimum leverage ratio (Tier 1 capital over total assets) of 4 percent.

25 March 2014: UK Financial Investments (UKFI) sells a further 7.5 percent of its holdings of Lloyds, bringing down its remaining stake to around 25 percent.

26 March 2014: Bank of America settles claims that it sold Fannie Mae and Freddie Mac defective mortgage bonds. The settlement

includes 6.3 billion dollars in cash and 3 billion in securities that Bank of America will repurchase. In a separate settlement, Bank of America and its former CEO, Kenneth Lewis, came to terms with New York City's attorney general for misleading investors about mounting losses at Merrill Lynch, about to be purchased by BofA. Lewis, who resigned in 2009, agreed to pay 10 million dollars and be barred for three years from serving as an officer or director of a public company. Neither Lewis nor Bank of America were forced to admit wrongdoing.

27 March 2014: The US government sells 95 million shares in Ally Financial (ex-GMAC), one of its few remaining holdings from the financial crisis of 2008. The IPO lowers its holding from 37 to 14 percent and this also means that taxpayers will have received back more than the 17.2 billion dollar bail-out.

2 April 2014: The ECB reports a huge build-up of sovereign debt among the assets of European banks. On average in February 2014, 5.8 percent of total bank assets consisted of sovereign bonds, an increase of 1.5 percentage points over two years. In Italy, the figure was 10.2 percent of total bank assets and 9.5 percent in Spain as contrasted to 4.6 percent in Germany.

15 April 2014: The European Parliament approves the two pieces of legislation for creating the Single Resolution Mechanism: the Bank Recovery and Resolution Directive (BRRD) and the corresponding Regulation.

16 April 2014: The former chairman of failed Anglo Irish Bank, Sean FitzPatrick, is acquitted of all 11 charges of criminal guilt in relation to lending by the bank.

29 April 2014: Greek Eurobank attracted more than 7 billion euro of orders from big institutional investors and hedge funds for a 2.9 billion rights issue that will return the country's third-largest bank to mostly private hands. The capital raising makes Eurobank the first of Greece's four big lenders to be largely privatized, with the stake held by the Hellenic Financial Stability Fund shrinking to 35 percent.

30 April 2014: Stress tests conducted by the Federal Housing Finance Agency as mandated under the Dodd–Frank legislation show that mortgage finance companies Fannie Mae and Freddie Mac would

need a government bailout of up to 190 billion dollars in a severe downturn, similar to the 188 billion they received under the latest crisis.

8 May 2014: The Swedish Financial Supervisory Authority decides on higher capital requirements for the four major banks. From 2015, they need to hold core equity in relation to risk-weighted assets for systemic purposes at a minimum of 3 percent under Pillar 1 and an additional 2 percent under Pillar 2. The countercyclical buffer will be activated at a level to be decided upon in autumn 2014. The floor weight for residential credits is also raised from 15 to 25 percent. A countercyclical buffer at 1 percent will also be applied for all banks irrespective of size from 2015.

8 May 2014: Barclays (which did not receive a bail-out during the crisis) plans to create a separate "bad bank" consisting of 115 billion pounds' worth of "non-core assets." The restructuring will cost 800 million pounds in addition to the 2.7 billion pounds announced earlier. The bulk of the bad bank will be made up of investment bank assets.

27 May 2014: As a consequence of the sharp turnaround in the Irish economy, having led Moody's to raise the country to Baa1, the national "bad bank" NAMA reports profits for the third year running, having during the year disposed of assets for 4.5 billion euro of the original 71.2 billion purchased in toxic assets during the crisis. It is expected to make a profit of perhaps 1 billion over its lifetime.

5 June 2014: The Sydney Appeals Court upholds the verdict of the lower court against ABN AMRO (now a part of RBS) and Standard & Poor's for misselling securities to Australian local authorities, calling the rating "unreasonable, unjustified and misleading" and charging the companies to compensate the investors for their 90 percent losses on these securities. A corresponding US case against S&P is still pending.

6 June 2014: In a stunning rebuke to prosecutors who earlier won cases against the chief executive and chairman of failed Kaupthing Bank, Icelandic courts find not guilty to the charges of breach of fiduciary duty and market manipulation, respectively, the former CEOs of Glitnir and Landsbanki, Larus Welding and Sigurjón Árnason, as

well as the major shareholder of Glitnir, Jón Ásgeir Jóhannesson. See also 26 March 2013 and 12 December 2013.

13 June 2014: The EU Commission sides with Denmark in opposing the treatment of covered bonds in the liquidity requirements proposed under the Basel III rules. The Danish mortgage bond market is at 400 billion euro, one of the largest in the world and the largest per capita. While Basel had assigned all covered bonds a so-called Level 2 status, limiting their use in banks' liquidity buffers to 40 percent, the Commission is set to split the securities into two classes. Banks will be free to use Level 1 covered bonds to fill 70 percent of their liquidity buffers, booked at 93 percent of their market value. As noted by Danish banks, there are too few Danish government bonds in circulation to fulfill the requirements, given a debt to GDP ratio less than half the EU average.

13 June 2014: Partly nationalized Commerzbank offloads Spanish and Portuguese commercial property loans worth over 5 billion euro to private equity groups including Lone Star. At the end of the first quarter of 2014, its portfolio of non-core assets was 102 billion euro, aiming for 75 billion by 2016.

13 June 2014: Uncertainty continues as regards the 5 billion dollar rights issue by Monte dei Paschi di Siena, and the continued risk of nationalization led to a fall of 20 percent in the share price in one day in the midst of the fundraising.

13 June 2014: In a surprise move, the Austrian government decides to bail in 890 billion euro in subordinated bonds in failed and nationalized Hypo Alpe Adria despite the fact that these bonds had been guaranteed by the state of Carinthia (Kärnten). The move led to the threat by Standard & Poor's to downgrade other major banks in Austria, including Erste Bank and Raiffeisen Bank International, which also have guarantees by regional authorities. The bank has already received 5.75 billion euro in support from the federal government. The government is also seeking an additional 800 billion euro payment from the previous owner Landesbank Bayern (LB), which has already lost 3.7 billion euro on the investment.

19 June 2014: Bank of America is ordered by a federal judge to face two government lawsuits in which it is accused of misleading investors about the quality of loans tied to 850 billion dollars

in residential mortgage-backed securities. The Justice Department broke off negotiations because it was dissatisfied with Bank of America's offer to pay more than 12 billion dollars, which included at least 5 billion in consumer relief. Bank of America and firms it purchased issued about 965 billion dollars of mortgage bonds from 2004 to 2008 (while JPMorgan Chase and companies it bought issued 450 billion).

20 June 2014: Lloyds, the UK's biggest mortgage lender, sells 175 million TSB shares, or 35 percent of the company, raising 455 million pounds. That's more than the 25 percent originally planned, "due to significant investor demand." Lloyds is being put under pressure the European Commission to divest TSB in its entirety. See 9 September 2013.

26 June 2014: The Bank of England's Financial Policy Committee proposes that banks' mortgage loans given at ratios of debt to income above 4.5 be limited to a maximum of 15 percent of the mortgage loan book.

30 June 2014: Monte dei Paschi di Siena completes its 5 billion euro share sale, enabling it to repay 3 billion of the 4.1 billion euro support received from the Italian state and thus avoiding the nationalization threatened by the EU Commission.

10 July 2014: In a clear indication that the European banking crisis is far from over, trading in the shares of Portugal's largest bank, Banco Espirito Santo, is halted after their price has fallen by 19 percent in a single day. Its CEO, Ricardo Salgado, is later arrested.

14 July 2014: Citigroup agrees to pay 7 billion dollars in fines and consumer relief to resolve government claims that it misled investors about the quality of mortgage-backed bonds sold before the 2008 financial crisis. JPMorgan Chase agreed in November to pay 13 billion dollars to resolve similar federal and state probes. The Citi accord includes a record 4 billion dollars in civil penalties to the Justice Department, 500 million to state attorneys general and the FDIC and about 2.5 billion dollars in various forms of consumer relief. The settlement covers securities issued, structured and underwritten between 2003 and 2008.

30 July 2014: Bank of America's Countrywide unit is ordered to pay 1.3 billion dollars in penalties for defective mortgage loans sold to

Fannie Mae and Freddie Mac in the run-up to the 2008 financial crisis in the first mortgage fraud case brought by the federal government to go to trial ("High-Speed Swim Lane"). The federal district court judge also directed Rebecca Mairone, a former mid-level Countrywide executive who was the only individual charged in the case, to pay 1 million dollars.

31 July – 4 August 2014: Troubled Portuguese bank Banco Espirito Santo (BES) reveals a loss of 3.6 billion euro for the first half-year, leading to a Tier 1 ratio of 5 percent, below the minimum 7 percent. The bank's share price has fallen by 75 percent since May. The government offered a capital bail-out from the 12 billion euro fund set aside for bank recapitalization during Portugal's EU support program. A new bridge bank, Novo Banco, will be set up, owned by the central bank and capitalized by 4.9 billion euro from the fund. It will receive deposits and viable assets and liabilities, whereas troubled assets (including intergroup loans) will remain in BES and written down by bailing in shareholders totally and owners of junior debt to at least 75 percent of face value according to market prices.

6 August 2014: The biggest Dutch bank, ING, plans to pay off early the 10 billion euro received in government aid after a profitable half-year. To date, it has already returned 9.3 billion euro of the capital injection and 3.2 billion euro in interest and premiums. The Dutch government came to the rescue after ING was hit with heavy losses on assets backed by US mortgages during the financial crisis. The payment also allows the bank to resume paying dividends.

21 August 2014: Bank of America will pay 16.65 billion dollars to end federal and state probes into its mortgage bond sales. The settlement, which includes 7 billion in consumer relief and 9.65 billion in cash, resolves remaining civil investigations by federal and state prosecutors. No criminal charges have been filed. The payment beats Citigroup's 7 billion dollar settlement in July 2013 and JPMorgan Chase's 13 billion dollar accord in November 2013. Bank of America's settlement also comes on top of its 9.5 billion agreement to resolve related Federal Housing Finance Agency (FHFA) claims. Bank of America has already booked more than 55 billion dollars in legal expenses tied to home loans, most of them linked to the 2008 takeover of the subprime lender Countrywide. In all,

the major banks have paid fines of 125 billion dollars for erroneous mortgage and mortgage bond sales.

22 August 2014: Goldman Sachs avoids trial by agreeing to a settlement of 1.2 billion dollars to resolve claims by the Federal Housing Finance Agency (FHFA) that the bank sold Fannie Mae and Freddie Mac faulty mortgage bonds. Under the settlement with the conservator for the two government-controlled mortgage finance companies, Goldman Sachs said it agreed to pay 3.15 billion dollars to repurchase mortgage-backed securities from Fannie and Freddie.

25 August 2014: In yet another failed attempt to bring to justice those responsible for the financial crisis, four leading executives of Bayern LB agree to pay between 5,000 and 20,000 euro without admitting criminal guilt for their involvement in the purchase of Austrian bank Hypo Alpe Adria.

1 September 2014: In a sign that the Spanish banking crisis is receding, Caixa Bank in Barcelona agrees to purchase the Spanish operations of Barclays for 0.8 billion euro. Its nationalized rival Calalunya Banc was acquired by BBVA on 21 July 2014 for 1.2 billion euro.

2 September 2014: In the largest issue yet of contingent convertible notes (CoCos), Santander sells 2.5 billion euro's worth of CoCos yielding 6.25 percent. They will convert to equity should the bank's CET1 ratio fall below 5.125 percent. Its CET1/RWA ratio at the end of 2013 (Basel II) was 11.71 percent.

3 September 2014: Following the Basel group, the three major regulatory authorities in the United States adopt rules forcing major banks to have enough liquidity reserves for a 30-day squeeze. In 2017, banks will have to hold 2,500 billion dollars in liquid assets, a total almost accomplished already in 2014, the shortfall being a mere 100 billion.

10 September 2014: As the first Swedish bank, Nordea (on the FSB's list of Global-SIFIs) issues CoCos to raise its capital base, the notes being transformed to equity if the bank's core Tier 1 ratio falls below 8 percent. Given its excellent capital position with a core Tier 1 ratio of 15.7 percent under Basel II and 13 percent under Basel III at the end of 2013, the required coupon was lower than the so far record low of 5.625 percent achieved by Belgian KBC

and 6.25 percent by Santander (see above). The five-year note was priced at a coupon of 5.5 percent and the 10-year note at 6.125 percent. The notes will be rated BBB+ by Standard & Poor's.

24 September 2014: RBS, majority-owned by the British state, sells shares worth 3 billion dollars in its US subsidiary Citizens Financial Group but still holds over 75 percent of the shares.

1 October 2014: A US District Court in Washington, DC dismisses claims from private investors concerning their loss of dividends from the mortgage giants Fannie Mae and Freddie Mac. Owned 80 percent by the government, their profits since the financial crisis have been almost exclusively used to repay the 187 billion dollar aid received from taxpayers rather than paying dividends to other shareholders. Including dividends, the two GSEs had by August 2014 repaid 216 billion dollars.

11 October 2014: The International Swaps and Derivatives Association (ISDA) and 18 major banks that dominate the market will from January 2015 allow supervisory authorities to apply temporary stays to prevent a rush to close derivatives contracts if a bank runs into trouble. A delay would give regulators time to ensure that critical parts of a bank, such as customer accounts, continue smoothly while the rest is wound down or sold off in an orderly way. Previously, derivatives counterparties could immediately close out collateral held. The agreement covers some 90 percent of the 700 trillion dollar market.

13 October 2014: The Financial Stability Board decides that from 2017, banks doing repo or securities lending business with non-banks must use a "haircut" of at least 6 percent in valuing the accompanying collateral.

26 October 2014: The ECB releases the results of the asset quality review and stress tests undertaken before it assumed supervision of the 130 largest banks in the euro area. Assuming a mild recession and a minimum 5.5 percent core Tier 1 equity ratio, only 25 banks failed. However, since the tests built on annual accounts for 2013 and a number of banks have raised capital and/or sold assets during 2014, 13 banks were ordered to raise a total of 7 billion euro. The worst "sinners" were Monte dei Paschi di Siena and Greek Eurobank, needing some 2 billion euro each. However,

should the rules have been a fully phased-in Basel III, a number of other banks would have failed, relying on the continued use of deferred tax assets, which are being phased out. The results may be compared with other estimates of capital shortfalls, ranging from 50 billion euro (Goldman Sachs) to 500 billion euro (Center for Risk Management in Lausanne).

31 October 2014: In one of very few legal cases in Europe, three former top executives of Italian bank Monte dei Paschi di Siena were convicted of obstructing regulators and misleading authorities on the bailed-out bank's finances, ordering former chairman Giuseppe Mussari, ex-general manager Antonio Vigni and former finance chief Gianluca Baldassarri to serve jail sentences of three years and six months. The case in question was a derivatives deal, "Alexandria," with Nomura Securities.

3 November 2014: The ECB becomes the overall supervisor for all euro area banks and the direct supervisor of some 130 banks.

10 November 2014: The Financial Stability Board (FSB) proposes that global banks should have a buffer of bonds or equity equivalent to at least 16 to 20 percent of their risk-weighted assets from January 2019. The banks' total buffer would include the minimum mandatory core capital requirements banks must already hold to bolster their defenses against future crises. The new buffer, formally known as "total loss-absorbing capacity" (TLAC), must be at least twice a bank's leverage ratio, a separate measure of capital to total assets regardless of the level of risk. These bonds would be converted to equity or written down to help shore up a stricken bank. Globally, the leverage ratio has been set provisionally at 3 percent but it could be higher when finalized in 2015; the United States has already set the leverage ratio at 6 percent for the major banks. The new rule will apply to 30 banks the regulators have deemed to be globally "systemically important."

19 November 2014: Joining the former executives of failed Icelandic banks Kaupthing and Glitnir, the former CEO of Landsbanki, Sigurjon Arnason, is sentenced to one year in prison, suspended for nine months, for market manipulation, having used loans from the bank to manipulate the bank's share price in the months leading up to its collapse in October 2008.

2 December 2014: A study finds that the stress test conducted by the ECB severely underestimated the true capital need of European banks. Should a 3 percent leverage ratio (Tier 1 capital to total assets) have been included, 12 additional banks would have failed the test and required a total of 66 billion euro in fresh equity.

18 December 2014: The US Treasury Department sells its remaining shares of Ally Financial (ex-GMAC) acquired under the government's TARP program bail-out. Taxpayers injected a total of 17.2 billion dollars into the lender during the financial crisis because of its mounting losses from subprime mortgages. The Treasury has already received 18.3 billion dollars and now gets a final 1.3 billion from its investment. The government sold the bulk of its stake when Ally went public last April.

PART II

Bail-out and/or bail-in of banks in Europe: a country-by-country event study on those European countries which did not receive outside support

In this and the next two parts of the book, a number of banks that were rescued, sold/merged or liquidated will be discussed. While there are most certainly a number of idiosyncratic factors at play in each individual case, five factors are common denominators in the crises, as shown in Figure 3 below.[1] The five factors are:

- Aggressive and ill-timed mergers and acquisitions (M&A);
- Too low capital bases;
- Risky funding structures with too little stable retail customer deposits;
- Bad lending;
- Bad investments/trading.

The bank with which we will start in the next chapter, Northern Rock, had too low capital due to its rapid growth, a risky funding structure with over heavy reliance on wholesale deposits and a loan book of dubious quality, due to the housing boom. Lloyds Bank on the other hand collapsed mainly on account of its untimely purchase of Halifax Bank of Scotland (HBOS). Royal Bank of Scotland (RBS) is the only bank which succeeded in hitting all the five factors!

Obviously not all countries or all banks that faced the financial crisis of 2007 onwards are studied. I focus on Western Europe and the United States since this is where the crisis hit the hardest (see the Introduction). And in particular, I study the choice of bail-out with

---

[1] Courtesy of *Financial Times*, Patrick Jenkins. Published in the FT on 9 September 2013.

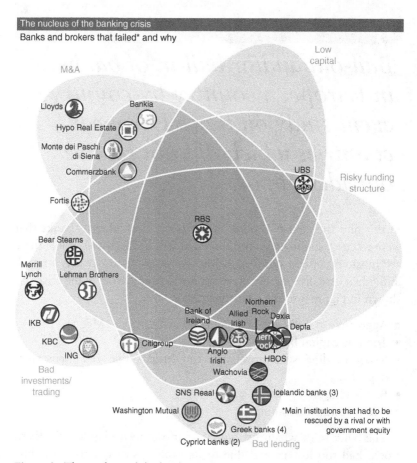

Figure 3. The nucleus of the banking crisis

taxpayers' money in contrast to bail-in with the money of creditors, depositors and other banks.

Some countries and banks such as Austrian Erste Bank and Hypo Group Alpe Adria, Swedish Carnegie Investment Bank and Latvian Parex Bank are mentioned in the Chronology (Part I) but omitted from the detailed study. Likewise, the injection of capital into French banks is not studied in detail since the banks involved were in no need of the rescue to the tune of 10.5 billion euro in fresh Tier 1 capital which was all the same (reluctantly) accepted by the EU Commission.[2] In the United States, I leave out a discussion of the mortgage giants Fannie Mae and Freddie Mac, firstly because their bail-outs were a foregone conclusion given their status as "Government-Sponsored Enterprises" (GSEs) and secondly because their resolution and future destiny lie somewhat outside the theme of this book and are still unclear as it goes to press (September 2015).

The errors on the part of management and supervisory authorities in creating and aggravating the problems are presented but the emphasis is on the resolution of the crisis: could it have been discovered and remedied earlier? How did the authorities (central banks, Treasury, Financial Supervisory Authority, Resolution Authority, the European Commission) handle the crisis? Were their actions effective and consistent? What was the end result? Have taxpayers been repaid? Is the end result a (more) viable banking system?

The actions taken to resolve the crisis (liquidity support, recapitalization, guarantees, sale/merger, setting up of a "bad bank," liquidation, changing of the guard, etc.) are graded on a standard academic scale of A–F where A is (almost) perfect and F stands for Fail. I am sure that many readers will disagree with my gradings but that is the way to start a discussion.[3] Figure 3 illustrates the factors that give high or low grades, respectively.

Factors leading to good grades (A–C):

- *Uninterrupted service:* if a bank is closed Friday afternoon (as is standard FDIC practice), depositors should not know the difference on Monday morning and transactions should flow normally.
- *Proactive supervision:* if regulatory authorities reacted before the situation became acute, they get extra points.
- *Speed of intervention:* a shorter time span from recognition of the problem to intervention is positive.
- *Liquidity:* did the Central Bank alleviate the inevitable liquidity crunch? How? When?

---

[2] http://europa.eu/rapid/press-release_IP-08-1900_en.htm
[3] A useful overview of the crisis and the reactions by the EU states is European Commission Competition, "The effect of temporary State aid rules adopted in the context of the financial and economic crisis," working paper, 5 October 2011, p. 17. http://ec.europa.eu/competition/publications/reports/working_paper_en.pdf

- *Guarantee for deposits:* in an acute crisis, stemming a bank run with a guarantee is vital to prevent a bank run.
- *Guarantee for other liabilities:* depending on the type of funding of the banking system, guaranteeing also other liabilities (as in Ireland and Germany) may be necessary but perhaps for a fee (as in the US Temporary Liquidity Guarantee Program run by the FDIC or in the Swedish guarantee program).
- *Was the guarantee for new debt only or total outstanding?* The first gives extra points.
- *Viability:* was a study undertaken and a decision made as to whether the bank was long-term viable or not or did the authorities just follow "the art of stumbling through"?
- *Long-run viability:* was the end result a viable bank? Did it improve the viability and stability of the financial system?
- *Systemic crisis:* was the crisis seen as involving only one or several banks or seen as systemic? When?
- *Ring-fencing and insuring of "toxic assets" for a fee:* were toxic assets separated and insured, as in Citibank and Bank of America?
- *Toxic assets:* did the authorities force or encourage the setting up of a "bad bank," internal or external?
- *Cooperation:* did the domestic authorities (FSA/OCC/OTS, Treasury, Central Bank, Deposit Insurance Agency) work well together? If so, they receive extra points.
- *International cooperation:* did host and home countries' regulators cooperate efficiently? If so, they receive extra points.
- *If taxpayers' money was involved, did they get their money back?* How? Outright nationalization, majority ownership, injection of common stock rather than preferred shares, warrants, all these give extra points.
- *Downsizing:* did the authorities put pressure on the saved bank to downsize, i.e. sell non-core assets, sell branches, sell foreign subsidiaries, cut down on staff?
- *Stigmatization:* did the authorities attempt to treat all banks equally in order to avoid stigmatizing the truly needy?
- *Legal assessment:* were leading figures of management brought to justice in events where clearly laws had been broken (insider trading, fraud, cover-up, breach of trust, false accounting, false testimony, perjury, etc.)?

- *Industry involvement:* were other, healthier banks involved in saving the failing ones, through fees for deposit insurance, stabilization funds or other arrangements, e.g. part-owning the "bad bank" as in Ireland and Spain or through a loss-sharing arrangement between banks as in Denmark?

Factors leading to bad grades (with some examples):

- Failure to guarantee continuity of service (Lehman Brothers)
- Failure to downsize a bank under resolution (RBS, Landesbanken, Bank of America)
- Failure to set up a bad bank, preferably external (RBS and Lloyds)
- Failure to establish whether the bank is viable (IKB, Commerzbank, Landesbanken)
- Failure to sell off non-core healthy assets (RBS, IKB, Dexia)
- Slow resolution/sale/wind-down (RBS, Hypo Real Estate)
- Infighting and/or lack of coordination between domestic regulators (Northern Rock, Washington Mutual, Bank of America)
- Infighting and/or lack of coordination between international regulators (Dexia, Fortis, Icelandic banks, Lehman Brothers)
- Overly hasty sale of non-core assets causing unnecessary losses (IndyMac)
- Imposing unnecessary losses on depositors[4] (Cyprus banks, IndyMac)
- Imposing losses on unsecured senior bondholders (Amagerbanken, IndyMac, Washington Mutual)
- Failure to try delinquent management in courts of law (RBS, IKB, Landesbanken, Dexia, Bear Stearns, Lehman Brothers, Washington Mutual, Wachovia, Citibank, Bank of America)

---

[4] This comment would apply to domestic deposits only since the legal background as concerns foreign-held deposits is not clear, as indicated by the verdict by the EFTA Court of Justice in the dispute between Iceland on the one hand and Britain and the Netherlands on the other. Nor does the US deposit insurance system cover foreign depositors.

1 | United Kingdom

Northern Rock, Royal Bank of Scotland (RBS),
Lloyds Banking Group

The United Kingdom story[1]

There appears to be no real consensus in the United Kingdom as to
whether the financial crisis was mainly occasioned by international
factors or mainly home-grown. The influential Turner review writes
(p. 29) that "at the core of the crisis lay an interplay between macro-
imbalances which had grown rapidly in the last ten years, and financial market developments and innovations which had been underway
for about 30 years but which accelerated over the last ten to 15, partly
under the stimulus of the macro-imbalances." British banks were basically following mainstream international developments – "the origins
of the crisis were to a significant degree global" – but influenced also by
the doubling of British residential property prices between 1997 and
2007 (only Ireland was worse at 250 percent!) and the rapid increase
in mortgage debt, from 50 percent of GDP in the year 2000 to 80 percent of GDP in 2006. While securitization of mortgages was far from
as prevalent as in the United States, it still rose from basically nothing
in 1995 to over 25 percent of mortgage lending in 2005 (including
mortgage-backed securities as well as covered bonds[2]).

---

[1] For overall descriptions of the British financial crisis, see e.g. Bank of England, "The
bank's response to the financial crisis," May 2012; Financial Services Authority,
"A regulatory response to the global banking crisis" (Turner review), Discussion
Paper 09/2, March 2009; HM Treasury, "Review of HM Treasury's management
response to the financial crisis," March 2012; Independent Commission on Banking
(ICB), "Final report, recommendations," September 2011 (Vickers report). Internet
sites for the above are provided in the list of literature. See also Hugh Pym, *Inside
the Banking Crisis: The Untold Story* (London: A&C Black, 2014).
[2] A mortgage-backed security (MBS) is a security where a number of individual
mortgages have been packed together and sold off to investors ("originate to
distribute" model). With the aid of an intervening special purpose vehicle (SPV),

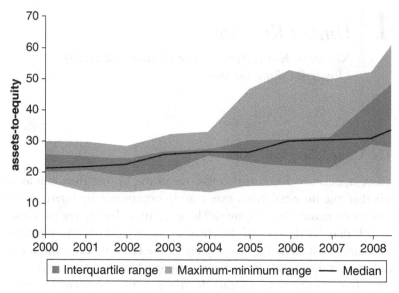

Figure 4. Leverage of UK banks, 2000–8
Source: Turner review, p. 39.

The Turner Review also blames the insufficient quantity and quality of capital under Basel II, as well as the over-reliance on model-based approaches to regulatory capital. While the major British banks had seemingly healthy BIS ratios at the end of 2007 in comparison with the required 8 percent (HSBC 13.60 percent, Royal Bank of Scotland 11.20 percent, Barclays 12.10 percent, Halifax Bank of Scotland 11.10 percent, Lloyds TSB 11.00 percent, Standard Chartered 16.70 percent, Northern Rock 11.60 percent),[3] in reality the underlying situation had deteriorated substantially, with the ratio of capital to (unweighted) assets falling dramatically from 4.7 percent in 2000 to 3.2 percent just six years later in 2006, implying an increase in leverage from 21 to 31 times. Obviously some banks, as shown in Figure 4, were much higher at a leverage ratio of 50 or even 60.

---

the credit risk is lifted from the originating bank. In a covered bond financing on the other hand, the bank refinances individual mortgages lumped together as a bond but retains the credit risk on its own books ("originate to hold" model).
[3] *The Banker*, July 2008.

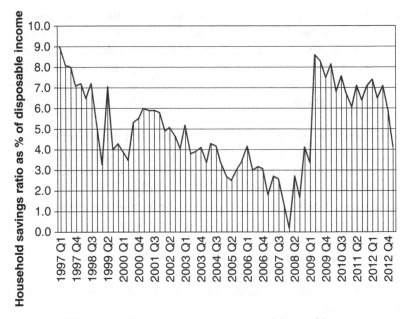

Figure 5. UK household savings ratio, percentage of disposable income
Source: ONS NRJS – nat income accounts Q1 2013.

If rising leverage ratios showed the increasing vulnerability of British banks to financial shocks, falling household savings ratios (Figure 5) indicated the parallel increasing vulnerability of households. From a healthy 9 percent (of disposable income) in 1997, personal savings fell to a low of zero at the end of 2007.

More idiosyncratic reasons for the crisis will be given in the stories below on individual banks in trouble.

Northern Rock[4]

In the early morning of 14 September 2007, UK mortgage bank Northern Rock experienced the first British bank run since 1866, with customers queuing in long lines to withdraw their money after

---

[4] Sources for the narrative are, among others, Alex Brummer, *The Crunch: The Scandal of Northern Rock and the Escalating Credit Crisis* (London: Random House, 2008); Franco Bruni and David T. Llewellyn, eds., *The Failure*

internet sites had broken down on account of the overloading. In three days, some 4.6 billion pounds in deposits were withdrawn, corresponding to 20 percent of the bank's retail deposits. Within a month, withdrawals would rise to 10.5 billion pounds, almost half of its retail deposit base, despite the fact that the government had in the meantime guaranteed all deposits not only of Northern Rock but of all UK banks.

Actually, the problems had started already on 30 July in the market for short-term interbank lending, when the German investment bank IKB Deutsche Industriebank AG, majority owned by the German federal state via Kreditanstalt für Wiederaufbau (KfW), found itself unable to roll (refinance) its liabilities in the form of asset-backed commercial paper (ABCP) and was rescued by a loan of 3.5 billion euro from Commerzbank, Deutsche Bank and KfW. The next step came on 6 August, when the largest French bank, BNP Paribas, froze three of its funds for withdrawals after the market for CDOs (collateralized debt obligations), based on US subprime mortgages, had fallen by 20 percent.

To alleviate the resulting lack of liquidity in the frozen interbank market, the major central banks in the world injected money into the system on 9–10 August: the Federal Reserve 43 billion dollars, the ECB 95 billion euro and the Bank of Japan 8 billion dollars (equivalent). The Bank of England was conspicuously absent from these interventions, for which it would later be severely criticized. The near bankruptcy of Countrywide Financial, the largest US mortgage bank, a few days later aggravated the lack of trust among banks and the liquidity squeeze worldwide. On 22 August, the ECB announced a further 40

of Northern Rock: A Multi-Dimensional Case Study (Vienna: SUERF – The European Money and Finance Forum, 2009); Financial Services Authority, "The supervision of Northern Rock: a lessons learned review," March 2008; HM Treasury, "The nationalisation of Northern Rock," report by the Comptroller Auditor General, HC 298 session 2008–9, 20 March 2009; House of Commons, "Fifth report" (on Northern Rock), 24 January 2008; Rosa M. Lastra, "Northern Rock, UK bank insolvency and cross-border bank insolvency," *Journal of Banking Regulation* 9:3 (May 2008), pp. 939–55; Song Shin Hyun, "Reflections on Northern Rock: the bank run that heralded the global financial crisis," *Journal of Economic Perspectives* 23:1 (Winter 2009), pp. 101–19; European Commission, "High level expert group on reforming the structure of the EU banking sector" (Liikanen report), October 2012.

billion euro liquidity support through the three-month scheme Longer-Term Refinancing Operation (LTRO). Until November, the ECB would inject a further 235 billion euro into the market.

Over the next month, Northern Rock in conjunction with its "tripartite" supervisory authorities (the Bank of England, the Financial Services Authority, FSA, and the Treasury) tried in vain to find a buyer for the bank. However, the bank's peculiar structure and its problems (see below) were well known. It was later revealed that Lloyds TSB had made an offer to buy the bank for 200 pence per share, approximately corresponding to the existing share price in the market. However, the offer was conditional on the Bank of England guaranteeing up to 30 billion pounds in emergency funding, a sum, as we shall see, corresponding to the overhang of short-term liabilities coming due. The Bank of England rejected the plan on 11 September, causing the planned merger to collapse (despite the positive attitude of the FSA and the Treasury towards the merger). This was a mere two days before events became acute, since, in the meantime, the liquidity situation of the bank had continued to deteriorate. In the late evening of 13 September 2007, the BBC reported that the Bank of England had, in its role as lender of last resort, given Northern Rock an extraordinary liquidity support to the tune of 21 billion pounds (later extended to over 55 billion including guarantees). The news led to the run on the bank the next morning, as described above.

A contributing feature to the run was the peculiar construction of British deposit insurance at that time. In order to avoid the perceived "moral hazard" of depositors being spared the burden of scrutinizing the bank in which they invested their savings, the UK practiced what was called "co-insurance." The state only guaranteed fully the first 2,000 pounds and only 90 percent of deposits over that amount up to a limit of 35,000 pounds. Hence even minor depositors had some money at risk and the only reasonable strategy, if in doubt about the bank's safety, was to withdraw all deposits over 2,000 pounds, shifting them to another bank. On 17 September, the chancellor of the exchequer, Alistair Darling, extended a government guarantee to all deposits in Northern Rock and, implicitly, to any other UK bank with problems (confirmed on 9 October but applicable only to deposits made after 19 September, thus introducing a further inducement to shifting the deposits from one bank to another in order to profit from the government guarantee on newly made deposits).

From 1 January 2011, Britain, in conjunction with other EU members, raised the ceiling to 85,000 pounds (100,000 euro), 100 percent of which will be compensated in the event of a bank failure, in the UK by the Financial Services Compensation Scheme (FSCS). In contrast to the former British system, there are also strict deadlines as to how quickly depositors will receive compensation.

As shown in Figure 6, Northern Rock had a funding situation that diverged markedly from other mortgage lenders. Before the run in September, the bank funded its liabilities of just over 100 billion pounds only to some 25 percent by retail deposits; the average for the sector at the time was 50 percent. Another 25 percent was wholesale, mainly banking, funding. The latter evaporated during August and early September in a "silent run," the former from 14 September onwards in a more visible and spectacular run. In just a few weeks, 51 billion pounds in deposits before the crisis had become 22 billion, necessitating the injection of the emergency loan from the Bank of England, eventually rising to 28 billion pounds.

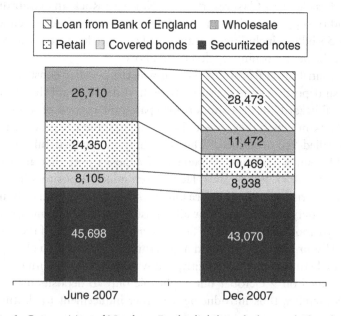

Figure 6. Composition of Northern Rock's liabilities before and after the run
Source: Northern Rock Annual report 2007.

Figure 6 also shows the extent of securitization of the mortgages lent. While the average securitization for British mortgage lenders had, as mentioned, risen to 25 percent, Northern Rock had securitized over 50 percent of the loans made. Some of the debt was held on its own books as covered bonds but the majority had been securitized through a Jersey-located special purpose vehicle (SPV) called Granite. This marked shift into "originate to distribute" from "originate to hold" had taken place just after the demutualization of Northern Rock in 1997 (see below).

The funding structure also implied a large maturity-gap problem for the bank. Long-term mortgages with fixed rates of interest were funded, in the main, by wholesale and retail borrowing with very short maturities, the duration being less than a year, and securitization with a duration of just three years. Hence, in a situation of rising interest rates, Northern Rock would be forced to pay higher interest on its funding with little or no possibility of raising interest rates on the asset side. In fact, as of September 2007, around 44 billion pounds on the liabilities side matured within 12 months as against only 8 billion pounds in assets, clearly a highly dangerous maturity mismatch.

There should have been a number of warning signals to awaken the diligence of the FSA, the funding gap being one of them. But there had been others, one of them being the rate of growth. Being the product of a number of mergers among (mutual) building societies, Northern Rock had converted into a joint-stock company in 1997 in order to facilitate growth. Over the next ten years, its total assets grew from 15.8 billion pounds to 114 billion pounds at the end of 2007, for a 23 percent average compound rate of growth. In 2007, it was the eighth largest bank in Britain but the fifth largest mortgage lender, having at the peak even occupied first place.

Its rapid growth had enabled it to join the prestigious FTSE-100 list in 2001, making it one of the 100 largest companies in the UK. Behind this rapid growth was an aggressive and innovative lending policy. Interest rate spreads were tighter than at other mortgage banks such as Halifax Bank of Scotland (HBOS) or Abbey National (owned by Santander) or Nationwide, the largest building society. A particular popular product was "Together loans" which were extended to cover up to 125 percent of the value of a newly bought house and up to six times the household's income, in contrast to the 2½-3 times income practiced generally. Not surprisingly, by the end of 2008, Together mortgages represented some 30 percent of the mortgage book of

Northern Rock but 50 percent of loans in default and 75 percent of repossessions (foreclosures).

A further warning sign to the FSA should have been the rapidly falling share price, going from 1,200 pence per share at the beginning of 2007 to 200 pence in September (and under 100 pence by December). Worldwide, stock markets were still on the rise and would peak only in October 2007, Dow Jones in the US as well as "Footsie" (FTSE) in Britain. Northern Rock was clearly going off in its own direction.

Despite these warnings, the FSA had on 29 June 2007 (barely five weeks before the acute crisis) authorized Northern Rock to move to the advanced IRB variant of the Basel II capital-adequacy regulation. This implied that instead of a standard 50 percent risk weight for mortgages under Basel I (with a minimum 8 percent capital-ratio requirement, this equals a 4 percent capital requirement for residential mortgages), its own internal models indicated a 15 percent risk weight and, correspondingly, a more than halving of capital requirements. The bank celebrated its regulatory success by deciding upon an extraordinary 59 million pound dividend to its shareholders in July 2007 (also approved by the FSA!). Fortunately, the amount had not been paid out when the crisis broke out and the payment was cancelled after the events in September, under pressure from the tripartite authorities.

Between September 2007 and February 2008, the tripartite authorities sought desperately to sell Northern Rock. Among the bidders were Sir Richard Branson's Virgin Money as well as private equity firms Cerberus and J. C. Flowers. But none of these bids was considered to give taxpayers a return for their money. Hence on 22 February 2008, Northern Rock was temporarily nationalized; the Office for National Statistics had ruled already on 6 February that the liabilities of Northern Rock must be added to the national debt, which thereby rose from 37 to 45 percent of GDP. A holding company, UK Financial Investments (UKFI), was created for the purpose of being the formal owner of the state's long-term holdings of bank shares. There has been a fierce debate whether the decision to nationalize the bank rather than selling it during the fall of 2007 was in the best interest of the taxpayer. The Treasury has defended its actions in a special report.[5]

---

[5] HM Treasury, "The nationalisation of Northern Rock," report by the Comptroller Auditor General, HC 298 session 2008–9, 20 March 2009.

Later the government holdings in Lloyds Banking Group and Royal Bank of Scotland (RBS) would be added to UKFI's books (see below). The UK Asset Resolution (UKAR) was created in 2010 as a "bad bank" for the remaining "toxic" mortgage assets of Northern Rock (and Bradford & Bingley). From 1 January 2010, the "old" Northern Rock had thus been split into a viable part, Northern Rock Bank plc, to be sold to the highest bidder, and a bad bank where the component loans would be sold separately over time. Existing shareholders were wiped out. Despite a court challenge (rejected by the Court of Appeals as well as by the House of Lords), the result of an independent expert evaluation made public on 8 December 2009 stood, namely that the correct value of compensation to the former shareholders of Northern Rock was nil. A similar result – nil – would, incidentally, be handed down half a year later to the ex-shareholders of failed Bradford & Bingley (see below).

On 17 November 2011, Northern Rock Bank plc, including 75 branch offices with one million customers, 14 billion pounds' worth of mortgage loans and 16 billion pounds in retail deposits, was sold to Sir Richard Branson's Virgin Money for an initial sum of 747 million pounds. This meant an immediate loss of 400 million pounds to the owner, UK Financial Investments, i.e. the British taxpayer, partly compensated by later payments from Virgin Money. The residual toxic (mortgage) assets remained with UKAR to be sold later. On 23 July 2012, it was announced that Virgin Money would be acquiring an additional 465 million pounds' worth of mortgage assets from UKAR. In addition, in July 2013, the private equity firm J. C. Flowers agreed to buy 450 million pounds' worth of the bank's loans from UKAR.

Overall grade of the handling of Northern Rock: B (on a scale of A to F=Fail)

In evaluating the response by the tripartite authorities to the crisis, it must be borne in mind that this was the first severe banking crisis to hit the UK since the Second World War. The collapse of BCCI in 1991 and Barings Bank in 1995 had been too small to matter systemically. In facing the problems of Northern Rock, the authorities discovered:

- A fundamental flaw in the deposit-insurance system, since corrected;
- The absence of a special bankruptcy regime for banks, since corrected;

- The absence of resolution regimes for handling banks in trouble, since corrected;
- An ineffective structure of financial supervision since 1997, whereby the FSA was responsible for micro prudential supervision and the Bank of England for systemic stability and the function as lender of last resort, creating an infighting between authorities as well as gaps in supervision. This has since been corrected by making the Bank of England (again) overall responsible for macro as well as micro prudential supervision.

It seems likely that the decision to reject the offer from Lloyds Banking Group in September of 2007 was the right one, not least in view of Lloyds' own later problems (see below). Whether it would have been more advantageous for the taxpayer to have accepted the bid from Virgin Money in 2007 rather than the (lower) bid from 2011 can be discussed. After the sale of Northern Rock Bank plc, the British National Audit Office on 18 May 2012 finalized the cost to the taxpayer of the nationalization of Northern Rock. Out of a total investment of 37 billion pounds into the two parts of the bank (the sold viable part and the retained "bad bank"), the government almost broke even, losing less than 0.5 billion pounds as a best estimate. At worst, the cost to the taxpayer might be 2 billion pounds.[6] However, even after repayments, the remaining debt of UK Asset Resolution to the government was still 43.4 billion pounds in March 2013, though paying a market-determined rate of interest.

Another way of seeing that the lesson had indeed been learnt, the resolution of Bradford & Bingley, a bank half the size of Northern Rock but with similar problems, was handled much more efficiently just one year later. On 29 September 2008, Bradford & Bingley was rescued after a run on the bank had cost it tens of millions of pounds. The bank received a bridge loan from the Bank of England of 17.9 billion pounds. The 197 branch offices, 2.7 million customers and 20 billion pounds' worth of deposits were sold the same day to Abbey National (owned by the Spanish bank Grupo Santander) for 612 million pounds, while the troubled mortgage book was taken over by the

---

[6] National Audit Office, "The Comptroller and Auditor General's report to the House of Commons," HC 34 2012–13, 12 July 2013, p. 13, www.nao.org.uk/wp-content/uploads/2013/07/HMT-Accounts-2012–13.pdf

state (UKAR). The offer from Santander was attractive since the last market valuation of the bank had only been 256 million pounds. Not only the mortgage book but also personal loan book, headquarters building, Treasury assets and its wholesale liabilities were taken into public ownership by UKAR.

The EU Commission accepted the actions taken on 28 October 2009, lauding in particular the split into a "good bank" and a "bad bank."[7]

The actions taken would have merited an "A," in particular the setting-up of a government-run "bad bank," were it not for the slow reaction of the FSA, allowing the bank to shift to model-based Basel II as well as authorizing an extra dividend during the summer of 2007 when the problems should have been evident.

Royal Bank of Scotland (RBS)[8]

At the end of 2007, the Royal Bank of Scotland Group (RBS) was by far the largest bank in the world, measured by assets, and the international number 3 in terms of Tier 1 capital. With total assets at 3.8 trillion dollars, it was way ahead of its nearest rivals, Deutsche Bank at 3 trillion and BNP Paribas at 2.5 trillion.[9] Even after some downsizing, it was still the world's largest bank by assets in 2008 at 3.5 trillion dollars.[10] A number of brand names were contained within the group, apart from the Royal Bank of Scotland itself. In 2000, RBS had acquired the much larger National Westminster Bank (NatWest) for 21 billion pounds in what was then the largest takeover in British financial history. RBS won out over rival Bank of Scotland

---

[7] http://europa.eu/rapid/press-release_IP-09-1600_en.htm

[8] Works used are, among others, Financial Services Authority, "The failure of the Royal Bank of Scotland," FSA Board report, December 2011, www.fsa. gov.uk/pubs/other/rbs.pdf; Ian Fraser, *Shredded: The Rise and Fall of the Royal Bank of Scotland* (Edinburgh: Birlinn, 2014); Iain Martin, *Making it Happen: Fred Goodwin, RBS and the Men who Blew up the British Economy* (London: Simon & Schuster, 2013); Jeroen Smit, *The Perfect Prey: The Fall of ABN AMRO, or What Went Wrong in the Banking Industry* (London: Quercus, 2010); European Commission, "High level expert group on reforming the structure of the EU banking sector" (Liikanen report), October 2012.

[9] *The Banker*, July 2008.

[10] *The Banker*, July 2009.

(BOS) by promising to retain the brand name and the bank intact whereas BOS intended to break up the bank. Ulster Bank is one of the major banks in Northern Ireland as well as in the Republic of Ireland. Wealth management is handled through Coutts private bank, one of the oldest in the world, with a history stretching back to 1692. In the United States, RBS/NatWest owns Citizens Financial Group, which ranked as the twelfth largest American bank in 2007. It also owns Greenwich Capital (now RBS Securities), a US broker-dealer and one of the only 21 primary dealers authorized to trade directly with the Federal Reserve. In 2005, it took a 5 percent stake in Bank of China (sold in 2009).

After the events in mid September 2008 which saw Lehman Brothers go bankrupt, a desperate Merrill Lynch, bought by the Bank of America and the world's largest insurance company, AIG, saved from ruin by the Federal Reserve by the largest bail-out ever of a private company, financial markets started to worry about RBS, which was seen as one of the worst-capitalized of the major banks. Finding normal supplies of liquidity insufficient, on 7 October the bank received support from the Bank of England under its Emergency Liquidity Assistance (ELA) program. On that day alone, the bank lost 6 billion pounds in customer deposits. On 13 October 2008 (the very same day that Treasury Secretary Paulson et consortes forced the major US banks to accept new capital), the British government announced injections of equity capital into RBS (20 billion pounds) as well as 17 billion pounds into Lloyds Banking Group (formed by a merger of Lloyds TSB and Halifax Bank of Scotland, HBOS, see below). The state thereby became a majority owner of RBS with 58 percent of the share capital and 43 percent of Lloyds.

By converting its 5 billion pounds' non-voting preference shares into ordinary common stock, the government's share of Royal Bank of Scotland rose from 58 to 70 percent on 19 January 2009. On 26 February 2009, RBS utilized the new state guarantee ("Asset Protection Scheme") to insure 325 billion pounds of assets (later reduced to 282 billion pounds). RBS would take the first 19.5 billion pounds in losses plus 10 percent of the residual. The fee to the government of 6.5 billion pounds in stock and a recapitalization of 13 billion pounds led to the state owning 83 percent of the bank. Moreover, a "bad bank" was to be set up to handle assets worth a nominal 540 billion pounds.

In the schematic graph above from the *Financial Times* (see Figure 3), the Royal Bank of Scotland (RBS) was the only one of the failed major banks in the world that merited being faulted on all of the five criteria: (1) aggressive and ill-timed mergers and acquisitions (M&A); (2) too low capital base; (3) risky funding structures with too little stable retail customer deposits; (4) bad lending; and (5) bad investments/trading.[11] How on earth did RBS get into such a position? Some data are to be found in Table 7.

The main event is evidently the purchase and carving up of Dutch bank ABN AMRO in 2007 (on which much more below), which resulted in a doubling of total assets of RBS in one year. When ABN AMRO's important trading positions were integrated into RBS, the net derivatives position trebled. For reasons explained below, a gross operating profit of 10 billion pounds in 2007 turned into a loss of 40 billion pounds, the largest ever in British corporate history.

While seemingly well capitalized with a BIS ratio of 11.2 percent in 2007 and 14.7 percent in 2008 (compared to an 8 percent minimum), this fact was mainly a result of a low proportion of risk-weighted assets

Table 7. *Selected data from Royal Bank of Scotland, 2006–10*

	2006	2007	2008	2009	2010
Total assets (billion pounds)	871	1,595	1,680	1,523	1,453
Derivatives position, net (billion pounds)	117	337	932	438	427
Gross operating profit (million pounds)	9,414	10,282	–40,836	–6,090	2,087
Return on equity (%)	19	18	neg.	neg.	13
Cost-income ratio (%)	42	41	79	69	60
Net interest margin (%)	2.47	2.46	2.08	1.76	2.01
Core Tier 1 capital ratio (%)	n.a.	4.0	6.1	11.0	10.7

Source: Annual accounts.

[11] Personally, I would have placed Bank of America in the same position; see below.

to total assets, in particular after being accepted for the Advanced IRB approach in June 2008, and an overreliance on hybrid and subordinated debt.[12] Its core Tier 1 ratio in 2007 was but 4 percent, a number the supervisor FSA wanted to see raised to at least 5 percent. Its core capital in relation to total assets (leverage ratio) was a low 2.33 percent in 2007 (according to *The Banker*), lower than most of its peers.

The FSA report (2011) has made an effort to see what the capital position of RBS would have been under the forthcoming Basel III rules. These stipulate a 4.5 percent absolute minimum of Core Equity Tier 1 (CET1) capital to risk-weighted assets (RWA) above which is added a conservation buffer of 2.5 percent for a total of 7 percent. If the 7 percent is breached, the bank faces restrictions on the payment of dividends as well as bonuses. RBS would also at the time have been placed by the Financial Stability Board (FSB) in the highest group of globally systemically important financial institutions (G-SIFI) with a 2.5 percent weight for a total of 9.5 percent,[13] to which may be added a countercyclical weight of up to 2.5 percent.

The FSA calculates that under Basel III, the actual CET1/RWA of RBS in 2006 would have been a low 2 percent (and 2.97 percent at end 2007). And as the report concludes, "if the Basel III standards had been in place, RBS would have been prevented from paying dividends at any time during the period reviewed in this Report (2005 onwards) and would have been unable to launch the bid for ABN AMRO" (p. 11).

Not only the lower-than-average capital ratio but the evolution of the share price of RBS should have given the FSA some food for thought. The bidding for ABN AMRO during spring and summer and the actual purchase on 17 October 2007 made only a minor impact on the stock price. However, on 6 December 2007, RBS made a first important write-down for credit losses. On 21 April 2008, RBS wrote down another 5.9 billion pounds and simultaneously issued new stock worth 12 billion pounds. The market was not impressed and the stock price fell 5 percent. In early October, the stock nosedived with the global and local problems.

---

[12] The shift to Basel II was expected to lower the capital base of British banks on average by 13 percent. The effect was, however, much larger for RBS which used a 96 percent confidence interval for its value-at-risk calculations rather than the usual and stipulated 99.9 percent.

[13] After the downsizing of the bank, the latest FSB classification gives RBS a SIFI weight of 1.5 percent.

For the year 2008, RBS posted a record loss before tax of 40.7 billion pounds, of which 30.1 billion was write-down of goodwill largely (22 billion pounds) related to the purchase of ABN AMRO. Losses on credit trading were 17.7 billion pounds, also to a large extent related to the CDS and CDO portfolios taken over from ABN AMRO. On the day of announcement, 19 January 2009, the share price of RBS fell by over 66 percent in just one day to 11 pence per share, compared to a year-high of 354 pence, a fall of 97 percent. Only HBOS did equally badly (to be discussed in the next section). See Figure 7.

"I don't think there can be any doubt that the key decision that led RBS to its difficulties was the acquisition of ABN AMRO. That is the painful reality that we can now do nothing to change. With the benefit of hindsight, it can now be seen as the wrong price, the wrong way to pay, at the wrong time and the wrong deal" (Chairman's introductory words at the Annual General Meeting of shareholders, 3 April 2009).

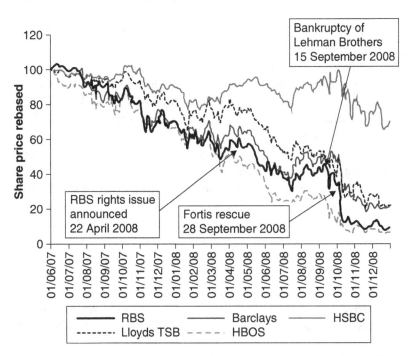

Figure 7. The share price of major UK banks June 2007 – December 2008
Source: FSA 2011, p. 202.

Table 8. *The carving up of ABN AMRO*

To RBS

Business unit North America (which had basically been sold)

Business unit Global Clients (except South America)

Dutch wholesale clients

Business unit Asia and Europe (excluding Italy and the Netherlands)

To Fortis

Business unit Netherlands (except wholesale)

Business unit private clients (except Latin America)

Business unit Asset Management

To Santander

Business unit Latin America

Private clients business in Latin America

Banca and asset management Banca Antonveneta (Italy)

On 17 October 2007, the Dutch bank ABN AMRO had been bought for 71 billion euro (easily the largest takeover in banking history) by a consortium consisting of the Benelux bank Fortis, the Spanish Santander and the Royal Bank of Scotland (RBS) which divided up the bank among them (see Table 8). The share of RBS was 38 percent of the total, which in turn corresponded to 61 percent of its actual Tier 1 capital at the end of 2006.

The price corresponded to 38 euro per share whereas an investment bank (Rothschild) had earlier calculated that a reasonable price would be 23 euro per share.[14] The competition with Barclays had cost RBS and the other members of the consortium dearly.

In August 2007, 95 percent of the shareholders of RBS had voted for the deal. However, the fight for ABN AMRO had begun already in March 2007, when Barclays revealed that it was in discussion with the Dutch bank concerning a possible merger among equals. In early April, the three-bank consortium made public their intention of a counterbid. For RBS, the main interest was the ABN AMRO subsidiary US bank LaSalle, headquartered in Chicago, which, while only

[14] Smit, *The Perfect Prey*, p. 350.

half its size, would complement RBS's Citizens Bank with its focus on the northeastern states of the United States. The combined bank would have become the fifth largest in the United States by assets. However, as a defensive maneuver, ABN AMRO sold LaSalle to Bank of America (effective 1 October), which should have made RBS pull out of the purchase plans, citing a material adverse change (MAC) as a motivation for breaking a bid made.[15]

The other interesting part was the wholesale (investment) banking of ABN AMRO which RBS saw complementing its own Global Banking and Markets (GBM), making it one of the leading banks in the world in fixed-income trading and securitization. In fact, this is where the major losses would originate (see below).

While RBS and Fortis would be bankrupted by the purchase of ABN AMRO, Santander complemented its Spanish (and British) operations by the South American acquisitions. The Italian Banca Antonveneta was almost immediately sold to Monte dei Paschi di Siena for 9 billion euro, corresponding to a profit for Santander of 36 percent for two months' holding. And as of 2014, it is Monte dei Paschi which is in need of state support and more capital, not Santander.

A second disastrous decision by RBS was to finance the ABN AMRO purchase mainly by debt instead of fresh share capital. RBS was already in a tight spot liquidity-wise before the purchase. The FSA (2011) has tried to estimate what the Liquidity Coverage Ratio (LCR) under Basel III would have been if it had been in place before the crisis. It estimated that at the end of September 2008, just before the acute liquidity crisis, the LCR of RBS would have been between 18 and 32 percent of requirements (one month liquidity coverage) as contrasted to the required 100 percent. The stock of unencumbered liquid assets would thus have had to rise by some 150 billion pounds to fulfill requirements.

---

[15] This was very clearly the position of RBS when the offer was considered in April–May. "At about eleven at night Groenink [CEO of ABN AMRO] and Martinez [ABN AMRO governor, i.e. chairman of the board] phoned Fred Goodwin [CEO of RBS]. They asked the chairman of the consortium whether they would now come up with an offer for the bank without LaSalle or perhaps one for LaSalle separately. Goodwin was astonished by the offer and phoned back half an hour later informing him that they weren't interested. The consortium wanted to buy the whole bank." Smit, *The Perfect Prey*, pp. 360–1.

A major cause of the loss in 2008 was credit trading, where losses rose from 1 billion pounds in 2007 to 12 billion pounds in 2008. Many of these losses actually stemmed from positions built up by RBS GBM before the acquisition of ABN AMRO but the additional positions squeezed core capital even further. A large proportion of the losses came from US subprime-related instruments: CDOs, CDO-squared, synthetic CDOs, hybrid CDOs, CDSs ...

The European Commission's competition commissioner ruled in November 2009 that RBS would have to sell its insurance divisions (Direct Line and Churchill) on account of the state aid received. The bank must also sell some branch offices in England and Wales, as well as its NatWest branches in Scotland (see below).[16] The bank also announced lay-offs of some 20,000 staff. The actual figure by 2013 would be 34,000 jobs cut (out of 220,000 at the end of 2007).

On 6 May 2012, RBS repaid the last 5.7 billion pounds of the liquidity support that at its peak had amounted to 75 billion (special liquidity and credit guarantee schemes). The state remains at 82 percent its main shareholder, however. On 17 October 2012, the bank exited from the Asset Protection Scheme agreed to in 2009, after having paid in to the Treasury 2.5 billion pounds in fees on covered assets of 282 billion pounds of loans and derivatives with no payments whatsoever from the Treasury. On September 2013, the RBS Group confirmed it had agreed to sell 308 RBS branches in England and Wales and 6 NatWest branches in Scotland to the Corsair consortium. The branches will be separated from the group by 2015 as a standalone business operating under the dormant William & Glyn's brand name.

Figure 8 shows that the potential losses of the government's holding (UKFI) of shares in RBS actually increased during 2012–13. Including funding costs on the government's injection of capital into RBS, the amount to be recovered stood at just over 50 billion pounds in March 2013, while the market value of the shares held had declined to 25 billion pounds.

Overall grade of the handling of Royal Bank of Scotland:
E (on a scale of A to F=Fail)

As acknowledged by the FSA and the National Audit Office in their reports, there were a number of errors committed in the handling

---

[16] http://europa.eu/rapid/press-release_IP-09-1600_en.htm

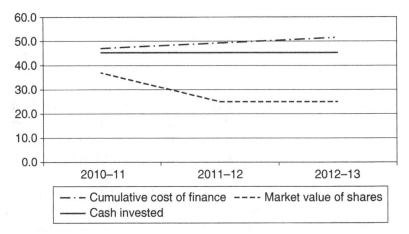

Figure 8. Value of shares in RBS held by UKFI and amount spent, billion pounds
Source: National Audit Office, "The Comptroller and Auditor General's report to the House of Commons," HC 34 2012–13, 12 July 2013.

of the RBS failure, here only summarized with my own comments added:

• The hands-off, "principles-based" approach to supervision was totally inadequate for a bank the size of RBS. In 2006–7, the FSA had allocated four full-time managers to supervise a bank of 3.8 trillion dollars in assets and 220,000 employees. This may be contrasted with 60 full-time OCC supervisors in a US bank of similar size, Citibank.

• The FSA allowed RBS to move to the advanced IRB approach under Basel II while not forcing the bank strongly enough to raise its already-low capital base, despite its own misgivings.

• While the FSA had no formal legal grounds for preventing the purchase of ABN AMRO, a strong supervisor could have marked its displeasure in such a way as to make the bank abstain, for instance by demanding substantially higher capital ratios under Pillar 2 of Basel II if the purchase went through.

• While total assets of RBS were wound down to 1.3 trillion pounds at the end of 2012, too little effort has been made by the supervisory authorities to force it to sell non-core assets such as the US, Asian or Irish subsidiaries.

- Only by 2015 will the Commission's ruling on the selling off of branches be completed (since an earlier deal with Santander fell through).
- An external "bad bank" was only set up five years after the crash, despite a decision to this effect already in February 2009.[17] The UK Treasury on 1 November 2013 finally decided that the bank was to set up an internal bad bank encompassing 38.3 billion pounds of assets.[18] This decision was far too little far too late. By the end of 2013, the "bad bank" had wound down assets to 29 billion.[19]
- However, Citizens' Bank in the United States as well as Ulster Bank still remained to be sold.
- Nor has any attempt been made to split up the bank along retail–wholesale lines of business as proposed by the Vickers commission in 2011[20] and included in the parliamentary bill on the reorganization of banks.[21]
- Out of 50 billion pounds spent on saving RBS, 25 billion pounds were a loss to the taxpayer as of March 2013, indicative of the fact that the market considers actions taken to bring the bank back to profitability so far totally inadequate. The share price has hovered in the 300–50 pence per share range since early 2013, much lower than the peaks of 550 achieved in 2009 and 2010.[22]

Lloyds Banking Group[23]

If Royal Bank of Scotland was a badly run bank where the purchase of ABN AMRO became the straw that broke the camel's back, Lloyds

---

[17] According to a newspaper report, the chancellor said on 18 October 2013, that RBS was "weeks" from setting up a bad bank for its toxic assets. www.telegraph.co.uk/finance/newsbysector/banksandfinance/10390168/RBS-bad-bank-due-in-weeks-says-George-Osborne.html

[18] Nigel (Lord) Lawson, "The decision not to break up RBS was wrong," *Financial Times*, 5 November 2013.

[19] "Five years on and the RBS pain is still far from over," *Financial Times*, 28 February 2014.

[20] Independent Commission on Banking (ICB), "Final report, recommendations," September 2011 (Vickers report), www.ecgi.org/documents/icb_final_report_12sep2011.pdf

[21] HM Treasury, Financial Services (Banking reform) Bill, 4 February 2013 (HC Bill 130), www.publications.parliament.uk/pa/bills/cbill/2012–2013/0130/2013130.pdf

[22] https://uk.finance.yahoo.com/q/bc?s=RBS.L&t=5y&l=off&z=l&q=l&c=

[23] This section builds, among others, on Ray Perman, *Hubris: How HBOS Wrecked the Best Bank in Britain* (Edinburgh: Birlinn, 2013); House of

TSB was a well-run and esteemed bank which made only one major error, namely buying Halifax Bank of Scotland (HBOS), and this at the worst possible time in October 2008.

Both future partners were the products of a number of previous marriages. A number of former savings banks, converted to joint-stock status, merged and were floated on the London Stock Exchange in 1986 as TSB (Trustee Savings Banks). In 1995, they combined with Lloyds, one of Britain's oldest banks, to create Lloyds TSB. HBOS was the product of the merger in 2001 of the former building society Halifax with the Bank of Scotland. In 2007, they were number 4 and 5 in terms of both assets and capital in the United Kingdom. Table 9 gives some of their characteristics. While their fundamental data in terms of BIS ratio, leverage, return on capital and cost–income ratio were rather similar in 2007, HBOS was evidently much more subjected to the liquidity squeeze of 2008 than was Lloyds TSB. The market's reaction was also evident from the movement of stock prices in Figure 7. From early 2008, HBOS was the worst performing stock of the major UK banks.

Table 9. *A comparison of Lloyds TSB and HBOS 2007–8*

	Lloyds TSB		HBOS	
	2007	2008	2007	2008
Total assets (billion pounds)	353.5	436.2	667.0	690.0
Profit before tax (million pounds)	4,089	825	5,474	–10,825
Tier 1 capital (billion pounds)	13.5	13.6	23.7	19.8
BIS ratio	11.0	11.2	11.1	10.3
Leverage (%)	3.95	3.14	3.66	2.87
Return on assets (%)	1.13	0.19	0.82	–1.57
Cost–income (%)	52	86	47	n.a.

Source: The Banker and annual accounts.

Commons, House of Lords, Parliamentary Commission on Banking Standards, "An accident waiting to happen, the failure of HBOS," Fourth report session 2012/13, 4 April 2013; Office of Fair Trading, "Anticipated acquisition by Lloyds TSB plc of HBOS plc," 24 October 2008. www.oft.gov.uk/shared_oft/press_release_attachments/LLloydstsb.pdf

Given the size of the two merging banks, the Office of Fair Trading (OFT) was hesitant to grant permission on competition grounds. However, the OFT also stated (p. 5) that its "review in this case involves a predictive merger assessment of financial markets in the UK (and also globally) that are currently experiencing extraordinary turbulence and change. These uncertain conditions, as exogenous forces affecting the market are being investigated, are a reason for caution ..." Indeed a very clairvoyant attitude!

However, the OFT also clearly indicates that it was pressured into giving its assent in a statement well worth quoting in full:

359. The OFT received submissions from the Bank of England, the FSA and HMT [Her Majesty's Treasury] (the Tripartite Authorities), all of whom argue that the necessity of the merger on financial stability grounds outweighs any potential competition concerns, and that the merger should not therefore be referred to the CC (Competition Commission). In particular:

360. The Bank of England notes the importance of HBOS as a major UK bank for the stability of the UK financial system as a whole. It contends that the sounder funding base and better quality of assets of Lloyds supports the merits of the merger in strengthening financial stability.

361. The FSA also notes the vulnerable position of HBOS leading up to announcement of the merger. It argues that a private sector acquirer of HBOS was and is the best way to promote financial stability in the UK, and that Lloyds was best placed to act quickly in making an offer for HBOS.

362. HMT agrees that the successful passage of the merger is crucial for financial stability. In particular, it argues that the benefits of the transaction for HBOS include increased confidence, an improved business model, a better capital base, a reduced reliance on wholesale funding, an improved credit rating, a broader business base, and the addressing of funding issues. All of these factors, it contends, will promote financial stability in the UK more generally.

This was written on 24 October 2008, five weeks after Lloyds TSB agreed to purchase HBOS for 12 billion pounds and 11 days after the British government announced injections of capital into Lloyds TSB and HBOS totaling 17 billion pounds, thereby making the state a minority owner of Lloyds Banking Group, which was the new name of the merged companies.

Not surprisingly, the first minister of Scotland, Alex Salmond, losing the second of his national flagships, on the day the merger was announced, criticized it, saying that any merger between the two should be based on measured discussion, not a "shotgun marriage" driven by unwarranted speculation. And he accused financial regulator the Financial Services Authority of leaving HBOS vulnerable to speculative attack by failing to act despite finding that the banking giant was properly funded and had a good capital ratio.[24]

If, on 13 October 2008, RBS and Lloyds Banking Group seemed equally vulnerable and dependent on the state for both its liquidity and its capital, the developments since then have been much more favorable for Lloyds. One wonders why. Is it because of superior management or the fact that Lloyds is only half the size of RBS? Or is it because the government and the other tripartite authorities have taken more actions to make Lloyds again a profitable and competitive bank, driven by a bad conscience over basically destroying a healthy bank by forcing it to take over a bank whose problems turned out to be even worse than the market in its judgment had thought?

On 6 March 2009, Lloyds Banking Group signed an agreement with the government, similar to the earlier RBS deal. Assets worth 260 billion pounds would be guaranteed by the state. Lloyds would take the first 25 billion pounds in losses and 10 percent of the rest. The fee to the government in the form of preference shares would lead to a government stake of 77 percent of the bank once the preference shares were converted into common stock; until then the state's share remained at 43 percent. However, on 24 November 2009 Lloyds issued the world's largest-ever rights issue of 13.5 billion pounds. While the government picked up its share and hence its ownership remained at 43 percent, Lloyds avoided having to pay for the asset insurance and never entered the Asset Protection Scheme. On top of shares, the bank also issued 7.5 billion pounds of "CoCo bonds," contingent convertible securities

---

[24] http://news.bbc.co.uk/2/hi/uk_news/scotland/edinburgh_and_east/7621153. stm. The statement concerning the health of the bank would turn out to be quite erroneous.

that automatically convert to equity should Lloyds' core Tier 1 ratio fall below 6 percent.

To gain the EU Commission's approval for the 17 billion-pound bail-out, Lloyds also committed to sell a retail banking unit with a 4.6 percent share of the current account market and 19 percent of the group's mortgage balances (see below).[25]

The National Audit Committee (see above and Figure 9) noted that at the end of March 2013, the capital support to Lloyds including funding costs had risen to 23 billion pounds while the value of shares held was 13 billion. However, the turnaround has led to a dramatic improvement in the share price of Lloyds. From a low of just over 20 pence in early 2012, the share rose to 45 pence at the time of the Audit Committee's report and continued to rise to 70–80 pence a share in 2013–14.[26] The government profited from the occasion. On

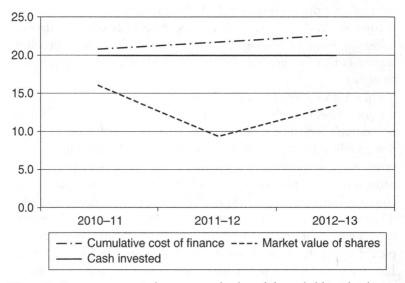

Figure 9. Government capital support and value of shares held in Lloyds Banking Group

[25] http://europa.eu/rapid/press-release_IP-09-1728_en.htm
[26] https://uk.finance.yahoo.com/q/bc?s=LLOY.L&t=5y&l=off&z=l&q=l&c=

16 September 2013, UK Financial Investments reduced its share of Lloyds from 38.7 percent to 32.7 percent. The price received in the marketplace slightly exceeded what the government had paid, leading to a profit of 60 million pounds for taxpayers. Two more tranches were scheduled for sale during 2014.

On 20 June 2013, the new Prudential Regulatory Authority (PRA) within the Bank of England decided that UK banks must raise an additional total of 13.4 billion pounds to overcome a capital shortfall by the end of the year in order to attain a ratio of 7 percent of equity to risk-weighted assets. Lloyds Banking Group must boost capital by 8.6 billion pounds.

Ordered by the EU competition authorities to downsize, Lloyds Banking Group has resuscitated the TSB (Trustee Savings Banks) brand name in creating a separate subsidiary with 631 branch offices in preparation for a sell-off in an IPO in 2014.[27] Interest in buying was declared by, among others, the private equity group J. C. Flowers. On 11 October 2013, Lloyds Banking Group sold its Australian business to Westpac for 860 million pounds.

Overall the new leadership of Lloyds (which is the new/old name for the group ex-TSB) has succeeded in downsizing both assets and risks. Dependency on wholesale funding with less than a year's maturity fell from 149 billion pounds at the end of 2012 to 51 billion at the end of June 2013. While total assets were reduced from 990 billion pounds to 877 billion in the same period, non-core assets fell from 195 billion to 83 billion. The cost–income ratio is down to what it was in 2007 and is scheduled to fall to 45 percent.[28]

Overall grade of the handling of Lloyds Banking Group: C (on a scale of A to F=Fail)

A "bad bank" to separate toxic assets is still lacking, assets could have been sold faster but in the main the response of the authorities has been quite acceptable after the disastrous decision by the former Labour government to force HBOS onto a hesitant Lloyds TSB. In the

---

[27] www.telegraph.co.uk/finance/newsbysector/banksandfinance/10293493/
Welcome-back-TSB-as-bank-splits-from-Lloyds.html
[28] "Lloyds chief builds on his baptism of fire," *Financial Times*, 14 October 2013.

view of the FSA already in 2004, as delivered to the board of HBOS by its group finance director: "The Group's [HBOS's] growth has outpaced the ability to control risks. The Group's strong growth, which is markedly different than the position of the peer group, may have given rise to 'an accident waiting to happen.'" Unfortunately, the FSA had forgotten its own message four years later in believing, with the Treasury, that a forced marriage with Lloyds could save HBOS.

2 | Germany
IKB, Hypo Real Estate, Commerzbank, Landesbanken

The German story

For many reasons, a financial crisis in Germany in 2007 seemed remote. While property prices had doubled in the ten years between 1997 and 2007 in most of the countries in Europe and risen by 200 percent or more in Ireland, the United Kingdom and Spain, they were flat in Germany.[1] Homeownership in Germany was and is also much lower than in most other European countries. While countries like Italy, Spain, Greece, Belgium and Ireland have around 80 percent of the population living in their own homes, only 46 percent of Germans owned their own homes in 2007, by far the lowest percentage in the EU (according to Eurostat).[2] German banks have also long since faced much stricter requirements as concerns loan-to-value (a maximum of 60 percent) than other European countries. Northern Rock's "Together loan" would not have been possible in Germany!

German banking is also much more fragmented and national than in most other European countries, especially in comparison with the smaller ones. Figure 10 shows that the share of the top five banks in terms of total banking assets in 1997 was only 16 percent in Germany as contrasted with 40 percent in France, 45 percent in Austria, 55 percent in Belgium and 80 percent in the Netherlands. The financial crisis (to be discussed in this chapter) and the demise of such banks as Dresdner Bank and several of the local Landesbanken led to a doubling of the ratio until 2010, which however still remained lower than in all the other countries presented in the figure.

---

[1] "Real estate doldrums: why the global housing market boom bypassed Germany," *Spiegel International*, 28 May 2008, www.spiegel.de/international/business/real-estate-doldrums-why-the-global-housing-market-boom-bypassed-germany-a-552901.html

[2] http://europa.eu/rapid/press-release_STAT-09-95_en.htm?locale=en

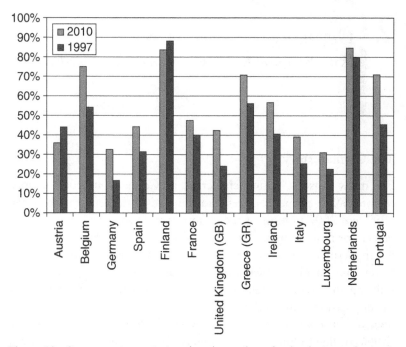

Figure 10. Concentration ratio (market share of top five banks in total assets)
Source: European Commission, "High level expert group on reforming the structure of the EU banking sector" (Liikanen report), October 2012, p. 18.

In another way of measuring dispersion, there were 1,893 financial institutions in Germany in 2012 but only 373 in the UK (Liikanen report, p. 119). In Germany, these were 95 percent domestically owned whereas half the credit institutions in the UK were foreign.

Nor is banking as dominant an industry in Germany as in some other countries. Figure 11 shows assets of financial institutions in the EU as a percentage of the home country's GDP. Ranging from 1,000 percent in Luxembourg, 800 percent in Ireland and Malta to figures below 100 percent in the former Communist states, we find Germany together with Belgium, Sweden, Austria and Spain at around 300 percent of GDP, half of the UK figure. Of the 25 largest banks in the world by assets in 2008, only one was German (Deutsche Bank) as contrasted to four British, three French, two Swiss and two Dutch, one Italian and one Spanish.

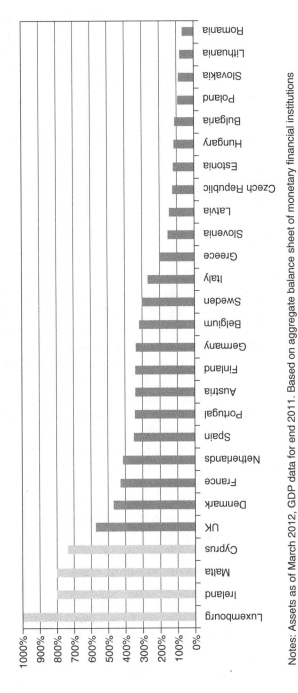

Figure 11. Banking in different EU countries, percentage of national GDP

Notes: Assets as of March 2012, GDP data for end 2011. Based on aggregate balance sheet of monetary financial institutions (MFIs). Vertical axis cut at 1000% (ratio for Luxembourg is 2400%). Data on MFI includes money market funds.

Source: Liikanen report, p. 13.

And to be honest, if any one bank in Germany was expected to face financial difficulties during the global financial crisis, the foremost candidate would have Deutsche Bank, which at the end of 2007 had a capital–asset ratio of 1.4 percent; i.e. the bank was leveraged 71 times, far above its peers. Yet Deutsche came through the crisis virtually unscathed (though with the share price even in mid 2014 at one-fourth of the level in 2007).[3]

It should also be pointed out that when the crisis struck, Germany, on 6 October 2008, just like Iceland, Ireland, Denmark and Austria, chose to protect German depositors in German banks, clearly excluding deposits in foreign subsidiaries and implicitly also deposits in foreign branches of German banks.[4]

IKB[5]

The Kreditanstalt für Wiederaufbau (KfW), owned by the German federal state (80 percent) and the states (20 percent), was set up after the war to handle the German part of the Marshall aid. In the 1990s, it was used to channel aid to the former East German states. By the beginning of the twenty-first century, its main role was to supplement other lenders, particularly with regard to small and medium enterprises ("Mittelstand"). Guaranteed by the federal state, it could borrow and hence lend on advantageous terms.

One of its subsidiaries, IKB Deutsche Industriebank AG, had, however, engaged in activities that were far from those intended. It had set up several Dublin-based subsidiaries, Rhinebridge/Rhineland Holding, constructed as Structured Investment Vehicles (SIV), borrowing on short-term asset-backed commercial paper (ABCP) and investing in US subprime mortgage-related CDOs as well as synthetic CDOs, such as Goldman Sachs' infamous Abacus 2007-AC1 (see the Chronology for 16 April 2010, 15 July 2010, 11 June 2011 and 1 August 2013). At the peak, it held a portfolio of 24 billion euro of various CDOs. After the freezing of markets for ABCP in June–July, it was unable to roll

---

[3] https://uk.finance.yahoo.com/q/bc?s=DBK.DE&t=1y&l=off&z=l&q=l&c=
[4] www.ft.com/intl/cms/s/0/d895ef54-92ef-11dd-98b5-0000779fd18c. html#axzz2jxX169s4
[5] See e.g. Dominik Schöneberger, *US Hypothekenkrise in Deutschland: Auswirkungen im Fall IKB* (Hamburg: Diplomica, 2009).

(refinance) its liabilities. Its liquidity position was restored by a loan of 3.5 billion euro by Commerzbank, Deutsche Bank and KfW, later increased to 5 billion euro, guaranteed by the federal state through SoFFin (Sonderfonds Finanzmarktstabilisierung). Since the ABCP had been sold with so-called liquidity put options guaranteed by KfW, the investors were able to sell the securities back to KfW, which thus took the loss onto its own books. The CEO of IKB, Stefan Ortseifen, was fired and later fined 100,000 euro for having covered up the losses in the Dublin subsidiaries in the financial reports during the first half of 2007, thus misleading investors.

For 2007, IKB took a write-down of 3 billion euro leading to a net loss of 1 billion euro. On 13 February 2008, it received a capital injection of 1.5 billion euro from the federal state. On 21 August 2008, the 91 percent of IKB owned by KfW was sold to private equity firm Lone Star for an undisclosed sum believed to be around 100 million euro, far lower than the market value of the company at the time. Lone Star, however, injected 225 million euro into the company as well as another 200 million in a separate "bad bank" to handle 3.3 billion euro of remaining securities related to the US subprime market.

Overall grade of the handling of KfW/IKB: B (on a scale of A to F=Fail)

While the German taxpayers have taken a severe hit, there was little else that could be done given the public ownership of KfW and its subsidiary IKB. Believing that the crisis was primarily one of liquidity, the government acted quickly and mainly with private money to aid IKB. When it turned out that the problem was deeper, it recapitalized the bank and sold it within a short time span, albeit at a loss.

However, given the development of the share price as set out in Figure 12, the German state and its taxpayers should have been happy to have been rid of the company. There was no upside to profit from the investment had the shares been retained in public hands. From a high of 32 euro per share in 2007, the price fell to 0.24 euro at the end of 2012 for a fall of over 99 percent and has never exceeded more than 1 euro since. The bank has continued to show losses for almost every period since 2009, although it has succeeded in repaying the 5 billion liquidity support guaranteed by SoFFin. The bank was evidently non-viable, so good riddance!

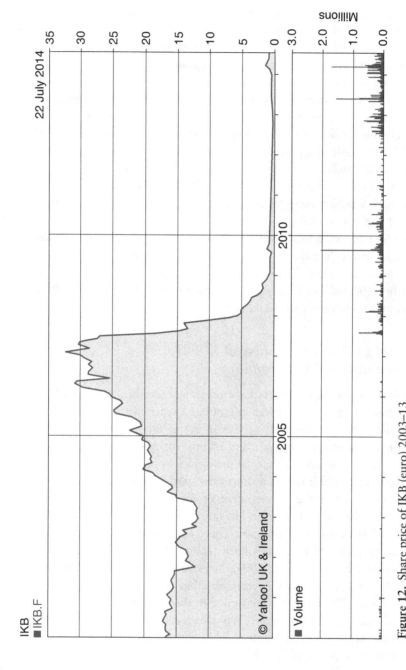

Figure 12. Share price of IKB (euro) 2003–13

Source: https://uk.finance.yahoo.com/q/bc?s=IKB.F&t=my&l=off&z=l&q=l&c=

The European Commission approved of the handling of IKB in two decisions in 2008 and 2009.[6]

Hypo Real Estate[7]

The Hypo Real Estate group (HRE), based in Munich, was spun off from HypoVereinsbank (which is today part of the Italian UniCredit group) in 2003, becoming the second largest commercial property lender in Germany. It made it into the DAX index in 2005, as one of the 30 largest companies in Germany by market capitalization. Its mistake, like so many other banks studied in this book (so far we have seen RBS and Lloyds and later in this chapter we will find Commerzbank), consisted in buying the wrong bank at the wrong time at the wrong price. On 1 October 2007, it took over the Dublin-based Depfa (Deutsche Pfandbriefanstalt), thereby increasing its total assets by 150 percent in one single year.

Depfa was a formerly state-owned bank which had been privatized in 1990, specializing in the financing of local authorities nationally as well as internationally, in particular being the largest German under-writer for public-sector covered bonds ("Öffentliche Pfandbriefe"). To obtain a more favorable regulatory and tax situation, the bank had moved its headquarters to Dublin, with special legislation from the Irish government established in 2002. Its main problem stemmed from having underwritten municipal bonds in the United States. After these had been downgraded in 2007–8, Depfa was required under the terms of the underwriting contracts to buy them back but the liquidity crisis made its financing impossible. On 29 September 2008, its new owner HRE received financial support to the tune of 35 billion euro from a consortium arranged by the German Bankers' Association and consisting of the ECB, the Bundesbank and several commercial banks. A week later, the loan volume was raised to 50 billion euro, of which 20 came from the Bundesbank, all guaranteed by SoFFin. The CEO of

---

[6] http://europa.eu/rapid/press-release_IP-08-1557_en.htm; http://europa.eu/rapid/press-release_IP-09-1235_en.htm

[7] See e.g. Matthäus Buder, Max Lienemeyer, Marcel Magnus, Bert Smits and Karl Soukup, "The rescue and restructuring of Hypo Real Estate," *EU Competition Policy Newsletter*, 3 (2011), pp. 41–4; Deutsche Bundesbank, "Fundamental features of the German bank restructuring Act," *Monthly Report*, June 2011, pp. 59–75.

HRE was forced to resign in October. On 21 January 2009, the total guarantee from SoFFin was raised to 62 billion euro. It would in the end become 145 billion euro, a higher figure than in any other state-aided European bank during the financial crisis.

As had been the case with IKB, the government soon realized that the problems of HRE were deeper than just lack of funding. On 30 March 2009, SoFFin purchased 8.7 percent of Hypo Real Estate for 600 million euro and on 3 June 2009, it took a majority position with a further 3 billion euro capital injection. On 5 October 2009, the German government bought the residual shares in Hypo Real Estate for 1.30 euro per share, thereby completing the nationalization. New legislation from March 2009 enabled it to force a nationalization, should the private shareholders resist. The private equity firm J. C. Flowers, which had a year earlier taken a 25 percent stake in the bank at 22.50 euro per share, lost out heavily.

The bank's "toxic assets," at 210 billion euro half of the balance sheet of HRE, were taken over by the newly started "bad bank" FMS Wertmanagement AöR (FMS-WM). Assets to be transferred were those without strategic value or containing larger-than-average risk or overly capital-intensive[8] or unsuitable for use as collateral. The German state through SoFFin has injected some 10 billion euro into HRE and FMS-WM, of which 7.7 billion went to HRE. The main active residual of HRE is presently its subsidiary Deutsche Pfandbriefbank (PBB), which has total assets of only 15 percent of HRE's at the peak. The EU Commission approved the state aid to HRE in July 2011 but on condition that Depfa be sold before 2014 and PBB reprivatized eventually. Consequently, on 26 August 2013, Hypo Real Estate put its subsidiary Depfa up for sale. As of September 2013, a number of potential buyers had shown an interest, among them private equity funds such as Lone Star and Bain Capital as well as hedge fund Third Point.[9] However, when by May 2014 a sale had not yet been realized, the German government canceled the sale and moved the 49 billion euro assets of Depfa bank to the FMS-WM "bad bank."[10]

---

[8] Since FMS-WM is not a bank, it does not have to follow the Basel capital requirements.

[9] www.ft.com/intl/cms/s/0/be31c644-2776-11e3-ae16-00144feab7de.html

[10] www.bloomberg.com/news/2014-05-13/germany-scraps-depfa-bank-sale-and-orders-lender-s-winddown.html

Overall grade of the handling of Hypo Real Estate: E (on a scale of A to F=Fail)

For several reasons, HRE has been handled much more slowly than was IKB. The main question – and the reason for the failing grade – is why IKB was deemed to be non-viable and sold whereas the equally non-viable HRE and Depfa bank have been retained rather than sold or liquidated. Along the line, there are a number of unacceptable lags: (a) it took the European Commission almost three years to accept the business plan, 18 July 2011;[11] (b) it took two to three years to transfer "toxic assets" to the new bad bank FMS-WM. The reason was said to be old and incompatible IT systems in the various subsidiaries of the bank, making the choice of which assets to transfer difficult; (c) why did it take over two years to put Depfa on the market after the EU Commission decision? And (d) nowhere has the long-term viability of HRE/PBB been studied and defended (at least publicly). It should have been sold much earlier, even at a loss, once the "toxic assets" had been shifted.

Commerzbank[12]

A new and expensive headquarters building has time and time again proved to be a good indicator of an extravagant company which will have future problems. Commerzbank in Frankfurt was no exception when it moved into the then-tallest building in Western Europe in 1997, 259 meters high and Europe's first ecological skyscraper.[13] Ten years later, the bank had to be saved by the German taxpayers to the tune of 18 billion euro in fresh equity. In the *Financial Times* analysis/ graph above (Figure 3), the bank was classified as encompassing three of the five problem areas: mergers & acquisitions, bad lending and bad trading. Fortunately, the problems of securities trading had already been solved by the 2005 closure of Commerzbank Securities (ComSec) after years of losses when more severe problems emerged in 2008.

---

[11] http://europa.eu/rapid/press-release_IP-11-898_en.htm

[12] Christopher Berg, *Analyse des Entstaatlichungsprozessus bei Kreditinstituten nach der Finanzkrise und dessen Chancen und Risiken am Beispiel der Commerzbank* (Norderstedt: GRIN Verlag, 2011).

[13] Ian Lambot and Colin Davis, eds., *Commerzbank Frankfurt: Prototype for an Ecological High-Rise* (Basel: Birkhäuser Verlag, 1997). The tower held its record until 2012 when it was supplanted by the Shard in London.

At the end of 2007, Commerzbank and Dresdner Bank (a subsidiary of the insurance company Allianz) were of about equal size, no. 2 and 3 ranked by assets among German banks. In other statistics, they diverged (according to *The Banker* July 2008):

- Dresdner had only two-thirds of the Tier 1 capital base of Commerzbank and thus lower capital–asset ratios (though actually its BIS ratio was higher than that of Commerzbank since the advantageous treatment in terms of Basel capital requirements of its important securities-trading operations in its investment bank Dresdner Kleinwort Benson implied a low ratio of risk-weighted assets to total assets).
- Return on assets in Dresdner were at 0.17 percent only half of that in Commerzbank.
- Return on equity was a healthy 15.7 percent in Commerzbank and only 7.1 percent in Dresdner.
- Commerzbank had a cost–income ratio of 64 percent whereas Dresdner was at a high 89 percent.

On 31 August 2008, Commerzbank nevertheless announced the purchase of Dresdner Bank for 9.8 billion euro, making the former owner Allianz with a stake of almost 30 percent the largest shareholder of Commerzbank. Dresdner wrote down 1.3 billion dollars (equivalent) in bad loans for the year which, however, turned out to be far too little as Dresdner made a loss of 6.5 billion dollars in 2008, losing over half of its equity. On 3 November 2008, Commerzbank received a capital injection of 8.2 billion euro from the German state, increased to 18.2 billion euro in January 2009. The state through SoFFin thereby became the largest shareholder of the bank with a 25 percent stake (the diluted equity demoting Allianz to second place).

A second bad acquisition was Eurohypo, active in mortgage lending and public finance and the issuer of "Pfandbriefe" (covered bonds) in the Commerzbank group. Originally started by the three major German banks together in 2003, Commerzbank became the sole owner of Eurohypo on 16 November 2005. When the financial crisis struck in 2007, Eurohypo was in its own right the eleventh largest bank in Germany with total assets over 200 billion euro. The bank was also active in a number of countries internationally. However, since 2011, no new lending was allowed except in Germany and from June 2012 the entire bank was in a wind-down mode, decreed by the

EU Commission, when it turned out that the original plan to sell the subsidiary could not be carried through.[14]

On 14 March 2013, Commerzbank issued 2.5 billion euro in new shares. This had the double advantage of lowering the German federal state's ownership from 25 percent, a blocking minority, to 17 percent (the limit being 20 percent), while simultaneously raising its capital ratio under Basel III rules from 7.6 to 8.6 percent.

In July 2013, it was announced that the German bank holding fund "Sonderfonds Finanzmarktstabilisierung" (SoFFin) was seeking to sell its remaining 17 percent share in Commerzbank to UBS. At the same time, Commerzbank succeeded in selling its UK commercial property unit for 5 billion euro in one of the largest property loan transactions in Europe. Its internal "bad bank" had run down assets by 36 billion euro to 124 billion.

As seen in Figure 13, the share price of Commerzbank fell sharply in 2008 and has continued to fall through 2014, for a total fall from the peak of over 98 percent.

Overall grade of the handling of Commerzbank: E (on a scale of A to F=Fail)

As was the case with Hypo Real Estate, one lacks a clear view from the authorities of what to do with the bank: is it long-term viable or not? Either it is viable and then you keep it until it can be sold at a profit to the taxpayers, or it is not, in which case you should get rid of it as quickly as possible and at a minimal cost to the taxpayers. Why should the German state step into Commerzbank at all with an injection of 18 billion euro in equity (plus 5 billion euro in guarantees) rather than leaving it to the market and Allianz to sort out their own problems, in particular in view of the overbanked situation in Germany? Instead, taxpayers injected 18 billion euro into a bank only to see the value of their stake fall to basically zero, moreover selling a substantial stake at a loss.

The main reason for the latter is probably the original decision by the EU Commission that the bank must shrink its balance sheet by 18 percent in four years and by 45 percent in six years.[15] The only reason

---

[14] http://europa.eu/rapid/press-release_IP-12-337_en.htm
[15] http://europa.eu/rapid/press-release_IP-09-711_en.htm?locale=en;

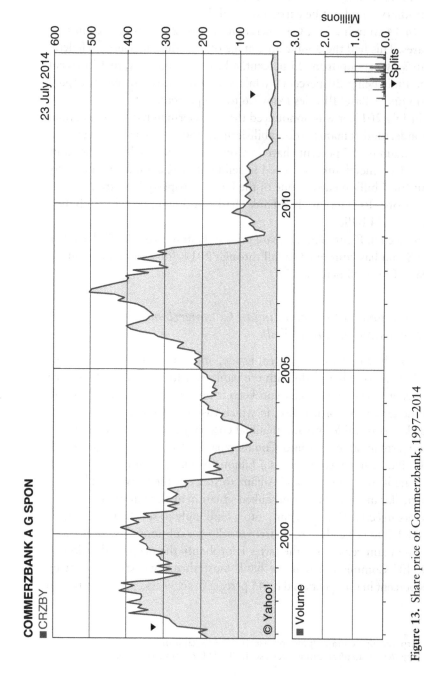

Figure 13. Share price of Commerzbank, 1997–2014

Source: http://finance.yahoo.com/q/bc?s=CRZBY&t=my&l=off&z=l&q=l&c=

not to award an "F" is the fact that the bank has set up an internal "bad bank" for non-core "toxic" assets such as Spanish property loans and is gradually winding it down.[16] In 2013, this restructuring was still ongoing but at a faster speed than anticipated, yet allowing for the return to profitability. The bank was also hoping to rid itself of its entire portfolio of Spanish property loans.[17] This was finally achieved in June 2014, when the bank offloaded Spanish and Portuguese commercial property loans worth over 5 billion euro to private equity groups including Lone Star. At the end of the first quarter of 2014, its portfolio of non-core assets was down to 102 billion euro, aiming for 75 billion euro by 2016.

The German independent monopolies commission recommended in July 2014 that the government sell its remaining 17 percent stake in Commerzbank as quickly as possible, even at a major loss to taxpayers. The commission states that "The government's stake represents an additional nuisance in a financial market already marked by numerous competitive distortions ... It makes no sense for the government to sit on the stake in hopes of a better share price."[18]

The Landesbanken[19]

German banking is, by assets, divided almost equally into three parts: commercial banks, cooperative banks and the so-called public banks. The latter consist of some 400+ savings banks (*Sparkassen*) and their regional Landesbanken-Girozentrale (LB). The LBs are owned by the savings banks and by their respective state (*Land*) and perform for the savings banks functions of clearing, asset management, investment banking, etc. Gradually, they have come to behave more like commercial banks in their own right, though with far less pressure for efficiency and profitability on account of their local and stable ownership.

---

[16] www.ft.com/cms/s/0/5dc4ea14-8f29-11e3-9cb0-00144feab7de.html#axzz2t CZ2bA99

[17] *Financial Times*, 14 February 2014: "Commerzbank to speed up sale of 'bad bank' assets."

[18] http://in.reuters.com/article/2014/07/09/commerzbank-sale-idINL6N0PK 36720140709?type=companyNews

[19] Among many sources, see the Liikanen report, pp. 64 ff., and *Financial Times*, 31 July 2014, "Bank balance."

It is a matter for debate whether this structure is viable in an internationally competitive world, as they claim themselves, or whether they constitute "zombie banks" that should be allowed to become extinct.[20] Be that as it may, in 2001 the European Commission decreed that their ability to borrow with a government or state guarantee (most often AAA/Aaa) constituted an unacceptable competitive advantage that had to disappear.[21] However, in the period of adjustment, until 2005, the Landesbanken not unnaturally borrowed all they could, raising money which was then invested in often less wise manners such as in US subprime MBSs or CDOs. Their balance sheets also swelled. In 2007, seven of the 15 largest banks in Germany were Landesbanken with combined total assets equal to the size of Deutsche Bank.

Theoretically there should be one Landesbank per state (*Land*). However, competition and the financial crisis have reduced them to basically five:

- Bayern LB, Munich (which also owns part of Landesbank Saar); it is 94 percent owned by the state of Bavaria;
- Norddeutsche LB, Hanover, in Niedersachsen, Mecklemburg-Vorpommern, Sachsen-Anhalt (which also owns most of Bremer LB); it is 59 percent owned by the state of Niedersachsen;
- HSH Nordbank LB, Kiel and Hamburg, Schleswig-Holstein; it is 65 percent owned by HSH Finanzfonds;
- LB Baden-Württemberg (LBBW) in Stuttgart (but which has also absorbed Sachsen LB and Rheinland-Pfalz LB since 2008);
- LB Hessen-Thüringen, Frankfurt/Erfurt ("Helaba") (which took over the viable parts of WestLB in 2012, see below) and also covers Nordrhein-Westfalen.

WestLB in Nordrhein-Westfalen (Düsseldorf) has been liquidated, as we shall see shortly. Landesbank Berlin Holding is a commercial bank, where the city of Berlin was forced by the European Commission to sell its stake.

In this book, we are mainly concerned with the reactions of the central supervisory authorities to the financial crisis: the central

---

[20] Yalman Onaran, *Zombie Banks: How Broken Banks and Debtor Nations Are Crippling the Global Economy* (Hoboken, NJ: John Wiley & Sons, 2012).
[21] http://europa.eu/rapid/press-release_IP-02-343_en.htm

bank, the financial supervisory authority (FSA) and the Treasury. The Landesbanken were, in the main, saved by their regional owners without federal intervention. The adventures of Sachsen LB and Bayern LB, which led to the demise of the former and the salvage of the latter to the tune of some 10 billion euro, are therefore not part of our story (though the essence can be found in the Chronology). Hence only the 6 billion euro guarantee to HSH Nordbank and the 3 billion in equity capital to WestLB from SoFFin are of relevance.

Already in the 1980s, WestLB started to change business model, going international in what would become an empire encompassing 11 countries in Europe, six countries in America, six countries in Asia, Australia and South Africa and also having important investment banking operations in New York, London, Luxembourg, Tokyo and Hong Kong, despite being only the 47th largest bank in the world by assets and the 103rd by capital in 2007. Its widespread operations and rapid growth made it unprofitable for most years of this century and had necessitated an equity injection in 2004 from its owners to the tune of 1.5 billion euro.

In 2009, this was not enough. In November, the German federal government through SoFFin injected 3 billion euro into the bank which, if converted into common stock, would give the state a 49 percent ownership of the bank. WestLB also agreed to offload some 85 billion euro in toxic assets to a new "bad bank," EAA ("Erste Abwicklungsanstalt"), with losses underwritten by the bank's owners, i.e. the state of Nordrhein-Westfalen and the local savings banks. As a condition for receiving the aid, the EU Commission decided that the bank must be wound down. And hence on 30 June 2012, the name West LB disappeared. The viable parts of the bank (in principle domestic residential mortgages) were taken over by the Landesbank Hessen-Thüringen (Helaba). The legal successor to WestLB is Portogon Financial Services which draws on the competence of the earlier staff to aid in the winding down of the portfolio of assets in EAA. It has been calculated that the total cost to the federal state and the local owners may be as high as 18 billion euro.[22]

---

[22] www.bloomberg.com/news/2012-06-29/westlb-s-fall-from-grace-is-lesson-in-investment-bank-hazards.html

Overall grade of the handling of WestLB:
F (on a scale of A to F=Fail)

The handling of West LB is graded mainly on the EU Commission since its winding down was decreed by the EU Commission and was not a decision for the government of Germany, the Bundesbank or the BaFin.[23]

There is no reason to believe that WestLB was worse run than some of the other expansionist Landesbanken (see Table 10), such as Bayern LB whose purchase of Austrian Hypo Group Alpe Adria and investments in US subprime CDOs cost the Bavarian state some 10 billion euro (see the Chronology) or Landesbank Baden-Württemberg (LBBW). In terms of profitability during the crisis (see below), WestLB was hit earlier than the others, being more international, but its record was hardly worse. In terms of capitalization, it lagged behind its peers but this is something for which the bank's owners should be blamed, not the bank and not the supervisory authorities. Hence the decisions by the EU Commission must be regarded as highly arbitrary, forcing the liquidation of WestLB while limiting the punishment of LBBW and HSH Nordbank to a shrinking of total assets while no action at all was taken against Bayern LB.[24,25]

Table 10. *Return on equity and capital–asset ratios of the major Landesbanken, percentage (according to* The Banker, *various issues)*

	Return on average equity, %			Capital–asset ratio, %		
	2007	2008	2009	2007	2008	2009
LBBW	3.0	−20.26	−9.02	2.80	2.73	3.67
Bayern LB	2.3	−43.27	−21.54	2.87	2.67	4.36
HSH Nordb	2.0	n.a.	−15.14	3.75	4.01	4.92
WestLB	*−23.6*	*0.45*	*−8.17*	*1.92*	*1.97*	*2.82*
Helaba	8.2	−0.96	2.39	2.90	3.09	3.69

[23] Bundesanstalt für Finanzdienstleistungsaufsicht, the German FSA.

[24] Taken from Cour des Comptes, *Dexia: un sinistre bancaire coûteux, des risques persistants* (Paris: La documentation française, 28 August 2013), table on state aid and Commission demands p. 92.

[25] http://europa.eu/rapid/press-release_IP-11-1576_en.htm (on WestLB); http://europa.eu/rapid/press-release_IP-09-1927_en.htm (on LBBW); www.nytimes.com/2008/12/01/business/worldbusiness/01iht-gbank.4.18298631.html?_r=0 (on Bayern LB).

3 | *Belgium, France, Luxembourg*
Dexia

Dexia[1]

If Commerzbank invited dire forecasts of future problems by its expensive new headquarters building, the managers of Belgian-French bank Dexia did even better: they built two new HQ at the same time! The "Tour Dexia" in the La Défense district of Paris (142 meters tall) was opened in 2005 and the "Dexia Tower" in Brussels (today, after Dexia's demise, called the Rogier Tower; at 137 meters, the third tallest building in Belgium) in 2006. In the latter building, its 4,200 windows were, at an unknown cost, equipped with 12 light bulbs each, which show red, green and blue LED light. Together, the 50,400 light bulbs allow various structures to be shown on the façade of the building, for instance the Dexia or the Olympics logo or a multi-colored light show.

From the time the Dexia Tower in Brussels was inaugurated in late 2006, the share price of Dexia on the Brussels exchange fell from a peak of 22.56 to 0.07 euro at the end of 2012 when the bank was broken up, a fall of 99.7 percent. The price of the residual part of the bank in July 2014 was 0.03 euro (after Dexia Banque Belgique was broken up and nationalized).

There is no particular French or Belgian or European story to the development of Dexia, just the story of a bank (or rather two banks) without political, supervisory, owner or management control, going off on an ambitious spending spree, with little relationship to the structure of banking activities in their respective home countries or the interest of their owners. Both its component companies had started as specialized

---

[1] Pierre-Henri Thomas, *Dexia: vie et mort d'un monstre bancaire* (Paris: Les petits matins, 2012); Cour des Comptes, *Dexia: un sinistre bancaire coûteux, des risques persistants* (Paris: La documentation française, 28 August 2013); Viral V. Acharya and Sascha Steffen, "The greatest carry trade ever? Understanding euro zone bank risks," NYU Stern School working paper, 18 November 2012.

banks, financing local authorities in their respective countries but had succumbed to higher ambitions. The Belgian Gemeentekrediet (Crédit Communal) began the international expansion in 1991 by taking a stake of 25 percent in the Banque Internationale de Luxembourg (BIL), the biggest bank in the duchy, increased to 51 percent the year after. The French Crédit Local took a majority stake in 1995 in the Hypothekenbank Berlin AG (becoming sole owner in 2003). In 1996, the two municipal-finance companies which were already represented in New York, London, Berlin and Vienna merged to become Dexia SA, with listing on the Brussels as well as Paris exchanges. Their important German subsidiary changed names in 2006 to become the (still existing) Dexia Kommunalbank Deutschland.

In subsequent years, expansion continued unabated. In 1997, Dexia took a stake of 40 percent in the Italian firm Crediop, which was then the biggest bank for financing Italian local authorities. The year after, the stake was raised to 60 percent. Dexia Crediop still exists, defying efforts to sell it. The year 2000 saw the purchase for 2.6 billion euro of the firm Financial Security Assurance (FSA) in the United States, a major player in lending to municipalities. The year after, Dexia acquired the Belgian bank Artesia Banking Corporation, a banking group with activities such as retail banking, insurance as well as asset management for a price tag of 3.3 billion euro. The same year, the stake in Crediop was increased to 70 percent.

In 2001, Dexia also started an important cooperation in Spain with Banco Sabadell in Barcelona in the form of Dexia Sabadell, where Dexia was the owner of 60 percent and the Spanish bank 40 percent. On 6 July 2012, Banco Sabadell exercised a put option to sell its 40 percent stake of Dexia Sabadell to Dexia, which since then is the sole owner. Dexia Sabadell has so far also defied attempts to find a buyer.

The year 2000–1 also saw the purchase of Dutch private bank Kempen & Co. for 1 billion euro (resold for 85 million euro in 2004) as well as asset manager Labouchère, renamed Dexia Bank Nederland, for 900 million euro (liquidated in 2005 for a cost of 400 million euro).

The years 2004–6 saw Dexia start subsidiaries in Canada, Mexico, the Czech Republic, Romania, Bulgaria, Poland, Australia, Japan, Hungary, Switzerland, India, China and South America. A major purchase in 2006 was the acquisition of the Turkish firm Denizbank for 3.3 billion dollars. Between 1999 and 2005, the balance sheet of Dexia had more than doubled from 245 to 508 billion euro (and to 651 billion euro by the end of 2008 when the bank had 38,000 employees). In 2008, it was the second largest bank in Belgium after Fortis and the 40th largest bank in the world measured by total assets. Dexia was, at that time, the world's leading bank in the market for financial services to local authorities.

Like many of the other banks studied in this book, it was the over-reliance on wholesale deposits that started its downfall after the crash of Lehman Brothers and AIG. In September 2008, Dexia needed to get wholesale funding of 260 billion euro, almost half its balance sheet, over the next 12 months, funds which were no longer available. On 29 September, news of liquidity and capital problems as well as doubts concerning the quality of its loans to Depfa and FSA led the stock price of Dexia to fall by 34 percent in one single day. In a short period of time, 15 billion euro, almost 10 percent of deposits, had been withdrawn in a silent bank run. Some help would come on 27 October when the Federal Reserve started its Commercial Paper Funding Facility (CPFF), creating a SIV which bought ABCB with highest rating. After UBS with borrowings of 72 billion dollars, the much smaller Dexia was the second largest borrower with 53 billion.[2]

The day after the dramatic fall of the share price, 30 September 2008, Dexia received an injection of fresh capital of 6.4 billion euro by the French (3 billion), Luxembourg (0.4 billion) and Belgian (3 billion) states. It also received guarantees for its borrowing of up to 150 billion euro (on 7 October), of which 60 percent was guaranteed by Belgium after fierce negotiations between the owner-states over how to share the burden. In return, Dexia was forced to sell assets in Spain, Italy, Austria and Slovakia, wind down its operations in the United States (FSA) and shrink its balance sheet by 35 percent, as decreed by the EU Commission. Dexia's chairman, Pierre Richard, and its CEO, Alex Miller, were both dismissed, the former being replaced by the respected former prime minister of Belgium, Jean-Luc Dehaene.

On 3 November 2008, the Austrian Kommunalkredit with assets of 40 billion euro, 49 percent owned by Dexia, was taken over by

---

[2] National Commission on the Causes of the Financial and Economic Crisis in the United States, *Financial Crisis Inquiry Report* (Washington, DC: Government Printing Office, January 2011), p. 373.

the Austrian state for the symbolic sum of 2 euro. On 13 November 2008, Dexia sold its US subsidiary FSA, one of the four big monoline insurers, to Assured Guaranty for 816 million dollars, but the deal specifically excluded the loss-making financial products division with a portfolio of 19 billion in asset-backed securities. During 2008, Dexia had already recapitalized its American subsidiary by 800 million dollars. The immediate loss from selling FSA was 1.6 billion euro; the Cour des Comptes (2013) would later place the total loss of the deal at 3.5 billion euro.

On 26 February 2010, Dexia was able to announce that the European Commission had, under certain conditions, approved the restructuring plan that was necessary to justify the government support for Dexia and to prevent unfair competition:[3]

- Some acquisitions had to be undone (Italian Dexia Crediop with total assets of 45 billion euro must be sold before 2012, part-owned Spanish Dexia Sabadell with 17 billion before 2013 as well as Dexia Banka Slovensko) but banking activities in Turkey, highly profitable to Dexia, could continue.
- By the middle of 2011, the state guarantee had to be abandoned.
- In total, Dexia had to be downsized by one-third by 2014 and its bond portfolio reduced to 125 billion euro.
- In the deal Dexia was also required to set up an internal "bad bank," Legacy Portfolio Management Division, encompassing assets of some 190 billion euro.

But the problems continued unabated. On 9 May 2011, Dexia revealed a loss for 2010 of 3.6 billion euro, in large part due to interest-rate swaps taken to hedge against increases in interest rates when actually they fell. A derivatives portfolio of no less than a notional 1,600 billion euro had been built up. For the second quarter of 2011, Dexia posted another 4 billion euro loss after writing down the value of its Greek debt in the "haircut" forced upon private holders of Greek sovereign debt (see the Chronology).

On 10 October 2011, Dexia had to be saved again by the involved governments. The bank had already received a capital injection of 6.4 billion euro in 2008. Now the Belgian retail bank part of Dexia,

---

[3] www.abbl.lu/de/node/2959

Dexia Banque Belgique, was nationalized at a price of 4.2 billion euro, creating a new bank, Belfius Banque et Assurance SA, a fact which led to a down-grading warning to the Belgian state by the rating agency Moody's. The residual holding company Dexia SA which still owned the French, Italian, Spanish, German and Turkish subsidiaries (and some more) received a guarantee of up to 90 billion euro, of which 60 came from Belgium, basically for the toxic assets in the "bad bank" which had yet to be set up.

On 8 June 2012, Dexia succeeded in finally selling its Turkish subsidiary Denizbank to the Russian Sberbank for 3 billion euro, registering a loss of 1 billion euro. On 13 December 2012, Dexia sold 90 percent of the shares in Dexia Banque Internationale in Luxembourg (BIL) to Precision Capital, owned by Qatar's royal family, for 730 million euro, the residual being held by the state of Luxembourg. The registered loss was 199 million euro. Precision also bought KBL, the Luxembourg subsidiary of Belgian KBC, for 1.05 billion euro.[4]

But losses had continued. On 9 November 2012, Dexia received another injection of 5.5 billion euro in preferred shares from its owners, leading the French and Belgian states to own 94 percent of the bank. The alternative would have been a default on 385 billion euro worth of liabilities. Losses for the year were 2.9 billion euro, down from 11.6 billion euro in 2011. Some 1.8 billion euro was lost in selling the French Dexia Municipal Agency (DMA) with assets of 94 billion euro to a French consortium for 1 euro. The Caisse Française de Financement Local, which started operations on 1 February 2013, is owned by a holding company 75 percent owned by the French state, 20 percent by the Caisse de Dépots et des Consignations and 5 percent by the Banque Postale. Basically owned and guaranteed by the French state, it has an Aaa rating from Moody's. This company will become the "new Crédit Local" for financing French local authorities while Dexia Crédit Local will be gradually wound down.[5]

In its scathing review of the rise and fall of Dexia, the French Cour des Comptes in an analysis published on 19 July 2013 estimated that Dexia, which had received around 11 billion euro in state aid as well

[4] www.bbc.co.uk/news/business-15235915.
[5] www.dexia.com/EN/journalist/press_releases/Documents/20121231_CP_ Accord%20def%20CE_EN.pdf

as state guarantees for (presently) 85 billion euro, may cost France alone 6.6 billion euro, to which should be added the risk of a need for further capital injections. The bank made a loss of almost 1 billion euro for the first half-year 2013 (p. 167).

On 13 September 2013, Dexia sold its Dexia Asset Management with 74 billion euro under management to New York Life Investments for 380 million euro. The company had been active in Brussels, Paris, Luxembourg and Sydney. Its half of the Canadian joint venture with RBC, named RBC Dexia Investor Services and located in London, had already been sold to RBC in July 2012 for 838 million euro, resulting in a small profit.

Overall grade of the handling of Dexia: F (on a scale of A to F=Fail)

"The major cause of the fall of Dexia was the Euro zone crisis," states Pierre-Henri Thomas in his book on Dexia, "*le monstre bancaire.*"[6] This is a far from convincing explanation of the fall of Dexia. It certainly did not convince the French Cour de Comptes in its review. The major cause of the demise of Dexia was its own expansionist policies, together with infighting in the board of directors and the board of management along nationalistic lines, as well as severe problems with internal communication, leading the boards to be ignorant of the risks taken in its subsidiaries.

Events after 2008 also demonstrated the incompatibility of national political pride in France and Belgium, each trying to save their own taxpayers from losses,[7] showing all too clearly the difficulties of the resolution of a transnational bank in today's eurozone as well as the additional barriers to an intelligent solution created by the EU Commission's competition commissioner. Focus on competition rather

---

[6] Thomas, *Dexia*, p. 139.

[7] The infighting sometimes took ridiculous forms. In September 2010, the Belgian FSA (Commissie voor Het Bank, CBFA) limited the ability of Dexia Banque Belgique (DBB), which held the treasury of the group, to lend to Dexia Crédit Local (DCL) in France. Likewise, when in December the same year, Dexia wanted to move 700 million euro's worth of Japanese bonds from DCL to DBB, the Belgian authorities refused to let the Belgian treasury take on the added risk. See Thomas, *Dexia*, pp. 174–5.

than viability has time and time again led the EU Commission down the wrong track. In the case of Dexia, it would have been better to force the bank back to its roots, namely the financing of local authorities in France and Belgium. This would have resulted in a much faster drive to get rid of irrelevant activities such as private banking, insurance, asset management, investor services etc. as well as forcing the sale of subsidiaries outside the two home markets. As it is, it seems rather idiotic to build a new organization in France, Caisse Française de

Table 11. *Bank restructuring plans and associated reductions in balance sheets*

Bank	Amount of aid (€ millions)	Reduction in balance sheet
Caja Castilla La Mancha	5.3	Liquidation
Caja Sur	2.7	Liquidation
Hypo Real Estate	30	85% in 3 years
WestLB 2	12	75%
Kommunalkredit	1.7	>60% in 2013
HSH Nordbank	13	61%
WestLB (May 2009)	5	50% in 3 years
Commerzbank	18.2	45% in 6 years / 18% in 4 years
Bank of Ireland	[4–5]	[30–40]% in 4 years
Fortis Bank	[8.1–8.6]	40%
Ethias	1.5	38% in 5 years
Dexia	8.4	35% in 6 years
ING	17	30% in 5 years
BAWAG	1.6	29%
LBBW	14.8	[25–30]% in 5 years
ATE	1.1	25.7% in 4 years
Lloyds	20.6	25% in 5 years
RBS	45.5	[>20]% in 5 years
Sparkasse Köln-Bonn	650	5%

Source: Cour des Comptes, *Dexia*, p. 92.

Financement Local, while at the same time winding down a formerly dedicated and competent organization, Crédit Local.

One also wonders why the EU Commission allowed the Belgian nationalization of Dexia Banque Belgique without any other demands than that the bank must not undertake any acquisitions until after 2014 nor pay dividends during this period. Likewise, the French state is directly or indirectly the sole owner of the holding company Société de Financement Local (SFIL) where the "toxic loans" from Dexia worth a nominal 4.2 billion euro have been parked.[8] See Table 11 for a number of state interventions and the resulting demands from the EU Commission.

---

[8] http://europa.eu/rapid/press-release_IP-12-1447_en.htm

4 | *Benelux*
Fortis, ING, SNS Reaal

The Dutch story

As shown above in Figures 10 and 11, the Netherlands has a strong presence in banking but also a highly concentrated one. With banking assets at 400 percent of GDP, it exceeds France, Germany or Belgium but not the UK or Luxembourg. In 2007, three of the 30 largest banks in the world by total assets were Dutch: ING, Rabobank and the then still-existing ABN AMRO. After the demise of the latter, the classification by the Financial Stability Board in 2012 of Globally Systemically Important Financial Institutions (G-SIFI) contained only one Dutch name, ING. The degree of concentration is high with the top five banks having 80 percent of all banking assets. Indeed, there are only some 20 banks altogether, to be contrasted with over 1,700 in neighboring Germany and, indeed, over 200 banks in (almost) neighboring Denmark, a country half the size of the Netherlands in terms of population.

As a seafaring and trading nation, it is hardly surprising that the Dutch should have a tradition in finance. Indeed, the Amsterdam Stock Exchange, started in 1602, is usually regarded to be the world's oldest stock exchange and the Amsterdamsche Wisselbank (Bank of Amsterdam), started in 1609, one of the world's oldest commercial banks.[1] But just like the story of present-day Dutch banking, there have also been periods of crises, such as the tulipmania speculation and crash in the 1630s[2] and the bankruptcy of the Dutch state in 1810,

---

[1] Only the Italian bank Monte dei Paschi di Siena (started in 1472) and German Berenberg Bank (started in 1590) are older. Both still exist.

[2] George A. Akerlof and Robert J. Shiller, *Animal Spirits: How Human Psychology Drives the Economy and Why It Matters for Global Capitalism* (Princeton University Press, 2009); Charles Mackay, *Extraordinary Popular Delusions and the Madness of Crowds* (New York: Harmony Books, 1841, 1852, 1980, 1995, 2003).

occasioned by the disastrous effect on Dutch trade of Napoleon's Continental System.

Fortis[3]

Established formally in 1990 with the merger of Dutch insurer AMEV, Belgian insurer AG and VSB, a Dutch bank, its real expansion began a few years later with the purchase in 1993 from the Belgian government of the Caisse Générale d'Épargne et de Retraite (CGER in French, ASLK in Flemish). In 1999, Fortis became the sole owner of CGER, which in the meantime had bought the Société National de Crédit à l'Industrie (SNCI). The year before, 1998, Fortis had bought Générale de Banque, its major competitor in Belgium. In 10 years, the group's total assets multiplied 10 times.

At the time, Fortis was the first major financial company in the Benelux countries to become a universal bank after changed legislation in 1991, encompassing retail banking, private banking, merchant (investment) banking as well as insurance. It also had a very special legal structure, with two parallel holding companies in Brussels and Utrecht, each owning 50 percent of the operative companies Fortis Bank and Fortis Insurance (see Figure 14). The main reason for Fortis Bank SA/NV being Belgian was a prerequisite condition when Fortis had bought CGER from the Belgian state that the bank would remain under Belgian law.

In contrast to many of the other banks studied in this book, venturing into a number of unfamiliar countries and continents, Fortis was always mainly a Benelux rather than an international group, although it had made some minor forays into Poland, Germany and Turkey. At the end of 2007, assets of 700 billion euro out of a total balance of 871 billion (80 percent) were held in Benelux-located subsidiaries of the group (Annual accounts 2007, p. 157).

---

[3] Jeroen Smit, *The Perfect Prey: The Fall of ABN AMRO, or What Went Wrong in the Banking Industry* (London: Quercus, 2010); Joan Condijts, Paul Gérard and Pierre-Henri Thomas, *La chute de la maison Fortis* (Paris: Éditions Jean-Claude Lattés, 2009); De Nederlandsche Bank, "Resolution framework for systemically important banks in the Netherlands," 11 July 2012. www. dnb.nl/binaries/Resolution%20Framework%20for%20Systemically%20 Important%20Banks%20in%20the%20Netherlands_tcm46-275579.pdf

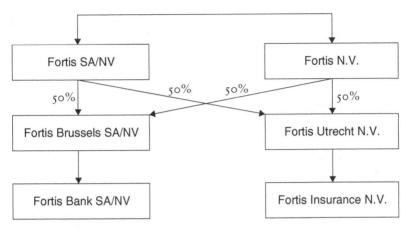

Figure 14. The operative structure of Fortis
Source: Fortis Annual accounts 2007, p. 16.

The story of how a three-bank consortium, including Fortis, bid for and conquered ABN AMRO on 17 October 2007 has already been told in connection with the story of RBS. In contrast to RBS, it appeared initially that Fortis had planned for and executed the deal well. Firstly, the parts of ABN AMRO received under the deal (mainly retail banking Netherlands and Asset Management) complemented well its existing Dutch and private-banking network. Secondly, Fortis financed a large part of the deal by a rights issue, concluded on 9 October 2007, whereby it sold no less than 13 billion euro (18 billion dollars) in fresh equity; at the time it constituted the second largest IPO in the world ever.[4]

Thirteen billion euro is a lot of money but Fortis' part of the 71 billion euro ABN AMRO bill was 24 billion euro, which was a substantial cost for a bank which at the time was worth 40 billion euro on the exchanges. Even worse was the fact that ABN AMRO had been purchased rather expensively, given the fierce bidding competition with Barclays.[5] The high price meant that Fortis was stuck with negative goodwill of no less than 19 billion euro which it was not

---

[4] IPO=Initial Public Offering. The record was held by the Industrial and Commercial Bank of China (ICBC) which the year before had sold a record 21.9 billion dollars' worth of new equity.
[5] The cost was 38 euro per share as contrasted with a fair price of 23 euro; see Smit, *The Perfect Prey*, p. 350.

allowed to carry on its books since the ABN AMRO name was still alive. It had to be written off. But how was this possible?

Despite having denied the necessity for additional capital, in June 2008 Fortis suddenly announced the need for an additional 8.3 billion euro, part of which would come from scrapping the dividend for 2007, saving 1.5 billion euro. Given earlier assurances, this was regarded as a breach of trust by its investors.[6] The share price of Fortis lost 19 percent in one single day when the announcement was made. The bank's long-time CEO, Jean-Paul Votron, was fired and replaced by Herman Verwilst (earlier CEO at CGER) on 11 July.[7] On the exchanges, the value of Fortis at the end of June was one-third of what it had been before the purchase of ABN AMRO nine months earlier.

The international events from mid September 2008 (Lehman Brothers, Merrill Lynch, AIG, Washington Mutual ...), together with newspaper reports of liquidity problems in Fortis, led to a run on the wholesale deposits of the bank on 26 September, the bank losing 20 billion euro in deposits that day. In one single week, the share price of Fortis dropped 35 percent to under 5 euro. The Lehman failure alone cost it 132 million euro.

On the verge of collapse, on 29 September, Fortis signed an agreement with the governments of Belgium, the Netherlands and Luxembourg, whereby Belgium purchased a 50[8] percent share in Fortis Bank Belgium for 4.7 billion euro in equity while Luxembourg injected 2.5 billion into its subsidiary, Fortis Banque Luxembourg. The Netherlands was to contribute 4 billion euro for its (almost) 50 percent part of Fortis Bank Netherlands. Maurice Lippens, chairman of Fortis since 1990, and the perceived author of the expansionist policies, was asked to step down. The agreement did little, however, to strengthen the confidence of the private investors in Fortis whose shares declined 23.7 percent that day to finish at 3.97 euro.

During the following days, the governments of Belgium and Luxembourg paid their share of the agreement but from the

---

[6] Condijts *et al.*, *La chute de la maison Fortis*, ch. 5, "Le mensonge" (the lie); Yves Fassin and Derrick Gosselin, "The collapse of a European bank in the financial crisis: an analysis from stakeholder and ethical perspectives," *Journal of Business Ethics* 102 (no. 2, 2012) pp. 169–91.

[7] He would have to step aside for health reasons already on 19 September, however.

[8] 49.93 percent to be exact.

Netherlands, nothing. The Dutch government had realized that they would lose control over the Dutch parts of the Fortis empire for a very low price, in particular as Fortis appears to have pledged Dutch assets as collateral for its Belgian borrowings.[9] The Dutch insurance business of Fortis had experienced no difficulties and should remain the jewel in the Dutch Fortis crown. Hence, on 3 October, the Dutch government reneged on the former agreement and purchased the entire Fortis Bank Netherlands as well as the remaining ABN AMRO assets, Fortis Insurance Netherlands and Fortis Corporate Insurance for 16.8 billion euro, of which 12.8 billion was payment for the banking activities and 4 billion for the insurance businesses. This in turn led the Belgian government on 10 October to buy the residual half of Fortis Bank Belgium for another 4.7 billion euro, i.e. 9.4 billion for the whole bank (or rather for 99.3 percent to be exact). Simultaneously, 75 percent of the Belgian bank was sold to BNP Paribas, making the Belgian state, with 11 percent of the equity capital, the largest shareholder in the French bank. BNP Paribas also purchased 66 percent of the Luxembourg subsidiary of Fortis Bank Belgium. Fortis Insurance Belgium was also to be sold to BNP Paribas for 5.5 billion euro. A "bad bank," capitalized partly by the Belgian state, was to be set up to manage and divest 10.4 billion euro in structured products (CDOs).

On 12 December, a Belgian appeals court unexpectedly stopped the purchase by BNP Paribas of Fortis Bank Belgium, awaiting shareholders' approval. On 19 December, the Belgian government was forced to resign on account of the "Fortis affair," the reason being an alleged attempt to interfere with the court's ruling or, as stated by the Supreme Court of Belgium in its investigation: "All the above [in the report] of course does not offer ... legal proof of an attempt to interfere with the judiciary, but there are undoubtedly significant indications which point in that direction."[10]

Shareholders duly rejected the deal, having seen the price of their investments in Fortis decline from 30 euro per share in April 2007, when the ill-fated offer for ABN AMRO was made, to around 1 euro in early 2009.

[9] Condijts *et al.*, *La chute de la maison Fortis*, p. 193.
[10] www.abc.net.au/news/2008-12-20/belgian-govt-collapses-over-fortis-affair/245854

Finally, on 6 March 2009, BNP Paribas and the Belgian state reached a new agreement concerning Fortis. BNP Paribas would, as before, purchase 75 percent of the nationalized bank but only 25 percent of the insurance company. The residual Fortis holding company would become in essence an insurance company with the remainder of the Fortis assets. The revised deal was approved at a general meeting of shareholders on 28 April (despite shoes being thrown at those members of the management who were present!).

In November 2013, the Belgian state sold its remaining 25 percent to BNP Paribas for 3.25 billion euro.

For the year 2008, the break-up of the Fortis group resulted in a write-down of 24.6 billion euro, basically wiping out the entire equity of the holding company. The residual company is today named Ageas Insurance, since ownership of the Fortis name passed to BNP Paribas with the sale of the bank. It is Belgium's largest insurance company, working mainly through the subsidiary AG Insurance, where Fortis BNP Paribas owns a 25 percent stake. Ageas also owned 45 percent of Royal Park Investments, the "bad bank" set up to manage the structured assets previously held by Fortis Bank. "Taking account of the very specific and uncommon circumstances in the case" [in particular the fact that a court ordered that the settlement be approved by shareholders], the EU Commission approved of the deal. The Commission noted in particular that the "bad bank", while mainly owned and guaranteed by the Belgian state, had taken over assets at such low prices that the loss would be borne mainly by the bank.[11] On 27 April 2013, Credit Suisse together with the American private equity firm Lone Star agreed to buy Royal Park Investments SA for 6.7 billion euro.

Since October 2010, BNP Paribas has been the sole owner of the former Luxembourg banking business of Fortis, renamed BGL BNP Paribas, the duchy having sold all of its part. It is the second largest bank in Luxembourg by assets.

For 2008, Fortis Bank Nederland announced a loss of 18.5 billion euro from the break-up of the group. On 1 July 2010, the Fortis name disappeared in the Netherlands when the two nationalized banks were combined and the name ABN AMRO was resuscitated. Fortis Insurance was spun off and continues operations under the name

---

[11] http://europa.eu/rapid/press-release_IP-09-743_en.htm

ASR Nederland; the corporate insurance business was sold. As of July 2014, the group ABN AMRO as well as the subsidiary bank remain 100 percent state owned. The group is, however, banned from making acquisitions under the terms of its agreement with the EU Commission on 5 April 2011.[12]

Overall grade of the handling of Fortis: E (on a scale of A to F=Fail)

The initial handling of Fortis shows very clearly the dictum of Lord (Mervyn) King, the former governor of the Bank of England that "banks may be international in life but are national in death." There are several contradictory stories of the events of 27 September – 3 October 2008 but they all show the acrimonious attitude between the two supervisory authorities and the two governments and their attempts to shift blame (and costs) onto the other party. Had the grading stopped at that point, it would have been a clear F (fail). However, in the end, events took a turn for the better with viable banks in the Netherlands, Belgium and Luxembourg and profitable insurance operations in the Netherlands and Belgium. Authorities are also to be commended for setting up a bad bank for the residual structured products as well as selling it within a reasonable period of time. What is lacking, however, is a timetable for selling the nationalized Dutch bank.

ING (Internationale Nederlanden Groep)

At the end of 2007, ING was not only the largest bank in the Netherlands but also the fifteenth-largest bank in the world by assets. Internationally active, the universal bank had fully acceptable ratios for leverage and BIS ratios. However, "just to make sure" under the existing uncertain circumstances, on 19 October 2008 the Dutch state injected 10 billion euro of new equity capital into ING Groep as well as giving it a guarantee for its US mortgage-related assets of 22 billion euro. To receive approval for the aid from the EU Commission, ING committed to divest its insurance and asset management business

---

[12] http://europa.eu/rapid/press-release_IP-11-406_en.htm

as well as the internet bank ING Direct USA.[13] In June 2011, Capital One Financial Corporation purchased ING Direct USA from ING for 9 billion dollars. Likewise, on 9 October 2012, ING Direct UK with 10.9 billion pounds in deposits was sold to Barclays at a loss of 320 million euro in order to exit the state aid.

By November 2013, all of the Tier 1 securities received from the state had been repaid except 2.2 billion euro by means not least of a share issue in December 2009 of 7.3 billion euro. After the last payment in May 2015, ING will have repaid 13.5 billion euro to the Dutch state for a return of 5 billion euro (12.5 percent) for the taxpayer.[14] At the same time, it had achieved a core Tier 1 ratio of 11.7 percent by the end of 2013. Figure 15 shows that the share price of ING after the fall in 2008 has held steady in the six years since then.

Overall grade of the handling of ING:
A (on a scale of A to F=Fail)

In order not to stigmatize weak banks, it is important that all banks, or at least as many as possible, participate in a government salvation in times of a systemic crisis. We will return to this theme in discussing the TARP program in the United States. ING received a safety buffer from the state while profiting from the circumstances to rationalize its operations.

SNS Reaal

The SNS Reaal group is the fourth largest financial group in the Netherlands. It had already received a capital injection from the Dutch state in November 2008 of 750 million euro. Hard hit by delinquent mortgage loans not only in its home country but also in Spain where it had major operations, it was nationalized on 1 February 2013. The initial cost of the nationalization was put at 3.7 billion euro, consisting of a capital injection of 2.2 billion euro and a 1.5 billion write-down as well as 5 billion euro in guarantees.

SNS Reaal would be uninteresting were it not for two new features which we have not encountered before in this book but to which we

---

[13] http://europa.eu/rapid/press-release_IP-09-1729_en.htm
[14] "Up and at 'em," *The Economist*, 4 October 2014.

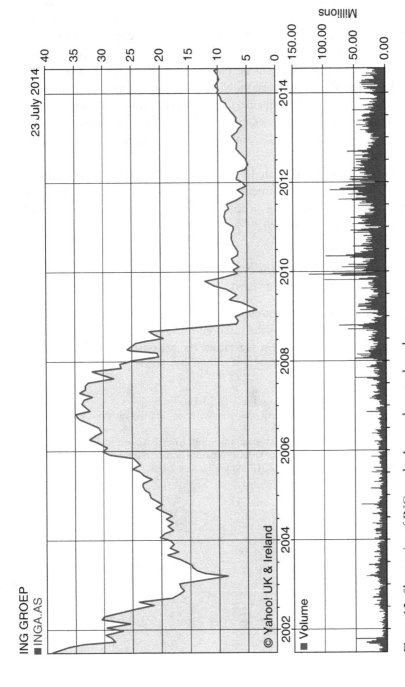

Figure 15. Share price of ING on the Amsterdam stock exchange

Source: https://uk.finance.yahoo.com/q/bc?s=INGA.AS&t=my&l=off&z=l&q=l&c=

will return in discussing Danish Amagerbanken, Anglo Irish Bank, Washington Mutual in the United States and the Cyprus banks. Firstly, the Dutch government levied a special 1 billion euro "contribution" on the Dutch financial system to help pay for the salvation, which given its concentration will be basically equally paid by ING, ABN AMRO and Rabobank. Secondly, not only were shareholders wiped out but so were 1.8 billion euro's worth of subordinated bonds. Senior bondholders were, however, protected. The EU Commission gave a temporary green light in December 2013[15] and approved the intervention on 27 May 2014.[16]

Interestingly enough, on 11 July 2013, a Dutch Court of Appeals ordered the Dutch government to compensate stockholders and investors in subordinated debt in the nationalized bank, though without giving an indication of level.

Overall grade of the handling of SNS Reaal: n/a (on a scale of A to F=Fail)

Since the legality of the action taken is still under dispute, it is not possible to pass judgment on the intervention. Action was taken speedily and the bailing-in of creditors follows the proposed EU rules.[17]

---

[15] http://europa.eu/rapid/press-release_IP-13-150_en.htm

[16] http://ec.europa.eu/competition/elojade/isef/case_details.cfm?proc_code=3_SA_36598

[17] European Commission, "On the application, from 1 August 2013, of state aid rules to support measures in favour of banks in the context of the financial crisis," Communication C(2013) 4119, 10 July 2013.

5 | *Italy*
Monte dei Paschi di Siena

The Italian story[1]

Just like Germany, Italy is dominated by a large number of banks (740 in 2012) and the five major banks had only 40 percent of total assets in 2010 (see Figure 10). However, the structure of banking is also influenced by the macroeconomic landscape, which is dramatically different from the German one. As shown in Figure 16, Italy suffers from having a government debt to GDP ratio of 135 percent, second only to Greece's 174 percent and in parallel with the debt ratios of Portugal and Ireland.[2]

However, as shown in Figures 17 and 18, the government debt in Italy is to a large extent held in domestic financial institutions, in turn nourished by a traditionally high household savings ratio. Almost 20 percent of the total financial assets of Italian financial institutions are held in domestic government bonds, a much higher percentage than in Greece, Ireland or Portugal where the debt is held to a larger extent by foreigners (even though the national share is rising). Looking only at banks, the share in their total assets of domestic government bonds rose from 6.8 percent in 2012 to 10 percent in August 2013, dominating Spain at 9.5 percent and Portugal at 7.6 percent.[3] During 2013, domestic banks absorbed 75 percent of net issues of Italian government bonds, as contrasted to 60 percent in Spain. Foreign investors

---

[1] See also Riccardo de Bonis, Alberto Franco Pozzolo and Massimiliano Stacchini, "The Italian banking system: facts and interpretations," Economics and Statistics Discussion Paper no 068/12, Università degli Studi del Molise, http://road.unimol.it/bitstream/2192/202/3/ESDP12068.pdf

[2] Ireland is for some reason missing from the Eurostat table but its debt to GDP ratio was 124 percent at the end of 2013.

[3] *Financial Times*, "Bank exposure to EU states' bonds on the rise," 13 October 2013, www.ft.com/intl/cms/s/0/9b6fb558-3270-11e3-b3a7-00144feab7de.html#axzz2jDlHy8X3

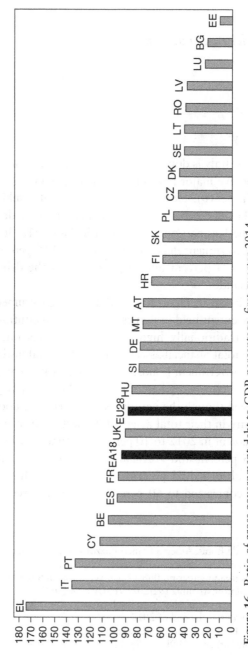

Figure 16. Ratio of gross government debt to GDP, percentage, first quarter 2014

Source: Eurostat http://epp.eurostat.ec.europa.eu/cache/ITY_PUBLIC/2-22072014-AP/EN/2-22072014-AP-EN.PDF

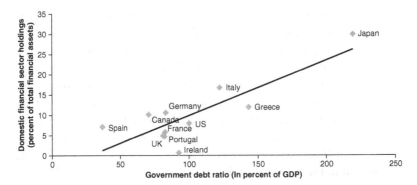

Figure 17. Government debt ratio to GDP and domestic financial sector holdings[4]

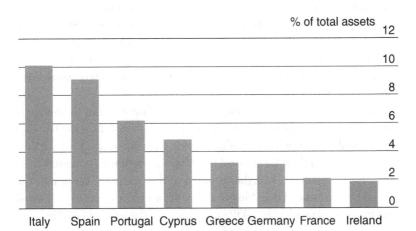

Figure 18. Percentage of banking assets held in domestic government bonds, July 2013
Source: ECB.

[4] Jochen R. Andritzky, "Government bonds and their investors: what are the facts and do they matter," IMF Working Paper WP 12/158, www.imf.org/external/pubs/ft/wp/2012/wp12158.pdf

are evidently reducing their exposure to the "PIIGS countries," forcing domestic institutions to pick up the slack.

The domestic dominance has advantages and disadvantages. The advantage is that domestic investors are more stable than fickle foreigners. But the disadvantage is firstly that banks may suffer from increased capital charges in the future or even write-downs or haircuts à la Greece. So far this has been avoided by the fact that government bonds in euro financed in euro have been regarded as risk-free under Basel II and hence have required no capital charges for credit risk if held in the banking book.[5] This treatment is, however, likely to change since it was an unintended exception to the Basel rules.

The second risk relates to the losses incurred when yields rise. As shown in Figure 19, the economic and political uncertainty in Italy led to a widening of the spread (difference) between Italian and German 10-year bonds from from just over 1 percentage point to over 5 percentage points during the European sovereign debt crisis in 2011 and 2012. The spread had fallen back to some 1.50 percentage points in mid 2014. Every single rise in yields will lead to a loss of market value of some 8 percent (for a 10-year bond), meaning that a 5 percentage point rise will evaporate approximately 40 percent market value if the bonds are marked to market.

The high correlation between government finances and the financial sector is a major cause for worry, according to the IMF, as is the fact that Italian banks are not very profitable, not least on account of the low yield received on their large bond holdings in relation to potential commercial lending rates.[6] A further problem is the continued economic and political uncertainty. Unstable governments and low consumer demand have led to a stagnation of GDP growth where the level of GDP in 2013 is 5 percent lower than in 2008 even before correcting for inflation. Non-performing loans have risen to 14 percent of all loans (September 2013).[7] Italian banks are also the biggest borrowers in the eurosystem

---

[5] Daniel Gros, "Banking union with a sovereign virus: the self-serving regulatory treatment of sovereign debt in the euro area," *CEPS Policy Brief* no. 289, 27 March 2013.

[6] IMF Survey, "Italy's financial system stabilized, still vulnerable," 27 September 2013. www.imf.org/external/pubs/ft/survey/so/2013/pol092713a.htm

[7] www.ft.com/intl/cms/s/0/17b6754c-3029-11e3-9eec-00144feab7de.html#axzz2j DlHy8X3

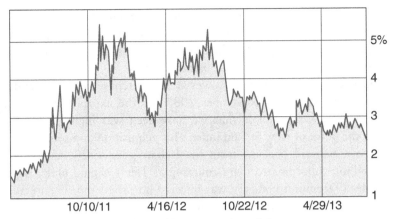

Figure 19. Ten-year yield spread between Italy and Germany
Source: http://blogs.marketwatch.com/thetell/2013/08/13/europes-haven-bond-yields-spike-as-economic-expectations-brighten/

with borrowings of 255 billion euro in June 2013. Moreover, the ECB has supported the Italian sovereign market by purchasing bonds for no less than 100 billion euro by the fall of 2013.

Monte dei Paschi di Siena[8]

The relative backwardness (if the term may be allowed) of the Italian banking sector with limited focus on international expansion and investment-banking activities had the advantage that Italy's banks were less affected by the financial crisis than banks in countries like the US, the UK or Germany. Instead they were harder hit by the European debt crisis from 2011 and the high interest rates that Italy had to pay.

The world's oldest bank, Monte dei Paschi di Siena (MPS), was introduced on the Milan exchange in 1999 but still with its *fondazione*

---

[8] www.bloomberg.com/news/2013-10-24/monte-paschi-born-out-of-black-death-struggles-to-survive.html

as major owner with one-third of the share capital. Over the next few years, it went on a shopping spree to acquire an increased presence in investment banking (MPS Finance) as well as asset management. In 2007, it was Italy's third largest bank by assets.

Its first major error was, however, the purchase from Santander of Antonveneta on 8 November 2007 for the exorbitant price of 10.3 billion euro, a price that we have seen was highly attractive from the point of view of Santander. This acquisition and some others led to a first-aid package from the Italian state in 2009, whereby 1.9 billion subordinated debt, counting as Tier 1 capital under Basel II rules ("Tremonti bonds"), was injected into the bank. The interest rate demanded by the state (according to EU competition rules) was, however, a high 9 percent.

The second error was the fact that MPS held government bonds in even greater proportion than the average Italian bank. This led to major losses when yields rose in 2011 (see Figure 6.4). For 2011, the bank recorded a loss of 4.7 billion euro, falling only marginally to a loss of 3.2 billion euro in 2012. These losses required a new aid package whereby MPS received 3.9 billion euro in aid ("Monti bonds"), of which part replaces the 2009 subordinated debt. It also received 13 billion euro in guarantees. The aid was approved by the European Commission on 17 December 2012 on condition that the bank issue 2.5 billion euro of new stock and shed 8,000 staff until 2017.[9] It is calculated to raise the bank's core Tier 1 ratio to 9 percent. It must also shrink its balance sheet from 240 billion euro to 180 billion.

In 2012, a third problem suddenly appeared. It turned out that from 2006 to 2009, the bank had entered into a number of derivative contracts ("Nota Italia" with JPMorgan Chase in 2006, "Santorini" with Deutsche Bank in 2008 and "Alexandria" with Nomura in 2009) with the purpose of shifting capital-demanding assets off-balance as well as hiding losses. These transactions had been hidden from the bank's supervisor, Banca d'Italia, as well as from its auditors. When revealed, they turned out to add 730 million euro in loss for the years covered: 152 million for Nota Italia, 305 million for Santorini and 274 million for Alexandria. The bank, in acknowledging the losses, also said there had been "mistakes" in reporting the trades. These "mistakes" forced

---

[9] http://europa.eu/rapid/press-release_IP-12-1383_en.htm

the then CEO of MPS, Giuseppe Mussari, to resign from the chairmanship of the Italian Bankers' Association, as well as being investigated for fraud. The bank's then finance director, Gianluca Baldassari, was temporarily jailed but released on technical grounds. Its director of communications committed suicide.

At the end of November 2013, the bank board approved an IPO of 3 billion euro to (partly) repay the loan from the state, exceeding the demand from the EU Commission. In April 2014, the issue was raised to 5 billion euro in order to pass the asset quality review and stress tests by the ECB. At the end of June 2014, Monte dei Paschi finally went through with a rights issue of 5 billion euro, which allowed it to repay 3.5 billion euro to the state and avoid nationalization. The dilution led, however, to a sharp fall in ths share price.

Overall grade of the handling of Monte dei Paschi: A (on a scale of A to F=Fail)

Given the precarious state of the Italian economy and the risk it entailed for the Italian banking system, the Italian authorities, primarily Banca d'Italia, reacted with commendable speed in 2009 under then governor Mario Draghi as well as in 2012 under the new governor Ignazio Visco. Setting up a bad bank would not have been helpful since the main troubled assets were "risk-free" Italian government bonds. Also, by that time, the undeclared derivatives losses were unknown. The state/taxpayers have not injected share capital but subordinated/hybrid debt for an attractive rate of interest, forcing the bank to replace this expensive financing in the equity market.

6 | *Denmark*

Roskilde Bank, Fionia Bank and the others vs.
Amagerbanken and Fjordbank Mors

The Danish story[1]

There are a number of reasons why the Danish banking sector and its way of handling failed banks is of interest. Firstly, the sector has undergone a dramatic consolidation in recent years with the number of banks falling to under one hundred under the influence of increased competition and the consequences of the financial crisis. Secondly, authorities have seized a number of banks and placed them under the holding company Finansiel Stabilitet. The FSA (Finanstilsynet) as well as the central bank have also been active in merging or liquidating failing banks.

Thirdly, and the reason for the country being included in this study, Denmark constitutes the first case in the European Union where even senior bondholders were forced to take "haircuts" when a bank was nationalized or merged. This possibility opened up in October 2010 when the unlimited guarantee for the domestic liabilities of Danish banks was allowed to lapse. Actually, already from 2007, a society was set up by the Danish Bankers' Association (Det Private Beredskab til Afvikling af Nødlidende Banker, Sparekasser og Andelskasser, translated as the Private Society for the Winding-down of Failing Banks, Savings Banks and Cooperative Banks), whereby the banking sector itself was supposed through fees to finance the resolution of its ailing member banks, helping them to merge with stronger partners. While membership in the society is in principle voluntary, all but a few small banks have signed up. The contribution of the state and the taxpayers

---

[1] The Committee on the Causes of the Financial Crisis in Denmark, "The financial crisis in Denmark: causes, consequences and lessons," www.evm.dk/english/publications/2013/~/media/oem/pdf/2013/2013-publikationer/18-09-13-rapport-fra-udvalget-om-finanskrisens-aarsager/conclusions-and-recommendations-170913.ashx

is thereby, as we shall see, limited in relation to the other countries which we have studied so far in this book.

Fourthly, Denmark has the world's largest mortgage market by capita or in relation to GDP and the second largest in Europe, after Germany, even in absolute numbers. Indeed, the mortgage bond market is four times the size of the domestic government bond market. This feature has, according to Denmark, to be taken into account when establishing Basel rules for the inclusion of liquid assets in the Liquidity Coverage Ratio (LCR) as well as limiting single counterparty exposures to 25 percent of Tier 1 capital. This is simply not feasible in a system dominated by four interconnected mortgage lenders (Nykredit, Realkredit Danmark, owned by Danske Bank, Nordea Kredit and BRF Kredit). The size of the mortgage market is obviously also of a great consequence for the development of "bubbles" and crashes.

From Roskilde Bank and Fionia Bank to Amagerbanken[2]

Over the 10 years to 2007, Danish house prices rose dramatically, as shown in Figure 20. The increase was far larger than in the other Nordic countries. It is interesting to note that the other three countries went through property-driven bubbles and consequent financial crises in the early 1990s.[3] Denmark was saved at that stage. But the countries having undergone earlier crises (the three Nordics as well as a number of Asian countries) had learnt the lesson and hence avoided problems this time whereas Denmark had not had this sobering experience.

Then house prices fell by over 25 percent in 2007–9. Only Ireland and Iceland suffered an even larger fall in property prices in such a short time. GDP in Denmark fell also by –1.2 percent in 2008 and by –4.7 percent in 2009. In combination with the large mortgage market,

---

[2] Finanstilsynet (Danish Financial Supervisory Authority), "Redogørelse fra Finanstilsynet om forløbet op til Amagerbanken A/S konkurs i henhold til § 352 a i lov om finansiel virksomhed," 24 August 2011; Danmarks Nationalbank (Ulrik Løgtholdt Poulsen and Brian Liltoft Andreasen), "Håndtering af nødlidende pengeinstitutter i Danmark"(Resolution of ailing financial institutions in Denmark), Kvartalsoversigt, 3. Kvartal 2011, pp. 79–94, http://nationalbanken.dk/DNDK/Publikationer.nsf/side/9EA7C855ACB 9BCAFC12579100034ACF8/$file/kvo_3_2011_del1_web.pdf
[3] See Johan A. Lybeck, *A Global History of the Financial Crash of 2007–2010* (Cambridge University Press, 2011), pp. 300 ff.

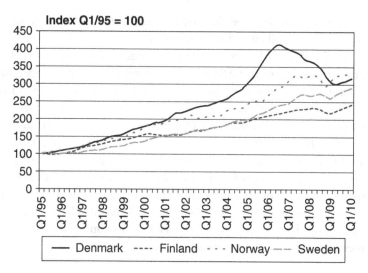

Figure 20. House price developments in the Nordic countries, 1995–2010
Source: Finanstilsynet, "Redogørelse fra Finanstilsynet," p. 36.

as described above, this meant that the Danish banking sector was among the worst hit in Europe. Profits were halved in major banks such as Nordea Denmark and Jyske Bank and turned into substantial losses in a number of small or medium-sized banks.

On 26 August 2008, the Danish central bank (Nationalbanken) took over Roskilde Bank, the sixth largest bank in Denmark, in the first Danish nationalization since 1928. Finansiel Stabilitet, the agency for handling failed banks, was set up only in October. Its branch network was sold in September to some other Danish banks, among them Nordea Denmark. With estimated losses of 37 billion DKK (5 billion euro), shareholders and holders of subordinated debt (Tier 2 capital) were wiped out, while senior unsecured bondholders were protected.

Responding to the financial crisis, on 10 October 2008 the Danish parliament adopted a law on financial stability ("Bankehjælpepakken I") whereby all domestic liabilities of Danish banks were guaranteed by the state. This guarantee was set to expire on 30 September 2010. The bank support agency Finansiel Stabilitet was set up to handle nationalized banks and aid the "private society" (see above) to merge failed banks.

On 24 February 2009, Finansiel Stabilitet injected 1 billion DKK in equity into the ninth largest bank, Fionia Bank on the island of Fyn, since the bank had failed in its efforts to issue equity to the market. This was, however, not sufficient and on 29 August, the viable parts of the bank were bought by Nordea for 900 million DKK, while loans of dubious quality for 10 billion DKK were taken over by Nova Bank Fyn, a subsidiary of Finansiel Stabilitet.

Ignoring a number of failed smaller banks (see, however, below), we turn to Amagerbanken, the tenth largest bank by assets. In 2010, it had succeded in raising almost 1 billion DKK in fresh equity on its own plus had it received 1.1 billion in hybrid capital from the state. However, criticism from the FSA on its valuations of real estate collateral and consequent requirements for write-downs of 3.1 billion DKK became too much. On 6 February 2011, Amagerbanken applied for bankruptcy and was taken over by the government agency Finansiel Stabilitet. The blanket guarantee for deposits as well as for other senior liabilities having been abolished in September 2010, unsecured senior bondholders lost 41 percent of their holdings, the first "bail-in" of creditors in the EU in the recent crisis. Shareholders and holders of subordinated debt were wiped out.[4] The viable residuals of the bank were later sold to BankNordik, a bank based on the Faroe Islands, on 18 May 2011. All in all, Amagerbanken cost Finansiel Stabilitet 15.2 billion DKK and the banking industry through the "private society" 2.2 billion DKK.

On 28 June 2011, the small failed regional bank Fjordbank Mors was taken over by Finansiel Stabilitet and later sold to Jyske Bank. Like Amagerbanken, investors of senior unsecured bonds had to take a haircut, here estimated at 26 percent.

The unexpected bailing-in of senior creditors led to an immediate reaction in the pricing of Danish bank debt vis-à-vis other Scandinavian banks, below Danske Bank, DNB (Norway), Nordea (Sweden), SEB (Sweden), Handelsbanken (Sweden), Swedbank (Sweden) and Pohjola (Finland). See Figure 21 (two alternative versions). It is quite apparent that the abolishing of the guarantee and the bailing-in of creditors cost Danish banks 100–200 basis points' extra yield. Swap spreads in the crisis rose from 100 basis points to 250 basis points compared to substantially less for the other major Nordic non-Danish banks.[5]

---

[4] http://dailybail.com/home/amagerbanken-28-billion-bank-failure-in-denmark-senior-bondh.html

[5] The holding company Nordea referred to in Figure 22 is Swedish based with subsidiary banks in the various Nordic countries (and elsewhere).

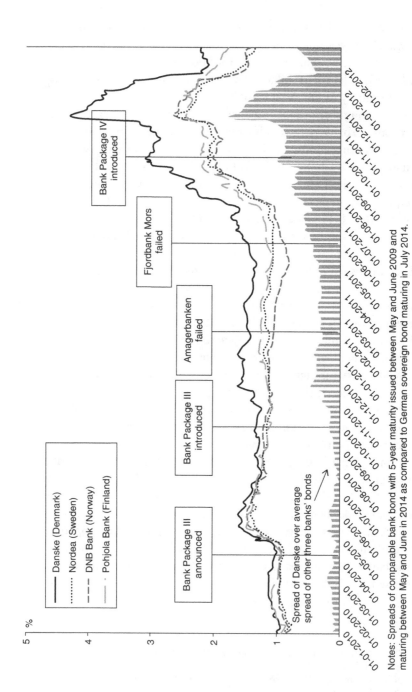

Notes: Spreads of comparable bank bond with 5-year maturity issued between May and June 2009 and maturing between May and June in 2014 as compared to German sovereign bond maturing in July 2014.

Figure 21a. Yield spread of selected Nordic bank bonds, 2010–12

Source: http://ekonomistas.se/2013/10/24/ena-bankens-stod-ar-den-andra-bankens-nod/

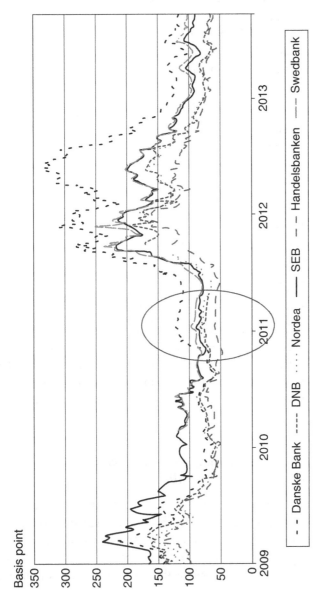

Figure 21b. CDS spread on senior unsecured debt in some Nordic banks, 2009–13
Source: Nationalbanken.

Even in July 2014, Danish banks reported continued problems in accessing wholesale funding as a result of the unexpected bail-in of senior creditors in 2011.[6]

All in all, between 2008 and 2012, Finansiel Stabilitet took over 11 banks and aided in the merger of another dozen banks as set out in the following table. Banks in *italics* have been discussed above.

Bankepakken I

EBH Bank	21 November 2008
Løkken Sparekasse	2 March 2009
Gudme Raaschou Bank	16 April 2009
Fionia Bank	*28 May 2009*
Capinordic Bank	11 February 2010
Eik Banki/Danmark	30 September 2010

Bankepakke III

Amagerbanken	*6 February 2011*
Fjordbank Mors	*24 June 2011*

Bankepakke IV

Max Bank	8 October 2011
Sparekassen Østjylland	21 April 2012

As can be seen from Figure 22, the total assets of Finansiel Stabilitet have been relatively stable since the nationalization of Fionia Bank in May 2009, implying that the company has succeeded in selling or liquidating assets at about the same pace as it has been forced to take on new engagements.

Overall grade of the handling of Danish banks: A or F (on a scale of A to F=Fail)

On one hand, the handling of failed banks in Denmark has been excellent. Authorities have been proactive both in aiding banks to raise capital and setting demands on write-downs and recapitalizations. When nationalizations have become necessary, the viable parts have been quickly sold to competitors while the government agency Finansiel

---

[6] www.bloomberg.com/news/2014-07-21/most-danish-banks-remain-cut-off-from-wholesale-funding.html

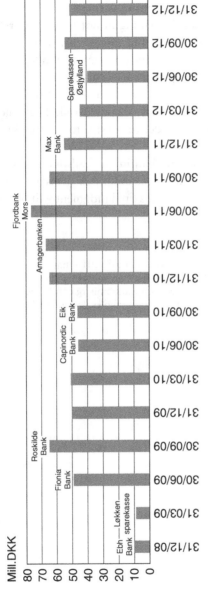

Figure 22. Total assets of recovered and disposed activities, 2008–12

Source: Finansiel Stabilitet, Annual report 2012, p. 5.

Stabilitet has taken on the role of "bad bank" to dispose of the rest. The banking sector has been called upon to help in the financing of ailing banks and helped to merge the viable parts of failing banks with healthier competitors. This merits an A.

But on the other hand, the bailing in not only of shareholders and investors of subordinated debt but also of investors in senior unsecured debt has created a worrisome uncertainty. While spreads on bank bonds or credit default swaps have basically returned to the same level as in other Nordic countries (all the four major Nordic countries are AAA/Aaa rated) in the next crisis, spreads would likely increase again in a crisis, making it even harder to survive for the banking system as a whole. This merits an F.[7]

However, the question of bail-in or bail-out of bondholders is not only a matter for individual countries' legislation but also the European Union as a whole. Thus final judgment will be reserved until the last part of the book.

---

[7] Bloomberg, the news agency, reported in July 2014 that most Danish banks were still having difficulty in funding as a result of the uncertainty created by the bail-in of senior creditors. See www.bloomberg.com/news/2014-07-21/most-danish-banks-remain-cut-off-from-wholesale-funding.html

Bail-out and/or bail-in of banks in Europe: a country-by-country event study on those European countries which received IMF/EU support[1]

---

[1] See also "Europe's zombie banks, blight of the living dead", *The Economist*, 13 July 2013.

7 | *Iceland*
Landsbanki, Glitnir and Kaupthing

The Icelandic story[1]

The Icelandic financial crisis is instructive for its own sake but it may also serve as a summary of the Asian crises in the 1990s, since Iceland committed exactly the same errors as the Asian countries had done 10 years earlier and at twice the scale (in relationship to the size of the economy). While the Asian crisis cost between 32 percent of GDP in Korea and 57 percent of GDP in Indonesia, the Icelandic crisis was originally estimated by the IMF to cost 80 percent of GDP. This was later (2012) lowered to an actual gross cost of 44 percent of GDP, beating even Ireland at 41 percent of GDP, the topic of the next chapter.[2]

On the macroeconomic plane, Iceland grew faster than surrounding countries in the first years of the new century, or by 4–8 percent per year. See Figure 23a. The focus of the government was aimed at achieving a better diversification of the economy, where the fishing industry still accounted for 20 percent of exports and 8 percent of employment. On the industrial side, Iceland wanted to utilize its cheap hydroelectric

---

[1] Már Gudmundsson and Thorstinn Thorgeirsson, "Fault lines in cross border banking: lessons from the Icelandic case," in P. Backé, E. Gnan and P. Hartmann, eds., *Contagion and Spillovers: New Insights from the Crisis*, SUERF Studies no. 5 (Vienna and Larcier: 2010); Willem H. Buiter and Anne Silbert, "The Icelandic banking crisis and what to do about it," Centre for Economic Policy Research, Policy Insight no. 26, October 2008; Richard Portes, "The Icelandic financial sector and the markets," Icelandic Chamber of Commerce, April 2008; Roger Boyes, *Meltdown Iceland: How the Global Financial Crisis Bankrupted an Entire Country* (London: Bloomsbury, 2009); Asgéir Jónsson, *Why Iceland? How One of the World's Smallest Countries Became the Meltdown's Biggest Casualty* (New York: McGraw-Hill, 2009); Michael Lewis, *Boomerang* (London: Penguin, 2011) ch. 1; Onaran, *Zombie Banks*, ch. 6; "Cracks in the crust," *The Economist*, 13 December 2008.
[2] International Monetary Fund (Luc Laeven and Fabian Valencia), "Systemic banking crises: a new database," IMF Working Paper 2008/224; updated June 2012, IMF Working Paper 2012/163.

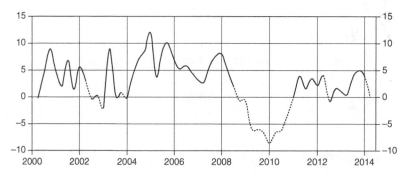

Figure 23a. Iceland GDP growth rate, 2000–14
Source: www.tradingeconomics.com/iceland/gdp-growth-annual

and geothermal energy for such energy-demanding industries as aluminum production. Service sectors such as tourism and banking were also in focus. The investment ratio in GDP was almost 30 percent and investments grew by over 20 percent annually.

The economic program was on the surface a spectacular success. Unemployment was negligible and Iceland rose in the "rich man's league" (measured by GDP per capita) to ninth position in the world, well ahead of countries such as Sweden, Denmark or the United Kingdom. But the high growth rate had its drawbacks. Just like in Asia, the deficit in the current account skyrocketed, to –25 percent of GDP in 2006, only to fall back somewhat to –15.5 percent in 2007. See Figure 23b. The reason for the improvement was increased exports, not least by the financial sector. Also just like in Asia, capital imports led to increases in house prices which more than doubled between 2001 and 2007, rising 35 percent in individual years.

The high growth rate had the additional advantage that the budget showed a surplus of 5–6 percent of GDP just before the crisis. The debt-to-GDP ratio in 2007 was but 28 percent, far lower than in other European countries. The euro area on average had a ratio of 66 percent, the European Union as a whole had a ratio of 59 percent. See Figure 23c. The crisis would lead the Icelandic debt to levels greater than the GDP, i.e. to a ratio above 100.

Yet, the rating agency Fitch had put Iceland on downgrade warning already in 2006, worried about the growing imbalances. In February 2008, Moody's downgraded all the three major Icelandic banks, "in

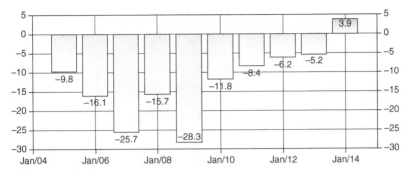

Figure 23b. Iceland current account as a percentage of GDP, 2004–13
Source: www.tradingeconomics.com/iceland/current-account-to-gdp

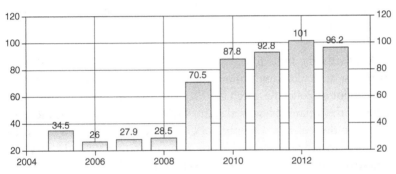

Figure 23c. Iceland government debt to GDP ratio, 2004–13, percentage
Source: www.tradingeconomics.com/iceland/government-debt-to-gdp

light of the weaker credit environment." In April 2008, Standard &
Poor's downgraded Iceland from A+ to A and Glitnir (the only bank
it rated) to a low BBB+. CDS spreads on the three Icelandic banks had
also started to widen markedly from the end of 2007.

Worries about the situation, in particular the current-account deficit, the persistent inflation rate and the size of the banking sector (see
below), led to two studies on Iceland being commissioned. The findings
of one study, commissioned by Landsbanki, the second largest commercial bank, were so negative and market-sensitive that the authors
(Professors Willem Buiter and Anne Sibert) were told to keep them

secret. The paper was published only after the crash in October. Their main conclusion in the paper, written in April 2008, was that (p. 17):

Iceland's economy is highly vulnerable to financial shocks. Iceland's banks have recently been exposed both to interruptions of funding liquidity and to interruptions of market liquidity in key markets for their assets. As regards shocks to funding liquidity, although Iceland's banks have not experienced classical bank runs (a sudden withdrawal of deposits), they have been subject to its credit market counterpart – the refusal of the bank's creditors to roll over maturing credit, secured or unsecured. As regards shocks to market liquidity, there have been wholesale financial market "strikes" – liquidity shortages in the wholesale financial markets in which banks and other highly leveraged financial institutions fund themselves to a growing extent. Exchange-rate volatility and instability, the huge spreads in the Icelandic banks' CDS markets and the de-facto exclusion of these banks from the international wholesale financial markets, are but the most visible manifestations of the financial difficulty Iceland finds itself in.[3]

At exactly the same time, April 2008, Richard Portes, a well-known professor at the London Business School and the founder of the Centre for Economic Policy Research (CEPR), dismissed as "rumors" any possibility of the Icelandic financial sector facing a meltdown. In a study presented to the Icelandic Chamber of Commerce, he concluded that while the three major banks were "aggressive and entrepreneurial," they also had strong competitive advantages such as "careful risk control, flat management structures and very capable management, unusual and strong business models." He also noted that the Financial Supervisory Authority (FME) was "highly professional" and that the central bank of Iceland (Sedlabanki) "achieves a high standard in its financial stability analyses."

The winner between these two highly contradictory evaluations would be selected just five months later ...

Landsbanki, Glitnir and Kaupthing

The three major Icelandic banks had been through a spectacular development. Kaupthing was started in the 1980s as a local broker-dealer

---

[3] Similar but academic conclusions were drawn in Robert Z. Aliber, "Monetary turbulence and the Icelandic economy," speech 20 June 2008, University of Iceland.

but grew to bank number 151 in the world by 2007 with total assets of 86 billion dollars through a series of aggressive mergers. JP Nordiska Bank was acquired in Sweden, in Norway the broker Sundal, in Britain the bank Singer & Friedlander, in the Netherlands NIBS and in Belgium Robeco Bank. The bank had activities in 13 countries. Funding was in the main through the internet under the name of Kaupthing Edge (which alluded to "cutting edge"). Most of these deposits were booked with Singer & Friedlander in the UK; however, in the Nordic countries as well as Germany, they were booked in Iceland with dire consequences for the depositors.

Landsbanki and Glitnir, with assets of 49 and 48 billion dollars, respectively, were somewhat smaller than Kaupthing but still number 204 and 212 in the world in 2007 by total assets. Like Kaupthing, Glitnir was really a broker-dealer with ambition. It purchased BN Bank in Norway, the brokerage firm Fischer Fondkommission in Sweden and FIM in Finland. Landsbanki had a different background, having been the central bank of Iceland, issuing currency notes, privatized as late as 2003. Just like Kaupthing, it then started purchasing aggressively, which led to its presence in 15 countries. Like Kaupthing, the main funding was through the internet under the brand name "Icesave." An attraction to British customers was the promise to always pay at least 25 basis points better interest than the Bank Rate. Icesave had more than 300,000 clients in the UK, many of them local authorities, with deposits over 5 billion euro (but also the universities of Oxford and Cambridge, as well as the Metropolitan Police). In just a few months, it acquired deposits of 1.7 billion euro in the Netherlands from 125,000 clients.[4] All in all, 116 British local authorities had deposited almost 1 billion pounds in the three Icelandic banks.

Together, the three banks had total assets at the end of 2007 of 184 billion dollars. This may be compared with Iceland's GDP of 20 billion dollars. Assets were almost ten times GDP, a ratio only achieved elsewhere by Luxembourg, which is a case by itself (see Figure 10). Liabilities in foreign currency were five times Iceland's GDP and even netting out foreign-currency assets, Iceland had liabilities in foreign currency amounting to 250 percent of GDP, over 40 billion dollars' worth of foreign debt. This may be compared with foreign-exchange

---

[4] Boyes, *Meltdown Iceland*, p. 133.

reserves of 2 billion dollars. How Iceland's central bank, Sedlabanki, could stand passively and witness this development is incredible. The mismatch in currency is evidenced by the foreign indebtedness. The mismatch in interest rate was just as severe, with investments in residential mortgages funded by short-term deposits, much of it wholesale.

The banks were on the surface stable and efficient, with BIS ratios of 11–12 percent (as compared to the minimum 8 percent) and cost–income ratios of 0.47–0.56 (2007), fully in line with the major British banks, which had BIS ratios from 11 (Lloyds TSB) to 13.6 (HSBC) and cost–income ratios of 0.47 (HBOS) to 0.57 (Barclays). But the problem was that a central bank cannot be lender of last resort in foreign currency. As stated well by Lord (Mervyn) King, then governor of the Bank of England, banks may be international in life but they are national in death.

The financial crisis was to expose mercilessly the mismatches in currency and interest of the Icelandic banks. Their subsidiaries in Europe were subjected to runs starting in September, in particular the British Singer & Friedlander. On 6 October 2008, the Icelandic government announced measures to combat the exploding financial crisis and the falling Krona (which had already fallen by 35 percent since the beginning of the year). Strict capital controls on outflows were instituted by the central bank. The Financial Supervisory Authority (FME) was given the right to nationalize banks or put them into receivership without nationalization. All deposits of *Icelandic* branches of Icelandic banks were to be guaranteed fully, thus excluding Landsbanki's "Icesave" accounts as well as Kaupthing Edge accounts, held by British, Dutch and German nationals. Trading in all bank shares was suspended.

On 7 October, the Icelandic FSA nationalized Landsbanki and Glitnir and the day after the Icelandic parts of Kaupthing. The Swedish subsidiary of Glitnir (ex-Fischer FK) was sold to HQ Bank and its Norwegian subsidiary to the Sparebank 1 group. Kaupthing's British subsidiary Singer & Friedlander was declared bankrupt and placed into administration by the UK Treasury, acting on advice from the FSA and the Bank of England. Its deposits were transferred to ING Direct, as were the deposits of Hardibanki, the much smaller British subsidiary of Landsbanki. Kaupthing Bank Sweden was nationalized under the Swedish National Debt Office[5] and later sold to the Finnish bank Ålandsbanken, which thereby entered the Swedish market. British, German and Dutch depositors lost an estimated 6.7 billion euro on their Landsbanki "Icesave" internet accounts, a sum in the main repaid by the respective governments, sparking a dispute on accountability between Iceland and the three governments (see below). In June 2009, Iceland declared itself legally responsible for depositors in these accounts, but lacking the possibility to repay.

Between 9 and 22 October 2008, the domestic parts of Iceland's three major banks were restarted with government money: NBI (Nýí Landsbanki) was set up with 200 billion krónúr in equity and 2,300 billion in assets, Nýí Glitnir with 110 billion krónúr in equity and 1,200 billion in assets, Nýja Kaupthing with 75 billion in equity and 700 billion in assets. Assets in foreign currency were left out and regarded as totally inadequate to repay foreign depositors. The combined assets of the three new banks, 4,200 billion krónúr or 35 billion dollars at the then ruling exchange rate (the krónúr having depreciated by 50 percent), may be compared to the 184 billion dollars the three banks held at year-end 2007 (according to *The Banker*, July 2008).

After having acknowledged in principle its debt to foreign depositors (a condition for the Netherlands approving the IMF aid), on 19 November 2008 Iceland received a support package of 5.1 billion dollars, of which 2.1 billion from the IMF and 3 billion in bilateral aid from the other Nordic countries. Iceland became the first West European country to receive IMF aid since Britain in 1976.

On 19 October 2009, after months of political haggling, Iceland agreed to borrow 2.35 billion pounds from the UK and 1.2 billion euro from the Netherlands to cover its deposit-insurance liabilities to depositors in the failed Landsbanki "Icesave." The president forced the issue to a referendum, however, refusing the payment of 3.8 billion euro to 320,000 Landsbanki Icesave investors in Britain and the Netherlands. On 6 March 2010, the Icelandic voters overwhelmingly (93-2) rejected the deal. On 9 December 2010, Iceland struck a new

---

[5] Just like the FDIC in the United States, the Swedish National Debt Office, an agency under the finance ministry, is responsible for bank resolution as well as the deposit guarantee system and the connected funds.

deal with the Netherlands and the UK concerning the Icesave accounts. While acknowledging the debt of almost 4 billion euro, the rate of interest to be paid was lowered to 3.3 percent rather than 5.55 percent in the previous agreement. However, on 9 April 2011, the population again rejected the agreement with Britain and the Netherlands concerning Icesave.

In a surprise move, the EFTA Court of Justice on 28 January 2013 supported entirely the claim by Iceland that it was not obligated to pay Britain and the Netherlands for payments made to investors in the failed Landsbanki online Icesave scheme, deposits booked in Iceland. The reason stated by the court was firstly the lack of clarity in international deposit-insurance cooperation and secondly the dire straits of the Icelandic economy after the crisis. Supported by this ruling, on 9 May 2013, the new Icelandic government said that foreign creditors in the failed banks Kaupthing, Landsbanki and Glitnir would lose their 3.8 billion dollar investments. These losses came on top of the refusal by Iceland to repay the United Kingdom and the Netherlands the amounts these countries had paid out for deposit insurance in the failed banks, in particular the Icesave accounts in Landsbanki (Singer & Friedlander, being a subsidiary, was of course covered by British deposit insurance).

From the middle of 2007 until June 2009, the Icelandic stock market index OMXI15 fell by 97 percent, from index 9,000 to 270. But on the other hand, it had risen 800 percent from 2001 to 2007. The currency fell from 90 Icelandic crowns to the dollar to a low point of 340 USD/ISK, a depreciation of 75 percent, but has since come back to 115 (July 2014), leaving the depreciation at a more normal 22 percent (equivalent to the Swedish depreciation after its financial crisis in 1992). GDP fell by 7 percent in 2009 while inflation rose to 17 percent (see Figure 23a).

On 31 August 2011, Iceland emerged officially from the IMF-led bail-out, being able to borrow on the markets again on its own. The IMF declared that Iceland had met all the fund's requirements. Growth had been restored, the fiscal balance improved by 10 percentage points of GDP and the banking sector restored to profitability, albeit at a much smaller size, total assets being some 200 percent of GDP and hence less than one-fifth of the amount before the crisis. The total gross fiscal cost of bank recapitalization and restructuring over the years 2008–11 amounted to 44 percent of GDP (as against initial IMF estimates of 80 percent), the net cost three years later had fallen to 20 percent.

Iceland was the first country outside the United States to hold former executives responsible for the crisis. On 24 April 2012, Geir Haarde, a former prime minister of Iceland, was found guilty of negligence in the (so far) only legal procedure against a major politician in the global financial crisis. However, no punishment was imposed and the government paid his legal costs. He was found innocent of the charge that he failed to attack the too-big-to-fail problem and two other charges.

In December 2012, two senior managers, the CEO Lárus Welding and the head of corporate finance Gudmundur Hjaltason, of failed Icelandic bank Glitnir were sentenced to nine months in prison for their role in the credit bubble. In March 2013, a number of former executives in failed Kaupthing and Landsbanki were charged, among them the two CEOs, with market manipulation in that the banks had lent money to be used to buy shares in the banks, in particular to members of their own boards. In December 2013, four former executives of failed Icelandic bank Kaupthing, among them the chairman Sigurdur Einarsson and the CEO Hreidar Mar Sigurdsson, were given prison sentences of three to five and a half years for fraud and manipulation in connection with an IPO where the capital injected into the bank was in fact financed by a loan from the bank.

Overall grade of the handling of Icelandic banks: A (on a scale of A to F=Fail)

While severe criticism could and should be levied at the central bank and the Financial Supervisory Authority (FME) for their inability to foresee and react to the vast build-up of assets and liabilities in the banking system, in particular in foreign currency, their handling of the crisis when it broke was exemplary. The banks were quickly nationalized, foreign-currency debt repudiated, new viable domestic banks set up within the time span of a few weeks. The residual of the "old banks" thus became in effect bad banks, containing deposits from foreigners and assets in the form of foreign-currency-denominated Icelandic mortgages, the latter (assets), however, being much smaller than the former (liabilities).

While the repudiation of debt of non-Icelandic depositors may strike a sour note, still it is in line with what other countries like Ireland,

Denmark and Germany did at the same time, which was to guarantee the deposits and (sometimes) other liabilities but only of their domestic banks.[6]

A recent study by the Central Bank of Iceland has considered by means of an econometric model whether alternative solutions might have produced superior results:[7]

- Adopting a more pro-cyclical fiscal policy;
- Allowing the krona exchange rate to drop without imposing capital controls;
- Paying the interest expense on the initial Icesave agreement;
- Rescuing the banking system à la Ireland.

However, all these four alternatives were found inferior to the one chosen.

---

[6] Ireland was, as we shall see below, forced to guarantee also the liabilities of foreign subsidiaries in Ireland since these were in effect Irish banks, but not branches of foreign-owned banks.

[7] Thorsteinn Thorgeirsson and Paul van den Noord, "The Icelandic banking collapse: was the optimal policy path chosen?" Central Bank of Iceland, Working Paper 62, March 2013.

8 | Ireland
Anglo Irish Bank, Bank of Ireland, Allied Irish Banks

The Irish story[1]

"This was not a problem confined to any individual bank. The problem was one for the system and caused entirely by the international market turmoil."[2] The sentence is taken from an e-mail, written on 30 September 2008 by the chief executive of the Irish FSA (the Financial Regulator, FR), Patrick Neary, to the Dublin correspondent of the *Financial Times*. And on the surface, one could believe his words. This was indeed the day after the TARP program had been rejected by the US House of Representatives, Wachovia Bank had agreed to be taken over by Citigroup, Bradford & Bingley had been nationalized in the United Kingdom, Glitnir had been almost totally nationalized by the Icelandic authorities, and Hypo Real Estate in Germany and Dexia in Belgium had been given extensive support by

---

[1] Patrick Honohan *et al.*, "The Irish banking crisis: regulatory and financial stability policy 2003–2008," A report to the Minister of Finance by the Governor of the Central Bank, 31 May 2010; Commission of investigation into the banking sector in Ireland (the Nyberg report), "Misjudging risks: the causes of the systemic banking crisis in Ireland," March 2011; Simon Carswell, *Anglo Republic: Inside the Bank that Broke Ireland* (London: Penguin, 2012); Donal Donovan and Antoin E. Murphy, *The Fall of the Celtic Tiger: Ireland and the Euro Debt Crisis* (Oxford University Press, 2013); Kenneth O'Sullivan and Stephen Kinsella, "Financial and regulatory failure: the case of Ireland," *Journal of Banking Regulation*, 14:1 (January 2013), pp. 1–15; Klaus Regling and Max Watson, *A Preliminary Report on the Sources of the Irish Banking Crisis* (Dublin: Government Publications Sales Office, 2010); Shane Ross, *The Bankers: How the Banks Brought Ireland to Its Knees* (London: Penguin, 2009); Maria Woods and Siobhán O'Connell, "Ireland's financial crisis: a comparative context," *Bank of Ireland Quarterly Bulletin* 4 (2012), pp. 97–118; Brian Cowen, "The euro: from crisis to resolution? Some reflections from Ireland on the road thus far," speech, 21 March 2012; Michael Lewis, *Boomerang: The Biggest Bust* (New York and London: Penguin, 2012), ch. 3.
[2] Carswell, *Anglo Republic*, p. 222.

their respective governments. And it was also the day when the Irish government promised to guarantee not only the deposits but almost all liabilities of the Irish banks.

Yet both statements are wrong. The problems in the Irish banks were mostly of their own doing, even if triggered by the international liquidity crisis, and there were major differences between the biggest banks. What is even worse is that the bank with the worst problems, Anglo Irish Bank, was working hand in glove with its supervisory authorities, the Central Bank of Ireland and the Financial Regulator, to present to the public the likes of the above-quoted statement. One could even say that Anglo Irish orchestrated the government's public statements, covering up its own precarious situation.

Neary added in a TV interview two days later that "by any estimate, the Irish banks are so well capitalized compared to any banks anywhere across Europe that I am confident that they can absorb any [bad] loans or any impairments that emerge in the ordinary course of business over the foreseeable future."[3] This was a third statement by the FR that would shortly be proven to be way off the mark.

Of all the country failures studied in this book, none – with the exception of the United States – has been so extensively discussed in the literature and subject to a number of official investigations, as footnote 1 to this chapter bears witness. Yet most of the attention has focused on why it happened, whereas the theme of this book is on how the resolution of the banking crisis was handled. For both these reasons, the presentation of events leading up to the crisis can be kept short.

There are many similarities but also many major differences between the Icelandic and the Irish stories of recent years. Both countries are small open economies that profited from the international liberalization of trade and capital movements to advance their position. Both were regarded as success stories to be imitated. In both cases, the rapid rate of growth in connection with benign regulators led to an overgrown banking sector with assets many times the country's GDP, 10 times in the case of Iceland, 8 times for Ireland. While avoiding the involvement in American subprime-related CDOs and derivatives that felled a number of other European banks and likewise avoiding, in the main, expensive international adventures, the Icelandic and

---

[3] Ibid. p. 232.

Irish banks were instead at the root of domestic property bubbles and became themselves the victims when the bubbles burst.

But here the similarities end. In Iceland, all the major banks were nationalized, whereas the picture for the Irish banks is more diverse, with the largest and most conservative bank, Bank of Ireland, almost making it through the crisis without government support. And as concerns resolution, there are wide differences. In Iceland, the fall in the exchange rate helped kickstart the economy, a path excluded to Ireland with its membership in the euro.[4] And perhaps most importantly, while Iceland bailed in the banks' foreign creditors, the Irish government went out of its way to protect creditors, even investors in subordinated debt, until the liquidation of the residual remnants of Anglo Irish Bank.

Figures 24a, 24b and 24c depict the major macroeconomic variables for Ireland. GDP growth in the beginning of the twenty-first century was high and stable at 4–6 percent. It followed 30 years of spectacular growth. When Ireland joined the European Union in 1973, its GDP per capita was only 74 percent of the EU average and only 57 percent of the OECD average. In 2007, just before the bubble burst, Ireland had a GDP per capita of 46,600 dollars, 59 percent above the EU average. Events during 2008–11 would see GDP fall by a cumulative 17 percent. Despite this fall, Irish GDP per capita was still 25 percent

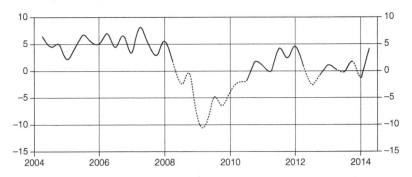

Figure 24a. Irish GDP growth rate, 2004–13
Source: www.tradingeconomics.com/ireland/gdp-growth-annual

---

[4] One may wonder why Ireland should choose to link itself to the euro area to which only some 40 percent of its exports are directed.

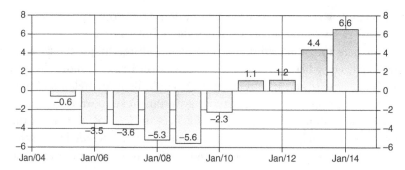

Figure 24b. Current account in Ireland as a percentage of GDP, 2004–13
Source: www.tradingeconomics.com/ireland/current-account-to-gdp

above the EU average in 2012 (according to the IMF). Unemployment rose from 4 to 15 percent but had by July 2014 fallen back to the Euroland average of 11.6 percent.

Figure 24b shows that the current account deteriorated with the overinvestment in property but not nearly as much as in Iceland. Instead, as described in more detail below, the Irish banks came to rely more and more on cheap lending from the ECB, where they became the largest borrowers. Irish banks' refinancing in the ECB rose to 40 billion euro in November 2008, to 80 billion euro in May 2009 and to 100 billion euro in January 2011, which meant that Ireland, with a share of 1 percent in the capital of ECB, accounted for 25 percent of the loans from ECB.[5] On top of this sum, the banks also took Emergency Liquidity Assistance (ELA) from the Irish Central Bank to the tune of 60 billion euro.

From mid 1990 to 2007, the price of residential property almost quadrupled. The reason was not least the growth of lending. In the five years up to 2006, loans from the three major banks increased at high rates: Bank of Ireland 28 percent on average per year, Allied Irish Banks 34 percent per year and Anglo Irish Bank 47 percent per year. On average, 80 percent of the new loans went into property, though as we shall see, Anglo was more focused on commercial property and construction than the others. The bubble was fed by increased

---

[5] Donovan and Murphy, *The Fall of the Celtic Tiger*, p. 238.

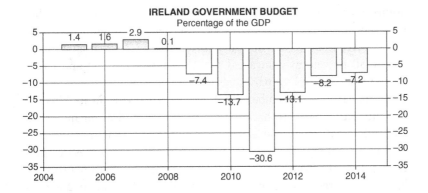

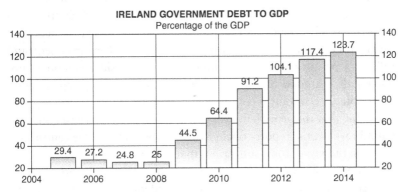

Figure 24c. The budget balance and government debt in Ireland, 2004–13, both expressed as a ratio to GDP
Source: www.tradingeconomics.com/ireland/government-budget and www.tradingeconomics.com/ireland/government-debt-to-gdp

competition from international lenders such as Ulster Bank (owned by RBS) and Bank of Scotland (Ireland). In a few years, margins on mortgages fell from 240 basis points to 50 basis points, hardly enough to cover the cost of capital charges and administration. Lending standards became more lax with loans up to four times income granted. From 2005, 100 percent mortgages were introduced without any reaction from the FR.[6] In a country with one of the highest rates of

[6] Ross, *The Bankers*, pp. 140–1.

homeownership in Europe, 75 percent in 2006, the resulting bubble was inevitable, as was the subsequent decline in homeownership to 70 percent by 2011. In five years, prices of residential property fell by 50 percent as contrasted to –18 percent in Spain and Greece and –15 percent in Denmark over the same period.

Yet as early as November 2004, the Central Bank in its Financial Stability Report (p. 10) had warned of "the risk of an unanticipated and sudden fall in residential prices, accompanied by an increase in the default rate among mortgage holders ... is the risk that poses the greatest threat to the health of the banking system." This warning seems to have been forgotten when three years later, in November 2007, the same report (p. 12) found that "against a more uncertain international backdrop, the indications are that the domestic economy continues to perform solidly. The overall picture for economic growth is generally satisfactory in the current uncertain international environment and follows a period of high growth. On the positive side, economic fundamentals – a good budgetary position, strong employment growth, an adaptable economy – continue to be sound."

Noting that the growth in property prices had slowed and gone into a mild reverse, the report concluded (same page) that "the central scenario is, therefore, for a soft rather than a hard, landing."

Figure 24c shows the impressive government finances, with a budget in surplus until 2008, and a government debt to GDP ratio of only 25 percent when the crisis started. The figures also show how the financial crisis changed these positive trends with remarkable speed. We will return to this below.

If the property bubble was much worse – both going up and going down – than in Iceland, the stock market reaction was milder. As shown in Figure 25, share prices fell by 81 percent from peak to bottom, as contrasted to 97 percent in Iceland (and by 54 percent worldwide, according to the International Federation of Exchanges) and started to recover by February 2009 in parallel with the rest of the world. This increase in share prices did not apply to Allied Irish Banks and Anglo Irish Bank, which had both been nationalized and shareholders wiped out, nor to Bank of Ireland whose share price fell from a peak of 23 euro at the peak in 2007 to 10 cents from which level it has recovered only marginally. In 2007, banks had constituted almost half of the capitalization of the Irish Stock Exchange. In November 2013, the corresponding figure was 6.7 percent.

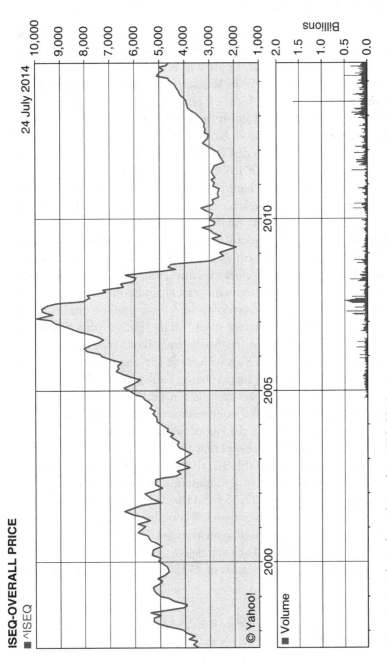

Figure 25. Irish stock market index, 1998–2014

Source: http://finance.yahoo.com/q/bc?s=%5EISEQ&t=my&l=off&z=l&q=l&c=

Anglo Irish Bank, Bank of Ireland, Allied Irish Banks[7]

The largest Irish bank by assets at the end of 2007 was, perhaps surprisingly, none of the four major "Irish" banks but Depfa. However, fortunately as it turned out, Depfa had been bought in October 2007 by Hypo Real Estate (HRE) in Munich (see Chapter 2) and had thus become mainly a problem for the German supervisory authorities and SoFFin when the roof fell in on the world's banks on 29 September 2008. Hence we focus here on Bank of Ireland with total assets at the end of 2007 of 312 billion dollars, Allied Irish Banks with 261 billion and Anglo Irish Bank with 137 billion. A special mention should be made of the fourth largest bank, Irish Life & Permanent, with 118 billion dollars in total assets, since this bank will play a rather peculiar role in our story of the Irish financial markets.

Like the FSA in the United Kingdom, the Irish Financial Regulator (FR) had adopted a "principles-based" approach to financial supervision. As described by its chief executive, Patrick Neary, this "places responsibility for the proper management and control of a financial service provider, and the intergrity of its systems, on the board of directors and its senior management."[8] The result of this benevolent attitude was that fast-growing Anglo Irish Bank was supervised by three managers from the FR, who were at the same time also responsible for supervision of the biggest bank, Bank of Ireland. In that same year, 2005, the FR carried out just eight inspections on the 48 financial institutions it supervised and none without advance warning.[9]

Given superficial data on the banks' financial stability, the FR might perhaps be forgiven for its belief that Irish banks were stable and well capitalized. As set out in Table 12, all the four major banks easily fulfilled the BIS requirement of a minimum 8 percent ratio of capital to risk-weighted assets in 2007. Nor did their overall capital–asset ratios shame them in relationship to their UK competitors. As set out in Figure 4, leverage in Britain had risen to an average of 35 before the crisis with some banks at a high 60. The capital–asset ratios of the Irish banks in 2007 would yield leverage ratios of 21 (Bank of Ireland), 17 (AIB), 14

---

[7] Patrick Honohan, "A plan to restore Ireland's banks to health," *Financial Times*, 31 March 2010.
[8] Ross, *The Bankers*, p. 79.
[9] Carswell, *Anglo Republic*, p. 74; Ross, *The Bankers*, p. 80.

Table 12. *Some data for Irish banks, 2007, 2008 and 2009*

Bank	Profit on average cap.%	Cost/income	BIS ratio	Capital–asset ratio[b]
Bank of Ireland[a]				
2007	20.5	50.9	11.10	4.8
2008	0	52.0	15.2	6.5
2009	−34.2	56.7	13.4	5.5
Allied Irish Banks (AIB)				
2007	24.3	51.8	10.1	5.9
2008	9.8	43.2	10.5	5.4
2009	−29.1	N/A	10.2	5.0
Anglo Irish Bank				
2007	21.4	22.3	12.0	7.0
2008	15.4	16.7	12.0	4.1
2009	N/A[c]	N/A	10.7	5.7
Irish Life & Permanent				
2007	18.1	52.2	10.4	3.8
2008	1.7	N/A	N/A	5.6
2009	N/A	N/A	9.2	2.3

[a]March 2008 and 2009, December 2009.
[b]Tier 1 capital over total assets.
[c]Anglo Irish had been nationalized in January 2009.
Source: The Banker, July 2008 to July 2010; Annual Accounts 2009 for Bank of Ireland.

(Anglo Irish) and 26 (Irish Life). With cost–income ratios of around 50, they were around average in efficiency worldwide, the explanation for the low figures for Anglo Irish being that as a bank exclusively directed at commercial customers, it had very few branch offices and likewise few clients (see below). The profitability levels were high but not exceptionally so in an international comparison in this the last international boom year before the crisis. Similar profit levels were reported by the major British banks for 2007: HSBC 25.1 percent, RBS 26.6 percent, Barclays 28.1 percent, HBOS 23.4 percent, Lloyds TSB 29 percent.

However, the above-quoted figures for the growth of lending volumes should have made the FR look a bit harder at the underlying statistics, in particular as regards Anglo Irish. Between 2000 and mid 2007, Anglo Irish had increased its market value (total capitalization) from 0.6 billion euro to 13.3 billion, an increase of 22 times or over 50 percent per year on average. At the annual Davos meeting in January 2007, consultancy Oliver Wyman had nominated Anglo Irish as the best bank in the world![10] In particular, it praised Anglo's focus on business lending and its small number of borrowers, making for efficiency (see above). It also noted its remarkable rate of growth of lending of 38 percent per year during the previous decade. The Nyberg report (p. 32) would add that the top 20 customers made up half of Anglo's loan book with an average loan per client of almost 1 billion euro, dominated by the property developer Sean Quinn and family, owing 2.3 billion euro in May 2008 (which, moreover, exceeded the legal limit for large exposures toward an individual borrower). Most of these borrowers were in property development or construction, paving the way for disaster when the bottom fell out of the property market. The Nyberg report (p. 32), however, also notes the criticism by its competitors of the lax lending standards at Anglo, "the mindset was 'there is a yes in there somewhere.'" Or otherwise stated, "[b]eing a relationship lender, Anglo found it quite difficult to decline a loan to any of its traditional top customers."

The Irish banks, heavily dependent on wholesale deposits and interbank loans, were hard hit by the worldwide loss of liquidity caused by the bankruptcy of Lehman Brothers on 15 September 2008. In a first move to prevent a bank run, the deposit guarantee was lifted to 100 percent of 100,000 euro, which stemmed a classic bank run by depositors but not the withdrawal of wholesale funding which continued unabated. On 19 September, the short-selling of Irish bank shares was forbidden but it stopped the continuous fall in their prices only momentarily.

On the evening of the chaotic 29 September, the government and the supervisory authorities were approached by the heads of the Bank of Ireland and AIB, who emphasized the seriousness of the global situation. They were, in particular, worried about contagion effects from Anglo Irish Bank (whose share price had tanked by 46 percent that very day) as well as from the other bank known to face liquidity problems, the Irish Nationwide Building Society (INBS). They suggested that both banks be nationalized.

---

[10] Carswell, *Anglo Republic*, p. 97.

Early in the morning of 30 September, as the first country in the European Union to take such a measure, the government of Ireland extended its backing guarantee of deposit insurance to cover an unlimited amount, including not only deposits but also bank bonds and dated subordinated debt (thus excluding only perpetual FRNs from counting as upper Tier 2 capital under Basel II). Liabilities worth 440 billion euro were guaranteed for two years in the six major domestic banks and building societies, a sum corresponding to 287 percent of Ireland's then-GDP.[11] Greece followed suit the same day. The European Commission claimed initially that this action was in violation of the free movement of capital but retracted when, a few days later, some other EU countries, including Austria, Germany, Belgium and Denmark, followed the example. Ireland was, however, forced after pressure from the UK to include also foreign-owned subsidiaries in the scheme, not only Irish-owned banks.

The decision has been subjected to a number of evaluations and questions:[12]

- Was the haste warranted? Could one not have waited to gather more information?
- Was the broad scope warranted, in particular the inclusion of subordinated debt?
- Should not a decision of this kind be taken in a spirit of national unity, involving also the opposition?
- Should not a decision of this kind be taken in consort with the ECB and other EU countries?

29 September 2008 was a day of international panic. It is hardly surprising that the Irish government felt that it had to come up with a solution in real time rather than wait and see. Like other governments, and supported by the confidence of the FR in the banks' solvency (see Table 12), the crisis was seen as exclusively a problem of lack of liquidity in otherwise healthy banks. Certainly it would have helped to take the time to accomplish a politically acceptable solution so as to avoid

---

[11] The actual amount guaranteed was later found to be 365 billion euro.
[12] In particular Donovan and Murphy, *The Fall of the Celtic Tiger*, pp. 197 ff. but also Honohan *et al.*, "The Irish banking crisis," pp. 119 ff. and the Nyberg report, pp. 77 ff.

the leader of the opposition being able to state that "[the guarantee] decision is an act of economic treason for which this country is now paying very dearly."[13] But there wasn't time!

The Nyberg report (p. 80) states that had the central bank and the Financial Regulator done their jobs, the crisis might have been avoided:

> In the Commission's view there is no question but that the Authorities should have had a much better idea of the underlying situation of the banks for some considerable time prior to September 29. This would have been a precondition for any crisis management approach based on the real underlying situation. On this basis, a much more systematic and rigorous assessment of the alternative measures suitable for the Irish situation could have been undertaken, possibly several years before. In particular, banks with impaired assets would probably have been required to raise additional capital prior to any guarantee on their liabilities.

But the point is that the central bank and the FR had not done their jobs and in the absence of information there was really no viable alternative to the guarantee.

The broad scope of the guarantee was also questioned. But as Honohan states (point 1.25, p. 14) "it is hard to argue with the view that an extensive guarantee needed to be put in place, since all participants (rightly) felt that they faced the likely collapse of the Irish banking system within days in the absence of decisive immediate action." There were also several historical precedents. Subordinated debt had been included in the guarantees given in the 1990s by Sweden, Finland and other countries. Furthermore, dated subordinated debt were a mere 12 billion euro or 3 percent of the sum guaranteed.

Donovan and Murphy (p. 219) also make the highly relevant point that had the Irish banking system been allowed to fail, the government would have had to pay depositors under the existing deposit guarantee scheme over 60 billion euro. This may be compared with the sum it eventually took to recapitalize the banks, 64 billion euro, as reckoned by the end of 2012 (and before AIB and Bank of Ireland are returned to the private sector which will lower the net cost even further).

---

[13] Donovan and Murphy, *The Fall of the Celtic Tiger*, p. 197.

Following the broad scope of the guarantee and the risk it entailed for the country's finances, on 8 October 2008, Moody's lowered the rating of the Republic of Ireland two steps, from Aa2 to A1.

Also following the haste of 29–30 September, a more thorough investigation was undertaken into the banks' situation, in particular into that of Anglo Irish. This investigation led to several dramatic events: the beginning of a bail-out of the major banks, the creation of a national "bad bank" (NAMA) and the "loans to directors affair," which in combination led to the fall of the senior management of Anglo Irish as well as of most of its board members and also the resignation of the chief executive of the Federal Regulator and of the governor of the Central Bank of Ireland.

It started on 15 December 2008 when Ireland proposed to use 10 billion euro to recapitalize its three biggest banks: 3.5 billion euro each for Bank of Ireland and Allied Irish Banks (AIB) and 1.5 billion for Anglo Irish Bank (raised the month after to 4 billion, see below).[14] The first two banks at that point in time claimed that they didn't need it but later changed their minds.[15] Table 13 shows the spiraling cost of the bail-out, eventually reaching a net of 64 billion euro by the end of

Table 13. *Increasing recapitalization requirements for Irish banks, 2009–11, billion euro*

	BOI	AIB	Anglo	INBS	EBS	IL&P
Phase 1 Early 2009	3.5	3.5	4.0			
Phase 2A March 2010		2.7	7.4	18.0	2.6	0.9
Phase 2B Sept. 2010		3.0	7.3	2.8		0.1
Phase 3 March 2011	5.2	13.3			1.5	4.0

Notes: BOI=Bank of Ireland; AIB=Allied Irish Banks; Anglo=Anglo Irish Bank; INBS=Irish Nationwide Building Society; EBS=Educational Building Society; IL&P=Irish Life & Permanent
Source: Donovan and Murphy, *The Fall of the Celtic Tiger*, p. 225; Honohan, "Recapitalisation of failed banks," p. 12.

---

[14] See also the discussion in Patrick Honohan, "Recapitalisation of failed banks: some lessons from the Irish experience," speech, 7 September 2012; Honohan, "A plan to restore Ireland's banks to health."
[15] Ross, *The Bankers*, p. 207.

2012, 40 percent of that year's GDP. The table itself sums to a gross of 80 billion euro but parts of the aid had been returned by the end of 2012. See also Table 1 where the corresponding data were expressed as a percentage of GDP and compared with other countries' support of their banking sectors. As noted earlier, Iceland and Ireland are in a class by themselves, only comparable to the Asian crises in the 1990s.

The originally proposed injection into Anglo Irish would have given the state a 75 percent stake in the bank. However, finding that the needs of the bank were far larger (the 4 billion euro later injected in May corresponding to its calculated loss for the first half of 2009), the bank was nationalized on 16 January 2009, shareholders losing all value from a company which had been worth 13 billion euro on the Irish Stock Exchange just a year before. But holders of senior bonds and dated subordinated debt were protected – for the time being.

The rest of the capitalizations were connected with "haircuts" on loans taken in connection with the transfer of bad loans to the national "bad bank" NAMA set up in the fall of 2009 and will therefore be discussed below.

For the year 2008, the Irish stock market's appreciation of its major banks had cooled appreciably. Stocks in the Bank of Ireland were down from 10.19 euro at the beginning of the year to 0.83 euro, a fall of 92 percent. Allied Irish Banks was down from 15.67 euro to 1.73 for a fall of 89 percent. Anglo's price went from 10.94 to 0.17 for a fall of 99 percent. And, as noted above and below, the last two were nationalized with shareholders as well as some other investors (see below) being wiped out.

The second issue, "loans to directors," was really three separate issues but stemming from the same business culture, one of profit-seeking, window-dressing, evasion and stealth. Together they led to the resignation on 19–20 December 2008 of Anglo's Chairman, Sean FitzPatrick, and CEO, David Drumm. The bank's finance director and chief risk officer, Willie McAteer, resigned on 7 January 2009 on account of the same affairs but also because of his own 8 million euro loan from the bank, borrowed at an interest of 1.4 percent.[16] On 9 January 2009, the chief executive of the Financial Regulator, Patrick

---

[16] The three will be criminally charged with "unlawful financial assistance" in trials starting in spring 2014.

Neary, resigned. And on 8 June 2009, the governor of the Central Bank of Ireland, John Hurley, announced his intention to retire prematurely in September, although he had been reappointed for a new term as recently as January. His successor, Dr. Patrick Honohan, was totally untainted by the events of recent years, having spent his career at the IMF and the World Bank and as a professor of economics at Trinity College in Dublin.

The first cover-up concerned the bank itself. Since the supervisory authorities preferred loans to be covered by (stable) customer deposits rather than (fickle) interbank borrowings, Anglo Irish had entered into a secret agreement with bank-insurer Irish Life & Permanent (IL&P). Every six months when accounts were to be established, Anglo Irish transferred 7.5 billion euro to IL&P's bank division as an interbank loan. The same amount was immediately returned to Anglo but from the insurance division of IL&P, allowing Anglo to register the transaction as a customer deposit rather than as an interbank borrowing. The size of the transaction is indicated by the fact that it corresponded to one-quarter of the entire loan book at IL&P. Anglo said "thanks" by lending IL&P 3.3 billion euro before its financial year ended on 30 June, thereby enabling it to lower its borrowings from the ECB. "You scratch my back, I'll scratch yours." The finance director of IL&P, Peter Fitzpatrick, as well as the bank's head of Treasury, David Gently, were fired on 12 February 2009; their counterparties at Anglo were already long gone. The CEO of IL&P, Denis Casey, survived temporarily but "resigned" in May 2009; its chair, Gillian Bowler, followed him in October 2010.

In December 2013, Peter Fitzpatrick and Denis Casey as well as the treasurer of Anglo Irish John Bowe were charged with conspiracy to defraud the public and (for Mr. Bowe) false accounting.

The second affair concerned the bank's "founding father" and dominant personality, CEO from 1986 until 2005 and then chairman of the board, Sean FitzPatrick. It turned out that he had personally borrowed no less than 155 million euro from his own bank, a loan which should have been declared under "loans to directors" in the annual accounts. However, before each 30 September (the bank's day of reckoning), he had seen to it that the loan was transferred to friends in the competitor bank Irish Nationwide. After a few weeks, the loan was returned to Anglo Irish and hence it was never reported either to the FR or to shareholders. This hiding of the true situation had taken place from 2000 to 2008. The chairman of Irish Nationwide, Dr. Michael Walsh, resigned his position on 17 February 2009.

The third problem was not of Anglo's own doing but the solution was. Anglo's biggest customer was Ireland's then-richest man, Sean Quinn. Unknown to the market and to Anglo, he had built up a speculative position in Anglo's shares. It was unknown, because he speculated through so-called Contracts for Difference (CFD), a derivative similar to a forward. Like a future/forward, the speculator only paid a margin but unlike a future, the underlying shares existed and were held by a broker. But like a future, if the price goes up you win and if the price falls you lose. Quinn's position in early 2008 turned out to be over 25 percent of the entire bank and as the share price had been falling since spring 2007, he had had to put up a gradually larger variation margin to the broker. He wanted out but as both he and the bank realized, dumping his 240 million shares onto the market when the price was already falling would spell disaster. The solution – revealed only after the bank's nationalization – was to lend money – 451 million euro – to a select group of 10 loyal customers, the "Golden Circle," also called the "Maple 10," who purchased the majority of Quinn's shares. The loans were non-recourse, meaning that the bank had no further claims on the borrowers other than the shares themselves, the value of which continued to fall. The bank held all the risk and had no upside. The board of Anglo Irish had approved the loans and the Financial Regulator was informed, a situation which cost most of them their jobs.

Connected with these scandals was the intimate involvement of the supervisors. In March 2008 after the forced sale of Bear Stearns to JPMorgan Chase, the shares of Irish banks in general and of Anglo Irish in particular came under pressure. The CEO of Anglo contacted the governor of the Central Bank to get a statement to calm speculators. The governor, before releasing his statement, sent it over to Anglo's CEO, who approved (sic) it. In the statement, the governor said that "the Irish banking sector remains robust and has no material exposures to the [US] sub-prime market."[17] He was out of a job a year later.

However, the bailing-out of the other two major banks from early 2008 (see below) also left its corpses. On 30 April 2009 the chairman,

---

[17] Carswell, *Anglo Republic*, p. 147.

CEO and finance director of Allied Irish Banks (AIB) all quit. On 19 May 2009, the chairman of the Bank of Ireland "resigned."

Having temporarily stopped the panic by its injection of capital into AIB and Bank of Ireland and the subsequent nationalization of Anglo Irish Bank (on 16 January 2009), the government turned to a more long-term solution for the banking system. On 8 April, finance minister Lenihan announced the setting up of a "bad bank," the National Asset Management Agency (NAMA) to purchase non-performing and toxic assets from the banks but at a discount to reflect their estimated long-run value. Since this meant a loss for the selling banks, they would have to be recapitalized by the state if they could not find fresh private capital. The reason for this set-up was, as we shall see below, that NAMA is owned only partly by the government, and partly by private investors.[18] The original plans were to purchase loans with a book value of 77 billion euro for 54 billion, implying an average discount of 30 percent. The actual discounts were to be far larger, as seen below. Of the total of 77 billion, 28 billion was to be taken from Anglo Irish, corresponding to 40 percent of the bank's loan book.

The promise to take over the banks' non-performing assets was very timely. On 29 May (2009), Anglo Irish revealed a loss of 4.9 billion euro for the past six-month period. Among the major write-downs were the loans to the "Golden Circle," 308 million euro, whose corresponding assets, Anglo shares serving as collateral for the loans, had become worthless with the nationalization and, as mentioned, the loans were non-recourse. Another 31 million euro was similarly written off, corresponding to "loans to directors" and senior management of Anglo to purchase, now worthless, Anglo stock. During that summer, Anglo received 4 billion euro in recapitalization, the first of many injections of fresh capital, as it would turn out. A year later, on 31 March 2010, Anglo Irish Bank reported results for the 15 months to December 2009 (having shifted its accounts from end September to annual). The losses for the period were 12.7 billion euro, caused by write-downs of 15.1 billion euro. The loss was the largest ever in Irish

---

[18] Sweden had handled the problem differently in 1992, transferring loans to the bad bank Securum at face value and then writing them down in Securum, which was then recapitalized. But since both Securum and the selling bank, Nordbanken, were 100 percent owned by the state, the transfer price was irrelevant.

corporate history, until Anglo itself struck a new record one year later. On 9 February 2011, Anglo announced a loss for 2010 of 17.6 billion euro. During the year 2010, it had also lost 16 billion euro in deposit withdrawals. In total, Anglo Irish would require the largest bail-out in the world, relatively speaking: 29 billion euro or 30 percent of its total assets. Second in this league of laggards worldwide was Hypo Real Estate with 15 percent of total assets in government support.

On 22 April 2010, the EU statistical agency Eurostat ruled that capital injections into the totally nationalized Anglo Irish Bank must be treated as government expenditure, hence raising both the budget deficit and the public debt. The projected Irish budget deficit for 2010 became an unheard of 32 percent of GDP (the actual deficit would later turn out to be 30.8 percent, falling to 13.4 percent in 2011 and 7.6 percent in 2012). See Figure 24c. The government debt-to-GDP ratio would continue to rise to well over 100 percent, landing at 125 percent in early 2014 (according to Eurostat), second only to Greece, Italy and Portugal.

Cognizant of the potential effect on Ireland's public debt, NAMA was set up with 49 percent public ownership, the majority of 51 percent being privatly owned (originally) by companies belonging to the spheres of Irish Life, Bank of Ireland and Allied Irish Banks.[19] Table 14 summarizes the situation as specified in the annual accounts for 2012. The dominance of Anglo, being responsible for almost one half of the assets transferred, is obvious, as is the fact that it encountered a higher discount on its assets than the other participating banks.

The losses on the asset transfers in combination with increased capital adequacy requirements ahead of the changes enforced by Basel III (a minimum core Tier 1 ratio of 8 percent, a minimum equity core Tier 1 ratio of 7 percent) led to banks having to raise more capital: Allied Irish Banks 7.4 billion euro, Bank of Ireland 2.7 billion euro, Irish Nationwide 2.6 billion euro, the Educational Building Society (EBS) 0.9 billion euro and the nationalized Anglo Irish Bank Corp 18.3 billion euro.

---

[19] Or, to be more precise, the publicly owned NAMA owns 49 percent and private investors 51 percent of NAMA Investment Ltd., which with subsidiaries owns the various loans taken over.

Table 14. *Loan acquisitions from participating institutions at end 2011, billion euro*

	AIB	Anglo	BOI	EBS	INBS	Total
Loan balances transferred	20.4	34.1	9.9	0.9	8.7	74.0
Price paid	9.0	13.4	5.6	0.4	3.4	31.8
Discount (%)	56	61	43	57	61	57
Loss to sellers	11.4	20.7	4.3	0.5	5.3	42.2

Source: www.nama.ie/about-our-work/key-figures/[20]

On 13 May 2010, the Irish government took an 18 percent equity stake in Allied Irish Banks (AIB) and on 9 June the government's position in Bank of Ireland rose to 36 percent after a capital injection of another 3.5 billion euro. This was, however, not sufficient for AIB (as the data in Table 14 indicate) and on 30 September, the government stated that it might have to inject more capital into the bank, thereby increasing the state's share to possible majority control. In June–July 2011, the Educational Building Society (EBS) was sold to AIB, the price being 1 euro. Simultaneously, the Central Bank in its renewed role as supervisor[21] required AIB to acquire an additional 14.8 billion euro in equity. These funds were raised from various government sources, leading to the state holding 99.8 percent of the common stock of AIB. Irish Life & Permanent, having absorbed Irish Nationwide in February, was nationalized in June.

Bank of Ireland, however, having been more conservative during the property boom, as Table 14 bears witness, escaped from the state's control. At the maximum, the state owned 36 percent of the bank, but equity raised from private investors reduced this share to 15 percent by the end of 2011.

On 1 July 2011, the two nationalized banks Anglo Irish Bank and Irish Nationwide Building Society were merged into the Irish Bank Resolution Corp., charged with the task of unwinding their assets. However, in February 2013, the Irish Parliament (Dail) voted to

---

[20] The Nyberg report, p. 54, has slightly different figures but I trust NAMA.

[21] The Financial Regulator had separated from the Central Bank as recently as 2003 but returned in October 2010.

liquidate the corporation. Remaining assets and 800 employees were transferred to the "bad bank" NAMA.

Since perpetual subordinated bonds had not been included in the guarantee from 2008, their holders together with shareholders were subject to losses. Between 2009 and 2011, "haircuts" of between 30 and 80 percent were administered to investors of subordinated bonds in AIB and Bank of Ireland. On average, the haircut was 55 percent, leading to a loss for investors of 14 billion euro.[22] When the assets of the two failed banks, Anglo Irish and INBS, were transferred to the Irish Bank Resolution Corp., the government proposed that even holders of senior unsecured bonds would be subjected to a haircut, an action strongly supported by the IMF. However, the government left the issue hanging, having failed to get the support from the ECB for such a potentially severe disruption of bond markets.

But despite the haircuts, the costs of the bank rescue were rapidly exceeding the means of the Irish government, in particular after the inclusion of the costs of recapitalizing Anglo Irish in the budget deficit and debt in April 2010 (see above). By September 2010, the cost of recapitalization was set at 50 billion euro, to which was added the increasing budget deficit even excluding the costs for saving the banks. Despite the denial from finance minister Lenihan of any need for an international bail-out as late as 9 November 2010, discussions were underway and on 28 November, Ireland formally applied for help from the "troika" (EU, ECB and IMF). Out of a total agreed bail-out sum of 85 billion euro, 35 billion would be used to recapitalize banks, aiming for a core Tier 1 ratio of 12 percent, and 50 billion to restore the consequences for the budget. The interest rate charged was, at 5.8 percent, some 3 percentage points above German levels; it was later reset to 3 percent. The sum of 22.5 billion euro came from each of the European Financial Stability Mechanism (EFSM), the European Financial Stability Facility (EFSF) and the International Monetary Fund (IMF). The sum of 17.5 billion euro was to be taken from the Irish National Pension Reserve Fund and the rest was bilateral support from the United Kingdom, Denmark and Sweden.

---

[22] http://namawinelake.wordpress.com/2013/01/21/burning-the-bondholders-by-how-much-have-they-been-singed/. See also Niall Lenihan, "Claims of depositors, subordinated creditors, senior creditors and Central Banks in bank resolutions," speech delivered at the AEDBF Conference, Athens, 5–6 October 2012.

Until mid 2007, there was virtually no spread between German and Irish bonds. Then the yield spread started rising to reach a peak of 11 percentage points in 2011, only to fall back with recovery to a spread (as of July 2014) of just over 1 percentage point, below the levels of both Italy and Spain. The Euro group of finance ministers decided on 14 November 2013 that Ireland could exit the program of close supervision as of 15 December 2013.

Overall grade of the handling of Irish banks: A (on a scale of A to F=Fail)

Much criticism can be levied at the Ministry of Finance, the Financial Regulator and the Central Bank for allowing one of the worst financial crises in recent history to develop unnoticed. But the purpose of this book is to evaluate the *response* to the crisis and, given the gravity of the situation, the initial lack of knowledge as to the size and scope of the problem, the reaction of the financial markets, the response of its EU partners and the ECB, most was handled correctly and in a reasonably timely manner.

- Ireland was first out in Europe with its all-encompassing guarantee in September 2008 and, given the nervousness of the markets, to include parts of junior (subordinated) debt was probably necessary.
- It took only a month of investigations to realize that the banks' situation was much more serious than mere liquidity and propose recapitalizations of the three major banks by the state.
- Anglo Irish was nationalized as early as January 2009 when the size of the capital support needed became evident, Allied Irish Banks and the two building societies followed later on.
- A "bad bank," NAMA, was proposed already in spring 2009 and was functional by the end of the year. It has been criticized for taking over large property loans irrespective of whether they were non-performing or not, but given the private involvement (which itself was necessary to avoid having the liabilities of NAMA added to those of the state), this was probably the best solution.[23]

---

[23] Onaran, *Zombie Banks*, p. 61.

- Through the construction of NAMA and the transfer of assets, the banking sector as a whole was forced to participate in the salvage operation (like in Denmark).
- When banks were found non-viable, in particular the remnants of Anglo Irish, they were liquidated. It could and should have happened sooner.
- Shareholders were wiped out but investors in subordinated debt also lost out.
- Senior management, board members, regulators who were responsible for the mess were forced to resign or retire; some of them are being sued for criminal liability.
- It remains to be discussed whether senior bond investors should also have been forced to take haircuts, but, as noted earlier, this decision was really taken away from the Irish government by the ECB and by its EU colleagues, in particular Germany, opposing subjecting investors in senior bank bonds to losses, fearing the contagion effects on bank bonds in other PIIGS countries. The decision to spare unsecured bondholders has later been criticized, in particular by the IMF.[24]

The most relevant grades are, in the current context, those of the market and they have also given an "A" to Ireland. Ten-year bond yields have come down from a peak of 14 percent to just over 2 percent, implying a doubling of prices since the crisis. As noted, Ireland was again rated investment grade by Standard & Poor's as well as by Moody's in July 2014. It has left the EU and IMF intensive care unit.[25]

---

[24] "Ireland 'unfairly treated' over bondholders in bust banks," interview with Alay Chopra, head of the IMF mission, *Financial Times*, 13 December 2013.
[25] *Financial Times*, 20 November 2013, "Ireland's comeback runs into growth test."

9 | *Greece*
Emporiki, Eurobank, Agricultural Bank

The Greek story[1]

In Iceland and Ireland, two prosperous economies with stable government finances were ruined by an excessive and opportunistic banking
sector. Greece constitutes the exact opposite: mostly healthy banks
were brought to ruin by a spendthrift state. The Greek story has been
told elsewhere and does not need to be repeated; here we are only
concerned with the effects of the sovereign debt crisis on its banks and
the resolution of its banking system.

Greece entered the euro area in 2001 by means of what have been
shown to be falsified statistics. Rather than fulfilling the Maastricht
criteria, Greece had a budget deficit in 2001 of 4.5 percent of GDP
(above the limit of 3 percent) and a government debt-to-GDP ratio of
103 percent, way above the 60 percent limit. It was also the only country in the euro area to break the required inflation threshold (a maximum of 1.5 percentage points above the average of the three countries
with the lowest inflation rate) every single year in the new century.[2]

Despite a healthy GDP growth rate of some 4 percent on average
during the years preceding the financial crisis, excessive government
spending, inefficiency in tax collection and lack of competitiveness led
to a budget deficit of 9.8 percent of GDP in 2008, rising to 15.7 percent
in 2009. Simultaneously, the government debt-to-GDP ratio exploded
to reach 130 percent of GDP in 2009 and 174 percent of GDP in 2014.
From the euro start year 1999 until 2009, unit labor costs in Greece
rose by 50 percent more than Germany's (and also 20 percent more

---

[1] Vicky Pryce, *Greekonomics: The Euro Crisis and Why Politicians Don't Get
It* (London: Biteback, 2012); Nikos Tsafos, *Beyond Debt: The Greek Crisis in
Context* (North Charleston, NC: CreateSpace, 2013); IMF Country Report
13/20, January 2013, www.imf.org/external/pubs/ft/scr/2013/cr1320.pdf
[2] Ales Bulir and Jaromík Hurník, "The Maastricht inflation criterion: how
unpleasant is purgatory," IMF Working Paper, WP/06/154, June 2006.

than Spain's and 30 percent more than Italy's, according to OECD data). In parallel, overconsumption and cheap borrowing led to a current-account deficit of 15 percent in 2007, second only to Iceland's.

During the adjustment phase, caused mainly by the cuts in public expenditures ordained by the "troika" (EU Commission, ECB, IMF), GDP fell a cumulative 20 percent until 2012 and a projected further fall of an additional 5 percent in 2013–14, returning to growth only in 2015. Unemployment rose to 28 percent with youth unemployment above 60 percent. As a result, on 27 April 2010, Standard & Poor's lowered the rating of Greece from BBB- to BB+, i.e. "junk," the first time this had happened to a eurozone country; Ireland and Portugal would follow. Fortunately, help was on its way. On 2 May 2010, the European Union's eurozone members, the ECB and the IMF agreed a 110 billion euro support package for Greece, conditional on austerity measures in the budget and the sale of 50 billion euro's worth of state assets. The interest rate was set at 5.5 percent. Of this sum, Greece set aside 10 billion euro to support its banking system as the austerity plan forced it to cut government expenditure by 13 percentage points of GDP in three years.

The ECB also helped by breaking its own rules in deciding that Greek banks could use Greek sovereign debt as collateral for borrowing even though the bonds had been downgraded to "junk." The ECB has also purchased over 30 billion euro's worth of Greek sovereign bonds. On 13 June 2010, Greece was again downgraded by Standard & Poor's to CCC, then the lowest rating in the world, on account of political unrest and uncertainty as to whether the necessary budget adjustments would be made.

On 21 February 2012, the "troika" agreed to a second bail-out of Greece worth 130 billion euro for a total of 240 billion euro for the two packages. However, as a precondition for the second aid package and to bring the debt/GDP ratio to a sustainable level, private holders of Greek government bonds, mainly banks, insurance companies and pension funds, were asked to take a "voluntary" "haircut" of 53.5 percent of the face value on their holdings, corresponding to a write-down of 75 percent of actual values or 107 billion euro. The operation would lower the Greek debt/GDP ratio by 30 percentage points.

During the discussions as to the size of the write-down and uncertainty over how many investors would accept the proposed debt swap, the Greek 10-year bond yield rose dramatically, reaching over 30 percent on some occasions (see Figure 26).

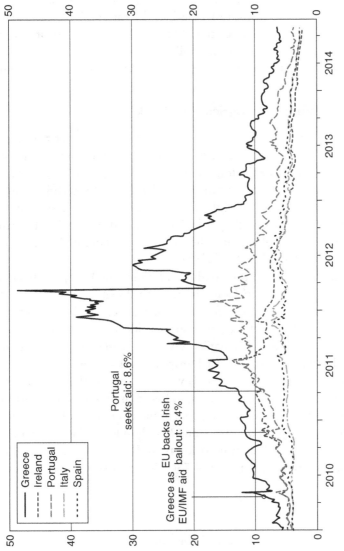

Figure 26. Ten-year bond yields in the euro area, 2010–14

Source: Reuters http://graphics.thomsonreuters.com/F/09/EUROZONE_REPORT2.html

Standard & Poor's cut the rating of Greece to "selective default" (SD) on account of the write-down of government debt. Also on account of this "haircut," but even more so because of the retroactive introduction of collective action clauses[3] forcing unwilling investors to participate in the debt restructuring, the International Swaps and Derivatives Dealers' Association (ISDA) declared a "credit event," leading to net payments of 3.5 billion euro for those investors who had bought credit default swap protection for Greek sovereign bonds.

Emporiki, Eurobank, Agricultural Bank

The Greek banking system is highly concentrated, with the five largest banks having over 70 percent of the market even before the mergers in recent years. While the four largest banks, judged to be viable "core banks" (National Bank of Greece, Alpha Bank, Eurobank Ergasias and Piraeus Bank), survived the first years relatively well, some of the smaller banks (such as Emporiki Bank, owned by the French bank Crédit Agricole, Probank and the Agricultural Bank of Greece) were hardest hit and lost over half of their capital base.

As part of the stress test conducted by the new European Banking Authority on European banks in July 2011, banks were forced to publish detailed information about their sovereign bond holdings, by country and by maturity, enabling outsiders to conduct their own stress tests on individual banks, given estimated write-downs and required capital ratios.[4] The 91 European banks surveyed held a total of 98 billion euro of Greek bonds which, valued at the going market rate, would lead to a combined capital need of 50 billion euro just for the Greek exposure. Adding haircuts in the banking book (assets held to maturity) also for Portuguese and Irish bonds would lead to a total capital need of 75 billion euro for these three sovereigns. Europe's banks at that time held a total of 736 billion euro in sovereign bonds

---

[3] Having reached agreement from a certain proportion of bondholders (66.7 percent), the rest of the investors in bonds following Greek law could be forced to accept the proposal. This did not apply to bonds issued under international law where nevertheless some 70 percent accepted the deal.

[4] Reuters constructed a highly useful capital-requirements calculator, available at http://graphics.thomsonreuters.com/11/07/BV_STRSTST0711_VF.html

issued by the "PIIGS" countries (Portugal, Ireland, Italy, Greece and Spain).

The National Bank of Greece, for instance, passed the stress test with a core Tier 1 capital ratio of 11 percent. But the bank held 12.9 billion euro of Greek sovereign bonds in its banking book which, if marked to market, would almost wipe out its entire core Tier 1 capital.[5] This was, moreover, before the crisis accelerated and before the rescheduling of the Greek debt. About one-third of the total write-down of 107 billion euro hit Greek banks, some of which also needed additional capital on account of the agreement with the troika that they attain a core Tier 1 ratio of 10 percent by mid 2013. The impacts were calculated *a priori* and may be compared with actual amounts spent in recapitalization as of 2012 (in billion euro) as shown in Table 15.

Accounting for the cost of mergers (see below), some 7 billion euro, the actual cost came to just over 41 billion euro, leaving a reserve of 9 billion, since 50 billion euro of the 240 billion had been allocated in bank support. This reserve is likely to be needed after the new stress

Table 15. *Estimated and actual capital[a] demand by Greek banks*

	Estimated capital demand	Actual amount spent
National Bank of Greece	8.1	8.5
Eurobank EFG	7.2	5.8
Piraeus	6.2	6.2
ATE (Agricultural Bank)	5.5	8.0
Alpha	4.2	4.0
Hellenic Postbank	3.1	4.2
Others	–	4.5
TOTAL (billion euro)	34.3	41.2

[a]http://graphics.thomsonreuters.com/11/07/BV_STRSTST0711_VF.html
Source: Hellenic Financial Stability Fund, Annual report 2012, p. 7. www.hfsf.gr/files/hfsf_annual_report_2012_en.pdf and *Financial Times*, 17 September 2013, "Third time lucky? The latest plan to rescue Greece."

[5] The actual loss turned out to be over 10 billion euro.

tests planned for 2014, this time conducted by the ECB. The recapitalizations have been approved by the EU Commission.[6]

During 2012–13, a number of smaller banks were absorbed into the four "core" banks, giving them a market share of 75 percent:

- The National Bank of Greece bought the viable parts of FBB and Probank.
- Piraeus Bank acquired the good parts of Agricultural Bank, Geniki Bank, Millennium Bank and the Greek subsidiaries of Cyprus banks Bank of Cyprus and Popular Bank.
- Alpha Bank purchased Emporiki Bank from Crédit Agricole, which before the sale was recapitalized by almost 3 billion euro by the French bank.
- Eurobank purchased the New Hellenic Post Bank and the New Proton Bank (the term "new" indicating nationalized and reconstructed banks, owned by the HFSF).

Three of the four "core" banks had, however, by the end of 2013 succeded in raising at least 10 percent of their capital needs from private sources, thereby avoiding being formally nationalized. Eurobank had been taken over in toto by the HFSF, however. On 29 April 2014, Greek Eurobank attracted more than 7 billion euro of orders from big institutional investors and hedge funds for a 2.9 billion rights issue that returned the country's third-largest bank to mostly private hands, with the stake held by the Hellenic Financial Stability Fund shrinking to 35 percent.

At least two of the core banks, National Bank of Greece and Piraeus Bank, have set up "bad banks" to handle non-performing loans, estimated to have risen to 29 percent of all loans by the end of 2013.

Overall grade of the handling of Greek banks:
F (on a scale of A to F=Fail)

The failing grade is not caused by any errors by the Greek government or the Central Bank of Greece, which is also the country's FSA, since the handling of the Greek crisis has been dictated entirely by the "troika." But the so-called PSI, private sector involvement, forcing a

---

[6] http://europa.eu/rapid/press-release_IP-12-860_en.htm

rescheduling of the Greek public debt on private investors, must be regarded as a major political error. Even with European banks' capital requirements (core Tier 1) set at a low 7.5 percent, the 107 billion euro wiped off the Greek government debt by the rescheduling is *entirely* met by a corresponding loss and hence need for (state) recapitalization of European banks: RBS 8.8 billion euro, Deutsche Bank 5.9 billion, Société Générale 5.5 billion, Commerzbank 5.1 billion, UniCredit 4.7, Bankia 4.6, Banco Popular 4.4, to take the largest needs. Also the continued fall in Greek GDP, now in its sixth year of recession, the rising unemployment rate, and the government debt which still stood at 174 percent of GDP at the end of the first quarter of 2014 according to Eurostat, all indicate a total failure of the program(s). To this should be added the uncertainty and hence increased interest cost for countries such as Spain, Portugal and Italy caused by the risk of a renewed "private sector involvement" for the other PIIGS countries.

To quote a report by the European Commission's own Joint Research Center (JRC):[7]

Results show that the haircuts on sovereign debts of EU MS [member states] in crisis would heavily worsen the stability of their banking systems but could also sometimes affect financial stability of other EU countries. We also show that the creation of a temporary capital buffer in the form of a capital target necessitated by the exceptional circumstances prevailing in some EU MS represent a step forward to Basel III rules.[8]

---

[7] European Commission (Stefano Zedda *et al.*), "The EU sovereign debt crisis: potential effects on EU banking systems and policy options," JRC Technical reports 2012, www.iadb.org/intal/intalcdi/PE/2013/11853.pdf

[8] Several academic studies also highlight the increased risk that large holdings of sovereign debt present to banks, in particular since sovereigns funded in the bank's home currency are regarded as risk free under Basel II and III. Capital requirements corresponding to the true risk could alleviate the situation. See James R. Barth, Apanard (Penny) Prabhavivadhana and Greg Yun, "The eurozone financial crisis: role of interdependencies between bank and sovereign risk," *Journal of Financial Economic Policy*, 4:1 (2012), pp. 76–97; Viral Acharya, Philipp Schnabl and Itamar Drechsler, "A tale of two overhangs: the nexus of financial sector and sovereign credit risks," Stern School of Business, April 2012; Daniel Gros, "Banking union with a sovereign virus: the self-serving regulatory treatment of sovereign debt in the euro area," *CEPS Policy Brief* no. 289, 27 March 2013.

As expected, the major effect of the haircut is within the country. Spillover important effects can be observed in the case of a haircut on Greek sovereign debts for Cyprus banks, and Italian sovereign debts for Belgian and Luxembourg banks. The effect is clearly non-linear in the amount of the haircut, due to the threshold effect exercised by the capital level of the bank owning the sovereigns.

10 | *Portugal*
Caixa Geral, Banco Espirito Santo, Millennium Bank

The Portuguese story

After Greece, Portugal is together with Italy and Spain the country with the highest ratio of government debt to GDP, over 130 percent at the beginning of 2014 as compared to 94 percent in the euro area as a whole (and a maximum of 60 percent according to the Maastricht criteria). Also, its competitiveness (relative unit labor cost) decreased since the formation of the euro area by 20 percent in relation to Germany, just like Spain and only slightly less than Italy. The budget deficit increased sharply in 2009 to 10 percent of GDP and the unemployment rate rose from 7 to a maximum of 18 percent before falling back somewhat.

What sets Portugal apart from some other PIIGS countries is firstly that just like Greece and Italy but in contrast to Spain, it already had a high debt ratio to begin with, 70 percent in 2008 as contrasted to Spain's 40 percent. Secondly, as was seen above in Figures 17 and 18, a much larger share of the government debt of Portugal was held by foreigners than in Italy or Greece. This means that the government has less control over the situation and must respond more quickly.

Hence the Portuguese government had little alternative but to demand a bail-out from its European colleagues when Moody's lowered the country's rating two notches to A1 in July 2010, by another three notches to Baa1 in April 2011 and by another four notches to Ba2 (i.e. "junk") in July 2011. In the agreement with the "troika" from 5 May 2011, 12 billion euro out of the 78 billion euro granted in aid from the IMF and the two EU Financial Stability funds would be used to recapitalize Portuguese banks, according to the agreement. Banks would have to attain a 9 percent core Tier 1 ratio by the end of 2011 and 10 percent by the end of 2012.

In December 2011, the European Banking Authority (EBA) published the amount of capital required for the EU banks in order to fulfill a core Tier 1 capital adequacy ratio of 9 percent. For Portugal this amounted to 7 billion in total and the figures shown in Table 16 for the major banks (in billion euro).

The first column represents the capital needs calculated by the EBA. The second column is taken from the Reuters capital-requirements calculator setting all "haircuts" to zero but the core Tier 1 ratio to 10 percent. The third column is taken from EU Commission documents approving the recapitalization, showing amounts actually transferred.

Ironically, the only one of the major banks not bailed out in Table 16 above turned out to need the largest bail-out when in August 2014 Banco Espirito Santo (BES) revealed a loss of 3.6 billion euro for the first half-year, leading to a Tier 1 ratio of 5 percent, below the minimum 7 percent. The bank's share price had fallen by 75 percent since May. The government offered a capital bail-out from the remainder of the 12 billion euro fund set aside for bank recapitalization during Portugal's EU support program. A new bridge bank, Novo Banco, has been set up, owned by the central bank and capitalized by 4.9 billion euro from the fund. It will receive deposits and viable assets and liabilities, whereas troubled assets (including intergroup loans) will remain in BES and written down by bailing in shareholders totally and owners of junior debt to at least 80 percent of face value according to market prices. Holders of senior debt were, however, spared and the price of the corresponding senior bonds reverted to (almost) par.[1]

Table 16. *Estimated and actual capital demand by Portuguese banks*

	To attain 9%	To attain 10%[a]	Received 2012–13[a]
Millennium BCP	2.1	3.2	3.0
Caixa Geral[a]	1.8	3.0	1.7
Banco Espirito Santo	1.6	n a	0[a]
Banco BPI	n a	n a	1.5
Banif	n a	n a	1.1

[a]http://graphics.thomsonreuters.com/11/07/BV_STRSTST0711_VF.html

[1] "Post-mortem begins into BES's fall from grace," *Financial Times*, 5 August 2014; www.bloomberg.com/news/2014-08-06/espirito-santo-shows-eu-s-need-for-speed-under-new-banking-rules.html

Overall grade of the handling of Portuguese banks: B (on a scale of A to F=Fail)

Portugal has made impressive attempts to adjust its imbalances. The budget deficit has been cut in half, even exceeding the ratios agreed in the bail-out. The unemployment rate has peaked and started to decline and the GDP growth was set to resume in 2014, according to OECD forecasts. The banking system is well capitalized after the injections of fresh equity but may suffer from the still-rising level of non-performing loans. The country has been able to return to the international bond market despite a continued "junk" rating, helped also by the purchase of sovereigns by the ECB to the tune of over 30 billion euro. Bond yields have come down but are still substantially higher than Spain's or Italy's. The reason is mainly the risk of a new bail-out and perhaps also the risk of a restructuring à la Greece.[2] What has been lacking in the bank resolution is also the setting up of banks for the non-performing loans. The problems faced by Banco Espirito Santo in summer 2014 show clearly that the problems are not totally over but also that the government and the central bank had learnt the lesson from the earlier bail-outs.[3]

---

[2] "Portugal edges closer to a second bailout," *Financial Times*, 22 November 2013.

[3] "Banco Espírito Santo storm stirs Portugal's bailout memories," *Financial Times*, 11 July 2014.

11 | *Spain*
*Bankia and the other ex-*cajas

The Spanish story[1]

As noted in the preceding chapter, Spanish bond yields are substantially below the Portuguese levels but similar to Italian, helped not least by large purchases by the ECB of sovereign bonds, 44 billion euro in the case of Spain in 2013 (as compared to 100 billion euro for Italy). This situation may change, however, as Spain is currently (July 2014) ranked at the second-lowest investment-grade level by both Moody's and Standard & Poor's, Baa2/BBB. Yet the eurozone finance ministers decided on 14 November 2013 that Spain, together with Ireland, may leave the intensive-care unit, and were able to borrow on their own. It should be remembered that the aid that Spain received (see below) was exclusively for recapitalization of the banking system, not for the state itself. Also the amount actually used, 41 billion euro, was much less than was granted, 100 billion.

Spain has two features that one would have thought should dampen the effect of the global financial crisis on the Spanish economy but also two factors which could make it worse. On the positive side, we have the government debt-to-GDP ratio which was below 40 percent when the crisis struck in 2008 and is only slightly above the euroland average even in 2014. The other positive feature was the system of capital "dynamic provisioning," forcing banks to increase capital cushions during the good years. Unfortunately, it was not enough.

On the bad side, there was firstly the loss of competitiveness vis-à-vis countries like Germany, unit labor costs (ULC) rising by over 30 percent more than Germany's during the decade. This in turn led

---

[1] Eloísa Ortega and Juan Peñalosa, "The Spanish economic crisis: key factors and growth challenges in the Euro area," Banco de España, Documentos ocasionales, nos. 1201, 2012, www.bde.es/f/webbde/SES/Secciones/Publicaciones/PublicacionesSeriadas/DocumentosOcasionales/12/Fich/do1201e.pdf

to a current-account deficit of 10 percent of GDP for several years, despite the booming tourist sector (61 million tourists in 2013, second in Europe only to France). However, the high unemployment rate at 27 percent led to an "internal devaluation" by 2013, forcing down relative ULC by over 15 percent from 2008.

The other problem, as any casual visitor to the Spanish Mediterranean coast could witness, was the construction boom. With house prices rising by 200 percent in the decade up to and including 2007, half a million new properties were built each year in a country of only 16 million households, half of them for foreigners and tourists. One of Europe's highest rates of homeownership helped feed the boom. Since the start of the crisis until 2013, house prices fell by 30 percent and construction come to a halt with a large number of buildings left unfinished for lack of demand.

Despite negative growth from mid 2008, Spain long avoided being downgraded on account of its strong starting position. But on 18 October 2011, almost to the day three years since the then prime minister Zapatero promised to guarantee Spanish banks' borrowing up to 100 billion euro, Moody's downgraded the sovereign debt of Spain from a high Aa2 to A1. The decision in June 2012 by the eurozone finance ministers to agree to a loan to recapitalize Spain's ailing banks of up to 100 billion euro (of which, however, only 41 billion has been drawn) led on 14 June 2012 to Moody's downgrading Spain to Baa3, just a notch above "junk."

Bankia and the other ex-*cajas*[2]

Like Germany, Spain has a very fragmented banking sector, where the five major banks had but 45 percent of total assets in 2010 (see Chapter 2). And just like Germany, the rest was dominated by local savings banks, *cajas de ahorro*. Somewhat ironically, one could say that the Spanish banking sector consisted of two giants (Banco Santander

---

[2] J. Carles Maixé-Altés, "Competition and choice: banks and savings banks in Spain," *Journal of Management History* 16:1 (2010), pp. 29–43; Fund for Orderly Bank Restructuring (FROB), Annual accounts, April 2013, www.frob.es/financiera/docs/20130425%20_Presentacion_abril2013.pdf; José Luis Heras Celemin, *El caso Bankia y algo más...o menos* (Madrid: Editorial Club Universitario, 2013).

and BBVA) and a large number of dwarfs. The first two banks were number 15 and 30 in the world by total assets in 2008 (according to *The Banker*, July 2009) and are among the G-SIFIs listed by the Financial Stability Board as requiring extra capital cushions under Basel III. The combined assets of these two banks were in 2008 equal to more than the total aggregate assets of the other 43 Spanish banks listed in that issue of *The Banker*, most of them *cajas*.

We have already encountered Grupo Santander in the consortium that bought ABN AMRO in October 2007 but coming out of the deal on the profitable side in contrast to the other two banks, RBS and Fortis, because it knew what it wanted. Santander got the South American and Italian operations of ABN AMRO but the latter (Banca Antonveneta) was immediately sold to Monte dei Paschi di Siena for 9 billion euro, with a profit of 36 percent for only two months' holding. Santander UK, operating in the United Kingdom as a subsidiary rather than a branch, bought Bradford & Bingley's 97 branch offices and 20 billion pounds' worth of deposits through its Abbey National subsidiary for 612 million pounds. It also bought failed mortgage lender Alliance & Leicester's viable operations. The bank is highly international, with only 13 percent of its customers and 15 percent of its profits coming from Spain (Annual accounts 2012). This fact, together with its focus on retail banking, may explain its having survived the Spanish crisis. Similarly, the second largest bank, BBVA (Banco Bilbao Viscaya Argentaria), has only 30 percent of its income coming from Spain. BBVA was also the first bank in setting up an internal "bad bank" in November 2011, into which it planned to deposit 30 billion euro in non-performing real estate assets. Both banks have survived the crisis with increased non-performing loans but without state aid, except for borrowing from the ECB.

So our main focus is on the savings banks, their problems and their resolution. Of the 47 *cajas de ahorro* existing in 2007, only two remain intact as such after the crisis, the rest having been merged and transformed into commercial banks or liquidated. As stated by Juan Maria Nin, CEO of the largest *caja*, the Barcelona-based La Caixa: "Spain enters this process about 18 months later than neighbouring countries. The system in Spain was better provisioned and much better supervised. But we had our own subprime."[3] That is, *cajas*.

---

[3] *Financial Times*, 9 May 2010.

The first bank to need support from the Bank of Spain was Caja de Ahorros Castilla La Mancha (later absorbed into Cajasur), which in March 2009 received a loan of 9 billion euro.

Anticipating that problems of solvency would be added to the problems of liquidity (as had already been seen in a number of European countries), Spain set up a 9 billion euro resolution fund in June 2009, in particular aimed at the ailing savings banks, "Fondo de Reestructuración Ordenada Bancaria," FROB. The fund may leverage itself tenfold and hence inject up to 90 billion euro in capital into the banks. The first support came in May 2010, when the Bank of Spain seized control over the ailing Cajasur de Andalusía, run (badly) by the Catholic Church.

In late 2010, Spain announced more encompassing plans for the ailing savings-bank sector. Problem savings banks were to be converted into commercial banks and, if necessary, recapitalized by the state bank resolution fund FROB. All Spanish banks were required to have a core Tier 1 ratio of 8 percent of risk-weighted assets as contrasted to a minimum of 7 percent under Basel III. First out was the Barcelona-based La Caixa, Spain's third largest bank, which, transformed into a commercial bank, would have a core Tier 1 ratio of 10.9 percent, becoming the tenth largest bank in Europe by capital.

Spain's number 4 bank, Caja de Madrid, owned by the city of Madrid, followed and merged with six smaller savings banks but with the city remaining as majority owner. The result was BFA Bankia, listed on the stock exchange from July 2011. It became the third largest bank in Spain but the leader in holding real estate assets, which would, within a year, lead to its downfall and nationalization. On 9 May 2012, the state bank support agency (FROB) became majority owner of Bankia after an injection of 4.5 billion euro. Bankia's chairman, the former minister of the economy and managing director of the IMF Rodrigo Rato, stepped down. On 25 May 2012, the capital need of the bank was raised to 23.5 billion euro after it lost over 19 billion euro for the year 2011 and FROB became the sole owner of the bank with heavy losses not only to shareholders but also to investors in subordinated debt (see below).

Having decreed that Spanish banks must attain a core Tier 1 ratio of 8 percent for listed banks and 10 percent for unlisted banks already by the end of 2011, the Bank of Spain estimated in March 2011 that the country's banks might need additional capital of 15 billion euro, concentrated to the major ex-savings banks such as Bankia, Nova Caixa Galicia (NCG) and Catalunya Caixa. Moody's at the same time set the shortfall at 40–50 billion euro, which would turn out to be a very exact forecast. Other banks, having failed to raise the necessary capital on their own, led to FROB spending almost 5 billion euro in recapitalizing and thus nationalizing Nova Caixa Galicia, Catalunya Caixa and Unnim. In November 2011, Banco de Valencia followed, after an injection of 1 billion euro in capital from FROB. This bank was sold in November 2012 to CaixaBank, the banking arm of La Caixa group, for 1 euro.

A "bad bank" was also created to handle up to 50 billion euro of failed loans. On 17 December 2012, the Spanish government started SAREB (*Sociedad de Gestión de Activos Procedentes de la Reestructuración Bancaria*). The state bank restructuring fund FROB contributed 45 percent of the capital and private interests 55 percent, among them Santander, Ibercaja, Bankinter, Unicaja, Cajamar, Caja Laboral, Banca March, Cecabank, CaixaBank, Banco Sabadell, Banco Popular, Kutxabank and Banco Caminos as well as foreign banks Deutsche Bank and Barclays and a number of insurance companies such as Generali, Zurich and AXA.

Out of a total volume of bad loans transferred, some 50 billion euro, Bankia is responsible for 22 billion, sold at an average 46 percent discount. SAREB has also bought assets worth a nominal 6.7 billion euro from nationalized Catalunya Banc as well as 5.7 billion from NCG Banco-Banco Gallego and 2 billion from Banco de Valencia. Altogether, SAREB's portfolio in 2013 consisted of 76,000 empty homes, 6,300 rented homes, 14,900 un-built plots of land and 84,300 individual loans.

In financing these write-downs, haircuts were imposed on owners of preference shares as well as subordinated debt, ranging from 36 percent on junior bonds to 61 percent on preference shares. Holders of common stock had been wiped out already at the nationalization. The bailing-in of investors was calculated to save the state some 10 billion euro in support.[4]

---

[4] See also Niall Lenihan, "Claims of depositors, subordinated creditors, senior creditors and Central Banks in bank resolutions," speech given at the AEDBF Conference, Athens, 5–6 October 2012.

The EU Commission approved of the bank aid in November 2012 but with conditions:[5]

In the case of BFA/Bankia, NCG Banco and Catalunya Banc, the Commission found that the proposed restructuring measures will ensure that the three banks return to long term viability as sound credit institutions in Spain. By 2017, the balance sheet of each bank will be reduced by more than 60% compared to 2010. In particular, the banks will refocus their business model on retail and SME lending in their historical core regions. They will exit from lending to real estate development and limit their presence in wholesale business. This will contribute to reinforcing their capital and liquidity positions and reduce their reliance on wholesale and central bank funding. The banks' transfer of assets to the asset management company "Sareb" will further limit the impact of additional impairments on the riskier assets and help to restore confidence. As regards NCG and Catalunya Banc, Spain committed to sell the banks before the end of the five-year restructuring period. Should a sale fail, Spanish authorities will present an orderly resolution plan.

These conditions were already in principle enshrined in the support of a maximum of 100 billion euro agreed by the euro finance ministers on 9 June 2012.

In attempting to give its ailing banks aid while circumventing new BIS and EU rules on capital adequacy, Spain decided on 12 September 2013 to allow its banks to reclassify "deferred tax assets" (DTA) as tax credits. The former are disallowed from core Tier 1 Capital under the new Basel III rules. DTA amounts to some 50 billion euro for the Spanish banking system, corresponding to no less than 83 percent of the total CET1 of nationalized Bankia, 64 percent of Banco Sabadell, 40 percent of Santander and Banco Popular, and 20–25 percent of BBVA and CaixaBank.[6]

Overall grade of the handling of Spanish banks: A (on a scale of A to F=Fail)

While the Bank of Spain in its capacity as macroprudential supervisor could and should be criticized for letting the property bubble develop,

---

[5] http://europa.eu/rapid/press-release_IP-12-1277_en.htm
[6] http://uk.reuters.com/article/2013/10/30/uk-spain-banks-idUKBRE99T0VK 20131030; www.ft.com/intl/cms/s/0/651e3222-1ac4-11e3-87da-00144feab7de. html#axzz2lIrdFWxV

its and the government's handling of the resulting crisis has been exemplary. Strong public finances and "dynamic provisioning" helped Spain delay its entrance into the European financial crisis. Since then, aid to the banking system sounds like a textbook example of "how to do it":

- October 2008: Guarantee of the banking system up to 100 billion euro;
- March 2009: Liquidity support for strained banks;
- June 2009: Bank support agency FROB started;
- December 2010: Reorganization of *cajas* into viable commercial banks;
- Banks were nationalized only if necessary, such as in the case of Bankia and Catalunya Caixa;
- When nationalized by the state, investors in common stock were wiped out while holders of preference shares and subordinated debt were subjected to haircuts. No holders of senior bonds were subjected to losses;
- December 2012: A "bad bank," SAREB, was set up, majority owned by private interests but with heavy involvement (45 percent) from FROB;
- Since Spain had also implemented the budget cuts demanded by the European Union and moreover had a relatively low debt-to-GDP ratio, its program for the banking sector has evolved in more harmony with the EU Commission and the ECB than has been the case in some other countries).

Appendix: Banking consolidation in Spain

Merging banks	Result	Share of Spanish banking assets (%)
Banco Santander	Banco Santander	18.9
Banesto		
BBVA	BBVA	14.9
Caixa Sabadell		
Caixa Terrasa		
Caixa Menlleu		
La Caixa	CaixaBank	12.1

Merging banks	Result	Share of Spanish banking assets (%)
Banco de Valencia		
Caixa Girona		
Cajasol		
Guadalajara		
Caja Navarra		
Caja Burgos		
Caja Canarias		
Caja Madrid	Bankia	11.9
Bancaja		
Caja Insular Canarias		
Caixa Laietana		
Caja Ávila		
Caja Segovia		
Caja Rioja		
Banco Sabadell	Banco Sabadell	5.6
Banco Guipuzcoana		
CAM		
Banco Popular		
Banco Pastor	Banco Popular	5.5

Source: Financial Times, 19 December 2013, "Spanish banks enjoy surge in popularity."

12 | *Cyprus*
Bank of Cyprus, Popular Bank (Laiki)

The Cyprus story[1]

The economy of Cyprus is only 0.1 percent of the GDP of the European Union, yet the financial crisis of 2012 and onwards has taken up proportionately much more time and effort for domestic and international decision-makers. We noted in the Introduction that the 10 billion euro received in support represented one-third of Cyprus's GDP. As will be presented in more detail below, Cyprus also represents the greatest failure of European bank resolutions among all the cases studied in this book.

Cyprus was in trouble already when it entered the euro zone on 1 January 2008. Its growth rate was declining and the country went into recession in the beginning of 2009, with GDP falling by 3 percent. Despite booming tourism (2 million tourists, yielding 11 percent of GDP in 2006), the current account worsened to a deficit of 12 percent of GDP in 2007 and 16 percent of GDP in 2008, occasioned in the main by a lack of competitiveness. It was (too) easily financed by a strong inflow of deposits, up to one-third stemming from outside the euro area, largely Russian.

The budget had been in deficit for a decade until 2007 when it showed a temporary surplus, only to fall back into a persistent deficit of around 6 percent of GDP for the following years, occasioned by a spending boom blamed on the incoming Communist president, Dimitris Christofias.[2] Fortunately, Cyprus had started the crisis with

---

[1] European Commission, "The economic adjustment program for Cyprus," *European Economy*, Occasional Papers 149, May 2013; "Eleven steps to a financial crisis," *Cyprus Mail*, 23 November 2013, http://cyprus-mail.com/2013/10/27/eleven-steps-to-a-financial-crisis/; Independent Commission on the Future of the Cyprus Banking Sector (David Lascelles *et al.*), Interim Report June 2013.

[2] www.ctvnews.ca/business/cyprus-financial-crisis-inquest-blames-country-s-economic-mess-on-ex-president-1.1486431

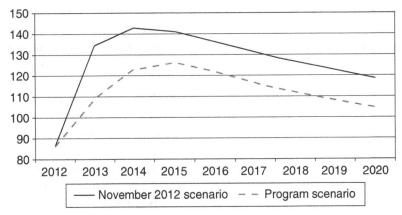

Note: The Nov. 2012 scenario is based on the Commission services winter 2013 forecast including EUR 10 bn recapitalization of the Cypriot banking system, while the "program" scenario is based on the agreed draft MOU (April 2013).

Figure 27. Forecast Cyprus debt-to-GDP levels, 2012–20
Source: European Commission, "The economic adjustment program for Cyprus," *European Economy,* Occasional Papers 149, May 2013, p. 56.

a debt-to-GDP level below 50 percent, but it rose to 88 percent at the beginning of 2013, just below the euro zone average. It is, however, forecast to continue its rapid increase, peaking at almost 130 percent of GDP by 2015, second only to Greece and in line with Portugal, Ireland and Italy (see Figure 27). However, with a debt-to-GDP ratio of 115 percent at the beginning of 2014, it appears that the actual trajectory may prove somewhat more positive than the forecast. On the other hand, it had risen by 25 percentage points in one single year.

Bank of Cyprus, Popular Bank (Laiki) and Hellenic Bank

As in so many other countries that we have studied, the problems created by the banking sector were firstly its outgrown size, 750 percent of GDP in 2010 in Cyprus (see Figure 10), and secondly the property boom. More original and worse was the situation in the banking system itself. Despite increasing property prices until the general financial crisis (after which house prices fell by 30 percent), Cypriot banks already had a relatively high level of non-performing loans as a ratio to total loans (NPL), as Table 17 indicates (from *The Banker* 2008–10 and the three banks' Annual accounts 2010–13).

These are the overall NPLs; for the banks' Greek operations, they had by 2012 risen to an average of 42 percent, i.e. almost one out of two loans was delinquent, amounting to 19 billion euro or 111 percent of Cyprus's GDP.

The second problem was liquidity. The ECB had supplied, in particular, Laiki Bank since 2011 with Emergency Liquidity Assistance (ELA). It exploded to 9 billion euro in the beginning of 2013, 50 percent of the island's GDP. This is a proportion greater than any ECB loan to any other country and a record for an individual bank. Total ELA at that point for Cyprus banks was 14 billion euro. On 13 March 2012, Moody's downgraded the sovereign debt of Cyprus to "junk." When on 25 June 2012 Fitch followed (downgrading Cyprus to BB+) and hence all the major rating agencies rated Cyprus as "junk," the ECB would not and could no longer accept Cyprus sovereign debt as collateral.

Since January 2012, Cyprus had been relying on a 2.5 billion euro emergency loan from Russia to cover its budget deficit. The "haircut" on holdings of Greek sovereign debt in February 2012 made this loan totally insufficient. The haircut of effectively 75 percent cost Cyprus banks 4.5 billion euro, 25 percent of GDP, of which Laiki Bank 2.3 billion and Bank of Cyprus 1.5 billion euro.

On the same day that Cyprus was downgraded, 25 June 2012, it asked for support from the European Stability Mechanism (ESM). After long and difficult negotiations, on 16 March 2013, the European

Table 17. *Ratio of non-performing loans (NPL) to total loans for Cyprus banks*

	2007	2008	2009	2010	2011	2012
Popular Bank (Laiki)	7.5	4.3	6.1	7.3	13.9	n a
Bank of Cyprus	5.6	3.8	5.6	7.3	10.2	23.7
Hellenic Bank	12.2	9.3	8.5	10.5	14.4	22.0

Union's euro area finance ministers agreed to support Cyprus with aid worth 10 billion euro. However, in an unprecedented move, uninsured depositors would lose 9.9 percent of their balances, insured depositors 6.75 percent, amounts transformed into stock holdings, to provide for 6 billion euro to recapitalize its banks. The plan was rejected by the Cypriot parliament on 19 March, with not a single legislator voting for the package.

In a total turn-around, on 25 March 2013, the final agreement between Cyprus and the international lenders (ECB, IMF and European Union) was signed, in which a bail-in of bank uninsured depositors was demanded as a precondition for a loan of 10 billion euro to the state of Cyprus, of which 1 billion came from the IMF. The 10 billion bail-out comprised 4.1 billion to spend on debt liabilities (refinancing and amortization), 3.4 billion to cover fiscal deficits, and 2.5 billion for the bank recapitalization. The second largest bank, Laiki Bank (also known as Cyprus Popular Bank), majority owned by the government, was to be wound down. Its good assets, together with deposits under 100,000 euro (the maximum amount guaranteed under EU deposit insurance), was to be transferred to the biggest bank, Bank of Cyprus. Bonds and higher-denomination deposits were converted into stock and, together with remaining assets, transferred to a "bad bank."

In Bank of Cyprus, insured deposits were safe but deposits above 100,000 were to be frozen until it could be established how much would have to be used to reach the sum necessary to capitalize the bank to 9 percent TCE1/RWA. An estimated 60 percent of these deposits would be compulsorily swapped into equity.

On 5 August 2013, the Cyprus financial authorities ruled that 47.5 percent of uninsured deposits in Bank of Cyprus would be forcibly converted into stock, leaving the bank with a 9 percent CET1/RWA ratio. However, most of the rest would be inaccessible for their owners for up to two more years. The revised agreement, expected to raise 4.2 billion euro in return for the 10 billion euro bail-out, did not require any further approval of the Cypriot parliament, as the legal framework for the implied solutions for Laiki Bank and Bank of Cyprus had been accounted for in the bill already passed by the parliament. The two banks' Greek operations as well as those of Hellenic Bank were sold to Piraeus Bank, which acquired net assets valued at 2.8 billion euro for a price of 524 million euro.

Overall grade of the handling of Cyprus banks:
F (on a scale of A to F=Fail)

Through its handling of the Cyprus crisis, the European Union has increased the risk of a bank run on uninsured and perhaps even insured depositors in the next crisis (Slovenia? Malta? Portugal?), increased financial volatility, increased skepticism, not to say hatred, against "Brussels" as well as made the road towards a banking union infinitely more difficult. To quote *The Economist* on the bailing-in of insured deposits:[3]

Whatever the rationale, it is a mistake for three reasons. The first error is to reawaken contagion risk elsewhere in the euro zone. Depositors have come through the financial crisis largely unscathed. Now they have been bailed in, some of them in breach of an explicit promise that they can be sure of getting their money back even if a bank goes belly-up.

Eurozone leaders will spin the deal as reflecting the unique circumstances surrounding Cyprus, just as they did the Greek debt restructuring last year. But if you were a depositor in a peripheral country that looked like it needed more money from the euro zone, what would your calculation be? That you would never be treated like the people in Cyprus, or that a precedent had been set which reflected the consistent demands of creditor countries for burden-sharing? The chances of big, destabilising movements of money (into cash, if not into other banks) have just shot up.

The second error is one of equity. There is an argument to be made over the principles of bailing in uninsured depositors. And there is a case for hitting everyone in Cypriot banks before any taxpayer in another country. But there is no moral imperative for whacking Cypriot widows and leaving senior bank bondholders untouched, as appears to be the case here; or not imposing any losses on sovereign-debt investors in Cyprus; or protecting depositors in the Greek operations of Cypriot banks, as has also happened. The euro zone may cloak this bail-out in the language of fairness but it is a highly selective treatment. Indeed, the euro zone's insistence that this is a one-off makes that perfectly plain: with enough foreigners at risk and a small enough country to push around, you get an outcome like Cyprus. (That is one reason why people are now wondering about the implications of this deal for little Latvia, also home to lots of Russian money and itself due to join the euro zone in 2014.)

---

[3] *The Economist*, 16 May 2013, www.economist.com/blogs/schumpeter/2013/03/cyprus-bail-out

The final error is strategic. The Cypriot deal has no coherence in the larger context. The euro crisis has been in abeyance for a few months, thanks largely to the readiness of the European Central Bank to intervene to help struggling countries. The ECB's price for helping countries is to insist they go into a bail-out programme. The political price of going into a programme has just gone up, so the ECB's safety net looks a little thinner.

The bail-out appears to move Europe further away from the institutional reforms that are needed to resolve the crisis once and for all. Rather than using the European Stability Mechanism to recapitalise banks, and thereby weaken the link between banks and their governments, the euro zone continues to equate bank bail-outs with sovereign bail-outs. As for debt mutualisation, after imposing losses on local depositors, the price of support from the rest of Europe is arguably costlier now than it ever has been.

It is also hard to square this outcome with the ongoing overhaul of finance. The direction of efforts to improve banks' liquidity position is to encourage them to hold more deposits; the aim of bail-in legislation planned to come into force by 2018 is to make senior debt absorb losses in the event of a bank failure. The logic behind both of these reform initiatives is that bank deposits have two, contradictory properties. They are both sticky, because they are insured; and they are flighty, because they can be pulled instantly. So deposits are a good source of funding provided they never run. The Cyprus bail-out makes this confidence trick harder to pull off.[4]

These are the principal criticisms. In the Cyprus case, they are enforced by a number of disturbing factors. Since the London and Moscow offices of the two banks remained open while those on Cyprus were closed, international depositors could withdraw their balances, shifting most of the effect onto Cypriot companies, retirees and other savers. Secondly, it has been claimed that a number of large depositors were tipped off by the president (and presumably other members of the government) and had had time to withdraw their balances.[5] So in contrast to Iceland where domestic savers were protected while foreign depositors suffered, in Cyprus the foreign and well-connected depositors were protected while domestic savers lost, in the case of Laiki Bank everything they had.

---

[4] See also "Injured island: the bail-out is working; the bail-in isn't," *The Economist*, 8 March 2014.
[5] http://hpub.org/criminals-in-government-cyprus-presidents-family-transferred-tens-of-millions-to-london-days-before-deposit-haircuts-by-zero-hedge/

Or, as was well stated by the Independent Commission:[6]

Although the terms of the MoU (memorandum of understanding between Cyprus and the Troika) have, in the end, only hit uninsured deposits in Cyprus' two largest banks, the inclusion of a deposit haircut and the accompanying capital controls will affect banking confidence in the eurozone more widely. For Cyprus, it will raise fears about the safety of deposits if the current round of financing proves insufficient, making it harder for Cyprus to lift capital controls. Also, the haircut arrangements radically alter the shareholding structure of Cyprus' largest bank with consequences that are hard to foresee. The selective way in which the haircut was applied raises questions of equity when depositors in foreign branches were spared, and other credit institutions in Cyprus receiving public money were not required to call on their depositors or members.

[6] Independent Commission on the Future of the Cyprus Banking Sector (Lascelles *et al.*), Interim Report, June 2013.

PART IV

The TARP program and the bailing out (and bailing in) of US banks

13 | The roles of the FDIC, the Treasury and the Fed in the crisis

The US story

During the Great Depression between 1929 and 1933, 9,759 US banks failed, leaving 16,096 surviving banks. In the drawn-out "third-world debt" and savings and loan crisis in the United States during the 1980s, 2,356 banks went belly-up, leaving 12,347 banks by 1990. In the recent Great Recession 2008–11, "only" 414 insured banks went bankrupt. Even in 2012 after the acute phase of the crisis, when another 51 banks failed, most of them were small and only three had total assets at around 1 billion dollars, leaving 6,096 banks as at the end of 2012. In 2013, another 25 banks failed but only one had assets above 1 billion dollars.[1]

From these data one could draw the (correct) conclusion that American banking has become more concentrated, the number falling mainly through mergers but also by liquidations of failed banks (see below). In 1995, the six largest banks or investment banks (Bank of America, JPMorgan Chase, Citigroup, Wells Fargo, Goldman Sachs and Morgan Stanley) held assets corresponding to just below 20 percent of GDP; less than 20 years later at the end of 2012, the same six banks had assets corresponding to 60 percent of GDP.[2] The six also accounted for 67 percent of all banking assets in the United States, placing the US among the most concentrated banking sectors in comparison with Europe (see Figure 10).

The declining number of failed banks could also lead to the (incorrect) conclusion that financial crises have become milder. Even in the worst year of the Depression, 1933, when 4,004 banks failed, their

---

[1] www.fdic.gov/bank/individual/failed/banklist.html

[2] Simon Johnson and James Kwak, *13 Bankers: The Wall Street Take-Over and the Next Financial Meltdown* (New York: Pantheon Books, 2010), p. 203 and own calculations.

combined deposits corresponded "only" to 6 percent of GDP. In the 1980s, no year's failure exceeded 2 percent of GDP measured by deposits/GDP. In the recent crisis, 353 of the 414 failed banks in 2008–11 were small, with assets of less than 1 billion dollars. Some, however, were large. The actual 2008 figure for deposits in failed banks was 3 percent of GDP, but adding the three major banks which survived solely due to government intervention (Wachovia, Citigroup and Bank of America), the figure would have been a whopping 16 percent of GDP, had these banks also been allowed to fail.

The year 2008 would see the largest bank failure in history, the collapse of Washington Mutual, with assets of 307 billion dollars, 2.1 percent of GDP by itself, thereby beating the 1984 record of the failure of Continental Illinois, which had assets of 40 billion dollars, "only" 1 percent of that year's GDP. The failure of Washington Mutual was also 10 times the size of the second largest failure, that of IndyMac the same year. The year 2008 would also see the largest corporate bankruptcy in history when the investment bank Lehman Brothers with assets of 639 billion dollars was allowed to fail. That year would as well witness the bailing-out of the world's largest insurance company, AIG, with total assets at over 1 trillion dollars.

We will return to the story of these failures in the next few chapters.

The financial crisis would lead to the worst economic development that the United States had witnessed since the 1930s. American households' net worth fell by 16 trillion dollars (or 25 percent) from the third quarter of 2007 to the first quarter of 2009. A large part of this was occasioned by the fall in share prices. The combined capitalization of NYSE (New York Stock Exchange) and NASDAQ fell from 20.7 trillion dollars in October 2007 to a low of 10.1 billion dollars in March 2009 (according to the World Federation of Exchanges). The value of households' real estate holdings fell from 22.7 trillion dollars at the end of 2006 to 16.1 billion at the end of 2011 after which a modest increase has taken place.[3]

Unemployment rose from 4 to 10 percent, the second worst episode after World War II. The fall in GDP, –2.8 percent in 2009 and an annualized –8 percent in the worst quarterly fall, was also the largest in the postwar era. The National Bureau of Economic Research declared a

---

[3] Federal Reserve Flow of Funds data, www.federalreserve.gov/releases/z1/20091210/z1r-5.pdf

recession between December 2007 and June 2009 which, at 18 months, was the longest since the Great Depression's 43 months, beating the two 16-month oil-price induced recessions of 1973–5 and 1981–2.

Figure 28 shows the result of a recent study on the output loss caused by the crisis. Even assuming that a faster rate of growth may eventually return GDP to the trend, i.e. what it would have been without the crisis – an assumption which is far from certain – the resulting loss will still correspond to almost a full year's production.

In various programs (capital injections, loans, purchases of securities, guarantees, swap arrangements) the American government accepted potential costs at a total of over 16 trillion dollars, more than the entire Gross Domestic Product and far more than the size of the national debt at the time. Of this potential sum, less than 3,000 billion dollars was used by September 2009 at the height of the crisis. See Table 18. Comparing the table with Figure 1 above, we see that the US and UK stories are largely similar as regards time line and the total size of interventions relative to GDP.

In direct outlays on capital injections and asset purchases, however, the main target of this book, the Treasury spent 4.8 percent of GDP, i.e. less than Britain's 6.7 percent of GDP and also less than Germany's 12.8 percent of GDP (according to the IMF data in Table 1). In sharp contrast to these two countries, most of the American support has

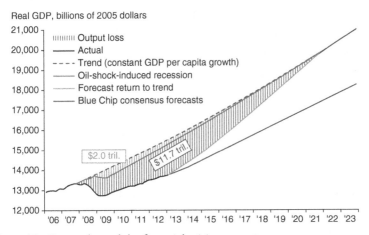

Figure 28. Output loss of the financial crisis
Sources: Bureau of Economic Analysis; Census Bureau; Blue Chip Economic Indicators; author's calculations.

Table 18. *Potential and actual amounts in the various US financial support programs at the peak by September 2009, billion dollars*

Program	Maximum amount	Used 30/09/2009
Federal Deposit Insurance Corporation (FDIC)		
Guarantee for insured deposits	4,800	n/a[a]
Guarantee for uninsured deposits	700	n/a
Guarantee for Public Private Invest.	800[a]	0
Temporary Liquidity Guarantee (TLGP)	1,500	308
Guarantee GE debt	65	55
FDIC part Citigroup guarantee	10	0
FDIC part Bank of America guarantee	3	0
FDIC cost of bank takeovers	n/a	45
Total FDIC	**7,878**	**408**
Federal Reserve		
Primary discount window	111	29
Secondary credit	1	0
Primary dealer facility	147	0[a]
Liquidity support asset-backed CP	146	0
Commercial paper program (CPFF)	1,800	14[a]
Term securities lending facility (TSLF)	250	0
Term Auction Facility (TAF)	500[a]	110[a]
Overnight securities lending	10	9
Term Asset Backed Loans (TALF)	1,000	44[a]
Money Market Funding Facility	600	0[a]
Purchases Bear Stearns assets[a]	29	26
Purchases AIG assets[a]	53	35
Credit AIG	60	39
Purchases of Fannie/Freddie MBS	1,250	776[a]
Purchases of Fannie/Freddie debt	200	150
Citigroup bail-out, Fed portion	220	0
Bank of America bail-out, Fed portion	97	0
Commitment to buy Treasuries	300	295
Foreign exchange swaps	unlimited!	29

Table 18. *Potential and actual amounts in the various US financial support programs at the peak by September 2009, billion dollars (cont.)*

Program	Maximum amount	Used 30/09/2009
Total Federal Reserve	6,774+ unlimited swaps	**1,556**
Troubled Assets Relief Program (TARP)		
Original bank capital purchase program	218	205
GM, Chrysler	80	78
Auto suppliers	5	4
AIG	70	70
"Make home affordable"	50	27
Bank of America additional amount	20	20
Citigroup additional amount	20	20
Citigroup asset guarantee	5	5
Bank of America asset guarantee	8	0
Guarantee for TALF	20	20
Guarantee for Public Private Invest.	100	27
Consumer lending initiative	50	0
Available for additional initiatives	54	0
Total TARP	**700**	**476**
Government		
New capital Fannie Mae/Freddie Mac	400	111
"Hope for homeowners"	320	20
"Neighborhood stabilization"	25	0
Treasury guarantee MMF	0	0
Total government	**745**	**131**
SUM TOTAL	*16,097*	*2,571*
US GDP IN THIRD QUARTER 2009	*14,384*	

[a]Not applicable since uses are paid by the insured banks themselves through fees. *Source:* CNN, 25 September 2009, Congressional Oversight Panel, press releases from Freddie Mac and Fannie Mae, TARP announcements on www.financialstability. gov/docs/transaction-reports/transactionReport051209.pdf, own calculations for deposit insurance.

also been recovered with a healthy return, a feature to which we will return below.

It is not altogether obvious which government programs should be included in "support to the financial system." The Special Inspector General for the Troubled Asset Relief Program (SIGTARP) found in his report to Congress in July 2009 (his Table 3.4) that the potential amount at stake was 23.7 trillion dollars or over 150 percent of GDP. He achieved this high number by adding several other agencies such as Veterans' Administration, Federal Housing Finance Agency and also assuming much wider potential losses on securities acquired by the Federal Reserve.[4] The question is why all potential support for housing should be regarded as costs of the financial crisis.

It would be erroneous to include also the various stimulus programs, such as the American Recovery and Reinvestment Act, student loan guarantees, Advanced Technology Vehicles, Car Allowance Rebate System, none of which was directly linked with aiding the financial sector. In all, these programs added another 1.2 trillion dollars in potential expenses by the government, of which about half had been drawn by September 2009.

We are not here concerned with all the various programs listed in Table 18 since the interest in this book is in TARP and in particular the Capital Purchase Program, CPP.[5] Bailing-out or bailing-in is the topic under study and bailing-out was exactly what CPP did!

Under the TARP program, a total of 707 banks received 205 billion dollars in capital injections. Of these, 196 billion had been repaid by December 2013, 2 billion had been written off and hence 7 billion dollars remained outstanding. During the lifetime of the program, taxpayers had also received dividends and other income of 47 billion dollars from the entire TARP program (of which 10 billion came from the CPP and the Systemically Failing Financial Institutions program).[6,7]

---

[4] The report is available at www.sigtarp.gov/reports/congress/2009/July2009_Quarterly_Report_to_Congress.pdf

[5] Presentation and discussions of the various programs may be found in, inter alia, Lybeck, A Global History of the Financial Crash of 2007–10, passim.

[6] SIGTARP, Office of the Special Inspector General for the Troubled Asset Relief Program, Quarterly Report to Congress, 29 January 2014, www.sigtarp.gov/Quarterly%20Reports/January_29_2014_Report_to_Congress.pdf

[7] An updated list of bail-out recipients, amounts received and repaid is to be found at http://projects.propublica.org/bailout/list

The purpose of the CPP was to recapitalize institutions which were judged to be long-run viable in order to promote financial stability and maintain public confidence in the financial system as a whole and in particular its banks.[8] While participation in the CPP was in principle voluntary, we will see that a number of major banks (like Wells Fargo) were force-fed to accept the common bail-out in order that the others, less well capitalized, would not be singled out and perhaps subjected to a "run." The Treasury department used TARP money mainly to buy preferred non-voting equity in the applying institutions, which paid a 5 percent dividend over the first five years, rising to 9 percent thereafter. This feature, together with limitations on executive pay in the participating institutions, led to the swift repayment of bail-out money received after the acute phase of the crisis was over. In addition, participating banks issued warrants to the Treasury to purchase common stock, which were later redeemed at a higher price as the financial institutions had returned to profitability.

When Goldman Sachs repaid its 10 billion dollars in TARP money received, the government had cashed in 318 million dollars in dividends on the preferred stock and an additional 1.1 billion dollars for the warrants held by the government and repurchased by the bank. The firm calculated that the TARP investment gave the taxpayer an annualized return of no less that 23 percent. More details on returns on bail-outs will be provided in the case studies below.

The roles of the FDIC, the Treasury and the Fed in the crisis

In order to better understand how the resolution of banks and investment banks in the following chapters was undertaken, a presentation of the US regulatory framework before Dodd–Frank is necessary.[9] We will come back later to the changes that the Dodd–Frank Act wrought and to the question whether it will diminish the risk of a new financial crisis in the US economy or at least make it milder.

---

[8] The evaluation of which banks are viable will obviously differ from person to person. See, for instance, Onaran, *Zombie Banks*, ch. 7, "U.S. zombies on IV drip."

[9] Dodd–Frank Wall Street Reform and Consumer Protection Act of 2010, H.R. 4173, signed into law 21 July 2010, www.gpo.gov/fdsys/pkg/BILLS-111hr4173 eh/pdf/BILLS-111hr4173eh.pdf

Banking in the United States can take a variety of different forms, leading to different regulation and supervision and sometimes to a choice of regulator by the regulated:

- National banks with a federal charter (which must be members of the Federal Reserve System);
- State member banks (i.e. banks with a state charter that have chosen to become members of the Federal Reserve);
- FDIC-insured state non-member banks;
- Non-FDIC insured state non-member banks;
- Insured federally chartered savings associations (i.e. insured by the FDIC);
- Insured state-chartered savings associations (savings banks and savings and loan associations);
- Non-FDIC insured state savings associations;
- Federally chartered credit unions;
- State-chartered credit unions;
- Bank holding companies (i.e. a company that owns banks but is not itself a bank);
- Savings association holding companies (i.e. a company that owns a savings association);
- Foreign branches of US banks;
- Edge Act corporations;[10]
- US branches and agencies of foreign banks.

At the time of the crisis (as well as now), US banks had/have a number of partially overlapping regulators. The *Federal Reserve* regulated state-chartered banks that were members of the Federal Reserve System as well as bank and other financial holding companies, foreign branches of US banks and state-chartered US branches of foreign banks. Nationally chartered banks must be members of the Federal Reserve System, but they were mainly regulated by the *Office of the Comptroller of the Currency* (OCC) within the Treasury department, whose mission is to charter, regulate and supervise all nationally

---

[10] An Edge Act corporation is a subsidiary of a Federal Reserve chartered bank or bank holding company or of a foreign-owned and foreign-chartered bank, started to engage in foreign banking activities. They may accept (non-insured) deposits and make loans but solely related to international transactions.

chartered banks as well as federally licensed branches and agencies of foreign banks. The *Office of Thrift Supervision* (OTS), also located in the Treasury, had as its main functions to charter, supervise and regulate all federally chartered and state-chartered savings banks and savings and loan associations as well as holding companies containing "thrifts." It was eliminated in July 2011 and its authorities were transferred to the OCC (for federally chartered savings associations), to the FDIC (for state savings associations) and to the Federal Reserve (for thrift holding companies and their subsidiaries).

Apart from managing the deposit-insurance system and the Deposit Insurance Fund (DIF), on which much more later, the *Federal Deposit Insurance Corporation* (FDIC) is also the primary regulator for state-chartered non-member banks and state-chartered thrifts (savings banks and savings and loan associations). It is also a secondary regulator for all FDIC-insured banks, a task which, as we shall see, sometimes brought it into conflict with the main bank regulator, the OCC or the OTS, when it felt that a bank was a threat to the FDIC and to the DIF while the primary regulator felt otherwise.

More importantly for the topic of this book, the FDIC had and has the sole power to act as receiver for failing and seized insured banks in order to protect (insured) depositors and then sell those banks and/or the viable parts of their assets to viable banks. See below.

Banks also have to conform to the rules and regulations of the Securities and Exchange Commission (SEC) which has a primary responsibility for regulating the securities industry in general as well as the stock and stock options exchanges, broker-dealers (investment banks), investment companies such as mutual funds and credit rating agencies. Apart from dealing with such issues as insider trading, we have seen from the Chronology that a number of US banks have been charged by the SEC with fraud or misleading information in connection with the sale of subprime mortgages or derivatives on these securities. We will return in the later chapters to the lack of adequate supervision by the SEC which allowed for the problems that felled Bear Stearns, Merrill Lynch and Lehman Brothers to arise.

Finally, the *Commodity Futures Trading Commission* (CFTC) has the authority to regulate the futures and options markets, corresponding exchanges as well as clearing organizations.

Table 19 tries to bring some order to this confusing story.

Table 19. *US regulatory authorities and those they supervise[a]*

Authority	Tasks	Supervised institutions, example
Federal Reserve System and its Board of Governors and the 12 regional Reserve Banks	Supervises financial holding companies, member banks and state-chartered foreign-owned banks. Gives liquidity support and supervises the stability of financial markets	Financial groups like Citigroup, JPMorgan Chase, KeyCorp, SunTrust Corp, PNC Financial Services, Wachovia, foreign banks such as Santander and Barclays USA
OCC (Office of the Comptroller of the Currency), a department within the Treasury	Supervises commercial banks with a national license ("national banks") but also federally chartered branches of foreign banks in the US	Banks like Citibank, PNC Bank, Key Bank, SunTrust Bank, National City. In all some 1,600 banks and 50 foreign-owned banks
FDIC (Federal Deposit Insurance Corporation)	Supervises those national and state commercial banks and savings banks who are not members of the Federal Reserve, responsible for banks in administration. Shares supervision of Fed member banks with the Fed	Bancorp South Bank, Bank of the West, GMAC Bank
OTS (Office of Thrift Supervision), a department within the Treasury (now abolished)	Supervises individual savings banks as well as financial conglomerates containing a savings bank	AIG, GE, Hartford, Countrywide and other groups containing savings banks, individual savings banks like IndyMac and Washington Mutual
National Credit Union Administration	Supervises credit unions	Navy Federal Credit Union, Pentagon Federal Credit Union, Columbia Credit Union etc

Table 19. *US regulatory authorities and those they supervise[a] (cont.)*

Authority	Tasks	Supervised institutions, example
States' "Department of Financial Institions"	Supervises state-chartered banks	Most of the bankrupt banks, such as Sanderson State Bank in Texas and Security Pacific in California, had a state license, not a national license
State "Insurance Departments"	Supervises insurance companies	AIG, Hartford Financial
FHFA (Federal Housing Finance Agency)	The supervisory authority for Federal Home Loan Banks	Ginnie Mae, Fannie Mae and Freddie Mac
SEC (Securities and Exchange Commission)	Supervises securities markets, stock exchanges, investment banks, broker-dealers, mutual funds, clearing houses, approves public prospectuses	Goldman Sachs, Merrill Lynch (before 2008), Lehman Brothers but also Citigroup Global Markets, New York Stock Exchange, NASDAQ, the Fixed Income Clearing Corporation (FICC) and the National Securities Clearing Corporation (NSCC)
CFTC (Commodity Futures Trading Commission)	Supervises exchange trades in derivatives in futures and options, some clearing houses	CME (Chicago Mercantile Exchange), CBOE (Chicago Board Options Exchange), New York Mercantile Exchange, Chicago Mercantile Exchange Clearing House, Options Clearing Corporation (OCC)

[a]FHFA was formed by the Housing and Economic Recovery Act on 30 July 2008.

Table 20. *Number of supervised institutions and their assets by major US regulator*

	Fed. Reserve	FDIC	OCC	OTS	Total
Number of supervised banks	878	5,205	1,635	826	8,544
Their assets in billion dollars	1,518	2,195	7,785	1,551	13,051

At the end of 2007, this implied the division of powers shown in Table 20, divided by primary regulator.[11]

The proposals by the Obama administration in June 2009, enacted by Congress in July 2010 in the Dodd–Frank Act (Wall Street Reform and Consumer Protection Act), however, did little to improve the situation. The major changes on the supervisory side are firstly the merger of the OCC and the OTS into a new National Banking Supervisor under the Treasury Department. Secondly, a new Federal Insurance Office was set up within the Treasury to provide for nationwide monitoring of the insurance industry, previously regulated solely by the individual states. The 50 states will, however, continue to do the actual supervision of insurance companies. The SEC (Securities and Exchange Commission) and the CFTC (Commodity Futures Trading Commission) will continue to co-exist, despite obvious overlaps and unclear boundaries. The CFTC seems the clear winner since it will in future regulate and supervise also all OTC derivatives, including credit default swaps (while the SEC is the major regulator for derivatives with underlying securities).[12]

---

[11] General Accountability Office (GAO), *Financial Institutions, Causes and Consequences of Recent Bank Failures*, Report to Congressional Committees, GAO 13–71, January 2013, p. 11.

[12] The CFTC had been expressly forbidden from regulating most OTC derivatives by the Futures Trading Practices Act of 1992 and the Commodity Futures Modernization Act of 2000 if the trades took place between "sophisticated parties." Transactions in OTC derivatives would not be regarded as futures as set out in the Commodity Exchange Act of 1936 and hence would not be regulated by the CFTC, nor would they be regarded as securities that would fall under the regulation of the SEC.

The power of the Federal Reserve was strengthened. It kept its supervisory role over banks, big as well as small, original proposals to rid it of the supervision of small banks having failed. The Federal Reserve Board includes a new vice chairman responsible for financial stability, reporting to Congress twice a year. It also got the responsibility for supervising financial holding companies deemed to pose systemic risk even if they don't contain any banks. Large financial companies such as AIG, Prudential and GE Capital that pose a systemic risk will also become subject to more stringent capital and liquidity requirements (see below). The new Consumer Financial Protection Bureau is an independent part of the Fed, set up to police the financial industry and protect consumers, especially as regards credit card fees and mortgage loans. Its director is a presidential appointee subject to confirmation by the Senate. The Fed also succeeded in eliminating the requirement that it reveal the names of banks who have borrowed from the Fed; this will now be required only with a two-year lag.

The FDIC gained the right to seize systemically important financial groups whether banks or not (AIG and Ally Financial, ex-GMAC, could thus have been seized by the FDIC had Dodd–Frank been in place). A new Financial Stability Oversight Council has been created to coordinate the various agencies as regards the macroprudential supervision and systemic risk. It consists of ten members from the Federal Reserve, the new Consumer Financial Protection Bureau, the Federal Deposit Insurance Corporation, the Federal Housing Finance Agency, the National Credit Union Agency, the Commodity Futures Trading Commission, the Securities and Exchange Commission, the Comptroller of the Currency and one independent member, all chaired by the Secretary of the Treasury. With a two-thirds vote, it may require a financial company, deemed to pose systemic threats, to divest assets. It is aided by a new Office of Financial Research within the Treasury.

This leads to the third of the functions of the FDIC (apart from insuring deposits and regulating and supervising some banks) and the one most relevant for this book, namely its role in the resolution of failed or failing banks, acting as receiver appointed by the main regulator (OCC, OTS or the Fed). Under existing legislation, the FDIC has the power to impose losses on unsecured creditors in resolving failed banks, such as happened with creditors of the failed thrift Washington Mutual (on which more below in later chapters). The Orderly Liquidation Authority (OLA) which was introduced by the

Dodd–Frank Act expands the resolution powers of the FDIC to bank holding companies and other financial holding companies deemed to be systemically important. The FDIC now also has the authority to choose which assets and liabilities to transfer to a third party. We will have much more to say on this later on.

The FDIC is required by law to resolve failed institutions using the method least costly to the Deposit Insurance Fund (DIF). The FDIC contacts qualified insured depository institutions to bid on deposits and the failing bank's assets. After all bids are received, the FDIC selects the option least costly to the DIF, which may include a purchase and assumption transaction with accompanying shared loss agreements. For this reason, the FDIC preferred Wells Fargo rather than Citigroup to purchase failed Wachovia despite the protests of the Treasury.

A problem with a large number of regulators – 50 states' regulators and eight national regulators – is inconsistency and bureaucratic infighting, making supervision as well as resolution more difficult. The Financial Crisis Inquiry Commission (FCIC) related several instances of how such inconsistencies and infighting between the regulatory authorities made the financial crisis unnecessarily dramatic and impeded resolutions.[13] For example:

For years, some states had tried to regulate the mortgage business, especially to clamp down on the predatory mortgages proliferating in the subprime market. The national thrifts and banks and their federal regulators – the Office of Thrift Supervision (OTS) and the Office of the Comptroller of the Currency (OCC), respectively – resisted the states' efforts to regulate those national banks and thrifts. The companies claimed that without one uniform set of rules they could not easily do business across the country, and regulators agreed ... In 2003, the OTS [issued] four opinion letters declaring that laws in Georgia, New York, New Jersey and New Mexico did not apply to national thrifts ... In January 2004, the OCC adopted a sweeping preemption rule applying to all state laws that interfered with or placed restrictions on national banks' ability to lend. Shortly afterward, three large banks ... said that they would convert from state charters to national charters, which

---

[13] Financial Crisis Inquiry Commission (FCIC), *Financial Crisis Inquiry Report: Final Report of the National Commission on the Causes of the Financial and Economic Crisis in the United States* (Washington, DC: Government Printing Office, January 2011).

increased the OCC's budget by 15 percent ... Several large national banks moved their mortgage-lending operations [from state charter] into subsidiaries and asserted that the subsidiaries were exempt from state mortgage lending laws. Four states challenged the regulation but the Supreme Court ruled aganist them in 2007. (pp. 111–12)

The Commission concluded its findings by stating that "the Office of the Comptroller of the Currency and the Office of Thrift Supervision preempted the applicability of state laws and regulatory efforts to national banks and thrifts, thus preventing adequate protection for borrowers and weakening constraints on this segment of the mortgage market" (p. 126). The Comptroller of the Currency, however, defended his actions by stating that "the agency has simply responded to increasingly aggressive initiatives at the state level to control the banking activities of federally chartered institutions" (ibid., p. 113).

But there was infighting also between the federal regulators. The Commission writes:

It also appeared that some institutions switched regulators in search of more lenient treatment. In December, 2006, Countrywide applied to switch regulators from the Fed and OCC to the OTS. Countrywide's move came after several months of evaluation within the company about the benefits of OTS regulation, many of which were promoted by the OTS itself over the course of an "outreach effort" initiated in mid-2005 ... An internal 2006 Countrywide briefing paper noted: "The OTS regulation of holding companies is not as intrusive as that of the Federal Reserve. In particular, the OTS rarely conducts extensive onsite examinations ... The OTS generally is considered a less sophisticated regulator than the Federal Reserve." (pp. 173–4)

The chairman of the FDIC during the crisis, Sheila Bair, has described vividly in her memoirs the fights with the Fed, especially the Federal Reserve Bank of New York and its then president Tim Geithner, concerning in particular Citigroup, and her similar fights with the OTS and its director John Reich, especially with regard to her concern for the troubled Washington Mutual (WaMu). It was when the FDIC, despite objections from the OTS, downgraded WaMu and put it on its troubled-bank list that Reich fired off his now-famous mail to a colleague that "I cannot believe the continuing audacity of this woman ...," prompting Bair's comments that "if only OTS had spent as much energy regulating WaMu as it had fighting us, we might have been able to avert a failure."[14]

Even after the failure of IndyMac in July 2008 (at 7 billion dollars, the most costly failure to the DIF during the whole crisis), Reich told the American Bankers' Association that:

> Selecting a strong regulator to monitor this new level playing field is critical for protecting consumers and restoring market confidence. I won't pretend to be a disinterested party, but I know that the OTS has the most extensive expertise of any regulatory agency in the oversight and supervision of mortgage banking operations and I believe the OTS is in the best position to assume federal authority to regulate the currently unregulated players in mortgage banking.[15]

John Reich "resigned" as director of the OTS on 12 February 2009 and the OTS itself was abolished by the Dodd–Frank Act with effect from 21 July 2011.

We will come back in more detail in Chapter 15 to the failures and near-failures of IndyMac, Wachovia, Countrywide and Washington Mutual.

---

[14] Sheila Bair, *Bull by the Horns: Fighting to Save Main Street from Wall Street and Wall Street From Itself* (New York: Free Press, 2012), pp. 89–90.
[15] http://files.ots.treas.gov/87169.pdf

14 | USA

Bear Stearns, Merrill Lynch and Lehman Brothers

Different rules of the game

The three investment banks mentioned in the headline all disappeared in the financial crisis. Bear Stearns was bought by JPMorgan Chase and Merrill Lynch by Bank of America, while Lehman Brothers was allowed to fail. We will provide more detailed descriptions of their demise later in this chapter. The other two major investment banks, Goldman Sachs and Morgan Stanley, were accepted by the Federal Reserve as commercial bank holding companies. A whole industry, created by the Glass–Steagall Act of 1933, had basically ceased to exist almost overnight. Some would say it was inevitable because their business model was no longer viable. Others would say that the lure of the TARP money on attractive conditions offered to banks (but not investment banks) was the main incentive for the shift.

Table 21 tries to spell out the different degrees of risk taken by the investment-bank sector in comparison with US commercial banks and European universal/investment banks. A first observation is that the American investment banks had substantially more risk (higher leverage ratio) when the crisis struck than the major US commercial banks. When the two remaining major investment banks converted to bank holding companies on 21 September 2008, their risk level had to be substantially reduced. There were two reasons for this forced change in behavior. Firstly, the investment banks were regulated by the SEC, not the OCC or the Fed, in what used to be characterized as "light touch" regulation. Regulation could, it had been concluded, be lighter since they did not take insured deposits from the public. Hence they had not the same need to be supervised and restricted in their activities since they did not pose the same degree of risk to overall financial stability, namely the risk of a "run" on their deposits. The fallacy of this argumentation will become apparent in the following. A run can ensue on wholesale funding through commercial paper and/or repos just as well as on deposits.

Table 21. *Leverage ratio^a (total assets/Tier 1 equity) in some universal and investment banks*

	2006	2007	2008	2009
US investment banks				
Bear Stearns	28.9	33.5	n a	n a
Lehman Brothers	26.2	30.7	n a	n a
Merrill Lynch	21.6	31.9	n a	n a
Morgan Stanley	31.7	33.4	13.0	16.5
Goldman Sachs	23.4	26.2	14.1	13.1
US major commercial banks				
Citigroup	20.7	24.5	16.3	14.6
JPMorgan Chase	17.6	16.6	16.0	15.3
Bank of America	16.0	20.6	15.0	13.8
Wells Fargo	13.1	15.7	15.1	13.2
European universal/investment banks				
UBS	59.1	69.4	61.9	42.2
Deutsche Bank	45.8	71.4	71.7	43.6
Barclays	43.2	44.8	49.8	27.7
BNP Paribas	41.8	49.7	45.0	32.7
Credit Suisse	35.7	39.2	36.2	28.5
RBS	29.0	42.9	34.4	22.2

^{a}It should be noted that the term "leverage" may mean both the capital/assets ratio and the assets/capital ratio.
Sources: David Stowell, *An Introduction to Investment Banks, Hedge Funds and Private Equity* (Waltham, MA: Academic Press, 2010), p. 187 for investment banks 2006–7, and own calculations from *The Banker*, various issues, for all other data.

Secondly, the capital requirements of banks vs. investment banks were vastly different. Investment banks in the US were permitted to shift to the Basel II framework, allowing them to calculate risks by their own internal models. Objections to Basel II from such bank regulators as Sheila Bair from the FDIC and influential academics such as Daniel Tarullo led to the situation whereby American banks and thrifts were still on Basel I (with its fixed risk weights) when the crisis began.[1] The FDIC had calculated that the median major bank shifting to Basel II would face 31 percent lower capital requirements and that overall capital required would fall by 22 percent. Implementation of Basel II was – fortunately – halted by the advancing financial crisis and hence US banks will make the jump directly from Basel I to Basel III.[2] In Europe, as we have seen, the migration to Basel II allowed banks to aggravate their already low capital situation.

The ability of US commercial banks and thrifts to reduce their capital levels was restricted also by other regulations, firstly by the requirements set by the FDIC through its "Prompt Corrective Action" (PCA) and secondly by the fact that US banks, in contrast to European banks, also had to follow rules limiting total assets in relation to capital (while Basel I and II only set restrictions on minimum capital to risk-weighted assets).[3] In order to be found "well-capitalized" under PCA, a bank would have to have a core Tier 1 capital/asset ratio of at least 5 percent, implying a maximum leverage ratio of 20. "Adequately capitalized" banks would similarly be limited to a ratio of 25. It is evident that – partly thanks to TARP/CPP – none of the banks in Table 21 was ever above 25 during the crisis.

In comparing US and European values, it should be noted that European banks mostly use IFRS (International Financial Reporting

---

[1] Bair, *Bull by the Horns*, ch. 3, "The fight over Basel II"; Robert A. Jarrow, "A critique of revised Basel II," *Journal of Financial Services Research* 32 (October 2007), pp. 1–11; Daniel K. Tarullo, *Banking on Basel: The Future of International Financial Regulation* (Washington, DC: The Peterson Institute for International Economics, 2008). Tarullo was at the time Professor of Law at Georgetown University. From 2009, he is a member of the board of governors of the Federal Reserve System and the governor in charge of bank supervision and regulation, overseeing the central bank's implementation of the Dodd–Frank financial regulation.

[2] The "Collins amendment" to the Dodd–Frank Act, inspired by Sheila Bair and originally proposed by the FDIC, will, however, prevent banks that shift to Basel III from having lower capital requirements than small banks still operating under Basel I, or lower than what insured institutions faced when the Act was adopted.

[3] In the implementation of Basel III (where a restriction on leverage is introduced with a minimum ratio of Tier 1 capital to assets of 3 percent) in the United States, the bank supervisors have decided that the eight major bank holding companies must hold at least 5 percent Tier 1 capital as a ratio to total (unweighted) assets and their bank subsidiaries at least 6 percent, corresponding to a "well-capitalized bank" under PCA.

Standards) while US banks (as well as Credit Suisse in the table and also Japanese banks) use GAAP (Generally Accepted Accounting Principles). If the calculations and comparisons made by the FDIC for 2012 are applicable, we should raise the US (and Credit Suisse) leverage ratios by some 50 percent to make them comparable with the European ratios. For that year, the leverage ratio of the major US banks was, on average, 16 under GAAP but would have been 23 under IFRS.[4] If we assume the same relationship for 2008, the four US commercial banks would have had a leverage ratio of 23 if translated into IFRS, as compared to 53 as average for the included European banks. Note in particular the ratios for UBS and Deutsche Bank![5]

Bear Stearns[6]

In discussing the American financial crisis and its main events, one is likely to mention the investment bank Lehman Brothers (the only one that was allowed to fail, with disastrous consequences) or the biggest investment bank of them all, Merrill Lynch (which was swallowed by

---

[4] Federal Deposit Insurance Corporation (Thomas Hoenig), "Capitalization ratios for global systemically important banks (G-SIB), data as of fourth quarter 2012." The main differences are firstly that GAAP but not IFRS allows netting of offsetting positions with the same counterparty and secondly that IFRS treats the market value of a derivative in gross terms when translating the credit value of a derivative into asset terms, while under GAAP, offsetting is allowed for the amount of collateral received against the claim, reducing the credit risk.

[5] In June 2013, the new Prudential Regulatory Authority (PRA) within the Bank of England, noting that Barclays had a capital–asset ratio of just 2.5 percent (corresponding to a leverage ratio of 40), in contrast to the minimum 3 percent, ordered it to raise a minimum of 3 billion pounds in fresh capital.

[6] Bill Bamber and Andrew Spencer, *Bear Trap: The Fall of Bear Stearns and the Panic of 2008* (New York: Brick Tower Press, 2008); Alan C. Greenberg and Mark Singer, *The Rise and Fall of Bear Stearns* (New York: Simon & Schuster, 2010); William Cohan, *House of Cards: A Tale of Hubris and Wretched Excess on Wall Street* (New York: Doubleday, 2009); Federal Reserve Board, "Bear Stearns, JPMorgan Chase and Maiden Lane LLC," *Regulatory Reform*, latest update 2 August 2013. www.federalreserve.gov/newsevents/reform_bearstearns.htm; Alan S. Blinder, *After the Music Stopped: The Financial Crisis, the Response and the Work Ahead* (New York: Penguin, 2013), ch. 5, "From Bear to Lehman: Inconsistency was the hobgoblin"; David Wessel, *In Fed We Trust: Ben Bernanke's War on the Great Panic and How the Federal Reserve Became the Fourth Branch of Government* (New York: Crown, 2009), ch. 9, "Unusual and exigent"; *Financial Crisis Inquiry Report* (Washington, DC: Government Printing Office, January 2011), esp. ch. 15; Henry M. (Hank) Paulson, *On the Brink: Inside the Race to Stop the Collapse of the Global Financial System* (New York: Business Plus, 2010), ch. 5, "Thursday, March 13, 2008."

Bank of America) or Washington Mutual (because it was the largest bank failure ever) or the insurance company AIG (because it was at the time the world's largest insurance company as well as the costliest bail-out ever).

But actually Bear Stearns should have the primary position for two reasons: firstly, it was the first major failure in the United States in the financial crisis of 2007–10 and secondly, because its failure and assumption by JPMorgan Chase drastically changed the rules of the game of resolution of financial firms in the United States.

As succinctly and provocatively stated by David Wessel in his *In Fed We Trust* (pp. 147–8, italics in original):

> *Before Bear Stearns*, no major financial institution had failed.
>
> *Before Bear Stearns*, the Fed was doing what central banks have done for generations: lending money for a few days, sometimes a few weeks, to solid commercial banks ...
>
> *After Bear Stearns*, potential buyers of any failing institution ... would ask the Fed not whether it would lend, but how much it was willing to kick in.
>
> *After Bear Stearns*, the debate would not be *whether* the Great Panic would require government bailouts but would instead be *who* would be bailed out and on what terms.
>
> *After Bear Stearns*, the line between Fed-protected, deposit-taking Main Street banks and the less tightly regulated, more leveraged Wall Street investment banks was obliterated.
>
> *After Bear Stearns*, the Fed's elastic interpretation of its powers to lend to almost anyone in "unusual and exigent circumstances" would lead the Bush administration to see the Fed as lender of *first* resort, rather than its traditional role as the lender of *last* resort.

Bear Stearns was the smallest of the five major investment banks and also one of the youngest. Conservatively run by its long-time CEO and later chairman of the board, Alan C. "Ace" Greenberg (the bank used to be called "the Sparta of Wall Street"), its expansion took entirely new dimensions and forms after his retirement in 2001.[7] In

---

[7] Born in 1927, Greenberg spent his entire 60-year career at Bear Stearns and was still chairman of the executive committee at Bear's demise in 2008 and the major player behind its sale to JPMorgan Chase, where he became a non-executive vice chairman at age 81.

2000, Bear had had total assets of 172 billion dollars. This doubled to 350 billion dollars in 2006 and rose again to 395 billion dollars at the end of 2007 when the bank's troubles began in earnest. At that time, it also had over 13 trillion dollars in notional value in derivative contracts, mostly OTC. These positions were supported by only 11 billion dollars of equity for a leverage ratio way above 30 even under GAAP (see Table 21). Its actual leverage ratio was, at around 38, even higher than the 33.5 stated in the table since Bear Stearns window-dressed its balance sheet every reporting quarter by selling assets which were then repurchased at the beginning of next quarter.[8]

The stock price of Bear Stearns had peaked at almost 173 dollars per share in January 2007. Just over a year later, JPMorgan Chase would offer to purchase the company for 2 dollars per share.

As we have seen earlier in the Chronology (Part I), some non-bank mortgage lenders had gone belly-up already during the spring of 2007. Some big international banks such as HSBC had also recorded huge losses on their American mortgage operations, especially on subprime mortgages. Yet it came as a surprise when, in June 2007, Bear Stearns Asset Management (BSAM), a firm controlled (but not guaranteed) by Bear Stearns, froze withdrawals from two of its hedge funds, the High-Grade Structured Credit Master Fund and the High-Grade Structured Credit Strategies Enhanced Leverage Fund. Bear Stearns had become one of the major originators of so-called private-label MBSs, i.e. such mortgage-backed securities which were not issued through the twin GSE agencies (government-sponsored enterprises) Fannie Mae and Freddie Mac. In the top year 2006, private-label issues at almost a trillion dollars were about equal to agency issues and Bear was one of the top three issuers. It also repackaged these MBSs into CDOs and CDO-squared, underwriting issues worth 36 billion dollars in 2006.[9] Most of these were sold to investors but some were retained for their own

---

[8] When asked by a colleague why the SEC could not simply order Bear Stearns to lower its leverage ratio, the SEC's Head of Consolidated Supervised Entities answered that "the SEC's job was not to tell the banks how to run their companies..." Quoted from the *Financial Crisis Inquiry Report*, p. 283.

[9] A (residential) mortgage-backed security ((R)MBS) is a security where the underlying assets are individual mortgages. A collateralized debt obligation (CDO) is a security with a number of MBSs as underlying assets; a CDO-squared is a security where the underlying assets consist of a number of CDOs.

BSAM funds. The two High-Grade funds at that time had 60 percent of their assets in CDOs backed by subprime mortgages, securities whose value had fallen sharply and would fall even more after the dramatic downgrading by the major rating firms (see the Chronology for 10 July 2007).

The head of BSAM, Ralph Cioffi, administered both 11 CDOs for Bear Stearns as well as running the two hedge funds. Since he picked the CDOs that the hedge funds would invest in, he was sitting on both sides of the transaction in a clear conflict of interest between his CDO investors and his hedge fund investors.

When banks funding BSAM through daily repo transactions started backing off and long-term trading partners refused to trade with BSAM, Bear Stearns itself took on the risk of funding BSAM by taking mortgage-related securities worth 1.6 billion dollars onto its own books. In an attempt to further rid the funds of risk, BSAM created a CDO-squared deal in the form of commercial paper which was sold to investors in May 2007. A critical condition for its success was that the deal was guaranteed by Bank of America with a liquidity put, enabling investors to sell the securities back if they could not be rolled (refinanced). This guarantee would eventually cost Bank of America more than 4 billion dollars as the underlying CDOs became worthless with the fall of subprime prices after the dramatic downgrading of hundreds of MBSs in early July. On 31 July 2007, both BSAM funds filed for bankruptcy.

In November 2007, Bear Stearns revealed a write-down of 1.9 billion dollars on subprime related securities, leading to its first-ever quarterly loss of 379 million dollars. Despite an investment of 1 billion dollars by China's sovereign wealth fund (SWF) Citic during the fall and despite an issue of 2.5 billion dollars' worth of unsecured bonds, the firm was facing not only liquidity problems (which were known to the market) but also an increasing lack of capital (which was not fully appreciated by the market at the time). As counterparties to its commercial-paper funding facilities dropped off one by one, Bear Stearns became more and more dependent on short-term financing through the repo market. At the end of 2007, it needed secured repo borrowing at over 100 billion dollars, most of it rolled over daily at gradually rising interest rates and gradually higher collateral demands from its counterparties, dominated by JPMorgan Chase and Bank of New York Mellon.

The crisis became acute on 10 March 2008, when Moody's downgraded a number of MBSs issued by Bear Stearns. The rumor spread that Bear Stearns itself had also been downgraded. Dutch Rabobank informed the company that it would not renew a 2 billion dollar line of credit. The OCC, the regulator of nationally chartered banks, was said to call around to the major banks to estimate their exposure to Bear Stearns in the event of a failure. A wholesale "bank run" ensued, involving mutual funds and other investors refusing to buy Bear's unsecured commercial paper as well as dried-up repo finance which was secured by MBSs, now worth much less than the day before. Bear had started the week with 18 billion dollars in liquid assets. On the evening of Thursday 13 March, the company informed its regulator, the SEC, that it would be unable to open next day, since the cash was virtually gone, only 2 billion dollars was left. That day the company was sharply downgraded by all the three rating agencies. Its stock price fell the same day by almost 50 percent, finishing below 30 dollars per share.

To survive the Friday, Bear Stearns received an emergency loan from the New York Fed of 12.9 billion dollars but it was made clear that it would not be renewed on Monday. The company had the weekend and no more to find a buyer. The only buyer potentially interested was JPMorgan Chase. Since Morgan was the clearing agent for Bear Stearns as well as its most important repo counterparty, it knew the company well, simplifying the compulsory "due diligence." JPMorgan, however, knowing that Bear's portfolio held some 26 billion dollars in securities backed by souring Alt-A and subprime mortgages, required the support from the Federal Reserve in order to make an offer. Invoking "unusual and exigent circumstances," the Federal Reserve used its authority under section 13(3) of the Federal Reserve Act to take almost 30 billion dollars' worth of securities off Bear Stearns' books. This was the first time since the Great Depression that the paragraph had been invoked. The procedure used was a loan from the New York Fed to JPMorgan of just under 29 billion dollars, while JPMorgan itself issued a subordinated loan for 1.15 billion dollars. Because of this construction, JPMorgan would take the first hit on Bear Stearns' loss, but after 1.15 billion the Fed would bear the losses up to 28.82 billion dollars. The loan was non-recourse, meaning that the Fed could not take any of JPMorgan's assets should losses appear, only the Bear securities it held as collateral for the loan. On that Sunday evening, JPMorgan made an offer to purchase Bear Stearns for 2 dollars per share; a month earlier, the stock had traded for 93 dollars per share. The price was raised to 10 dollars per share a week later because of the risk that the shareholders would otherwise not agree to the takeover. Even so, the price paid corresponded roughly to the value of the recently built 47-story Bear Stearns Building on 383 Madison Avenue in New York, valuing the entire operations of Bear Stearns and its franchise at zero. That the offer was attractive for the buyer was also seen in the fact that the share price of JPMorgan rose 10 percent the day the agreement was made public.[10]

The collateral for the loan, i.e. the securities taken from Bear's portfolio, were parked in a newly started Fed-owned special purpose vehicle (SPV) called Maiden Lane LLC (limited liability company), named for the street next to the one in New York where the New York Fed has its address. Over time, there would be also Maiden Lane II and III, when a similar procedure was used to aid AIG, on which we will have more to say later on. The gradual disposal of the collateral would repay the loan to Morgan. As of September 2013, the loan had been repaid in full with interest, while still leaving a balance of securities worth 1.5 billion dollars in Maiden Lane.[11]

On the very same day that JPMorgan Chase made public its offer to purchase Bear Stearns, Sunday 16 March 2008, the Fed approved the primary dealer credit facility (PDCF), by which the Fed could lend to all its primary dealers, whether banks or not. As stated by the earlier CEO of Bear Stearns, Jimmy Caine, the PDCF came "just about 45 minutes" too late to save his firm.[12] He was probably wrong, since the problems of Bear Stearns were not only lack of liquidity but also solvency where the Fed facility would not have helped.

Overall grade of the handling of Bear Stearns:
A (on a scale of A to F=Fail)

A number of critical comments have been made on the Fed's innovative decision to help bailing out Bear Stearns, or to be more precise,

---

[10] As CEO of Chicago-based Bank One, Jamie Dimon, the same Dimon who was now CEO of JPMorgan Chase, had offered to pay around 100 dollars per share for Bear Stearns in 2000 just before the stockmarket crash (Cohan, *House of Cards*, p. 273).

[11] www.newyorkfed.org/markets/maidenlane.html

[12] Blinder, *After the Music Stopped*, p. 114.

to bail out its creditors while the shareholders suffered.[13] The former chairman of the Federal Reserve, Paul Volcker, stated in a speech to the Economic Club of New York that the Fed had taken "actions that extend to the very edge of its lawful and implied powers."[14] Vincent Reinhart, at the time secretary to the Federal Open Market Committee, later called it "the worst policy mistake in a generation."[15] Donald Kohn, the Fed's vice chairman, called it "an irreversible decision that would have consequences that were very hard to say at the time."[16] Anna Jacobson Schwarz, co-author of Milton Friedman in their classic *A Monetary History of the United States*, called it a "rogue operation."[17]

The chairman of the Federal Reserve, Ben Bernanke, later called it "the toughest decision during the financial crisis" (FCIC, *Financial Crisis Inquiry Report*, p. 105). In his statement to the Senate Committee on Banking, Housing, and Urban Affairs on 3 April 2008, he stated:

Our financial system is extremely complex and interconnected, and Bear Stearns participated extensively in a range of critical markets. The sudden failure of Bear Stearns likely would have led to a chaotic unwinding of positions in those markets and could have severely shaken confidence. The company's failure could also have cast doubt on the financial positions of some of Bear Stearns' thousands of counterparties and perhaps of companies with similar businesses. Given the exceptional pressures on the global economy and financial system, the damage caused by a default by Bear Stearns could have been severe and extremely difficult to contain. Moreover, the adverse

---

[13] One of the major shareholders of Bear Stearns was the ex-CEO Jimmy Cayne. His billion-dollar holding in the company was ultimately sold for 61 million dollars.

[14] Niall Ferguson, *The Ascent of Money: A Financial History of The World* (New York: Allen Lane/Penguin 2008), p. 395; Blinder, *After the Music Stopped*, p. 110.

[15] Blinder, *After the Music Stopped*, p. 110. Vincent Reinhart is today chief US economist at Morgan Stanley. He is the husband of Carmen Reinhart, co-author of Carmen M. Reinhart and Kenneth S. Rogoff, *This Time Is Different: Eight Centuries of Financial Folly* (Princeton University Press, 2009).

[16] Blinder, *After the Music Stopped*, p. 105. After his retirement from the Fed, Donald Kohn became a non-executive member of the Financial Policy Committee of the Bank of England.

[17] Ibid., p. 110.

impact of a default would not have been confined to the financial system but would have been felt broadly in the real economy through its effects on asset values and credit availability.

To prevent a disorderly failure of Bear Stearns and the unpredictable but likely severe consequences for market functioning and the broader economy, the Federal Reserve, in close consultation with the Treasury Department, agreed to provide funding to Bear Stearns through JPMorgan Chase. Over the following weekend, JPMorgan Chase agreed to purchase Bear Stearns and assumed Bear's financial obligations.[18]

High-level politicians, members of the Senate's Committee on Banking, Housing and Urban Affairs, supported the decision. Senator Charles Schumer (D-NY) said that "when you are staring into the abyss, you don't quibble about details." Senator Christopher Todd (D-CT), of Dodd–Frank fame, said similarly that "I believe this is the right action that was taken over the weekend. To allow this to go into bankruptcy, I think, would have created some systemic problems that would have been massive."[19]

It is difficult not to agree with the above statements. Bear Stearns was "too interconnected to fail," if not "too big to fail." It was the prime broker to hundreds of hedge funds (executing trades, holding collateral, etc). In total, it had some 5,000 trading partners. It was the counterparty in some 750,000 derivatives transactions (remember its 13 trillion dollars in nominal derivative positions). It was a critical actor in the 2.8 trillion dollar overnight repo market, in itself responsible for almost 5 percent of the market. Had it failed, the dominoes might have tumbled (as indeed they did five months later when Lehman Brothers was allowed to fail).

Not only the innovative character of the rescue, invoking an almost forgotten paragraph in the Federal Reserve Act, but also the speed of action, merits an "A." From the first call for help by Bear Stearns to the New York Fed to the offer from JPMorgan, it took only 72 hours.[20]

---

[18] www.federalreserve.gov/newsevents/testimony/bernanke20080403a.htm
[19] Cohan, *House of Cards*, p. 98.
[20] Kate Kelly, *Street Fighters: The Last 72 Hours of Bear Stearns, the Toughest Firm on Wall Street* (New York: Portfolio Trade/Penguin, 2010); "Inside the Fall of Bear Stearns," *Wall Street Journal*, 9 May 2009.

Merrill Lynch[21]

One may perhaps wonder why Merrill Lynch is included in this chapter and in this book at all since – officially – the government was in no way involved in the purchase by Bank of America of Merrill Lynch in September 2008. Yet, as we shall see, by sticks and carrots, the US Treasury and the Federal Reserve were very much responsible for the merger taking place, thus saving the largest of the American investment banks from probable bankruptcy. "A shotgun wedding" was a later characteristic of the event.[22]

There were many similarities between Bear Stearns and Merrill Lynch, only Merrill was much larger. Like Bear, it had had a traditionally conservative attitude, being called "the Catholic firm of Wall Street." It never catered to the very rich but focused, as its founder Charlie Merrill had stated, on "the modest sums of the thrifty," for whom its 700 regional branch offices and the 15,000 strong salesforce ("the thundering herd") were visible everywhere just like any local bank branch office. This gave Merrill not only a family name over the whole country but the ability to market on its own the CDOs and other products it created rather than relying on independent brokers. Merrill was also known for taking care of its own people, the image of "Mother Merrill" giving rise to many life-time careers.

All this changed when Stanley O'Neal became president in 2001 and then CEO and chairman in 2003. Potential rivals to his power were rapidly dismissed and the internal image changed to one of cutthroat competition for promotions, perks and bonuses. In his first year as president, more than 20,000 jobs were abolished. Clients with less than 100,000 dollars to invest lost their private broker and were shunted to common call centers. The risk appetite increased dramatically, the bank's exposure to mortgage-based CDOs increasing tenfold. During the first half of 2007 alone, Merrill produced 34 billion

---

[21] Apart from literature cited above for Bear Stearns, see Greg Farrell, *Crash of the Titans: Greed, Hubris, the Fall of Merrill Lynch and the Near-Collapse of Bank of America* (London: Random House, 2010); Gretchen Morgenson, "How the thundering herd faltered and fell", *New York Times*, 8 November 2008; Bethany McLean and Joe Nocera, *All the Devils Are Here: The Hidden History of the Financial Crisis* (New York: Portfolio/Penguin, 2010).

[22] It was said by Congressman Edophus Towns from New York. *Financial Crisis Inquiry Report*, p. 384.

dollars' worth of CDOs, beating the nearest rival Citibank by 4 billion. The downside of this huge volume was that the collapsing subprime market and falling house prices had led to bonds being forcibly retained on Merrill's own books. As of 30 June 2007, Merrill had a net exposure to CDOs of over 30 billion dollars and rising.

The image of Merrill and its profitability from 2002 to mid 2007 had, however, whetted the appetite of the largest commercial bank in the US in terms of deposits, Bank of America. On 30 September 2007 (when, as we remember, the two Bear Stearns funds had recently filed for bankruptcy and a number of subprime lenders had gone belly-up), O'Neal met in secret with the CEO of Bank of America, Ken Lewis. Given Merrill's focus on faltering CDOs and the known fact that it had doubled its balance sheet over the last two years to over a trillion dollars, Lewis thought that Merrill might be tempted to accept a merger proposal. He was willing to pay 90 dollars per share, which represented a 26 percent premium over the current price in the market. Despite the fact that – unknown to Lewis – Merrill was about to make public a dramatic downturn in its revenues and a huge loss for the third quarter, O'Neal turned the offer down as being insufficient. A year later, his successor would sell the company to the same Lewis for 29 dollars per share, less than a third of the price offered in 2007.

The third quarter would add to both exposures and write-downs. On 24 October 2007, Merrill Lynch announced reservations for credit losses of 7.9 billion dollars for the third quarter alone (later increased to 8.4 billion). This led to a net quarterly loss of 2.3 billion dollars, about the same size as its profit just one quarter before. The losses occurred despite the fact that the investment bank had retained mainly the super senior tranches (rated AAA–AA) in the CDOs they had constructed, selling the lower-rated tranches. But subprime valuations had collapsed after the general ratings downgrade in July; even the senior tranches were being valued at perhaps 60 cents in the dollar.

At the end of September, the bank held a gross position of 55 billion dollars in CDO-related paper of which almost 40 billion was unhedged. This should be compared with the fact that at the end of 2006, Merrill's shareholder equity had been but 39 billion dollars. It hadn't helped its solvency that the firm had also bought back 21 billion dollars' worth of its own stock since 2004 in order to increase the price of its shares, which in turn was the main driver behind the senior management's bonus payments. In early October, the head of Merrill's

Fixed Income (FICC), Osman Semerci, who had engineered the extensive CDO production as well as hidden the extent of the resulting exposure, was fired. On 30 October, he was followed by Stan O'Neal himself, "resigning" both on account of the losses but also since he had approached Bank of America as well as Wachovia with merger proposals without informing his board of directors. His replacement was John Thain, presently CEO of the New York Stock Exchange, but with a long career at Goldman Sachs. He would himself "resign" just over a year later.

In late 2007 and early 2008, the situation appeared to be stabilizing under the new CEO. Certainly, Merrill Lynch had to write down an additional 14.1 billion dollars of the CDOs, leading to a net loss for the year 2007 of a massive 8.6 billion dollars. But it had also received a capital injection of 6.2 billion dollars from Davis Advisors and Temasek Holdings, Singapore's Sovereign Wealth Fund, later increased by another 3.4 billion, as well as 6.6 billion dollars in fresh capital from the sovereign wealth funds of Kuwait and South Korea and Japanese bank Mizuho, in total over 17 billion dollars.

But the company continued to bleed in synchronization with the deteriorating US economy, officially in recession since December 2007. For the first quarter of 2008, Merrill wrote down another 4.5 billion dollars and lost 2 billion. For the second quarter, the loss increased to 4.7 billion dollars. However, it also sold its share in the Bloomberg news agency and other assets for almost 8 billion dollars, thereby more than making up for the loss in the half-year. At the end of July, it also sold CDOs once having been valued at 30.6 billion dollars to the private equity firm Lone Star Funds for 1.7 billion dollars in cash and a loan of 5.1 billion dollars. The consequence would be a writedown in the third quarter of 2008 of 4.4 billion dollars. But it also succeeded in raising over 7 billion fresh dollars from the market in a secondary offering, the largest ever for a financial institution.

If things looked reasonably manageable, the impending fall of Lehman Brothers changed all that. The meeting at the New York Fed on Friday, 12 September 2008 with the heads of the major banks and investment banks (except the one most concerned, Dick Fuld from Lehman Brothers) made it clear that the Treasury and the Fed had no intention of bailing out Lehman like they had bailed out Bear Stearns and expected its brethren to perform that task, just as they had bailed out Long Term Capital Management (LTCM) in 1998. But the hole this time was ten times larger and there was no way that the banks, given their own present conditions, would give away the 30 billion dollars needed to fill the hole.

The meeting, however, resulted in John Thain, CEO of the firm which would evidently be next in line if Lehman Brothers went under, calling Ken Lewis of Bank of America. Like a schoolboy, he had been summoned – twice – to the office of Hank Paulson, US Treasury Secretary, a former senior colleague from Goldman Sachs[23] and told that he should consider a merger with BofA while it was still interested. The fall of Lehman would probably make a potential deal even worse and aggravate the already serious fall in Merrill's stock price.

But to the general surprise of the negotiating team from Merrill Lynch, the offer they received was 29 dollars per share, way above Friday's closing price of 17 dollars, in an all-stock bid worth 50 billion dollars. At year end 2006, Merrill's share price had been 256 dollars ... But now the offer was generous and at midnight, 14 September, it was accepted by both Boards of Directors and signed by the two CEOs. The deal would close on 1 January 2009. Merrill Lynch was no more.[24]

But the story of government intervention doesn't end here. Rather, it begins now. Two issues cropped up, risking the entire deal: the escalating losses at Merrill and the question of bonuses for the Merrill people.

At least the latter was easy to solve short-term but would come back to haunt the bank later on. Since investment banking firms rewarded their performers with bonuses to a much higher degree than commercial banking, it was important that the Merrill people could themselves allocate bonuses for 2008. After the merger was completed at year end, it would be up to the BofA board to decide. So with the tacit agreement of the leadership of BofA, Merrill decided to pay out the bonuses before year end rather than in February as was customary. A clause in the merger agreement specified that the bonus pool could

---

[23] Thain had been co-chief operating officer (COO) to Paulson's CEO until he had left for the New York Stock Exchange in 2004.

[24] It would remain a separate subsidiary of Bank of America until December 2013 when the accounts were integrated, although BofA continues to use the Merrill Lynch name for its investment banking activities, including commercial lending, M&A, wealth management, private banking and retail brokerage.

not exceed 5.8 billion dollars, the same amount as for 2007. The financial situation of the company was, however, vastly different in 2008 and should have merited much smaller amounts, if any. Indeed, the executive committee members of Goldman Sachs with its CEO, Lloyd Blankfein, had made public that they would not accept bonuses for 2008. The three top figures at Morgan Stanley with its CEO, John Mack, did likewise. Yet Thain demanded 40 million dollars for himself, a demand later scaled back to 10 million. He got zero. Total bonuses paid out, however, were still 4 billion dollars. The issue had become especially sensitive since firms receiving TARP money would be restricted in setting salaries and bonuses. Merrill Lynch was set to receive 10 billion dollars of TARP money but only once the merger with Bank of America was completed. Hence the board's compensation committee had double reasons to see to it that the bonuses were paid out before year end.

Bank of America would pay a fine to the SEC of 150 million dollars to settle the charge that shareholders of BofA were not informed before their vote of the formulation in the takeover contract concerning bonuses.

When the shareholders of BofA voted on the deal in early December, they were not told either of the exploding losses in the recently bought investment bank. In early November, it became apparent that losses for October alone would be over 7 billion dollars, almost equivalent to the loss for the entire year 2007. In the week before Christmas, Lewis contacted both Bernanke and Paulson, saying that his board of directors was having second thoughts about the deal. Losses for the fourth quarter at Merrill Lynch were now estimated at 22 billion dollars. Even after tax, they would amount to 16 billion dollars, half Merrill's equity, which in the board's mind motivated breaking off the deal, invoking MAC (material adverse change), i.e. changes that had taken place after the deal was made but before it would be finalized.

In April 2013, Bank of America would pay a fine of 2.43 billion dollars to the SEC to settle the charge that it had misled investors, knowing full well the magnitude of the escalating losses in Merrill Lynch, since they were reported daily to the new owners of the company. No individuals have, however, been charged, neither from Merrill nor from BofA.

In fact, it was not BofA's board that was driving the issue but Lewis himself. Citigroup had just received an additional 20 billion dollars in TARP money plus a guarantee from the government for 306 billion dollars' worth of "toxic assets," since the failure of the largest bank in the United States would run the risk of creating a systemic crisis. Many thought, including Bernanke and Paulson, that Lewis was making an idle threat to cancel the deal just to get a similarly favorable TARP treatment. At a meeting at the Fed, the two government officials strongly advised Lewis against invoking MAC. Firstly, the wording of the MAC in the contract in question specifically ruled out cancelation on account of a general deterioration in market conditions, making it highly unlikely that a break-off would be accepted by the courts. Secondly, displaying openly such incompetence might lead to a run on both banks. However, the question of a support package, similar to the one received by Citi, was raised.

A few days later, on 21 December, Lewis was back on the phone to Paulson, threatening to undo the deal. Paulson in his memoirs vividly describes his actions word for word.[25] Sticks and carrots! First he threatened. The regulator of Bank of America, the Fed, could and probably would replace the entire board and management of BofA, should it display such a "colossal lack of judgment" as to invoke MAC, Paulson said. Secondly, however, the government would not let any systemically important institution fail; implying that a support package just might be available after the deal had been consummated.

He refused, however, to supply the letter demanded by Lewis promising government help, since the Treasury would have had to make such a letter public which in itself might lead to a run on both institutions. But lo and behold, two weeks after the merger had been completed, on 15 January 2009, Bank of America, which had already received 25 billion dollars of TARP money (15 billion for itself and 10 billion for Merrill), got a further injection of 20 billion dollars in preferred stock from the government, plus a guarantee for 118 billion in "toxic assets," on and off balance, mainly the heritage of Merrill Lynch.

[25] *On the Brink*, pp. 429–30.

Overall grade of the handling of Merrill Lynch:
B (on a scale of A to F=Fail)

It is difficult to see what the government could have done better. It had identified economies; were the two institutions to merge, it encouraged the merger. The Financial Crisis Inquiry Commission was broadly supportive of the actions taken (p. 386) although noting that the resulting increase in concentration in banking "places great responsibility on regulators for effective oversight of these institutions."

The main negative voice was that of Sheila Bair, chair of the FDIC, questioning correctly whether the extra infusion of TARP money into BofA and the guarantee for its toxic assets were really necessary.[26] It turned out she was (probably) right: Bank of America soon wanted to exit the program. However, the US Treasury and the FDIC still gained 425 million dollars for a never-used guarantee.

As indicated by the chapter heading in her book where the events are discussed, "Bailing out the boneheads," she is also highly critical of the bailing out of incompetent banks in general and Merrill Lynch in particular. She regarded Merrill as "clearly insolvent with no options for accessing capital from nongovernment sources."[27] While her statement would have been partly correct if Merrill had been a commercial bank, subject to the leverage limits under Prompt Corrective Action, it was not, being an investment bank not subject to regulation by the FDIC. Also it had succeeded up to the end in raising a surprising amount of fresh private capital, only it wasn't enough given mounting losses.

Her second worry was the effect of the acquisition of Merrill Lynch on the insured deposits of Bank of America and hence the effect on the FDIC itself. After all, BofA had 800 billion dollars of deposits. She writes:

Frankly, I wasn't wild about the idea of BofA buying Merrill Lynch. I didn't think its management and board knew much about running a major securities firm, and Merrill had really loaded up on toxic mortgage investments. My view was that holding companies and their subsidiaries should be sources of strength for insured banks, not the other way around. Like so many of the other major securities firms, Merrill had relied excessively on short-term, unstable funding and had taken on extremely high levels of

[26] *Bull by the Horns*, pp. 126 ff.
[27] Ibid., p. 114.

leverage. It needed BofA, with its stable insured deposit base and thicker capital cushion, not the other way around.[28]

Yet one wonders what would have happened if Merrill Lynch had been allowed to fail at the same time as, or slightly after, Lehman Brothers. The impact of the fall of Lehman was bad enough, as we shall see in the next section of this chapter, in particular in combination with the subsequent failures of AIG and Washington Mutual. Also one wonders if it is the role of government agencies to prevent privately agreed mergers, not requiring any government assistance (it was only long after the agreement was signed that BofA tried to involve the government). The Federal Reserve most certainly had to give its permission for the merger since it regulated the Bank of America holding company but what would have happened if it had said "no"? A bank run is the most probable answer.

I will still give regulators a "B" rather than an "A" because they were too passive in the treatment of the investment banks. They reacted quickly in the case of Bear Stearns but then let things develop during the summer at Merrill (and Lehman Brothers) without taking any initiatives until very late in the day. The assumption was that the failure of Bear Stearns would teach the others a lesson to deleverage. It didn't and they didn't and the authorities should have realized that. The investment banks had, of course, been allowed to borrow vast amounts from the Fed in their capacity as primary dealers through the Fed's Term Securities Lending Facility and the Primary Dealer Credit Facility. Yet, the remaining investment banks might have been saved, had they been given direct access to TARP money and had their (newly issued) liabilities, for a fee, been guaranteed just like the FDIC's Temporary Guarantee Liquidity Program (TLGP) did for FDIC-insured banks. Invoking the "systemic exception" (see below), TGLP could have been extended also to investment banks.

Lehman Brothers[29]

The biggest bankruptcy in history is paradoxically the easiest to describe from the point of view of this book since the regulatory authorities, the SEC, the Treasury, the Fed, did nothing, or at least next

---

[28] Ibid., p. 127.
[29] Apart from earlier cited literature, see Lawrence J. McDonald, *A Colossal Failure of Common Sense: The Inside Story of the Collapse of Lehman*

to nothing to prevent it. And the view of the FDIC was well known. If Sheila Bair was against the marriage between Bank of America and Merrill Lynch, she would have objected even more to one of "her" insured banks taking over the much more exposed Lehman Brothers, especially a weak bank like Citi.

Lehman Brothers was the second smallest of the five major investment banks on Wall Street but still twice the size of Bear Stearns. Much more internationally oriented than the other four, it had over 50 percent of its revenue from outside the United States, operating under 2,895 legal identities in 80 different markets around the globe with branch offices or subsidiaries in 12 countries. At the time of its demise, it had 22,000 counterparties, 26,000 employees, more than 100,000 creditors, 906,000 outstanding derivative contracts and 839,000 pending trades.[30] Its bankruptcy would lead to 80 insolvency proceedings in 18 different countries (apart from the United States). Some 66,000 claims totaling 873 billion dollars would be made against Lehman Brothers.[31] Five years later, it is all still being sorted out (see below). Even its inhouse-made securities were international to an extreme degree. One MBS constructed by Lehman had as underlying 5,200 different commercial real estate properties in 11 different legal jurisdictions.[32]

On the surface, Lehman was about as leveraged as the other investment banks. The true situation was, however, far worse, as would be revealed only during the bankruptcy proceedings.[33] It had hidden assets by so-called "regulatory arbitrage" in utilizing differences between American and British accounting standards. By the internal program "Repo 105," the bank transferred bonds at the end of each quarter to its British subsidiary, Lehman Brothers International Europe, registering them as a final sale instead of the repo it really was,

Brothers (New York: Three Rivers, 2010); Andrew Ross Sorkin, *Too Big to Fail: Inside the Battle to Save Wall Street* (London: Allen Lane, 2009).

[30] Lehman Brothers International (Europe) in administration, Joint administrators' progress report for the period 15 September 2008 to 14 March 2009, www.pwc.co.uk/assets/pdf/lbie-progress-report-140409.pdf; www.stanfordlaw review.org/online/misconceptions-about-lehman-brothers-bankruptcy

[31] FCIC, *Financial Crisis Inquiry Report*, p. 340.

[32] Ibid., p. 29.

[33] United States Bankruptcy Court, Southern District of New York, in re Lehman Brothers Holdings Inc., Report of Anton R. Valukas, Examiner, Jenner & Block LLP, http://jenner.com/lehman/

using the proceeds to pay back debt. "105" alluded to the fact that it sold assets worth 105 million dollars to produce a cash inflow of 100 million; for this reason it could be treated as a sale rather than a repo under US accounting rules. There was also a "Repo 108" with similar connotations. In the British subsidiary, however, the same transaction was registered as a repo. At the beginning of the next quarter, Lehman borrowed money in the market to repurchase the "sold" securities. In this way, Lehman had transferred off-balance 50.4 billion dollars' worth of unreported assets at the end of the second quarter of 2008, just before its collapse, a substantial fraction of the 275 billion dollar assets under management.

In this way and others, it hid the fact that its leverage ratio was far higher than reported. At the time of its collapse, after large losses in the second and third quarters, its tangible equity was a mere 1.3 percent of total assets, for a leverage ratio of 76, beating even Deutsche and UBS in Table 21.[34] An additional reason for the increased leverage in comparison with the 2007 data in Table 21 was a stock repurchase of 19 percent of its outstanding public shares as late as January 2008, just before the crash of Bear Stearns. All this was done to raise the stock price and hence improve bonuses.

Even though Lehman was still formally profitable for the first quarter of 2008, it was seen as the next weakest of the five investment banks and hence the problems faced by Bear Stearns on Friday, 14 March 2008, led to a fall of 14.6 percent of Lehman's stock price. From a high of over 80 dollars per share in May 2007, its price reached 30 dollars after Bear Stearns' fall. Half a year later the price would be zero.

The first public major inkling of trouble ahead came on 16 June 2008, when the bank reported a quarterly loss of 2.8 billion dollars, the first negative quarter in the 14 years that had passed since it was spun off from American Express in 1994. The stock price fell an immediate 20 percent to a low of 12 dollars per share. It had started the year at almost 60 dollars.

The next unfavorable piece of news came unfortunately the same weekend that the government had placed Fannie Mae and Freddie Mac into conservatorship. On the morning of Tuesday, 9 September, news agencies reported that the deal between Lehman Brothers and

---

[34] Lehman Brothers in administration, report, p. 5.

the Korea Development Bank (KDB) had fallen through. Perhaps it had been a forlorn hope since it should have been apparent that KDB was never going to pay anything close to what the CEO of Lehman, Dick Fuld, was asking. The next day, the company announced an estimated quarterly loss of 3.9 billion dollars, beating the second quarter loss by over a billion. The news led to a 45 percent fall over the day in Lehman Brothers' share price, which finished below 8 dollars per share.

It became evident that Lehman must be sold, whole or in parts. Interested buyers in the beginning were Bank of America and British bank Barclays, represented by the CEO of Barclays Capital, Bob Diamond, who was American by birth. Interestingly enough, the initiative had come from an old friend of Diamond's, Robert Steel, formerly of Goldman Sachs but now Under Secretary of the Treasury. He had also served on the board of Barclays and hence knew the company well. Ken Lewis from BofA made clear, however, that without a government guarantee for some 40 billion dollars' worth of toxic commercial and residential mortgages on Lehman's books, he would not make an offer. As we saw above, he was really more interested in Merrill Lynch, though at this stage keeping all options open.

The government, through the Treasury Secretary Hank Paulson, made clear, inside the administration as well as publicly, that a bail-out à la Bear Stearns was not on the cards. Firstly, as he stated repeatedly, he did not want to be known as "Mr. Bailout" and, given the mood in Congress, he thought he might even be impeached for doing another Bear Stearns. Secondly, there were political risks. The president's brother, Jeb Bush, ex-governor of Florida, as well as their cousin, George H. Walker IV, worked for Lehman in different capacities and a bail-out could easily become "a public relations nightmare" for the administration.[35] Thirdly, Dick Fuld, nicknamed "the Gorilla," remained on very difficult personal terms with the Treasury Secretary after a disastrous dinner together right after the fall of Bear Stearns, which the always over-sensitive Fuld interpreted as an order from Paulson to sell Lehman Brothers.[36] Fourthly, it must be remembered that the full extent of Lehman's leverage was not known since "Repo

[35] Sorkin, *Too Big to Fail*, p. 284.
[36] McDonald, *A Colossal Failure of Common Sense*, p. 306.

105" had hidden a large sum of its assets. Fifthly, this impression was reinforced by Fuld's attitude to the bitter end that "we are doing fine." Sixthly, the general and public view was that the situation was not as bad as in March. With the Fed's discount window open to investment banks, the risk of a liquidity squeeze à la Bear Stearns was seen as much smaller, while another bail-out would give the impression that "we will no longer have exceptions forged in a crisis. We will have a new de facto federal policy of underwriting Wall Street that will encourage even more reckless risk-taking."[37]

However, the regulators were at this stage finally realizing the full precarious situation of Lehman Brothers, not least in knowing that it had borrowed an unprecedented 230 billion dollars in the repo market on Thursday, 11 September. Counterparties such as JPMorgan Chase were also asking Lehman in vain for more collateral and several counterparties had notified Lehman that they would no longer deal with the firm. The stock fell another 10 percent on Friday, 12 September, to 3.70 dollars, meaning that the employees of Lehman which owned a quarter of the company were basically broke. The CEO, Dick Fuld, had himself lost close to a billion dollars. Hence the "heads of the ten families," i.e. the CEOs of the major banks and investment banks, were called to a meeting in the evening of that Friday at the New York Fed to see if it was possible to save Lehman. Dick Fuld was notoriously absent from those invited.

Acting on the belief that Barclays would buy Lehman, provided that some guarantee could be found for its toxic assets, the CEOs and their assistants set to work over the weekend. Alternatively, they were to suggest actions to mitigate the effects should Lehman have to file for Chapter 11 on Monday. It was noted that John Thain of Merrill Lynch soon disappeared from the proceedings and the remaining CEOs drew the (correct) conclusion that he was in negotiations with Bank of America, leaving only Barclays as a potential suitor.

By Sunday, it was all over and for two reasons. Firstly the group had evaluated Lehman's assets, finding that some 70 billion dollars' worth of assets in commercial and residential real estate would perhaps only be worth half that amount, easily wiping out Lehman's equity, which

---

[37] Leader, *Wall Street Journal*, 12 September 2008, "Lehman's fate," http://online.wsj.com/news/articles/SB122117590254125801

stood at 28 billion dollars at the time. The bankers could see no reason to come up with the planned 33 billion dollars to buy the bad bank containing the toxic assets ("ShitCo" as it was immediately called by the participants), while the healthy parts of Lehman would be bought by Barclays for a garage-sale price, thereby immediately creating a strong new competitor for themselves.

And anyway, it was all in vain since the regulatory authorities of the United States and the United Kingdom had not understood each other. The US Treasury was convinced that Barclays wanted to do the deal since they had expressed an interest in the discussions way back in March. But much had happened since then and Barclays' regulator, the Financial Services Authority (FSA), under its chairman Sir Callum McCarthy was becoming increasingly skeptical. It invoked a formality, however, in order to paint itself out of the political corner of not offending its US counterparts. It insisted on the technicality that a purchase by Barclays required a shareholders' vote, which could take weeks or months to organize, and in the meantime, someone had to guarantee and fund the liabilities of Lehman. Only the British government could waive that formality and the chancellor of the exchequer, Alistair Darling, made clear that he would not help Barclays to "import America's cancer" into Britain.[38] Nor could or would the Federal Reserve extend a guarantee to a British bank in order to help it purchase an American financial institution. End of story.

In the early hours of Monday, 15 September 2008, Lehman Brothers Holdings Inc. filed for protection under Chapter 11. With 639 billion dollars in total assets, it is easily the biggest bankruptcy ever worldwide. Since assets in the London-based Lehman Brothers International Europe were frozen under British bankruptcy laws, own funds as well as customer funds, European and Asian Lehman customers faced severe liquidity problems in not being able to recover their money.

And then the firesale started. Barclays Bank got what it wanted, the healthy parts of the company's North American operations, its Times Square headquarters (by itself, worth close to a billion dollars at the time) and about 9,000 employees. As the only bidder, it paid a miserly 1.3 billion dollars for the package. Nomura Holdings paid 200 million dollars for Lehman's Asian operations. The trickiest businesses to sell

---

[38] Sorkin, *Too Big to Fail*, p. 348.

have been in Europe, where claims in the German subsidiary worth a nominal 2.4 billion dollars were sold for just 500,000 dollars.[39]

As of 2013, the sorting out of claims was expected to take another few years. However, the payback is much better than originally estimated. Lawyers for the Lehman estate have estimated that 70,000 creditors with claims totaling 309 billion dollars may get back 80 billion, having already (in March 2013) received 47 billion, for an estimated payout of 26 percent.[40]

In an interesting paper, the FDIC has studied what would have happened had the Orderly Liquidation Authority (OLA) under the Dodd–Frank Act of 2010 been operative at the time of Lehman's collapse. The FDIC would then have had the authority to seize and wind down not only insured banks but any "financial company" whose demise was deemed to have systemic implications. The FDIC claims that had OLA been invoked, using the normal procedures that the FDIC has established for failing banks, 97 percent of the claims might have been recovered rather than 26 percent. Others have, however, doubted these calculations.[41]

The day of Lehman's bankruptcy and the following two weeks were driven by one panic after an other. On that Monday, S&P 500 fell by 4.7 percent. But Lehman was soon overshadowed by new dramatic events. The day after, the Reserve Primary Fund which had invested heavily in Lehman's commercial paper "broke the buck" and the world's largest insurance company, AIG, had to be bailed out by the Federal Reserve. Washington Mutual created the largest bank bankruptcy ever when it collapsed on 25 September. On 29 September, the negative vote in the House of Representatives on the TARP proposal led to a fall in the S&P of 8.9 percent for the day.

Hence, given these events, it is difficult to say exactly which event caused the ensuing crisis. But, as shown in Figure 29, the spreads

---

[39] "German move raises hopes over unwinding of Lehman's assets," *Financial Times*, 12 July 2010.

[40] http://money.cnn.com/2013/09/16/investing/lehman-brothers/

[41] Federal Deposit Insurance Corporation (FDIC), "The orderly liquidation of Lehman Brothers Holdings Inc. under the Dodd–Frank Act," *FDIC Quarterly* 5:2 (2011), pp. 31–49; William F. Kroener III, "Comment on orderly liquidation under Title II of Dodd–Frank and Chapter 14," in Kenneth E. Scott and John B. Taylor, eds., *Bankruptcy not Bailout: A Special Chapter 14* (Stanford, CA: Hoover Institution Press, 2012).

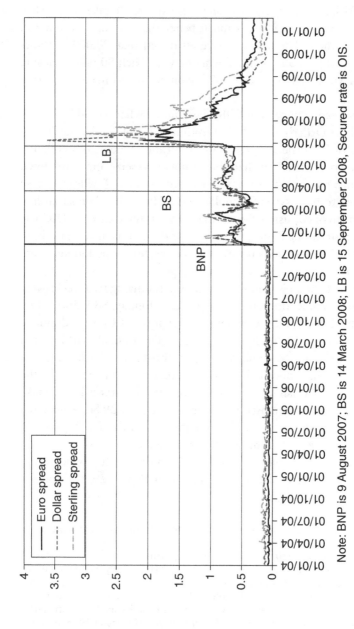

Figure 29. Spreads between three-month interbank money market rates and official rates, percentage

Source: Antonio De Socio, "The interbank market after the financial turmoil," Banca d'Italia Working Paper 819, September 2011.

Note: BNP is 9 August 2007; BS is 14 March 2008; LB is 15 September 2008; Secured rate is OIS.

between interbank market rates and official rates, normally 5–10 basis points, had reached about 100 basis points at some instances the previous year, for instance at the time Bear Stearns was sold. In the week following the collapse of Lehman Brothers, they rose to records: 350 basis points in dollar, 300 basis points in sterling and 200 basis points in euro.

The so-called "fear index," the VIX volatility on the Chicago Board Options Exchange, rose sharply with the bankruptcy of Lehman on Monday to 69 percent from 55 the trading day before and reached a high of 70 on 17 September before falling back. Interestingly enough, just like the interest spread, the highest level of fear was reached on 24 and 27 September when VIX attained 79 and 80 percent respectively, the highest ever both before and after the financial crisis. On the 25th, Washington Mutual was seized by the OTS. Figure 30 depicts the monthly averages where September 2008 at 67 percent beats all other months with ease.

Overall grade of the handling of Lehman Brothers: F (on a scale of A to F=Fail)

The verdicts on the government's decision to let Lehman fail are highly different from person to person, as might be expected. Was it a "colossal failure of common sense" as claimed by McDonald or was it necessary to quench the rising feeling that the salvation of Bear Stearns, Fannie Mae and Freddie Mac had created a "moral hazard" situation where everybody in trouble could expect to be bailed out? The question would soon be academic after the government's bail-out of an insurance company, AIG, as well as two major auto companies, GM and Chrysler, and their respective finance vehicles, reinforcing the question in many people's minds as to why on earth Lehman had been allowed to go bust and not the others. Or was it simply, as stated by the Fed's Ben Bernanke, that neither the government nor the Fed could really do very much under the existing legislation at the time? In contrast to Bear Stearns, the assets held by Lehman, said Bernanke, were of such low quality that they could not be accepted as collateral for a loan from the Fed except at such a large haircut as to make the loan insufficient to save Lehman. And there was no white knight to save it either.

On the positive side, supporting the government's decision, we find the CEOs of competitors Goldman Sachs and JPMorgan Chase.

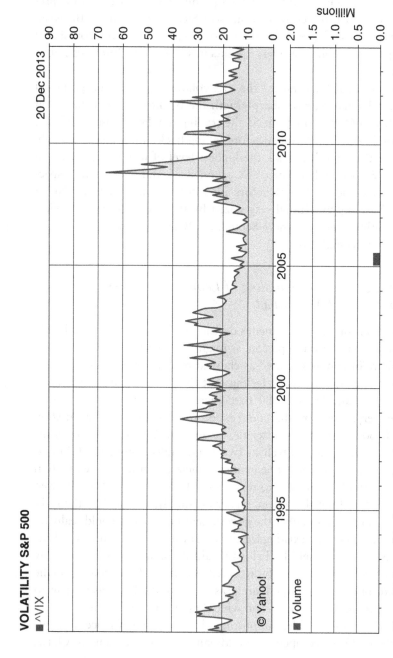

Figure 30. VIX volatility on the Chicago Board Options Exchange (implied volatility of the S&P 500 futures option, standard deviation of annualized daily percentage changes, monthly averages)

Source: http://finance.yahoo.com/q/bc?s=%5EVIX&t=my&l=off&z=l&q=l&c=

Neither thought that Lehman's failure was *the* trigger behind the cataclysmic events that followed, just one event among many. Dimon told the Financial Inquiry Commission (FDIC, p. 342):

I didn't think it was so bad. I hate to say that ... But I thought it was almost the same if on Monday morning the government had saved Lehman ... You still would have had terrible things happen ... AIG was still going to have the runs on the other banks and you were going to have absolute fear and panic in the global markets. Whether Lehman itself got saved or not ... the crisis would have unfolded along a different path, but it probably would have unfolded.

We saw above the contemporaneous commentary from the *Wall Street Journal*, warning the regulatory authorities against "encouraging even more reckless risk-taking" by bailing out Lehman.

John Thain, CEO of Merrill Lynch, thought otherwise, stating that "allowing Lehman to go bankrupt was the single biggest mistake of the whole financial crisis" (FDIC, p. 342). Fed chairman Ben Bernanke, while claiming that the regulatory authorities could not have intervened, shared the opinion as to the Armageddon that Lehman's bankruptcy wreaked:

We never had any doubt about that. It was going to have huge impacts on funding markets. It would create a huge loss of confidence in other financial firms. It would create pressure on Merrill and Morgan Stanley, if not Goldman, which it eventually did. It would probably bring the short-term money markets into crisis, which we didn't fully anticipate; but, of course, in the end it did bring the commercial paper market and the money market mutual funds under pressure. So there was never any doubt in our minds that it would be a calamity, catastrophe, and that, you know, we should do everything we could to save it.

Sheila Bair points in particular to Lehman's presence in the derivatives markets as the main reason why its bankruptcy became so dramatic since, under the bankruptcy code, derivatives partners are given the choice of canceling their contracts and selling the collateral posted, further driving down the price of these assets.[42]

---

[42] Bair, *Bull by the Horns*, p. 194.

A critical voice was also that of Alan Blinder, a professor at Princeton where he had been a colleague of Bernanke's but also an earlier member of the board of governors. The title of the relevant chapter in his book says it all: "From Bear to Lehman: inconsistency was the hobgoblin." In particular, he is critical of the attitude of the Fed that the collateral that Lehman could raise was insufficient, making it clear that this decision was highly subjective and the judge – the only judge – of the issue was the Fed itself. It said no, not because it had to but because it wanted to.

It is apparent that the US regulatory authorities merit an "F" over the handling of Lehman Brothers, irrespective of whether its bankruptcy was *the* event that caused the panic of 2008 or just *one* of the events behind the crisis.

Firstly, it was naïve to take for granted that the markets had had time to prepare after the sale of Bear Stearns. The message was obviously different from the emitting end to the recipients, who saw the saving of Bear Stearns as a sign that they too would be saved. Inspection of the books of Lehman or Merrill during the summer would have shown that they had not wound down positions, rather the opposite.

Secondly, not only was the SEC totally incompetent in its role as supervisor but the interaction between supervisors failed completely. A stress test conducted by the Fed in June 2008 after the Fed's decision to fund primary dealers, whether banks or not, revealed severe problems of liquidity at Lehman, yet New York Fed officials were "very reluctant" to obtain information that would shed light on Lehman's counterparties, since such a request would send a "huge negative signal." It was important to collect the information but "without risks" (FDIC, p. 329).

Thirdly, there was a total break-down in communications between the US and UK authorities. Remember that the original suggestion that Barclays should buy Lehman had come from the US Treasury. Alistair Darling would later claim that "Paulson told him that the FRNBY [Federal Reserve Bank of New York] might be prepared to provide Barclays with regulatory assistance to support a transaction if it was required" (FDIC p. 334). For Paulson, however, such a guarantee to Barclays was out of the question (ibid., p. 336). A follow-up on the March conversation between Steel at the Treasury and McCarthy at the British FSA should have sorted out this misunderstanding from the beginning. Perhaps the reason for the lack of contact was that Steel had left the Treasury in July to become CEO of Wachovia.

And yet, at least from the outside, a solution would have appeared so simple, had the will existed. Barclays Capital had a US subsidiary, Barclays Capital Inc., which was (and is) a broker-dealer and also a Primary Dealer to the Fed. This organization, which was an American incorporated company, could have purchased Lehman Brothers with the aid of a guarantee from the New York Fed on the toxic assets since it was a US company, later converting into a US incorporated bank holding company under the supervision of the Fed. It might seem like a midge merging with an elephant, but in mid September 2008, the entire operation of Lehman Brothers could be bought for, at most, a couple of billion dollars, peanuts compared to the total assets of Barclays at 2,459 billion dollars at the end of 2007. Remember that Barclays later bought Lehman's American operations for just over a billion dollars.

Fourthly and finally, the authorities merit an "F" for making no attempts to bring responsible parties to justice for what was obviously an illegal attempt at window-dressing the accounts of Lehman. False accounting and/or fraud should have been the criminal charge directed at a number of individuals from the CEO through the CFO down. Instead they live a life of comfort in retirement.[43]

---

[43] www.publicintegrity.org/2013/09/10/13326/ex-wall-street-chieftains-living-large-post-meltdown-world

15 | USA

Countrywide, IndyMac, Washington Mutual and Wachovia

There is only one difference between the four banks studied in this chapter and the three financial institutions discussed in the next chapter. The four banks mentioned in the title above were indeed big financial institutions, but they were not too big to fail. And fail they did or would have had they not been saved by merger with a "white knight." AIG, Citigroup and Bank of America, on the other hand, were "too big to fail." Hence the treatment they (and their creditors) received was vastly different. In one case discussed in this chapter (Washington Mutual), even senior creditors lost out, in another (IndyMac) not only creditors but even uninsured depositors were hit; in the second case, everybody was saved, including counterparties to derivative transactions, unsecured bondholders and even shareholders.

Countrywide

By the end of 2006, 20 percent of new mortgage lending in the United States consisted of subprime loans and the biggest subprime lender was Countrywide Financial Services. The holding company contained one subsidiary for mortgage banking, Countrywide Mortgage Banking, which originated and securitized mortgages but which was not a bank. Its sister, the savings bank Countrywide Bank, had a national banking license; it was supervised by the Office of Thrift Supervision (OTS), financing mortgage lending by its own deposits.[1] Together they were by far the largest mortgage lender in the United States in 2006 with one-quarter of the entire US market for new residential mortgages and 17 percent of the stock outstanding. Another subsidiary in the group, Countrywide Financial Markets, was licensed as a broker-dealer,

---

[1] As we saw earlier, it had recently shifted to the OTS from the Federal Reserve since OTS was seen as a more benign and "understanding" regulator.

financed by issuing asset-backed commercial paper (ABCP), trading and underwriting mortgage-backed securities. Thus one subsidiary in the Countrywide Financial Services group underwrote issues of another subsidiary, a very risky combination as it would turn out when markets crashed in 2007. The fourth member of the group was Countrywide Warehouse Lending, which provided short-term lines of credit to mortgage bankers which used these funds to originate loans later sold to Countrywide.

A large part of mortgage loans originated by Countrywide Mortgage Banking was securitized and sold to investors. The major purchaser of Countrywide's loans was Fannie Mae. In 2004, Countrywide supplied 26 percent of all loans purchased by Fannie; in 2007, the figure had risen to 28 percent. "Billions of dollars in toxic mortgages went straight from Countrywide to the government-sponsored enterprise [GSE] that would just four years later become a ward of the state."[2] Countrywide had achieved this symbiotic existence with Fannie in two ways. Firstly, it got extremely advantageous rates on the guarantees extended by Fannie on its MBSs, 13 basis points, 10 basis points below other major mortgage originators, given on the condition that Countrywide promise not to do any business with Fannie's brother GSE and fiercest competitor, Freddie Mac. Secondly, two former CEOs of Fannie, James A. Johnson (CEO 1991–8) and Franklin Raines (CEO 1998–2004), as well as a number of other helpful well-placed individuals, were "friends of Angelo," meaning that they could borrow from Countrywide Bank at very favorable rates of interest.[3] Johnson had, for example, six personal loans totaling over 10 million dollars with Countrywide. He was also permitted the use of the Countrywide corporate jet.[4]

By 2006, two-thirds of the subprime loans originated by Countrywide had loan-to-value ratios of 100 percent or above, i.e. the buyer had put nothing down in order to purchase a house. That very

---

[2] Gretchen Morgenson and Joshua Rosner, *Reckless Endangerment: How Outsized Ambition, Greed and Corruption Led to Economic Armageddon* (New York: Times Books/Henry Holt, 2011), p. 183.

[3] "Angelo" was of course Angelo Mozilo, founder of Countrywide and CEO from 1969 to 2008.

[4] Other "friends of Angelo" included Alfonso Jackson, the secretary of housing and urban development, as well as a number of politicians including Senator Chris Dodd, of Dodd–Frank fame (Morgenson and Rosner, *Reckless Endangerment*, p. 187).

same year CEO Angelo Mozilo e-mailed a colleague on the company's practices, stating that "in all my years in business I have never seen a more toxic product."[5] He would soon be proven right, when the nationwide delinquency rate on subprime mortgages with adjustable interest rates (ARM) rose from 5 to 45 percent, led by Countrywide.

The liquidity problems of the group started in earnest on 6 August 2007 when American Home Mortgage filed for bankruptcy, unable to roll its funding on commercial paper. Problems increased further on 9 August, when BNP Paribas stopped withdrawals in three funds which had mainly invested in US subprime mortgages and subprime-based MBSs. One of the first victims was the repo market, despite injections of liquidity into the system by the major central banks: the Federal Reserve 43 billion dollars and the ECB 95 billion euro that same day. A primary victim was Countrywide which was heavily dependent on the repo market for its financing, also becoming more and more important as subprime credits were increasingly more difficult to sell and loans remained on its books, swelling total assets. The company asked its regulator, the OTS, if the Fed would intervene by allowing the bank in the group to borrow on behalf of the holding company through the discount window and supply other members of the group (Mortgage Banking as well as Warehouse Lending). The Fed refused, saying that it "had not lent to a nonbank in decades and such lending in the current circumstances seems highly improbable."[6] The Fed would strike a very different note half a year later with Bear Stearns.

From March to December 2007, Countrywide also increased its borrowing from its Federal Home Loan Bank from 27 to 48 billion dollars.[7]

On 15 August, Bank of New York Mellon notified the New York Fed that unless Countrywide came up with more collateral, it would stop lending to the firm and sell the existing collateral held. Risking a fire sale in an already nervous market, Tim Geithner, the head of the New York Fed (and later finance minister under President Obama), brokered a deal to both parties' satisfaction. The price was, however, that Countrywide had to draw down 11 billion dollars of emergency bank credit lines to stabilize its liquidity. When this became known the

---

[5] Wessel, *In Fed We Trust*, p. 117.
[6] FCIC, *The Financial Crisis Inquiry Report*, p. 249.
[7] Ibid., p. 274.

next day, the company was immediately downgraded by the rating companies, even its senior unsecured debt becoming almost "junk." Its shares fell by 11 percent on that single day and 8 billion dollars in deposits were lost in a bank run. The stock which had begun the year at 42 dollars per share fell to 21 dollars that day and would end the year at 9 dollars. A few days later, a white knight appeared in the form of Bank of America investing 2 billion dollars in convertible preferred stock which, if converted, would give it 16 percent of the company. While, at the time, the two parties denied the possibility of a full merger, on 11 January 2008, Countrywide was purchased by Bank of America for 4.1 billion dollars. The company had been valued at 24 billion dollars one year earlier.

So far we have seen little of the regulatory authorities and one may wonder why Countrywide is included in this book at all. Yet, after the merger was completed in the summer of 2008, the authorities became active both as concerns personal misdeeds by its senior management and fraud committed by the company. It began in October 2010, when the former CEO Angelo Mozilo, charged by the SEC with insider trading and securities fraud, having received a total compensation of close to 500 million dollars, reached an agreement with the SEC to avoid criminal charges for having sold his own shares while knowing of the bank's problems. He paid a fine of 67.5 million dollars (20 million of which was paid by his Countrywide insurance) and accepted a lifetime ban on serving as an officer or director of any publicly owned company. The former chief operating officer of Countrywide paid a fine of 5.5 million dollars and its chief financial officer 130,000 dollars.

In January 2011, Bank of America agreed to pay 2.6 billion dollars to Fannie Mae as compensation for faulty information on substandard loans sold by Countrywide, the US Justice Department adding a fine of 1 billion dollars for false mortgage claims. In January 2013, when a number of major US banks agreed to pay over 20 billion dollars on home loans, the major payer was Bank of America who agreed to pay Fannie Mae 11.6 billion dollars for misstating the quality of mortgage loans sold and securitized by Countrywide. In May 2013, monoline insurer MBIA received a 1.7 billion dollar settlement from Bank of America for misrepresentation of mortgages originated by Countrywide included in MBSs insured by MBIA.

So far by 2013, the purchase of Countrywide in 2008 for 4.1 billion dollars had cost Bank of America 16.9 billion dollars in fines and other legal settlements. But worse is perhaps to come when Bank of America heads to trial over claims that Countrywide knowingly approved substandard loans in a process called "Hustle," defrauding Fannie Mae at a cost of close to a billion dollars. "Hustle" stood for the High-Speed Swim Lane (HSSL) action that Countrywide undertook in 2007 to counter the tightened underwriting standards at Fannie Mae, streamlining and speeding up loan origination by basically abandoning loan quality checks. A mid-level executive, Rebecca Mairone, was found guilty of fraud in connection with "Hustle" in October 2013 and fined 1.1 million dollars, wiping out her assets since she was not covered by the firm's insurance for higher-level executives.

Overall grade of the handling of Countrywide: C (on a scale of A to F=Fail)

In the handling of Countrywide's fall, there is little to criticize. The New York Fed tried to ease its liquidity constraint and the Federal Reserve accepted its merger with Bank of America. The FDIC was not involved at all, even though Sheila Bair in her memoirs calls the deal "overpriced," a statement that later events would prove to be more than correct (see above).[8] She was positive, however, toward the merger itself and "relieved that a larger, more profitable commercial bank had taken it over." The criticism that can be directed against the authorities will be repeated in most other cases to follow in this book, namely the inability of the US regulatory authorities to bring criminal charges against individuals who knowingly "cooked the books" in misrepresenting mortgages sold to, in particular, Fannie Mae or Freddie Mac, or committed other crimes such as insider dealing. Many of the individuals participating in the club "Friends of Angelo" could and should have been prosecuted for improper behavior. Here the United States has much to learn from Iceland and Ireland, even though attitudes appear to have hardened since 2013, not least by the appointment of Mary Jo White, an experienced US attorney and prosecutor, to head the SEC.[9]

---

[8] Bair, *Bull by the Horns*, pp. 2, 76.
[9] "Mary Jo White Is the Woman Who Makes Wall Street Admit Guilt," *Business Week*, 16 October 2013.

IndyMac[10]

Total assets of IndyMac were only some 30 billion dollars at the time of the seizure by its regulator, the OTS, but it was still the third largest savings and loan institution in the United States and the largest in the Los Angeles area, as well as the seventh largest American mortgage originator. Its collapse would also lead to the single largest loss to the FDIC Deposit Insurance Fund during the crisis, over 7 billion dollars.[11]

Its name, IndyMac, was an abbreviation of the Independent National Mortgage Corporation, obviously trying to insinuate that it was a government-sponsored enterprise like Freddie Mac.

It had been spun off from Countrywide in 1997 (see above), focusing on the most risky products in mortgage lending. Having few branch offices, it acquired its deposit base through independent brokers, offering higher interest rates than its competitors. Mortgages were also made primarily through brokers with emphasis on Alt-A loans (so called "liar loans" since the income and asset statements by the borrower were not verified). It also offered interest-only loans as well as option ARM, i.e. loans with adjustable interest rates where the borrower could choose not to pay interest at all for certain months but add the interest due to the capital value of the debt.

The growing problems of IndyMac were well known to the regulators, not least since it was a heavy borrower with its local Federal Home Loan Bank. In spring 2008, the FDIC succeeded in finally getting the OTS to downgrade the bank from "well capitalized" to "adequately capitalized" and start planning for its ultimate resolution since it was apparent that problems were growing. The downrating would have occurred already in the first quarter, had not the local OTS representative allowed the bank to backdate capital received as if it had arrived already before the 31 March report date. Otherwise, the bank would have been downgraded or perhaps even seized three months earlier than it actually was. During late spring also, rating companies had downgraded a number of MBSs originated by IndyMac but which were retained in its own portfolio for lack of investor interest.

The issue of resolution was, however, accelerated on 27 June 2008 by a surprising open letter by Senator Chuck Schumer (D-NY) to the

---

[10] www.fdic.gov/bank/individual/failed/IndyMac.html
[11] Bair, *Bull by the Horns*, p. 80.

FDIC and other regulatory authorities, expressing concern over the bank whose "financial deterioration poses significant risks to both tax payers and borrowers … and that the regulatory community may not be prepared to take measures that would help prevent the collapse of IndyMac or minimize the damage should a failure occur."[12] The letter, for obvious reasons, led to a run on the bank's deposits, 1.3 billion dollars being withdrawn in the week that followed. The downgrading by the OTS had led as well to the bank losing its right to borrow in the Home Loan Bank system. The bank was effectively facing both an acute liquidity crisis and insolvency. It was downgraded by Standard & Poor's to CCC, just one notch above default, two days before the seizure. It was seized by the OTS on 12 July 2008. Its share price had fallen from a peak of 50 dollars to 31 cents.

Since the normal "purchase and assumption" was not feasible, the precipitated seizure not having allowed time to find a buyer wanting to take over the entire bank, the FDIC set up a bridge bank, IndyMac Federal Bank FSB ("New IndyMac"), in order that customers should not suffer a breakdown of their banking facilities. In January 2009, parts of the bank were sold to a private equity group, IMB HoldCo LLC, led by Dune Capital Management and J. C. Flowers. This group started a new savings institution, One West Bank FSB, to take over the healthy parts of IndyMac. The FDIC also agreed together with the sale to share losses on a portfolio of qualifying loans, with IMB HoldCo assuming the first 20 percent of losses, with the FDIC sharing losses 80/20 for the next 10 percent of losses and 95/5 thereafter. One West Bank also promised to continue the program of mortgage modification begun by the FDIC.[13]

Shareholders and investors of subordinated debt were naturally wiped out. But uniquely, the FDIC, in selling the remaining assets, found that the proceeds did not cover liabilities by far. Hence unsecured bondholders lost their entire investments as did partly also uninsured depositors (those with deposits above 100,000 dollars, the limit at the time), losing in the aggregate some 270 million dollars.[14]

The leading officers of IndyMac would be charged by the SEC in February 2011 for securities fraud for not adequately informing

---

[12] Ibid.
[13] Blinder, *After the Music Stopped*, pp. 330–1.
[14] www.fdic.gov/bank/individual/failed/indymac_q_and_a_no_value.html

investors about the declining financial condition of the bank. The CEO, Michael W. Perry was, with 15.92 million dollars in total compensation, one of the highest paid CEOs in the United States in 2006. In a civil settlement with the SEC on 28 September 2012, he agreed to pay a penalty of 80,000 dollars (sic!) without either admitting or denying the allegations.[15] On 14 December 2012, he agreed to pay the FDIC 1 million dollars, another 11 million dollars being paid from the bank's insurance. Three other officers of the bank were ordered to pay the FDIC a total of 168 million dollars for "breach of fiduciary duty." No criminal charges were filed against Perry or against anybody else.[16]

Overall grade of the handling of IndyMac: E (on a scale of A to F=Fail)

It is quite obvious that regulators failed miserably in checking the abuses at IndyMac. The resolution of the bank would have merited an "F" were it not for the gravity of the problems inherited from the negligence and incompetence of the OTS. Allowing the bank to backdate capital received postponed the seizure by at least three months, aggravating the problem. Yet the senior OTS regulator responsible for the decision was allowed to retire prematurely with his full pension. The setting up of a bridge bank allowed customers to continue their banking business as before. Sheila Bair and the FDIC also merit commendation for the mortgage modification program initiated by the FDIC.

Yet one wonders if it was necessary to hit uninsured depositors. The FDIC sold remaining assets quickly and in the worst possible market just to be rid of the burden. As shown not least by Sweden's "bad bank" Securum, cleaning up the toxic loans of Nordbanken in the 1990s, taking your time and giving markets time to recover can lead to vastly improved prices on these assets. It took Securum five years to sell off the loan book and, indeed, the remaining government-held shares in the nationalized bank (today Nordea) were ultimately sold only in 2013, 20 years after the crash. But taxpayers did in the end come out on top. Similarly, the "nationalized" New IndyMac could

---

[15] www.sec.gov/litigation/litreleases/2012/lr22502.htm

[16] www.lexisnexis.com/legalnewsroom/litigation/b/litigation-blog/archive/ 2012/12/17/former-indymac-ceo-agrees-to-12-million-settlement-with-fdic. aspx

have sold the good assets but retained the toxic assets in a bad bank under the FDIC's umbrella until markets had recovered. Alternatively, since the TARP program had been approved in early October, the government could have done it "the Swedish way," setting up a government-run bad bank since, after all, the original purpose of TARP was to purchase toxic assets from otherwise healthy banks. Only later was the focus shifted to recapitalizing banks (CPP).

Another reason to give regulators an "E" rather than an "F" is also that the FDIC Insurance Fund took a large hit on IndyMac and became precariously low. See the discussion on Washington Mutual below and the next two chapters.

Washington Mutual[17]

Since Lehman Brothers was not a bank but an investment bank, the failure of Washington Mutual (WaMu) with assets of 307 billion dollars was by far the largest bank failure of the recent crisis. It was at the time the sixth largest bank in the United States and the largest savings institution. Its name was misleading since it had converted from a mutual savings bank to a stock savings bank (Washington Mutual Bank) already in 1983, wholly owned by the listed holding company Washington Mutual Inc. Since then, it had acquired some 30 financial institutions, continuing to add on average one bank per year up to the very end. The most disastrous acquisition would turn out to be Long Beach Financial Corp., bought in 1999. Long Beach had been one of the earliest banks to offer subprime loans and while small, it would change the entire culture of Washington Mutual. By acquisitions and aggressive lending, WaMu's assets increased from 149 billion dollars in 1990 to 194 billion in 2000 and to 328 billion in 2007.[18]

---

[17] Apart from earlier quoted literature, see United States Congress, Senate Permanent Subcommittee on Investigations, *Wall Street and the Financial Crisis: Anatomy of a Financial Collapse*, section III, "High risk lending: case study of Washington Mutual," pp. 48–161, 13 April 2011; Kirsten Grind, *The Lost Bank: The Story of Washington Mutual, the Biggest Bank Failure in American History* (New York: Simon & Schuster, 2013); Josh Rosner, "The Washington Mutual story," 13 March 2013, www.ritholtz.com/blog/2013/03/jpmorgan-chase-out-of-control-introduction/

[18] Source: Annual accounts.

In perennial competition with Countrywide as to who would be the largest mortgage originator in the country, its share of so-called non-traditional mortgages (Alt-A, subprime, option ARM) was seemingly not alarming. A study by the Federal Reserve in 2005 showed non-traditional originations at Washington Mutual at 31 percent of total new mortgages which could be compared with 59 percent at Countrywide and 58 percent at Wells Fargo.[19] Unfortunately for the reliability of the study, at about the same time, Washington Mutual decided to dramatically increase the share of non-traditional loans where the margins were far higher than on traditional mortgages. The margin in extending and securitizing a classic fixed-rate mortgage was at the time 19 basis points as compared to 109 basis points for an Option ARM and 150 basis points for a subprime loan.[20] At the end of 2007, the share of subprime and option ARM mortgages had risen to almost 70 percent.[21]

Nor could the Fed study delve into the quality of the mortgages, most of which Washington Mutual had securitized, getting rid of the credit risk (or so one thought until litigation started after the crisis). An internal study undertaken a year before that by the Fed revealed that only about a quarter of mortgages originated in the Long Beach subsidiary were of a quality sufficient to be sold to outside investors.[22] It does not seem that the results were shared with the OTS, the regulator of Washington Mutual Bank, nor with the state bank regulator of California which regulated its sister, the Long Beach subsidiary of the common holding company Washington Mutual Inc.

In July 2007, Standard & Poor's and Moody's both began a severe downgrading of AAA/Aaa rated residential mortgage-backed securities (RMBS) and corresponding CDOs (collateralized debt obligations). On one single day, Standard & Poor's downgraded 498 subprime-related issues with a nominal value of around 6 billion dollars and Moody's 399 issues worth 5.2 billion. During the second half of 2007, Standard & Poor's downgraded more than 9,000 RMBS ratings. Over 90 percent of RMBS originally rated AAA/Aaa in 2006 and 2007 would by 2010 have been downgraded to junk status. Among

---

[19] FCIC, *Financial Crisis Inquiry Report*, p. 20.
[20] *Wall Street and the Financial Crisis*, p. 64.
[21] Grind, *The Lost Bank*, p. 158.
[22] *Wall Street and the Financial Crisis*, p. 76.

the worst performers was Washington Mutual and, in particular, its subsidiary Long Beach Mortgage Corp, the latter being responsible for 6 percent of mortgage securities issued in 2006 but 14 percent of the downgrades.[23] All of the 75 RMBS issued by Long Beach that year would be downgraded to junk status within a year.

Having lost two of its three major supervised national savings banks to the OCC (Golden West to Wachovia, Countrywide to Bank of America), the OTS was anxious to retain Washington Mutual in its fold. This set up a conflict with the FDIC which regarded the management of the thrift as totally incompetent to manage a bank with some 50,000 employees and over 300 billion dollars in assets. Facing difficulties selling off their loans, the bank had increased its borrowing in the Federal Home Loan Bank system from 28 to 73 billion dollars between the first and fourth quarters of 2007 (and to 83 billion by June 2008).[24] The FDIC also noted the loss of 1.9 billion dollars for the final quarter of 2007 and a projected loss of 1 billion dollars for the first quarter of 2008. The OTS had downgraded the bank from 2 to 3 (on a scale of 1 to 5). A study by the FDIC had also revealed that the hedging strategies undertaken by the bank were old-fashioned and insufficient.

The FDIC encouraged a merger offer from JPMorgan Chase (at the same time as this bank was acquiring Bear Stearns in March 2008) of 8 dollars per share. The offer was, however, rejected by the board of directors of WaMu (probably with the eager support of the OTS) and instead, on 7 April 2008, WaMu received a capital injection of 7.2 billion dollars from private-equity investors led by TPG Capital. It would all be lost just half a year later. This sum corresponded to 8.75 dollars per share.[25] A factor in the board's decision was probably that in this way both the members of the board and the management could remain in their lucrative positions, WaMu being one of the banks in the country that paid its board members best.

On 22 July 2008, Washington Mutual reported a loss of 4.4 billion dollars for the first half of 2008 due mainly to credit losses of 9.4 billion dollars. Moody's downgraded the company to Baa3, just one

---

[23] Ibid., p. 124.
[24] FCIC, *Financial Crisis Inquiry Report*, p. 274.
[25] Bair, *Bull by the Horns*, pp. 75–8; Grind, *The Lost Bank*, p. 235.

notch above "junk." Coming right after the seizure of IndyMac, the news set off a run over the next week, depositors withdrawing over 9 billion dollars (6 percent) of deposits. Six weeks later, the long-term CEO and president of WaMu, Kerry Killinger, was fired by the board of directors, though leaving with a 15.3 million dollar severance payment. Its stock price had fallen from a peak of 45 dollars per share in 2006 to under 2 dollars (and would shortly become worthless). Simultaneously, WaMu signed a memorandum of understanding with its regulators, the OTS and the FDIC, on improving risk management and raising more capital.

On 11 September 2008, Moody's downgraded the debt of Washington Mutual to "junk" status with negative outlook, citing the bank's "reduced financial flexibility," "deteriorating asset quality" and "expected franchise erosion." Together with the events over the coming days (Lehman Brothers, AIG), it led to a new run on the bank, 17 billion dollars' worth of deposits (12 percent of total deposits remaining after the earlier run, 9 percent of deposits as of June 2008) being withdrawn in the two weeks remaining until the bank was seized. Its liquidity would not have lasted another week and the Federal Home Loan Bank had also lowered to 30 percent the valuation of the WaMu collateral it held, leading to demands for more collateral that WaMu did not have.

A week later, on 18 September 2008, the FDIC downgraded Washington Mutual's CAMELS[26] rating from a 3 to a 4, thereby putting it on the problem bank list. Although banks are not named on the list, the addition of a 300-billion-dollar-asset institution would pinpoint WaMu and most certainly bring down the bank when the list was published at the end of October. Sheila Bair told the new CEO, Alan Fishman, that he had one month to find a buyer. But the acute liquidity crisis did not leave room even for this period of grace. Regulators had to intervene.

On Thursday 25 September, the Office of Thrift Supervision (OTS) seized Washington Mutual, placing it in receivership under the FDIC. Normally seizures would occur on Fridays after bank closing to give the FDIC the weekend to find a buyer, but rumors of the forthcoming

---

[26] Capital adequacy, Asset quality, Management quality, Earnings, Liquidity, Sensitivity to market risk.

seizure made the Thursday action necessary. Also a buyer was already available. The next day, JPMorgan Chase purchased the banking activities from the FDIC for 1.9 billion dollars in cash while assuming full responsibility for the branch network of Washington Mutual Bank, as well as most of the bank's assets (leaving out only the option ARMs), all deposits (188 billion dollars), insured as well as uninsured, and covered and secured bonds. No other bidders had appeared after having been scared away by the low quality of WaMu's mortgage assets. The holding company Washington Mutual Inc. filed for bankruptcy under chapter 7 of the Bankruptcy Code.

In sharp contrast to the handling of creditors of Bear Stearns, Fannie Mae, Freddie Mac and AIG (see next chapter), unsecured and subordinated creditors in WaMu were not bailed out, even senior creditors receiving only 55 percent of the nominal value of their bonds; 20 billion dollars' worth of senior bonds being wiped out, together with 2 billion dollars in preferred shares and common stock still worth a nominal 7 billion dollars.[27] There was no cost to the FDIC's Deposit Insurance Fund (DIF), also in sharp contrast to the recent failure of IndyMac.

The new CEO of Washington Mutual, Alan Fishman, resigned after only 17 days in his post with salary and signing bonus of 7.5 million dollars, amounting to half a million dollars in salary per working day. He abstained, however, from the severance pay to which he was formally entitled.

In March 2011, the FDIC sued the former chief executive and other top executives of the failed bank, accusing them of reckless lending. In December of the same year, the three executives (former CEO Kerry Killinger, former president Steve Rotella and the former president of Home Loans David Schneider) agreed to pay 65 million dollars without admitting or denying guilt. The FDIC had originally sought 900 million dollars! Most of their payments under the settlement were covered by Washington Mutual's insurance policy. In December 2013, the same individuals were reputed to settle claims from the OCC for

---

[27] Grind, *The Lost Bank*, p. 311; www.fdic.gov/bank/individual/failed/wamu. html; Paulson, *On the Brink*, p. 293.

an undisclosed amount.[28] Neither of them nor anybody else has been criminally charged by any supervisory authority.

The treatment meted out to the assuming bank has, however, been different. In February 2012, JPMorgan Chase was fined 275 million dollars by the Federal Reserve for "unsafe and unsound" practices in residential loan servicing and processing, mainly the result of its purchase of WaMu. In November 2013, JPMorgan Chase came to an agreement to pay a total of 13 billion dollars for mortgage business stemming from the purchases of Bear Stearns and Washington Mutual. The deal resolved civil probes by three US attorneys, two state attorneys general and three federal regulators. It included 4 billion dollars in relief for consumers and 9 billion dollars in fines and other payments. The payouts would cover a separate 5.1 billion accord with the Federal Housing Finance Agency over the bank's sale of mortgage-backed securities to Fannie Mae and Freddie Mac. In anticipation of a deal, JPMorgan took a 7.2 billion dollar charge after tax for expenses tied to regulatory matters and litigation in the third quarter of 2013, leading the bank to announce a 380 million dollar loss on 11 October. It is still unclear whether JPMorgan will also face criminal charges in relation to the mortgages and mortgage-backed securities sold. With the settlement, the bank had to admit having sold substandard mortgages without sufficient due diligence.[29]

On 18 December 2013, JPMorgan Chase sued the FDIC in a federal court, charging that the agency should be responsible for more than 1 billion dollars in costs that JPMorgan still faces over its purchase of Washington Mutual from the FDIC in 2008. The bank also wants the FDIC to help pay for the lawsuits it faces from private investors who bought mortgage securities from WaMu. JPMorgan argues those are also the responsibility of the FDIC as the original owner, not the bank. According to the suit, JPMorgan is not seeking funds from the FDIC's operating budget, only from a pool of WaMu assets still held by the FDIC. JPMorgan's suit demands that these

---

[28] www.bloomberg.com/news/2013-12-03/ex-wamu-ceo-killinger-said-to-be-near-settlement-in-bank-failure.html

[29] www.bloomberg.com/news/2013-11-20/jpmorgan-13-billion-mortgage-deal-seen-as-lawsuit-shield.html

assets, valued at almost 3 billion dollars, should be used primarily to pay its claims.

Overall grade of the handling of Washington Mutual: F (on a scale of A to F=Fail)

Just as was the case with Lehman Brothers, the protracted legal battles, continuing in 2013, show that the handling of the bankruptcy of Washington Mutual was badly flawed. For obvious reasons, its main author, FDIC chair Sheila Bair, defends the actions by the FDIC on moral-hazard grounds and thought that the operation had been "successful." She writes:[30]

> WaMu had been horribly mismanaged and was a major player in the kind of abusive, unaffordable, and at times potentially fraudulent lending that had driven the subprime mortgage crisis. WaMu's bondholders and shareholders had a duty to monitor risk taking at the institution and assure management's accountability. The responsibility was theirs, not the tax payers. It is amazing to me that those who lost money on the WaMu failure tried to assign blame to the FDIC and Chase instead of the WaMu management.

She would also tell the Financial Crisis Inquiry Commission (p. 367) that WaMu's failure "was practically a nonevent. It was below the fold if it was even on the front page…barely a blip given everything else that was going on."

The run on Wachovia by uninsured depositors and unsecured bondholders the day after Washington Mutual was seized tells a different story, to which we will return in the next section.

Others have offered different interpretations of the handling of WaMu. The then-secretary of the Treasury, Hank Paulson, writes:[31]

> The WaMu solution wasn't perfect although it was handled smoothly using the normal FDIC process. JPMorgan's purchase cost tax payers nothing and no depositors lost money, but the deal gave senior WaMu debt holders about 55 cents on the dollar, roughly equal to what the securities had been trading for. In retrospect, I can see that, in the middle of a panic, this was

[30] Bair, *Bull by the Horns*, p. 93.
[31] Paulson, *On the Brink*, pp. 292–3.

a mistake. WaMu, the sixth-biggest bank in the country, was systemically important. Crushing the owners of preferred and subordinate debt and clipping senior debt holders only unsettled debt holders in other institutions [in particular in Wachovia, my note], adding to the market's uncertainty about government action. Banks were even less willing to lend to one another.

Neel Kashkari, at the time assistant secretary of the Treasury for Financial Stability, speaks in a similar vein:[32]

And so, I think, in my judgment it was a mistake… At the time, the economy was in such a perilous state, it was like playing with fire. In my view we should have found a way to allow somebody to acquire WaMu pre-bankruptcy.

And this evaluation comes from Alan Blinder, professor of economics at Princeton University and a former member of the board of governors of the Fed:[33]

History will long debate the wisdom of Bair's decision. Was it wise (Bair's view) or foolish (Geithner's view) to strike a blow against moral hazard in the midst of a panic? Probably not wise, not without loud and clear prior warning. After all, after Bear, Fannie, Freddie and AIG, investors had come to expect the opposite.

For obvious reasons, market participants were scathingly critical. "This is an unprecedented destruction of senior bond holders such that bank bond investors may be thinking to themselves, why bother?" and "There is now a precedent set which is tax payer friendly and 100 percent risk asset hostile."[34]

While understanding that it must have been frustrating for the FDIC working with a regulator (OTS) who was bent on saving the bank up to the very end to protect its own interests (apart from the reputational consequences for OTS of a WaMu failure, the bank also paid 15 percent of OTS's budget!), the overall grade must still be an "F." Just as the clumsy handling of IndyMac set in motion the bank run

---

[32] FCIC, *Financial Crisis Inquiry Report*, p. 366.
[33] Blinder, *After the Music Stopped*, p. 157
[34] Wessel, *In Fed We Trust*, p. 221.

that killed Washington Mutual, so the unjust treatment meted out to senior bondholders in WaMu led to the near-collapse of an even larger institution, Wachovia.

The FDIC, citing "systemic risk," could have saved senior creditors from losses rather than saving itself and the DIF, according to the FDIC Improvement Act (FDICIA) of 1991 which states:

> Under the law, the FDIC may bypass the least cost test in certain extraordinary circumstances. This is referred to under FDICIA as the "systemic risk exception." This exception allows the FDIC to bypass the least cost method if it "would have serious adverse effects on economic conditions or financial stability" and if bypassing the least cost method would "avoid or mitigate such adverse effects."
>
> A high standard is set in the law in order to exercise this authority. The systemic risk exception requires the approval of two thirds of the members of the FDIC's Board of Directors, two thirds of the members of the Board of Governors of the Federal Reserve System, and the Secretary of the U.S. Treasury, who must first consult with the President. This requires therefore a process for interagency coordination and collaboration, including protocols for communication and the criteria the responsible agencies will use to make such a determination.[35]

Refused for Washington Mutual, the "systemic risk exception" would be invoked just a few days later for Wachovia (next section). Where is the logic?

Moreover, any losses to the Deposit Insurance Fund (DIF) occasioned by bailing out senior bondholders would anyway be borne by the industry itself, not by taxpayers. The DIF had a balance of 52 billion dollars at the end of 2007, corresponding to 1.22 percent of insured deposits, just above the then required minimum of 1.15 percent (increased to 2 percent by the Dodd–Frank Act). This balance had a year later shrunk to a bare 19 billion dollars, corresponding to just 0.4 percent of insured deposits. The sum may also be compared with deposits in banks that failed during 2007–8 of 213 billion dollars.

This did not mean the DIF was bankrupt. Firstly, not all deposits in the failed banks were covered and secondly, most bank failures were

---

[35] Martin J. Gruenberg, FDIC vice chairman, speech, 3 May 2007, www.fdic.gov/news/news/speeches/archives/2007/chairman/spmay0307.html

solved by another bank accepting responsibility for the failed bank's deposits and depositors, like JPMorgan Chase did for WaMu. Still, to reattain the required minimum, the FDIC doubled the fee it collects from the insured banks for the guarantee. From 2009, banks had to pay an amount of between 12 and 45 basis points (0.12–0.45 percentage points) on insured deposits, depending on their perceived risk, as measured by their capital strength (CAMELS rating). Moreover, on 30 June 2009, all banks were charged a one-off sum of 0.20 percent in order to restore the insurance fund. They also had to pay their insurance premiums for the next three years in advance. By these methods, the FDIC avoided having to use its borrowing rights of 500 billion dollars in the Treasury throughout the entire crisis. [36]

Adding an extra one-off charge to the insured banks of 20 billion dollars to save the senior bondholders in WaMu would have been worth it, to the FDIC as well as to the banking community, judging by later events.

Regulators also deserve an "F" for the almost complete lack of interest shown in charging individuals responsible for, as Bair writes, "abusive, unaffordable, and at times potentially fraudulent lending." Individuals have been allowed to settle by paying ridiculously low fines, without admitting guilt and no criminal charges have been made as regards senior management, only against small fry, middle or low level executives.[37]

This stands in sharp contrast to the efficiency of SIGTARP (the Special Inspector General of the TARP program) in catching frauds in the program, e.g. selling non-existent mortgages which allow the

---

[36] Two changes have been made since. Firstly, the risk-based fee structure now (2014) ranges from 2.5 to 45 basis points. Secondly, the basis has been changed from insured deposits to all liabilities (i.e. total assets minus tangible equity) in order to avoid penalizing community banks financed basically by deposits while subsidizing large ex-investment banks like Goldman Sachs or Morgan Stanley with few deposits. www.fdic.gov/deposit/insurance/index.html

[37] Sometimes, the perpetrators have instead been rewarded. Despite widespread allegations of mortgage fraud in Ameriquest Mortgage Banking, having led to a 325 million dollar settlement in 2005, with financial regulators in 49 states and the DC accusing Ameriquest of misrepresenting and failing to disclose loan terms, charging excessive loan origination fees and inflating appraisals to qualify borrowers for loans, the founding father and former CEO of Ameriquest, Roland Arnall, was appointed by President George W. Bush as US Ambassador to the Netherlands.

purchasing bank to claim TARP money, covering up the true condition of the applicant bank or using the TARP money received for private purposes. In her report for the fourth quarter of 2013, SIGTARP reports that 65 individuals have been sentenced and are serving prison sentences for fraud in connection with the TARP program and another 112 have been convicted by the courts but await sentencing, 154 individuals are still awaiting trial and 60 have been banned for life from serving in financial companies.[38]

Would that the FDIC, the Fed, the OCC and the SEC had been equally efficient!

Wachovia

In 2007, Charlotte-based Wachovia was the fourth-largest bank in the United States and number 30 in the world with its 783 billion dollars in total assets. In the United States, only Citigroup, JPMorgan Chase and Bank of America were larger. In terms of deposits, it was even number

---

[38] www.sigtarp.gov/Quarterly%20Reports/October_29_2013_Report_to_
Congress.pdf "This report summarizes notable SIGTARP investigations that illustrate how tone at the top can breed a criminally corrupt culture. SIGTARP's investigation resulted in convictions against four bank officers at TARP-applicant Bank of the Commonwealth and six co-conspirators for crimes to hide past-due loans and the bank's near-failure condition. Six have been sentenced to prison including the vice president (sentenced to 17 years) and president of a subsidiary (sentenced to eight years). The CEO and another officer await sentencing. SIGTARP uncovered an alleged six-year criminal enterprise at failed Premier Bank that led to the indictment against its chairman and three officers/directors. More than 6 million dollars in TARP money was lost when Premier failed. SIGTARP found that the officers of failed United Commercial Bank (UCB) allegedly engaged in fraudulent accounting tricks to conceal the bank's condition resulting in criminal charges against three officers. All of UCB's 298 million dollars in TARP funds are lost. SIGTARP's investigation resulted in prison sentences of 12, 7 and 3 years for three senior officers of failed TARP-applicant FirstCity Bank for fraudulently tricking the loan committee into approving millions in loans to buyers of the CEO's property and for siphoning millions. SIGTARP's investigation of failed TARP applicant Appalachian Community Bank resulted in a five-year prison sentence for the vice president for criminal self-dealing and concealing bad loans. SIGTARP's investigation into TARP-applicant First Community Bank led to the CEO being sentenced to two years in prison for criminally covering up bad loans. SIGTARP's investigation of Mainstreet Bank resulted in a guilty plea by the CEO for lying to SIGTARP about his use of TARP funds to purchase a vacation condo days after receiving the funds."

three. When it was purchased by Wells Fargo in early October 2008, government money was not involved. But as we shall see, the Treasury and the FDIC had learnt a lesson from the treatment of Washington Mutual and were prepared to step in to prevent a follow-up to that disaster with a bank more than double the size of WaMu, even if in the end, their help was not necessary.

Wachovia with its home in North Carolina had the advantage of having its main base in the eastern parts of the United States where housing speculation had not been as intense as in the "sand states" of California, Nevada, Arizona and Florida, where the majority of bank failures would take place. In 2008, the four sand states accounted for over 42 percent of mortgage-related home foreclosures while having only 24 percent of the nation's total mortgages.[39] Out of 414 bank failures 2008–11, the four states accounted for 29 percent while having only 21 percent of the population. And this understates their importance since the failed banks in these states were the mammoths. Five of the ten bank failures involving more than 10 billion dollars in assets occurred in these states: 3 in California, 1 in Nevada and 1 in Florida. We have already met some of them: IndyMac in Pasadena, California (32 billion dollars in assets) and Washington Mutual Bank (307 billion) which was licensed in Henderson, Nevada (although the WaMu Inc. holding company was headquartered in Seattle, Washington). The other three were Downey Savings and Loan in Newport Beach, California (13 billion), Bank United FSB in Coral Gables, Florida (13 billion) and United Commercial Bank in San Francisco, California (11 billion).[40]

A second factor of importance is that Wachovia was originally a well-run bank. As late as 2007, with the accelerating financial crisis, its non-performing loans (NPL) were only 1.21 percent of total loans which may be compared with 2.50 percent at Washington Mutual and a terrifying 6.49 percent at IndyMac and 6.96 percent at Countrywide.[41]

---

[39] www.fdic.gov/bank/analytical/quarterly/2009_vol3_1/AnatomyPerfectHousing.html

[40] General Accountability Office (GAO), *Financial Institutions, Causes and Consequences of Recent Bank Failures*, Report to Congressional Committees, GAO 13–71, January 2013.

[41] Source: *The Banker*, July 2008 for the first three and the 10-K filing by Countrywide to the SEC at www.sec.gov/Archives/edgar/data/25191/000104746908002104/a2182824z10-k.htm

This good-boy image changed with its acquisition in 2006 of Golden West based in Oakland, California, then the second largest thrift institution in the United States, operating under the inventive name "World Savings Bank." It held assets of 125 billion dollars and had 12,000 employees operating in the 10 western states, where the presence of Wachovia so far had been minimal. The problem was that its portfolio of mortgages was almost entirely option ARM, a product sold under the name of "Pick-a-Pay." In other words, you pay interest when you feel like it.

Wachovia shows clearly the complex interaction between regulators. The bank holding company was regulated by the Fed, Wachovia Bank by the OCC and the other subsidiary, Golden West, by the OTS since it was a federally chartered savings institution. And the two insured banks had the FDIC as a secondary regulator. As described by Sheila Bair, the main regulator OCC had failed to inform the FDIC of the mounting problems in Wachovia and the gradual loss of deposits. The FDIC had trusted the information from the OCC and not put a monitor of its own into the bank, as it had done in WaMu, not trusting the OTS. [42]

The bank's problems began in earnest during the summer of 2008. In June, it ousted its CEO since 2000, Kennedy "Ken" Thompson, replacing him with Robert K. "Bob" Steel, who had been the Treasury's under secretary for domestic finance. On 22 July, it reported a whopping 8.9 billion dollar loss for the second quarter, having shown a small loss for the first quarter. Most of the losses stemmed from the purchase of Golden West, where credit losses on its option ARM were expected to rise to 22 percent of the balance outstanding. [43] But it also succeeded in raising 7 billion dollars in new equity during the summer, almost making up for the loss. The OCC simultaneously downgraded the bank, assessing its risk profile as "high."

The seizure of Washington Mutual in the evening of Thursday, 25 September, and the loss enforced upon unsuspecting unsecured creditors led to a run on Wachovia the day after. In one single day, it lost 5.7 billion dollars of deposits, 1.1 billion in commercial paper and faced demands from unsecured creditors for immediate repayment

---

[42] Bair, *Bull by the Horns*, p. 84.
[43] FCIC, *Financial Crisis Inquiry Report*, p. 304.

of long-term bonds of 50–60 billion dollars. The value of its 10-year unsecured bonds fell from 73 to 29 percent of the nominal value as investors feared a repeat of WaMu; its share price fell by 27 percent, wiping out 8 billion dollars in market value.[44]

On Monday, 29 September 2008, a deal was brokered by the New York Fed, the FDIC and the Treasury. The board of Wachovia agreed to be taken over by Citigroup for 2.2 billion dollars in cash, corresponding to 1 dollar per share. Apart from all deposits (450 billion dollars), Citi would also take over responsibility for 53 billion dollars of senior and subordinated unsecured debt. Citi would acquire the commercial and retail banking operations, while the money management and brokerage operations would be left to existing shareholders in a rump-Wachovia. Citi would take the first 42 billion dollars in losses out of a loan portfolio of 312 billion and the FDIC only losses above that amount, receiving preferred stock of 12 billion dollars in Citi in return. This was the first time since the passing of the FDIC Improvement Act in 1991 that the "systemic risk exception" had been invoked.

While the FDIC involvement seemed relatively risk-free, the FDIC estimating expected losses at 35 billion to a maximum of 52 billion dollars, in principle its losses could go up to 270 billion (312–42) dollars, dramatically increasing the involvement of the FDIC. With the deal, FDIC-insured deposits at Citibank would also rise from 150 billion to 600 billion dollars. It is no wonder that Sheila Bair was worried, feeling that "Citi was a very sick institution" which might not be able to take on the additional burden of such a large addition as Wachovia.[45] The potential losses must be placed in conjunction with the 34.6 billion dollars sitting in the Deposit Insurance Fund at the time. To overcome Bair's resistance and win FDIC approval for the deal, the Treasury took the unusual step of promising to fund all potential losses arising from the transaction without involving the DIF. Normally the Treasury was only expected to extend a loan to the DIF if it was totally broke.

While shareholders at Wachovia felt that "their" bank had been sold too cheaply, they realized that the alternative was a seizure by the

---

[44] Ibid., p. 367.
[45] Ibid., p. 101.

OCC, placing the bank into receivership with the FDIC, which would turn around and sell it to Citi for an even smaller amount.

However, it never got that far. On 2 October, Wells Fargo bid 15.4 billion dollars (in its own stock), 7 dollars per share, a bid which moreover did not require the support by the FDIC or the Treasury. Wells would also purchase the entire bank, whereas Citi would, as we have seen, leave some parts out of the deal. The reason for the renewed interest by Wells Fargo in Wachovia was a new ruling by the Internal Revenue Service (IRS) that an acquiring bank could offset its operating profits by losses sustained by the acquired bank even prior to the acquisition. Under the old rule, Wells Fargo would have had the possibility of deducting only 18.6 billion of Wachovia's losses but spread out over 20 years. With the new rule, it could utilize all of Wachovia's 74 billion dollar loss for an immediate tax saving of 19.4 billion (to be compared with the 15.4 billion it paid for Wachovia).[46]

Despite the fury of Vikram Pandit, Citi's CEO, and Tim Geithner from the New York Fed, and a court challenge by Citi, the deal went through. Geithner was, however, right in that Citi would suffer reputational damage from the failed deal which would have increased its weak domestic deposit base. Its share price fell by 18 percent on the day the Wells announcement was made and by 43 percent within the week.[47] A relieved Sheila Bair noted that the decision was not hers anyway but the Fed's since it was one bank holding company acquiring another.

Overall grade of the handling of Wachovia: B (on a scale of A to F=Fail)

Scared by the market's reactions to the inept handling of IndyMac and WaMu, regulators were far more proactive this time and willing to bet taxpayers' money, although Sheila Bair wanted to do another WaMu. She writes on the invoking of the systemic risk exception:

> But that was only the beginning of a profound philosophical disagreement between me and Tim Geithner. He did not want creditors, particularly bond holders, in those large, failing financial institutions to take losses. I did. For

---

[46] In practice Wells could only offset 1 billion since the IRS repealed its own Notice 2008-83 in 2009.

[47] Blinder, *After the Music Stopped*, p. 160.

years, those poorly managed institutions had made huge profits and gains from their high-flying ways, and large institutional bond investors had provided them with plenty of cheap funding to do so. Their primary regulators, the NY Fed and OCC, had stood by as bond investors extended credit to the behemoths based on the implied assumption that if anything went wrong, the government would bail them out. But we do not have an insurance program for big bond investors. They are sophisticated and well heeled and can fend for themselves. There is no reason for the government to protect them.[48]

She should have realized that firstly, as pointed out above, "moral hazard" should be stemmed before a crisis, not when you are already in the crisis. Secondly, behind those "large institutional bond investors" she wants to punish were ordinary people who had put their entire pensions and other savings into insurance companies, mutual funds, pension funds and endowment funds that they believed were perfectly safe, the little people she was so sorry to see hit by the failure of Wachovia and the "haircut" to uninsured deposits, of whom she writes:

There were some really heartbreaking stories about many of those uninsured accounts; the mother of an Afghanistan soldier, killed in action who had deposited all of his life insurance, a police woman who had just sold her home and had deposited the proceeds...[49]

The same kind of people had been hit by the haircut to unsecured creditors at WaMu and the same kind of people would have been similarly adversely affected had the same treatment been meted out to creditors of Wachovia. Fortunately, she was persuaded to yield, not least since "her" FDIC's DIF would be protected from any losses arising from the Citi–Wachovia deal. In the end, the resolution became a private affair between Wells Fargo and Wachovia without government intervention, except for the Fed's blessing of the merger.

One would have liked to give the handling of Wachovia an "A" but the continued misunderstanding and infighting among the regulatory authorities must be criticized in some way so I'll give them a "B." Nor, by the way, does Dodd–Frank clear up the regulatory mess, a question to which we will return in the next part of the book.

---

[48] Bair, *Bull by the Horns*, pp. 99–100.
[49] Ibid., p. 81.

16 | USA

AIG, Citibank and Bank of America:
zombies too big to fail?

Too big to fail[1]

A too-big-to-fail firm is one whose size, complexity, interconnectedness and critical functions are such that, should the firm go unexpectedly into liquidation, the rest of the financial system and the economy would face severe adverse consequences. Governments provide support to too-big-to-fail firms in a crisis not out of favoritism or particular concern for the management, owners, or creditors of the firm, but because they recognize that the consequences for the broader economy of allowing a disorderly failure greatly outweigh the costs of avoiding the failure in some way. Common means of avoiding failure include facilitating a merger, providing credit, or injecting government capital, all of which protect at least some creditors who otherwise would have suffered losses (Ben S. Bernanke, chairman of the board of governors of the Federal Reserve System).[2]

Which institutions are too big to fail (TBTF) and why? Big in terms of total assets or deposits is one thing. JPMorgan Chase would have had total assets of 3.7 trillion dollars at the end of 2012 rather than the stated 2.4 trillion had it reported under international IFRS standards rather than GAAP; Bank of America would have had assets of 3.1 trillion instead of 2.1 trillion, Citigroup 2.7 trillion instead of 1.9 trillion. They would have dominated the European giants: HSBC with total assets of 2.6 trillion, Deutsche Bank and Crédit Agricole 2.5 trillion,

---

[1] Onaran, *Zombie Banks*, ch. 7, "US banks on IV drop"; "Europe's zombie banks, blight of the living dead," *The Economist*, 13 July 2013, www.economist.com/news/leaders/21581723-europes-financial-system-terrible-state-and-nothing-much-being-done-about-it-blight

[2] Ben S. Bernanke, testimony before the Financial Crisis Inquiry Commission, 2 September 2010, "Causes of the recent financial and economic crisis," www.federalreserve.gov/newsevents/testimony/bernanke20100902a.htm

BNP Paribas and Barclays 2.4 trillion.[3] It is, however, probably more relevant to ask, big in relationship to what? A number of alternatives open up: its home banking market or share of different markets, total world banking market, its home country's deposit insurance fund or GDP.[4] In 2012, UBS had "only" 1.2 trillion dollars in total assets, a dwarf in relation to the giants cited above, but it was still 1.9 times Switzerland's GDP, whereas the largest American bank, JPMorgan Chase, at double the size of UBS "only" had assets corresponding to 23 percent of the GDP of the United States. Which is the more relevant figure? And what can be done about it?

In the terminology of the Basel Group's Financial Stability Board (FSB), these behemoths are called Globally Systemically Important Financial Institutions (G-SIFIs). In November 2013, 29 banks world-wide were pinpointed by the FSB as G-SIFIs, eight of which were American banks, which thus face the extra capital surcharges to their risk-weighted capital requirements on top of the minimum 7 percent decided-upon under Basel III (as listed in the parentheses): JPMorgan Chase (an extra 2.5%), Citibank (2%), Bank of America, Goldman Sachs and Morgan Stanley (1.5%), Bank of New York Mellon, State Street Bank and Wells Fargo (1%).[5]

In a similar vein, the Federal Reserve, acting together with the FDIC and the OCC, has decided that these eight banking groups must have a leverage ratio (core equity Tier 1 capital/total unweighted assets) of no less than 5 percent at the holding company level and 6 percent in the subsidiary bank(s), whereas Basel III only stipulates a 3 percent lever-age ratio. Bank holding companies with more than 50 billion dollars

---

[3] Federal Deposit Insurance Corporation, "Capitalization ratios for global sys-temically important banks (G-SIB), data as of fourth quarter 2012."

[4] James R. Barth and Apanard Prabha, "Too big to fail: a little perspective on a large problem," Federal Reserve Bank of Chicago, 15th Annual Banking Conference, 15–16 November 2012; James R. Barth, Apanard (Penny) Prabha and Phillip Swagel, "Just how big is the too-big-to-fail problem?" *Journal of Banking Regulation* 13 (November 2012), pp. 265–99.

[5] Basel III specifies a minimum ratio of core equity Tier 1 (CET1) to risk-weighted assets (RWA) of 4.5 percent on top of which comes a capital-conservation buffer of 2.5 percent, making for a minimum of 7 percent. Above these, individual countries may add a countercyclical buffer of 1–2.5 percent. JPMorgan Chase would thus potentially face a demand for CET1/RWA of 12 percent under Basel III. This is similar to what Switzerland demands of its two major banks except that these also face an additional demand for 9 percent CoCo bonds.

in total assets will also be scrutinized more intensively by the Fed. The Financial Stability Oversight Council (FSOC) has also designated three non-bank holding companies (AIG, Prudential and GE Capital) as being of sufficient size to having systemic financial impact, warranting increased supervision by the Federal Reserve and the possibility of their resolution by the FDIC under its new Dodd–Frank powers.

In view of the fact that the increased capital requirement goes hand in hand with the promise under Dodd–Frank not ever again to use taxpayers' money for a bank bail-out, in November 2013, Moody's lowered the rating of four major US banks by one notch. Bank of New York Mellon was cut to A1 from Aa3; Goldman Sachs was lowered to Baa1 from A3. JPMorgan Chase was cut to A3 from A2, and Morgan Stanley was downgraded to Baa2 from Baa1.

A first observation is that too big to fail is a statement of fact, not a desirable feature of banking or regulation.[6] Most studies would agree that there are few economies of scale in banking above, at most, 100 billion dollars in total assets and if there are, they are due to the existence of the TBTF syndrome, allowing these banks to borrow at lower rates than other, smaller banks, since there is a high likelihood that they will be bailed out.[7] It can be argued that the actions by the FSB and the Federal Reserve have unwittingly increased this borrowing advantage for the 29 anointed G-SIFI banks and the corresponding American TBTF banks since it made clear that they would be saved one way or another, whereas before, there was some uncertainty as to which banks would be saved.[8] A prerequisite is, of course, that the home country has the financial ability to bail out its TBTF banks. A recent study has found that the CDS (credit default swaps) market prices the TBTF banks quite differently depending on the stability of public finances in their home state.[9]

---

[6] For a contrary view, see Richard X. Bove, *Guardians of Prosperity: Why America Needs Big Banks* (New York: Penguin, 2013).

[7] A good summary of the issue and references is given in Andrew G. Haldane, "On being the right size," Bank of England speeches, 25 October 2012. www.bankofengland.co.uk/publications/Documents/speeches/2012/speech615.pdf

[8] Peter J. Wallison, "Too big to ignore: the future of bailouts and Dodd-Frank after the 2012 election," American Enterprise Institute, 24 October 2012.

9 Asli Demirgüç-Kunt and Harry Huizinga, "Are banks too big to fail or too big to save? International evidence from equity prices and CDS spreads," *Journal of Banking and Finance* 37 (March 2013), pp. 875–94; Morris Goldstein and

When the financial crisis struck at the end of 2007, there were some 120 banks worldwide exceeding the limit of 100 billion dollars in total assets. Of these banks, 19 were American. As noted earlier, the six largest banks (Bank of America, JPMorgan Chase, Citigroup, Wells Fargo, Goldman Sachs and Morgan Stanley) held assets corresponding to 60 percent of US GDP in 2012.[10] The six also accounted for 67 percent of all banking assets in the United States.

But even more importantly, banks' (and insurance companies') derivative transactions tend to dwarf these numbers while making interconnections even more important and resolutions even more complex. We saw earlier that Lehman Brothers had 906,000 outstanding or pending derivative contracts at the time of its bankruptcy.

On 30 June 2008, American banks held the following nominal OTC derivatives positions:

- JPMorgan Chase 94,500 billion dollars (60 times its total on-balance assets)
- Bank of America 37,700 billion dollars (22 times its total on-balance assets)
- Citigroup 35,800 billion dollars (16 times its total on-balance assets)
- Wachovia 4,100 billion dollars (5 times its total on-balance assets)[11]
- Goldman Sachs 45,900 billion dollars (52 times its total on-balance assets)
- Morgan Stanley 37,000 billion dollars (56 times its total on-balance assets)[12]

These six US financial institutions alone were responsible for 37 percent of the world total OTC derivatives volume outstanding (684,000 billion dollars).

During and after the financial crisis, a number of voices have been raised to insist that resolution of the next financial crisis requires

Nicolas Veron, "Too big to fail: the transatlantic debate", Peterson Institute Working Paper no. 2, 2011.

[10] Simon Johnson and James Kwak, *13 Bankers, The Wall Street Take-Over and the Next Financial Meltdown* (New York: Pantheon Books, 2010) p. 203 and own calculations.

[11] FCIC, *Financial Crisis Inquiry Report*, p. 300.

[12] The ex-investments banks' holdings are of the first quarter of 2009 after their conversion to banks.

solving the too-big-to-fail problem. In his above-quoted testimony, the Fed's Ben Bernanke concluded that "if the crisis has a single lesson, it is that the too-big-to-fail problem must be solved." Similarly, lord (Mervyn) King, ex-governor of the Bank of England said: "It is not in our national interest to have banks that are too big to fail, too big to jail or simply too big."[13] And former Fed chairman Alan Greenspan agreed: "If they're too big to fail, they're too big."[14]

Daniel Tarullo, the Fed governor overseeing the central bank's supervision efforts, has argued that current efforts under Dodd–Frank to reduce the risk a big bank's failure would pose to the US economy may fall short. They "would leave more too-big-to-fail risk than I think is prudent."[15]

While the Basel group has proposed and both the European Union and the United States have enacted rules to persuade the TBTF banks gradually to shrink since they face additional capital charges, some voices propose a formal break-up of the biggest banks, similar to what the anti-trust Sherman Act of 1890 did to some manufacturing companies.

Federal Reserve Bank of Dallas president Richard Fisher:

The 2010 Dodd–Frank Act hasn't fixed a system in which the biggest banks are seen as critical to the proper functioning of our economy and deserve rescues. Less than a dozen of the largest and most complex banks are each capable – through a series of missteps by their management – of seriously damaging the vitality, resilience and prosperity that has personified the US economy. Any of these megabanks, given their systemic footprint and interconnectedness with other large financial institutions, could threaten to bring down the economy, again. The government should break up the biggest institutions to safeguard the financial system on account of the too-big-to-fail advantage that large firms have over smaller rivals.[16]

[13] www.bbc.co.uk/news/business-22980749
[14] www.bloomberg.com/apps/news?pid=newsarchive&sid=aJ8HPmNUfchg
[15] www.huffingtonpost.com/2013/05/03/daniel-tarullo-too-big-to-fail_n_3210863.html
[16] www.bloomberg.com/news/2013-06-25/fed-s-fisher-urges-bank-breakup-amid-too-big-to-fail-injustice-.html

US Senator Elizabeth Warren (earlier Professor of Law at Harvard University and chair of the Congressional Oversight Council, "COP," of the TARP program):

Where are we in making sure behemoth institutions on Wall Street can't bring down the economy again? And make wild gambles that suck up all the profits in the good times? And stick the taxpayer with the bill when it goes wrong? Three years since Dodd–Frank was passed, the biggest banks are bigger than ever, the risks to the system have grown and the market distortions continue. It is time to act: the last thing we should do is wait for another crisis. We have got to get back to running this country for American families, not for its largest financial institutions.[17]

And Sheila Bair, earlier chair of the FDIC, says:

It would surely be in the government's interest to downsize megabanks. Sen. Sherrod Brown (D-Ohio) continues to push his bill to split apart the largest institutions. Regulators have new authority to order divestitures under the Dodd-Frank financial reform law. From a shareholder standpoint, government breakups have a pretty good outcome. It worked out well for John D. Rockefeller, whose shares in Standard Oil doubled after it was ordered to break up.[18]

Similarly, Hank Paulson, summing up his period as Treasury Secretary during the crisis:

The largest financial institutions are so big and complex that they pose a dangerously large risk. Today the top financial institutions in the US hold close to 60 percent of financial assets, up from 10 percent in 1990. This dramatic concentration, coupled with much greater interconnectedness, means that the failure of any of a very few large institutions can take down a large part of the system and, in domino fashion, topple the rest. The concept of 'too big to fail' has moved from the academic literature to reality and must be addressed.[19]

---

[17] www.theguardian.com/world/2013/nov/12/elizabeth-warren-obama-banks
[18] http://finance.fortune.cnn.com/2012/01/18/big-banks-break-up-bair/
[19] Paulson, *On the Brink*, p. 440. Among other articles urging a break-up of the TBTF banks we find: "Ex-Citi chief Weill urges bank break-up," *Financial Times*, 25 July 2012; several articles by Simon Johnson (professsor at MIT and

American International Group, AIG[20]

Not only was AIG in 2007 the world's largest insurance company, with total assets of over 1 trillion dollars, operating in 130 countries around the globe and having over 120,000 employees. Unknown to most, especially to its banking regulator, the OTS, which oversaw AIG's banking activities as a thrift holding company, it was also one of the world's largest hedge funds with a book of OTC derivatives of 12,000 contracts worth a nominal 2.7 trillion dollars. Of these, 1 trillion was with 12 counterparties only, implying that AIG was not only too big to fail but also, like Bear Stearns, too interconnected to be allowed to fail. Most devastatingly, the London-based AIG Financial Products division (AIGFP), headed by Joseph Cassano, had entered into credit default swaps (CDS) to insure a nominal 441 billion dollars' worth of mortgage securities originally rated AAA, as well as credits. This was a substantial part of the total CDS market worth 58.2 trillion dollars at the end of 2007.

As a counterparty in these derivatives transactions, it profited from being one of a very small number (six to be exact) of US companies who had an AAA/Aaa rating from Standard & Poor's as well as Moody's. This meant that it did not have to put up any collateral when it entered a deal with a counterparty, which most often was one of the major investment banks in the world such as Goldman Sachs, Merrill Lynch, Société Générale or Barclays.

A CDS contract is really nothing but an insurance contract, where the buyer insures a certain credit risk for a periodic premium. If a

former chief economist at IMF): "Too big to fail not fixed despite Dodd-Frank," *Bloomberg*, 9 October 2011; "Breaking up four big banks," *New York Times*, 19 May 2012; "Banks' living wills don't defuse systemic risk," *Bloomberg*, 8 July 2012; "Big banks are hazardous to the US economic health," *Bloomberg*, 2 September 2012; "Fed should push to cut biggest banks down to size," *Bloomberg*, 15 October 2012; "Breaking up big banks is a severely conservative project," *Bloomberg*, 28 October 2012; "Who decided the US megabanks are too big to jail?" *Bloomberg*, 4 February 2013; Johan A. Lybeck, "It is time to consider breaking up the banking behemoths," *Financial Times*, 19 March 2009.

[20] Apart from earlier cited literature, see Ron Shelp and Al Ehrbar, *Fallen Giant, the Amazing Story of Hank Greenberg and the History of AIG* (Hoboken, NJ: John Wiley & Sons, 2009); "AIG's rescue, size matters," *Financial Times*, 18 September 2008. Unless otherwise stated, the story of AIG draws upon the FCIC, passim.

credit event is declared, he pockets the value of the contract, else he has paid his premium in vain. In contrast to ordinary insurance, it is quite possible to insure something one doesn't own ("naked default swap"). Also in sharp contrast to an ordinary insurance contract where the insurance company is obliged to have reserves corresponding to a certain fraction of policies written, AIG was not obligated to have any reserves whatsoever since the derivatives markets were almost totally unregulated. Recall that the Commodity Futures Trading Commission (CFTC) had been expressly forbidden to regulate most OTC derivatives by the Futures Trading Practices Act of 1992 and the Commodity Futures Modernization Act of 2000 if the trades took place between "sophisticated parties."

From the viewpoint of the counterparty bank, most of these deals were caused by regulatory arbitrage as the counterparty after entering into the CDS contract now had a claim against a bank, AIGFP, which carried a 1.6 percent capital charge under Basel I rather than the standard 8 percent charge for a commercial credit or 4 percent for a residential mortgage. In June 2008, AIGFP had insured 294 billion dollars in corporate debt, 141 billion dollars in European residential mortgages and 78 billion dollars in CDOs, the latter mostly written on securities with subprime mortgages as underlying.

The head of AIGFP was not unduly worried about the lack of reserves, stating in August 2007 that: "It is hard for us, and without being flippant, to even see a scenario within any realm of reason that would see us losing \$1 in any of those transactions."[21]

Just one month later, the AIGFP had to book an unrealized loss of 352 million dollars on its CDS contracts. The fact that the derivative contracts now had a positive value for the counterparty led to AIG having to start delivering collateral. Likewise, it was formally committed to put up collateral to the counterparty if the company was downgraded, as indeed it was starting from spring 2005, gradually falling from AAA to A- on the day it was bailed out, 16 September 2008. Some firms, in particular Goldman Sachs, also started having cold feet about the future ability of AIG to deliver and bought CDS protection on the CDSs written by AIGFP.

---

[21] www.nytimes.com/2008/09/28/business/28melt.html?pagewanted=all&_r=1&

However, no actual collateral margin calls were made until July 2007, after the demise of Bear Stearns' hedge funds, when Goldman Sachs requested 1.8 billion dollars. Its evaluation of the underlying bonds indicated a 15 percent fall in value of the underlying securities, whereas the models of AIGFP indicated no long-term decline (hence the statement by its president, Joe Cassano, above). While the insurance regulators for such monocline (credit) insurers as MBIA did not allow collateral to be put up until an actual loss had been suffered, no such restrictions applied to the unregulated AIGFP. A further problem in finding an agreement was that other counterparties to AIGFP such as Merrill Lynch were not equally negative on the "true" value of the underlying securities as Goldman was. On 10 August, AIGFP finally sent over 450 million dollars, its first collateral posted. The parties continued to disagree as to the correct size of the collateral, though not on the principle. On 2 November, Goldman demanded 2.8 billion dollars' worth of collateral, on 23 November, an additional 3 billion and in February 2008 an additional 2.5 billion dollars. The noose had begun to tighten around the neck of AIGFP. By the weekend Lehman crashed, posted collateral had risen to 19 billion dollars, of which 7.6 billion had gone to Goldman.[22]

On 28 February 2008, AIG reported an 11.1 billion dollar write-down on subprime mortgages for the fourth quarter of 2007, leading to an annual loss of over 5 billion dollars. The share price dipped by 12 percent for the day to 45 dollars; at the peak in 2002, it had been close to 2,000 dollars (or around 145 dollars correcting for secondary offerings). It would not return and exceed 45 dollars until May 2013 after having been as low as 5 dollars per share (see Figure 31). Its president and CEO, Martin J. Sullivan, was later ousted (15 June). AIG's regulator, the OTS, finally downgraded the company from a "2" to a "3."

With all attention focused first on IndyMac, then Fannie Mae and Freddie Mac, then Lehman, the rapidly rising problems at AIG went unnoticed by the public as well as by the regulatory authorities. While aware of the problem during "Lehman weekend," there was no time to consider also AIG. On the Monday morning when Lehman filed for bankruptcy, all the three major rating firms downgraded AIG,

---

[22] Blinder, *After the Music Stopped*, p. 135.

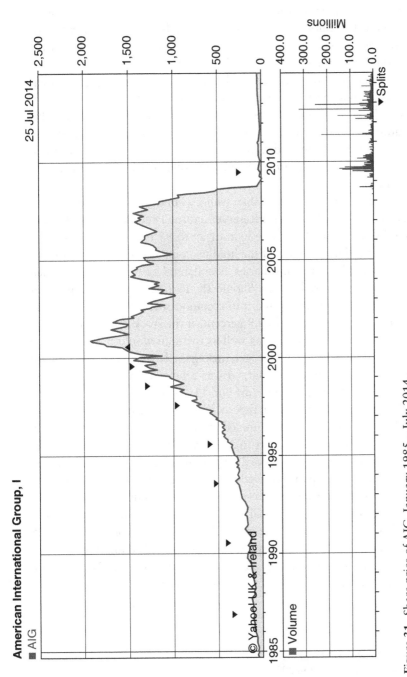

Figure 31. Share price of AIG, January 1985 – July 2014

Source: http://uk.finance.yahoo.com/q/bc?s=AIG&t=my&l=off&z=l&q=l&c=

triggering collateral demands for an additional 13 billion dollars above the 19 billion that the firm had already posted. Its already low share price nosedived 60 percent to below 5 dollars during the day.

Should the regulatory authorities intervene when they had let Lehman go only the day before? Both companies were big and interconnected but there were two major differences. Firstly, while important, AIGFP was only a (destructive) part of a lucrative and stable insurance business which could be partly sold to pay off any debt to the government.[23] Secondly, in contrast to Lehman, the Fed regarded the assets of AIG as sufficient-quality collateral for the size of the loan needed.

Hence, on 16 September 2008, using, as in the case of Bear Stearns, Section 13(3) of the Federal Reserve Act, the Federal Reserve Bank of New York extended a bridge loan of up to 85 billion dollars to AIG, taking as collateral assets of the holding company and the majority of its stock holdings in subsidiaries as collateral as well as being issued convertible preferred shares. Should the loan (a so-called equity participation note) be converted into common stock, it would make the government the owner of 79.9 percent of the stock outstanding (over 80 percent and the holding as well as the loan would have had to be integrated into the federal budget, raising the federal debt by 85 billion dollars). The interest rate charged was a hefty LIBOR plus 8.50 percentage points or, at the time, around 11.50 percent.

While AIG had said that they needed an immediate loan of only 4 billion dollars, in fact they immediately withdrew 14 billion. Already on 10 November, the support to AIG was extended and changed after the company reported losses of 24.5 billion dollars for the third quarter. The insurance company received a capital injection of 40 billion dollars and the credit line was increased to 112.5 billion dollars, a large part of which was used to repay CDS and securities lending counterparties (see below). The interest rate charged was lowered from LIBOR + 8.5 percent to LIBOR + 3 percent. Support from the Fed and the Treasury in the form of capital and loans would ultimately reach 182.5 billion dollars. Of these, 68 billion came from the TARP program, which was

---

[23] At its height, AIGFP has contributed 7 percent of AIG's operating income in 2005 and 17 percent in 2006.

eventually repaid with a 5 billion dollar profit to the government (see below).

In March 2009, AIG got another 30 billion dollars from the Fed. At the same time, the government converted its 70 billion dollars' worth of preference shares to common stock in order to strengthen its control over the company. AIG's loss for the year 2008 was reported at almost 100 billion dollars, the largest loss ever reported by any company in the world.

Three years later, in June 2012, AIG repaid the original 45 billion dollar loan from the New York Fed by drawing on TARP money. The rescue operation had netted the Fed 17.7 billion dollars in profit, mainly because of the capital gain on the securities held as collateral and sold. The 79.9 percent public shareholder stake in AIG was also gradually sold on the market. In September 2012, when the government's stake fell to 21.5 percent, the Federal Reserve became AIG's main regulator in its capacity as a financial holding company under Dodd–Frank legislation. In December 2012, the US Treasury sold off its last shares in AIG at a total profit of 5 billion dollars. Total return to the taxpayer was thus 22.7 billion dollars. In 2013, the AIG ran a widespread publicity campaign called "Thank you, America." The taxpayers could have responded "Thank you, AIG."

The company had during the five years shrunk from 1 trillion dollars in total assets to 540 billion and its headcount from 116,000 to 64,000. In both 2012 and 2013, it made a profit of over 6 billion dollars after tax as contrasted to a profit of 2 billion in 2011 and a loss of 1.5 billion in 2010.

Overall grade of the handling of AIG: A (on a scale of A to F=Fail)

The bail-out of AIG will forever remain contentious. Should taxpayers really take a risk of 182 billion dollars to bail out a company which wasn't even a bank? A company that had been badly mismanaged, evaded supervision, helping banks avoid capital requirements ("regulatory arbitrage"), paying hundreds of millions of dollars in bonuses to incompetent top management?

Firstly, AIG was a bank, or more precisely a thrift holding company regulated by the OTS since it had savings banks as subsidiaries. Hence it was in this respect no different from, say, Washington Mutual Inc.

Secondly, one must remember the uncertainty at the time, coming just after the Lehman collapse, as well as the haste with which everything had to be decided. The FCIC inquiry has stated the dilemma well (p. 433):[24]

For a policymaker, the calculus is simple: if you bail out AIG and you are wrong, you will have wasted taxpayer money and provoked public outrage. If you don't bail out AIG and you're wrong, the global financial system collapses. It should be easy to see why policymakers favored action – there was a chance of being wrong either way, amd the costs of being wrong without action were far greater than the costs of being wrong with action.

Thirdly, the policy makers did most things right. They ousted the existing management, in particular the CEO Robert Willumstad (despite the fact that he had been CEO for only three months). They made it very clear to the board of AIG that the harsh terms were not negotiable and that the alternative was bankruptcy. They separated the collateral assets to a special Fed-run company (Maiden Lane II and III). They took their time, over four years, to sell the collateral securities as well as the stock received and were rewarded by a nice capital gain. In this way, the taxpayers profited handsomely. They put pressure on the company in their capacity as the dominant shareholder to make AIG shrink and focus on its core business, selling or liquidating non-core or overly risky business, in the process unwinding the entire book of AIG Financial Products.

This brings us to the first of the really contentious issues. During November–December 2008, the Fed and the Treasury allowed AIG to repay its counterparties in securities lending operations and Credit Default Swaps in full, 100 cents on the dollar, no "haircuts": 71 billion dollars plus the 35 billion that the institutions already held in collateral for a total of 106 billion dollars (see Table 22). A public outcry ensued, in particular since some of the major receivers were foreign banks such as Société Générale (receiving 17.4 billion dollars), Deutsche Bank (14.9 billion), Barclays (8.5 billion), BNP Paribas (4.9 billion) or "Wall Street" investment banks, recently converted to banks, such as Goldman Sachs (18.8 billion).

---

[24] Actually, to be fair, the statement is taken from the dissenting views of Keith Hennessy, Douglas Holtz-Eakin and Bill Thomas rather than from the Commission's majority.

Table 22. *Payments to AIG counterparties, billion dollars*

Securities lending counterparties	Credit default swap counterparties	Payment	New payments	Collateral held
Barclays	7.0	Société Générale	6.9	9.6
Deutsche Bank	6.4	Goldman Sachs	5.6	8.4
BNP Paribas	4.9	Merrill Lynch	3.1	3.1
Goldman Sachs	4.8	Deutsche Bank	2.8	5.7
Bank of America	4.5	UBS	2.5	1.3
HSBC	3.3	Calyon	1.2	3.1
Citigroup	2.3	D. Genoss. Bank	1.0	0.8
Dresdner Kleinwort	2.2	Bank of Montreal	0.9	0.5
Merrill Lynch	1.9	Wachovia	0.8	0.2
UBS	1.7	Barclays	0.6	0.9
ING	1.5	Bank of America	0.5	0.3
Morgan Stanley	1.0	RBS	0.5	0.6
Société Générale	0.9	Dresdner Bank	0.4	0.0
AIG International	0.6	Rabobank	0.3	0.3
Credit Suisse	0.4	LB Baden-Würt	0.1	0.0
Paloma Securities	0.2	HSBC	0.0	0.2
Citadel	0.2			
TOTAL	43.7		27.1	35.0

Source: FCIC, *Financial Crisis Inquiry Report*, p. 377.

The uproar in the papers can be imagined but other critical voices were also heard. Not surprisingly, Sheila Bair from the FDIC claimed that "there is no reason in the world why [AIG's] counterparties couldn't have taken a 10 percent haircut."[25]

---

[25] Blinder, *After the Music Stopped*, p. 139.

Robert C. Pozen, at the time at the Brookings Institution as well as a senior lecturer at Harvard Business School, later chairman of MFS Investment Management, wrote:[26]

During the first week of November, 2008, the Federal Reserve Bank of New York – with the current Treasury Secretary Timothy Geithner as its then president – took over the negotiations with the large banks owning CDS contracts with AIG. After a week of negotiations, the New York Fed instructed AIG to settle these CDS contracts by paying the full face value of all the relevant bonds – $62 billion, as compared to their then market value of less than $30 billion.

In my view, these $62 billion in AIG payments were unjustified gifts to sophisticated investors, who had made an error of investment judgment in choosing a weak counterparty for their CDS contracts. The choice of appropriate counterparties is a critical component of risk management at all financial institutions. Even the vice-chair of the New York Fed admitted that the payments "will reduce their incentive to be careful in the future."

Since federal officials have not explained why they chose to pay in full instead of negotiating discounts, we can only speculate. One theory is that the US Treasury wanted to provide financial assistance to foreign banks suffering the fallout of the American credit crisis. These foreign banks received roughly $40 billion of the $62 billion in payouts from AIG. Perhaps this was an indirect way to achieve the US Treasury's objective since Congress would not authorize a direct bailout of foreign banks.

There are conspiracy theories as well. Some observers point out that Stephen Friedman, the chairman of the New York Fed, is a director of Goldman Sachs. Goldman received almost $13 billion in settlement from AIG and Friedman bought 50,000 shares of Goldman shortly after the federal takeover of AIG. Goldman claims that it was fully hedged against any losses if AIG had failed, but the reliability of these hedges has been questioned by the federal auditor.

SIGTARP, Neil Barofsky, was even more critical, writing:[27]

Even worse than the bonus payments [see below], at least in terms of financial cost, was the subject of our other AIG audit, which explore the reasons

---

[26] Robert C. Pozen, "AIG: the secret bailout," *Harvard Business Review*, 23 November 2009, http://blogs.hbr.org/2009/11/aig-the-secret-bailout/

[27] Barofsky, *Bailout*, pp. 183 ff.

for Geithner's agreement to effectively pay full value to the banks for the CDOs [sic][28] the government purchased from them. These beneficiaries included Société Générale ($16.5 billion in CDOs bought), Goldman Sachs ($14 billion), Deutsche Bank ($8.5 billion), Merrill Lynch ($6.2 billion), UBS ($4.3 billion), Wachovia ($1 billion) and Bank of America ($800 million). Our audit sought to find out why Geithner hadn't negotiated a lower price on behalf of the public.

On its face, it seemed unfair and unnecessary that the government would so grossly overpay for the bonds, particularly to those banks that had already received so much TARP money … [The] approach resulted in a departure from the normal workings of the marketplace, where concessions on debts owed by struggling companies are not uncommon.

Joseph Stiglitz, Nobel-prize winning professor at Columbia University and a former chief economist at the World Bank, said AIG's settlement of credit default swaps following its bail-out by the US government looks like "grand larceny."[29]

Alan Blinder, however, defends the payment on the grounds that there were numerous counterparties, many of them foreign.[30] What right had the American government to impose losses on foreign banks? What would have happened if, as in the case of the Greek "haircut", some banks accepted a write-down and others would not? The result would have been numerous lawsuits. To this, one could add that had AIG, aided and goaded by the government and the Fed, not paid up in full, ISDA[31] would have declared a credit event, allowing the counterparties to liquidate the collateral held. Another 35 billion dollars of securities would have been dumped onto an already panicky securities market.

The other scandal was, in terms of absolute amounts, peanuts, 165 million dollars. But it concerned bonus payments to 418 members of the now wound-down AIG Financial Products division, those responsible for bringing the company down and potentially costing taxpayers 182 billion dollars. An angry President Obama, asking "How do they justify this outrage to the taxpayers who are keeping the company

---

[28] He meant CDSs rather than CDOs or perhaps he didn't know the difference. See Table 22.
[29] www.bloomberg.com/apps/news?sid=asZ6r4QWJz_A&pid=newsarchive
[30] Blinder, *After the Music Stopped*, p. 139.
[31] The International Swaps and Derivatives Association.

afloat?", ordered his finance minister Tim Geithner to block the payment. However, it had been decided by the board already in March 2008 long before the government's intervention and was thus fully legal and untouchable.

Public pressure led, however, to a number of the recipients returning the money. Newspaper commentators said inter alia: "I would deny them the bonuses if possible. I would be for an exemplary hanging or two. Have it in Times Square, invite Madame Defarge. You borrow a guillotine from the French and we could have a party" and "I was going to recommend boiling them in oil in Times Square."[32] New York Attorney General Andrew Cuomo, investigating the bonuses, also subpoenaed data on credit derivatives to determine banks' improperly received taxpayer funds.

> Our investigation into corporate bonuses has led us to an investigation of the credit-default swap contracts at AIG. CDS contracts were at the heart of AIG's meltdown. The question is whether the contracts are being wound down properly and efficiently or whether they have become a vehicle for funneling billions in taxpayer dollars to capitalize banks all over the world.[33]

Cuomo's pressure ultimately led to about half the bonuses being returned.

Yet, apart from the clumsy handling of the bonuses, to my mind the regulators' resolution of AIG was exemplary. Its failure on top of Lehman's bankruptcy would in all likelihood have crashed the markets. The Fed and the Treasury deserve an "A."

Citigroup[34]

For those who have a conspiratorial bent, one could claim that the entire TARP/CPP program was directed at saving one TBTF bank and one bank only, namely Citigroup/Citibank. All the others became free riders, profiting from Citi's problems and the regulatory solution. While this statement may prove an exaggeration, it does expose a

---

[32] http://en.wikipedia.org/wiki/AIG_bonus_payments_controversy
[33] www.bloomberg.com/apps/news?sid=asZ6r4QWJz_A&pid=newsarchive
[34] Over and above earlier cited literature, see "Shrunken ambition," *Financial Times*, 19 December 2013.

fundamental difference between the way the United States handled problems in its TBTF banks and how they were handled in Europe. On the "Old Continent," problem cases were handled one by one; only those banks that needed support were bailed out. Commerzbank was bailed out, Deutsche Bank wasn't. UBS was, Credit Suisse wasn't. Erste Bank in Austria was, Bank Austria wasn't. Amagerbanken and some others in Denmark were, Danske Bank and Jyske Bank weren't. Monte dei Paschi di Siena was, UniCredit and Intesa Sanpaolo weren't. The Spanish *cajas* were, Santander and BBVA weren't.

A particular point can be made for Britain, where the conditions attached to government aid were much more stringent than those in the United States: change of management, frozen bonuses, high (12 percent) interest on the injected preferred shares. The rate of interest in question became irrelevant, however, when the government converted its holdings in RBS to common stock in January 2009 but the conditions had in the meantime deterred more healthy banks such as Barclays, Standard Chartered and HSBC from seeking government support. Lloyds Banking Group would be the only bank except RBS to seek state aid.

The US approach was entirely different from that in Europe; all megabanks were forcefed in order not to stigmatize the one bank or the few banks that truly needed the money. "What do I need $25 billion more capital for?" asked the outspoken Dick Kovacevich, chairman of Wells Fargo at the famous Treasury meeting on 13 October 2008.[35] Yet in the end, as we shall see in a moment, he was also forced to accept the capital injection (which was repaid by Wells with a 2.2 billion dollar gain to the government already in December 2009). He would later state that "[e]veryone understood who needed the money and why," arguing that only those firms that were in trouble should have been bailed out. "TARP caused the crisis to get much greater since it conveyed the message that the entire industry was in deep, deep trouble."[36] It is quite obvious that the "who" he alluded to was Citi.

The only country in Europe to use the "US model" was France, distributing a total of 10.5 billion euro to all its major banks: Crédit Agricole (3 billion), BNP Paribas (2.5 billion), Société Générale

---

[35] Paulson, *On the Brink*, p. 364.
[36] Interview 13 September, 2013, www.cnbc.com/id/101032772

(1.7 billion), Crédit Mutuel (1.2 billion), Caisses d'épargne (savings banks, 1.1 billion) and Banque Populaire (950 million). But then, since France did not have a financial crisis and none of the mentioned banks really needed the money, it was all a show to make French banks more competitive, a game plan ultimately but reluctantly accepted by the EC Commission.[37] The Commission, however, insisted on such harsh terms on the subordinated debt furnished by the state that its decision led to an immediate repayment of the money by the recipient banks during October–November 2009.[38] But then they had enjoyed their capital advantage for a full year.

At the same meeting, Sheila Bair also presented the FDIC's Temporary Liquidity Guarantee Program (TLGP). TLGP helped bring stability to financial markets and the banking industry during the crisis period. The TLGP consisted of two components: (1) the Transaction Account Guarantee Program (TAGP), an FDIC guarantee of noninterest-bearing transaction accounts; and (2) the Debt Guarantee Program (DGP), an FDIC guarantee of certain newly issued senior unsecured debt. The TAGP guaranteed in full all domestic noninterest-bearing transaction deposits and *now* accounts held at participating banks through 31 December 2010. Over the course of the DGP's existence, 122 entities issued TLGP debt. At its peak, the DGP guaranteed 346 billion dollars of outstanding debt. The DGP guarantee on all TLGP debt that had not already matured expired on 31 December 2012. Therefore, at the end of 2012, no debt guaranteed by the DGP remained. The FDIC collected 10.4 billion dollars in fees and surcharges under the DGP with small losses.

As concerns Citigroup, the bank turned out to be a good source of revenue for the public purse. On a total TARP injection of 45 billion dollars received plus a government guarantee for its "toxic assets" (see below), the taxpayer received 13.4 billion dollars interest and capital gain on top of repayment of principal.

Citibank was in 2007 the biggest bank in the United States, by assets as well as capital, although like Lehman, it had a high international presence, operating in 140 countries with a total workforce of almost

[37] http://europa.eu/rapid/press-release_IP-08-1900_en.htm
[38] www.ft.com/intl/cms/s/0/85a0649e-b893-11de-809b-00144feab49a.html#axzz2pssBV4bC

400,000. Two-thirds of its deposit base came from non-American holders and over half of its gross revenue was earned overseas. It held almost 2.2 trillion dollars in assets, even as measured under GAAP, and an additional 1.2 trillion off-balance as well as a notional 35.8 trillion dollars in derivatives positions.

The problems at Citi surfaced in October 2007, when Citigroup reported a write-down of 5.9 billion dollars for the third quarter. In November, it was forced to make a new reservation of 11 billion dollars on top of the one taken just a month earlier. It succeeded, however, at the same time in attracting a share infusion of 7.5 billion dollars from the sovereign wealth fund of Abu Dhabi which thereby became the bank's largest shareholder. Its total subprime exposure was stated at 55 billion dollars at the time, 42 billion more than the bank had told investors just three weeks before. The bank's CEO and chairman Charles "Chuck" Prince was forced to resign.

Actually, the problems should have been known internally much earlier. Already in 2005, the OCC as supervisor of Citibank had stated that "earnings and profitability growth have taken precedence over risk management and internal control ... The findings of this examination are disappointing, in that the business grew far in excess of management's underlying infrastructure and control processes," referring not least to the group's over 2,000 subsidiaries.[39] Yet regulators took no concrete action. In 2006, the person responsible for verifying the quality of loans to be sold to the GSEs for securitization found that 60 percent of the loans that CitiFinancial, the lending arm of Citibank, bought were inferior to the standards set by Fannie Mae and Freddie Mac and could result in a forced buy-back.[40] Next year, the ratio rose to 80 percent. He would ultimately be proven right. In July 2013, Citigroup came to an agreement with the Federal Housing Finance Agency (FHFA) to pay 968 million dollars to Fannie Mae for defective mortgages. In September, a similar agreement concerning loans sold to Freddie Mac cost Citi another 395 billion dollars. It also paid a fine of an undisclosed size to the FHFA.

During spring 2008, the problems accelerated. On 15 January 2008, Citigroup wrote down credits for 18 billion dollars for the fourth

---

[39] FCIC, *Financial Crisis Inquiry Report*, p. 199.
[40] Ibid., p. 19.

quarter of 2007. In April, it reported a 5.1 billion dollar loss for the first quarter due to new write-downs of 12 billion dollars. Ultimately, write-downs of mortgages and mortgage-related CDOs (of which Citi used to retain the AAA and supersenior tranches, selling the rest) would reach 58 billion dollars, more than half Citigroup's equity in 2007, which was moreover far lower than its competitors' even to begin with. That year, Citigroup reported a leverage (capital/assets) ratio of just 4.08 percent to be contrasted with Wells Fargo's 6.37 percent, JPMorgan's 5.68 percent, Wachovia's 5.56 percent and Bank of America's 4.86 percent (*The Banker*, July 2008). In other words, in the terminology of the FDIC, Citi was on the borderline of becoming an "undercapitalized" bank rather than an "adequately capitalized" bank.[41] Also in April 2008, both the OCC and the FDIC lowered Citi's CAMELS rating from a 2 ("satisfactory") to a 3 ("less than satisfactory"), again citing weaknesses in the bank's risk management.

Yet losses continued: 2.5 billion dollars for the second quarter of 2008, 2.8 billion dollars for the third quarter, 8.3 billion dollars for the fourth quarter, leading to a cumulative loss of 27.7 billion dollars for the entire year 2008. On top of the rising losses came the defeat over Wachovia in early October. While there was no run on any particular day, the bank suffered a continuing haemorrhage of deposits. It was a humiliated Citi that participated in the meeting on 13 October 2008 with the Treasury's Hank Paulson, FDIC's Sheila Bair, Ben Bernanke and Tim Geithner from the Fed and John Dugan, the Comptroller of the Currency. During this meeting, the CEOs of nine major US banks agreed to accept a combined 125 billion dollars in new capital under the TARP program: Jamie Dimon, JPMorgan Chase (25 billion), Richard Kovacevich, Wells Fargo (25 billion), Vikram Pandit, Citigroup (25 billion), Kenneth Lewis, Bank of America (15 billion), John Thain, Merrill Lynch (10 billion), Lloyd Blankfein, Goldman Sachs (10 billion), John Mack, Morgan Stanley (10 billion), Robert Kelly, Bank of New York Mellon (3 billion), Ronald Logue, State Street Bank (2 billion).

All banks had been forced to participate to avoid stigmatizing those who really needed the injection, especially Citi. The Treasury would hold preferred non-voting stock yielding 5 percent interest (rising to

---

[41] www.fdic.gov/regulations/laws/rules/2000-4500.html

9 percent after five years) plus warrants to purchase common stock. Pay and bonuses of participating banks would be severely curtailed. The markets responded to the news with thumbs up, Dow Jones rising 11 percent over the day. By December 2010, all the nine banks had repaid the TARP money with a good return to the taxpayer. Of the nine participating CEOs, four were gone within the year and only two remained in power six years later in 2014, Jamie Dimon of JPMorgan Chase and Lloyd Blankfein of Goldman Sachs.

But despite the injection, problems mounted at Citi. On 19 November 2008, Citibank transferred CDOs worth over 17 billion dollars from an off-balance SIV (structured investment vehicle) onto its own books. The group's share price dropped by 23 percent the next day and by 60 percent for the week. The market for Credit Default Swaps indicated a 25 percent probability that Citigroup would become bankrupt within five years. Hence a second salvage operation became necessary. On 23 November, Citigroup received a further 20 billion dollars in TARP capital on top of the earlier 25 billion. The government would also guarantee 306 billion dollars of "toxic assets," Citi taking the first 37 billion dollars of losses; thereafter the FDIC would bear 90 percent of further losses, maximized at 10 billion dollars, with the Federal Reserve taking any further losses. The taxpayer was paid by receiving 7 billion dollars' worth of preference shares, yielding 8 percent interest, plus warrants corresponding to over 4 percent of common stock. The share price of Citigroup rose 62 percent on the news (but it had fallen from 60 dollars per share to under 4 dollars at this time). In February 2009, however, when 25 billion dollars of preference shares held by the government were converted to common stock, raising the stake of the government in the bank to 36 percent, Citi's share price fell by the same number.

Thereafter the situation stabilized. In May 2009, results of the stress test of 19 US banks conducted by the Federal Reserve and the FDIC revealed that they needed an additional 74.6 billion dollars in capital. Bank of America alone needed 33.9 billion dollars (a result of overpaying for Merrill Lynch), Wells Fargo 13.7 billion, GMAC 11.5 billion and Citigroup 5.5 billion. Nine of the banks, among them Goldman Sachs and JPMorgan Chase, were judged to already have sufficient capital. Since the stress tests – in sharp contrast to those conducted in Europe – were held to be tough and trustworthy, confidence in the American banking system rose.

In December 2009, Citigroup repaid the last 20 billion dollars of support given under the TARP program in order to escape from the imposed pay limits. It also terminated the guarantee given to its "toxic assets." The US government's equity stake was reduced to 27 percent from a 36 percent majority stake after Citigroup had sold 21 billion dollars' worth of common stock in the largest single share sale in US history, beating the earlier record set by Bank of America just one month before (see below).

In July 2010, the US Treasury sold in the market parts of its holdings in Citigroup, bringing down its stake from 27 percent to 18 percent of total equity. The price per share, 4.03 dollars, gave the taxpayer a handsome profit, since at the bottom of the crisis the shares were worth less than one dollar. In October 2010, the Treasury reduced its stake in Citigroup to 12 percent by selling 1.5 billion ordinary shares at a profit of just over 1 billion dollars. And finally, on 6 December 2010, the US government sold off its remaining shares in Citigroup for 4.35 dollars, marking an exit from ownership in the bailed-out banking giant with a total of 12 billion dollars' gross profit for taxpayers. During these years, the taxpayer had received over 3 billion dollars in dividend payments, 7.5 billion dollars in capital gains on shares held and sold the rest from the repurchase of warrants held by the Treasury.

On 9 September 2013, the FDIC sold to the public 2.4 billion dollars' worth of subordinated notes in Citigroup, originally used as payment for the federal guarantee on 306 billion dollar assets, thereby ending all public support for the banking group from the FDIC, the Treasury and the Federal Reserve.

Overall grade of the handling of Citigroup:
A (on a scale of A to F=Fail)

As in so many of the cases we have studied, the supervision of the failing bank up to the acute crisis left much to be desired, despite the fact that the OCC had allocated 60 full-time supervisors to Citibank. But the grade given concerns actions taken after the crisis exploded and here it is difficult to fault the involved regulatory authorities. Apart from stabilizing the bank in the ways described above, they also put pressure on it to shrink, its workforce falling from 375,000 at the peak to 251,000 at the end of 2013. Total assets had fallen from 2.2 trillion to 1.9 trillion dollars.

On top of that, Citi had also split off some 600 billion dollars' worth of toxic assets into an internal "bad bank" which by fall 2013 had succeeded in selling off assets so that only 122 billion dollars remained.[42] Something for the more leisurely RBS to copy!

The lone dissenting voice was, as so often, that of Sheila Bair at the FDIC. She would have preferred to see Citi closed, split up and sold, noting in particular that the majority of the deposits were foreign-owned and thus not insured by the FDIC.[43] There may, however, have been similar thoughts at higher political levels. Ron Suskind in his book on "confidence men" claims that President Obama had decided to break up Citibank. Geithner and Obama's chief economic advisor Larry Summers told Obama, however, that the government probably lacked the powers to nationalize and dismantle a bank that was neither bankrupt nor inadequately capitalized.[44] This may (perhaps) change with the Dodd–Frank Act, on which much more later on.

Be that as it may, I will still give the regulators an "A" for their handling of Citi. I would perhaps have liked them to put more pressure on the bank to shrink but, on the other hand, that would have been a bit unfair in comparison with the other TBTF banks which have been allowed to grow unhindered during the crisis, as shown in Table 23 for the 10 largest banks in 2007 and 2013, respectively.

Bank of America

We have encountered Bank of America several times before in this book, always on the lookout to acquire more banks ("a snake gobbling up poisoned rats," as Yalman Onaran so succinctly puts it in his book on Zombie banks).[45] In April 2007, it had purchased Chicago-based LaSalle Bank with assets of 116 billion dollars for 21 billion dollars in cash from Dutch bank ABN AMRO. In January 2008, Countrywide, the largest mortgage bank in the United States,

---

[42] www.ft.com/intl/cms/s/0/5a329e10-431a-11e3-9d3c-00144feabdc0. html#axzz2pssBV4bC
[43] Paulson, *On the Brink*, p. 411.
[44] Ron Suskind, *Confidence Men, Wall Street, Washington and the Education of a President* (New York: HarperCollins, 2011), pp. 219 ff.; Robert Kuttner, *A Presidency in Peril* (White River Junction, VT: Chelsea Green, 2010), pp. 62 ff.
[45] Onaran, *Zombie Banks*, p. 85.

was bought by Bank of America for 4.1 billion dollars. And finally, in September 2008, it took over the largest US investment bank, Merrill Lynch, for 50 billion dollars or 29 dollars per share, a 70 percent premium over the latest closing price of 17 dollars per share. The bank's capital was beginning to become hard pressed, something that even the CEO of Bank of America, Ken Lewis, began to realize after his expensive purchase of Merrill.[46]

Sheila Bair from the FDIC was also becoming concerned:[47]

And in truth, I started to worry a bit about Bank of America. I thought it had overextended itself with acquisitions, including the planned purchase of Merrill Lynch. BofA's deposit base was over $800 billion. If the press started seriously scrutinizing our ability to protect the depositors of an institution that size with only a $30 billion credit line, we were going to have a serious public confidence problem on our hands.

Both would have reason to be relieved when, as a result of the meeting of the "nine families" on 13 October 2008, Bank of America was allocated an infusion of preferred shares from TARP money, 15 billion dollars for itself and 10 billion dollars for Merrill Lynch. The latter would, however, only be paid out after the merger was consummated on 1 January 2009. The host at the meeting, Treasury secretary Hank Paulson, describes vividly the role played by Bank of America's Ken Lewis in getting his colleagues to accept the money, having him say that "I don't think we should talk about this too much. We're all going to do it, so let's not waste anybody else's time … Let's cut the BS and get this done." Vikram Pandit, CEO of the neediest institution, Citi, seconded enthusiastically: "this is very cheap capital. I'm in."[48]

The Congressional Oversight Council (COP) under the chairmanship of (now Senator) Elizabeth Warren would later agree with his statement, finding that the terms of the state aid gave the TARP bank recipients and, in particular the eight largest banks, a subsidy of 22 percent. The addition of AIG and the second infusion into ailing Citibank under the Systemically Significant Failing Institutions (SSFI) Program

---

[46] Greg Farrell, *Crash of the Titans: Greed, Hubris, the Fall of Merrill Lynch and the Near-Collapse of Bank of America* (London: Random House, 2010) p. 332.
[47] Bair, *Bull by the Horns*, p. 110.
[48] Paulson, *On the Brink*, pp. 365–6.

Table 23. *The 10 major US banks by assets 2007 and 2013*

	Total assets 2007 (bill.)	Total assets 2013 (bill.)
Citigroup	2,188	1,880
Bank of America	1,716	2,102
JPMorgan Chase	1,562	2,515
Goldman Sachs	–	912
Wachovia	783	–
Morgan Stanley	–	833
Wells Fargo	575	1,527
Washington Mutual	328	–
US Bancorp	237	364
Bank of New York Mellon	198	374
Suntrust Banks	180	173
Capital One	151	297
SUM	7,918	10,977
10-bank share of US bank assets	56%	75%

increased the average subsidy even further to 31 percent, costing tax-payers 78 billion dollars, as set out in Table 24.[49] COP comments: "The valuation report concludes that Treasury paid substantially more for the assets purchased under the TARP than their then-current market value. The use of one-size-fits-all investment policy, rather than the use of risk-based pricing more commonly used in market transactions, underlies the magnitude of the discount."

The table does not include the second infusion of capital into Bank of America in January 2009. We recall from the discussion of Merrill Lynch above that Messrs Paulson and Bernanke dissuaded Ken Lewis from backing out of the deal by firstly threatening to fire him and his

---

[49] Congressional Oversight Panel, Oversight report, 6 February 2009, "Valuing Treasury's acquisitions," p. 6, www.gpo.gov/fdsys/pkg/CPRT-111JPRT47178/pdf/CPRT-111JPRT47178.pdf

Table 24. *Capital received under TARP/CPP and implicit subsidy (billion dollars)*[a]

Recipient	Face value	Estimated value	Subsidy %	Subsidy dollars
CPP				
Bank of America	15.0	12.5	17	2.6
Citigroup	25.0	15.5	38	9.5
JPMorgan Chase	25.0	20.6	18	4.4
Morgan Stanley	10.0	5.8	42	4.2
Goldman Sachs	10.0	7.5	25	2.5
PNC Financial	7.6	5.5	27	2.1
US Bancorp	6.6	6.3	5	0.3
Wells Fargo	25.0	23.2	7	1.8
Subtotal	124.2	96.9	22	27.3
311 other banks	70.0	54.6	22	15.4
SSFI				
AIG	40.0	14.8	63	25.2
Citigroup	20.0	10.0	50	10.0
Subtotal	60.0	24.8	59	35.2
TOTAL	254.2	176.2	31	78.0

[a]Systemically significant failing institutions (SSFI).
Source: Congressional Oversight Panel, Oversight report, 6 February 2009, "Valuing Treasury's Acquisitions," p. 6. www.gpo.gov/fdsys/pkg/CPRT-111JPRT47178/pdf/CPRT-111JPRT47178.pdf

entire board of directors if he did and secondly by promising to hand out more "candy." Bank of America, which had already accepted 25 billion dollars of TARP money, hence received a further injection of 20 billion dollars in preferred stock plus a guarantee for 118 billion in its "toxic assets," on and off balance. BofA would take the first 10 billion in losses and 10 percent above that, the FDIC and the Treasury would take the next 20 billion. The guarantee quickly turned out to be unnecessary (as Sheila Bair had already estimated[50]) but the government insisted on its fee (425 million dollars) anyway.

To my mind, the criticism from COP is not fair and not really relevant to the evaluation of the success or failure of the TARP program. Firstly, the action was taken in the middle of the battle to save the US (and world) financial system; there was no time for an unbiased outside evaluation of true values. Secondly, treating the institutions similarly, one size fits all, was the stated intention in order not to stigmatize the two neediest recipients, Citigroup and Bank of America. The table shows clearly the enormous differences between the banks. In Wells Fargo, the government bought assets worth 23.2 billion dollars for 25 billion, well within the margin of error. In Citigroup on the other hand, the same 25 billion dollars brought only 15.5 billion in assets. It was precisely this type of discrepancy that the program wanted to cover up in order to avoid a run on Citi (and BofA).

Thirdly, the possible subsidy at the time is irrelevant since the banks repaid the nominal aid (including the possible subsidy) with a healthy return to the taxpayer. When Bank of America repaid its share in December 2009, the government had received 4,566,857,694 dollars in dividends and capital gains on the 45 billion dollars injected, hence paying back also the "subsidy." In order to effect the repayment, Bank of America had issued 19.3 billion dollars' worth of new preferred shares, a new record, being beaten, however, the month after by an even larger issue by Citigroup. Of the profits to the taxpayer, 1.9 billion dollars were dividends and the residual capital gains. When, on 3 March 2010, Bank of America repurchased the warrants connected with the TARP program at a total of over 1.5 billion dollars, it was the biggest such sale yet. This dwarfed the 1.1 billion raised from a similar warrant sale by Goldman Sachs and the 950 million dollars by JPMorgan Chase.

However, the problems of BofA were not quite over. In May 2009, results of the stress test of 19 US banks conducted by the Federal Reserve and the FDIC revealed that they needed an additional

---

[50] Bair, *Bull by the Horns*, pp. 126 ff.

74.6 billion dollars in capital. Bank of America alone needed almost half of the total, 33.9 billion dollars.

In January 2011, Bank of America agreed to pay 2.6 billion dollars to Freddie Mac and Fannie Mae in compensation for faulty information on loans sold by Countrywide, the lender that BofA acquired in 2008, followed up by a fine to the US Justice Department of 1 billion dollars for false mortgage claims originating in its Countrywide division.

In January 2013, Bank of America (mainly on account of its Countrywide purchase) agreed to pay Fannie Mae an additional 11.6 billion dollars for misstating the quality of mortgage loans sold and securitized. In December, it reached a similar deal with Freddie Mac, paying 404 million for faulty mortgages sold 2000–2009. The reason for the difference between Fannie and Freddie is, as we saw above, its symbiotic relationship with Fannie, more or less excluding making business with Freddie. In May 2013, it also paid monoline insurer MBIA 1.7 billion dollars for misrepresentation of mortgages included in MBSs insured by MBIA.

In January 2014, Bank of America agreed to pay 8.5 billion dollars in compensation to mortgage-bond investors such as BlackRock to compensate for misleading or erroneous information as to their quality, again mainly a result of BofA's purchase of Countrywide Financial. And in March 2014, the bank settled renewed claims that it sold Fannie Mae and Freddie Mac defective mortgage bonds. The settlement included 6.3 billion dollars in cash and 3 billion in securities that Bank of America would repurchase.

And with a tougher attitude from the new attorney general Eric Holder and the courts, in June 2014, Bank of America was ordered by a federal judge to face two government lawsuits in which it is accused of misleading investors about the quality of loans tied to 850 billion dollars in residential mortgage-backed securities. The Justice Department broke off negotiations because it was dissatisfied with the offer by Bank of America to pay more than 12 billion dollars in compensation, which included at least 5 billion in consumer relief. Bank of America and firms it purchased (mainly Countrywide) issued about 965 billion dollars of mortgage bonds from 2004 to 2008 (while JPMorgan Chase and companies it bought issued 450 billion).

Hence even before the outcome of the pending lawsuit, Bank of America has paid a total of over 35 billion dollars for the errors of a company it purchased for 4.1 billion dollars in 2008, a sum set to rise to some 50 billion dollars or perhaps more if new suits are added.[51]

Overall grade of the handling of Bank of America: B (on a scale of A to F=Fail)

The evaluation of BofA follows that of Citi: timely, effective and utterly necessary. By 2012, the bank had returned to profitability although it was still feeble, earning 1.5 billion dollars in 2011 (1 percent return on equity), 4.2 billion (2.6 percent return on equity) in 2012 and 11.4 billion in 2013 (7 percent return on equity).[52]

Its BIS III capital ratio (CET1/RWA) had risen from 5.99 percent in 2010 to 6.64 percent in 2011 to 6.74 percent in 2012 and to 9.96 percent in 2013, well above the 7 percent required under Basel III.

The bank has also, like Citi, split off its toxic assets into an internal "bad bank." No less than 6.7 million loans totaling around 1 trillion dollars, including delinquent loans and riskier option ARM and sub-prime loans, have been separated and will gradually be wound down.[53]

The handling by the authorities would merit an "A" were it not for the fact that the balance sheet of BofA has held steady at 2.1–2.3 trillion dollars since 2009. Its total staff count shrank marginally from 284,000 at the end of 2009 (remember Merrill Lynch was not integrated until January so we cannot use the 2008 figures) to 245,000 at the end of 2012. One would have hoped and expected that the US government with its upper hand would have forced a more substantial reduction of at least one of its TBTF banks. It didn't.

[51] www.businessweek.com/articles/2014-04-30/u-dot-s-dot-finally-ready-to-charge-banks-for-crimes-as-long-as-theyre-foreign-banks
[52] Annual accounts, http://investor.bankofamerica.com/phoenix.zhtml?c=71595& p=irol-irhome&cm_re=EBZ-Corp_SocialResponsibility-_-Enterprise-_-EI38LT 0005_AboutSite_InvestorRelations#fbid=5_gqvbf3Ggs
[53] www.bloomberg.com/news/2011-03-08/bofa-segregates-almost-half-its-mort gages-into-bad-bank-under-laughlin.html

PART V

Summary of the micro studies

The studies in Parts II–IV of the book give rise to a number of questions which will be helpful in drawing conclusions as to what would be useful approaches to resolutions in the next crisis, amending Dodd–Frank and the European BRRD (Bank Recovery and Resolution Directive) where necessary, and what actions should be avoided.[1]

How did the authorities (Central Bank, Treasury, Financial Supervisory Authority, Deposit Insurance Agency, international organs such as the EU Commission and the IMF) handle the crisis? Were their actions effective and consistent? What was the end result for the bank in question? Was the end result a (more) stable banking system? What went wrong? Was it bad management, bad environment or both? Should the problems have been obvious earlier? What did supervisory authorities do and when? How was the bank resolved: resurrection, sale/merger or liquidation? Were "toxic assets" separated into a "bad bank," inside or outside the bank? Was senior management ousted? Were culprits criminally or civilly charged? Could the resolution have been handled faster/more efficiently? Was taxpayer money involved? Have taxpayers been repaid? How was the upside for taxpayers achieved once a bank has returned to profitability? Were unsecured creditors and uninsured depositors hit?

---

[1] The International Monetary Fund has published a number of useful papers summarizing the financial crisis and individual countries' responses. See, in particular, Stijn Claessens, Giovanni Dell'Ariccia, Deniz Igan and Luc Laeven, "Cross-country experiences and policy implications from the global financial crisis," *Economic Policy* 62 (April 2010), pp. 267–93, also at http://relooney. fatcow.com/SI_FAO-Asia/Global-Crisis_2.pdf; Stijn Claessens *et al.*, "Crisis management and resolution: early lessons from the financial crisis," IMF Staff Discussion Note, 9 March 2011, www.imf.org/external/pubs/ft/sdn/2011/ sdn1105.pdf. See also Dirk Schoenmaker, *Governance of International Banking: The Financial Trilemma* (Oxford and New York: Oxford University Press, 2013), esp. ch. 4.

Table 25. *Track record of the regulatory authorities in 15 countries*

Rating	No. of countries
A	8 (9)
B	7
C	2
D	–
E	4
F	7 (6)[a,b]
n r	1

[a] The number depends on the grade allocated to Amagerbanken. See above.

[b] Greece was given an "F" despite an almost perfect handling by the domestic authorities but on account of the totally inappropriate policies of the "troika," in particular the write-down of privately held Greek sovereign debt which created a Greek banking crisis and severe write-downs in other (mainly) European banks, enforcing the need for government-aided recapitalizations.

We have studied 29 cases of government resolutions of failed or failing banks during the 2007–13 financial crises, grading the interventions according to the generally accepted academic scale of A–F. Table 25 shows the track record of the regulatory authorities in 15 countries.

The criteria for distributing these grades have been the following (to repeat the table from earlier for greater simplicity).

Factors leading to good grades (A–C)

Uninterrupted service: if a bank is closed Friday afternoon (as is standard FDIC practice), depositors should not know the difference on Monday morning and transactions should flow normally;[2]

---

[2] See also Financial Stability Board, "Guidance on identification of critical functions and critical shared services," Bank for International Settlements,

Proactive supervision: if regulatory authorities reacted before the situation became acute, they get extra points;

Speed of intervention: a shorter time span from recognition of the problem to intervention is positive;

Liquidity: did the central bank alleviate the inevitable liquidity crunch? How? When?

Guarantee for deposits: in an acute crisis, stemming a bank run with a guarantee is vital to prevent a bank run;

Guarantee for other liabilities: depending on the type of funding of the banking system, guaranteeing also other liabilities (as in Ireland and Germany) may be necessary but perhaps for a fee (as in the US Temporary Liquidity Guarantee Program run by the FDIC or in the Swedish guarantee program);[3]

Was the guarantee for new debt only or total outstanding? The first gives extra points;

Viability: was a study and decision undertaken as to whether the bank was long-term viable or not or did the authorities just follow "the art of stumbling through?"

Long-run viability: was the end result a viable bank? Did it improve the viability and stability of the financial system?

Systemic crisis: was the crisis seen as involving only one or several banks or seen as systemic? When?

Ring-fencing and insuring of "toxic assets" for a fee: were toxic assets separated and insured, as in Citibank and Bank of America?

Toxic assets: did the authorities force or encourage the setting up of a "bad bank," internal or external?

Cooperation: did the domestic authorities (FSA/OCC/OTS, Treasury, Central Bank, Deposit Insurance Agency) work well together? If so, they receive extra points;

International cooperation: did host and home countries' regulators cooperate efficiently? If so, they receive extra points;

If taxpayers' money was involved, did they get their money back? How? Outright nationalization, majority ownership, injection of

"Guidance papers on recovery and resolution planning," 16 July 2013, www.financialstabilityboard.org/press/pr_130716.pdf

[3] www.swedbank.com/idc/groups/public/@i/@sbg/@gs/@treasury/documents/article/cid_609402.pdf

common stock rather than preferred shares, warrants, all these give extra points;

Downsizing: Did the authorities put pressure on the saved bank to downsize, i.e. sell non-core assets, sell branches, sell foreign subsidiaries, cut down on staff?

Stigmatization: did the authorities attempt to treat all banks equally in order to avoid stigmatizing the truly needy?

Legal assessment: were leading figures of management brought to justice in events where clearly laws had been broken (insider trading, fraud, cover-up, breach of trust, false accounting, false testimony, perjury, etc.)?

Industry involvement: were other, healthier banks involved in saving the failing ones, through fees for deposit insurance, stabilization funds or other arrangements, e.g. part-owning the "bad bank" as in Ireland and Spain or through a loss-sharing arrangement between banks as in Denmark?

Factors leading to bad grades (with some examples)

Failure to guarantee continuity of service (Lehman Brothers)

Failure to downsize a bank under resolution (RBS, Landesbanken, Bank of America)

Failure to set up a bad bank, preferably external (RBS and Lloyds)

Failure to establish whether the bank is viable (IKB, Commerzbank, Landesbanken)

Failure to sell off non-core healthy assets (RBS, IKB, Dexia)

Slow resolution/sale/wind-down (RBS, Hypo Real Estate)

Infighting and/or lack of coordination between domestic regulators (Northern Rock, Washington Mutual, Bank of America)

Infighting and/or lack of coordination between international regulators (Dexia, Fortis, Icelandic banks, Lehman Brothers)

Overly hasty sale of non-core assets causing unnecessary losses (IndyMac)

Imposing unnecessary losses of depositors[4] (Cyprus banks, IndyMac)

---

[4] This comment would apply to domestic deposits only since the legal background as concerns foreign-held deposits is not clear, as indicated by the verdict of the EFTA Court of Justice in the dispute between Iceland on the one hand and Britain and the Netherlands on the other. Nor does the US deposit insurance system cover foreign depositors.

Imposing unnecessary losses on unsecured senior bondholders (Amagerbanken, IndyMac, Washington Mutual)

Failure to try delinquent management in courts of law (RBS, IKB, Landesbanken, Dexia, Bear Stearns, Lehman Brothers, Washington Mutual, Wachovia, Citibank, Bank of America).

We will remember these traits in commenting in the next chapter on the Dodd–Frank Act and on the changes in regulation and supervision in the European Union in the chapter after that.

A question for the reader to bear in mind: how come the TARP/CPP program in the United States was a success in the sense that taxpayers got their money back with a decent return, whereas in most European bail-outs, taxpayers have yet to see their money returned? For the European countries all together, some 700 billion dollars had by 2013 been returned from support actions worth 1,500 billion (see Table 1).

PART VI

Political and regulatory responses to the crisis: to bail out or to bail in, that's the question

17 | *Future bail-outs in the United States under Dodd–Frank and OLA*

Dodd–Frank Wall Street Reform and Consumer Protection Act of 2010: what it doesn't do

Many believe, as I do, that the Dodd–Frank Act in its present form will neither prevent a future financial crisis nor alleviate its resolution in comparison with experiences from the recent crisis. Rather it risks making it worse. A number of comments supporting this view will be stated below.

One could also note that at 848 pages, it easily surpasses the 32 pages of the Federal Reserve Act of 1913 and the 37 pages of the Glass–Steagall Act of 1933, the earlier major pieces of banking legislation. However, the Financial Institutions Reform, Recovery, and Enforcement Act (FIRREA) of 1989 ran to 371 pages, showing the rising trend. Increasing complexity is the rule of the day. However, there are also rising demands from central bankers for less complexity.[1]

And this is only the primary legislation which must then be translated into actual rules. At latest count, only just over one half of the 398 pieces of detailed rules that must be adopted by the Federal Reserve, the SEC, the CFTC, the FDIC and the other regulators had been finalized by mid 2014, four years after President Obama's signing of the Act.[2] The final product will run to tens of thousand pages of rules by which the financial industry must abide.[3] It has been estimated

---

[1] See the speech by the Bank of England's then director of financial stability, today chief economist, Andy Haldane, on "Turning the red tape tide," 10 April 2013, www.bankofengland.co.uk/publications/Documents/speeches/2013/speech646.pdf

[2] http://blogs.wsj.com/cfo/2014/04/08/nearly-half-of-dodd-frank-rules-still-unwritten/; http://online.wsj.com/articles/peter-wallison-four-years-of-dodd-frank-damage-1405893333

[3] www.davispolk.com/Dodd-Frank-Rulemaking-Progress-Report/

that 2,600 new supervisors are needed.[4] The largest US banks have hired 10,000 new compliance officers since the Dodd–Frank Act was adopted. The House of Representatives Financial Services Committee has estimated that the Dodd–Frank regime would impose at least 27 billion dollars in new assessments annually on financial firms and require more than 2.2 million annual labor hours to comply with just the first 10 percent of rules issued.[5] As a percentage of revenue, small banks will bear costs under the new regulation that far exceed those borne by the megabanks.[6,7]

Dodd–Frank has indeed created a monster whose appetite is yet to be determined. Box 1 presents some highly relevant criticisms of the Dodd–Frank legislation, coming from lawyers as well as economists (all *italics* in the quotes are mine to stress the main points).

These are harsh words but they are unfortunately true. While creating an enormously complex financial architecture and requiring millions of additional person-years for supervisors as well as for the supervised, creating vast additional costs to the banking industry and society,[8] the Dodd–Frank Act does little to attack and remedy the underlying causes of the recent financial crisis, such as:

(a) *The ability by a borrower to purchase a house in which he/she has no intention of ever living.* It has been calculated that 28 percent of all residential house purchases in 2005 and 22 percent in 2006 were undertaken on pure speculation by persons who never intended to live there or even use it as a secondary home.[9]

(b) *The possibility of borrowing the entire purchase price of the house* or sometimes even more. We have encountered in the case studies a number of instances where the borrower could pay interest-only on a loan or even add the interest charge to the capital owed (option

---

[4] http://financialservices.house.gov/dodd-frank/

[5] Ibid.

[6] http://mercatus.org/publication/how-are-small-banks-faring-under-dodd-frank

[7] www.stlouisfed.org/banking/community-banking-conference/PDF/Marsh_Norman_Reforming_Regulation.pdf

[8] While required by law to estimate benefits and costs of proposed legislation, the GAO could not even begin to put numbers on the various positive and negative effects. See General Accountability Office (GAO), "Financial crisis losses and potential impacts of the Dodd–Frank Act," 16 January 2013.

[9] Alan Greenspan, *The Age of Turbulence: Adventures in a New World* (New York: Penguin, 2007, 2008), p. 231.

Box 1   Criticisms of Dodd–Frank legislation

The heated debate in Congress over the proper response [to the financial crisis] continued until July 2010, culminating in the The Dodd–Frank Wall Street Reform and Consumer Protection Act (Pub. L. 111–203). This massive statute runs for 848 pages, contains 16 titles, requires 386 more agency rulemakings, and mandates 67 studies. *Most of it was a collection of assorted changes to the financial system that various groups had been advocating for some time, unrelated to the causes of the panic.*

(Kenneth E. Scott, Professor of Law and Economics Emeritus, Stanford Law School)[10]

I will argue that the effort crafted by Congress to correct the problems of TBTF [too big to fail] – known as the 2010 Dodd–Frank Wall Street Reform and Consumer Protection Act (Dodd–Frank) – *is, despite its best intentions, ineffective, burdensome, imposes a prohibitive cost on the non-TBTF banking institutions and needs to be amended. It is an example of the triumph of hope over experience.*

(Richard W. Fisher, president, Federal Reserve Bank of Dallas)[11]

This has been the story since 2008. True, laws have been changed and regulations have been tightened to curb the most egregious dice games. Capital requirements have been raised a tad, lowering slightly the insurance risk to governments and reducing by the same small amount the implicit taxpayer subsidies that pay for the bankers' bonuses. The

---

[10] Kenneth E. Scott, "A guide to the resolution of failed financial institutions," in Kenneth E. Scott and John B. Taylor, eds., *Bankruptcy not Bailout: A Special Chapter 14* (Stanford, CA: Hoover Institution Press, 2012), pp. 3–4.

[11] Richard W. Fisher, "Correcting 'Dodd–Frank' to actually end 'too big to fail,'" statement before the Committee on Financial Services, US House of Representatives, hearing on examining how the Dodd–Frank Act could result in more taxpayer-funded bailouts, 26 June 2013, http://financialservices.house.gov/uploadedfiles/hhrg-113-ba00-wstate-rfisher-20130626.pdf

Dodd–Frank legislation has increased compliance burdens on Wall Street.

Welcome as they are, these represent changes at the margin. The basic structure of the system – with its perverse incentives, too-big-to-fail institutions and too-powerful-to-jail executives – remains untouched. The universal banks, combining straightforward commercial banking with high-risk trading, live on. The result is that the organising purpose of banking – to provide essential lubrication for the real economy – remains entangled with dangerous and socially useless speculation.

Taxpayers are still providing big subsidies in the form of guarantees that, perversely, encourage banks to take more risks. In the absence of real competition, a self-sustaining oligopoly of senior bankers continues to set its own rewards. Banks complain about the fatter rule books, but what we have seen is a series of "tweaks" rather than the radical shake-up needed to make the system safe. What Paul Volcker, the former US Federal Reserve chairman, has called the "unfinished business" of reform remains just that.

(Philip Stevens, Financial Times*)*[12]

It seems that overregulation has been chosen as the right response to the recent financial crisis and the Wall Street Reform and Consumer protection Act (Dodd–Frank Act) is its archetype. With its 848 pages, only corporate lawyers may not complain about its prolixity and complexity, but there are many reasons for criticism in choosing the path of complex and abundant regulation.

Overregulation has significant costs not only to the private business regulated, which will have to devote more time and money to compliance, but also to the regulators and supervisors themselves, at least for two reasons.

First, it has to be taken into account that more regulation eventually leads to an additional burden for the supervisors. For every rule created, one more duty of supervision will be

---

[12] Philip Stevens, "Nothing can dent the divine rights of bankers," *Financial Times*, 17 January 2014.

added and one more potential violation appears. The second reason for being critical towards overregulation has to do with the aftermath of oversight. It has been overlooked that the job of supervisors does not end with the confirmation of compliance with the rules or the identification of violations. What will be the consequences if a financial institution fails to observe the regulation?

On the one hand, creating new rules without setting any negative consequence if they are not observed is the same as declaring their ineffectiveness from the beginning. Rules that demand a positive or negative behavior must be followed by a sanction, or they tend to be discredited. It is not possible to count on the good will of the financial institutions on that matter. On the other hand, administrative sanction seems to be the natural consequence to the violation of financial regulation, since criminalization should only be used to preserve the most important values for society and to prevent and punish the most serious violations.

(Marcelo Madureira Prates, attorney,
Banco Central do Brasil)[13]

The Dodd–Frank Wall Street Reform and Consumer Protection Act, which was heralded as a landmark in establishing financial industry responsibility and consumer protection, is in fact a disaster in the making for the people of this country and the banks that serve them. Every American is now paying more for banking services and getting fewer of them. Millions of people are at risk of losing their bank accounts or credit cards altogether. In spite of record low mortgage rates, home loans are more difficult, and for some impossible, to procure. Small businesses are facing a devastating financial climate, with high interest and financing costs – assuming they can even get loans in the first place.

On a broader scale, the United States financial system itself has been harmed by antibank activity. While Congress fiddles with ideas to appease an angry populace, it risks the position

---

[13] Marcelo M. Prates, "Why prudential regulation will fail to prevent financial crises: a legal approach," Central Bank of Brazil Working Paper no. 335, 1 November 2013.

of the United States in the global economy ... The United States has been the strongest nation in the world for a century. In part, it is because our nation's financial system is the best in the world. It is also due to the fact that the global financial system is based in the United States.

(Richard X Bove, bank analyst at Rochdale Securities)[14]

From the standpoint of providing a sound and robust regulatory structure, the [Dodd–Frank] Act falls flat on at least four important counts:

The Act does not deal with the mispricing of pervasive government guarantees throughout the financial sector. This will allow many financial firms to finance their activities at below-market rates and take on excessive risk.

Systemically important firms will be made to bear their own losses but not the costs they impose on others in the system. *To this extent, the Act falters in addressing directly the primary source of market failure in the financial sector, which is systemic risk.*

In several parts, the Act regulates a financial firm by its form (bank) rather than function (banking). This feature will prevent the Act from dealing well with the new organizational forms likely to emerge in the financial sector – to meet the changing needs of global financial markets, as well as to respond to the Act's provisions.

The Act makes important omissions in reforming and regulating parts of the shadow banking system that are systemically important. It also fails to recognize that there are systemically important markets – collections of individual contracts and institutions – that also need orderly resolution when they experience freezes.

(Viral V. Acharya is Professor of Finance
at the Stern School, New York University)[15]

---

[14] Richard X. Bove, *Guardians of Prosperity: Why America Needs Big Banks* (New York: Penguin, 2013), pp. 5–6.
[15] Viral V. Acharya *et al.*, "A bird's eye view: the Dodd–Frank Wall Street Reform and Consumer Protection Act," in Viral V. Acharya *et al.*, eds., *Regulating Wall Street: The Dodd–Frank Act and the New Architecture of Global Finance* (Hoboken, NJ: John Wiley, 2011), p. 8.

Today, the effect of Title I and Title II of Dodd–Frank is to re-create a class of special public companies that, because of their ties to the government, receive the benefit of a GSE-like "implied government guarantee". For background, for the better part of the first decade of this millennium, market participants were increasingly convinced the GSEs (Fannie and Freddie) could become unstable. Nevertheless domestic and foreign bondholders and foreign central banks viewed the companies as low credit risks. It was assumed that if they got into trouble they would be bailed out with taxpayer dollars and without significant losses being forced upon bondholders.

As a result, the GSEs had a significantly lower cost of capital than their non-"special" and fully private competitors. They also benefit from a government-imposed monopoly on the best credits in the mortgage sector, leaving the subprime world to private lenders. No matter how frequently the Treasury, the Fed, the White House or Congress said that the government did not stand behind the obligations of the GSEs, the markets did not accept that view. When push came to shove in September 2008, the GSEs were taken over by the government, placing taxpayers on the hook for any potential GSE losses. GSE creditors walked away from the accident and even equity holders, who had always been paid to take the first loss, were not wiped out.

So, are we expected to believe that today's TBTF institutions are not provided a lower cost of capital, by the markets and rating agencies, based on the understanding that the government will always stand ready to fund their losses? Moreover, from where in history can we draw comfort that when a macro crisis hits, regulators and policymakers will assess to other TBTF institutions the realized losses rather than arguing that that might lead to a contagion risk?

(Joshua Rosner, managing director,
Graham Fisher & Co.)[16]

---

[16] Statement of Joshua Rosner, managing director, Graham Fisher & Co., before the House Committee on Financial Services, Subcommittee on Oversight and Investigations, "Who is too big to fail: does Title II of the Dodd–Frank Act enshrine taxpayer funded bailouts?" 14 May 2013, also at www.scribd.com/doc/141572927/Rosner-Testimony-on-Title-II-05-14-2013

Critically, Dodd–Frank fails to reconfigure in any significant way the fragmented US regulatory structure. Rather than consolidating existing agencies into one or two regulators, each able to act quickly and efficiently, we now require regulators with a history of disagreement and difficulty in operating together to sit collegially around the Council's table and make key decisions by a vote of a majority or two-thirds of its members, depending on the issue. A single federal regulator may not be the answer, but the number of federal regulators we now have is surely not the right result either. The notion of one bank regulator, one markets regulator and one consumer regulator for all products remains, unfortunately, wishful thinking in the US.

But, more importantly, Dodd–Frank does not address adequately the issue of moral hazard. Despite the many provisions to monitor and reduce systemic risk, it remains unlikely that the Government will allow an institution that is the size of one of the US's five largest financial institutions to fail, especially in the absence of effective coordinated and consistent resolution mechanisms in key markets. The market will likely make that judgment as well, and those firms will continue to have financing advantages that only increase the likelihood of their failure.

There is also a serious question about whether Dodd–Frank will undermine the competitive position of major US financial institutions. Certain of its provisions, clearly, will not be followed in other key jurisdictions such as the EU – for example, the Volcker Rule. The universal bank model is now accepted globally as the way to do business, and the Volcker Rule is not consistent with that model and is not likely to be replicated elsewhere. Furthermore, the size limitation imposed with respect to growth by acquisition could disadvantage US institutions if the industry consolidates globally.

Regulatory arbitrage remains a real issue as nations enact their financial reforms. Funding resolution and bailout expenditures have been a point of international divergence. As noted earlier, the OLA [Orderly Liquidation Authority, see below] is not pre-funded, given the desire to avoid the appearance of a bailout. Further, Dodd–Frank restricts regulators' other tools for financial assistance, such as government guarantees. Meanwhile, the IMF and European governments seem to be moving in the direction of imposing bank taxes to create resolution funds. Thus, the US may face a challenge in coordinating to resolve failing, international institutions if its only choice is liquidation, but other countries have a fund available to provide financial assistance to stave off insolvency.

(Edward F. Greene, a partner at Cleary Gottlieb,
formerly the General Counsel of the Securities
and Exchange Commission)[17]

The Dodd–Frank Act compounds the problem [of TBTF banks] by declaring that every banking organization larger than $50 billion is "systemically important." This is pure fiction, but it signals that these banks – simply because of their size – are more likely than others to be rescued if they are in danger of failing. The same will apply to nonbanks like insurance companies [AIG, Prudential], finance companies [GE Capital], hedge funds, and money-market funds if they are designated as "systemically important financial institutions" by the Financial Stability Oversight Council [as the three mentioned companies have been].

We've seen this movie before, where private companies use public backing to reduce their borrowing costs. It was called "Fannie Mae and Freddie Mac Take the Taxpayers for a Ride." Then, as now, the subsidy was real and measurable. Lowering their costs of funding and allowing creditors to infer government support made Fannie and Freddie immune to competition and prone to take extraordinary risks.

Today's systemically important firms reap the same financial benefit of the government's implicit backing. That benefit is not just some vague, "I'll-be-here-for-you-tomorrow" feel-good thing. No, it's a hard-edged financial leg-up that separates winners from losers, acquirers from acquirees, and in the end will determine whether our financial system consists of many large and small firms or only a few behemoths.

Increasingly, policymakers are paying attention to the benefit systemically important banks enjoy and are calling it for what it is – a taxpayer subsidy. To name a few, Federal Reserve

---

[17] Edward F. Greene, "Dodd–Frank and the future of financial regulation," *Harvard Business Law Review* 79 (2011), also at http://hblr. org/?p=1728

Bank of Dallas President Richard Fisher and FDIC director and former Federal Reserve Bank of Kansas City President Thomas Hoenig. Even Fed Chairman Bernanke now uses the "S" word. This, from Bernanke at a recent press conference: "In other words, a bank which is thought to be too big to fail gets an artificial subsidy in the interest rate that it can borrow at ..."[18] ...

These regulators are talking about banks, but the same benefits will accrue to nonbanks that the FSOC [Financial Stability Oversight Council] singles out as systemically important. These subsidies are slow-motion bailouts in the present tense.

Regulators, following the dictates of Dodd–Frank, are painted into a corner. Either they go light on the systemically important firms and allow them, by virtue of their size and the taxpayer subsidy, to wipe out all competition; or they bring the regulatory hammer down on them, crippling a large part of the financial system and dashing the hopes for economic recovery.

A way out of this corner is to shift the focus away from past and future bailouts and onto the continuing bailouts. It is the ongoing bailout – the taxpayers' subsidies of the TBTFs – that is preventing market discipline from playing its customary role of determining winners and losers. *The government should not signal to the market that* any *firm – bank or nonbank – is too-big-to-fail. Instead of enshrining our TBTF firms, we should be seeking ways to reduce or eliminate their federal subsidies.*

One way of accomplishing this is to require the TBTFs to identify the portion of their earnings that is attributable to their subsidy. Another approach would be the use of a "bail-in" mechanism forcing creditors to absorb the losses of a failure thus reducing or eliminating the TBTFs' funding advantage.

Prior to the financial crisis, the policy option of the government intervening to save a systemically important firm was called "constructive ambiguity." It provided creditors with just enough uncertainty to keep the biggest banks from being subsidized. But

---

[18] For a list of people – bankers, lawyers, regulators, academics, journalists – who have spoken out on TBTF, see www.toobighasfailed.org/too-big-to-fail/

the financial crisis and the Dodd–Frank response have turned
government intervention into a perceived entitlement. Hyper-
regulation and living wills do not change that perception.

(Peter Wallison and Cornelius K. Hurley,
Senior Fellows at American Enterprise Institute and
Professor of Law at Boston University School of Law,
respectively)[19]

Sir, You have correctly pointed out that fines are not the
answer to supersized banks. Too-big-to-fail banks benefit from
the lethal combination of a public subsidy, inert shareholders
and criminal prosecutors cowed by the prospect of bringing
any of the financial behemoths before the bar of justice.

We cannot give our prosecutors the spine they lack. We can,
however, begin to measure with some certainty the financial
subsidy taxpayers are bestowing on these elite institutions.
Andrew Haldane at the Bank of England has made significant
contributions here. In the US, if the General Accountability
Office does its job properly, it will soon produce a study quantifying the enormity of the subsidy.

Placing that number before a disgusted public and its elected
representatives may well be a step toward finally achieving a
"more muscular intervention" as you have called for. Clearly,
the speeding tickets are not having any effect.

(Cornelius K. Hurley, director, Boston University
Center for Finance, Law and Policy)[20]

In an on-camera interview, which aired recently, Breuer [Assistant
Attorney General Lanny Breuer, the head of the criminal division
at the Justice Department and the man responsible for determining whether anyone should be prosecuted for the financial
crisis of 2008] stated plainly that *some financial institutions*
are too large and too complex to be held accountable before
the law. Bipartisan pressure is now being applied on the Justice
Department to reveal exactly how this determination was made.

[19] "Too big to fail has become a permanent bailout program," *Forbes*,
14 August 2012.
[20] Cornelius K. Hurley, "Why are banks being let off the hook?" *Financial*
Times, 17 January 2014.

Breuer made the comments for a documentary aired by the PBS program "Frontline." The investigative report, titled "The Untouchables,"asked why no senior Wall Street executive has been prosecuted for apparently well-documented illegal acts, such as authorizing document forging, misleading investors and obstructing justice. Breuer was shockingly candid.

"Well, I think I am pursuing justice," he said. "And I think the entire responsibility of the department is to pursue justice. But in any given case, I think I and prosecutors around the country, being responsible, should speak to regulators, should speak to experts, because if I bring a case against Institution A, and as a result of bringing that case, there's some huge economic effect – if it creates a ripple effect so that suddenly, counterparties and other financial institutions or other companies that had nothing to do with this are affected badly – it's a factor we need to know and understand.

> *(Simon Johnson, professor at MIT and*
> *former chief economist at IMF)*[21]

The major flaw of the federal banking regulatory system is that it treats a community bank with $165 million in assets (the mediansized American bank) as the same essential creature as JPMorgan Chase or Bank of America. A bank with $165 million in assets and a bank with $2 trillion in assets may both take deposits and make loans, but the similarities end there. Since the 1999 Gramm–Leach–Bliley Act, which reduced barriers between depository banks and investment banks, the gap between community banks and large, complex financial institutions has grown and the focus of federal regulatory activity has been on large institutions. It is simply not a principled policy choice to regulate them both under the current "one size fits all" approach. As discussed in Part II(A), it is an accident of history that we do so. *Dodd–Frank continues the historical trend of regulating small, traditional banks and large, complex financial institutions under the same rubric and will have an impact on shaping the market in ways that are*

---

[21] Simon Johnson, "And who decided US megabanks are too big to jail?" *Bloomberg*, 4 February 2013.

> counterproductive to the goals of Dodd-Frank and which are
> against our common interests.
>
> *(Tanya Marsh, associate professor of law,*
> *Wake Forest University School of Law,*
> *Winston-Salem, NC; Joseph Norman,*
> *attorney at K&L Gates LLP, Charlotte, NC)*[22]

ARM loans). Two-thirds of the subprime loans originated by Countrywide in 2006 had loan-to-value ratios of 100 percent or above. Golden West, later bought by Wachovia, had its own option ARM, sold under the illuminating name of "Pick-a-Pay." In July 2009, Freddie Mac and Fannie Mae received permission to refinance residential mortgages up to a limit of 125 percent loan-to-value (LTV), this in an effort to stem the rising wave of foreclosures (now lowered to 95 percent). Most banks would, after the crisis, demand at least 5 percent downpayment but there is (in contrast to most European countries) no law that requires it.[23,24]

(c) The legal right to walk away from a house with negative equity (LTV>100 percent) with no further legal claims from the bank (*non-recourse loan*).

---

[22] Tanya D. Marsh and Joseph W. Norman, "Reforming the regulation of community banks after Dodd–Frank," Federal Reserve Bank of St. Louis symposium, www.stlouisfed.org/banking/community-banking-conference/PDF/Marsh_Norman_Reforming_Regulation.pdf, p. 7.

[23] For a summary of LTV maxima rules worldwide, see IMF, *Global Financial Stability Report*, no. 1, April 2011, table 3.1, https://www.imf.org/external/pubs/ft/gfsr/2011/01/pdf/chap3.pdf. The FDIC has, however, in its role as supervisor set a limit for LTV of 85 percent. See http://www.fdic.gov/regulations/laws/rules/2000-8700.html

[24] The Consumer Financial Protection Bureau, acting under Title XIV of the Dodd–Frank Act, has instituted some restrictions in response to the factors which led to the financial crisis, such as required borrower information (doing away with Alt-A loans), restrictions on negative amortizations, maximum recommended payment-to-income ratio (43 percent), the requirement for the lender to calculate monthly cost on highest interest rate not teaser rates, a ban on payments by banks to mortgage brokers, etc. See http://files.consumerfinance.gov/f/201401_cfpb_mortgages_consumer-summary-new-mortgage.pdf

(d) The ability to arrange a loan *through a mortgage broker* with no physical contact between ultimate lender and borrower.

(e) The ability by investment banks operating under Basel II and III rules to measure the risks in their portfolios by means of *internal models,* understood only by themselves (Advanced IRB). A study by BIS of 15 internationally active megabanks found that the average risk weighting of their *trading assets* varied from 10 percent to nearly 80 percent with most banks between 15 and 45 percent. Even with a hypothetical model portfolio, applied identically to all the banks, and where therefore supervisory differences and banks' trading activity was held constant, the value at risk (VaR) of a well-diversified portfolio varied between 75 and 175 percent or by a factor of more than 2, with corresponding effects on capital requirements. Portfolios for individual market risks (equity, interest rate, exchange rate, credit spreads) showed far larger variations between banks.[25]

Similar differences were found when a sample of 32 major international banks was asked to model the *risk in their banking book* (corporate, banking and sovereign credit risk exposures). The difference between the extremes was up to some +/-2 percentage points in capital ratio around an assumed average of 10 percent, i.e. from 7.8 to 11.8 percent. Applied to the entire banking book, these differences would translate into a range from 5.9 to 15.7 percent ratio of capital to risk-weighted assets.[26]

This ability of banks to "game" the capital requirements continues under Basel III, in the United States applied now also to commercial banks and thrifts.[27,28,29,30]

---

[25] Bank for International Settlements, "Regulatory consistency assessment programme (RCAP) – analysis of risk-weighted assets for market risk," January 2013.

[26] Bank for International Settlements, "Regulatory consistency assessment programme (RCAP) – analysis of risk-weighted assets for credit risk in the banking book," July 2013.

[27] See, however, below for mitigating circumstances, especially the Collins amendment to Dodd–Frank.

[28] Clifford Rossi, "Banks model risk worse than ever, thanks to Basel III," *American Banker*, 11 July 2013, www.americanbanker.com/bankthink/model-risk-worse-than-ever-thanks-to-basel-iii-1060517-1.html

[29] Darryl G. Getter, "US implementation of the Basel capital regulatory framework," Congressional Research Service, November 2012.

[30] See also Johan Lybeck, "Forget Basel III and head straight for Basel IV," *Financial Times*, 2 February 2012.

(f) The absence of sufficient retained "skin in the game" when a bank repackages a mortgage into a mortgage-backed security (MBS) or a collateralized debt obligation (CDO). Under Dodd–Frank, this participation is set at a low 5 percent.[31]

(g) The continued ability by investment banks to create *innovative (toxic) derivative products* (such as "CDO-cube" or synthetic CDSs) that defy analysis by rating agencies as well as by investors, with no required approval by the Securities and Exchange Commission or the new Consumer Financial Protection Bureau within the Federal Reserve as long as the products are sold only to professional investors.[32]

(h) The *lack of consistency between risk weights and true risk* in capital requirements. Sovereign debt is still regarded as risk-free under Basel III and in the corresponding CRD IV package in the EU and carries a zero risk weight in the calculation of risk-weighted assets, in turn leading to an overinvestment in true risk/reward terms in these instruments.[33]

(i) The continued ability of unsupervised or less supervised *"shadow-banking"* actors such as hedge funds, private equity funds, structured investment vehicles (SIVs), money market funds, broker-dealers, exchange-traded funds (ETF), finance companies or even non-financial companies to mimic banking activities.[34] While the Financial Stability Board (FSB) estimates the size of

---

[31] Dodd–Frank, note 5, § 941, Section 15G(c) (1) (B) (i). See also www.global-businesslawreview.org/wp-content/uploads/2012/04/2gThompson.pdf

[32] This stands in sharp contrast to e. g. the Netherlands where under new legislation the Financial Supervisory Authority (AFM) must check whether new investment products serve a purpose, whether they are cost-efficient and whether they are intelligibly described to the average investor. Similarly, the French securities-market supervisor, the AMF, has forbidden the marketing of "complex" financial products to investors. See Niamh Moloney, "The legacy effects of the financial crisis on regulatory design in the EU," ch. 2 in Eilís Ferran *et al.*, *The Regulatory Aftermath of the Global Financial Crisis* (Cambridge University Press, 2012), pp. 188, 190.

[33] See e.g. Daniel Gros, "Banking union with a sovereign virus: the self-serving regulatory treatment of sovereign debt in the euro area," *CEPS Policy Brief* no. 289, 27 March 2013.

[34] See e.g. Ben Bernanke, "Some reflections on the crisis and the policy response" (speech, 13 April 2012 at the Russell Sage Foundation and the Century Foundation Conference on "Rethinking Finance"), reprinted in Alan S. Blinder, Andrew Lo and Robert Solow, eds. *Rethinking the Financial Crisis* (New York: Russell Sage Foundation, 2013), pp. 3–13.

shadow-banking at 60–70 trillion dollars, other estimates go as high as over 100 trillion dollars, almost equal to the total assets of the world's 1,000 largest banks in 2012 (*The Banker*, July 2013).

(j) The continued *quantity-related remuneration/bonus structures.* While companies receiving TARP money were subject to pay limits on salaries and bonuses and while Dodd–Frank (§951) mandates shareholders' "say on pay," these restrictions apply solely to the highest echelon of executives. While these rewards were and are exorbitantly high, they did not cause the financial crisis. Instead, it was the remuneration of lower echelons, which rewarded quantity over quality, that was one of the main reasons behind the crisis and where little has changed.[35]

(k) Dodd–Frank's almost purely *domestic* character. In particular, Dodd–Frank leaves out regulation of cross-border derivative trades. It does not enhance the cooperation between regulatory authorities, the lack of which permitted AIG Financial Products to roam freely, nor does it help the messy resolution of failed companies such as Lehman Brothers.[36] Large foreign-owned banks with assets above 50 billion dollars must in the future conduct their US banking operations under an intermediate US-licensed bank holding company, supervised by the Federal Reserve and subject to the same increased demands concerning capital, liquidity, stress tests, enhanced supervision and "living wills" placed on the major US banks. This insulates the United States and may make foreign banks less willing to enter into the US banking market.

(l) Nor does Dodd–Frank do much for the *proliferation of regulatory authorities and their lack of coordination.* Certainly, the Office of Thrift Supervision (OTS) has been abolished and a coordinating Financial Stability Oversight Council created, but will it be

---

[35] The over 100 billion dollars paid so far by banks in litigation over substandard mortgages might hopefully have brought a change in culture that the law has not been able to do.

[36] The United States has, however, entered into bilateral agreements with the UK and Canada concerning resolution of cross-border financial companies. See Bank of England, "Resolving globally active, systemically important financial institutions," a joint paper with the Federal Deposit Insurance Corporation, 12 December 2012. This agreement appears a bit one-sided, however, in view of the US decision to require that major foreign banks operate in the United States as separately capitalized intermediate holding companies.

enough when the same incentives for turf fighting between the regulatory authorities still operate?

(m) *Regulatory capture.* The Dodd–Frank Act does nothing to prevent the continued symbiotic existence between supervisors and supervised, characterized by the "revolving-door," whereby high-level executives move back and forth between the private and public sectors.[37]

(n) Through the *Volcker rule*, Dodd–Frank eliminates (or at least tries to) banks' proprietary trading and limits severely their ability to own or fund hedge and private equity funds. Yet neither of these phenomena was at the root of the financial crisis and their restriction may lead to the proscribed activities going into the less-supervised shadow-banking sector or abroad.

(o) Nor has Dodd–Frank in any way attacked the *too-big-to-fail problem.* Rather, as pointed out above, by explicitly naming a number of TBTF institutions that will merit special treatment, it has ennobled them to a state where there is no longer any doubt that they will be saved.[38] More on this in the following.

(p) Finally, Dodd–Frank may have decreed that management causing "their" bank to fail should be removed but it does nothing to aid the deplorable lack of interest in *bringing potential wrongdoers to justice.*

To summarize the results of the micro studies in Parts II–IV, banks failed in the recent crisis because they were badly managed and badly

---

[37] Some examples: Robert Rubin went straight from being co-chairman of Goldman Sachs to Treasury secretary and then back to chairman and director at Citigroup. Hank Paulson was CEO and chairman at Goldman Sachs before becoming Treasury secretary. Paulson's successor, Tim Geithner, became president of private equity firm WarburgPincus after his term ended. To this could be added that the boards of directors of the 12 regional Federal Reserve Banks contain a number of senior bankers. The CEO of Lehman Brothers, Dick Fuld, is one example, Jamie Dimon of JPMorgan Chase another. Steve Friedman was simultaneously chairman of the board of the Federal Reserve Bank of New York and a member of the board of Goldman Sachs when the latter applied to the former to change status to bank holding company. See also Kuttner, *A Presidency in Peril*, pp. 137 ff.

[38] In a recent study, the IMF finds that the implicit subsidy of TBTF banks has probably not fallen after the introduction of Dodd–Frank, indeed depending on the approach used, it may even have risen. In the worst case, it amounted to an annual 580 billion dollars, of which 310 billion in the euro area, 110 billion each in the UK and Japan and 50 billion in the US. See ch. 3, "How big is the implicit subsidy for banks considered too important to fail?" in International Monetary Fund, *Global Financial Stability Report*, April 2014, www.imf.org/external/pubs/ft/gfsr/2014/01/pdf/text.pdf

supervised. Megabanks such as Royal Bank of Scotland, Washington Mutual and Citigroup failed (or were on the verge of doing so); so did hundreds of small banks. Specialized banks such as Northern Rock, Hypo Real Estate, Dexia or Countrywide failed or had to be rescued, as did universal banks such as Fortis, UBS or Commerzbank. Privately owned banks as well as public and publicly sponsored banks, such as the German Landesbanken or Fannie Mae and Freddie Mac, failed.

While "Wall Street" banks (investment banks) certainly aggravated the crisis as well as spreading it worldwide through their creation of innovative securities and derivatives, they did not originate "the panic of 2008," "Main Street" banks did.

This is what any proposed legislation should take (or should have taken) as its starting point.

The FDIC and prompt corrective action (PCA)

Before looking at what Dodd–Frank has improved (or at least changed) as concerns the resolution of failed/failing financial institutions, it is necessary to see how and in what manner the FDIC in its role as resolution manager performed under previous legislation.

As we have seen above in the micro studies, after a financial institution is seized by its primary regulator (the FDIC, the OCC, the OTS, the Federal Reserve or state regulators), it may be placed in receivership or conservatorship with the FDIC. According to section 11(c) of the Federal Deposit Insurance Act, the FDIC acts as a receiver in order to liquidate and wind up the affairs of the failed financial institution. The FDIC is required to do this in a manner that creates the least cost to the Deposit Insurance Fund (DIF). While Washington Mutual Bank was sold to JPMorgan Chase, unwanted assets and liabilities were put into receivership under the FDIC for the time being before being disposed of. The holding company, Washington Mutual Inc., filed for bankruptcy under chapter 11 of the bankruptcy code.

If, on the other hand, the purpose is to preserve the institution as a going concern, the FDIC will act as conservator. In the case of IndyMac where no buyer for the bank could be found, a bridge bank was set up, IndyMac Federal Bank FSB, under the conservatorship of the FDIC and later sold. IndyMac Bank with residual unwanted assets and liabilities was placed in receivership under the FDIC and wound down, too quickly as we have seen, imposing losses even on uninsured depositors.

The fact that conservatorship remains the exception is seen by the fact that at the end of 2008, there was only one bank in conservatorship while there were 41 banks in receivership from failures occurring in 2007 and 2008. At the end of 2009, the number of receiverships had risen to 179 and to 344 at the end of 2010 while there were no banks left in conservatorship.[39,40]

Under its legislation, the FDIC has a statutory mandate to perform a least-cost solution, i.e. it may not take actions that would yield higher losses to the deposit insurance fund by protecting depositors above the insured amounts or by protecting unsecured creditors more than depositors. Such a calculation of the optimal solution takes into account a number of factors such as:

- The difference between the book value of assets and liabilities;
- Estimated market value of assets;
- Dollar value of insured and uninsured deposits, resp., and of other liabilities;
- Losses on contingent claims;
- Value of collateral extended and received in derivatives transactions and repos and guarantees extended and received.

Only by invoking the systemic risk exception whereby it is deemed that a failed institution's closure "would have serious adverse effects on economic conditions or financial stability" may the FDIC override the least-cost requirement (Deposit Insurance Act §1823 (c)(4)(G)(i)(I)). However, a decision required a two-thirds majority of the FDIC Board as well as of the board of governors of the Federal Reserve System and the approval of the secretary of the Treasury who must first consult with the president.[41]

---

[39] FDIC, Annual reports 2008, 2009 and 2010.
[40] Ironically, the major evaluation of the handling by the FDIC under Prompt Corrective Action (PCA) was undertaken in January 2007, just before the BIG crisis started, noting that between June 2004 and January 2007, no bank or thrift failed. See www.fdic.gov/deposit/insurance/initiative/AssessmentofRegulators.pdf
[41] A good description of the process from just before the crisis is the speech given by Martin J. Gruenberg, then vice chairman of the FDIC, before a Basel Symposium on Deposit Insurance Cross Border Issues on 3 May 2007, "The FDIC's approach to large bank resolution implementation issues," www.fdic.gov/news/news/speeches/archives/2007/chairman/spmay0307.html

As we saw above in the micro studies, the systemic risk exception was invoked for the first time ever in the planned takeover of Wachovia by Citigroup. It turned out not to be necessary as Wachovia was instead purchased by Wells Fargo without FDIC support. However, the later guarantee to Citi itself where the FDIC bore part of the risk required a systemic risk exception, the second one. The third instance was the establishment of the Temporary Liquidity Guarantee Program (TLGP) on 13 October 2008 whereby the FDIC guaranteed certain unsecured bank debt issued through October 2009 as well as some uninsured deposits of participating institutions through December 2010. The participants were charged a fee of 75 basis points for debt and 10 basis points for uninsured deposits. It should be specially noted that participants were warned that "a special assessment will be collected to cover any losses not covered by the fees to ensure no impact on the Deposit Insurance Fund or the U.S. taxpayer."[42]

The use of the systemic risk exception was later criticized by the General Accountability Office (GAO) for creating "moral hazard" in that qualified investors would have less incentive to critically investigate the quality of the financial institutions in which they proposed to invest.[43]

The FDIC has two primary types of closing transactions, with multiple variations of both, to resolve failing institutions, namely (a) Purchase and Assumption or (b) Deposit Payoff:[44]

Purchase and Assumption (P&A) is a resolution transaction in which a healthy institution purchases some or all of the assets of the failed financial institution and assumes some or all of the liabilities, including all insured deposits.

1. *Basic Purchase and Assumption.* Assets transferring to the acquiring institution (AI) are limited to cash and cash equivalents.
2. *Modified Purchase and Assumption.* Cash and a portion of the loan portfolio (loan pools) are transferred to the acquiring institution.

---

[42] www.fdic.gov/news/news/financial/2008/fil08103a.html
[43] GAO, "Regulators' use of systemic risk exception raises moral hazard concerns and opportunities exist to clarify the provision," April 2010, www.gao.gov/assets/310/303248.pdf
[44] The list below is taken from General Accountability Office (GAO), *Financial Institutions, Causes and Consequences of Recent Bank Failures*, Report to Congressional Committees, GAO 13–71, January 2013, pp. 65–6.

3. *Whole Bank Purchase and Assumption.* The acquiring institution assumes essentially all assets and liabilities.
4. *Whole Bank Purchase and Assumption with Shared Loss Agreements* (SLA). Specific assets assumed by the assuming institution are covered in that the FDIC reimburses the acquiring institution or shares in loan losses.
5. *Bridge Bank Resolution Transaction.* A type of purchase and assumption transaction for which the FDIC itself acts temporarily as the assuming institution (example: IndyMac).

Deposit Payoff Transaction. A resolution strategy that occurs when there is no assuming institution, the bank is liquidated and the FDIC directly pays the insured amounts to the depositor and becomes the holder of the claim.

1. *Straight Deposit Payoff.* This is only executed if the FDIC does not receive a bid for the purchase and assumption transaction, thus no liabilities are assumed and no assets are purchased by an acquiring institution.
2. *Insured Deposit Transfer.* The deposits and secured liabilities of a failed institution are transferred to a healthy institution which assumes the reponsibility for them. This means no assets are purchased.
3. *Deposit Insurance National Bank* (DINB) – Insured deposits are transferred to a newly chartered federal financial institution, which is operated for a limited period of time by the FDIC to permit depositors to make an orderly withdrawal of funds.
4. *Open Bank Assistance.* The FDIC determines it is least costly to the DIF to provide assistance rather than close the failing bank.

Of the 414 failed banks during 2008–11 for which the FDIC was named receiver, it used the P&A procedure to resolve 394, corresponding to 98 percent of assets in these failing institutions. However, FDIC was only able to resolve these banks with purchase and assumption agreements because it offered to share in the losses incurred by the acquiring institution. At the height of the financial crisis in 2008, FDIC sought bids for whole bank purchase and assumption agreements with little success. Potential acquiring banks did not have sufficient capital to take on the additional risks that the failed institutions' assets represented. Because shared loss agreements had worked well during the savings and loan crisis of the 1980s and early 1990s, the FDIC decided to use this method to solicit bids to provide potential buyers some protection on the purchase of failed bank assets, reduce immediate cash needs, keep assets in the private sector, and minimize disruptions to banking customers.

Under the agreements, the FDIC generally agreed to pay 80 percent for covered losses with the acquiring bank covering the remaining 20 percent. From 2008 to the end of 2011, the FDIC resolved 281 of the 414 failures (68 percent) by providing a shared loss agreement.[45] By comparing the estimated cost of the shared loss agreements versus the estimated cost of directly liquidating the failed bank, the FDIC claims that the use of shared loss agreements saved the DIF over 40 billion dollars.

As we saw above, at the cost of having to charge insured institutions a one-off fee, the FDIC came through the crisis without having to resort to borrowing in the Treasury. But then, it was helped by the infusion of over 200 billion dollars of TARP money into problem banks. What would have happened without them? What will happen next time when/if TARP-like taxpayer bail-outs are ruled out by Dodd–Frank?

Figure 32 shows how quickly the deposit insurance fund was depleted from the end of 2007 to September 2009. It was partially restored by member banks prepaying 45 billion dollars of future assessments. Among the biggest payers were Bank of America (3.5 billion dollars), Wells Fargo (3.2 billion), JPMorgan Chase (2.4 billion) and Citigroup (1.2 billion). Still the Fund only returned to positive territory in June 2011 and stood at only 0.44 percent of insured deposits even at the end of 2012 and at 0.79 percent at the end of 2013.[46]

The conclusion is firstly that the insurance fund must be made larger and the required reserve ratio has since been raised from 1.22 to 1.35 percent of insured deposits by Dodd–Frank, too low but at least a step in the right direction. Internally, the FDIC specifies a Designated Reserve Ratio of 2 percent.[47] Secondly, the FDIC must have an unlimited line of credit in the Treasury to establish confidence that it will always be capable of repaying depositors in failed financial institutions.

Thirdly, the resolution of Washington Mutual and the near resolution of Wachovia showed clearly that the FDIC was in no condition to undertake a resolution of a megabank like Citi without subjecting

[45] GAO, *Financial Institutions*, pp. 40–1.
[46] FDIC, *Annual Report 2013*, p. 14, www.fdic.gov/about/strategic/report/ 2013annualreport/AR13final.pdf
[47] Ibid., p. 13.

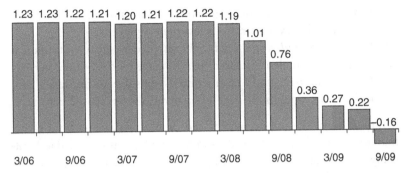

Figure 32. Ratio of the Deposit Insurance Fund to insured deposits, March 2006 – September 2009
Source: Financial Times, http://ftalphaville.ft.com//2009/11/24/85041/fdics-insurance-in-the-red-problem-banks-hit-16-year-high/

bondholders and probably also uninsured depositors to major losses. As noted by Sheila Bair,[48] the proposed merger between Citi and Wachovia could theoretically have cost the FDIC 270 billion dollars; this is a situation where the insurance fund contained 34 billion and would soon show a deficit. The sum may also be compared with the over 5 trillion dollars in insured deposits, of which a combined Wachovia+Citi alone would have been responsible for some 600 billion.

Under section 38 in the Federal Deposit Insurance Corporation Improvement Act (FDICIA) of 1991, defining and dealing with Prompt Corrective Action, the FDIC is required to divide its insured banks according to the following five capital categories, defined by (a) total risk-based capital ratio (Tier 1 + Tier 2 capital divided by risk-weighted assets), (b) Tier 1 risk-based capital ratio and (c) leverage capital ratio, i.e. Tier 1 tangible equity divided by total (unweighted) assets. Following the leverage ratio, a bank is considered:

1. *Well capitalized:* an insured depository institution is "well capitalized" if its leverage ratio significantly exceeds 5 percent.
2. *Adequately capitalized:* an insured depository institution is "adequately capitalized" if it meets a 4 percent leverage ratio.

---

[48] Bair, *Bull by the Horns*, p. 102.

3. *Undercapitalized:* an insured depository institution is "undercap-italized" if its leverage ratio is less than 4 percent.
4. *Significantly undercapitalized:* an insured depository institution is "significantly undercapitalized" if its leverage ratio is below 3 percent.
5. *Critically undercapitalized:* an insured depository institution is "crit-ically undercapitalized" if its leverage ratio is less than 2 percent.

Indicative of the importance placed on leverage, using total rather than unweighted assets in the denominator, a bank is regarded as "crit-ically undercapitalized" if its tangible equity is less than 2 percent of total assets, irrespective of its capital ratios under the first two alter-natives which use risk-weighted assets. This is in sharp contrast to the European regulatory framework under Basel II which continues under Basel III, where the newly introduced leverage ratio is seen as a com-plement to the risk-based ratios and, moreover, set at a low 3 percent, corresponding to an "undercapitalized" bank in the United States. We will return in the last chapter in the book to the importance of ade-quate capital and the inadequacy of Basel III.

Under Prompt Corrective Action (PCA), the FDIC issues a warning to the bank when it becomes "undercapitalized." If the leverage ratio drops below 3 percent, the FDIC can change management and force the bank to take other corrective actions, viz. to sell assets and/or issue new capital or arrange for its sale to a healthy bank. When the bank becomes critically undercapitalized, the FDIC must declare the bank insolvent unless the situation is rectified within 90 days, and can take over the management of the bank as receiver.

In its report to Congress in 2011, the Financial Stability Oversight Council noted that despite these measures, the Deposit Insurance Fund suffered major losses during the latest crisis (as we saw above), suggesting that capital ratios alone were not sufficient as triggers for corrective action.[49] The Financial Stability Board has since suggested a number of additional qualitative and quantitative triggers for man-agement and supervisors, such as:

- Ratings downgrades;
- Profit & loss statements;

---

[49] Financial Stability Oversight Council, "Report to Congress on prompt correc-tive action," December 2011, www.treasury.gov/initiatives/fsoc/studies-reports/Documents/FSOC%20PCA%20Report%20FINAL.pdf

- Credit risk limits;
- Ratio of delinquent loans;
- Ratio of retail to wholesale funding;
- Percentage renewal of wholesale funding;
- Withdrawal of deposits and other funding;
- Increased collateral requirements;
- Senior debt spreads;
- CDS spreads, if available;
- Short-term interest rates such as three-month LIBOR.[50]

Dodd–Frank Wall Street Reform and Consumer Protection Act of 2010: what it does do[51]

"In an economic crisis, the question is not whether government 'picks winners,' but whether it does so competently and transparently."[52]

In at least three ways, enumerated and discussed below, changes wrought by the Dodd–Frank Act will make solving the next financial crisis more difficult, not easier. Perhaps even worse is the fact that

---

[50] Financial Stability Board, "Recovery and resolution planning, making the key attributes requirements operational," November 2012.

[51] Among several hundred books and articles presenting and discussing the Dodd–Frank Act, I would like to recommend the following: John C. Coffee, "The political economy of Dodd-Frank: why financial reform tends to be frustrated and systemic risk perpetuated," in Eilís Ferran *et al.*, *The Regulatory Aftermath of the Global Financial Crisis* (Cambridge University Press, 2012); William D. Cohan and David Skeel, *The New Financial Deal: Understanding the Dodd–Frank Act and Its (Unintended) Consequences* (Hoboken, NJ: John Wiley & Sons, 2011); Financial Stability Board, "Implementing the FSB key attributes of financial resolution regimes – how far have we come?" 15 April 2013; Edward F. Greene, "Dodd-Frank and the future of financial regulation," *Harvard Business Law Review* 79 (2011); International Monetary Fund, "A fair and substantial contribution by the financial sector," Final report for the G-20, June 2010; David Mayes, "Who pays for bank insolvency?" *Journal of International Money and Finance* 23 (2004), pp. 515–51; Thomas Philippon and Philipp Schabl, "Efficient recapitalization," *Journal of Finance* 68:1 (February 2013), pp. 1–42; Kenneth E. Scott, "A guide to the resolution of failed financial institutions," in Kenneth E. Scott and John B. Taylor, eds., *Bankruptcy not Bailout: Special Chapter 14* (Stanford, CA: Hoover Institution Press, 2012); United States Congress, House of Representatives, Committee on Financial Services, "Who is too big to fail: does Title II of the Dodd–Frank Act enshrine taxpayer-funded bailouts?" Hearing, 15 May 2013.

[52] Kuttner, *A Presidency in Peril*, p. 72.

the Act adds significantly to the uncertainty as to how the regulatory authorities will react in a crisis in their handling of the too-big-to-fail firms to be resolved under the Act, thereby risking creating widespread panics and runs, on banks as well as on other non-bank financial companies that are subject to the Orderly Liquidation Authority (OLA).

Firstly, the Act severely curtails the ability of the Federal Reserve to extend emergency credits to non-banks, even to holding companies that the Fed is itself supervising.[53] Box 2 shows what the Act says on this issue.

By abolishing the previous emergency lending authority by the Federal Reserve under section 13(3) of the Federal Reserve Act to lend to individual firms, Dodd–Frank makes such lending as occurred to Bear Stearns and AIG illegal. Likewise, the Act forbids the creation of such companies as Maiden Lane I, II and III which took over and gradually liquidated assets taken over from these two companies. Even if a company is formally solvent and not involved in any resolution or bankruptcy proceeding, as was the case with Bear Stearns, and even if adequate collateral is available, as in the case of AIG, the Fed may still not extend an emergency loan. As we saw above, JPMorgan Chase would not have purchased Bear Stearns without a risk-sharing arrangement with the Fed. We saw earlier that the speed with which the Fed reacted was essential in avoiding a market panic. It could act quickly since it could take the necessary decisions on its own, albeit by a qualified majority of the Board. The market appreciated the actions and the speed, only 72 hours from the first call for help to find a solution. While the S&P 500 index fell by some 3 percent on the two days (Friday, 14 March and Monday, 17 March 2008) when the future of Bear Stearns was unknown, on Tuesday, 18 March the market recovered, rising by over 4 percent in a single day of trading. Similarly, concerning aid to AIG, panic was avoided and order restored by the 85-billion dollar loan extended by the Fed on 16 September 2008. The stock market finished the tumultuous week virtually unchanged, having been down 5 percent at the worst.

---

[53] See also Thomas Cooley *et al.*, "The power of central banks and the future of the Federal Reserve System," ch. 2 in Acharya *et al.*, eds., *Regulating Wall Street*.

Box 2   The Dodd–Frank Act: Federal Reserve System
Provisions

TITLE XI. FEDERAL RESERVE SYSTEM PROVISIONS

SEC. 1101. FEDERAL RESERVE ACT AMENDMENTS ON
EMERGENCY LENDING AUTHORITY

FEDERAL RESERVE ACT – The third undesignated paragraph
of section 13 of the Federal Reserve Act (12 U.S.C. 343) … is
amended –

(2) by striking "individual, partnership, or corporation" the
first place that term appears and inserting the following: "participant in any program or facility with broad-
based eligibility";

(6) (B) (i) As soon as is practicable after the date of enactment of this subparagraph, the Board shall establish,
by regulation, in consultation with the Secretary of
the Treasury, the policies and procedures governing
emergency lending under this paragraph. Such policies and procedures shall be designed to ensure that
any emergency lending program or facility is for
the purpose of providing liquidity to the financial
system, and not to aid a failing financial company
and that the security for emergency loans is sufficient to protect taxpayers from losses and that any
such program is terminated in a timely and orderly
fashion …

(ii) The Board shall establish procedures which pro-
hibit borrowing from programs and facilities by
borrowers that are insolvent. Such procedures …
A borrower shall be considered insolvent under this
subparagraph if the borrower is in bankruptcy, resolution under Title II of the Dodd–Frank Wall Street
Reform and Consumer Protection Act or any other
Federal or State insolvency proceeding.

(iii) A program or facility that is structured to remove assets from the balance sheet of a single and specific company or that is established for the purpose of assisting a single and specific company avoid bankruptcy, resolution under Title II of the Dodd–Frank Wall Street Reform and Consumer Protection Act or any other Federal or State insolvency proceeding shall not be considered a program or facility with broad-based eligibility.

(iv) The Board may not establish any program or facility under this paragraph without the prior approval of the Secretary of the Treasury.

Proposal 1

While avoiding the moral hazard involved in being allowed to extend credit to just any individual financial company, as was the case under the old version of section 13(3), it would seem that a workable compromise between systemic risk and moral hazard is to extend Dodd–Frank to allow for (adequately secured) lending at the Fed's own discretion not only to banks but also to such non-bank financial holding companies and other financial companies that are directly supervised by the Fed, these companies having been decreed by the Financial Stability Oversight Council to be systemically important. This would at the time of writing (2014) include only AIG, Prudential and Ally Financial but would allow for the addition of other systemically important non-bank financial companies over time.

This will also counter the criticism that Dodd–Frank regulates "banks" but not "banking" since it would allow for the gradual addition of a number of companies in the "shadow banking sector" deemed to be of systemic importance. And by inference, the Fed would hence be allowed to lend to money market mutual funds, private equity and hedge funds, SIFs, finance companies, etc., and, perhaps most importantly, to clearing houses that assume gradually more systemic importance after Dodd–Frank in the United States and EMIR in Europe but without a lender of last resort to back them up. It would be easy to add the Fed as a secondary regulator to these clearing houses, together with the CFTC, allowing for borrowing facilities at the Fed for these clearing houses.[54]

The moral hazard created by this widening of the circle of potential borrowers should be addressed by a risk-based pricing of these facilities, not by outlawing them outright.

References to the secretary of the Treasury should be removed. The Federal Reserve is and should be an independent institution responsible only to Congress, not to the government. The present setup risks slowing down the necessary speed of reaction in an emergency. It should be quite sufficient to demand that the Fed receives sufficient collateral for any loan extended. Since it will only have the authority to lend to supervised banks or to such non-banks that it itself supervises, evaluation under due diligence of the value of any proposed collateral should not be too difficult.

The second important change that Dodd–Frank brought is the Orderly Liquidation Authority (OLA).[55] Box 3 shows what the Act says on this issue.

Under previous FDIC legislation, still applicable for non-systemic financial companies, a resolution (seizure) begins with a decision by the financial company's primary regulator to seize the company (bank) and put it into receivership or conservatorship under the FDIC. As concerns the resolution of TBTF banks and other systemically important financial institutions, the board of the primary regulator (the Fed for bank holding companies) together with the board of the FDIC makes a recommendation, taken by a two-thirds majority in both cases, to the Treasury secretary who, after having consulted with the president, will decide why handling the failure under the normal bankruptcy code (chapter 7 or chapter 11) would have severe negative implications for the country's financial stability. He/she must also determine whether the company is in imminent danger of default due to insufficient capital (insolvency) or inability to pay its obligations (insufficient liquidity). If the board of the company agrees, the company is placed under receivership with the FDIC. If not, the matter is referred to the

---

[54] See also Johan Lybeck, "Too-big-to-fail clearers should be publicly owned," *Financial Times*, 13 September 2013.

[55] See in particular Viral V. Acharya *et al.*, "Resolution authority," chapter 8 in Acharya *et al.*, eds., *Regulating Wall Street*.

Box 3 The Dodd–Frank Act: Orderly Liquidation
Authority

TITLE II. ORDERLY LIQUIDATION AUTHORITY

SEC. 204. ORDERLY LIQUIDATION OF COVERED FINANCIAL COMPANIES.

(a) Purpose of Orderly Liquidation Authority.– It is the purpose of this title to provide the necessary authority to liquidate failing financial companies that pose a significant risk to the financial stability of the United States in a manner that mitigates such risk and minimizes moral hazard. The authority provided in this title shall be exercised in the manner that best fulfills such purpose, so that –

   (1) creditors and shareholders will bear the losses of the financial company;

   (2) management responsible for the condition of the financial company will not be retained; and

   (3) the Corporation [the FDIC] and other appropriate agencies will take all steps necessary and appropriate to assure that all parties, including management, directors, and third parties, having responsibility for the condition of the financial company bear losses consistent with their responsibility, including actions for damages, restitution, and recoupment of compensation and other gains not compatible with such responsibility.

(b) Corporation as Receiver.– Upon the appointment of the Corporation under section 202, the Corporation shall act as the receiver for the covered financial company, with all of the rights and obligations set forth in this title.

(c) Consultation.– The Corporation, as receiver –

   (1) shall consult with the primary financial regulatory agency or agencies of the covered financial company and its covered subsidiaries for purposes of ensuring an orderly liquidation of the covered financial company;

District of Columbia district court which must take a decision within 24 hours after a closed hearing. The petition must be granted unless the company can show that it is indeed solvent/liquid.

We saw above that the FDIC normally has a number of options available on how to handle a failed bank, from liquidating the bank and paying off its depositors from the Deposit Insurance Fund (DIF), to assisting a purchase and assumption with or without a shared loss with the purchasing institution, to setting up a temporary bridge bank to Open Bank Assistance, where the FDIC determines that it is least costly to the DIF to provide assistance for the continued running of the bank rather than closing it.

Under Title II of the Dodd–Frank legislation, it is mandated that the financial company shall be liquidated (as the term OLA clearly specifies). Period. If a bridge bank is set up, it must be temporary; an absolute maximum of five years is allowed. The bank may not be continued, nor may it be reorganized. There is no mention that the liquidation must proceed in a manner that will be cost efficient. Nor does the FDIC as receiver need to follow normal bankruptcy priorities of claims. The FDIC may transfer or sell selected assets and liabilities of the failed company at will, provided that creditors receive no less than what they would have received under bankruptcy (however, that value is to be determined a priori, *vide* the continued problems in establishing the validity of and paying off claims on Lehman Brothers).

The Act makes clear that losses are to be borne by shareholders and creditors and, if necessary, by the failed megabank's surviving TBTF colleagues; they may not involve taxpayers (see below). Some creditors will, however, nevertheless be protected, namely those who have entered into so-called "qualified financial contracts" with the company in question, by which is meant all types of transactions where collateral has been transferred or margin placed: secured credits and repos, credit default swaps as well as interest and currency swaps, futures, forwards and options, irrespective of whether they be exchange traded or OTC. The problems of settling Lehman Brothers' vast derivatives book would thus not have changed under Dodd–Frank and the favored correspondents of AIG's derivatives transactions would be just as favored under the Dodd–Frank Act.

There are numerous problems with the present formulation of the OLA. The very fact that a number of institutions have been classified as TBTF (G-SIFI) by the Financial Stability Oversight Council and/or the Financial Stability Board most likely means that they will continue to borrow at below-market interest rates, especially in a renewed crisis, hence receiving a taxpayer-financed subsidy. The threat to break them up under a "living will" rather than continue operations under an FDIC-supervised bridge bank (see below) is simply not trustworthy in a renewed situation of general panic as in 2008.[56] The market continues to believe that they will be saved.

Another risk is a bank run. The very fact that unsecured creditors of systemically important institutions could – as they did in the bankruptcy of Washington Mutual – lose part of their investments in an entirely unpredictable manner, given the freedom given to the FDIC to select which liabilities to protect, would most certainly lead to a run (wholesale and/or retail) on a bank suspected of being on its way to an OLA. Its unsecured debt will be dumped, as will securities held as collateral, risking a fall in value. Deposits above the insured limit will be withdrawn in panic. Hence the very rumor of a potential liquidity crisis in a TBTF institution, true or not, will create one.

Proposal 2

Title II should be renamed the Orderly Resolution Authority (ORA) since it should be made clear that liquidation is only one of several alternatives made available to the FDIC. The text should provide for the seizure of banks as well as bank or non-bank holding companies in distress and placing them under the resolution authority of the FDIC, thereby extending its powers under the Federal Deposit Insurance Act. Losses to stakeholders should follow normal bankruptcy order.

---

[56] See among many contributions, Richard W. Fisher [President of the Federal Reserve Bank of Dallas], "Correcting 'Dodd–Frank' to actually end 'too big to fail,'" statement before the Committee on Financial Services, US House of Representatives, hearing on "Examining how the Dodd–Frank Act could result in more taxpayer-funded bailouts," 26 June 2013; United States Congress, House of Representatives, Committee on Financial Services, "Who is too big to fail: does Title II of the Dodd–Frank Act enshrine taxpayer-funded bailouts?", hearing, 15 May 2013, especially the statement by David A. Skeel.

The FDIC should have full flexibility in choosing the resolution model it thinks best. However, in so doing, the Deposit Insurance Fund should not be made available for other purposes than paying off depositors in liquidated banks. See below. While the FDIC should have the possibility of bailing in unsecured creditors and uninsured depositors, legislation should make clear that this is an outcome to be avoided. See below for the Orderly Resolution Fund.

The third feature of Title II that needs to be amended is the construction of what Dodd–Frank calls the Orderly Liquidation Fund.

One part of this legislation tries to maintain Chinese walls between the traditional roles of the FDIC as bank supervisor, manager/defender of the Deposit Insurance Fund and caretaker of (small) banks placed under its umbrella as receiver. The addition of its role under Title II of Dodd–Frank should seemingly not change any of these old roles. The Deposit Insurance Fund may not be used to assist the resolution/ liquidation of "covered financial companies," i.e. TBTF banks and bank and non-bank holding companies under Fed supervision. Nor may the Orderly Liquidation Fund in the Treasury be used to assist in the resolution of failing banks under the existing Federal Deposit Insurance Act.

One might ask whether this separation of tasks is feasible and whether it is desirable.

The use of the same term "fund" for the two phenomena is also highly misleading. The DIF is an existing pre-paid fund, paid for by risk-based fees on the liabilities of the insured institutions (changed from a fee on deposits by the Dodd–Frank Act). The Act also raised the required long-term reserve ratio of the DIF to insured deposits to 1.35 percent. This ratio will, however, only be reached in the long-run, the actual value in 2013 being, as noted above, 0.79 percent of insured deposits (or 47 billion dollars on some 6 trillion dollars insured deposits).

By contrast, the so-called Orderly Liquidation Fund (OLF) is not a pre-paid fund but essentially an overdraft facility in the Treasury by the FDIC. On being appointed as receiver of a TBTF financial institution, the FDIC may issue obligations to the Treasury, making available 10 percent of the estimated value of assets of the company for which it is acting as receiver. After 30 days, the facility rises to 90 percent of the value of consolidated assets. The obligations to the Treasury must be repaid after an absolute maximum of 5 years. Should liquidated

Box 4 The Dodd–Frank Act: Orderly Liquidation Fund

(n) ORDERLY LIQUIDATION FUND

    (1) ESTABLISHMENT – There shall be established in the Treasury of the United States a separate fund to be known as the "Orderly Liquidation Fund," which shall be available to the Corporation [FDIC] to carry out the authorities contained in this title, for the cost of actions authorized by this title, including the orderly liquidation of covered financial companies, payment of administrative expenses, the payment of interest and principal by the Corporation on obligations issued under paragraph (5), and the exercise of the authorities of the Corporation under this title.

(5) AUTHORITY TO ISSUE OBLIGATIONS

    (A) CORPORATION AUTHORIZED TO ISSUE OBLIGATIONS-

    Upon appointment by the Secretary [of the Treasury] of the Corporation as receiver for a covered financial company, the Corporation is authorized to issue obligations to the Secretary.

(6) MAXIMUM OBLIGATION LIMITATION – The Corporation may not, in connection with the orderly liquidation of a covered financial company, issue or incur any obligation, if after issuing or incurring the obligation, the aggregate amount of such obligations outstanding under this subsection for each covered financial company would exceed –

    (A) an amount that is equal to 10 percent of the total consolidated assets of the covered financial company, based on the most recent financial statement available, during the 30-day period immediately following the date of appointment as receiver ...

    (B) the amount that is equal to 90 percent of the fair value of the total consolidated assets of each covered financial company that are available for repayment, after the time period described in subparagraph (A).

(8) RULE OF CONSTRUCTION –
(A) IN GENERAL – Nothing in this section shall be construed to affect the authority of the Corporation under ... the Federal Deposit Insurance Act, the management of the Deposit Insurance Fund by the Corporation, or the resolution of insured depository institutions, provided that –
(i) the authorities of the Corporation contained in this title shall not be used to assist the Deposit Insurance Fund or to assist any financial company under applicable law other than this Act;
(ii) the authorities of the Corporation relating to the Deposit Insurance Fund, or any other responsibilities of the Corporation under applicable law other than this title, shall not be used to assist a covered financial company pursuant to this title, and
(iii) the Deposit Insurance Fund may not be used in any manner to otherwise circumvent the purposes of this title.

(o) ASSESSMENTS –
(1) RISK-BASED ASSESSMENTS
(A) ELIGIBLE FINANCIAL COMPANIES DEFINED – For purposes of this subsection, the term "eligible financial company" means any bank holding company with total consolidated assets equal to or greater than $50,000,000,000 and any non-bank financial company supervised by the Board of Governors.
(B) ASSESSMENTS – The Corporation shall charge one or more risk-based assessments in accordance with the provisions of subparagraph (D), if such assessments are necessary to pay in full the obligation issued by the Corporation to the Secretary under this title within 60 months of the date of issuance of such obligations.

assets of the company not suffice for the repayment, holders of subordinated debt, unsecured bonds and uninsured deposits will be forced to cover the difference, in this order. Should even this not be sufficient, the FDIC is obligated to levy an assessment on the other remaining TBTF financial institutions (defined as banks and financial holding companies with more than 50 billion dollars in consolidated assets) to make up the difference.

Interestingly enough, no mention is made of maximizing the value of the borrowing from the Fed. The DIF can borrow a maximum of 100 billion dollars from the Treasury (to be compared with some 6 trillion dollars in insured deposits) but the OLF may borrow an amount limited only by the assets of the company under resolution (but subject to a qualified vote in the Fed board and the agreement of the Treasury secretary and the president). On 31 December 2013, the 33 bank holding companies which had more than 50 billion dollars in assets, qualifying them for TBTF status, together held assets of 12.4 trillion dollars.[57]

It should be obvious that the FDIC – administratively and financially – would soon be overwhelmed by the resolution of even one of these megabanks, in particular since financial crises tend to affect several banks at the same time, the underlying problem factors (e.g. a drying up of the interbank market) tending to be common.

For the same reason it should be obvious that the repayment mechanisms legislated by Dodd–Frank will not be put into practice in a new crisis. Forcing losses on unsecured debt holders in a bank under resolution in the middle of a financial crisis will lead to a firesale by holders of unsecured debt in other banks, just like the handling of Washington Mutual led to rapidly falling prices for Wachovia's debt. Similarly, to expect a financial industry already on its knees to pay a fee to the OLF to repay the debt of the FDIC would also aggravate the crisis.

To this comes the free-rider problem. Why would any megabank have an incentive to cut down on its risks if it knows that it will be "the others" that will have to clean out the Augean stables?

---

[57] http://blogs.wsj.com/moneybeat/2014/03/03/ranking-the-50-biggest-banks-from-j-p-morgan-to-firstmerit/

Proposal 3

While rejected by Congress, it is obvious that a resolution fund must be built up by risk-based fees on the involved banks in good times. This fund should be managed by the FDIC but separate from the Deposit Insurance Fund. It should be used for the recapitalization of banks that the FDIC deems long-term viable as well as for the reorganization and liquidation of the others. Hence the fund should be called the Orderly Resolution Fund rather than the Orderly Liquidation Fund. In order to be credible, it should correspond to the costs of recent financial crises in the US as well as in Europe, i.e. 3–4 percent of GDP or at present 500–600 billion dollars, well in line with the 700 billion dollars allocated by Congress under the TARP program.

While the Orderly Resolution Fund (ORF) is being built up, the FDIC should have borrowing rights of 500 billion dollars for this Fund in the Treasury. The same borrowing limit should be set for the Deposit Insurance Fund. The borrowing capability of the DIF is presently restricted to 100 billion dollars under section 14 of the Federal Deposit Insurance Act but should be raised back to the 500 billion dollars that was in force between 20 May 2009 and 31 December 2010. The use of both facilities would be subject to the qualified approval by the Federal Reserve, the Treasury and the president.

The FDIC should have full flexibility to use the funds under the ORF at will, lending to institutions for which it acts as receiver or conservator as well as injecting capital. It should in each case be forced to submit a plan to the Treasury as to how the bank would repay the capital injected and how taxpayers would earn a profit. In order to get control over a bank placed under conservatorship under the FDIC, injecting common stock would normally be preferred to buying preferred shares.[58]

The setting up of such a Resolution Fund corresponds to what is being done in the euro area, as well as in some other EU countries such as Sweden and Germany (see the next chapter).[59] It is also in line with the recommendations by the IMF.[60]

---

[58] See also the discussion in Robert Pozen, *Too Big to Save: How to Fix the US Financial System* (Hoboken, NJ: John Wiley & Sons, 2010), pp. 226 ff.

[59] European Commission, "Bank resolution funds," COM (2010) 254 Final, 26 May 2010 http://eur-lex.europa.eu/LexUriServ/LexUriServ.do?uri=COM:2010:0254:FIN:EN:PDF

[60] International Monetary Fund, "A fair and substantial contribution by the financial sector," 27 June 2010, www.imf.org/external/np/g20/pdf/062710b.pdf

Furthermore, there seems to be no reason to separate the handling of TBTF banks from other banks, the line of demarcation of 50 billion dollars in assets being totally arbitrary. The United States has four megabank holding companies with assets (under GAAP) of 1.5–2.5 trillion dollars: JPMorgan Chase, Bank of America, Citigroup, Wells Fargo. Then there is a vast gap to number 5, Bank of New York Mellon, with assets under 400 billion dollars. And going down the list, why should E*Trade Financial Corp. with assets of 47 billion dollars be resolved differently from Zions Bancorp with assets of 56 billion dollars?

It seems much more logical to apply the same well-practiced methodology to all banks as well as to financial holding companies, using the same Single Point of Entry at the holding company level that Sheila Bair wanted to use for Citi during the crisis but was (probably) prevented from doing by then-existing legislation, now changed by Dodd–Frank.

If something ain't broken, don't fix it

It should be apparent from the micro studies in this book that, overall, the United States handled and survived the financial crisis better than most European countries. One first reason was that its banks started off in a better condition. The FDIC's Prompt Corrective Action (PCA), focusing on minimum leverage ratios, had led to American banks being better capitalized than their European counterparts. Furthermore, they had avoided the disaster that Basel II brought to European banks (and American investment banks) by staying on Basel I with its fixed risk weights.

Thirdly, the long built-up experience by the FDIC in the efficient resolution of failing banks had few similarities in Europe where virtually everything had to be learnt and built from scratch (except in such countries as Sweden that had been through a similar storm in the 1990s). Fourthly, despite the occasional infighting among American regulators, most failing US banks were national, thus avoiding the problems of the lack of cooperation between the regulatory authorities that prevented effective responses in many of the European cases studied, with Dexia and Fortis being among the worst examples. The continuing problems of resolving Lehman Brothers was an exception, not the rule!

In their response to the crisis, the US regulatory authorities also made a number of decisions that turned out to have made a difference. Firstly, after the inept handling of IndyMac, Lehman Brothers and Washington Mutual, there was never any doubt that banks' uninsured depositors and unsecured creditors would be saved one way or another. Banks might disappear on a Friday but come Monday, depositors would still be able to access their accounts and creditors could still sell their bank bonds. Transitions were mostly seamless, a testimony to the skill of FDIC staff.

Secondly, not knowing a priori whether a particular bank's problem was one of lacking confidence and liquidity or one of solvency, the authorities attacked both simultaneously, hence the two-pronged decision to guarantee bank liabilities through the Temporary Liquidity Guarantee Program of the FDIC and the capital injections through the Capital Purchase Program of TARP. Both were originally priced relatively cheaply in order to persuade as many as possible to sign up; indeed, the major banks were, as we have seen, more or less forced to take their share of the TARP money. Rising interest costs and restrictions on executive pay led to their being repaid as soon as possible and with a nice profit to the taxpayer.

With the rapid response to the crisis came a rapidly returned confidence, aided not least by the harsh and hence credible stress tests carried out by the Federal Reserve, forcing a number of banks to raise a substantial amount of new capital. The European stress tests, on the other hand, were treated as a joke and had probably more of a negative effect on confidence in the Old Continent's banking system.

The gradual return to growth in the United States, contrasted with the disastrous effect on confidence and growth of the European debt crisis, led to quite different outcomes for their respective banks. While the US banking system had already returned to profitability by the beginning of 2010, their European colleagues were mostly in negative territory way into 2013.[61] More on this aspect will be discussed in the next chapter.

---

[61] See for instance the Deutsche Bank research, "Bank performance in the US and Europe, an ocean apart," 27 September 2013, www.dbresearch.com/PROD/ DBR_INTERNET_EN-PROD/PROD0000000000320825/Bank+performance+ in+the+US+and+Europe%3A+An+ocean+apart.pdf. See also recent FDIC

The return to profitability led to the possibility to raise equity capital. We have seen how giants like Bank of America and Citi repaid the government by issues of equity larger than ever seen before, some 20 billion dollars each in common stock. Overall, between 2007 and mid 2013, European banks raised an estimated 248 billion euro in new equity vs. 190 billion euro in the US.[62] But the comparison is defective, firstly since total assets of European banks are some five times those of US banks.[63] Secondly, the profitability of US banks gave them an advantage denied to European banks, namely to increase capital from retained earnings. The level of profitability also allowed them to increase loan loss provisions at a much faster rate.

Overall, the US handling of the financial crisis, while frequently improvised, turned out quite well. Instead of dismantling the structure, as Dodd–Frank largely does, it should be improved upon in ways suggested by this chapter.

reports, www2.fdic.gov/qbp/index.asp?source=govdelivery&utm_medium=
email&utm_source=govdelivery
[62] Ibid.
[63] Fifteen trillion dollars in the United States as against 75 trillion dollars in
Europe (of which 62 in the European Union), according to the European
Banking Federation, Facts and Figures 2012. Recall that of the world's 30 largest banks by assets, 15 are European and only 5 American. www.relbanks.com/
worlds-top-banks/assets

18 | Future bail-outs in the European Union under the Single Resolution Mechanism and the Bank Recovery and Resolution Directive

Europe and the US contrasted

The last section of Chapter 17 tried to enumerate some of the things that distinguished and separated the handling of the financial crisis on the two sides of the Atlantic, thereby trying to begin to give an answer to the question as to why the American bail-out money has, in the main, been repaid while the European hasn't, and why US banks appear to be recovering from the crisis much faster than their European competitors.[1]

American banks were already to begin with better capitalized than their European counterparts, thanks to the US focus on minimum leverage ratios rather than on capital in relation to risk-weighted assets.

---

[1] Among many useful references, see Viral V. Acharya and Sascha Steffen, "The greatest carry trade ever? Understanding Euro zone bank risks," NYU Stern School Working Paper, 18 November 2012; Thorstein Beck, ed., *Banking Union for Europe: Risks and Challenges* (London: CEPR and VoxEU.org, 2012); Claudia M. Buch, Tobias Körner and Benjamin Weigert, "Towards deeper financial integration in Europe: what the Banking Union can contribute," Sachverständigenrat (German Council of Economic Experts), Working Paper 2/2013, August 2013; Jacopo Carmassi, Carmine de Noia and Stefano Micossi, "Banking union: a federal model for the European Union with prompt corrective action," CEPS Policy Brief no. 282, 18 September 2012; James R. Barth, Apanard (Penny) Prabha and Greg Yun, "The Eurozone financial crisis: role of interdependencies between bank and sovereign risk," *Journal of Financial Economic Policy* 4:1 (2012), pp. 76–97; Douglas J. Elliot, "Key issues on European banking union: trade-offs and some recommendations," Working Paper 52, November 2012, Brookings institution; Rishi Goyal *et al.*, "A banking union for the euro area," IMF Staff Discussion Note, 13 February 2013; Niamh Moloney, "The legacy effects of the financial crisis on regulatory design in the EU,", ch. 2 in Eilís Ferran *et al.*, *The Regulatory Aftermath of the Global Financial Crisis* (Cambridge University Press, 2012); Nicolas Verón, "A realistic bridge towards European banking union," Petersen Institute for International Economics Policy Brief 13–17, June 2013. The EU Commission publishes regular updates on where the process of forming a European Banking Union stands.

Table 21 showed asset/capital ratios of the major European megabanks being double those of the included US banks, even correcting for the difference between IFRS and GAAP accounting principles. When the crisis struck in 2007, large North American banks had, on average, a ratio of Tier 1 capital to risk-weighted assets of 9.42 percent which may be contrasted with 4.74 percent in Germany, 5.69 percent in Italy and 6.29 percent in Spain (but 11.68 percent in Britain).[2] Obviously, adequate capital is only part of the story, albeit an important one.

Thanks not least to the opposition by the FDIC and its chair Sheila Bair, American (commercial) banks had avoided the disaster that Basel II brought to European banks from 2004 onwards by being forced to stay on Basel I with its fixed risk weights, a blessing in disguise as it turned out.

The long built-up experience by the FDIC in the efficient resolution of failing banks had few similarities in Europe where virtually everything – legal as well as institutional frameworks – had to be learnt and built from scratch. The FDIC had lived through the Latin American crises and the thrift crisis in the 1980s as well as the Asian and Russian crises in the 1990s, and the relevant pieces of legislation in the form of the FDIC Improvement Act of 1991 and the Federal Deposit Reform Act of 2005 were the happy results, as well as the changes brought to the bankruptcy legislation by the Bankruptcy Abuse Prevention and Consumer Protection Act of 2005.

As a consequence of the existence for the last 75 years of a credible safety net for insured deposits, there were no major retail bank runs in the United States during the crisis (but certainly wholesale runs until the establishment of the Temporary Liquidity Guarantee Program and other measures to rebuild confidence in the wholesale and repo markets). By contrast, deposit insurance in the European Union was only introduced in 1995 by Directive 94/19/EC and was untested. Moreover, even in 2014, a number of important EU countries (Austria, Italy and the UK among others) still lacked pre-funded deposit insurance.[3]

---

[2] *The Banker*, July 2008.
[3] International Monetary Fund, "European Union: publication of financial sector assessment program documentation – technical note on deposit insurance," IMF Country Report no. 13/66, March 2013.

While European regulatory authorities in most countries lacked a macrostability view during the crisis, chasing individual failing banks one after the other, the US authorities were more inclined to see the crisis in systemic terms, as a crisis of the banking industry.[4] Thus, while in Europe only needy banks were recapitalized (except in France...), the TARP program was available to all viable banks (and probably to some non-viable banks), all the US megabanks being forced to participate. In this way, panic and runs were avoided since the public had no way of knowing which TARP recipients really were in need of the money and which weren't; everybody was treated alike. In Europe, the major state-aided and/or state-owned "zombies" still stand out, to be occasionally flogged in the press: RBS, Bankia, Commerzbank, Monte dei Paschi, ABN AMRO, Eurobank, etc.[5]

With the rapid response to the crisis in the US came a rapidly returned confidence, aided not least by the harsh and hence credible stress tests carried out by the Federal Reserve, forcing a number of banks to raise a substantial amount of new capital. The European stress tests, on the other hand, were treated as a joke and had probably more of a negative effect on confidence in the Old Continent's banking system.

The gradual return to growth in the United States, contrasted with the disastrous effect on confidence and growth of the European debt crisis (see below), led to quite different outcomes for their respective banks. While the US banking system had already returned to profitability by the beginning of 2010, their European colleagues were mostly in negative territory way into 2013.[6]

---

[4] See e.g. Randall S. Krozner, "Making markets more robust," ch. 2 in Randall S. Kroszner and Robert J. Shiller, *Reforming US Financial Markets, Reflections Before and Beyond Dodd–Frank* (Cambridge, MA: MIT Press, 2011).

[5] For instance, "Five years on and the RBS pain is still far from over," *Financial Times*, 28 February 2014; "German competition body urges govt to sell Commerzbank," http://uk.reuters.com/article/2014/07/09/uk-commerzbank-sale-idUKKBN0FE1AJ20140709; "Pireaus Bank escapes state control, Eurobank does not," www.reuters.com/article/2013/04/22/us-piraeusbank-millennium-idUSBRE93L0XF20130422; "Dutch bank ABN AMRO's top salaries hike plan sends wrong signal," www.forbes.com/sites/marcelmichelson/2014/06/18/dutch-bank-abn-amros-top-salaries-hike-plan-sends-wrong-signal/

[6] See, for instance, the Deutsche Bank research, "Bank performance in the US and Europe, an ocean apart," 27 September 2013, www.dbresearch.com/PROD/DBR_INTERNET_EN-PROD/PROD0000000000320825/Bank+performance+in+the+US+and+Europe%3A+An+ocean+apart.pdf and Dirk Schoenmaker

The return to profitability by US banks led to the possibility of raising more equity capital. See the enormous difference between the United States and Europe in Figure 33. From 2007 to mid 2013, European banks raised a total of 248 billion euro in new equity as against 190 billion euro for US banks but we must remember that total assets in European banks are five times those of US banks, American corporations relying much more on direct access to the capital market than their European counterparts.

The profitability of US banks also gave them an advantage denied to European banks, namely to increase capital from retained earnings. The level of profitability furthermore and thirdly allowed them to increase loan loss provisions at a much faster rate, putting the problems behind them.

Overall, the US handling of the financial crisis, while frequently improvised, turned out quite well. Instead of dismantling it, as

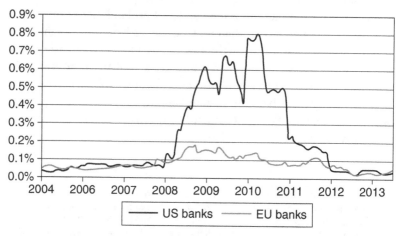

Figure 33. Bank equity issues in the US and Europe, 2004–13, percentage of total assets
Source: Dirk Schoenmaker and Toon Peek, "The state of the banking sector in Europe," OECD Economics Department Working Paper 1102, 27 January 2014, p. 19.

and Toon Peek, "The state of the banking sector in Europe," OECD Economics Department Working Paper 1102, 27 January 2014.

Dodd–Frank largely does, it should be improved upon as suggested by this and the former chapter. Europe's leaders, however, have a lot to learn from their US counterparts and this chapter will look at how/if they have learned their lesson.

Figure 34a–d spells out the development between 2007 and 2012 of the 7,861 banks which existed in the European Union of 27 countries in 2012.

Return on equity. Having recovered from the financial crisis itself, profitability in the European banking sector suffered by the sovereign debt crisis in the PIIGS countries spilling over into northern Europe, not least the forced write-down of Greek debt. US banks had a return on equity of 8.8 percent in 2012 as compared to –1.6 percent in the EU.[7]

Capital adequacy. With government aid and by shrinking assets (and to some extent by issuing new capital), European banks improved their Tier 1 BIS ratio from 8 to 12 percent. US banks had, however, a Tier 1 ratio of 13.1 percent in 2012, despite assets having risen from 13.4 trillion dollars to 14.4 trillion dollars in the five-year period.[8]

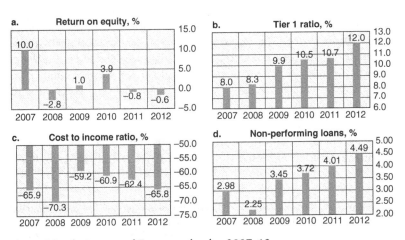

Figure 34a–d. Aspects of European banks, 2007–12
Source: European Banking Federation, March 2014 www.ebf-fbe.eu/publications/statistics/

---

[7] Source for the US: Federal Reserve Bank of St. Louis, http://research.stlouisfed.org/fred2/series/USROE
[8] Source for the US: www.bankregdata.com/allHMmet.asp?met=ONE

Efficiency. In terms of cost-to-income ratios, the US and Europe were surprisingly identical at around 66 percent.[9]

NPL ratio. In a stagnating Europe, non-performing loans as a share of total loans doubled between 2008 and 2012 to 4.5 percent and were still rising in 2013 whereas US banks had non-performing loans at 3.3 percent (and falling from 5 percent in 2009).[10]

Competition vs. stability aspects[11]

While both American and European national regulatory authorities did some infighting, the national European authorities (and their banks) also had to fight a supranational hydra in the form of the EU Commission. One of the major contentions of this chapter is that the Commission's focus on a "level-field" competition and the Single Market to the detriment of stability was (and is) one of the major reasons why Europe has fared worse than the United States in getting its banks back on their feet. I take a clear exception to the statement by Professor Eilís Ferran (in her otherwise excellent review) that

Pre-crisis, the primary aim of EU financial services policy was to "consolidate dynamically towards an integrated, open, inclusive, competitive, and economically efficient EU financial market." The need to address at EU level the negative side-effects of removing internal barriers was not ignored, but nor was it the number one priority. Now, EU financial services regulation is all about improving safety and soundness.[12]

As the dictata of the European Commission concerning the legality of the national aid efforts, quoted in Parts II and III of the book,

---

[9] McKinsey data for the US from "The triple transformation," McKinsey Annual Review of the Banking Industry, October 2012.

[10] Source: World Bank http://data.worldbank.org/indicator/FB.AST.NPER.ZS. The data bank of St. Louis Fed shows US NPL falling from a peak of 5.6 percent in 2009 to 2.7 percent in the final quarter of 2013: http://research.stlouisfed.org/fred2/series/NPTLTL

[11] See also Stefano Micossi, Ginevra Bruzzone and Miriam Cassella, "Bail-in provisions in state aid and resolution procedures: are they consistent with systemic stability?" CEPS Policy Briefs no. 318, 21 May 2014, http://papers.ssrn.com/sol3/papers.cfm?abstract_id=2445900

[12] Eilís Ferran, "Crisis-driven regulatory reform: where in the world is the EU going?" ch. 1 in Eilís Ferran *et al.*, *The Regulatory Aftermath of the Global Financial Crisis* (Cambridge University Press, 2012), pp. 80–1.

should already have made clear, the Commission was throughout the crisis and to this day almost exclusively focused on competition to the detriment of macroeconomic stability. Indeed, the EU Commission has acknowledged that after the initial period of accepting state aid in the name of financial stability, it started to tighten conditions for state aid to the financial sector from the second half of 2010. The Commission writes (boldface in original):

All in all, in the second semester of 2010 the Commission considered that there was a sufficient level of stabilization in the financial sector to embark on a gradual exit path, with a tightening of conditions to grant aid. That process started with tighter conditions for government guarantees from 1 July 2010, and was then extended to the other temporary rules governing aid to both financial institutions and the real economy from 1 January 2011. In particular, from that date, every beneficiary of a recapitalization or impaired asset measure has been obliged to submit a restructuring plan to the Commission's approval, irrespective of the level of aid it received...

The tightening of the conditions for approving aid conveys the signal that banks have to prepare for a return to normal market mechanisms without State support when market conditions permit such a return. In particular, they should accelerate the still necessary restructuring. At the same time, the applicable rules afford sufficient flexibility to duly take account of the potentially diverse circumstances affecting the situation of different banks or national financial markets, and also cater for the possibility of an overall or country-specific deterioration of financial stability.[13]

This period – mid 2010 – is precisely the time when the sovereign debt crisis entered into its most critical phase, putting pressure not only on the sovereigns and states in the so-called PIIGS countries (see below) but also on banks in northern Europe, having invested in the sovereign debt from these countries and being severely hit by the

---

[13] European Commission–Competition, "The effects of temporary State aid rules adopted in the context of the financial and economic crisis," Working paper, 5 October 2011, p. 17, http://ec.europa.eu/competition/publications/reports/working_paper_en.pdf
See also European Commission, "On the application, from 1 August 2013, of state aid rules to support measures in favour of banks in the context of the financial crisis," Communication C(2013) 4119, 10 July 2013, http://eur-lex.europa.eu/LexUriServ/LexUriServ.do?uri=OJ:C:2013:216:0001:0015:EN:PDF

write-down of Greek debt.[14] Below is the timeline of major events (see also the more detailed Chronology in Part I):

Box 5   A chronology of major events in the sovereign debt crisis, 2010–14

29 January 2010	Spain decides on an austerity plan to save 4 percent of GDP in public spending.
9 February 2010	Greece endorses its first austerity plan, freezing public-sector wages.
27 April 2010	Standard & Poor's downgrades the sovereign debt of Greece to "junk."
2 May 2010	Greece and the ECB, EU and the IMF (the "troika") agree on the first aid package of 110 billion euro, of which 10 billion is to be used to recapitalize the Greek banking system.
3 May 2010	The ECB says it will accept Greek debt as collateral even though rated "junk."
9 May 2010	Eurozone countries create the European Financial Stability Facility (EFSF) with 440 billion euro in capital. Together with support from the IMF, the Facility can muster 750 billion euro in aid.
25 May 2010	Italy decides on a 25 billion euro reduction in public spending.
27 May 2010	The Spanish parliament decides on a 15 billion euro reduction package.

---

[14] For an insightful and critical assessment of the reaction of the various EU authorities to the debt crisis, see Philippe Legrain, *European Spring: Why Our Economies and Politics Are in a Mess – and How to Put Them Right* (New York: CB Books, 2014).

14 June 2010	Moody's cuts the rating of Greece to "junk."
28 November 2010	Ireland and the "troika" agree an 85 billion euro bail-out, of which 35 billion will be used to recapitalize its banks.
17 May 2011	Portugal agrees a 78 billion euro bail-out with the "troika" members, of which 12 billion is earmarked for recapitalization of the banking sector.
5 July 2011	Moody's downgrades the sovereign debt of Ireland to "junk" on account of the rising costs of the banking crisis.
15 July 2011	The Italian parliament agrees on a new austerity package.
18 September 2011	S&P lowers the ratings of all major Italian banks as well as of the state, from A+ to A-.
27 October 2011	The EFSF is allowed to leverage up to 1 trillion euro.
16 December 2011	The Italian parliament increases the size of the austerity package to 50 billion euro.
13 January 2012	France and Austria as well as the EFSF lose their AAA rating from S&P.
21 February 2012	Greece receives an additional 130 billion euro in promised aid. A plan is approved for a write-down of Greek debt of almost 100 billion euro, mainly affecting European bank investments.
28 February 2012	The ECB refuses to accept Greek bonds as collateral and S&P declares Greece in selective default on account of the write-down of debt.

29 February 2012	The ECB lends a total of 1,018.7 billion euro to some 800 European banks.
9 March 2012	ISDA declares that the restructuring of Greek debt constituted a "credit event," leading to pay-outs on Credit Default Swaps.
13 March 2012	Moody's downgrades the debt of Cyprus to "junk."
10 July 2012	Spain reaches a deal with the EU to receive a maximum of 100 billion euro to recapitalize its banks (of which actually only 41 billion was used).
27 July 2012	Greece and the EU agree on an 18 billion euro recapitalization plan for the four major Greek banks.
27 September 2012	The eurozone countries agree on a permanent aid facility, the European Stability Mechanism (ESM), with a lending capacity of 500 billion euro.
5 December 2012	Fifty billion euro of the 240 billion total are dedicated to support the Greek banking system.
28 February 2013	Italy's Banca Monte dei Paschi di Siena receives a bail-out of 4.1 billion euro from the Italian state via Banca d'Italia.
25 March 2013	A package of 10 billion euro is arranged for Cyprus on condition that bail-ins are used to recapitalize its major bank, the other being liquidated.
14 November 2013	Ireland and Spain are allowed to exit the "intensive care."
27 May 2014	As a consequence of the sharp turnaround in the Irish economy, having led Moody's to raise the country to Baa1, the national "bad bank" NAMA reports profits for the

	third year running, having during the year disposed of assets of 4.5 billion euro of the originally 71.2 billion purchased in toxic assets during the crisis. It is expected to make a profit of perhaps 1 billion euro over its lifetime.
10 July 2014	In a clear indication that the European banking crisis is far from over, trading in the shares of Portugal's largest bank, Banco Espirito Santo, is halted after their price has fallen by 19 percent in a single day. Its CEO, Ricardo Salgado, is later arrested. The bank reveals a loss for the first half-year of 3.6 billion euro, leading to its core Tier 1 ratio falling to 5 percent.
1 August 2014	Moody's upgrades the sovereign rating of Greece to Caa1, still one of the lowest ratings in the world, only Cyprus is even worse at Caa3.
4 August 2014	Banco Espirito Santo is split into a new "good bank," Novo Banco, capitalized from Portugal's bank support fund and owned by the central bank, and a "bad bank" containing non-performing and intergroup loans which will be written down and wiping out shareholders (among them Crédit Agricole) and holders of subordinated debt. Senior bondholders are not bailed in.

The timeline shows clearly that stability had not returned by 2010 when the Commission unilaterally decided that it had. The Commission did not change its policies even as the sovereign debt crisis intensified over the coming years, nor has it acknowledged its mistakes since, even though it claimed to have had "financial stability as overarching objective."[15] This reluctance to face up to its mistakes stands in sharp contrast to the "mea culpa" of both the OECD and the IMF, accepting responsibility for the fact that they gravely underestimated the effects of policies that aggravated the underlying sovereign and banking crisis.

In a technical but highly influential paper, the chief economist of the IMF, Professor Olivier Blanchard, reported that the effects of fiscal consolidation on such variables as GDP growth and unemployment were far higher than had previously been thought. Instead of fiscal multipliers being around -0.5, he found that during the sovereign debt crisis, while variable, they were 2–3 times higher than previously assumed. Had these facts been known, it is likely that far less austere policies would have been prescribed for such countries as Greece.[16]

In a similar vein, the OECD's Economic Department has recently acknowledged that it substantially overestimated future GDP growth both in the 2007–9 downturn and in the subsequent recovery. Interestingly enough, the major errors were committed for countries that were more open to trade and capital flows, in countries where the product and labor markets were relatively more regulated, where banking sectors were largely foreign-owned and where banks had low capital ratios pre-crisis, such as Greece and Cyprus.[17]

However, the Commission continued to stress competition above financial stability and wrote in 2013 (italics are mine):

In the meantime, an increasing divergence in economic recovery across the Union, the need to reduce and consolidate public and private debt, and the existence of pockets of vulnerability in the financial sector have led to persistent tensions in the financial markets and fragmentation with increasing

---

[15] European Commission, "Communication from the Commission on the application, from 1 August 2013, of State aid rules to support measures of favour of banks in the context of the financial crisis" ("Banking Communication"), 2013/C 216/01, 13 July 2013, http://eur-lex.europa.eu/LexUriServ/LexUriServ.do?uri=OJ:C:2013:216:0001:0015:EN:PDF

[16] IMF, "Growth forecast errors and fiscal multipliers," Working paper 13/1, January 2013, www.imf.org/external/pubs/ft/wp/2013/wp1301.pdf. See also www.washingtonpost.com/blogs/wonkblog/wp/2013/01/03/an-amazing-mea-culpa-from-the-imfs-chief-economist-on-austerity/

[17] OECD, "OECD forecasts before and after the financial crisis: a post mortem," OECD Economics Department Policy Notes, no. 23, February 2014, www.oecd.org/eco/outlook/OECD-Forecast-post-mortem-policy-note.pdf

distortions in the single market. *The integrity of the single market needs therefore to be protected including through a strengthened State Aid regime.*
The Crisis Communications clearly spell out that even during the crisis the general principles of State aid control remain applicable. In particular, in order to limit distortions of competition between banks and across Member States in the single market and adress moral hazard, aid should be limited to the minimum necessary and an appropriate own contribution to restructuring costs should be provided by the aid beneficiary. The bank and its capital holders should contribute to the restructuring as much as possible with their own resources. State aid should be granted on terms which represent an adequate burden-sharing by those who have invested in the bank.
Such differerences in the approach to burden-sharing between Member States have led to divergent funding costs between banks depending on the perceived likelihood of a bail-in as a function of the Member State's fiscal strength. They pose a threat to the integrity of the single market and risk undermining the level playing field which State aid control aims to protect.[18]

We will see below how the Commission has imposed its conditions on bail-in before a bail-out is allowed, all in the name of equal competition aspects of the Single Market, even while inviting a macroprudential disaster.

What the European Union wants to achieve in terms of bail-out vs. bail-in[19]

We notice firstly that the emphasis of the Commission is still on the Single Market and the competitive aspects of the Union and only secondarily on stability concerns. Hence parsimonious states with stable government finances are to be prevented from aiding their domestic banks in relation to prodigal states without sufficient domestic financial resources. The lack of sufficient common financial backstops has, however, forced a political compromise on this point, as we shall see below.
This Commission focus on competition and disregard for the need for a credible financial backstop has received a severe rebuke from the European Central Bank, although framed in unobtrusive language so as to not insult a sister EU institution. Unfortunately, as we shall see

---

[18] Commission, "Communication... ", pp. 5–6, passim.
[19] See also Ferran, "Crisis-driven regulatory reform."

Box 6   Remarks by EU internal-markets Commissioner
Michel Barnier, 27 June 2013 (italics are mine)[20]

I am very pleased that finance ministers of the Member States
have managed a few minutes ago to reach broad political agreement on the future rules for how to restructure and resolve
failing banks. These rules are of utmost importance to protect
taxpayers from having to bail-out banks in the future. *They will*
be instrumental to deal with the threat of banks which today are
"too-big-to-fail" and to help overcome links between states and
banks which continue to weigh on economic growth.

The agreement represents a balanced compromise. I am
pleased that the fundamental principles and provisions in the
Commission's proposal have been accepted by Member States.

1. A comprehensive and credible framework

My first priority has been to ensure that the framework is robust
and clear. This has largely been secured. All banks will have to
prepare plans for times of distress and authorities will have
to ensure that all preventative steps are taken to deal with bank
failure. Authorities will have a broad range of powers and
tools to ensure that any failing bank can be restructured and
resolved in a way which preserves financial stability and pro-
tects taxpayers. *Critically, a harmonised rulebook is established*
for how the costs of bank failure are allocated – starting with
bank shareholders and creditors, and backed by financial sup-
port from resolution funds sourced from the banking sector and
not taxpayers.

---

[20] http://europa.eu/rapid/press-release_MEMO-13-601_el.htm; see
also remarks by Herman van Rompuy, president of the European
Council, "Towards a genuine economic and monetary union," 26 June
2012, EUCO 120/12, http://ec.europa.eu/economy_finance/crisis/docu
ments/131201_en.pdf and Rishi Goyal *et al.*, "A banking union for the
euro area," IMF Staff Discussion Note, SDN 13/01, 13 February 2013.

2. Integrity and unity of the Single Market

There is no divergence in the fundamental concepts of the framework between Member States, for example those in the Euro Area and those outside. *Banks in all Member States will be subject to harmonised provisions governing how resolution is carried out and how the costs are shared. No Member State will be able to subject banks to less onerous resolution arrangements, for example based on its fiscal strength.* As a result there will be no discrimination between investors in the EU and fragmentation in funding conditions for banks operating in different Member States will decrease. *A degree of necessary flexibility to carve out certain categories of creditors in order to protect financial stability has been given to national resolution authorities but it is sufficiently framed so that the integrity of the Single Market is not undermined.*

3. A strong regime for financing resolution

Discussions today focussed on the all-important details of how the costs of resolution are shared. From the start, I have insisted that the regime must convince markets and citizens that we are serious about ending public bailouts of banks. To the furthest extent possible, bank losses must be covered by private bank investors and the banking sector as a whole. As established in the run-up to today's meeting, there is an inextricable link between how much capacity there is within a bank to allocate losses to shareholders and creditors, how much flexibility is given to exclude one or other creditor from having to bear losses, and how much money has to be available in resolution funds sourced from the banking sector to cover any shortfall. Fortunately, the outcome ensures an appropriate equilibrium between these variables and I am confident the solution found is credible.

Today's agreement also paves the way for us to move forward with stage two of the Banking Union: the Single Resolution Mechanism. With the rulebook for how bank resolution across the EU well on the way to be finalised in coming months, the specific institutional mechanism necessary to carry it out in the most effective way for Member States participating in the Banking Union can be developed. This mechanism will complement the powers already conferred on the European Central Bank to supervise banks in Member States participating in the Banking Union, starting with all those in the Euro Area. The Single Resolution Mechanism will integrate critical aspects of decision-making and financing so that, notwithstanding greater supervisory scrutiny by the ECB, a possible bank failure can be managed in the most efficient and least disruptive way. The Commission will make a proposal accordingly in the coming weeks.

below, its critique fell on deaf ears as the compromise result on access to the common public purse is far too small to make an impact.

The ECB is of the view that, while subject to the principle of fiscal neutrality, access to fiscal resources would be an essential element of the SRM's [Single Resolution Mechanism] backstop arrangements. This is because private sources of funding may, especially at the start of the SRM, be scarce and temporarily dry up under acute financial market turmoil. The ECB understands that the Commission had not included an obligation on participating Member States to grant access to public funds as this could interfere with Member States' fiscal sovereignty which cannot be encroached upon under the legal basis of the proposed regulation. Against this background, the ECB considers it important that participating Member States cater for a joint and solid public backstop to be available upon the entry into force of the proposed regulation.[21]

And (ibid., p. 10, the emphasis is mine)

The ECB acknowledges that the State aid framework has proved essential in defining common parameters for national public support within the context

---

[21] European Central Bank, "Opinion of the European Central Bank of 6 November 2013 on a proposal for a Regulation of the European Parliament and of the Council..." (CON/2013/76), p. 9.

of bank resolution across the Union. However, the ECB is of the view that the impact of the application of State aid control and its impact on resolutions undertaken by the SRM should be carefully assessed. Once the SRM is fully operational, resolution decisions will be taken at the Union level, thus preserving the level playing field and not distorting the single market. In view of this, the parallel assessment under the State aid procedure should not delay, duplicate or hinder the resolution process. The aim of preserving the internal market and not distorting competition between the participating Member States and non-participating Member States can be achieved within the resolution process. Integration of State aid aspects into the resolution process may, in particular, be envisaged given that the Commission has the final decision-making power. *In any event, the application of the proposed regulation should ensure that State aid control neither results in any undue delays nor hinders the achievement of the resolution objectives, in particular given the need to protect financial stability.*

In a slightly earlier, leaked private letter to the Commission in July 2013, ECB president Mario Draghi sought – in vain – to modify the proposed rules limiting the possibility of taxpayer bail-outs. Draghi said in the letter that mandatory burden-sharing with shareholders and junior bondholders was warranted when a bank was on the brink of collapse or its capital had fallen below the minimum regulatory threshold. There could be cases, however, when a bank had a viable business model and its capital was above the minimum threshold, but its supervisor still required it to raise additional funds. In such cases, if the bank could not raise the capital needed in the market quickly enough, the ECB president said state aid should be possible without junior bondholders getting hit first. The letter also said incentives should be in place to ensure that banks did their best to raise private capital before resorting to state aid.[22]

Secondly, we note the similarity with the US situation after Dodd–Frank. Should a bail-in of (unsecured) creditors prove insufficient, the banks under supervision will be subject to an *ex post* levy to pay for the failures of other banks' risky adventures. This hardly creates the best incentive for careful and cautious bank management. And, moreover, it is hardly a credible policy in the midst of a systemic financial

---

[22] See http://m.ft.com/cms/s/0/13cc9614-397f-11e3-a3a4-00144feab7de.html and http://uk.reuters.com/article/2013/10/19/uk-banks-bondholders-draghi-idUKBRE99I03220131019

crisis. Since it is not credible, it invites speculation over what would really happen in a (new) crisis.

Resolution as an integral part of a European banking union[23]

Broadly viewed, a true banking union needs five legs. They must also be consistently and simultaneously put in place and applied; else it is like a stool with legs of uneven length.[24]

1. *A common currency and a common central bank acting as a reliable lender of last resort*

   In the United States, the Federal Reserve has been in existence since 1913; in Europe, the ECB was started only in 1999. However, aggressive actions ("quantitative easing" in the United States, "long-term refinancing operations," LTRO, and, from September 2012, "outright monetary transactions", OMT, in Europe) taken over the past crisis have given both central banks immense credibility, at the cost of a dramatic growth of their balance sheets, rising three to four times. Neither of them may, after the adoption of the Dodd–Frank Act in the US, lend to individual non-banks. This may create a problem if the origin of the next crisis is located in the "shadow banking sector," say a large hedge fund or an insurance company or even a large non-financial corporation, facing liquidity problems. It does seem rather illogical that the Federal Reserve Board is given the power to supervise non-bank holding companies deemed to be of systemic importance for financial stability but it may not lend to them individually.

2. *Common minimum rules for solvency and liquidity*

   A world-wide standardized basis is provided through the adoption of the Basel III rules, introduced in the United States by

---

[23] European Commission, "Communication from the Commission to the European Parliament and the Council, 'A roadmap towards a banking union,'" COM (2012) 510, 12 September, 2012; European Commission, "A blueprint for a deep and genuine economic and monetary union, launching a European debate," COM(2012) 777 final/2, 30 November 2012; European Council, "Towards a genuine economic and monetary union," Herman Van Rompuy, EUCO 120/12, 26 June 2012.

[24] See e.g. Nicolas Véron, "A realistic bridge towards European banking union," Petersen Institute for International Economics, Policy Brief 13–17, June 2013; Elliot, "Key issues on European banking union."

Dodd–Frank[25] and by the CRD IV package (Directive and Regulation) in the European Union. The US has, however, chosen to demand more stringent leverage (capital-to-total assets) ratios of its too-big-to-fail (TBTF) banks (6 percent as compared to Basel's 3 percent). Some countries in the European Union such as Sweden may fully utilize their right to charge its TBTF banks an extra capital charge in relation to risk-weighted assets of 5 percent rather than the 1–2.5 percent agreed upon by Basel's Financial Stability Board (FSB).[26] Banks must also fulfill the requirements by 2015 rather than 2018, as decreed by Basel.

We will have more to say on the sufficiency of capital ratios in the Conclusion.

3. *A Single Supervisory Mechanism (SSM)*[27]

There are clear similarities between the US and the EU in setting up a revised system of supervision. In Europe, the ECB is charged with the direct supervision of around 130 TBTF banks with assets corresponding to some 85 percent of total eurozone banking assets, with the characteristics stated below. It will also be the secondary supervisor to the 6,000 or so smaller banks supervised nationally in the euro area but not to the residual 2,000 banks chartered by non-euro member states, unless these countries choose to voluntarily join the Single Supervisory Mechanism (SSM).

The ECB will supervise banks from the eurozone and other participating countries:

If the value of their assets exceeds € 30 billion.

If the value of their assets exceeds both € 5 billion and 20 percent of the GDP of the member state in which it is located.

If the bank is among the three most significant banks of the country in which its headquarters is located.

If the bank has large cross-border activities.

If the bank receives assistance from a eurozone bail-out fund.

---

[25] But modified by the Collins Amendment to Dodd–Frank; see Chapter 17 and the Conclusion.

[26] However, only 3 percent can be charged under Pillar 1 and hence anything above will have to be charged under Pillar 2.

[27] See also Eilís Ferran and Valia S. G. Babis, "The European Single Supervisory Mechanism," University of Cambridge Faculty of Law Research Paper no. 10/2013, http://papers.ssrn.com/sol3/papers.cfm?abstract_id=2224538

In the United States, the Federal Reserve will supervise just over 30 domestic bank holding companies which have assets above 50 billion dollars, the other banks and bank holding companies being supervised by the OCC, the FDIC or by state supervisors, depending on their charter. Just as in Europe, these 30 banks have around 85 percent of total banking assets. In contrast to the ECB, however, the Fed will also supervise such non-bank holding companies as are deemed systemically important by the Financial Stability Oversight Council. The ECB will have no such rights. In sharp contrast also to the United States, there will, for the foreseeable future, exist no common Deposit Insurance Authority in Europe, acting as a secondary supervisor (and resolution authority; see below) to the central bank or to federal/state supervisors like the FDIC does in the US.

4. *Common Deposit Guarantee Authority and common Deposit Guarantee Fund*

   This is perhaps where the major difference between the United States and the European Union will exist over the coming years. Whilst there are rules for how much of deposits are guaranteed in both areas (250,000 dollars vs. 100,000 euro), the FDIC is the sole and unique deposit insurance authority in the US, whereas the deposit-insurance system in Europe is and will continue to be nationally fragmented. Furthermore, in the US, there exists a common ex ante bank-financed Deposit Insurance Fund (DIF), aiming at reaching 1.35 percent of covered deposits in the years to come. In Europe, many countries still lack pre-funded systems at all and they will only be required to attain the desired 0.8 percent of covered deposits by 2024. The critical difference is thus that banks in California may have paid their insurance fees to the DIF in order to compensate depositors in a crashed Florida bank, whereas in Europe, the only cooperation among the national deposit-insurance funds will be bilaterally arranged loans on a voluntary basis.

5. *A Single Resolution Authority, a Single Bank Resolution Fund and a common backstop under the Single Resolution Mechanism (SRM)*

   In the US, a decision on the resolution of a failing TBTF bank requires a vote with qualified majority by the FDIC and the Federal Reserve boards and the agreement of the secretary of the Treasury. Once the decision is taken, however, the FDIC is in sole and total control of the process, as described in the previous chapter. In the European Union, as developed in more detail later in this chapter, a resolution decision is a complex process involving the ECB as supervisor, the newly created Single Resolution Board (SRB), the EU Commission, the European Banking Authority (EBA), national regulators and ultimately the ECOFIN Council of (Finance) Ministers if the Board and the Commission have different opinions.

A common feature in Europe and the US is the insistence that not only shareholders but also unsecured creditors, junior as well as senior, be bailed in before any resolution fund or taxpayers' money is used. Or rather, in the United States as we have seen, there is no fund strictly speaking to correspond to the Orderly Liquidation Fund and in Europe, the resolution funds, while prefunded by bank fees on a risk-based basis, will be national for the time being and only gradually communalized and will attain only 1 percent of covered deposits, or an estimated 70 billion euro (of which 55 billion in the Euro area). A minimum of 8 percent of banks' total liabilities and equity must be bailed in before the resolution fund is to be accessed. See below.

As a final backstop, the existing 500 billion euro European Stability Mechanism (ESM) may be used, but only partly (up to 60 billion euro), to recapitalize bridge banks directly and only once the single supervisory mechanism is in place and only provided that the ECB takes over the supervision of the bank in question, if it is not already the supervisor. The ESM would then become the (temporary) partial owner of the distressed bank, a role for which it has no prior experience.[28]

The 55 billion euro single resolution fund corresponds to approximately 0.1 percent of total banking assets in the European Union, according to statistics from the European Banking Federation (EBF), and a slightly higher proportion of euro area bank assets, comprising 72 percent of the total. This corresponds to some 0.4 percent of the

---

[28] "In the meantime, a country could request aid from the European Stability Mechanism. Yet policymakers say they purposefully made that option very hard to take. The chances of the ESM stepping in are 'very, very small,' Dutch finance minister Jeroen Dijsselbloem told lawmakers in The Hague on 2 July." www.bloomberg.com/news/2014-08-06/espirito-santo-shows-eu-s-need-for-speed-under-new-banking-rules.html

area's GDP. We recall that costs of recapitalization during the last crisis have been, on average, 3–4 percent of GDP in the majority of countries even after repayments and an average of 7 percent of GDP gross, i.e. during the crisis phase (see Table 1). The conclusion speaks for itself.

An additional complicating factor is that since member states could not agree, the Single Resolution Fund (SRF) will not be guided entirely by EU rules but its gradual mutualization is decided upon by a separately agreed mechanism among the participating countries outside of normal EU legislation.[29,30] The European Parliament objected to this feature, demanding that the Fund be created through normal EU treaties, subject to the Parliament's decision.[31]

The five legs of the Banking Union are obviously interdependent and should ideally be introduced simultaneously. In particular, it might be highly dangerous if the ECB starts its activity as planned in October–November 2014 with an Asset Quality Review of the 130 banks under its supervision, followed by a tough stress test under the supervision of the EBA. Without a resolution authority, the Single Resolution Board, and a sufficient financial backstop in place, markets may well panic, while pondering over where the necessary new capital infusion to banks that failed the test will come from. As detailed more below and in the references in the footnote, the Single Resolution Board must be able to draw primarily on the resources of the ESM with the involved countries' taxpayers as ultimate back-up.[32]

---

[29] The InterGovernmental Agreement (IGA) on mutualizing the Single Resolution Fund was signed by 26 of the 28 members, Britain and Sweden abstaining. See http://europa.eu/rapid/press-release_STATEMENT-14-165_en.htm

[30] In the Council agreement in December 2013, the Irish finance minister Michael Noonan pleaded the case for a backstop to underpin the bank-failure fund given its limited capacity, saying markets need a sign that a plan's in place. "When you think of European banks having multi-trillions of assets on their balance sheets, the fund itself is quite small," Noonan said. "Maybe if we could bring forward the date of consideration of the backstop, or if we had an agreement that a backstop would be in place by a certain date, that might help the credibility of the system." www.irishtimes.com/business/economy/proposals-to-break-deadlock-on-bank-fund-put-forward-at-ecofin-1.1696134

[31] www.ft.com/intl/cms/s/0/7c1d0dda-7ec0-11e3-8642-00144feabdc0.html; www.bloomberg.com/news/2014-03-10/eu-bank-crisis-talks-resume-as-draghi-watches-attentively.html

[32] Stefano Micosse, Ginevra Bruzzone and Jacopo Carmassi, "The new European framework for managing bank crises," CEPS Policy Brief 304, 21 November 2013; Thorsten Beck, Daniel Gros and Dirk Schoenmaker, "On the design

The OECD has calculated that the 200 largest eurozone banks will need to raise an additional 300–400 billion euro in new equity to pass.[33] This may be compared with the 30 billion euro actually raised in the first half-year of 2014. We will come back to this issue in the Conclusion.

Detailed analysis of the proposed treaties

The proposed new treaties consist of a Regulation on the Single Resolution Mechanism (SRM) and a Directive on Bank Recovery and Resolution (BRRD), partly overlapping. The Regulation applies formally to all the members of the European Union but is applicable only to the eurozone (and other participating) countries whose banks are supervised directly or indirectly by the ECB under the SSM while the Directive is applicable for all EU member states.

The Regulation puts in place the path resolution authorities under the Single Resolution Mechanism (SRM) must follow.[34] The procedure of how a resolution is to be conducted is spelled out in article 16 of the SRM Regulation.

The ECB in its role as the overall supervisor, aided by national supervisors for smaller banks, would give the alarm when a bank supervised

of a single resolution mechanism," in European Parliament, "Banking union: the Single Resolution Mechanism," Monetary Dialogue, 18 February 2013 (Nicolas Véron *et al.*); Charles Wyplosz, "Banking union as crisis management tool," in Thorstein Beck, ed., *Banking Union for Europe, Risks and Challenges* (London: CEPR and VoxEU.org, 2012); Dirk Schoenmaker, *Governance of International Banking: The Financial Trilemma* (Oxford and New York: Oxford University Press, 2013); "From bail-out to bail-in," *The Economist*, 14 December 2013, www.economist.com/blogs/freeexchange/2013/12/european-banks

[33] www.bloomberg.com/news/2013-07-23/european-banks-face-capital-gap-with-focus-on-leverage.html

[34] Regulation (EU) no. 86/2014 of the European Parliament and of the Council of 15 July 2014 establishing uniform rules and a uniform procedure for the resolution of credit institutions and certain investment firms in the framework of a Single Resolution Mechanism and a Single Bank Resolution Fund and amending Regulation (EU) no. 1093/2010, see http://eur-lex.europa.eu/legal-content/EN/TXT/HTML/?uri=OJ:L:2014:225:FULL&from=EN. See also www.europarl.europa.eu/news/en/news-room/content/20140411IPR43458/html/Parliament-lifts-bank-bailout-burden-fromtaxpayers%E2%80%99-shoulders and www.consilium.europa.eu/uedocs/cms_data/docs/pressdata/en/ecofin/143925.pdf

under the SSM mechanism finds itself in trouble and is likely to fail. The Single Resolution Board with its five executive members and including representatives from the relevant national authorities (as well as representatives of the ECB and the European Commission as observers) would prepare for the resolution of the bank. Is the bank viable? What are its assets really worth? Can the bank be sold? Should a bridge bank be set up? Should good and bad assets be separated? Should the bank be continued after a bail-in of creditors, with unsecured bank debt being converted to equity or written off? Will resolution involve the Single Resolution Fund?

On the basis of the Board's recommendation, the EU Commission will decide whether and how to place a bank in resolution and it would also spell out a framework for the use of resolution tools (bridge bank, sale, asset separation, bail in). See below on the Directive. The Commission's role would normally be limited to the formal decision to trigger the resolution of a bank and the decision on the resolution framework, thereby ensuring its consistency with the Single Market and with EU rules on state aid.[35]

The reason is the following. Under existing EU treaties, neither the Single Resolution Board nor any other agency such as the European Banking Authority (EBA) may take such as decision at the EU level, which is reserved for an EU institution such as the Commission, the ECB or the Council. This limit on the delegation of power follows the so-called "Meroni doctrine," named after a case where the European Court of Justice (ECJ) in 1958 challenged a decision by the High Authority of the European Coal and Steel Community (the predecessor of the Commission). In 2005, the ECJ gave a clear signal that the distinctions outlined in the doctrine still apply. Referring directly to *Meroni*, the Court upheld the conferral of power to one of the organs of the European Central Bank, stating that

[w]ith regard to the conditions to be complied with in the context of such delegations of powers, it should be recalled that, as the Court held in *Meroni*, first, a delegating authority cannot confer upon the authority to which the powers are delegated powers different from those which it has

---

[35] If within 24 hours the Commission has failed to react, the Board's proposal is put into action.

itself received. Secondly, the exercise of the powers entrusted to the body to which the powers are delegated must be subject to the same conditions as those to which it would be subject if the delegating authority exercised them directly, particularly as regards the requirements to state reasons and to publish. Finally, even when entitled to delegate its powers, the delegating authority must take an express decision transferring them and the delegation can relate only to clearly defined executive power.[36]

If the Commission objects to the proposal by the SRB, the matter is referred to the Council of Ministers which takes a decision by simple majority. The Board is obligated to set out a revised resolution plan following the decision by the Council. After the first 24 hours, the Board has 8 hours to formulate an alternative, for a total of 32 hours, making it in the early hours of Sunday if the process is started as it should on Friday evening.

Proposal 4

Given the lack of financial and economic competence of the Commission on banking issues as well as its almost exclusive focus on the Single Market and competition aspects, it would be preferable to create the Single Resolution Board within the ECB, thereby creating a parallel institution to the ECB in its role as the operator of the Single Supervisory Mechanism. This would echo the Bank of England's setting up a Special Resolution Unit within the Bank in parallel to its Prudential Regulatory Authority (PRA), the country's main financial supervisor together with the Financial Policy Committee.[37] This would leave the Commission to focus on competition matters, just as the Financial Conduct Authority does in the UK.

It would have been preferable to house the Single Resolution Board within a common Deposit Insurance Authority as in the United States (and other countries such as Sweden) but given the absence of such a common Deposit Insurance Authority for the foreseeable future, the ECB solution seems to be the only feasible alternative.

[36] www.publications.parliament.uk/pa/cm200809/cmselect/cmeuleg/19xxx/1905.htm

[37] www.bankofengland.co.uk/FINANCIALSTABILITY/Pages/role/risk_reduction/srr/default.aspx

Let us turn now to the issue of bail-in and bail-out. Box 7 shows the salient features of the Directive on the Recovery and Resolution of credit institutions (BRRD), in particular as concerns the conditions for bail-out and bail-in (italics are mine).[38]

Evaluation

Despite the words of Commissioner Barnier, quoted above, that only the banking industry itself and bank owners and creditors should bear the costs of bank failures, a taxpayer bail-out is not outlawed but made more difficult. Bail-in of shareholders and other creditors must amount to 8 percent of total assets of the institution before a bail-out is allowed. And the injection of capital must in the first place come from the built-up resolution (stabilization) funds and may only amount to 5 percent of the total balance sheet of the saved institution.

Given that the ratio of risk-weighted assets to total assets in European banks is, on average, around one-third the demand for an 8 percent bail-in would mean that only banks with Basel III CET1/ RWA ratios higher than 24 percent will be able to avoid bailing in subordinated and senior creditors. It may be compared with an actual average core Tier 1 ratio to risk-weighted assets of 11.7 percent in December 2013.[39] Even the largest SIFI banks will not be required to have more than 12 percent equity in relation to risk-weighted assets by 2018.[40,41]

---

[38] European Union, Directive 2014/59/EU of the European Parliament and of the Council of 15 May 2014 establishing a framework for the recovery and resolution of credit institutions and investment firms and amending Council Directive 82/891/EEC, and Directives 2001/24/EC, 2002/47/EC, 2004/25/EC, 2005/56/ EC, 2007/36/EC, 2011/35/EU, 2012/30/EU and 2013/36/EU, and Regulations (EU) no. 1093/2010 and (EU) no. 648/2012, of the European Parliament and of the Council, *Official Journal* L 173/190, 12.6.2014. http://eur-lex.europa.eu/ legal-content/EN/TXT/HTML/?uri=OJ:L:2014:173:FULL&from=EN

[39] Source: www.ft.com/cms/s/0/e4d05a72-0141-11e4-9750-00144feab7de. html#axzz39L5Hspwf

[40] Basel III establishes a 4.5 percent minimum capital charge of Common Equity Tier 1 (CET1) to risk-weighted assets (RWA) on top of which comes a capital-conservation buffer of 2.5 percent, a cyclical buffer of a maximum of 2.5 percent and a SIFI charge of 2.5 percent for the largest institutions.

[41] www.bloomberg.com/news/2013-12-16/eu-banks-shrink-assets-by-1-1-trillion-as-capital-ratios-rise.html

Box 7 Directive on the recovery and resolution of credit institutions (BRRD)

The conditions for state aid are spelled out already in the Preamble to the Directive, stating:

(73) Where those exclusions are applied, the level of write down or conversion of other eligible liabilities may be increased to take account of such exclusions subject to the 'no creditor worse off than under normal insolvency proceedings' principle being respected. Where the losses cannot be passed to other creditors, *the resolution financing arrangement may make a contribution to the institution under resolution subject to a number of strict conditions including the requirement that losses totalling not less than 8% of total liabilities including own funds have already been absorbed, and the funding provided by the resolution fund is limited to the lower of 5% of total liabilities including own funds or the means available to the resolution fund and the amount that can be raised through ex-post contributions within three years.*

(74) In extraordinary circumstances, where liabilities have been excluded and the resolution fund has been used to contribute to bail-in in lieu of those liabilities to the extent of the permissible cap, the resolution authority should be able to seek funding from alternative financing sources.

(75) *The minimum amount of contribution to loss absorption and recapitalisation of 8% of total liabilities including own funds or, where applicable, of 20% of risk-weighted assets should be calculated based on the valuation for the purposes of resolution in accordance with this Directive.* Historical losses which have already been absorbed by shareholders through a reduction in own funds prior to such a valuation should not be included in those percentages.

Article 34

General principles governing resolution

1. Member States shall ensure that, when applying the resolution tools and exercising the resolution powers, resolution authorities take all appropriate measures to ensure that the resolution action is taken in accordance with the following principles:

   (a) *the shareholders of the institution under resolution bear first losses;*

   (b) *creditors of the institution under resolution bear losses after the shareholders in accordance with the order of priority of their claims under normal insolvency proceedings, save as expressly provided otherwise in this Directive;*

Article 37

General principles of resolution tools

1. Member States shall ensure that resolution authorities have the necessary powers to apply the resolution tools to institutions and to entities referred to in point (b), (c) or (d) of Article 1(1) that meet the applicable conditions for resolution.

2. Where a resolution authority decides to apply a resolution tool to an institution or entity referred to in point (b), (c) or (d) of Article 1(1), and that resolution action would result in losses being borne by creditors or their claims being converted, the resolution authority shall exercise the power to write down and convert capital instruments in accordance with Article 59 immediately before or together with the application of the resolution tool.

3. *The resolution tools referred to in paragraph 1 are the following:*

   (a) *the sale of business tool;*

   (b) *the bridge institution tool;*

(c) *the asset separation tool;*

(d) *the bail-in tool.*

4. *Subject to paragraph 5, resolution authorities may apply the resolution tools individually or in any combination.*

5. Resolution authorities may apply the asset separation tool only together with another resolution tool.

Article 43

The bail-in tool

1. In order to give effect to the bail-in tool, Member States shall ensure that resolution authorities have the resolution powers specified in Article 63(1).

2. Member States shall ensure that resolution authorities may apply the bail-in tool to meet the resolution objectives specified in Article 31, in accordance with the resolution principles specified in Article 34 for any of the following purposes:

   (a) to recapitalise an institution or an entity referred to in point (b), (c) or (d) of Article 1(1) of this Directive that meets the conditions for resolution to the extent sufficient to restore its ability to comply with the conditions for authorisation (to the extent that those conditions apply to the entity) and to continue to carry out the activities for which it is authorised under Directive 2013/36/EU or Directive 2014/65/EU, where the entity is authorised under those Directives, and to sustain sufficient market confidence in the institution or entity;

   (b) to convert to equity or reduce the principal amount of claims or debt instruments that are transferred:

      (i) to a bridge institution with a view to providing capital for that bridge institution; or

      (ii) under the sale of business tool or the asset separation tool.

Article 44

Scope of bail-in tool

1. Member States shall ensure that the bail-in tool may be applied to all liabilities of an institution or entity referred to in point (b), (c) or (d) of Article 1(1) that are not excluded from the scope of that tool pursuant to paragraphs 2 or 3 of this Article.

2. Resolution authorities shall not exercise the write down or conversion powers in relation to the following liabilities whether they are governed by the law of a Member State or of a third country:

   (a) covered deposits;

   (b) secured liabilities including covered bonds and liabilities in the form of financial instruments used for hedging purposes which form an integral part of the cover pool and which according to national law are secured in a way similar to covered bonds;

   (c) any liability that arises by virtue of the holding by the institution or entity referred to in point (b), (c) or (d) of Article 1(1) of this Directive of client assets or client money including client assets or client money held on behalf of UCITS as defined in Article 1(2) of Directive 2009/65/EC or of AIFs as defined in point (a) of Article 4(1) of Directive 2011/61/EU of the European Parliament and of the Council, provided that such a client is protected under the applicable insolvency law;

   (d) any liability that arises by virtue of a fiduciary relationship between the institution or entity referred to in point (b), (c) or (d) of Article 1(1) (as fiduciary) and another person (as beneficiary) provided that such a beneficiary is protected under the applicable insolvency or civil law;

   (e) liabilities to institutions, excluding entities that are part of the same group, with an original maturity of less than seven days;

   (f) liabilities with a remaining maturity of less than seven days, owed to systems or operators of systems designated according to Directive 98/26/EC or their participants and arising from the participation in such a system;

(g) a liability to any one of the following:

   (i) an employee, in relation to accrued salary, pension benefits or other fixed remuneration, except for the variable component of remuneration that is not regulated by a collective bargaining agreement;

   (ii) a commercial or trade creditor arising from the provision to the institution or entity referred to in point (b), (c) or (d) of Article 1(1) of goods or services that are critical to the daily functioning of its operations, including IT services, utilities and the rental, servicing and upkeep of premises;

   (iii) tax and social security authorities, provided that those liabilities are preferred under the applicable law;

   (iv) deposit guarantee schemes arising from contributions due in accordance with Directive 2014/49/EU.

Article 57

Public equity support tool

1. *Member States may, while complying with national company law, participate in the recapitalisation of an institution or an entity referred to in point (b), (c) or (d) of Article 1(1) of this Directive by providing capital to the latter in exchange for the following instruments, subject to the requirements of Regulation (EU) No. 575/2013:*

   (a) Common Equity Tier 1 instruments;

   (b) Additional Tier 1 instruments or Tier 2 instruments.

2. Member States shall ensure, to the extent that their shareholding in an institution or an entity referred to in point (b), (c) or (d) of Article 1(1) permits, that such institutions or entities subject to public equity support tool in accordance with this Article are managed on a commercial and professional basis.

3. Where a Member State provides public equity support tool in accordance with this Article, it shall ensure that its holding in the institution or an entity referred to in point (b), (c) or (d) of Article 1(1) is transferred to the private sector as soon as commercial and financial circumstances allow.

Article 99

European system of financing arrangements

A European system of financing arrangements shall be established and shall consist of:
   (a) national financing arrangements established in accordance with Article 100;
   (b) the borrowing between national financing arrangements as specified in Article 106;
   (c) the mutualisation of national financing arrangements in the case of a group resolution as referred to in Article 107.

Article 100

Requirement to establish resolution financing arrangements

1. Member States shall establish one or more financing arrangements for the purpose of ensuring the effective application by the resolution authority of the resolution tools and powers.

   Member States shall ensure that the use of the financing arrangements may be triggered by a designated public authority or authority entrusted with public administrative powers.

   The financing arrangements shall be used only in accordance with the resolution objectives and the principles set out in Articles 31 and 34.

2. Member States may use the same administrative structure as their financing arrangements for the purposes of their deposit guarantee scheme.

3. Member States shall ensure that the financing arrangements have adequate financial resources.

4. For the purpose of paragraph 3, financing arrangements shall in particular have the power to:
   (a) raise *ex-ante* contributions as referred to in Article 103 with a view to reaching the target level specified in Article 102;
   (b) raise *ex-post* extraordinary contributions as referred to in Article 104 where the contributions specified in point (a) are insufficient; and
   (c) contract borrowings and other forms of support as referred to in Article 105.
5. Save where permitted under paragraph 6, each Member State shall establish its national financing arrangements through a fund, the use of which may be triggered by its resolution authority for the purposes set out in Article 101(1).

Article 101

Use of the resolution financing arrangements

1. The financing arrangements established in accordance with Article 100 may be used by the resolution authority only to the extent necessary to ensure the effective application of the resolution tools, for the following purposes:
   (a) to guarantee the assets or the liabilities of the institution under resolution, its subsidiaries, a bridge institution or an asset management vehicle;
   (b) to make loans to the institution under resolution, its subsidiaries, a bridge institution or an asset management vehicle;
   (c) to purchase assets of the institution under resolution;
   (d) to make contributions to a bridge institution and an asset management vehicle;
   (e) to pay compensation to shareholders or creditors in accordance with Article 75;
   (f) to make a contribution to the institution under resolution in lieu of the write down or conversion of liabilities of certain creditors, when the bail-in tool is applied and the resolution

authority decides to exclude certain creditors from the scope of bail-in in accordance with Article 44(3) to (8);

(g) to lend to other financing arrangements on a voluntary basis in accordance with Article 106;

(h) to take any combination of the actions referred to in points (a) to (g).

The financing arrangements may be used to take the actions referred to in the first subparagraph also with respect to the purchaser in the context of the sale of business tool.

2. *The resolution financing arrangement shall not be used directly to absorb the losses of an institution or an entity referred to in point (b), (c) or (d) of Article 1(1) or to recapitalise such an institution or an entity.* In the event that the use of the resolution financing arrangement for the purposes in paragraph 1 of this Article indirectly results in part of the losses of an institution or an entity referred to in point (b), (c) or (d) of Article 1(1) being passed on to the resolution financing arrangement, the principles governing the use of the resolution financing arrangement set out in Article 44 shall apply.

Article 102

Target level

1. *Member States shall ensure that, by 31 December 2024, the available financial means of their financing arrangements reach at least 1% of the amount of covered deposits of all the institutions authorised in their territory. Member States may set target levels in excess of that amount.*

Article 103

Ex-ante contributions

1. In order to reach the target level specified in Article 102, Member States shall ensure that contributions are raised at least annually from the institutions authorised in their territory including Union branches.

2. The contribution of each institution shall be pro rata to the amount of its liabilities (excluding own funds) less covered deposits, with respect to the aggregate liabilities (excluding own funds) less covered deposits of all the institutions authorised in the territory of the Member State.

   Those contributions shall be adjusted in proportion to the risk profile of institutions, in accordance with the criteria adopted under paragraph 7.

7. The Commission shall be empowered to adopt delegated acts in accordance with Article 115 in order to specify the notion of adjusting contributions in proportion to the risk profile of institutions as referred to in paragraph 2 of this Article, taking into account all of the following:

   (a) the risk exposure of the institution, including the importance of its trading activities, its off-balance sheet exposures and its degree of leverage;

   (b) the stability and variety of the company's sources of funding and unencumbered highly liquid assets;

   (c) the financial condition of the institution;

   (d) the probability that the institution enters into resolution;

   (e) the extent to which the institution has previously benefited from extraordinary public financial support;

   (f) the complexity of the structure of the institution and its resolvability;

   (g) the importance of the institution to the stability of the financial system or economy of one or more Member States or of the Union;

   (h) the fact that the institution is part of an IPS.

Article 104

Extraordinary ex-post contributions

1. Where the available financial means are not sufficient to cover the losses, costs or other expenses incurred by the use of the financing arrangements, Member States shall ensure

that extraordinary ex-post contributions are raised from the institutions authorised in their territory, in order to cover the additional amounts. Those extraordinary ex-post contributions shall be allocated between institutions in accordance with the rules laid down in Article 103(2).

Extraordinary ex-post contributions shall not exceed three times the annual amount of contributions determined in accordance with Article 103.

Article 109

Use of deposit guarantee schemes in the context of resolution

When the bail-in tool is applied, the deposit guarantee scheme shall not be required to make any contribution towards the costs of recapitalising the institution or bridge institution pursuant to point (b) of Article 46(1).

For countries such as Sweden which has already built up a resolution (stabilization) fund in excess of 3 percent of covered deposits, the requirement may be lowered to 20 percent of risk-weighted assets.[42,43] However, in no case must the resolution fund or taxpayers inject more than 5 percent of total assets into a bank as new capital and the money must be repaid within five years (the same time frame as for the use of the US Orderly Liquidation Fund).

The possibility of bailing in senior unsecured creditors has also been brought forward to 2016 from the original 2018.[44]

---

[42] The exception requires that the fund is entirely prepaid which is not yet the case in Sweden, the government's start-up injection of 15 billion SEK not having been paid up.

[43] As of the end of 2013, the Swedish stabilization fund contained 49 billion SEK which divided by some 1,300 billion in covered deposits yields a ratio of 3.7 percent. This corresponds to 1.3 percent of GDP and will, in the absence of payouts, increase with the annual charge of 0.036 percent on bank liabilities, the earlier ceiling for the fund of 2.5 percent of GDP having been scrapped.

[44] www.ft.com/intl/cms/s/0/555f3ade-6303-11e3-a87d-144feabdc0.html?siteedition=uk#axzz2vvM638At

Should a bail-in prove insufficient, the possibility exists of ex post charges on the supervised financial institutions, just like under Dodd–Frank.

Despite the optimistic proposal of the Commission in 2010, the result in the form of a common financial backstop (Single Bank Resolution Fund) is much more limited.[45] Only after 10 years will the Resolution Fund reach 1 percent of covered deposits (around 55 billion euro in the euro area) and it will stay national and only be gradually communalized during these 10 years. It will be financed by a risk-based fee on the liabilities of the participating institutions.

The fund may be used to:

guarantee assets or liabilities of the bank under resolution, or a
    bridge bank or an asset-management vehicle ("bad bank");
make loans to the above-mentioned institutions;
purchase assets from the banks under resolution;
contribute capital to a bridge bank or asset-management vehicle.

The fund may not, however, be used to recapitalize a going concern and any amount spent must, as noted above, be repaid within five years.

The other and more important reason why taxpayers are likely to be involved in the next crisis is that the proposed structure is not credible, as indicated also by the comments below. Neither domestic resolution funds nor the common fund will be sufficient; nor is the threat to bail in also senior bondholders and uninsured depositors. As well stated by Oliver Burrows from Dutch Rabobank: "If you bail in senior bondholders, capital markets will freeze … and the bank concerned will not be able to fund itself again. If you're a regulator, the answer is not to drop a nuclear bomb but to find a diplomatic solution."[46,47]

---

[45] European Commission, "Bank resolution funds," COM (2010) 254 Final, 26 May 2010.

[46] *Financial Times*, 8 August 2014: "Bank bond investors sleepwalk into bail-ins."

[47] It is remarkable that the Commission document on which the proposal is based makes no mention of possible runs by creditors as a bail-in becomes anticipated. See DG Internal Market, "Discussion paper on the debt write-down tool – bail-in," undated, http://ec.europa.eu/internal_market/bank/docs/crisis-management/discussion_paper_bail_in_en.pdf

Proposal 5

As the US secretary of the Treasury, Jack Lew, succinctly put it, the proposed European resolution fund is "too little, too late."[48] Nor will it break the "doom loop" between sovereign risk and bank risk.

National funds are natural elements in those countries which prefer to stay out of the common resolution mechanism. These funds also need a financial backstop. As indicated earlier, Sweden's stabilization fund already corresponds to 1.3 percent of GDP and will ultimately attain at least 3 percent of GDP. For these countries, it must be possible to use the national fund to recapitalize banks much earlier than present restrictions allow. The national stabilization fund must also, as does the Swedish one, have an unlimited borrowing right in the Treasury (in the Swedish case, the National Debt Office, an authority under the Treasury).

For banks participating in the SSM and SRM, in the absence of a common Single Resolution Fund, the Single Bank Resolution Board must be given the financial means to fulfill its mission. For the time being, this can only mean using the resources of the European Stabilization Mechanism (ESM), 500 billion euro. At the demand of the SRB, it must be made possible for the ESM to lend to individual banks in the euro area directly rather than to their sovereign. However, as noted above, the ESM does not constitute an ideal owner of failing banks (even though it will create a subsidiary for that purpose). Hence, as regards recapitalizations, the ESM should extend the necessary funds to the Bank Resolution Board which will then inject fresh capital into the ailing banks, a subsidiary of the Board becoming the partial and temporary owner of the (bridge) bank.

However, in order to avoid subsidizing "zombie banks," the present restriction that the ESM may only participate in recapitalizations of banks having a minimum of 4.5 percent CET1/RWA is sensible. Normally, this minimum amount would be expected to be provided by bail-ins or by the member state in question. The member state will also share 20/80 with the ESM in a further recapitalization, in order to attain the capital ratio decreed by the relevant supervisor.[49]

---

[48] www.reuters.com/article/2014/01/07/us-france-lew-idUSBREA060M 120140107

[49] European Stability Mechanism, "ESM direct bank recapitalisation instrument," Luxembourg, 20 June 2013, www.consilium.europa.eu/uedocs/cms_data/docs/ pressdata/en/ecofin/137569.pdf

Major criticisms against the SSM/SRM/SRF structure have begun to appear (this is written in September 2014). Comments mimic much of the critique enumerated above. Firstly, the resolution mechanism is unwieldy and too politicized. Secondly, without common deposit insurance and a deposit insurance fund, bank runs will be an inevitable part of the next crisis, in particular since deposits above 100,000 euro may also be bailed in. Thirdly, there is no requirement for banks to hold sufficient amounts of bailable instruments like subordinated debt and CoCos. Fourthly, in particular on account of the limited size of the resolution funds, there must be a backstop in the form of the ESM and, ultimately, the taxpayers. Fifthly, the link between sovereigns and banks through banks' holdings of sovereign bond remains and is becoming a gradually larger threat.

As Professor Emilios Avgouleas from the University of Edinburgh Law School commented:

[The paper] explains why bail-in regimes will fail to eradicate the need for an injection of public funds where there is a threat of systemic collapse, because a number of banks have simultaneously entered into difficulties, or in the event of the failure of a large complex cross-border bank, except in those cases where failure was clearly idiosyncratic.[50]

Another critical voice is Lorenzo Bini-Smaghi, a former member of the ECB Executive Board:

The mechanism is unsatisfactory from several viewpoints. The decision-making process is cumbersome and involves too many bodies. The funds are insufficient to tackle a big banking problem. The ability of the mechanism to borrow in the markets is still unclear. The period of transition to the final system is too long, at least compared to the frequency of banking crises. Overall, the separation between banking and sovereign risk – which was the main goal of the union – has not been achieved. [51]

---

[50] Emilios Avgouleas and Charles Goodhart, "A critical evaluation of bail-in as a bank recapitalization tool," paper prepared for the conference on "Bearing the losses from bank and sovereign default in the eurozone," organized by Franklin Allen, Elena Carletti and Joanna Gray at the European University Institute, Florence, 24 April 2014.

[51] http://blogs.ft.com/the-a-list/2013/12/19/the-european-banking-union-is-a-disappointment/

Among critical articles that still show a way forward we find this from Jeffrey N. Gordon and Wolf-Georg Ringe:

The project of creating a Banking Union is designed to overcome the fatal link between sovereigns and their banks in the Eurozone. As part of this project, political agreement for a common supervision framework and a common resolution scheme has been reached with difficulty. However, the resolution framework is weak, underfunded and exhibits some serious flaws. Further, Member States' disagreements appear to rule out a federalized deposit insurance scheme, commonly regarded as the necessary third pillar of a successful Banking Union.

This paper argues for an organizational and capital structure substitute for these two shortcomings that can minimize the systemic distress costs of the failure of a large financial institution. We borrow from the approach the Federal Deposit Insurance Corporation (FDIC) has devised in the implementation of the "Orderly Liquidation Authority" under the Dodd Frank Act. The FDIC's experience teaches us three important lessons: first, systemically important institutions need to have in their liability structure sufficient unsecured (or otherwise subordinated) term debt so that in the event of bank failure, the conversion of debt into equity will be sufficient to absorb asset losses without impairing deposits and other short term credit; second, the organizational structure of the financial institution needs to permit such a debt conversion without putting core financial constituents through a bankruptcy or other resolution process, and third, a federal funding mechanism deployable at the discretion of the resolution authority must be available to supply liquidity to a reorganizing bank. On these conditions, a viable and realistic Banking Union would be within reach – and the resolution of global financial institutions would be greatly facilitated, not least in a transatlantic perspective.

The Single Resolution Mechanism (SRM) just enacted by the European Parliament will fail in its essential mission of managing the failure of a systemically important bank in a way that overcomes the fatal link between sovereigns and their banks. The SRM simply provides no strategy to avoid contagion from a bank failure because depositors and short-term creditors are not adequately protected, due to an insufficient resolution fund and the absence of a credible, centralized deposit insurance scheme. If bank resolution is not a credible threat, then the Single Supervisory Mechanism of the European Banking Union will be a paper tiger. (*Jeffrey N. Gordon, Richard Paul Richman Professor of Law, Columbia Law School; Wolf-Georg Ringe, Professor of International Commercial Law, Copenhagen Business School & University of Oxford*)[52]

---

[52] Jeffrey N. Gordon and Wolf-Georg Ringe, "Bank resolution in the European banking union: a transatlantic perspective," Columbia Law and Economics

Other experts have been seemingly more positive. Eilís Ferran writes:

Yet it is important not to lose sight of how far the EU, or more especially the euro area, has come in financial regulation since 2008. The overhaul of prudential regulation and supervision has been far-reaching. There has been a remarkable shift of power from national to supranational (EU and euro area) authorities. The links between banks and sovereigns may not have been fully broken but they have certainly been considerably weakened. From being a topic that was not even on the regulatory policy radar prior to the crisis, a sophisticated EU regime for the resolution of failing banks has been agreed, and it includes an array of procedures and tools, including bail-in powers that, in time, should reduce considerably the likelihood of a need to call upon public funding. An apparatus for industry funding of resolution processes is emerging. Innovative legal thinking is continuing to refine approaches to resolution planning, including a much richer understanding of the interrelationship between the structure of banking groups and the choice of resolution strategies. There is even already a common public sector back-stop of sorts for the euro area in the form of the ESM, which, albeit subject to strict conditionality and only up to a limited amount, will be available once the SSM is effective to recapitalize ailing banks directly as well as to stabilize the public finances of ESM Members. The ESM has the potential to play a role in resolution funding support as well, at least for an interim period.

The conclusion that this points to is that there has been put in place a legal framework that, on balance, is sufficiently robust to equip the institutional apparatus of EBU with sufficient authority and credibility to begin to rebuild confidence and, in that way, to contribute to the reversal of the trend towards EU financial market disintegration. That is progress.[53]

But a caveat is that she is mostly concerned with the stability of the *legal* foundations of the treaties (SSM and SRM), not their *economic stability*. Or as she writes: "From this analysis the paper builds the case for the claim that the legal framework for the two mechanisms is sufficiently robust for the new arrangements to have the authority and credibility to rebuild confidence and, in that way, to contribute to the reversal of the trend towards EU financial market disintegration."

Working Paper no. 465, 22 July 2014 http://papers.ssrn.com/sol3/papers. cfm?abstract_id=2361347

[53] Eilís Ferran, "European banking union: imperfect but can it work?" University of Cambridge Faculty of Law Research Paper, no. 30, 2014, http://papers.ssrn. com/sol3/papers.cfm?abstract_id=2426247

Another highly competent observer, Daniel Gros, director of the Centre for European Policy Studies (CEPS), has recently concluded: "This compromise on the SRM is an inelegant step in the right direction. It leaves as many problems unresolved as it addresses. The riders on the European bicycle will have to continue to pedal for some time."[54]

Another observer, Thierry Philipponnat, secretary general of the Brussels-based Finance Watch research group, has said: "It is clear that important flaws remain in the design of banking union, not least the presence of banking structures that are incompatible with a credible bail-in and resolution mechanism."[55]

What he was referring to, in particular, was the continued preferential treatment of sovereign debt in the banking book which means that the "doom loop" between sovereign and bank risk is far from broken: "The current regulatory preference for sovereign debt gives rise to "moral suasion," a situation in which large banks hold undue influence over their governments through the purchase of their governments' debt. When this is combined with doubts about the behaviour of the SRM in a systemic crisis, it is clear that important flaws remain in the design of Banking Union."[56]

The consulting and accountancy firm Price Waterhouse Coopers labeled their analysis "EU bank recovery and resolution directive: triumph or tragedy."[57]

The final word has not been said on the European banking union.

---

[54] Daniel Gros, "The bank resolution compromise: incompete but workable?", CEPS Commentary, 18 December 2013, www.ceps.eu/book/bank-resolution-compromise-incomplete-workable. See also his www.project-syndicate.org/commentary/daniel-gros-examines-the-inelegant-but-fundamental-innovation-that-is-the-single-resolution-mechanism

[55] www.ft.com/intl/cms/s/0/7c3c8cd8-cee2-11e3-8e62-00144feabdc0.html#axzz38vvhivHT

[56] www.finance-watch.org/press/press-releases/858

[57] www.pwc.com/et_EE/EE/publications/assets/pub/pwc-eu-bank-recovery-and-resolution-directive-triumph-or-tragedy.pdf

Conclusion
Toward host-country supervision and resolution?

As a result of the financial crisis which began in 2007 and continues to this day in 2014 (vide Portugal, Slovenia, Bulgaria, etc.), a number of measures have been taken to make a repeat of a crisis of a similar magnitude less likely. Foremost among measures to increase the resistance of banks to financial stress are the Basel III rules for increasing the quality and quantity of capital as well as the introduction of liquidity coverage ratios, implemented by the Dodd–Frank legislation in the United States and by the CRD IV package in the European Union (Directive and Regulation).

Additional measures to improve stability are enhanced supervision, in particular of the too-big-to-fail (TBTF) banks, and a focus on stringent stress tests of banks. Other important measures include increasing the transparency and stability of the OTC derivatives market, forcing most trades to pass through clearing houses and increasing the capital requirements on those that don't. The Dodd–Frank Act places restrictions on the ability of US banks to own hedge and equity funds and forbids banks' proprietary trading, a half step back to the Glass–Steagall division into banks and investment banks. In Europe, countries such as the UK and France are forcing banks to ring-fence their core activities, especially insured deposit-taking, from riskier investment-bank activities. As this is written in September 2014, the European Commission has recently put forward its proposal on ring-fencing, following the Liikanen report.[1] As discussed earlier in this book, while helpful if the overall level of capital in the banking system is raised, domestic

---

[1] European Commission, "Proposal for a regulation of the European Parliament and of the Council on structural measures improving the resilience of EU credit institutions," 29 January 2014, COM 2014 (43) final. http://eur-lex.europa.eu/LexUriServ/LexUriServ.do?uri=COM:2014:0043:FIN:EN:PDF; European Commission, "High level expert group on reforming the structure of the EU banking sector" (Liikanen report), October 2012. http://ec.europa.eu/

ring-fencing would not by itself have prevented the recent financial crisis, nor will it prevent a new one.[2] The global financial crash was not started by "Wall Street" (even though investment banks helped spread and aggravate the impulses) but by "Main Street's" residential mortgage bankers.

An international form of ring-fencing may, however, prove helpful.

Capital requirements

A number of central bankers and academics have criticized the new capital requirements as being far too low, following both theoretical and empirical points of departure.[3] According to the Modigliani-Miller (M-M) theorem, banks' funding costs should in principle be indifferent to the choice of equity vs. debt.[4] Even lifting the unrealistic assumptions behind the strict version of the M-M theorem, a number of studies have found that the socially optimal ratio of equity to risk-weighted assets should be far higher than the 7 percent proposed by Basel III, 12–20 percent depending on assumptions.[5] An empirical

internal_market/bank/docs/high-level_expert_group/liikanen-report/final_
report_en.pdf

[2] See also Anat Admati and Martin Hellwig, "Comments to the UK Independent Commission on Banking," Working Paper, Stanford University, July 2011.

[3] See, for instance, Anat R. Admati *et al.*, "Fallacies, irrelevant facts, and myths in capital regulation: why bank equity is *not* expensive," Stanford University Working Paper no. 186, 2010; Anat Admati and Martin Hellwig, *The Bankers' New Clothes: What's Wrong with Banking and What to Do about It* (Princeton University Press, 2013); Anat Admati and Martin Hellwig, "Does debt discipline bankers? An academic myth about bank indebtedness," Working Paper, Stanford University, 18 February 2013; Andrew G. Haldane, "The $100 billion question," comments given at the Institute of Regulation & Risk, Hong Kong, 30 March 2010; Andrew Haldane, "Capital discipline," speech before the American Economic Association, Denver, January 2011; Simon Johnson, "Why higher bank capital is in the public interest" (review of Admati and Hellwig), *Bloomberg*, 4 March 2013; Rym Ayadi, Emrah Arbak and Willem Pieter de Groen, "Regulation of European banks and business models: towards a new paradigm," Centre for European Policy Studies (CEPS), 2012, http://peches bancaires.eu/pdf/Bank_Regulation_in_the_EU.pdf

[4] Franco Modigliani and Merton H. Miller, "The cost of capital, corporation finance and the theory of investment," *American Economic Review* 48 (June 1958), pp. 261–97.

[5] Bank of England, "The long-term economic impact of higher capital levels," *Financial Stability Report* 2010:2 (June 2010), pp. 55–72; David Miles, Jing

observation is that banks, before the government safety net was put in place, had much higher capital ratios than today, 15–25 percent.[6] Another observation, noted earlier in the critique of the Dodd–Frank Act, is that the continued lower funding costs for the global systemically important financial institutions (G-SIFIs) indicate that investors still regard these banks as being too big to fail, which is tantamount to stating that their levels of equity are not believed to be sufficient to weather a new serious financial crisis. The IMF has recently estimated that this annual subsidy, worth an estimated 150–590 billion dollars annually, continued well into 2012, i.e. even after the adoption of the Dodd–Frank Act.[7]

Some countries have therefore gone further in demanding more capital from their banks than Basel III does. In Sweden, the four major banks (of which one, Nordea, is on the list of the Financial Stability Board as a G-SIFI) will be required to have a 5 percent SIFI charge on domestic exposures instead of the 1–2.5 percent mandated by Basel III and the FSB.[8] Adding a cyclical charge of 1 percent, this implies a ratio of core equity Tier 1 (CET1) to risk-weighted assets (RWA) of 13 percent (minimum 4.5% + capital conservation buffer 2.5% + countercyclical buffer 1.0% + SIFI charge 5%). To this will be added a – so far unspecified – level of bailinable debt, consisting of subordinated debt and conditional convertible (CoCo) bonds in order to never have to bail in holders of senior unsecured bank bonds or depositors.[9]

Yang and Gilberto Marcheggiano, "Optimal bank capital," Bank of England Discussion Paper no. 31, April 2011 (revised 2013); Sveriges Riksbank, "Lämplig kapitalnivå i svenska storbanker – en samhällsekonomisk analys" (Optimal level of capital in the Swedish major banks – an economic analysis), report 2011. For an opposing view, see e.g. Douglas J. Elliot, "Higher capital requirements would come at a price," Working Paper, Brookings Institution, 20 February 2013, www.brookings.edu/research/papers/2013/02/20-bank-capital-requirements-elliott

[6] Andrew G. Haldane, "Banking on the state," *BIS Review* 139/2009.
[7] www.ft.com/cms/s/0/60f1c218-b8b2-11e3-835e-00144feabdc0.html#axzz2y5rZaOsW
[8] Sveriges regering, lagrådsremiss av den 3 april 2014 avseende förstärkta kapitaltäckningsregler, www.regeringen.se/content/1/c6/23/81/30/053c5f8e.pdf
[9] Finansinspektionen (Swedish Financial Supervisory Authority), "Promemoria: Förslag till högre kapitaltäckningskrav för de större svenska bankgrupperna" (Proposal for higher capital adequacy ratios for the major Swedish banking groups), November 2011.

Similarly, the Danish Financial Supervisory Authority (Finanstilsynet) and the Central Bank will also be demanding a 13 percent CET1/RWA ratio for its systemically important banks, including the cyclical buffer, to which will be added an unspecified level of bailinable debt.[10] Denmark as well as Sweden may thus eventually land close to what Switzerland already requires from its two major banks: 19 percent total capital, of which 10 percent must be CET1 and the rest may be CoCos (not including the cyclical capital charge).

In the UK, the supervisory authorities have yet to specify what the CRD IV implementation will imply for the British megabanks.[11] Analysts expect the demands to be risk-adjusted, meaning perhaps a core (CET1) capital ratio for HSBC at about 13.5 percent and at 13 percent for Barclays, 12.5 percent at RBS and 11.5 percent at Lloyds.[12]

Figure 35 shows the CET1/RWA ratios for the major European banks at the end of 2013. It is quite evident that a number of banks will have to raise equity to pass the stress test by the EBA and the ECB at the end of 2014, even though the level of capital required in a stressed situation has not yet been spelled out by the EBA.

In the United States, as noted earlier, the Federal Reserve Board has specified a 5 percent leverage ratio (equity over total assets) for the systemically important banking groups under its supervision and a 6 percent ratio of their banking subsidiaries. The United States is also bound by the Collins Amendment to the Dodd–Frank Act, applicable to all banking institutions with assets above 500 million dollars. Specifically, section 171(b)(2) of the Collins Amendment to the Dodd–Frank Act states:

[10] Utvalget om systemisk vigtige finansielle institutter i Danmark, "Systemisk vigtige finansielle institutter i Danmark: identifikation, krav og krisehåndtering" (Systemically important financial institutions in Denmark: identification, requirements and crisis resolution), 11 March 2013, p. 10, www.evm.dk/~/media/oem/pdf/2013/2013-publikationer/14-03-13-sifi-udvalgets-rapport/rapport-sifi-udvalget.ashx

[11] Bank of England/Prudential Regulation Authority, Consultation Paper | CP5/13, "Strengthening capital standards: implementing CRD IV," August 2013, www.bankofengland.co.uk/pra/Documents/publications/policy/2013/implementingcrdivcp513.pdf

[12] www.ft.com/intl/cms/s/0/c39f7d8c-58f5-11e3-9798-00144feabdc0.html#axzz2wKSnc31x;http://uk.reuters.com/article/2013/10/18/uk-banks-capital-britain-idUKBRE99H0Q220131018

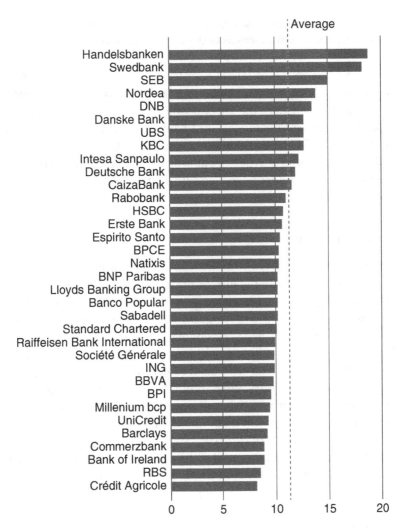

Figure 35. CET1/RWA ratios for the major European banks at the end of 2013
Source: www.ft.com/cms/s/0/e4d05a72-0141-11e4-9750-00144feab7de.
html#axzz39L5Hspwf

the minimum risk-based capital requirements established under this paragraph shall not be less than the generally applicable risk-based capital
requirements, which shall serve as a floor for any capital requirements
that the agency [the FDIC] may require, nor quantitatively lower than the

generally applicable risk-based capital requirements that were in effect for insured depository institutions as of the date of enactment of this Act.

Hence, large US banks cannot have lower capital requirements than smaller ones (being on Basel I when the Dodd–Frank Act was adopted in July 2010), nor may the introduction of Basel III lead to a lower capital requirement for the included banks, mainly banks with assets between 500 million and 50 billion dollars. For the largest banks, the Federal Reserve's new requirement will be tougher than what these banks had before under Basel I and II (the latter only partially introduced into the US).

Deposit insurance

Despite the early efforts by the EU Commission, it has turned out to be impossible to furnish the European Union with the other leg of the necessary support for its banking system apart from a strong capital base, namely a common deposit guarantee scheme comparable to the American FDIC, with a corresponding common Deposit Insurance Fund.[13] Agreement has been reached on principles of payout and on a fund to attain 0.8 percent of covered deposits but these funds will stay national for the foreseeable future.[14] Hence there is no possibility of creating in Europe, as in the United States, a common Deposit Guarantee Authority which is also the Common Resolution Authority as desired by a number of experts.[15]

Some countries, such as Sweden, have already built up a national Deposit Insurance Fund of over 2 percent of insured deposits.

---

[13] European Commission, "Proposal for a Directive of the European Parliament and the Council on Deposit Guarantee Schemes," COM (2010) 369, 12 July 2010.

[14] www.eu2013.lt/en/news/pressreleases/lithuanian-presidency-reaches-political-agreement-on-deposit-guarantee-schemes; "Till default do us part" (on banking union and deposit insurance), *The Economist*, 8 June 2013.

[15] For instance, Dirk Schoenmaker and Daniel Gros, "A European Deposit Insurance and Resolution Fund", CEPS Working Document no. 364, May 2012. For a contrary view, see however Claudia M. Buch, Tobias Körner and Benjamin Weigert, "Towards deeper financial integration in Europe: what the banking union can contribute," Sachverständigenrat (German Council of Economic Experts), Working Paper 2/2013, August 2013.

However, most other countries are severely lacking. According to the IMF, covered deposits as a percentage of GDP in the euro area ranged from 1.3 percent in countries such as Luxembourg and Malta to a low of 0.4 percent in Italy and Estonia. Most countries were between 0.5 and 0.8 percent of GDP. Prefunded guarantee systems were, however, far more variable, ranging from over 1 percent of GDP in Estonia and Portugal to zero or basically zero in countries like Austria, France, Italy and the Netherlands (to which we could add the UK which so far lacks a prefunded system).[16]

Conclusion: toward a system of host country supervision and resolution?

While stressing the importance of common rules for capital ratios, supervision and resolution, it appears that important countries have in fact lost faith in the process and prefer to go it alone, being as independent as possible of others' mistakes. In the United States, as we have seen, major international banks must in the future operate as local separately capitalized subsidiaries under the supervision of the Federal Reserve, whereas up untill now, the Fed only looked at the banks' total (global) level of capital irrespective of where it was held. Sometimes, giant Deutsche Bank even had negative capital in the United States; now it has to find 20 billion dollars in additional capital or shrink assets by some 100 billion dollars. Other banks hard hit by the new rules are major investment banks such as Barclays and Société Générale.[17]

It appears that a number of European countries are drawing similar conclusions, in particular the UK.[18] In the future, the Prudential Regulation Authority (PRA) will take a hard look at whether the supervisor in the bank's home country is a sufficiently tough regulator;

---

[16] International Monetary Fund, "European Union: Publication of Financial Sector Assessment Program Documentation-Technical Note on Deposit Insurance," IMF Country Report no. 13/66, March 2013, p. 3, www.imf.org/external/pubs/ft/scr/2013/cr1366.pdf

[17] www.ft.com/cms/s/0/1a1110d4-9d7c-11e3-a599-00144feab7de.html

[18] "The Balkanisation of banking, the island defence," *The Economist*, 1 March 2014; "Regulators may disagree but should say who calls the shots" (Gillian Tett), *Financial Times*, 27 February 2014.

else the bank will have to enter Britain as a subsidiary, regulated and supervised by the PRA, rather than as a home-country supervised branch office.[19] Some banks such as Spanish Santander already operate on this business model. Indeed, between 1997 and 2011, the share of cross-border assets in Europe held by subsidiaries rather than branches rose from 40 to almost 70 percent.[20]

Wouldn't it be a lovely compliment to the European Union's financial integration if the PRA were to decide that the ECB is not a sufficiently strong supervisor and hence, all major euro area banks have to enter the UK as subsidiaries!

Others have drawn even more drastic conclusions concerning the (failed) trajectory toward a European banking union.[21] Perhaps host country control is the answer if the EBU were to fail? It would provide for an increase in average capital levels worldwide as well as facilitate the resolution of cross-border banks.

---

[19] Bank of England, "Supervising international banks, the Prudential Regulation Authority's approach to branch supervision," Consultation Paper CP4/14, February 2014.

[20] Dirk Schoenmaker, *Governance of International Banking: The Financial Trilemma* (Oxford and New York: Oxford University Press, 2013), p. 44.

[21] Wolfgang Münchau, "Europe should say no to a flawed banking union", *Financial Times*, 17 March 2014.

Addendum

As this book goes to press, the Financial Stability Board has complemented the earlier work by the Basel Committee on Banking Supervision with a proposal for minimum levels of bailinable debt in the banks regarded as too big to fail, or in Basel-speak, globally systemically important financial institutions (G-SIFIs).[1] Since the proposal is still on the drawing-board, I will limit myself to the bare bones as regards this new concept, total loss-absorbing capital (TLAC).

Above the presently decided capital requirements under Basel III, i.e.

- 4.5% minimum CET1[2]/RWA
- 2.5% Capital Conservation Buffer in the form of CET1
- 1% other Tier 1 capital
- =8% Minimum Tier 1 capital

will be added an additional

- +8–12% Loss absorbing capital (subordinated debt, CoCos...)

Since the large banks are also subject to a

- 1–2.5% SIFI charge[3]

and may be subject to a

- 0–2.5% countercyclical buffer[4]

---

[1] Financial Stability Board, "Adequacy of loss-absorbing capacity of global systemically important banks in resolution," Consultative Document, 10 November 2014, www.financialstabilityboard.org/wp-content/uploads/TLAC-Condoc-6-Nov-2014-FINAL.pdf; www.bloomberg.com/news/2014-11-10/banks-face-25-loss-buffer-as-fsb-fights-too-big-to-fail.html

[2] Core Equity Tier 1.

[3] Sweden plans to introduce a 5 percent SIFI charge for its four major banking groups; however, only 2.5 percent may be included under Pillar 1, the rest being added under Pillar 2.

[4] Sweden proposed in the fall of 2014 to demand a 1 percent countercyclical buffer from its banks.

It implies that the G-SIFIs will have to hold, at the discretion of the supervisory authority, 17–25 percent capital in relation to risk-weighted assets. They must also hold a minimum of 6 percent TLAC in relation to total (unweighted) assets, of which at least 3 percent must be CET1.

It has been calculated that there will be a need to issue 480–1,600 billion dollars in Contingent Convertible securities (CoCos) and other Basel III-approved bailinable debt to satisfy the new requirements.[5]

However, it is difficult to see that the proposal, while a step in the right direction, solves the problems highlighted in this book. Foremost, the threat to bail in even senior debt holders in a systemic crisis is not credible. As a bank reaches a position where a bail-in becomes possible, a run on its debt will ensue which will increase funding costs for all (large) institutions. Some evidence of the nervousness of investors in bailinable debt has already begun to appear.[6] The solution, as put forward by Anat Admati, Martin Hellwig, Andy Haldane and many others, is to demand a much higher proportion of equity in the capital requirements.[7]

---

[5] www.reuters.com/article/2014/11/20/banks-capital-idUSL6N0TA2V720141120

[6] "S&P warns of higher risk in bank bail-in bonds," *Financial Times*, 6 February 2014, www.ft.com/intl/cms/s/0/4d6efa3c-8f57-11e3-be85-00144feab7de.html #axzz3L759BfTY
"Fannie Mae debt too risky? Only when investors share pain," www.bloomberg.com/news/2014-12-04/fannie-mae-debt-too-risky-only-when-investors-share-pain.html; "Bank holding company bonds fray as traders fret over risk," www.bloomberg.com/news/2014-11-27/bank-holding-company-bonds-fray-as-traders-fret-over-risk.html

[7] Anat Admati *et al.*, "Fallacies, irrelevant facts, and myths in capital regulation: why bank equity is *not* expensive," Stanford University Working Paper no. 186 (2010), https://gsbapps.stanford.edu/researchpapers/library/RP2065R1&86. pdf; Anat Admati and Martin Hellwig, *The Bankers' New Clothes: What's Wrong with Banking and What to Do about It* (Princeton University Press, 2013); Anat Admati and Martin Hellwig, "Does debt discipline bankers? An academic myth about bank indebtedness," Stanford University Working Paper, 18 February 2013, www.gsb.stanford.edu/sites/default/files/research/documents/Academic%20myth-rev2%202-19-13.pdf; Anat Admati and Martin Hellwig, "The parade of the bankers' new clothes continues: 23 flawed claims debunked," 3 June 2013, http://bankersnewclothes.com/wp-content/uploads/2013/06/parade-continues-June-3.pdf; Andrew G. Haldane, "Capital discipline," speech before the American Economic Association, Denver, January 2011, www.bankofengland.co.uk/publications/Documents/speec2011/speech484.pdf

Bibliography

Legal instruments

European Union

European Commission, "From financial crisis to recovery: a European framework for action," COM (2008) 706 Final, 29 October 2008, http://eur-lex.europa.eu/LexUriServ/LexUriServ.do?uri=COM:2008:07 06:FIN:EN:PDF

"Driving European recovery," COM (2009) 114 Final 4 April 2009, http://eur-lex.europa.eu/LexUriServ/LexUriServ.do?uri=COM:2009:01 14:FIN:EN:PDF

"European financial supervision," COM (2009) 252 Final, 27 May 2009, http://eur-lex.europa.eu/LexUriServ/LexUriServ.do?uri=COM:2009:02 52:FIN:EN:PDF

"Bank resolution funds," COM (2010) 254 Final, 26 May 2010, http://eur-lex.europa.eu/LexUriServ/LexUriServ.do?uri=COM:2010:0254:FI N:EN:PDF

"Proposal for a Directive of the European parliament and the Council on deposit guarantee schemes," COM (2010) 369, 12 July 2010, http://ec.europa.eu/internal_market/bank/docs/guarantee/20100712_ proposal_en.pdf

"An EU framework for crisis management in the financial sector," COM (2010) 579 Final, 20 October 2010, http://eur-lex.europa.eu/ LexUriServ/LexUriServ.do?uri=COM:2010:0579:FIN:EN:PDF

"Proposal for a Regulation of the European Parliament and of the Council on prudential requirements for credit institutions and investment firms," submitted on 20 July 2011, COM 2011/0452 http://eur-lex.europa

"Proposal for a Directive of the European Parliament and of the Council on the access to the activity of credit institutions and the prudential supervision of credit institutions and investment firms and amending Directive 2002/87/EC of the European Parliament and of the Council on the supplementary supervision of credit institutions, insurance undertakings and investment firms in a financial conglomerate," submitted on 20 July 2011, COM 2011/453, http://eur-lex.europa.eu/ LexUriServ/LexUriServ.do?uri=COM:2011:0453:FIN:EN:PDF

"Proposal for a Directive of the European Parliament and of the Council establishing a framework for the recovery and resolution of credit institutions and investment firms and amending Council Directives 77/91/ EEC and 82/891/EC, directives 2001/24/EC, 2002/47/EC, 2004/25/ EC, 2005/56/EC, 2007/36/EC and 2011/35/EC and Regulation (EU) no. 1093/2010, COM(2012) 280/3," 6 June 2012, http://ec.europa.eu/ internal_market/bank/docs/crisis-management/2012_eu_framework/ com_2012_280_en.pdf. See also Commission Staff Working Document, "Impact assessment accompanying the document proposal for a directive of the European Parliament and of the Council establishing a framework for the recovery and resolution of credit institutions and investment firms and amending Council Directives," 77/91/EEC and 82/891/EC, Directives 2001/24/EC, 2002/47/EC, 2004/25/EC, 2005/56/ EC, 2007/36/EC and 2011/35/EC and Regulation (EU) no. 1093/2010; {COM(2012) 280 final}; {swd(2012) 167 final}," http://ec.europa.eu/ internal_market/bank/docs/crisis-management/2012_eu_framework/ impact_assessment_final_en.pdf

"Proposal for a Regulation of the European Parliament and the Council establishing uniform rules and a uniform procedure for the resolution of credit institutions and certain investment firms in the framework of a Single Resolution Mechanism and a Single Bank Resolution Fund," preliminary draft 11 July 2013, http://eur-lex.europa._e_u_/_L_e_x_U_ r_i_S_e_r_v_/_L_e_x_U_r_i_S_e_r_v_._d_o_?_u_r_i_=_C_O_M_:_2_0_1_ 3_:_0_5_2_0_:_F_I_N_:_E_N_:_P_D_F_ _

"On the application, from 1 August 2013, of state aid rules to support measures in favour of banks in the context of the financial crisis," Communication C(2013) 4119, 10 July 2013, http://eur-lex.europa.eu/ LexUriServ/LexUriServ.do?uri=OJ:C:2013:216:0001:0015:EN:PDF

"Proposal for a Regulation of the European Parliament and of the Council establishing uniform rules and a uniform procedure for the resolution of credit institutions and certain investment firms in the framework of a Single Resolution Mechanism and a Single Bank Resolution Fund and amending Regulation (EU) no. 1093/2010 of the European Parliament and of the Council, (COM/2013/76)," 10 July 2013, COM 2013 520 Final, http://eur-lex.europa.eu/LexUriServ/LexUriServ.do?uri=COM:20 13:0520:FIN:EN:PDF

"Proposal for a Regulation of the European Parliament and of the Council on structural measures improving the resilience of EU credit institutions," 29 January 2014, COM 2014 (43) Final, http://eur-lex.europa.eu/ LexUriServ/LexUriServ.do?uri=COM:2014:0043:FIN:EN:PDF

European Council, "Proposal for a Directive of the European Parliament and of the Council establishing a framework for the recovery and resolution of credit institutions and investment firms and amending Council Directives 77/91/EEC and 82/891/EC, Directives 2001/24/EC, 2002/47/EC, 2004/25/EC, 2005/56/EC, 2007/ 36/EC and 2011/35/EC and Regulation (EU) no. 1093/2010, 11148/1/13," 28 June 2013, http://register.consil ium.europa.eu/doc/srv?l=EN&t=PDF&gc=true&sc=false&f=ST%20 11148%202013%20REV%201

European Union, Directive 2009/14/EC of the European Parliament and of the Council of 11 March 2009 amending Directive 94/19/ EC on deposit-guarantee schemes as regards the coverage level and the payout delay, http://ec.europa.eu/internal_market/bank/docs/ guarantee/200914_en.pdf

Directive 2013/36/EU of the European Parliament and of the Council of 26 June 2013 on access to the activity of credit institutions and the prudential supervision of credit institutions and investment firms, amending Directive 2002/87/EC and repealing Directives 2006/48/EC and 2006/49/EC

Directive 2014/59/EU of the European Parliament and of the Council of 15 May 2014 establishing a framework for the recovery and resolution of credit institutions and investment firms and amending Council Directive 82/891/EEC, and Directives 2001/24/EC, 2002/47/ EC, 2004/25/EC, 2005/56/EC, 2007/36/EC, 2011/35/EU, 2012/30/ EU and 2013/36/EU, and Regulations (EU) no. 1093/2010 and (EU) no. 648/2012, of the European Parliament and of the Council, Official Journal L 173/190, 12.6.2014, http://eur-lex.europa.eu/legal-content/ EN/TXT/HTML/?uri=OJ:L:2014:173:FULL&from=EN

Regulation (EU) no. 1093/2010 of the European Parliament and of the Council of 24 November 2010 establishing a European Supervisory Authority (European Banking Authority), amending Decision no. 716/2009/EC and repealing Commission Decision 2009/78/EC, http:// eur-lex.europa.eu/LexUriServ/LexUriServ.do?uri=OJ:L:2010:331:0012 :0047:EN:pdf

Regulation (EU) no. 648/2012 of the European Parliament and of the Council of 4 July 2012 on OTC derivatives, central counterparties and trade repositories (European Markets Infrastructure Regulation, "EMIR"), http://eur-lex.europa.eu/LexUriServ/LexUriServ. do?uri=OJ:L:2012:201:0001:0059:EN:PDF

Regulation (EU) no. 575/2013 of the European Parliament and of the Council of 26 June 2013 on prudential requirements for credit institutions and investment firms and amending Regulation (EU) no. 648/2012 (1), http:// eur-lex.europa.eu/legal-content/EN/ALL/?uri=OJ:L:2013:176:TOC

Regulation (EU) no. 86/2014 of the European Parliament and of the Council of 15 July 2014 establishing uniform rules and a uniform procedure for the resolution of credit institutions and certain investment firms in the framework of a Single Resolution Mechanism and a Single Bank Resolution Fund and amending Regulation (EU) no. 1093/2010, http://eur-lex.europa.eu/legal-content/EN/TXT/HTML/?uri=OJ:L: 2014:225:FULL&from=EN

Sweden

Regeringen, *Offentlig administration av banker i kris*, SOU 2000:66
Regeringens proposition 2009/10:30, Stabilitetsavgift, www.riksdagen.se/sv/Dokument-Lagar/Forslag/Propositioner-och-skrivelser/prop-20091030-Stabilitetsavg_GX0330/. Available in English: Government bill 2009/10:30, "Stability fee," www.government.se/content/1/c6/14/74/26/d5f73aef.pdf
Sveriges regering, *Lagrådsremiss av den 3 april 2014 avseende förstärkta kapitaltäckningsregler*, www.regeringen.se/content/1/c6/23/81/30/053c5f8e.pdf

United Kingdom

Banking Act 2009, adopted 21 February 2009, www.legislation.gov.uk/ukpga/2009/1/contents?view=plain
Capital Requirements Regulations 2006, SI 2006 no. 3221
Financial Services Act 2012, adopted19 December 2012, www.legislation.gov.uk/ukpga/2012/21/contents/enacted
Financial Services (Banking Reform) Act 2013, adopted 18 December 2013, www.legislation.gov.uk/ukpga/2013/33/pdfs/ukpga_20130033_en.pdf
HM Treasury, Financial Services (Banking reform) Bill, 4 February 2013 (HC Bill 130), www.publications.parliament.uk/pa/bills/cbill/2012-2013/0130/2013130.pdf
"Sound banking, delivering reform," Bill, October 2012, Cm 8453, www.hm-treasury.gov.uk/d/icb_banking_reform_bill.pdf

United States

Dodd–Frank Wall Street Reform and Consumer Protection Act of 2010, H.R. 4173, passed 5 January 2010, www.gpo.gov/fdsys/pkg/PLAW-111publ203/pdf/PLAW-111publ203.pdf

Books and articles, supervisory authorities, consultancies[1]

Accenture, Basel III handbook, www.accenture.com/SiteCollectionDocuments/PDF/Accenture-Basel-III-Handbook.pdf

Acharya, Viral V., "A theory of systemic risk and design of prudent bank regulation," *Journal of Financial Stability* 5 (September 2009), pp. 224–55, also at http://pages.stern.nyu.edu/~sternfin/vacharya/public_html/correlation-jfs.pdf

Acharya, Viral V. *et al.*, *Guaranteed to Fail: Fannie Mae, Freddie Mac and the Debacle of Mortgage Finance* (Princeton University Press, 2011)

Acharya, Viral V. *et al.*, eds., *Regulating Wall Street: The Dodd–Frank Act and the New Architecture of Global Finance* (Hoboken, NJ: John Wiley & Sons, 2011)

Acharya, Viral V., Iamar Drechsler and Philipp Schnabl, "Bank bailouts and sovereign credit risk," Stern School of Business Working Paper, April 2013, http://pages.stern.nyu.edu/~idrechsl/ADS_4april2013.pdf

Acharya, Viral V., Robert Engle and Matthew Richardson, "Capital shortfall: a new approach to ranking and regulating systemic risk," *American Economic Review* 102 (May 2012), www.voxeu.org/article/capital-shortfall-new-approach-ranking-and-regulating-systemic-risks

Acharya, Viral V. and Matthew Richardson, eds., *Restoring Financial Stability, How to Repair a Failed System* (Hoboken, NJ: John Wiley & Sons, 2009)

Acharya, Viral V., Philipp Schnabl and Itamar Drechsler, "A tale of two overhangs: the nexus of financial sector and sovereign credit risks," Stern School of Business, April 2012, also at www.voxeu.org/article/tale-two-overhangs-nexus-financial-sector-and-sovereign-credit-risks

Acharya, Viral V. and Sascha Steffen, "Falling short of expectations? Stress-testing the European banking system," NYU Stern School presentation, January 2014, also at http://pages.stern.nyu.edu/~sternfin/vacharya/public_html/pdfs/AQR%20presentation%20-%2015%20Jan%202014.pdf

"The greatest carry trade ever? Understanding Euro zone bank risks," Stern School of Business Working Paper, 18 November 2012, also at http://financeseminars.darden.virginia.edu/Lists/Calendar/Attachments/153/Acharya%20paper%20for%202013%20-%20Carry%20Trade.pdf

---

[1] See also http://businesslibrary.uflib.ufl.edu/financialcrisesbooks and www.investorhome.com/crisisbooks.htm, which lists over 300 books on the crisis.

Acharya, Viral V. and Rangarajan K. Sundaram, "The financial sector bailout: sowing the seeds of the next crisis?" In Viral V. Acharya and Matthew Richardson, eds., *Restoring Financial Stability: How to Repair a Failed System* (Hoboken, NJ: John Wiley & Sons, 2009), ch. 15

Acharya, Viral V. and Tanju Yorulmazer, "Too many to fail: an analysis of time-inconsistency in bank closure policies," *Journal of Financial Intermediation* 16 (2007), pp. 1–31, also at www.bankofengland. co.uk/publications/Documents/workingpapers/wp319.pdf

Admati, Anat R. *et al.*, "Fallacies, irrelevant facts, and myths in capital regulation: why bank equity is not expensive," Stanford University Working Paper no. 186, 2010, https://gsbapps.stanford.edu/researchpapers/library/RP2065R1&86.pdf

Admati, Anat and Martin Hellwig, *The Bankers' New Clothes: What's Wrong with Banking and What to Do about It* (Princeton: Princeton University Press, 2013)

"Comments to the UK Independent Commission on Banking," Working Paper, Stanford University, July 2011, www.gsb.stanford.edu/sites/default/files/research/documents/ICB_Admati_Hellwig.pdf

"Does debt discipline bankers? An academic myth about bank indebtedness," Working Paper, Stanford University, 18 February 2013, www. gsb.stanford.edu/sites/default/files/research/documents/Academic%20myth-rev2%202-19-13.pdf

"The parade of the bankers' new clothes continues: 23 flawed claims debunked," 3 June 2013, http://bankersnewclothes.com/wp-content/uploads/2013/06/parade-continues-June-3.pdf

Adrian, Tobias and Hyun Song Shin, "The changing nature of financial intermediation and the financial crisis of 2007–2009," *Annual Review of Economics* 2 (September 2010), pp. 603–18, also at www.newyork fed.org/research/staff_reports/sr439.pdf

Ahamed, Liaquat, *Lords of Finance: The Bankers Who Broke the World* (New York: Penguin, 2009)

Alexander, Gordon J. and Alexandre M. Baptista, "Does the Basle Bank Accord reduce bank fragility? An assessment of the value-at-risk approach," *Journal of Monetary Economics* 53: 7 (2006), pp. 1631–60, www.sciencedirect.com/science/article/pii/S0304393206000699

Allen, Franklin and Douglas Gale, *Understanding Financial Crises* (Oxford University Press, 2007, 2009)

Allen, William A., *International Liquidity and the Financial Crisis* (Cambridge University Press, 2013)

Aliber, Robert Z., "Monetary turbulence and the Icelandic economy," speech, 20 June 2008, University of Iceland, www.hi.is/files/skjol/ice landlecutre-May-2008.pdf

Allison, Herbert M., *The Megabank Mess* (Seattle: Amazon Digital Services, 2011)

Amri, Puspa, Apanard Ankinand and Clas Wihlborg, "International comparisons of bank regulation, liberalization and banking crises," *Journal of Financial Economic Policy* 3: 4 (2011), pp. 322–39, also at www.cgu.edu/PDFFiles/SPE/CIEP%20working%20paper/Intl_comp_regulations_AmriEtal.pdf

Angkinand, Apanard P., Clas Wihlborg and Thomas D. Willett, "Market discipline for financial institutions and markets for information," in James R. Barth, Lin Chen and Clas Wihlborg, eds., *Research Handbook on International Banking and Governance* (Northampton, MA: Edward Elgar, 2012), pp. 1–51

Arnold, Bruce, Claudio Borio, Luci Ellis and Fariborz Moshirian, "Systemic risk, macro-prudential policy frameworks, monitoring financial systems and the evolution of capital adequacy," *Journal of Banking and Finance* 36:12 (December 2012), pp. 3125–32, also at www.asb.unsw.edu.au/research/instituteofglobalfinance/Documents/Sytemic%20risk,%20Macroprudential%20polices.pdf

Association for Financial Markets in Europe (AFME), "Prevention and cure: securing financial stability after the crisis," September 2010

Avgouleas, Emilios and Charles Goodhart, "A critical evaluation of bail-in as a bank recapitalization tool," paper prepared for the conference on "Bearing the losses from bank and sovereign default in the Eurozone," organized by Franklin Allen, Elena Carletti and Joanna Gray at the European University Institute, Florence, 24 April 2014

Ayadi, Rym and Rosa M. Lastra, "Proposals for reforming deposit guarantee schemes in Europe," *Journal of Banking Regulation* 11:3 (June 2010), pp. 210–22, www.palgrave-journals.com/jbr/journal/v11/n3/pdf/jbr20109a.pdf

Ayadi, Rym, Emrah Arbak and Willem Pieter de Groen, "*Regulation of European banks and business models: towards a new paradigm*," Centre for European Policy Studies, 2012, http://pechesbancaires.eu/pdf/Bank_Regulation_in_the_EU.pdf

Backé, Peter, Ernest Gnan and Philipp Hartmann, eds., *Contagion and Spillovers: New Insights from the Crisis*, SUERF Studies no. 5/2010 (Brussels and Vienna: Larcier, 2010), www.suerf.org/download/studies/study20105.pdf

Bair, Sheila, *Bull by the Horns: Fighting to Save Main Street from Wall Street and Wall Street From Itself* (New York: Free Press, 2012)

"Testimony before the House Committee on Financial Services," 26 June 2013, http://financialservices.house.gov/uploadedfiles/hhrg-113-ba00-wstate-sbair-20130626.pdf

"Why it's time to break up the 'too big to fail' banks," *Fortune*, 6 February 2012, http://finance.fortune.cnn.com/2012/01/18/big-banks-break-up-bair/

Baker, Dean, *Plunder and Blunder: The Rise and Fall of the Bubble Economy* (Sausolito: PoliPoint Press, 2009)

Baker, Dean *et al.*, "The value of the 'too-big-to-fail' big bank subsidy," CEPR September 2009, www.cepr.net/documents/publications/too-big-to-fail-2009-09.pdf

Bamber, Bill and Andrew Spencer, *Bear Trap: The Fall of Bear Stearns and the Panic of 2008* (New York: Brick Tower Press, 2008)

Bank for International Settlements, "Adjustments to the Basel II market risk framework," 18 June 2010, revised February 2011, www.bis.org/publ/bcbs193.pdf

"Assessing the macroeconomic impact of higher loss absorbency for global systemically important banks," October 2011, www.bis.org/publ/bcbs202.pdf

"Assessing the macroeconomic impact of the transition to stronger capital and liquidity requirements," August 2010, www.bis.org/publ/othp10.pdf

"An assessment of the long-term economic impact of stronger capital and liquidity requirements," August 2010, www.bis.org/publ/bcbs173.pdf

"Basel III: a global regulatory framework for more resilient banks and banking systems," December 2010, www.bis.org/publ/bcbs189_dec2010.pdf

"Basel III: international framework for liquidity risk measurement, standards and monitoring," December 2010, www.bis.org/publ/bcbs188.pdf

"Basel III regulatory consistency assessment, preliminary report (level 2): European Union," October 2012, www.bis.org/bcbs/implementation/l2_eu.pdf

"Basel III regulatory consistency assessment, preliminary report (level 2): United States of America," October 2012, www.bis.org/bcbs/implementation/l2_us.pdf

"Basel Committee announces steps to strengthen the resilience of the banking system," press release, 16 April 2008, www.bis.org/press/p080416.htm

"The Basel Committee's response to the financial crisis: report to the G20," October 2010, www.bis.org/publ/bcbs179.pdf

"Calibrating minimum capital requirements and capital buffers: a top-down approach," October 2010, www.bis.org/publ/bcbs180.pdf

"Central bank governance and financial stability," a report by a study group, May 2011, www.bis.org/publ/othp14.pdf

"Core principles for effective deposit insurance systems," March 2009, www.bis.org/publ/bcbs151.htm

"Enhancements to the Basel II framework," July 2009, www.bis.org/publ/bcbs157.pdf

"Fundamental review of the trading book," May 2012, www.bis.org/publ/bcbs219.pdf

"Global systemically important banks: assessment methodology and the additional loss absorbency requirement," November 2011, www.bis.org/publ/bcbs207.pdf

"Guidance papers on recovery and resolution planning," 16 July 2013, www.financialstabilityboard.org/press/pr_130716.pdf

"International Convergence of Capital Measurement and Capital Standards: a revised framework, comprehensive version," June 2006, www.bis.org/publ/bcbs128.pdf

"International framework for liquidity risk measurement, standards and monitoring," December 2009, www.bis.org/publ/bcbs165.pdf

"The liquidity coverage ratio and liquidity risk monitoring tools," January 2013, www.bis.org/publ/bcbs238.pdf

"Margin requirements for non-centrally cleared derivatives," July 2012, www.bis.org/publ/bcbs226.pdf

"Principles for sound stress testing practices and supervision," March 2009, www.bis.org/publ/bcbs147.pdf

"Regulatory consistency assessment programme (RCAP): analysis of risk-weighted assets for credit risk in the banking book," July 2013, www.bis.org/publ/bcbs256.pdf

"Regulatory consistency assessment programme (RCAP): analysis of risk-weighted assets for market risk," January 2013, www.bis.org/publ/bcbs240.pdf

"Revised Basel III leverage ratio and disclosure requirements," June 2013, www.bis.org/publ/bcbs251.pdf

Semi-annual OTC Derivatives Statistics, various issues

"Strengthening the resilience of the banking sector," December 2009, www.bis.org/publ/bcbs164.pdf

Bank for International Settlements, Committee on the Global Financial System (CGFS), "Operationalising the selection and application of macroprudential instruments," December 2012, www.bis.org/publ/cgfs48.pdf

Bank for International Settlements, Financial Stability Forum, "Addressing procyclicality in the financial system," April 2009, www.financialstabilityboard.org/publications/r_0904a.pdf

Bank of England, "The bank's response to the financial crisis," May 2012, www.bankofengland.co.uk/about/Pages/response/index.aspx

Financial Stability Report, various issues

"Instruments of macro prudential policy," discussion paper, December 2011, www.bankofengland.co.uk/publications/Documents/other/financialstability/discussionpaper111220.pdf

"The long-term economic impact of higher capital levels," *Financial Stability Report* 2010:2 (June 2010), pp. 55–72, www.bankofengland. co.uk/publications/Documents/fsr/2010/fsr27sec5.pdf

"The Prudential Regulatory Authority's approach to bank supervision," April 2013, www.bankofengland.co.uk/publications/Documents/praapproach/bankingappr1304.pdf

"Regulating international banks," speech before the British Bankers' Association, 17 October 2013, by Andrew Bailey, deputy governor, www.bankofengland.co.uk/publications/Documents/speeches/2013/speech687.pdf

"Resolving globally active, systemically important financial institutions," a joint paper with the Federal Deposit Insurance Corporation, 12 December 2012, www.bankofengland.co.uk/publications/documents/news/2012/nr156.pdf

"The role of macroprudential policy: a discussion paper," November 2009, www.bankofengland.co.uk/publications/other/financialstability/roleofmacroprudentialpolicy091121.pdf

"Supervising international banks, the Prudential Regulation Authority's approach to branch supervision," Consultation Paper CP4/14, February 2014, www.bankofengland.co.uk/pra/Documents/publications/policy/2014/branchsupcp4-14.pdf

The Banker, Top 1000 World Banks, various issues

Barofsky, Neil, *Bailout: How Washington Abandoned Main Street while Rescuing Wall Street* (New York: Free Press, 2012)

Barth, James R., Gerard Caprio Jr. and Ross Levine, *The Guardians of Finance: Making Them Work for Us* (Cambridge, MA: MIT Press, 2012)

Rethinking Bank Regulation (Cambridge University Press, 2006)

Barth, James R., Gerard Caprio Jr. and Ross Levine, "Bank regulation and supervision in 180 countries from 1999 to 2011," *Journal of Financial Economic Policy* 5:2 (2013), pp. 111–219, also at http://faculty.haas.berkeley.edu/ross_levine/Papers/Bank_Regulation_and_Supervision_Around_the_World_15JAN2013.pdf

Barth, James R., Lin Chen and Clas Wihlborg, eds., *Research Handbook on International Banking and Governance* (Northampton, MA: Edward Elgar, 2012)

Barth, James R. and Apanard Prabha, "Too big to fail: a little perspective on a large problem," Federal Reserve Bank of Chicago, November 2012, www.chicagofed.org/digital_assets/others/events/2012/international_conference/barth_111512.pdf

Barth, James R., Apanard (Penny) Prabha and Phillip Swagel, "Just how big is the too-big-to-fail problem?" *Journal of Banking Regulation* 13 (November 2012), pp. 265–99, also at www.milkeninstitute.org/publi cations/publications.taf?function=detail&ID=38801315&cat=

Barth, James R., Apanard (Penny) Prabha and Greg Yun, "The eurozone financial crisis: role of interdependencies between bank and sovereign risk," *Journal of Financial Economic Policy* 4:1 (2012), pp. 76–97, also at http://papers.ssrn.com/sol3/papers.cfm?abstract_id=1966295

Beck, Thorstein, ed., *Banking Union for Europe, Risks and Challenges* (London: CEPR and VoxEU.org, 2012), www.voxeu.org/sites/default/files/file/Banking_Union.pdf

Benes, Jaromir and Michael Kumhof, "The Chicago plan revisited," IMF Working Paper 12/202, August 2012, www.imf.org/external/pubs/ft/wp/2012/wp12202.pdf

Benston, George J. *et al.*, *Perspectives of Safe and Sound Banking: Past, Present and Future* (Cambridge, MA: MIT Press, 1986)

Berd, Arthur M., ed., *Lessons from the Financial Crisis* (London: RISK Books, 2010)

Berg, Christopher, *Analyse des Entstaatlichungsprozessus bei Kreditinstituten nach der Finanzkrise und dessen Chancen und Risiken am Beispiel der Commerzbank* (Norderstedt: GRIN Verlag 2011)

Berger, Allen N., Richard J. Herring and Giorgio P. Szegö, "The role of capital in financial institutions," *Journal of Banking & Finance* 19:3–4 (1995), pp. 393–430, also at http://fic.wharton.upenn.edu/fic/papers/95/9501.pdf

Berger, Allen N., Richard J. Herring and Giorgio P. Szegö, "The role of capital in financial institutions," *Journal of Banking and Finance* 19:3–4 (June 1995), pp. 393–430, also at http://fic.wharton.upenn.edu/fic/papers/95/9501.pdf

Bernanke, Ben, *The Federal Reserve and the Financial Crisis: Lectures* (Princeton University Press, 2013)

"Some reflections on the crisis and the policy response" (speech 13 April 2012 at the Russell Sage Foundation and the Century Foundation Conference on "Rethinking Finance"), reprinted in Alan S. Blinder, Andrew Lo and Robert Solow, eds., *Rethinking the Financial Crisis* (New York: Russell Sage Foundation, 2013), pp. 3–13, also at www.federalreserve.gov/newsevents/speech/bernanke20120413a.htm

Better Markets, "The cost of the financial crisis," September 2012, http://bet termarkets.com/sites/default/files/Cost%20Of%20The%20Crisis_1.pdf

Black, Lamont and Lieu Hazelwood, "The effect of TARP on bank risk-taking," FDIC/JFSR Annual Conference, September 2011, www.fdic.gov/bank/analytical/cfr/2011/sept/Black_presentation.pdf

Blinder, Alan S., *After the Music Stopped: The Financial Crisis, the Response and the Work Ahead* (New York: Penguin, 2013)

Blinder, Alan S., Andrew Lo and Robert Solow, eds., *Rethinking the Financial Crisis* (New York: Russell Sage Foundation, 2013)

Blundell-Wignall, Adrian *et al.*, "The current financial crisis: causes and policy issues," *OECD Financial Market Trends* 2 (2008), pp. 1–21, www.oecd.org/finance/financial-markets/41942872.pdf

Blundell-Wignall, Adrian, Gert Wehinger and Patrick Slovik, "The elephant in the room: the need to deal with what banks do," *OECD Financial Market Trends* 2 (2009), pp. 11–35, www.oecd.org/datao ecd/13/8/44357464.pdf

Bookstaber, Richard, *A Demon of Our Own Design: Markets, Hedge Funds and the Perils of Financial Innovation* (Hoboken, NJ; John Wiley & Sons, 2007)

Borio, Claudio, "The financial turmoil of 2007–? A preliminary assessment and some considerations," BIS Working Paper no. 251 (2008), www.bis.org/publ/work251.pdf

Borio, Claudio, Mathias Drehman and Kostas Tsatsaronis, "Stress testing macro stress testing: does it live up to expectations?" BIS Working Paper no. 369, January 2012, www.bis.org/publ/work369.pdf

Boston University, Center for Finance, Law and Policy, "Too big to be efficient? The impact of implicit funding subsidies on scale economies in banking," January 2013, www.bu.edu/bucflp/files/2013/01/Draft-Announcement-1-14-20131.pdf

Bove, Richard X., *Guardians of Prosperity: Why America Needs Big Banks* (New York: Penguin, 2013)

Boyd, John H. and Amanda Heitz, "The social costs and benefits of too-big-to-fail banks," Federal Reserve Bank of Cleveland, August 2011, www.clevelandfed.org/research/Seminars/2011/heitz.pdf

Boyes, Roger, *Meltdown Iceland: How the Global Financial Crisis Bankrupted an Entire Country* (London: Bloomsbury, 2009)

Brown, Elizabeth F., "A comparison of the handling of the financial crisis in the United States, the United Kingdom, and Australia," *Villanova Law Review* 55:3 (2010), pp. 509–76, http://papers.ssrn.com/sol3/papers.cfm?abstract_id=1864898

"The new laws and regulations for financial conglomerates: will they better manage the risks than the previous ones?" *American University Law Review* 60 (May 2011) pp. 1339–1415, http://papers.ssrn.com/sol3/papers.cfm?abstract_id=1864928

Brownell, Charles, *Subprime Meltdown: From US Liquidity Crisis to Global Recession* (New York: Ingram, 2008)

The Crunch: The Scandal of Northern Rock and the Escalating Credit Crisis (London: Random House, 2008)

Brummer, Alex, *Bad Banks: Greed, Incompetence and the Next Global Crisis* (London: Random House, 2014)

Bruni, Franco and David T. Llewellyn, eds., *The Failure of Northern Rock: A Multi-Dimensional Case Study* (Vienna: SUERF – The European Money and Finance Forum, 2009), www.suerf.org/download/studies/study20091.pdf

Brunnermeier, Markus, "Deciphering the liquidity and credit crunch, 2007–08," *Journal of Economic Perspectives* 23:1 (Winter 2009), pp. 77–100, www.princeton.edu/~markus/research/papers/liquidity_credit_crunch.pdf

Brunnermeier, Markus *et al.*, "The fundamental principles of financial regulation," Geneva Report on the World Economy 11, Conference report, CEPR 2009, www.princeton.edu/~markus/research/papers/Geneva11.pdf

Buch, Claudia M., Tobias Körner and Benjamin Weigert, "Towards deeper financial integration in Europe: what the Banking Union can contribute," Sachverständigenrat (German Council of Economic Experts), Working Paper 2/2013, August 2013, www.sachverstaendigenrat-wirtschaft.de/fileadmin/dateiablage/download/publikationen/Arbeitspapier_02_2013.pdf

Buckley, Adrian, *Financial Crisis: Causes, Context and Consequences* (London: Financial Times/Prentice Hall, 2011)

Buder, Matthäus *et al.*, "The rescue and restructuring of Hypo Real Estate," *EU Competition Policy Newsletter* 3 (2011), pp. 41–44, http://ec.europa.eu/competition/publications/cpn/2011_3_9_en.pdf

Buiter, Willem H. and Anne Silbert, "The Icelandic banking crisis and what to do about it," Centre for Economic Policy Research, Policy Insight no. 26, October 2008, www.cepr.org/sites/default/files/policy_insights/PolicyInsight26.pdf

Bulir, Ales and Jaromík Hurník, "The Maastricht inflation criterion: how unpleasant is purgatory," IMF Working Paper, WP/06/154, June 2006, www.imf.org/external/pubs/ft/wp/2006/wp06154.pdf

Buttimer, Richard J., "The financial crisis: imperfect markets and imperfect regulation," *Journal of Financial Economic Policy* 3:1 (2011), pp. 12–32, www.deepdyve.com/lp/emerald-publishing/the-financial-crisis-imperfect-markets-and-imperfect-regulation-XJkRr40pzC

Caprio, Gerard, Asli Demirgüç-Kunt and Edward J. Kane, "The 2007 meltdown in structured securitization: searching for lessons, not scapegoats," *World Bank Research Observer* 25:1 (2010), pp. 125–55, http://siteresources.worldbank.org/INTFR/Resources/KaneCaprioDemirgucKunt-The2007Meltdown.pdf

Carmassi, Jacopo, Carmine de Noia and Stefano Micossi, "Banking union: a federal model for the European Union with prompt corrective action," CEPS Policy Brief no. 282, 18 September 2012, http://ceps.be/book/banking-union-federal-model-european-union-prompt-corrective-action

Carswell, Simon, *Anglo Republic: Inside the Bank that Broke Ireland* (London: Penguin, 2012)

Case, Karl E. and Robert Shiller, "Is there a bubble in the housing market?" *Brookings Papers on Economic Activity* 2 (2003), also at www.econ. yale.edu/~shiller/pubs/p1089.pdf

Cecchetti, Stephen, "Crisis and responses: the Federal Reserve in the early stages of the financial crisis," *Journal of Economic Perspectives* 23:1 (Winter 2009), pp. 51–75, www.ucl.ac.uk/~uctpnpa/cecchetti.pdf

Celemin, José Luis Heras, *El caso Bankia y algo más...o menos* (Madrid: Editorial Club Universitario, 2013)

Central Bank of Ireland and the Financial Regulator, *Financial Stability Report*, years 2004–7, www.centralbank.ie/publications/documents/ 1.%20financial%20stability%20report%202007%20-%20part% 201.pdf

Chadha, J. S. and S. Holly, eds., *Interest Rates, Prices and Liquidity: Lessons from the Financial Crisis* (Cambridge University Press, 2011)

Cheng, Siwey, *The US Financial Crisis: Analysis and Interpretation* (San Francisco, CA: Long River Press, 2012)

Chow, Julian T. S. and Jay Surti, "Making banks safer: can Volcker and Vickers do it?" IMF Working Paper 2011/236, November 2011, www. imf.org/external/pubs/ft/wp/2011/wp11236.pdf

Claessens, Stijn *et al.*, "Crisis management and resolution: early lessons from the financial crisis," IMF Staff Discussion Note, 9 March 2011, www.imf.org/external/pubs/ft/sdn/2011/sdn1105.pdf

"Resolving systemic crises: policies and institutions," World Bank Policy Research Working Paper 3377, August 2004, in Patrick Honohan and Luc Læven, eds., *Systemic Financial Crises, Containment and Resolution* (Cambridge University Press, 2005), www-wds.worldbank. org/external/default/WDSContentServer/WDSP/IB/2004/09/07/00016 0016_20040907154538/additional/126526322_20041117165058.pdf

Claessens, Stijn, Richard Herring and Dirk Schoenmaker, "A safer world financial system: improving the resolution of systemic institutions," Centre for Economic Policy Research (CEPR), London, 2010, www. cepr.org/pubs/books/cepr/booklist.asp?cvno=P210

Claessens, Stijn, Giovanni Dell'Ariccia, Deniz Igan and Luc Laeven, "Cross-country experiences and policy implications from the global financial crisis," *Economic Policy* 62 (April 2010), pp. 267–93, also at http:// relooney.fatcow.com/SI_FAO-Asia/Global-Crisis_2.pdf

Coffee, John C., "Bail-ins vs. bail-outs: using contingent capital to mitigate systemic risk," Columbia Law and Economics Working Paper 380, October 2010 http://papers.ssrn.com/sol3/papers.cfm?abstract_id=1675015

"The political economy of Dodd–Frank: why financial reform tends to be frustrated and systemic risk perpetuated," in Eilís Ferran *et al.*,

The Regulatory Aftermath of the Global Financial Crisis (Cambridge University Press, 2012)

Cohan, William D., *House of Cards: A Tale of Hubris and Wretched Excess on Wall Street* (New York: Doubleday, 2009)

Money and Power: How Goldman Sachs Came to Rule the World (New York: Anchor, 2012)

Cohan, William D. and David Skeel, *The New Financial Deal: Understanding the Dodd–Frank Act and Its (Unintended) Consequences* (Hoboken, NJ: John Wiley & Sons, 2011)

Commission of Investigation into the Banking Sector in Ireland (the Nyberg report), "Misjudging risks: the causes of the systemic banking crisis in Ireland," March 2011, www.bankinginquiry.gov.ie/Documents/ Misjuding%20Risk%20-%20Causes%20of%20the%20Systemic%20 Banking%20Crisis%20in%20Ireland.pdf

Committee on the Causes of the Financial Crisis in Denmark, "The financial crisis in Denmark, causes, consequences and lessons," 18 September 2013, www.evm.dk/english/publications/2013/~/media/oem/pdf/2013/2013- publikationer/18-09-13-rapport-fra-udvalget-om-finanskrisens- aarsager/conclusions-and-recommendations-170913.ashx

Condijts, Joan, Paul Gérard and Pierre-Henri Thomas, *La chute de la maison Fortis* (Paris: Éditions Jean-Claude Lattés, 2009)

Congdon, Tim, "Drive for higher capital-asset ratios is deflationary," weekly letter, 14 September 2009

Connaughton, Jeff, *The Payoff: Why Wall Street Always Wins* (New York: Prospecta Press, 2012)

Cooper, George, *The Origin of Financial Crises: Central Banks, Credit Bubbles and the Efficient Market Fallacy* (Petersfield: Harriman House, 2008)

Copeland, Laurence, "The death of the credit markets: suicide, homicide or accidental death?" *Investment Research and Analysis Journal* 3:1 (Spring 2008), pp. 14–22

Council of the European Union, "Proposal for a Directive of the European Parliament and of the Council establishing a framework for the recovery and resolution of credit institutions and investment firms," 11148/1/13, 28 June 2013, http://register.consilium.europa.eu/ doc/srv?l=EN&t=PDF&gc=true&sc=false&f=ST%2011148%20 2013%20REV%201

Cour des Comptes, *Dexia: un sinistre bancaire coûteux, des risqué persistants* (Paris: La documentation française, 28 August 2013), www.ccomptes.fr/ Actualites/A-la-une/Dexia-un-sinistre-couteux-des-risques-persistants

Cowen, Brian, "The euro: from crisis to resolution? Some reflections from Ireland on the road thus far," speech, 21 March 2012, www.corkeco nomics.com/wp-content/uploads/2012/03/3.21.12-Cowen-Speech.pdf

Danmarks Nationalbank (Ulrik Løgtholdt Poulsen and Brian Liltoft Andreasen), "Håndtering af nødlidende pengeinstitutter i Danmark" (Resolution of ailing financial institutions in Denmark), *Kvartalsoversigt* 3 (2011), pp. 79–94 (The Quarterly Review of the central bank is only available in Danish), http://nationalbanken.dk/DNDK/Publikationer. nsf/side/9EA7C855ACB9BCAFC12579100034ACF8/$file/ kvo_3_2011_del1_web.pdf

Das, Satyajit, *Traders, Guns and Money: Knowns and Unknowns in the Dazzling World of Derivatives* (Englewood Cliffs, NJ: Prentice-Hall, 2010)

Davies, Howard, *The Financial Crisis: Who Is to Blame?* (Cambridge: Polity Press, 2010)

Davies, Richard and Belinda Tracey, "Too big to be efficient? The impact of implicit funding subsidies on scale economies in banking," discussion paper, June 2012, www.tilburguniversity.edu/research/institutes-and-research-groups/ebc/events/2012/post-crisis/daviestracey.pdf

DeAngelo, Harry and René M Stulz, "Why high leverage is optimal for banks," NBER and European Corporate Governance Institute, working paper, August 2013, http://fic.wharton.upenn.edu/fic/papers/13/13-20.pdf

De Bonis, Riccardo, Alberto Franco Pozzolo and Massimiliano Stacchini, "The Italian banking system: facts and interpretations," Economics and Statistics Discussion Paper no. 068/12, Università degli Studi del Molise, http://road.unimol.it/bitstream/2192/202/3/ESDP12068.pdf

De Socio, Antonio, "The interbank market after the financial turmoil," Banca d'Italia Working Paper no. 819, September 2011, www.bancaditalia.it/ pubblicazioni/econo/temidi/td11/td819_11/en_td819/en_tema_819.pdf

Demirgüç-Kunt, Asli and Enrica Detragiache, "Does deposit insurance increase banking system stability? An empirical investigation," *Journal of Monetary Economics* 49 (October 2002), pp. 1373–1406, also at http://siteresources.worldbank.org/INTFR/Resources/475459-11080 66643741/asli_enrica.pdf

Demirgüç-Kunt, Asli, Enrica Detragiache and Ouarda Merrouche, "Bank capital: lessons from the financial crisis," IMF Policy Research Working Paper Series 5473, December 2010, www.imf.org/external/pubs/ft/ wp/2010/wp10286.pdf

Demirgüç-Kunt, Asli and Harry Huizinga, 2010, "Are banks too big to fail or too big to save? International evidence from equity prices and CDS spreads," *Journal of Banking and Finance* 37 (March 2013), pp. 875–894, also at www.ebs.edu/fileadmin/redakteur/funkt.dept.economics/ Colloquium/Too_big_to_save_May_14.pdf

Demirgüç-Kunt, Asli, Edward Kane and Luc Laeven, eds., *Deposit Insurance around the World: Issues of Design and Implementation* (Cambridge, MA: MIT Press, 2008)

De Nederlandsche Bank, "Resolution framework for systemically important banks in the Netherlands," 11 July 2012, www.dnb.nl/binaries/ Resolution%20Framework%20for%20Systemically%20Important%20 Banks%20in%20the%20Netherlands_tcm46-275579.pdf

Deutsche Bundesbank, "Fundamental features of the German bank restructuring Act," Monthly Report, June 2011, pp. 59–75, www. bundesbank.de/Redaktion/EN/Downloads/Publications/Monthly_ Report_Articles/2011/2011_06_%20fundamental_features_german_ bank_restructuring_act.pdf?__blob=publicationFile

Donovan, Donal and Antoin E. Murphy, *The Fall of the Celtic Tiger: Ireland and the Euro Debt Crisis* (Oxford University Press, 2013)

Dudley, William C., "Solving the too big to fail problem," remarks at the clearing house's Second Annual Business Meeting and Conference, New York City, 15 November 2012, www.newyorkfed.org/newsevents/ speeches/2012/dud121115.html

Duffie, Darrell, *How Big Banks Fail and What to Do About It* (Princeton University Press, 2011)

Dunbar, Nicholas, *The Devil's Derivatives: The Untold Story of the Slick Traders and Hapless Regulators who Almost Blew up Wall Street … and Are Ready to Do It Again* (Cambridge, MA: Harvard Business Review Press, 2011)

Elliot, Douglas J., "Higher capital requirements would come at a price," Brookings Institution Research Paper, 20 February 2013, www.brook ings.edu/research/papers/2013/02/20-bank-capital-requirements-elliott

"Key issues on European banking union: trade-offs and Some recommendations," Brookings Institution Working Paper 52, November 2012, www.brookings.edu/~/media/research/files/papers/ 2012/11/european%20banking%20union%20elliott/11%20 european%20banking%20union%20elliott

"A primer on bank capital," Brookings Institution Research Paper, January 2010, www.brookings.edu/~/media/Files/rc/papers/2010/0129_capital_ elliott/0129_capital_primer_elliott.pdf

Ellis, Luci, "The housing meltdown, why did it happen in the United States?" BIS Working Paper no. 259, September 2008, www.bis.org/ publ/work259.pdf

Estrella, Arturo, "The cyclical behavior of optimal bank capital," *Journal of Banking and Finance* 28:6 (2004), pp. 1469–98, also at www.bis.org/ bcbs/events/oslo/estrella.pdf

Estrella, Arturo, Sangkyun Park and Stavros Peristiani, "Capital ratios as predictors of bank failure," *Federal Reserve Bank of New York Economic Policy Review*, 6:2 (July 2000), pp. 33–52, www.ny.frb.org/ research/epr/00v06n2/0007estr.html

European Banking Authority (EBA), "Overview of the EBA 2011 EU-wide stress test," 18 March 2011, www.eba.europa.eu/cebs/media/Publications/ Other%20Publications/2011%20EU-wide%20stress%20test/EBA-ST-2011-003--(Overview-of-2011-EBA-EU-wide-stress-test).pdf

"2011 EU-wide stress test: aggregate report," 15 July 2011, www.eba. europa.eu/pdf/EBA_ST_2011_Summary_Report_v6.pdf

European Central Bank, *Financial Stability Review*, various issues

"Opinion of the European Central Bank of 6 November 2013 on a proposal for a Regulation of the European Parliament and of the Council establishing uniform rules and a uniform procedure for the resolution of credit institutions and certain investment firms in the framework of a Single Resolution Mechanism and a Single Bank Resolution Fund and amending Regulation (EU) No. 1093/2010 of the European Parliament and of the Council (CON/2013/76)," www.ecb.europa.eu/ecb/legal/ pdf/en_con_2013_76_f_sign.pdf

European Commission, "The economic adjustment program for Cyprus," European Economy, Occasional Papers 149, May 2013, http://ec.europa.eu/ economy_finance/publications/occasional_paper/2013/pdf/ocp149_en.pdf

"Facts and figures on State aid in the EU Member States – 2012 update," Staff Working Paper, SEC (2012) 443 final, 21 December 2012, http:// ec.europa.eu/competition/state_aid/studies_reports/2012_autumn_ working_paper_en.pdf

"High level expert group on reforming the structure of the EU banking sector" (Liikanen report), October 2012, http://ec.europa.eu/ internal_market/bank/docs/high-level_expert_group/liikanen-report/ final_report_en.pdf

"The high-level group on financial supervision in the EU" (de Larosière Committee), report 25 February 2009, http://ec.europa.eu/ internal_market/finances/docs/de_larosiere_report_en.pdf

"Press release, CRDIV – frequently asked questions," MEMO 11/527, 20 July 2011, http://europa.eu/rapid/press-release_MEMO-11-527_en.htm?locale=en

European Commission (Zedda, Stefano *et al.*), "The EU sovereign debt crisis: potential effects on EU banking systems and policy options," JRC Technical Reports 2012, www.iadb.org/intal/intalcdi/PE/2013/11853.pdf

European Commission–Competition, "The effect of temporary State aid rules adopted in the context of the financial and economic crisis," Staff Working Paper, 5 October 2011, http://ec.europa.eu/competition/ publications/reports/working_paper_en.pdf

European Council (Herman van Rumpuy), "Towards a genuine economic and monetary union," EUCO 120/12, 26 June 2012, http://ec.europa. eu/economy_finance/focuson/crisis/documents/131201_en.pdf

European Economic Advisory Group (EEAG), *Report on the European Economy*, February 2009, ch. 2, "The financial crisis," www.cesifo-group. de/ifoHome/policy/EEAG-Report/Archive/EEAG_Report_2009.html

European Parliament, "Banking Union: the Single Resolution Mechanism," Monetary Dialogue, 18 February 2013 (Nicolas Véron *et al.*), www. europarl.europa.eu/document/activities/cont/201304/20130422ATT 64861/20130422ATT64861EN.pdf

European Union, "Bank capital rules: the council endorses agreement with EP (European Parliament)," 5 March 2013, www.consilium.europa.eu/ uedocs/cms_Data/docs/pressdata/en/ecofin/135823.pdf

"EU Bank Recovery and Resolution Directive (BRRD): frequently asked questions," European Commission – MEMO/14/297 15/04/2014, http://europa.eu/rapid/press-release_MEMO-14-297_en.htmEvanoff, Douglas D. and George G. Kaufman, eds., *Systemic Financial Crisis: Resolving Large Bank Insolvencies* (Hackensack, NJ: World Scientific Publishing, 2005)

Fahlenbrach, Rüdiger and René M. Stulz, "Bank CEO incentives and the credit crisis," *Journal of Financial Economics* 99:1 (January 2011), pp. 11–26, http://papers.ssrn.com/sol3/papers.cfm?abstract_id=1439859

Farlow, Andrew, *Crash and Beyond, Causes and Consequences of the Global Financial Crisis* (Oxford University Press, 2013)

Farrell, Greg, *Crash of the Titans: Greed, Hubris, the Fall of Merrill Lynch and the Near-Collapse of Bank of America* (London: Random House, 2010)

Fassin, Yves and Derrick Gosselin, "The collapse of a European bank in the financial crisis: an analysis from stakeholder and ethical perspectives," *Journal of Business Ethics* 102:2 (2012) pp. 169–91, www.feb.ugent. be/nl/Ondz/wp/Papers/wp_11_726.pdf

Federal Deposit Insurance Corporation (FDIC), "Capitalization ratios for global systemically important banks (G-SIB), data as of fourth quarter 2012," www.fdic.gov/about/learn/board/hoenig/capitalizationratios.pdf

"The orderly liquidation of Lehman Brothers Holdings Inc. under the Dodd–Frank Act," *FDIC Quarterly* 5:2 (2011), pp. 31–49, www.fdic.gov/ bank/analytical/quarterly/2011_vol5_2/Article2.pdf, www.ft.com/cms/ 0a72e3a2-6948-11e0-9040-00144feab49a.pdf

Federal Reserve Bank of Dallas (Atkinson, Tyler, David Luttrell and Harvey Rosenblum), "How bad was it? The costs and consequences of the 2007–09 financial crisis," Staff Paper no. 20, July 2013, http://dallasfed. org/assets/documents/research/staff/staff1301.pdf

Federal Reserve Board, "Bear Stearns, JPMorgan Chase and Maiden Lane LLC," Regulatory Reform, latest update 2 August 2013, www.federal reserve.gov/newsevents/reform_bearstearns.htm

Ferran, Eilís, "European Banking Union: imperfect but can it work?", University of Cambridge Faculty of Law Research Paper no. 30, 2014, http://papers.ssrn.com/sol3/papers.cfm?abstract_id=2426247

Ferran, Eilís *et al.*, *The Regulatory Aftermath of the Global Financial Crisis* (Cambridge University Press, 2012)

Ferran, Eilís, Niamh Moloney and Jennifer Payne, eds., *Oxford Handbook of Financial Regulation* (Oxford University Press, 2015)

Financial Crisis Inquiry Commission (FCIC), *Financial Crisis Inquiry Report: Final Report of the National Commission on the Causes of the Financial and Economic Crisis in the United States* (Washington, DC: Government Printing Office, January 2011), also at www.gpo.gov/fdsys/pkg/GPO-FCIC/pdf/GPO-FCIC.pdf

Financial Services Authority, "The failure of the Royal Bank of Scotland," FSA Board report, December 2011, www.fsa.gov.uk/pubs/other/rbs.pdf

"A regulatory response to the global banking crisis (the Turner review)," Discussion Paper 09/2, March 2009, www.fsa.gov.uk/pubs/discussion/dp09_02.pdf. www.fsa.gov.uk/pubs/other/turner_review.pdf

"Strengthening liquidity standards," Policy statement 09/16 plus feedback, www.fsa.gov.uk/pages/library/policy/policy/2009/09_16.shtml

"The supervision of Northern Rock: a lessons learned review," March 2008, www.fsa.gov.uk/pubs/other/nr_report.pdf

Financial Stability Board, "Effective resolution of systemically important financial institutions: recommendation and timelines," July 2011, www.financialstabilityboard.org/publications/r_110719.pdf

"Implementing the FSB key attributes of financial resolution regimes – how far have we come?" 15 April 2013, www.financialstabilityboard.org/publications/r_130419b.pdf

"Key attributes of effective resolution regimes for financial institutions," 4 October 2011, www.financialstabilityboard.org/publications/r_111104cc.pdf

"Macro-prudential policy tools and frameworks," February 2011, www.financialstabilityboard.org/publications/r_1103.pdf

"Recovery and resolution planning, making the key attributes requirements operational," November 2012, www.financialstabilityboard.org/publications/r_121102.pdf

"Strengthening oversight and regulation of shadow banking, an integrated overview of policy recommendations," November 2012, consultative document, www.financialstabilityboard.org/publications/r_121118.pdf

"Thematic review on deposit insurance systems," February 2012, www.financialstabilityboard.org/publications/r_120208.pdf

"Update of group of global systemically important banks (G-SIBs)," November 2012, www.financialstabilityboard.org/publications/r_121118.pdf

Financial Stability Oversight Council, "Report to Congress on Prompt Corrective Action," December 2011, www.treasury.gov/initiatives/fsoc/studies-reports/Documents/FSOC%20PCA%20Report%20FINAL.pdf

"Study and recommendations on prohibitions on proprietary trading and certain relationships with hedge funds and private equity funds," January 2011, www.treasury.gov/initiatives/Documents/Volcker%20sec%20%20619%20study%20final%201%2018%2011%20rg.pdf

Finansdepartementet, "Offentlig administration av banker i kris," SOU 2000:66, www.regeringen.se/content/1/c4/17/06/69d6831d.pdf

Finansinspektionen (Swedish Financial Supervisory Authority), "Promemoria, Förslag till högre kapitaltäckningskrav för de större svenska bankgrupperna," November 2011, www.fi.se/upload/30_Regler/50_Kapitaltackning/2011/FoS_kapital_25nov11ny.pdf

"Promemoria, Riskviktgolv för svenska bolån," November 2012, www.fi.se/upload/43_Utredningar/40_Skrivelser/2012/riskvikter_pm_sve.pdf

Finansinspektionen, "Risks in the financial system," various years, reports

Finansmarknadskommittén, "Efter finanskrisen: några perspektiv på finansmarknaden," SOU December 2012, www.sou.gov.se/fmk/pdf/Rapport%20Efter%20finanskrisen.pdf

Finanstilsynet (Danish Financial Supervisory Authority), "Redogørelse fra Finanstilsynet om forløbet op til Amagerbanken A/S konkurs i henhold til § 352 a i lov om finansiel virksomhed," 24 August 2011, www.dfsa.dk/~/media/Tal-og-fakta/2011/Redegoerelse_352a_Amagerbanken.ashx

Firzli, Nicolas J., "A critique of the Basel Committee on Banking Supervision," *Revue Analyse Financière*, 10 November 2011 and Q2 2012

Fisher, Richard W., "Correcting 'Dodd–Frank' to actually end 'too big to fail,'" statement before the Committee on Financial Services, US House of Representatives, hearing on "Examining how the Dodd–Frank Act could result in more taxpayer-funded bailouts," 26 June 2013, http://financialservices.house.gov/uploadedfiles/hhrg-113-ba00-wstate-rfisher-20130626.pdf

Foster, George Bellamy and Fred Magdoff, *The Great Financial Crisis: Causes and Consequences* (New York: Monthly Review Press, 2009)

Franklin, Allen and Douglas Gale, *Understanding Financial Crises* (Oxford University Press, 2007)

Fraser, Ian, *Shredded: The Rise and Fall of the Royal Bank of Scotland* (Edinburgh: Birlinn, 2014)

French, Kenneth *et al.*, *The Squam Lake Report: Fixing the Financial System* (Princeton University Press, 2010)

Friedman, Jeffrey and Wladimir Kraus, *Engineering the Financial Crisis, Systemic Risk and the Failure of Regulation* (Philadelphia, PA: University of Pennsylvania Press, 2011)

Gandhi, Priyank and Hanno N. Lustig, "Size anomalies in US bank stock returns," NBER Working Paper 16553, 2010 (forthcoming *Journal of Finance*), www.nber.org/papers/w16553

Garnaut, Ross, *The Great Crash of 2008* (Melbourne University Press, 2009)

Geithner, Timothy F., *Stress Test: Reflections on Financial Crises* (London and New York: Random House, 2014)

General Accountability Office (GAO), "Financial crisis losses and potential impacts of the Dodd–Frank Act," 16 January 2013, www.gao.gov/assets/660/651322.pdf

"Financial institutions, causes and consequences of recent bank failures," report to Congressional Committees, GAO 13–71, January 2013, www.gao.gov/assets/660/651154.pdf

"Proprietary trading: regulators will need more comprehensive information to fully monitor compliance with restrictions when implemented" (Washington, DC: GAO) (July 2011), also at www.gao.gov/assets/330/321006.pdf

Gerhardt, Maria, "Consumer bankruptcy regimes and credit default in the US and Europe: a comparative study," CEPS Working Paper, 318/July 2009, also at http://aei.pitt.edu/11336/1/1887.pdf

Getter, Darryl G., "US implementation of the Basel capital regulatory framework," Congressional Research Service, November 2012, http://assets.opencrs.com/rpts/R42744_20121114.pdf

Global Markets Institute (Goldman Sachs), "Measuring the TBTF effect on bond pricing," May 2013, www.goldmansachs.com/our-thinking/public-policy/regulatory-reform/measuring-tbtf-doc.pdf

Goldstein, Morris and Nicolas Veron, "Too big to fail: the transatlantic debate," Peterson Institute Working Paper no. 2, 2011, www.iie.com/publications/interstitial.cfm?ResearchID=1745

Goodhart, Charles and Jean-Charles Rochet, "Evaluation of the Riksbank's monetary policy and work with financial stability 2005–2010," Reports from the Riksdag 2010/11: RFR5, www.riksbank.se/Upload/Dokument_riksbank/Kat_publicerat/Rapporter/2011/Goodhart%20Rochet%20engelska.pdf

Gordon, Jeffrey N. and Wolf-Georg Ringe, "Bank resolution in the European banking union: a transatlantic perspective," Columbia Law and Economics Working Paper no. 465, 22 July 2014, http://papers.ssrn.com/sol3/papers.cfm?abstract_id=2361347

Gordy, Michael and Bradley Howells, "Procyclicality in Basel II: can we treat the disease without killing the patient," *Journal of Financial Intermediation* 15:3 (2006), pp. 395–417, also at www.bis.org/bcbs/events/rtf04gordy_howells.pdf

Gorton, Gary B., *Misunderstanding Crises: Why We Don't See Them Coming* (Oxford University Press, 2012)

Slapped by the Invisible Hand: The Panic of 2007 (Oxford University Press, 2010)

Gorton, Gary B. and Andrew Metrick, "Regulating the shadow banking system," *Brookings Papers on Economic Activity* 41:2 (2010), pp. 261–312, also at www.brookings.edu/~/media/projects/bpea/fall%20 2010/2010b_bpea_gorton.pdf

Goyal, Rishi *et al.*, "A banking union for the euro area," IMF Staff Discussion Note, SDN 13/01, 13 February 2013, www.imf.org/external/pubs/ft/sdn/2013/sdn1301.pdf

Greenberg, Alan C. and Mark Singer, *The Rise and Fall of Bear Stearns* (New York: Simon & Schuster, 2010)

Greenspan, Alan, *The Age of Turbulence: Adventures in a New World* (New York: Penguin, 2007, 2008)

Grind, Kirsten, *The Lost Bank: The Story of Washington Mutual, the Biggest Bank Failure in American History* (New York: Simon & Schuster, 2013)

Gros, Daniel, "Banking union with a sovereign virus: the self-serving regulatory treatment of sovereign debt in the euro area," CEPS Policy Brief no. 289, 27 March 2013, www.ceps.eu/book/banking-union-sovereign-virus-self-serving-regulatory-treatment-sovereign-debt-euro-area

"Too interconnected to fail = too big to fail, what is in a leverage ratio?" VOX, January 2010, www.voxeu.org/article/too-interconnected-fail-too-big-fail

Group of 30 (G-30), "Financial reform: a framework for financial stability," report, 15 January 2009, www.group30.org/images/PDF/Financial_Reform-A_Framework_for_Financial_Stability.pdf

Gudmundsson, Már and Thorstinn Thorgeirsson, "Fault lines in cross border banking: lessons from the Icelandic case," in P. Backé, E. Gnan and P. Hartmann, eds., *Contagion and Spillovers: New Insights from the Crisis*, SUERF Studies no. 5/2010 (Vienna and Brussels: Larcier)

Gulliver, John, "Fed's bank stress tests make dubious assumptions," *Bloomberg*, 13 March 2013, www.bloomberg.com/news/2013-03-12/fed-s-bank-stress-tests-make-dubious-assumptions.html

Haldane, Andrew G., "Banking on the state," BIS Review 139/2009, www.bis.org/review/r091111e.pdf

"The $100 billion question," comments given at the Institute of Regulation & Risk, Hong Kong, 30 March 2010, www.bankofengland.co.uk/publications/Documents/speeches/2010/speech433.pdf

"Capital discipline," speech before the American Economic Association, Denver, January 2011, www.bankofengland.co.uk/publi cations/Documents/speeches/2011/speech484.pdf

"On being the right size," speech, October 2012, www.bankofeng land.co.uk/publications/Documents/speeches/2012/speech615.pdf

"Turning the red tape tide," speech, April 2013, www.bankofeng land.co.uk/publications/Documents/speeches/2013/speech646.pdf

Haldane, Andrew G. (and Vasileios Madouros), "The dog and the fris-bee," speech, August 2012, www.bankofengland.co.uk/publications/ Documents/speeches/2012/speech596.pdf

Hamilton Place Strategies, "Banking on our future: the value of big banks in a global economy," February 2013, www.hamiltonplacestrategies.com/ wp-content/uploads/2013/02/Banking-on-Our-Future-vF.pdf

Hanson, Samuel, Anil K. Kashyap and Jeremy C. Stein, "A macro-pruden-tial approach to financial regulation," *Journal of Economic Perspectives* 25:1 (Winter 2011), pp. 3–28, http://pubs.aeaweb.org/doi/pdfplus/ 10.1257/jep.25.1.3 or www.economics.harvard.edu/faculty/stein/files/ JEP-macroprudential-July22-2010.pdf

Helleiner, Hubert, Stefano Pagliari and Hubert Zimmerman, eds., *Global Finance in Crisis: The Politics of International Regulatory Change* (London: Routledge, 2009)

Hellwig, Martin F., "Systemic risk in the financial sector: an analysis of the subprime-mortgage financial crisis," *De Economist* 157:2 (2009), pp. 129–207, http://link.springer.com/content/pdf/10.1007% 2Fs10645-009-9110-0.pdf

Herndon, Thomas, Michael Ash and Robert Pollin, "Does high public debt consistently stifle economic growth? A critique of Reinhart and Rogoff," University of Massachusetts Amherst, Political Economy Research Institute, Working Paper no. 322, April 2013, www.peri.umass.edu/file admin/pdf/working_papers/working_papers_301-350/WP322.pdf

HM Treasury, "Banking reform, a new structure for stability and growth," 4 February 2013, www.hm-treasury.gov.uk/d/banking_reform_040213. pdf

"The Financial Services Bill: the Financial Policy Committee's macro prudential tools," September 2012, Cm 8434, www.hm-treasury.gov. uk/d/condoc_fpc_tools_180912.pdf

"The nationalisation of Northern Rock," report by the Comptroller Auditor General, HC 298 session 2008–2009, 20 March 2009, www. nao.org.uk/wp-content/uploads/2009/03/0809298.pdf

"A new approach to financial regulation: the blueprint for reform," Cm 8083, June 2011, www.hm-treasury.gov.uk/d/consult_finreg__new_ approach_blueprint.pdf

"Review of HM Treasury's management response to the financial crisis," March 2012, www.hm-treasury.gov.uk/d/review_fincrisis_response_290312.pdf

Hoenig, Thomas M., "Back to basics: a better alternative to Basel capital rules," speech to the American Banker Regulatory Symposium, September 2012, www.fdic.gov/news/news/speeches/archives/2012/spsep1412_2.html

"Restructuring the banking system to improve safety and soundness," FDIC, December 2012, www.fdic.gov/about/learn/board/Restructuring-the-Banking-System-05-24-11.pdf

Honohan, Patrick and Daniela Klingebiel, "Controlling fiscal costs of banking crises," World Bank, May 2000, www1.worldbank.org/finance/assets/images/depins02.pdf

Honohan, Patrick and Luc Læven, eds., *Systemic Financial Crises, Containment and Resolution* (Cambridge University Press, 2005)

Honohan, Patrick, "A plan to restore Ireland's banks to health," *Financial Times*, 31 March 2010, www.ft.com/intl/cms/s/0/da83ac20-3cfd-11df-bbcf-00144feabdc0.html?siteedition=intl#axzz2knNJrO3S

"Recapitalisation of failed banks: some lessons from the Irish experience," speech, 7 September 2012, www.bis.org/review/r120907j.pdf?frames=0

Honohan, Patrick *et al.*, "The Irish banking crisis: regulatory and financial stability policy 2003–2008," a report to the minister of finance by the governor of the Central Bank, 31 May 2010, http://mpra.ub.uni-muenchen.de/24896/1/MPRA_paper_24896.pdf

House of Commons, "Fifth report" (on Northern Rock), 24 January 2008, www.publications.parliament.uk/pa/cm200708/cmselect/cmtreasy/56/5602.htm

House of Lords, Parliamentary Commission on Banking Standards, "An accident waiting to happen, the failure of HBOS," Fourth report session 2012/13, 4 April 2013, www.publications.parliament.uk/pa/jt201213/jtselect/jtpcbs/144/144.pdf

Hudson, Michael W., *The Monster: How a Gang of Predatory Lenders and Wall Street Bankers Fleeced America – and Spawned a Global Crisis* (New York: Times Books, 2010)

Huertas, Thomas F., *Crisis: Cause, Containment and Cure* (Basingstoke: Palgrave Macmillan, 2010)

Independent Commission on Banking (ICB), "Final report: recommendations," September 2011 (Vickers report), www.ecgi.org/documents/icb_final_report_12sep2011.pdf

Independent Commission on the Future of the Cyprus Banking Sector (David Lascelles *et al.*), Interim report, June 2013, www.centralbank.gov.cy/media//pdf/LSE_ICFCBS_INTERIM_REPORT_06_13.pdf

Ingves, Stefan and David S. Hoelscher, "The resolution of systemic bank-
ing crises: the way forward," in Douglas D. Evanoff and George G.
Kaufman, eds. *Systemic Financial Crisis: Resolving Large Bank
Insolvencies* (Hackensack, NJ: World Scientific Publishing, 2005)

Institute of International Finance, "Interim report on the cumulative impact
on the global economy of proposed changes in the banking regulatory
framework," June 2010, www.ebf-fbe.eu/uploads/10-Interim%20NCI_
June2010_Web.pdf

"Response to the global financial crisis 2007–2012" (Washington,
DC: IIF, 2012), also as pdf document www.iif.com/about/article+
1156.php

International Monetary Fund, "European Union: publication of financial
sector assessment program documentation – technical note on deposit
insurance," IMF Country Report 13/66, March 2013, www.imf.org/
external/pubs/ft/scr/2013/cr1366.pdf

"A fair and substantial contribution by the financial sector," final report
for the G-20, June 2010, www.imf.org/external/np/g20/pdf/062710b.
pdf

"Fiscal adjustment in an uncertain world," Fiscal Monitor, April 2013,
www.imf.org/external/pubs/ft/fm/2013/01/pdf/fm1301.pdf

Global Financial Stability Report, various issues, 2008–13, www.imf.org/
External/Pubs/FT/GFSR/2013/01/pdf/text.pdf

Global Financial Stability Report, April 2014, ch. 3, "How big is the
implicit subsidy for banks considered to important to fail?" www.imf.
org/external/pubs/ft/gfsr/2014/01/pdf/text.pdf

"Macro-prudential policy: an organizing framework," 14 March 2011,
www.imf.org/external/np/pp/eng/2011/031411.pdf

World Economic Outlook, various issues, 2008–13

Jaffee, Dwight M. and Johan Waldén, "The impact of Basel III and Solvency 2
on Swedish banks and insurers – an equilibrium analysis," Report to the
Swedish Financial Markets Committee (Finansmarknadskommittén),
Report no. 3, December 2010, www.sou.gov.se/fmk/pdf/Rapport%20
3%20engelsk%20ny.pdf

Jarrow, Robert A., "A critique of revised Basel II," *Journal of Financial
Services Research* 32 (October 2007), pp. 1–11, www.fdic.gov/bank/
analytical/cfr/2006/sept/JarrowR.pdf

Johnson, Simon, "Banks' living wills don't defuse systemic risk," *Bloomberg*,
8 July 2012

"Betrayed by Basel," *New York Times*, 13 January 2013

"Big banks are hazardous to the US economic health," *Bloomberg*, 2
September 2012

"Breaking up big banks is a severely conservative project," *Bloomberg*,
28 October 2012

"Breaking up four big banks," *New York Times*, 19 May 2012

"Fed should push to cut biggest banks down to size" (on Fed governor Daniel Tarullo), *Bloomberg*, 15 October 2012

"Too big to fail not fixed despite Dodd–Frank," *Bloomberg*, 9 October 2011

"Who decided the US megabanks are too big to jail?" *Bloomberg*, 4 February 2013

"Why higher bank capital is in the public interest" (review of Admati and Hellwig), *Bloomberg*, 4 March 2013

Johnson, Simon and James Kwak, *13 Bankers: The Wall Street Take-Over and the Next Financial Meltdown* (New York: Pantheon Books, 2010)

Jónsson, Asgéir, *Why Iceland? How One of the World's Smallest Countries Became the Meltdown's Biggest Casualty* (New York: McGraw-Hill, 2009)

Kane, Edward, "Missing elements in US financial reform: a Kübler-Ross interpretation of the inadequacy of the Dodd–Frank Act," *Journal of Banking and Finance* 36:3 (2012), pp. 654–61, http://papers.ssrn.com/sol3/papers.cfm?abstract_id=1654051&download=yes

Kapan, Tümer and Camelia Minoiu, "Balance sheet strength and bank lending during the global financial crisis," IMF Working Paper 13/102, May 2013, www.imf.org/external/pubs/ft/wp/2013/wp13102.pdf

Kaufman, George G. and Kenneth E. Scott, "What is systemic risk and do bank regulators retard or contribute to it?" *Independent Review* 7:3 (Winter 2003), pp. 371–91, also at www.independent.org/pdf/tir/tir_07_3_scott.pdf

Kaufman, Henry, *The Road to Financial Reformation, Warnings, Consequences, Reforms* (New York: John Wiley & Sons, 2009)

Kashyap, Anil K. and Jeremy C. Stein, "Cyclical implications of the Basel II capital standards," *Economic Perspectives* Q1 (2004), pp. 18–31, also at www.economics.harvard.edu/faculty/stein/files/basel-chicago-fed-04.pdf

Kashyap, Anil K., Jeremy C. Stein and Samuel G. Hanson, "An analysis of the impact of 'substantially heightened' capital requirements on large financial institutions," Harvard Business School and University of Chicago, May 2010, www.people.hbs.edu/shanson/Clearinghouse-paper-final_20100521.pdf

Kay, John, "Narrow banking: the reform of banking regulation," Centre for the Study of Financial Innovation, September 2009, www.johnkay.com/wp-content/uploads/2009/12/JK-Narrow-Banking.pdf

KBW (Keefe, Bruyette and Woods), "Financial stocks weekly: US bank leverage, is better than Europe good enough?" *Equity Strategy*, 16 June 2013, http://dealbreaker.com/2013/06/banks-might-be-undercapitalized-depending-how-you-count/kbw-exh-2/

"Financial stocks weekly: will the US close the loophole on Basel leverage?" *Equity Strategy*, 28 May 2013, https://kbw3.bluematrix.com/docs/pdf/fb489291-6323-4823-ab9f-b8e18b46ba0f.pdf?

Kelly, Brian, Hanno Lustig and Stijn van Nieuwerburgh, "Too-systemic-to fail: what option markets imply about sector-wide government guarantees," NBER Working Paper 17615, 2012, http://papers.ssrn.com/sol3/papers.cfm?abstract_id=1762312

Kelly, Kate, *Street Fighters: The Last 72 Hours of Bear Stearns, the Toughest Firm on Wall Street* (New York: Portfolio Trade/Penguin, 2010)

King, Stephen D., *When the Money Runs Out* (New Haven, CT: Yale University Press, 2013)

Kluth, Michael and Kennet Lynggaard, "Explaining policy responses to Danish and Irish banking failures during the financial crisis," *West European Politics* 36:4 (2013), pp. 771–88

Kotlikoff, Laurence J, *Jimmy Stewart Is Dead: Ending the World's Financial Plague with Limited Purpose Banking* (Hoboken, NJ: John Wiley & Sons, 2010)

Kroszner, Randall S. and Robert J. Shiller, *Reforming US Financial Markets, Reflections Before and Beyond Dodd–Frank* (Cambridge, MA: MIT Press, 2011)

Krugman, Paul, *The Return of Depression Economics and the Crisis of 2008* (New York: W. W. Norton, 2009)

"Too big to fail fail," *New York Times*, 11 January 2010

Kubarych, Roger, *Stress Testing the System: Simulating the Global Consequences of the Next Financial Crisis* (New York: Council on Foreign Relations Press, 2001)

Kuttner, Robert, *A Presidency in Peril* (White River Junction, VT: Chelsea Green, 2010)

Labonte, Marc, "Systemically important or 'too big to fail' financial institutions," Congressional Research Service, 30 July 2013, www.fas.org/sgp/crs/misc/R42150.pdf

Laeven, Luc and Fabian Valencia, "Resolution of banking crises: the good, the bad and the ugly," IMF Working Paper no. 10/146, June 2010, www.imf.org/external/pubs/ft/wp/2010/wp10146.pdf

"Systemic banking crises: a new database," IMF Working Paper 2008/224, www.imf.org/external/pubs/ft/wp/2008/wp08224.pdf, updated June 2012, IMF Working Paper 2012/163, www.imf.org/external/pubs/ft/wp/2012/wp12163.pdf

Langohr, Herwig and Patricia Langohr, *The Rating Agencies and Their Credit Ratings: How They Work and Why They Are Relevant* (New York: Wiley, 2008)

Lastra, Rosa M., "Legal and regulatory responses to the financial crisis," University of London, Legal Studies Research Paper 100/2012, March 2012, http://papers.ssrn.com/sol3/papers.cfm?abstract_id=2020553

"Northern Rock, UK bank insolvency and cross-border bank insolvency," *Journal of Banking Regulation* 9:3 (May 2008), pp. 939–55

Lenihan, Niall, "Claims of depositors, subordinated creditors, senior creditors and central Banks in bank resolutions," speech at AEDBF Conference, Athens, 5–6 October 2012, www.aedbf.eu/fileadmin/eu/pictures/news/2012/athens/presentations/LENIHAN.pdf

Levich, Richard M. *et al.*, *Ratings, Rating Agencies and the Global Financial System* (Dordrecht: Kluwer Academic, 2002)

Levine, Ross, "An autopsy of the US financial system: accident, suicide or negligent homicide," *Journal of Financial Economic Policy* 2:3 (2010), pp. 196–213, also at www.econ.brown.edu/fac/Ross_Levine/other%20files/Autopsy-4-13.pdf

Levy, Aviram and Sebastian Schich, "The design of government guarantees for bank bonds: lessons from the recent financial crisis," *OECD Financial Market Trends* 1(2010), pp. 1–32, www.oecd.org/finance/financial-markets/45636972.pdf

Lewis, Michael, *The Big Short: Inside the Doomsday Machine* (New York: W. W. Norton, 2010)

Boomerang: The Biggest Bust (New York and London: Penguin, 2012)

Litan, Robert E., "The political economy of financial regulation after the crisis," in Alan S. Blinder, Andrew Lo and Robert Solow, eds., *Rethinking the Financial Crisis* (New York: Russell Sage Foundation, 2013), pp. 269–302, also at www.russellsage.org/sites/all/files/Rethinking-Finance/Litan.%20Political%20Economy%20of%20Financial.pdf

Llewellyn, David T., "A framework for crisis prevention and management: where is Pillar 4?" paper presented at the Annual Colloquium of the Belgian Financial Forum, 10 November 2010, http://vorschau.bwg.at/bwg/bwg_v3.nsf/sysPages/xEFE05EE2CA609AECC1257904002F0ADA

Lo, Andrew W., "Reading about the financial crisis: a 21-book review," *Journal of Economic Literature* 50: 1 (March 2012), pp. 151–78, also at http://mitsloan.mit.edu/finance/pdf/Lo-20120109c.pdf

"Regulatory reform in the wake of the financial crisis of 2007–2008," *Journal of Financial Economic Policy* 1:1 (2009), pp. 4–43, www.emeraldinsight.com/journals.htm?articleid=1790056

Lowenstein, Roger, *The End of Wall Street* (New York: Penguin, 2010)

Lui, Alison, "Single or twin? The UK financial regulatory landscape after the financial crisis of 2007–2009," *Journal of Banking Regulation* 13:1

(January 2012), pp. 24–35, www.palgrave-journals.com/jbr/journal/
v13/n1/pdf/jbr201118a.pdf

Lybeck, Johan A., "Finance ministers take note: bailouts are often better
than bailin," *Financial Times*, 14 April 2013

"Forget Basel III and head straight for Basel IV," *Financial Times*,
2 February 2012

"Glass–Steagall would not have stopped the crash," *Financial Times*, 16
July 2013

A Global History of the Financial Crash 2007–2010 (Cambridge
University Press, 2011)

"It is time to consider breaking up the banking behemoths," *Financial
Times*, 19 March 2009

Mackay, Charles, *Extraordinary Popular Delusions and the Madness of
Crowds* (New York: Harmony Books, 1841, 1852, 1980, 1995, 2003)

Marques, Luis Brandao, Ricardo Correa and Horacio Sapriza, "International
evidence on government support and risk taking in the banking sector,"
IMF Working Paper 13/94, May 2013, www.imf.org/external/pubs/ft/
wp/2013/wp1394.pdf

Martin, Iain, *Making It Happen: Fred Goodwin, RBS and the Men who
Blew Up the British Economy* (London: Simon & Schuster, 2013)

Mayer, Thomas, "A Copernican turn for banking union," CEPS Policy Brief
no. 290, 14 May 2013, http://aei.pitt.edu/42201/1/A_Copernican_
Turn_for_Banking_Union.pdf

Mayes, David, "Moral hazard, bank resolution and the protection of depos-
itors," in James R. Barth, Lin Chen and Clas Wihlborg, eds., *Research
Handbook on International Banking and Governance* (Northampton,
MA: Edward Elgar, 2012), ch. 14

"Who pays for bank insolvency?" *Journal of International Money and
Finance* 23 (2004), pp. 515–51, http://ideas.repec.org/a/eee/jimfin/
v23y2004i3p515-551.html

Mayes, David and Aarno Liuksila, eds., *Who Pays for Bank Insolvency?*
(New York: Palgrave MacMillan, 2004)

Mayo, Mike, *Exile on Wall Street: One Analyst's Fight to Save the Big Banks
from Themselves* (Hoboken, NJ: Wiley, 2011)

McDonald, Lawrence J., *A Colossal Failure of Common Sense: The Inside
Story of the Collapse of Lehman Brothers* (New York: Three Rivers, 2010)

McKenzie, George and Stephen Thomas, *Financial Instability and the
International Debt Problem* (London: Macmillan, 1992)

McLean, Bethany and Joe Nocera, *All the Devils Are Here: The Hidden
History of the Financial Crisis* (New York: Portfolio/Penguin, 2010)

Merkley, Jeff and Carl Levin, "The Dodd–Frank Act restrictions on proprietary trading and conflicts of interest: new tools to address evolving

threats," *Harvard Law and Policy Review* 48:2 (2011), pp. 515–53, www.harvardjol.com/wp-content/uploads/2011/07/Merkley-Levin_ Policy-Essay.pdf

Micossi, Stefano, "Do we need a resolution fund paid for by financial institutions?" EuropEos Commentary, May 2010, www.ceps.be/book/ do-we-need-resolution-fund-paid-financial-institutions

Micossi, Stefano, Ginevra Bruzzone and Jacopo Carmassi, "The new European framework for managing bank crises," CEPS Policy Brief 304, 21 November 2013, www.ceps.be/book/new-european-framework-managing-bank-crises

Micossi, Stefano, Ginevra Bruzzone and Miriam Cassella, "Bail-in provisions in state aid and resolution procedures: are they consistent with systemic stability?" CEPS Policy Brief 318, 21 May 2014, http://papers. ssrn.com/sol3/papers.cfm?abstract_id=2445900

Miles, David, Jing Yang and Gilberto Marcheggiano, "Optimal bank capital," Bank of England Discussion Paper no. 31, April 2011 (revised 2013), www.bankofengland.co.uk/publications/Documents/externalmpc papers/extmpcpaper0031.pdf

Miller, Merton H., "Does the M&M proposition apply to banks?" *Journal of Banking and Finance* 19 (June 1995), pp. 483–9, http://econ.queensu. ca/faculty/milne/870/Merton%20Miller%20on%20banking% 20and%20the%20MM%20theorem.pdf

Milne, Alistair, *The Fall of the House of Credit: What Went Wrong in Banking and What Can Be Done to Repair the Damage* (Cambridge University Press, 2009)

Mishkin, Frederic S., "How big a problem is too big to fail?" *Journal of Economic Literature* 44:4 (2006), pp. 988–1004, also as www.nber.org/ papers/w11814.pdf?new_window=1

"Over the cliff: from the subprime to the global financial crisis," *Journal of Economic Perspectives* 25:1 (Winter 2011), pp. 49–70, also at http:// pubs.aeaweb.org/doi/pdfplus/10.1257/jep.25.1.49

Modigliani, Franco and Merton H. Miller, "The cost of capital, corporation finance and the theory of investment," *American Economic Review* 48 (June 1958), pp. 261–97

Moody's Analytics, "Basel III new capital and liquidity standards – FAQ," 19 January 2012, www.moodysanalytics.com/~/media/Insight/Regulatory/ Basel-III/Thought-Leadership/2012/2012-19-01-MA-Basel-III-FAQs. ashx

Moosa, Imad A., "Basel II as a casualty of the global financial crisis," *Journal of Banking Regulation* 11:2 (March 2010), pp. 95–114, also at www. doc88.com/p-214942407649.html

The Myth of the Too Big to Fail (London: Palgrave Macmillan, 2010)

Morgenson, Gretchen and Joshua Rosner, *Reckless Endangerment: How Outsized Ambition, Greed and Corruption Led to Economic Armageddon (on Fannie Mae and Freddie Mac)* (New York: Times Books/Henry Holt, 2011)

Morris, Charles R., *The Trillion Dollar Meltdown: Easy Money, High Rollers, and the Great Credit Crash* (New York: Public Affairs, 2008)

Morris, Stephen and Hyun Song Shin, "Financial regulation in a system context," *Brookings Papers on Economic Activity* 39 (Fall 2008), pp. 229–74, www.brookings.edu/~/media/Projects/BPEA/Fall%202008/2008b_bpea_morris.PDF, also at www.princeton.edu/~hsshin/www/BPEA2008.pdf

Muolo, Paul and Matthew Padilla, *Chain of Blame: How Wall Street Caused the Mortgage and Credit Crisis* (Hoboken, NJ: John Wiley & Sons, 2010)

Münchau, Wolfgang, *Kernschmelze im Finanzsystem* (Munich: Carl Hanser Verlag, 2008)

Nichols, Mark W., Jill M. Hendrickson and Kevin Griffith, "Was the financial crisis the result of ineffective policy and too much regulation? An empirical investigation," *Journal of Banking Regulation* 12:3 (June 2011), pp. 236–51, www.palgrave-journals.com/jbr/journal/v12/n3/full/jbr20113a.html

Nolle, Daniel E., "Global financial system reform: the Dodd–Frank Act and the G-20 agenda," *Journal of Financial Economic Policy* 4:2 (2012), pp. 160–97

Norges Bank *et al.*, "Macroprudential supervision of the financial system – Organisation and Instruments," report, January 2012, www.regjerin gen.no/pages/36861944/report_makropru.pdf

Noss, Joseph and Rhiannon Sowerbutts, "The implicit subsidy of banks," Bank of England Financial Stability Paper 15, May 2012, www.bank ofengland.co.uk/publications/Documents/fsr/fs_paper15.pdf

Nyberg, Peter, see Commission of Investigation into the Banking Sector in Ireland

OECD, *Banks under Stress* (Paris: OECD, 1992)
    The Financial Crisis: Reform and Exit Strategies (Paris: OECD, 2009)
    "The subprime crisis: size, deleveraging and some policy options" (April 2008)

Onaran, Yalman, *Zombie Banks: How Broken Banks and Debtor Nations Are Crippling the Global Economy* (Hoboken, NJ: John Wiley & Sons, 2012)

O'Sullivan, Kenneth and Stephen Kinsella, "Financial and regulatory failure: the case of Ireland," *Journal of Banking Regulation* 14:1 (January

2013), pp. 1–15, www.ucd.ie/geary/static/publications/workingpapers/gearywp201136.pdf

Ötger-Robe, Inci, Aditya Narain, Anna Ilyina and Jay Surti, "The too-impor tant-to-fail conundrum: impossible to ignore and difficult to resolve," IMF Staff Discussion Note, SDN 11/12, 27 May 2011, www.imf.org/external/pubs/ft/sdn/2011/sdn1112.pdf

Oura, Hiroko and Liliana Schumacher, "Macro-financial stress testing – principles and practices," IMF Staff Report, August 2012, www.imf.org/external/np/pp/eng/2012/082212.pdf

Pagliari, Stefano, ed., *Making Good Financial Regulation: Towards a Policy Response to Regulatory Capture* (Guildford: Grosvenor House, 2012)

Partnoy, Frank, *Infectious Greed: How Deceit and Greed Corrupted the Financial Markets* (New York: Public Affairs, 2009)

Paulson, Henry M. (Hank), *On the Brink: Inside the Race to Stop the Collapse of the Global Financial System* (New York: Business Plus, 2010)

Pazarbasioglu, Ceyla, Jianping Zhou, Vanessa Le Leslé and Michael Moore, "Contingent capital: economic rationale and design features," IMF Staff Position Note no. SDN/11/01, 25 January 2011, www.imf.org/external/pubs/ft/sdn/2011/sdn1101.pdf

Perman, Ray, *Hubris: How HBOS Wrecked the Best Bank in Britain* (Edinburgh: Birlinn, 2013)

Pfleiderer, Paul, "Reducing the fragility of the financial sector: the impor tance of equity and why it is not expensive," speech at Norges Bank conference, 29 November 2012, www.gsb.stanford.edu/sites/default/files/research/documents/Norges%20Bank%20Macroprudential%20Regulation%20Workshop%20Pfleiderer%20For%20Distribution%20%281%29.pdf

Philippon, Thomas and Philipp Schabl, "Efficient recapitalization," *Journal of Finance* 68:1 (February 2013), pp. 1–42, http://onlinelibrary.wiley.com/doi/10.1111/j.1540-6261.2012.01793.x/full or http://pages.stern.nyu.edu/~pschnabl/public_html/PhilipponSchnablFeb2012.pdf

Piskorski, Tomasz, Amit Seru and James Witkin, "Asset quality mis-representation by financial intermediaries: evidence from RMBS market," Working Paper, Columbia Business School and Chicago Booth School of Business, 2013, http://papers.ssrn.com/sol3/papers.cfm?abstract_id=2215422

Portes, Richard, "The Icelandic financial sector and the markets," Icelandic Chamber of Commerce, April 2008, http://faculty.london.edu/rportes/Iceland%20international%20financial%20sector.pdf

Posner, Richard A., *A Failure of Capitalism: The Crisis of '08 and the Descent into Depression* (Cambridge, MA: Harvard University Press, 2009)

Pozen, Robert, *Too Big to Save: How to Fix the US Financial System* (Hoboken, NJ: John Wiley & Sons, 2010)

Prates, Marcelo M., "Why prudential regulation will fail to prevent financial crises: a legal approach," Central Bank of Brazil Working Paper no. 335, 1 November 2013, http://papers.ssrn.com/sol3/papers.cfm?abstract_id=2375470

Pro Publica, List of bailout recipients and repayments, http://projects.propublica.org/bailout/list

Pryce, Vicky, *Greekonomics: The Euro Crisis and Why Politicians Don't Get It* (London: Biteback, 2012)

Puspa, Amri, Apanard P. Angkinand and Clas Wihlborg, "International comparisons of bank regulation, liberalization and banking crises," *Journal of Financial Economic Policy* 3:4 (2011), pp. 322–39, also at http://papers.ssrn.com/sol3/papers.cfm?abstract_id=1903510

Pym, Hugh, *Inside the Banking Crisis: The Untold Story* (London: A&C Black, 2014)

Quagliarello, Mario, *Stress Testing the Banking System: Methodologies and Applications* (Cambridge University Press, 2009)

Rajan, Raghuram G., *Fault Lines: How Hidden Fractures still Threaten the World Economy* (Princeton University Press, 2010)

Ratnovski, Lev, "Competition policy for modern banks," IMF Working Paper 13/126, May 2013, www.imf.org/external/pubs/ft/wp/2013/wp13126.pdf

Read, Colin, *Global Financial Meltdown: How We Can Avoid the Next Economic Crisis* (Basingstoke: Palgrave Macmillan, 2009)

Regling, Klaus and Max Watson, *A Preliminary Report on the Sources of the Irish Banking Crisis* (Dublin: Government publications Sales Office, 2010), www.bankinginquiry.gov.ie/Preliminary%20Report%20into%20Ireland's%20Banking%20Crisis%2031%20May%202010.pdf

Reinhart, Carmen M. and Kenneth S. Rogoff, "The aftermath of financial crises," *American Economic Review*, May 2009, also at www.nber.org/papers/w14656.pdf

"Is the 2007 US sub-prime financial crisis so different? An international historical comparison," NBER Working Paper 13761, January 2008, www.nber.org/papers/w13761

This Time Is Different: Eight Centuries of Financial Folly (Princeton University Press, 2009)

Repullo, Rafael, "Policies for banking crises, a theoretical framework," in Patrick Honohan and Luc Læven, eds., *Systemic Financial Crises, Containment and Resolution* (Cambridge University Press, 2005)

Riksgäldskontoret (Swedish National Debt Office), "Riksgäldens årgärder för att stärka det finansiella systemet," 9 August 2013, www.riksgalden.se/Dokument_sve/om_riksgalden/rapporter/ bankstod/Riksg%c3%a4ldens%20%c3%a5tg%c3%a4rder%20 f%c3%b6r%20att%20st%c3%a4rka%20stabiliteten%20i%20 det%20finansiella%20systemet%202013_2.pdf

Riksrevisionsverket, Stabilitetsfonden, RiR 2011:26, www.riksrevisionen. se/PageFiles/14507/Anpassad_11_26%20Stabilitetsfonden.pdf

Ritholtz, Barry, *Bailout Nation* (Hoboken, NJ: John Wiley & Sons, 2009)

Rochet, Jean-Charles, *Why Are there So Many Banking Crises? The Politics and Policy of Bank Regulation* (Princeton University Press, 2008)

Rogoff, Kenneth, "Ending the financial arms race," Project Syndicate, 7 September 2012, www.project-syndicate.org/commentary/ending-the-financial-arms-race-by-kenneth-rogoff

Rogoff, Kenneth S. and Carmen M. Reinhart, "This time is different: a panoramic view of eight centuries of financial crises," NBER Working Paper 13882 (March 2008), www.economics.harvard.edu/files/faculty/ 51_This_Time_Is_Different.pdf

Rosner, Josh, "The Washington Mutual story," 13 March 2013, www.ritholtz. com/blog/2013/03/jpmorgan-chase-out-of-control-introduction/

Ross, Shane, *The Bankers: How the Banks Brought Ireland to Its Knees* (London: Penguin, 2009)

Roubini, Nouriel, "The current US recession and the risks of a systemic financial crisis," US House of Representatives Financial Services Committee, 26 February 2008, http://msnbcmedia.msn.com/i/msnbc/ sections/tvnews/nightly%20news/roubini022608.pdf

Roubini, Nouriel and Stephen Mihm, *Crisis Economics: A Crash Course in the Future of Finance* (New York and London: Allen Lane, 2010)

Roubini, Nouriel and Brad Setser, *Bail-outs or Bail-ins: Responding to Financial Crises in Emerging Markets* (Washington, DC: Institute for International Economics, 2004)

Santomero, Anthony M. and Paul Hoffman, "Problem bank resolution: evaluating the options," University of Pennsylvania, the Wharton School, Financial Institutions Center, Working Paper no. 98.05, 1998, http://fic. wharton.upenn.edu/fic/papers/98/9805.pdf

Santomero, Anthony M. *et al.*, *Challenges for Central Banking* (Boston: Kluwer Academic, 2001)

Santow, Leonard, *Do They Walk on Water? Federal Reserve Chairmen and the Fed* (New York: Praeger, 2008)

Sapir, André, "Europe after the crisis: less or more role for nation states in money and finance?" *Oxford Review of Economic Policy* 27:4 (Winter

2011), pp. 609–19, http://oxrep.oxfordjournals.org/content/27/4/608.
abstract

Schoenmaker, Dirk, *Governance of International Banking: The Financial Trilemma* (Oxford and New York: Oxford University Press, 2013)

Schoenmaker, Dirk and Daniel Gros, "A European deposit insurance and resolution fund," CEPS Working Document no. 364, May 2012, www.ceps.eu/book/european-deposit-insurance-and-resolution-fund

Schoenmaker, Dirk and Toon Peek, "The state of the banking sector in Europe," OECD Economics Department Working Paper 1102, 27 January 2014, www.oecd-ilibrary.org/docserver/download/5k3 ttg7n4r32.pdf?expires=1394983777&id=id&accname=guest& checksum=65C45A9C4A143FE59D71C61312F70424

Schöneberger, Dominik, *US Hypothekenkrise in Deutschland: Auswirkungen im Fall IKB* (Hamburg: Diplomica, 2009)

Scott, Hal C., ed., *Capital Adequacy Beyond Basel: Banking, Securities and Insurance* (Oxford University Press, 2005)

The Global Financial Crisis (New York: Foundation Press, 2009)

Scott, Kenneth E. and John B. Taylor, eds., *Bankruptcy not Bailout: A Special Chapter 14* (Stanford, CA: Hoover Institution Press, 2012)

Shelp, Ron and Al Ehrbar, *Fallen Giant: The Amazing Story of Hank Greenberg and the History of AIG* (Hoboken, NJ: John Wiley & Sons, 2009)

Shiller, Robert J., *Finance and the Good Society* (Princeton University Press, 2012)

Irrational Exuberance (Princeton University Press, 2000, 2005)

The Subprime Solution: How Today's Global Financial Crisis Happened and What to Do about It (Princeton University Press, 2008, 2012)

Shin, Hyun Song, "Reflections on Northern Rock: the bank run that heralded the global financial crisis," *Journal of Economic Perspectives* 23:1 (Winter 2009), pp. 101–19, http://isites.harvard.edu/fs/docs/icb. topic470237.files/articles%20spring%202009/Shin_2009.pdf

SIGTARP, Office of the Special Inspector General for the Troubled Asset Relief Program, *Quarterly Report to Congress*, 29 October 2013, www.sigtarp.gov/Quarterly%20Reports/October_29_2013_Report_ to_Congress.pdf

Quarterly Report to Congress, 29 January 2014, www.sigtarp.gov/ Quarterly%20Reports/January_29_2014_Report_to_Congress.pdf

Sinclair, Timothy J., *The New Masters of Capital: American Bond Rating Agencies and the Policy of Credit Worthiness* (Ithaca, NY: Cornell University Press, 2005)

Sinn, Hans-Werner, *Kasino-Kapitalismus: Wie es zur Finanzkrise kam, und was jetzt zu tun ist* (Berlin: Econ Verlag, 2009)

Skeel, David, *The New Financial Deal: Understanding the Dodd–Frank Act and Its Unintended Consequences* (Hoboken, NJ: John Wiley & Sons, 2011)

Smit, Jeroen, *The Perfect Prey: The Fall of ABN AMRO, or What Went Wrong in the Banking Industry* (London: Quercus, 2010)

Sommer, Reine, *Die Subprime-Krise. Wie einige faule US-Kredite das internationale Finanzsystem erschüttern* (Hanover: Telepolis, 2008)

Sorkin, Andrew Ross, *Too Big to Fail: Inside the Battle to Save Wall Street* (London: Allen Lane, 2009)

Soros, George, *The New Paradigm for Financial Markets: The Credit Crisis of 2008 and What It Means* (New York: Public Affairs, 2008)

Sowell, Thomas, *The Housing Boom and Bust* (New York: Basic Books, 2009)

Stern, Gary H. and Ron J. Feldman, *Too Big to Fail: The Hazards of Bank Bailouts* (Washington, DC: Brookings Institution, 2004, 2009)

Stiglitz, Joseph, *Freefall: America, Free Markets and the Sinking of the World Economy* (New York: W. W. Norton, 2010)

Suskind, Ron, *Confidence Men: Wall Street, Washington and the Education of a President* (New York: HarperCollins, 2011)

Sveriges Riksbank, *Finansiell stabilitet*, various issues

  "Lämplig kapitalnivå i svenska storbanker – en samhällsekonomisk analys," report 2011, www.riksbank.se/Upload/Rapporter/2011/rap_lamplig_kapitalniva_i_svenska_storbanker_111206_sve.pdf

  "Riksbanken och finansiell stabilitet," report February 2013

Swagel, Philip, "The financial crisis: an inside view," *Brookings Papers on Economic Activity* 40: 1(April 2009), pp. 1–78, http://muse.jhu.edu/journals/brookings_papers_on_economic_activity/v2009/2009.1.swagel.pdf

Swiss Financial Markets Supervisory Authority (FINMA), "Ordinance of the Swiss Financial Markets Supervisory Authority on the insolvency of banks and securities dealers," 22 October 2012, www.admin.ch/ch/e/rs/9/952.05.en.pdf

Taleb, Nassim N., *The Black Swan: The Impact of the Highly Improbable* (New York: Random House, 2007)

Tarr, David G., "The political, regulatory and market failures that caused the US financial crisis: what are the lessons?" *Journal of Financial Economic Policy* 2:2 (2010), pp. 163–86, also at https://openknowledge.worldbank.org/bitstream/handle/10986/3810/WPS5324.pdf?sequence=1

Tarullo, Daniel K., *Banking on Basel: The Future of International Financial Regulation* (Washington, DC: Peterson Institute for International Economics, 2008)

Taylor, John B., *Getting off Track: How Government Actions and Interventions Caused, Prolonged and Worsened the Financial Crisis* (Stanford: Hoover Institution Press, 2009)

Taylor, Mark P. and Richard Clarida, eds., *The Global Financial Crisis* (Abingdon: Routledge, 2013)

Tett, Gillian, *Fool's Gold: The Inside Story of J. P. Morgan and How Wall Street Greed Corrupted Its Bold Dream and Created a Financial Catastrophe* (New York: Little, Brown and Co., 2009)

Thomas, Pierre-Henri, *Dexia: vie et mort d'un monstre bancaire* (Paris: Les petits matins, 2012)

Thorgeirsson, Torsteinn and Paul van den Noord, "The Icelandic banking collapse: was the optimal policy path chosen?" Central Bank of Iceland Working Paper 62, March 2013, www.cb.is/library/ Skr%C3%A1arsafn---EN/Working-Papers/WP%2062.pdf

Thornton, Daniel L., "The Federal Reserve's response to the financial crisis: what it did and what it should have done," Federal Reserve Bank of St. Louis Working Paper 2012/050-A, http://research.stlouisfed.org/ wp/2012/2012-050.pdf

Todd, Jonathan H., *Crisis+5: A Survey of the American Economy Five Years post-Lehman Brothers* (private issue, Amazon 2013)

Tsafos, Nikos, *Beyond Debt: The Greek Crisis in Context* (North Charleston, NC: CreateSpace, 2013)

Turner, Adair, *Economics after the Crisis: Objectives and Means* (Cambridge, MA: MIT Press, 2012)

Turner, Adair et al., *The Future of Finance* (London: London School of Economics, 2010)

Tuttle, Robert and Chong Pooi Koon, "The world's strongest banks," *Bloomberg*, 1 May 2013, www.bloomberg.com/slideshow/2013-05-01/ the-world-s-strongest-banks.html

Ueda, Kenichi and Beatrice Weder di Mauro, "Quantifying structural subsidy values for systemically important financial institutions," IMF Working Paper 128, 2012, www.imf.org/external/pubs/ft/wp/2012/ wp12128.pdf

United States Bankruptcy Court, Southern District of New York, "In Re Lehman Brothers Holdings Inc., report of Anton R. Valukas, Examiner, Jenner & Block LLP," http://jenner.com/lehman/lehman/VOLUME%201.pdf

United States Congress, Committee on Banking, Housing and Urban Affairs, US Senate, "A breakdown in risk management: what went wrong at JPMorgan Chase?" hearing, 13 June 2012 (Washington, DC: US Government Printing Office, 2013), also at www.gpo.gov/fdsys/pkg/ CHRG-112shrg78850/pdf/CHRG-112shrg78850.pdf

United States Congress, House of Representatives, Committee on Financial Services, "Who is too big to fail: does Title II of the Dodd–Frank Act enshrine taxpayer-funded bailouts?" hearing, 15 May 2013, http://financialservices.house.gov/calendar/eventsingle.aspx?EventID= 333122

United States Congress, Senate Permanent Subcommittee on Investigations, "Wall Street and the financial crisis: anatomy of a financial collapse," 13 April 2011, www.hsgac.senate.gov//imo/media/doc/Financial_Crisis/ FinancialCrisisReport.pdf?attempt=2

United States Department of the Treasury, "*Blueprint for a modernized financial regulatory structure*" (Washington, DC: Department of the Treasury, March 2008), www.treasury.gov/press-center/press-releases/ Documents/Blueprint.pdf

United States General Accountability Office, "Financial regulatory reform: financial crisis losses and potential impact of the Dodd–Frank Act," GAO 13–180, www.gao.gov/assets/660/651322.pdf

Utvalget om systemisk vigtige finansielle institutter i Danmark, "Systemisk vigtige finansielle institutter i Danmark: identifikation, krav og krise-håndtering" (Systemically important financial institutions in Denmark: identification, requirements and crisis resolution), 11 March 2013, www.evm.dk/~/media/oem/pdf/2013/2013-publikationer/14-03-13-sifi-udvalgets-rapport/rapport-sifi-udvalget.ashx

Verhelst, Stijn, "The Single Supervisory Mechanism: a sound first step in Europe's banking union," Royal Institute for International Affairs Working Paper, March 2013, www.egmontinstitute.be/papers/13/ eur/1303-Single-Supervisory-Mechanism.pdf

Véron, Nicolas, "A realistic bridge towards European banking union," Petersen Institute for International Economics Policy Brief 13–17, June 2013, www.iie.com/publications/pb/pb13-17.pdf

Vickers report, see Independent Commission on Banking (ICB) "Volcker rule, once simple, now boggles," *New York Times*, 22 October 2011, www.nytimes.com/2011/10/22/business/volcker-rule-grows-from-simple-to-complex.html?pagewanted=all&_r=1&

Wæchter, Philippe and Martial You, *Subprime, la faillite mondiale? Cette crise financière qui va changer votre vie* (Monaco: Éditions Alphée, 2008)

Wallison, Peter J., "Too big to ignore: the future of bailouts and Dodd–Frank after the 2012 election," American Enterprise Institute, 24 October 2012, www.aei.org/outlook/economics/financial-services/banking/too-big-to-ignore-the-future-of-bailouts-and-dodd-frank-after-the-2012-election/

Wessel, David, *In Fed We Trust: Ben Bernanke's War on the Great Panic and How the Federal Reserve Became the Fourth Branch of Government* (New York: Crown, 2009)

Wheelock, David C. and Paul W. Wilson, "Do large banks have lower costs? New results of returns to scale for US banks," Federal Reserve Bank of St. Louis Working Paper, http://research.stlouisfed.org/wp/2009/2009-054.pdf

Wihlborg, Clas, "Developing distress resolution procedures for financial institutions," paper presented at the International Conference on Improving Financial Institutions: "The Proper Balance between Regulation and Governance," Helsinki, 19 April 2012, www.virtusinterpress.org/IMG/pdf/Helsinki_conference_paper_3.pdf

"The organization of banking and supervision: introduction and overview," *Journal of Financial Economic Policy* 5:4 (2013), pp. 1–11

Wilmarth, Arthur E., "The Dodd–Frank Act: a flawed and inadequate response to the too-big-to-fail problem," *Oregon Law Review* 89 (2011), pp. 951–1057, www.law.gwu.edu/Academics/research_centers/C-LEAF/Documents/WilmarthDFAct.pdf

Wolf, Martin, *Fixing Global Finance* (Baltimore: Johns Hopkins University Press, 2008)

The Shifts and the Shocks: What We Have Learned – and Have Still to Learn – from the Financial Crisis (London and New York: Allen Lane and Penguin, 2014)

Woods, Maria and Siobhán O'Connell, "Ireland's financial crisis: a comparative context," *Bank of Ireland Quarterly Bulletin* 4(2012), pp. 97–118, www.centralbank.ie/publications/documents/ireland's%20financial%20crisis%20a%20comparative%20context.pdf

Woods, Thomas E. Jr., *Meltdown: A Free-Market Look at Why the Stock Market Collapsed, the Economy Tanked and the Government Bailout Will Make Things Worse* (Washington, DC: Regnery, 2009)

Woodward, Bob, *Maestro: Greenspan's Fed and the American Boom* (New York: Touchstone, 2000)

Wymeersch, Eddy, Klaus J. Hopt and Guido Ferrarini, *Financial Regulation and Supervision: A Post-Crisis Analysis* (London: Edward Elgar, 2011)

Zandi, Mark, *Financial Shock: A 360° Look at the Subprime Mortgage Implosion and How to Avoid the Next Financial Crisis* (Upper Saddle River, NJ: Pearson Education, 2009)

Zhou, Jianping *et al.*, "From bail-out to bail-in: mandatory debt restructuring of systemic financial institutions," IMF Staff Discussion Note 12/03, 24 April 2012, www.imf.org/external/pubs/ft/sdn/2012/sdn1203.pdf

The Economist, *various issues from July 2007*

"AAAsking for trouble," 12 July 2007
"Bond insurers: a monoline meltdown," 26 July 2007
"Asset-Backed Securities sold down the river Rhine," 9 August 2007
"A liquidity squeeze: bankers mistrust," 16 August 2007
"Banks in trouble: the game is up," 16 August 2007
"American investment banks: shots in the dark," 30 August 2007
"Houses built on sand," 13 September 2007
"Bank mergers: three's company," 13 September 2007
"British banks: the great Northern run," 20 September 2007
"America's housing giants: don't free Fannie and Freddie," 4 October 2007
"When to bail out," 4 October 2007
"Curing SIV," 8 October 2007
"CDOh no!" 8 November 2007
"Bank capital, tightening the safety belt," 27 November 2007
"American house prices, fantasy or phobia," 29 November 2007
"Central banks: a dirty job but someone has to do it," 13 December 2007
"Bond insurers: Buddy can you spare us $ 15 billion?" 24 January 2008
"Credit derivatives, gross exaggeration," 31 January 2008
"Société Générale: no défense," 31 January 2008
"Credit-rating agencies: restructured products," 7 February 2008
"Northern Rock: now make it work," 1 February 2008
"The credit crunch: mark it and weep," 6 March 2008
"Credit markets, if at first you don't succeed," 13 March 2008
"Wall Street's crisis," 19 March 2008
"Investment banks: the $ 2bail-out," 19 March 2008
"The financial system: what went wrong?" 19 March 2008
"American banks: not so thrifty," 10 April 2008
"Derivatives: taming the beast," 17 April 2008
"Derivatives: clearing the fog," 17 April 2008
"Deposit insurance: when the safety net fails," 1 May 2008
"European banks: Austria 1, Germany 0," 15 May 2008
"Insurance: is AIG the Citigroup of insurance?" 15 May 2008
"Paradise lost," 5 May 2008
"Cycle clips," 15 May 2008
"Black mark," 15 May 2008
"Bank of America and Countrywide," 26 June 2008
"Fannie Mae and Freddie Mac: end of illusions," 17 July 2008
"Aftermath of a megamerger," 17 July 2008
"Bank losses: hall of shame," 7 August 2008
"American housing: ticking time bomb?" 4 August 2008

"Auction-rate securities: kick in the ARS," 14 August 2008

"Capital ideas," 28 August 2008

"German banking," 4 September 2008

"European banks: cross-border contagion," 18 September 2008

"AIG's rescue: size matters," 18 September 2008

"Investment banking: is there a future?" 18 September 2008

"American finance: and then there were none," 18 September 2008

"Echoes of the Depression: 1929 and all that," 2 October 2008

"Accounting: fair cop," 2 October 2008

"Global banks: on life support," 2 October 2008

"When fortune frowned (special survey)," 11 October 2008

"Global finance: lifelines," 11 October 2008

"America's bail-out: TARP priority," 11 October 2008

"Link by link," 18 October 2008

"Rescuing the banks, but will it work?" 18 October 2008

"Hedge funds in trouble," 25 October 2008

"Mewling and puking: how damaged is the Basel 2 accord?" 25 October 2008

"A helping hand to homeowners," 25 October 2008

"Cracks in the crust" (on Iceland), 13 December 2008

"Greed – and fear, a special report on the future of finance," 24 January 2009

"Move over, subprime," 7 February 2009

"A ghoulish prospect" (nationalization of banks), 28 February 2009

"Stress-test mess," 28 February 2009

"Rebuilding the banks," 16 May 2009

"In defence of the dismal science" (by Robert Lucas), 8 August 2009

"The toxic trio" (Fannie Mae, Freddie Mac, AIG), 15 August 2009

"Where it all began" (house prices), 22 August 2009

"Death warmed up" (on letting banks fail), 3 October 2009

"Over the counter, out of sight," 4 November 2009

"Cheap as chips," 16 January 2010

"Base camp Basel," 23 January 2010

"From bail-out to bail-in," 30 January 2010

"They might be giants," 15 May 2010

"Repent at leisure: a special report on debt," 26 June 2010

"A decent start" (US financial reform), 3 July 2010

"Coming in from the cold," 18 December 2010

"Chained but untamed: special report on international banking," 14 May 2011

"America's bail-out math," 11 June 2011

"Patchwork planet," 2 July 2011

"Too big not to fail" (on Dodd–Frank), 18 February 2012

"Playing with fire, a special report on financial innovation," 25 February 2012

"Light touch no more" (on UK financial regulation), 1 December 2012

"Blind justice" (on jailing/fining bankers), 4 May 2013

"Twilight of the gods" (on international banking), 11 May 2013

"System reboot" (on Greek banks), 25 May 2013

"Till default do us part" (on banking union), 8 June 2013

"Blight of the living dead" (on Europe's zombie banks), 13 July 2013

"Giant reality check" (on China's big banks), 31 August 2013

"Riding high" (on Wells Fargo), 14 September 2013

"Capital punishment," 14 September 2013

"Putting Humpty together again" (on international resolution), 23 November 2013

"Banking on a new union," 14 December 2013

"The inevitability of instability, a welcome burst of new thinking on financial regulation," 25 January 2014

"The slumps that shaped modern finance," 12 April 2014

"Capital punishment," 5 July 2014

"Up and at 'em" (on ING), 4 October 2014

"Buffering" (on FSB's Total Loss Absorbing Capacity), 15 November 2014

Financial Times, *various issues from August 2007 (only survey articles, not news per se)*

"A crash history lesson in crashes for Wall Street," 27 August 2007

"Credit write-downs," 20 February 2008

"Turmoil reveals the inadequacy of Basel II," 27 February 2008

"IMF points to high cost of credit crisis," 9 April 2008

"Triple A rating does not guarantee against default," 3 May 2008

"Credit turmoil shows how Basel II must be improved," 8 May 2008

"New Basel consensus in need of fundamental rethink," 9 May 2008

"Moody's error gave top ratings to debt products," 21 May 2008

"Who rates the rating agencies?" 29 May 2008

"Do away with rating-based rules," 9 July 2008

"Brussels outlines ratings agencies plan," 31 July 2008

"EU criticized for ratings proposal," 3 September 2008

"Credit ratings agencies," 28 September 2008

"Europe's banking crisis needs a common solution," 2 October 2008

"Global financial crisis," 11–12 October 2008

"Influence of ratings agencies questioned," 17 October 2008

"US regulators and what they do," 22 October 2008

"In the face of fragility," 15 December 2008

"Britain and Spain: a tale of two house market bubbles," 6 January 2009
"Europe's banks need a Federal fix" (by Howard Davies), 14 January 2009
"Error-laden machine," 3 March 2009
"To nationalise or not to nationalise is the question," 4 March 2009
"The Fed's moral hazard maximizing strategy" (by Willem Buiter), 6 March 2009
"Hypo Reality," 20 March 2009
"Ten principles for a Black Swan proof world" (by Nassim Nicholas Taleb), 7 April 2009
"Subprime explosion: who isn't guilty?" 6 May 2009
"How greed turned to panic," 9 May 2009
"America's triple A rating is at risk," 13 May 2009
"Financial reform, re-spinning the web," 22 June 2009
"The cautious approach to fixing banks will not work," 1 July 2009
"Houses to put in order" (on Fannie Mae and Freddie Mac), 4 September 2009
"In defence of financial innovation" (by Robert Shiller), 28 September 2009
"How to tame the animal spirits" (by John Plender), 30 September 2009
"UK bank chief doubts curbs will stop future crises," 21 October 2009
"Payback time," 27 October 2009
"A three-way split is the most logical," 29 October 2009
"An eclectic aviary" (on the Federal Reserve), 13 November 2009
"Smoke signals," 26 November 2009
"Citi [of London] limits," 14 December 2009
"Latest saga hardens lack of faith in Landesbanks," 15 December 2009
"How America let banks off the leash," 17 December 2009
"Banks face revolutionary reform," 22 January 2010
"Tripped up," 25 January 2010
"Government rescue packages for banks," 25 January 2010
"Use of clearers to rein in OTC derivatives," 15 January 2010
"The hindered haircut" (on AIG), 27 January 2010
"A disorderly descent," 2 February 2010
"Banks concede reform is inevitable," 4 February 2010
"Eroded authority" (on British bank supervision), 12 February 2010
"Markets fear end of easy money era," 20/21 February 2010
"A business decision" (on leaving your house to the bank), 23 February 2010
"Lehman file rocks Wall Street," 13 March 2010
"A [property] market to prop up," 23 March 2010
"Goldman versus the regulators," 19 April 2010
"The challenge of halting the financial doomsday machine," 21 April 2010
"A new broom" (on Irish banking), 10 May 2010

"A wider divide [between bankers and politicians]," 26 May 2010

"Accounting standards divide set to widen," 27 May 2010

"That sinking feeling," 2 June 2010

"Leaning lenders," 4 June 2010

"A tricky pick" (on Goldman Sachs and Abacus CDO), 10 June 2010

"Worries over [European] banking stress tests fuel anxiety," 15 June 2010

"Banks win battle to tone down Basel III," 25 June 2010

"A line is drawn," 1 July 2010

"EU sets new pay practices in stone," 2 July 2010

"Short measures," 19 July 2010

"Banks find exercise relatively painless," 24–25 July 2010

"Seven lenders fail stress tests," 24–25 July 2010

"A test cynically calibrated to fix the result," 26 July 2010

"Stressed but not blessed," 26 July 2010

"Derivative dilemmas," 12 August 2010

"Suspense over," 19 August 2010

"Bailout doubts unnerve investors," 26 August 2010

"The money moves on," 15 September 2010

"Basel: the mouse that did not roar," 15 September 2010

"Germany's weak link," 28 September 2010

"The long hangover," 4 October 2010

"The best bet to curb too big to fail," 14 October 2010

"Room to improve," 2 November 2010

"Paper weight," 2 November 2010

"Pressure mounts over derivatives clearing," 3 November 2010

"A garden to tame," 15 November 2010

"A punt too far," 20/21 November 2010

"Don't dismiss Modigliani-Miller *Logic in Bank Funding*" (by David Miles), 30 November 2010

"America must start again on financial regulation" (by Henry Kaufman), 17 December 2010

"Brussels plans bondholder 'bail-ins,'" 7 January 2011

"Overarching problems," 27 January 2011

"Elusive information," 16 February 2011

"The debt net," 21 February 2011

"Higher capital ratios talk cuts banks' appeal" (by Patrick Jenkins and Brooke Masters), 27 March 2011

"Visibility needed" (on German banks), 6 April 2011

"Lenders pressed on capital raising," 7 April 2011

"A shield asunder," 20 May 2011

"German regulator hits at bank stress tests," 7 June 2011

"Conduits of contention," 16 June 2011

"Biggest banks face new capital clampdown," 17 June 2011
"Ledger domain" (on accounting rules), 27 June 2011
"Again under strain," 8 July 2011
"A disappearing act (Dodd–Frank)," 21 July 2011
"The price of protection," 12 September 2011
"Why breaking up is so hard to do" (by Martin Wolf), 21 September 2011
"Bankers versus Basel," 3 October 2011
"Banks contemplate shrunken future," 14 October 2011
"Shadow banking hits new peak," 28 October 2011
"Banks buoyant as capital needs clarified," 28 October 2011
"Barnier Commission set to consider break-up of banks," 23 November 2011
"Crunch time arrives for troubled lenders," 19 January 2012
"New capital framework 'biased against US,'" 30 January 2012
"Conflicting signals," 2 April 2012
"Shadow banking," 10 April 2012
"Banks are on a euro zone knife edge" (by Martin Wolf), 25 April 2012
"Investors lose faith in risk measures," 24 May 2012
"Pressure rises for break-up of US banks," 24 May 2012
"Risk waiting," 25 May 2012
"High pay persists despite poor performance," 25 June 2012
"Break up big banks, says ex-Citi chief Weill," 26 July 2012
"Regulators should keep it simple," 5 September 2012
"Wide variation in banks' risk estimates," 26 September 2012
"M. Stanley shows the flaky side of value at risk model," 19 October 2012
"An improbable profit" (AIG), 23 October 2012
"Collateral damage," 25 October 2012
"Warning over steps to reform biggest banks," 27–28 October 2012
"Big banks' capital needs under microscope," 30 November 2012
"Banks in the UK face threat of forced break-up," 17 December 2012
"Basel move aims to stoke recovery" (on the liquidity coverage ratio, LCR), 8 January 2013
"Republicans join liberals to control rise of the 'megabank,'" 11 January 2013
"Outlook unchanged" (on ratings companies), 15 January 2013
"Brussels retreat on key bank reform" (Liikanen report), 30 January 2013
"Risk models fuel fears for bank safety," 1 February 2013
"The long climb back (on US house prices)," 19 February 2013
"US raises stakes on bank crisis plans," 28 February 2013
"EU poised to unveil revamped banking rule book," 28 February 2013
"Bonuses are only a symptom of banking's true problem," 4 March 2013
"Doubts cast on Icelandic model to handle crisis," 4 March 2013

"Wall Street's latest idea" (on collateral transformation), 5 March 2013

"Risk management, financial institutions," 19 March 2013

"Cut down to size" (on executive pay), 25 March 2013

"Bank built on flawed business model" (on HBOS), 5 April 2013

"Financial sins" (on late reactions to the crisis), 10 April 2013

"US cannot pay for Europe's capital sin," 24 April 2013

"Clock is ticking in fight over banking union," 30 April 2013

"Brussels to clamp down on 'shadow banking,'" 6 May 2013

"Finance ministers face bail-in conundrum," 13 May 2013

"Banks in cash calls to meet Basel III," 14 May 2013

"Cloud lifts from UK banks as review ends," 23 May 2013

"The UK's capital disagreement," 6 June 2013

"Professor of doom is 'waiting for the next crisis,'" 10 June 2013

"Rush to EU banking union hits road works and diversions," 27 June 2013

"Britain is leading the world when it comes to bank reform" (by John Kay), 26 June 2013

"Regulators are finally catching up with banks" (by John Gapper), 4 July 2013

"Banks feeling bruised by new capital ratios," 5 July 2013

"Basel fuels bank safety metric fears," 6/7 July 2013

"Strain over bank rules spills into transatlantic trade talks," 8 July 2013

"Brussels treads on thin legal ice" (on resolution powers), 12 July 2013

"Upsetting the narrative" (on Goldman Sachs), 15 July 2013

"Banks need 'to shrink' balance sheets," 22 July 1013

"UBS," 23 July 2013

"RBS weighs its strategies from crossroads," 2 August 2013

"Banks' living wills start to take form," 5 August 2013

"Balance sheet battle," 15 August 2013

"Back from the bailouts" (on Fannie Mae and Freddie Mac), 4 September 2013

"Banks adapt to being kept in check," 9 September 2013

"Lehman bankruptcy saga enters its final chapters," 13 September 2013

"Insane financial system lives on post-Lehman," 13 September 2013

"Five bitter pills" (on banking reform), 13 September 2013

"'Too big to fail' still a threat to the financial system" (by Bob Diamond, ex-CEO of Barclays), 16 September 2013

"Stop encouraging banks to load up on state debt" (by Jens Weidmann, Bundesbank), 1 October 2013

"EU banking union plans run up against legal concerns," 9 October 2013

"Crash course" (on Alan Greenspan), 26/27 October 2013

"Day of reckoning as banks' bill for misconduct mounts," 30 October 2013

"'Bail-in' fear looms over bank bond investors," 5 November 2013
"Funds jostle for Fannie and Freddie spoils," 14 November 2013
"Regulator warns on nationalism over banks," 18 November 12013
"Lights come back on for European banks," 20 November 2013
"Main Street fights back," 4 December 2013
"Five years on, Lehman still haunts us" (by Martin Wolf), 9 December 2013
"Volcker comes of age in spite of protests," 11 December 2013
"Credibility test," 12 December 2013
"Project on survival of banks nears fruition" (on bank resolution), 18
      December 2013
"Spanish banks enjoy surge in popularity," 19 December 2013
"Banking union falls short of EU goal," 20 December 2013
"EU banking plan raises anxiety," 30 January 2014
"Dodd-Frank is not tough; it is impossible" (by John Dizard), 24 February
      2014
"Time to modernize" (on Italian banking), 5 March 2014
"Europe should say no to a flawed banking union" (by Wolfgang Münchau),
      17 March 2014
"A highy imperfect banking union," 23 March 2014
"Fed's stress tests set bar high for Europe," 28 March 2014
"EU banking reforms mark biggest shake-up for 20 years," 16 April 2014
"'Too big to fail' is too big to ignore" (by Martin Wolf), 16 April 2014
"German banks line up to join coco party," 24 April 2014
"European banking union: foundations laid but bricks still to fall in place,"
      8 May 2014
"Shadow and substance (on shadow banking)," 10 May 2014
"Stresses and messes" (lunch with Tim Geithner), 17 May 2014
"Hurrah before the storm," 14/15 June 2014
"Risky business, global threat" (on Chinese shadow banking), 16 June 2014
"Taking another path" (on shadow banking), 17 June 2014
"A man walks out of a bank" (lunch with Vikram Pandit), 12/13 July 2014
"Britain versus the banks," 19/20 July 2014
"Flowers warns tighter rules leave banks vulnerable to next crisis," 21 July
      2014
"Bank balance" (on Landesbanken), 31 July 2014
"Bank bond investors sleepwalk into bail-ins," 8 August 2014
"Banks horse-trade on ringfence fine print," 15 August 2014
"Financial reforms make the next failure even messier," 2 September 2014
"Moody's to rejig bank ratings," 10 September 2014
"Europe's bank bail-in rules change the game," 11 September 2014
"ECB health checks carry a wobbly prognosis," 18 September 2014

"The biggest show in town" (on NAMA), 23 September 2014
"Roman bankers protest at stress test results," 27 October 2014
"Alternative stress tests find French banks are weakest in Europe,"
    28 October 2014
"Bank stress tests fail to tackle deflation spectre," 28 October 2014
"'Too big to fail' fears reach clearing houses," 3 December 2014

Index

AAA ratings, 10–12, 14, 18, 31–32, 47
Abacus, 4, 57–58, 63, 178–179
Abbey National (Santander), 11,
    20–22, 158–159, 272
ABCP (asset-backed commercial
    paper), 4, 19, 54–55, 152,
    178–179, 335
ABN AMRO, 3, 6–7, 50, 63, 98, 135,
    161–166, 199, 201–205, 272,
    381–382
ABS (asset-backed bonds), 14
ACA, 8
ACA Management LLC, 57–58
Ackermann, Josef, 77
ACPR (Prudential Supervisory and
    Resolution Authority), 116
Admati, Anat, 488
Adoboli, Kweku, 84
Affordable Housing Program, 54
Agius, Marcus, 95
Agricultural Bank of Greece, 96,
    262–264
AIA, 55–56
AIB (Allied Irish Banks), 33, 36,
    41–42, 51, 56–57, 59–60, 67–68,
    71–72, 74, 77, 79–80, 84, 92,
    240–257, 257
    bank data, 245
AIG (American International Group),
    xvi, xxix, 11–12, 18, 20, 25–27,
    30–31, 37–38, 52–56, 68, 70,
    74, 96–97, 99, 111–112, 160,
    193, 327, 359–360, 364–374,
    422–424
    crisis handling grades, 369–374
AIG counterparties, payments to,
    370–374
AIGFP (AIG Financial Products),
    364–368, 373–374
Alandsbanken, 232–233

Alexandria derivatives contract,
    141, 208–215
Alliance & Leicester, 272
Allianz, 34, 184
Ally Financial, xxix, 92, 105–106, 130,
    134, 142
Alpha Bank, 102, 132, 262–263
Alt-A loans, 339, 343
Altor, 30
Amagerbanken, 69, 74–75, 80,
    219, 375
Ambac, 10, 14, 71
American Express, 42–43
American Home Mortgage, 4, 336
American Mortgage Bankers
    Association, 50
Ameriquest, 5
AMF, 69
Amsterdam Stock Exchange, 199–200
Anglo Irish Bank, 33, 35, 37, 43–44,
    56–58, 67–68, 71–72, 79–81, 96,
    103, 132, 134, 238, 240–257
    bank data, 245
    contagion by, 246
    market value, 246
Anti-Terrorism, Crime and Security
    Act (2001), 24–25
antibank activity, 401
Applegarth, Adam, 9
ARM (adjustable mortgage rate),
    335–336, 343, 354
Arnall, Roland, 5
Arnason, Sigurjòn, 135–136, 141, 235
Artesia Banking Corporation, 192
ASLK (Caisse Générale d'Épargne et
    de Retraite), 200
Asset Protection Scheme, 35, 49, 97,
    160, 166, 171–172
Asset Quality Review, 132,
    140–141, 458

Australia, deposit guarantee, 25
Austria
  bank levy, 55
  bank nationalization, 53
  ratings, 490
  sovereign debt crisis, timeline, 442
Avgouleas, Emilios, 475
AXA, 274

Baden-Württemberg (LBBW) LB, 5,
  15, 69, 103, 188, 190
BaFin, 48, 79, 111
bail-ins
  of creditors, xxvii–xxviii
  and TBTF, 406
  of unsecured bondholders, xvi–xvii
bail-outs
  by private investors, xxviii
  conditions, xxvii–xxviii
  taxpayer-funded, xxv–xxxii,
    xxix–xxx
Bailey, Arthur, 109
bailing-in system, 111
Bain Capital, 182
Bair, Sheila, xxv, 45, 50, 301–302,
  304–305, 320–322, 331, 341–342,
  345, 348–349, 354–357, 363,
  371, 376, 378–379, 381–382,
  419, 434, 438
balance sheet reductions, 197
Baldassari, Gianluca, 141, 208–215
BAMC, 129
Banca d'Italia, 104–105, 208–215
Banca Antonveneta, 6–7, 214, 272
Banca March, 274
Banco BPI, 268
Banco Caminos, 274
Banco de Valencia, 88, 98–99, 104, 274
Banco Gallego, 274
Banco Grupo Caja, 3, 107
Banco Mare Nostrum, 107
Banco Popular, 39, 120, 274–275
Banco Sabadell, 129, 192, 194, 274–275
Banco Santander, 6–7, 11, 20–22, 85–86,
  88, 112–113, 120, 139–140, 165,
  271–272, 274–275
Banif, 268
Bank of America, 3, 8, 10, 14, 17,
  23–27, 34–37, 41–42, 47–48,
  52–54, 56, 73, 83–84, 92, 94,
    96–97, 101–102, 105–106, 110,
    114–116, 118–119, 131, 133–134,
    136–139, 260, 287–288, 304,
    318–319, 337–338, 358–361,
    379, 381–387, 434, 436
  crisis handling grades, 387
Bank of Amsterdam, 199–200
Bank Austria, 375
bank bankruptcy regimes, 157–158
Bank of Canada, 9, 20–22, 124
bank CEOs
  pay, 113, 115
  pay-back salaries/bonuses, 79–80
Bank of Clark County, 35
Bank of Commerce, 28–29
bank crisis handling, xxviii
  AIG, 369–374
  Bank of America, 387
  Bear Stearns, 311–313
  Citigroup, 380–381
  Commerzbank, 185–187
  Countrywide, 338
  Cypriot banks, 173–174
  Danish banks, 222–224
  Dexia, 196–198
  factors in, 143–145, 390–393
  Fortis, 185–187
  good/bad grade factors, 145–147,
    390–393
  Greek banks, 264–266
  HRE (Hypo Real Estate), 183
  Icelandic banks, 235–236
  IKB, 179–181
  IndyMac, 340–342
  ING, 206
  Irish banks, 257–258
  KfW, 179–181
  Lehman Brothers, 329–333
  Lloyds Banking Group, 173–174
  Merrill Lynch, 320–321
  MPS (Monte dei Paschi de
    Siena), 215
  Northern Rock, 157–159
  Portuguese banks, 269
  RBS, 161, 166–168
  Spanish banks, 275–276
  Wachovia Bank, 356–357
  Washington Mutual, 348–352
  WestLB, 190
  see also *individual banks*

Bank of Cyprus, 108, 117, 264,
    279–281
Bank of Denmark, 20–22
Bank of England, 6, 13–14, 18–19,
    20–22, 24–25, 34, 36, 42, 45, 49,
    59, 74–76, 85, 109, 111–113,
    123–124, 137, 157–158, 160, 461
Bank Gospodarki Zywnosciowej, 127
Bank for International Settlements, 80
Bank of Ireland, 33, 36, 42, 51, 55–57,
    61, 79–80, 83, 92, 103, 240–257
    bank data, 245
Bank of Japan, 4, 20–22, 124, 152–153
Bank of New York Mellon, 25–27, 43,
    83, 126, 336–337, 359–360
Bank of Norway, 20–22
bank runs, 303, 428
Bank of Scotland (Ireland), 240–241
Bank Secrecy Act, 99
Bank of Spain, 60, 76, 118, 273–274
Bank of Sweden, 18–22, 24–25
bank undercapitalization, 419–420
Bank United FSB, 353
bank viability, 146, 149, 391
Banka Solvensko, 194
bankers' bonuses, Great Britain, 52–53
Bankia, 76, 94–95, 98–99, 104,
    110–111, 120, 132, 273–276
Banking Reform Act, 129
Banking Union, xvii, 454–459
Bankinter, 274
BankNordik, 219
Bankruptcy Abuse Prevention and
    Consumer Protection Act, 438
banks, stress testing see stress testing
Banque de France, 124
Banque Populaire, 108, 375–376
Banque Postale, 85
Barclays Bank, xxviii, 8, 14, 17–18,
    29, 31, 55–56, 83–84, 95, 97,
    108–109, 112–113, 116–117,
    122, 126–127, 135, 201, 274,
    304, 332–333, 358–359, 375
Barnier, Michel, 88, 102, 130–131, 462
    remarks by, 450–452
Barofsky, Neil, 44–45, 372–373
Basel I, 59–60, 86, 88, 156, 304–305,
    438, 484
Basel II, 47, 59–60, 86, 88, 136,
    139–140, 150, 156, 158–159,

    212, 214, 247–249, 304–305,
    410, 420, 438, 484
Basel III, xv, 59–60, 62, 67, 72, 74,
    78–79, 84, 86, 88–89, 106–109,
    111–114, 116–118, 120, 123,
    130, 139–141, 162–163, 165,
    272–273, 275, 304–305, 359–360,
    410, 420, 454, 462, 479–481,
    484, 487–488
Bayern LB, 12, 32–33, 136, 139,
    188–190
BB&T, 28–29, 43, 46
BBVA (Banco Bilbao Viscaya
    Argentaria), 86, 88, 123, 139,
    272, 375
BCBS (Basel Committee on Banking
    Supervision), 44, 47, 53, 66,
    73–74, 77, 80, 86–88, 101,
    487–488
    see also Basel I; II; III
Bear Stearns, xvi, 3–4, 9, 12–13, 20,
    119, 122–123, 303–304,
    306–313, 422–424
    BSAM (Bear Stearns Asset
        Management), 3, 308–309
    crisis handling grades, 311–313
Belfius Banque et Assurance SA,
    194–195
Belgium
    ratings, 85, 194–195
    state bank ownership, 126
Berkshire Hathaway, 77
Bernanke, Ben, 33–35, 37, 312–313,
    318–319, 329, 331, 358, 362,
    378–379, 383–385, 405–406
BES (Banco Espirito Santo),
    137–138, 268
Bharara, Preet, 3, 186
BIL (Banque Internationale de
    Luxembourg), 192
Bini-Smaghi, Lorenzo, 475
BlackRock, 131
Blanchard, Olivier, 488
Blankfein, Lloyd, 13, 25–27, 31, 94,
    113, 318, 378–379
Blavatnik, Len, 118
Blesa, Miguel, 110–111
Blinder, Alan, 332, 349, 373
Bloomberg's, 15, 20–22, 88, 119
BN Bank, 231

BNP Paribas, xxviii, 4, 23, 31, 33, 38–39, 47–48, 81–83, 88, 108, 126–127, 152, 203–205, 304, 358–359, 375–376
Borgen, Thomas E., 120–121
Boston Consulting Group, 89
Bove, Richard X., 402
Bowe, John, 251
Bowler, Gillian, 251
Bradford & Bingley, 11, 20–22, 44, 56, 63, 117, 157–159, 237–238, 272
Braunstein, Douglas, 95
Bremer LB, 188
Breuer, Lanny, 407–408
BRF Kredit, 122, 132
bridge banks, 428
Britain *see* United Kingdom
Brown, Gordon, 37
Brown, Sherrod, 109, 363
BRRD (Bank Recovery and Resolution Directive), xvi, xxvi, xxxiv–xxxv, 127, 134, 389, 459–461, 463–472
  Article 34 (general principles governing resolution), 463
  Article 37 (general principles of resolution tools), 464–465
  Article 43 (bail-in tool), 465
  Article 44 (scope of bail-in tool), 466–467
  Article 57 (public equity support tool), 467–468
  Article 99 (European system of financing arrangements), 468
  Article 100 (requirement to establish resolution financing arrangements), 468–469
  Article 101 (use of the resolution financing arrangements), 469–470
  Article 102 (target level), 470
  Article 103 (*ex ante* contributions), 470–471
  Article 104 (extraordinary *ex post* contributions), 471–472
  Article 109 (use of deposit guarantee schemes in the context of resolution), 472
  evaluation, 462–473
  preamble, 463
BSAM (Bear Stearns Asset Management), 3, 308–309

Buffet, Warren, 19–20, 77
Buiter, Willem, 229–230
Bundesbank, 20–22, 48, 181–182
Bure Equity, 30
Burrows, Oliver, 473
Bush, George W., 5, 23
Bush, Jeb, 324–325

Caine, Jimmy, 311
Caisse de Dêpots et des Consignations, 195
Caisse Française de Financement Local, 195, 197
Caisses d'epargne, 375–376
Caixa Geral, 268
CaixaBank, 74, 88, 98, 104, 139, 273–274
caja CAM, 129
Caja de Ahorros Castilla La Mancha, 40, 273
Caja de Ahorros de Mediterràneo, 125
Caja de Madrid, 273
Caja La Mancha, 40
Caja Laboral, 274
Caja Madrid, 94, 110–111
Cajamar, 274
cajas, private investor bail-outs, xxviii
cajas de ahorro, 272
Cajastur, 40
Cajasur de Andalusía, 60
Camdessus, Michel, 46–47
CAMELS, 18–19
capital adequacy, 108–109, 114
capital buffers, 111–112
Capital One, 28–29, 43, 206
capital ratios, 86, 88
capital requirements, 89–91, 304–305, 480–484
capital-asset ratios, xxxv
Carnegie Investment Bank, 20, 144–145
Carney, Mark, 114
Casey, Denis, 251
Cassano, Joseph, 38, 364
Catalunya Banc, 98–99, 104, 139, 274–275
Catalunya Caixa, 76, 85, 273–274, 276
Cayne, James, 9
CBO (Congressional Budget Office), 66, 97

CCP (central counterparty
    clearing), 94
CDC (Caisse des Depôts et
    Consignations), 85
CDOs (collateralized debt obligations),
    3–4, 6–7, 11–12, 29, 57–58, 64,
    69, 102–103, 152, 178–179,
    343–344, 411
CDS (credit default swaps), 8, 11–12,
    31–32, 41, 56, 65, 67–69, 71,
    360, 364
CDS contracts, 364–366
Cecabank, 274
Center for Risk Management, 140–141
Central Bank of China, 58
Central Bank of Greece, 132
Central Bank of Iceland *see* Sedlabanki
Central Bank of Ireland, 238, 240,
    242, 252
Cerberus, 54, 156
CET1 (Core Equity Tier 1) capital,
    xxxv
CET1/RWA ratios, 481–484
CFD (contracts for difference), 252
CFTC (Commodity Futures Trading
    Commission), 68, 100–101, 121,
    295–298, 365
CGER (Caisse Générale d'Épargne et
    de Retraite), 200
chairman/CEO split, 94
Chicago Board Options Exchange,
    28, 329–330
China
    capital adequacy rate, 50
    cash reserve requirement, 59
    CDS market, 71
Christofias, Dimitris, 278–279
Chrysler Corporation, 25–27, 33,
    41–42, 52–53, 124, 127
    and Fiat, 79
Chrysler Financial, xxix, 34, 52–53
Churchill, 166
CIC (China Investment
    Corporation), 9
Cioffi, Ralph, 3, 309
CIT, 49
Citic Bank, 123
Citigroup, 5–10, 13, 20–22, 25–27, 32,
    37–38, 42, 47–48, 51–53, 63, 69,
    72, 74, 83–84, 88, 92, 94, 96–97,

    105–106, 114, 116, 118–119,
    121–122, 126–127, 133, 137–139,
    237–238, 287–288, 304, 319,
    358–361, 374–385, 434, 436
    crisis handling grades, 380–381
Citizens' Bank, 168
Citizens Financial Group, 140
City National Bank of Florida,
    110–111
City National Corp, 28–29
co-insurance, 153–154
CoCo (contingent convertible) bonds,
    xvi–xvii, 50–51, 69, 75–76, 84,
    107, 111–112, 116–117, 127,
    139–140, 171–172, 475, 481,
    487–488
Colonial Bank of Alabama, 46
Colonial Bank of Arkansas, 81
Comeria, 28–29
Commerzbank, 29, 34, 75, 86, 88, 103,
    107, 116, 136, 152, 178–179,
    183–187, 375
    capital support, xxix
    ComSec, 183
    crisis handling grade, 185–187
    and Dresdner Bank, 184
    and Eurohypo, 184–185
    share issue, 185
    share prices, 180–181, 185–186
Commodity Futures Modernization
    Act, 365
Community First Bank of Oregon, 45
complex debt securities, 69
Conference of State Bank
    Supervisors, 56
Connor, Mark O., 96
constructive ambiguity, 406
Consumer Financial Protection
    Agency, 43
Consumer Financial Protection Bureau,
    299, 411
Consumer Protection and Markets
    Authority, 61
continuity of service *see* uninterrupted
    service
cooperation, 146, 391
COP (Congressional Oversight
    Council/Panel) for TARP, 74, 363,
    382–385
Corbat, Mike, 113

Corker, Bob, 114
corrective action triggers, 420–421
Corsair, 166
Corzine, Jon, 86
countercyclical capital buffers, 73–74, 104, 135
Countrywide, 5, 10, 23–24, 37, 69, 73, 91–92, 101–102, 110, 119, 131, 137–139, 152–153, 334–338, 344, 381–382, 386, 398, 409
  crisis handling grades, 338
Cour des Comptes, 193–196
Coutts, 159–160
Cowen, Brian, xxvi
CPDOs (constant proportion debt obligations), 98
CPFF (Commercial Paper Funding Facility), 54–55, 193
CPP (Capital Purchase Program), xxix, xxix, 97, 124, 292–293, 305, 342
CRD IV (Capital Adequacy Directive), xv, 105, 130, 479
CRD (Capital Requirements Directive), 110
Crediop, 192, 194
Crédit Agricole, 102, 108, 126–127, 358–359, 375–376
Crédit Communal, 192
credit events, 260–262
Crédit Locale, 192, 197
credit losses, global financial crisis, xxviii
Crédit Mutuel, 375–376
credit risk mitigation, 71
Credit Suisse, 6–7, 11, 33, 43, 69, 83–84, 110, 304, 375
credit trading, 166
Credit Watch, 10
crisis of confidence in Europe crisis phase, 1–2
crisis handling grades *see* banking crises
Crosby, Sir James, 109–110
cross-border systemic risk supervision, 51
CRR (Capital Requirements Regulation), 110
Cucchiani, Enrico Tommaso, 121
Cunliffe, Sir John, 124
Cuomo, Andrew, 36, 374

currency-swap tool (Federal Reserve), 59
Cyprus, 278–284
  bank liquidity, 280
  budget deficit, 278–279
  crisis handling grades, 282–284
  debt/GDP ratio, 278–279
  The Economist insured deposits bailing-in errors, 282–283
  ELA (Emergency Liquidity Assistance), 280
  ESM support, 280–281
  financial aid, 107–108, 280–281
  financial/banking background, 278–279
  financial/banking crisis, xxviii
  growth/GDP decline, 278
  insured/uninsured deposits, 281
  NPL (non-performing loans), 279–280
  ratings, 280, 490
  Russian emergency loan, 280
  sovereign debt, xxviii, 280
  crisis timeline, 442
  see also Bank of Cyprus; Hellenic Bank; Popular Bank

Danish Bankers' Association, 216–217
Danske Bank, 112, 120–122, 219–221, 375
Darling, Alistair, 6, 52–53, 153–154, 326, 332–333
Davis Advisors, 9, 316
Davis Square Funding VI, 69
DAX, 23–24
Debt Guarantee Program, 27
debt guarantees, 146
Dehaene, Jean-Luc, 22, 193
DeKaBank, 73
Denizbank, 95, 195
Denmark, 216–224
  bank debt, 74–75
  bank deposit guarantees, 23–24
  bank liabilities guarantee, 216–217
  bank nationalization, 37
  banks crisis handling grades, 222–224
  deposit guarantees, 56
  financial stability law, 218
  financial/banking background, 216–217

Denmark (cont.)
Finansiel Stabilitet *see* Finansiel
Stabilitet
GDP, 217–218
house prices, 217–218
LCR (Liquidity Coverage
Ratio), 217
mortgage bond market, 136, 217
mortgage market per capita, 217
SIFI rules, 122
Depfa, 6, 118–119, 181–183, 193, 244
deposit guarantees, 145–146, 391,
435, 484–485
deposit insurance
in banking union, xvii
common rules, 128
Europe, 438, 484–485
FDIC proposals, 71
Northern Rock, 157–158
Deposit Insurance Act, 415
Deposit Insurance Authority, 461
derivative transactions *see* OTC
derivatives
Deutsche Bank, xxviii, 6–7, 10, 13, 29,
31, 75, 81–84, 94, 103, 126–127,
152, 178–179, 208–215, 274,
304–306, 358–359
Dexia, 22, 31, 78, 85, 95, 98–100, 104,
116, 191–198, 237–238, 434
crisis handling grade, 196–198
overseas subsidiaries, 192–193
restructuring plan, 194
Dexma, 85
DGP (Debt Guarantee Program), 376
Diamond, Bob, 95, 120–121, 324–325
DIF (Deposit Insurance Fund), 295,
300–301, 345–346, 350–351,
355, 414, 418–419, 420–421,
427, 429–433, 484–485
Dillon Read Capital Management, 3
Dimon, Jamie, 25–27, 94, 113,
117–118, 329–331, 378–379
Direct Line, 166
DLR Kredit, 122
DMA (Dexia Municipal Agency), 195
DNB NOR, 108, 219–221
Dochow, Darrel, 33
Dodd–Frank Act, xv, xxv, xxxiv–xxxv,
xxxvi, 49, 59–60, 62–63, 70, 84,
89, 93, 100, 105–106, 115, 123,

127, 134–135, 293, 298, 327,
350, 360, 362–363, 389, 479–480
Collins amendment, 482–484
compliance with, 360
criticisms of, 399–409
domestic character of, 412
Federal Reserve System
Provisions, 422
and management wrongdoing, 413
OLF (Orderly Liquidation Fund),
xxxvi, 429–432, 472
overregulation, 400–401
Proposal 1, 424
Proposal 2, 428–432
Proposal 3, 433–434
and regulatory authorities,
412–413
and regulatory capture, 413
repayment mechanisms, 432
risk-based capital requirement,
482–484
section 165, 131
size of, 397
and TBTF problem, 413, 421–422,
426–428
see also TBTF
Title I, xxv, 403
Title II (Orderly Liquidation/
Resolution Authority), xvi, 403,
426–429
Title XI (Federal Reserve System
Provisions), 422
and underlying causes of financial
crisis, 398–414
and Volcker rule, 413
see also FDIC
Donovan, Donal, 248
Douglass National Bank, 10
Dow Jones stock market index, 4, 6–7,
20–24
Downey Savings, 353
downsizing, 149–151, 391
Draghi, Mario, 86, 453
Dresdner Bank, 29, 34, 184
Drew, Ina, 95
Drumm, David, 250–251
DTA (deferred tax assets), 120, 275
Dugan, John, 378–379
Dune Capital Management, 34, 340
dynamic provisioning, 270–271

E*Trade Financial Corp., 434
EAA, 50–51
EBA (European Banking Authority),
  68, 73, 76, 78, 81, 85, 89–91,
  107–108, 128, 262–263,
  267–268, 460
EBF (European Banking
  Federation), 457
EBH Bank, 25–27
EBS (Educational Building Society),
  56–57, 255
ECB (European Central Bank), 8–9,
  13, 18–19, 20–22, 24–27, 29,
  38–39, 42, 44, 59, 73, 103, 141,
  152–153
  Asset Quality Review, 132, 140–141
  banking union, 99
  bilateral swap agreements, 124
  eurozone bonds, 60
  LTRO (longer-term refinancing
    operation), 5–6
  OMT (outright monetary
    transactions), 96
  SSM (Single Supervisory
    Mechanism), xvii, 459–461
  Systemic Risk Board, xxxv
ECJ (European Court of Justice),
  460–461
ECNs (enhanced capital notes), 49–50
ECOFIN Council, xxxvi, 52, 59–60,
  99, 105, 128
economic crisis phase, 1–2
The Economist, insured deposits
  bailing-in errors, 282–283
EFSF (European Financial Stability
  Facility), 59, 61, 71–72, 256,
  489–490
EFSM (European Financial Stability
  Mechanism), 71–72, 256
EFTA Court of Justice, 102, 234
Einarsson, Sigurdur, 128, 235
EIOPA (European Insurance and
  Occupational Pension Authority),
  68, 73
ELA (Emergency Liquidity Assistance),
  24, 160, 240, 280
Emergency Economic Stabilization
  Act, 23
EMIR (European Market Infrastructure
  Regulation), 94, 131

Emporiki Bank, 102, 262–264
Enhanced Leverage Fund, 3
equity capital, 436
equity participation note, 368
Erste Bank, 38, 114, 131, 136,
  144–145, 375
ESM (European Stability Mechanism),
  71–72, 81, 99, 113, 280–281,
  456–457, 474–475, 477
ESMA (European Securities and
  Markets Authority), 60–61, 68,
  73, 120
ESRB (European Systemic Risk Board),
  72–73
ESRC (European Systemic Risk
  Council), 68
EU banking union, 120
  see also SSM (Single Supervisory
  Mechanism)
EU Commission, 30
EU Parliament, financial regulation/
  supervision, 68, 111
Euribor markets, 126–127
euro stabilization fund *see* EFSF
Eurobank, 115–116, 132, 134,
  140–141, 262–264
Eurobank Ergasias, 112
Eurohypo, 184–185
European banking union,
  xvii, 454–459
  common central bank, 454
  common currency, 454
  common solvency/liquidity rules,
    454–455
  European Stability Mechanism,
    71–72, 81, 99, 113, 280–281,
    456–457
  Single Resolution Authority,
    456–458
  Single Supervisory Mechanism, xvii,
    107, 120, 132–133, 455–456
European banks
  aid conditions, 442, 452–453
  bank equity issues, 440
  bank resolution, 438
  capital adequacy, 441–442
  capital requirements, 89–91,
    480–484
  CET1/RWA ratios, 481–484
  compared to US banks, 437–441

European banks (cont.)
  deposit insurance, 438
  and the EC, 441–442
  efficiency, 442
  NPL ratio, 442
  profitability, 439
  return on equity, 441
  see also individual banks
European Commission, 44, 59
  bank levy, 60
  state aid, 448–449
  trading rules, 67–68
European Council, Directive
  2009/14/EC, 39
European Deposit Insurance Funds,
  484–485
European regulatory authorities, 439
European Resolution Board,
  xxxv–xxxvi
European Single Market, 441–442
European sovereign debt crisis,
  timeline, 442
European treaties, proposed, 459–461
European Union
  bank remuneration, 62–63
  deposit guarantee scheme, 24
  failing banks resolution/restructuring
    proposals, 450–452
  hedge funds, 62–63, 70
  ratings, 129
European Union banks, state aid to,
  xxxii, xxxiii
Eurostat, 58, 254
Euroyen markets, 126–127
EverBank, 93

failed bank resolution rules, 114
False Claims Act, 94
Fannie Mae, 9, 12, 15–17, 29–30, 32,
    37–40, 44–45, 61, 63, 66, 70, 73,
    83–84, 91–92, 101–102, 109–110,
    114, 116–117, 122–125, 129,
    133–135, 137–140, 144–145,
    291, 308–309, 323–324, 335,
    337–338, 347–348, 366–368,
    377, 386, 403, 405
  capital support, xxix
Farkas, Lee B., 81
FASB (Financial Accounting Standards
  Board), 41, 60, 62

FCIC (Financial Crisis Inquiry
  Commission), 300–301, 320,
  348, 370
FDIC (Federal Deposit Insurance
  Corporation), xvi, xxxv–xxxvi,
  xxxvi, 13, 15, 17–22, 27, 31–32,
  34, 40, 42, 44–45, 47–48, 50, 56,
  64–65, 71, 75–77, 81, 89–91, 93,
  99–100, 113–115, 119, 137, 290,
  293–302, 305, 327, 339–342,
  345–350, 355, 359–360, 380, 476
  bank capitalization, 437–438
  bank equity issues, 440
  bank resolution, 433, 438
  as bank supervisor, 429
  bank undercapitalization, 419–420
  banks, aspects of, 441
  closing transaction types, 416–418
  as conservator, 414–415
  Deposit Payoff closing
    transactions, 417
  least-cost solutions, 415
  P&A (Purchase and Assumption)
    closing transactions, 416–417
  PCA (Prompt Corrective
    Action) *see* PCA
  as receiver/liquidator, 414,
    426–427, 428
  resolution funds, 433
  Single Market, 441–442
  and TBTF institutions, 429–432
  see also Dodd–Frank
FDICIA (FDIC Improvement Act),
  349–350, 355, 419–420, 438
fear index, 329–330
Fed Funds, 6
Federal Deposit Insurance Act
  (section 11), 414
  (section 14), 433
Federal Deposit Reform Act, 438
Federal Home Loan Bank, 336–337,
  339, 344–345
Federal Insurance Office, 65, 298
Federal Open Market Committee, 71
Federal Reserve, xxxvi, 4, 6–10,
  12–14, 17–27, 30–32, 40, 42,
  44–46, 50, 54–57, 59, 63–64, 77,
  92–93, 100, 105–106, 113–114,
  123–125, 152–153, 193, 290,
  294–299, 336, 359–360, 435

Federal Reserve Act
  (section 13(3)), xvi, 12, 310,
    368–369, 422–424
  size of, 397
Federal Reserve Bank of Dallas, 88
Federal Reserve Bank of Kansas
  City, 76
Federal Reserve Bank of New York,
  97, 368–369
Federal Trust, 31
Feinberg, Kenneth, 52–53
Feldstein, Martin, 71
FEM (Financial Supervisory
  Authority), of Iceland, 230
Ferran, Eilís, 441–442
FHFA (Federal Housing Finance
  Agency), 16–17, 29, 63, 70,
    83–84, 116, 121–124, 134–135,
    138–139, 296–298, 347–348, 377
Fifth Third Bank, 28–29
FIM, 231
Financial Company Resolution
  Fund, 45
Financial Conduct Authority, 120
financial crises, post-World War II,
  xxvii–xxviii
financial crisis (2007–14)
  full timeline, 1–2
  (2007), 2–9
  (2008), 9–34
  (2009), 34–54
  (2010), 54–73
  (2011), 73
  (2012), 92–101
  (2013), 101–129
  (2014), 130–142
  Dodd–Frank limitations, 398–414
  underlying causes, 398–414
  see also individual institutions
financial sector support, as percentage
  of GDP, xxx
Financial Supervisory Authority
  (Denmark), 482
Financial Supervisory Authority
  (Sweden), 59, 76–77,
    118–119, 135
Finansiel Stabilitet Bank Support
  Agency, 25–27, 69, 74–75, 80,
    216, 218–219, 222–224, 482
Fionia Bank, 25–27, 37, 218–219

FIRREA (Financial Institutions
  Reform, Recovery, and
  Enforcement Act), 102–103, 397
First City Bank of Georgia, 96
First Franklin Financial Corp., 12
First Horizon National, 28–29
First Niagara Financial, 28–29
Fischer Fondkommission, 231
Fisher, Richard, 88, 362, 399–400,
  405–406
Fishman, Alan, 20, 345–346
Fitch rating agency, 10, 19,
  228–229, 280
FitzPatrick, Peter, 251
FitzPatrick, Sean, 96, 103, 134, 250–252
Fjordbank Mors, 69, 80, 219
FME (Financial Supervisory
  Authority), 23–24, 232, 235
FMS WM, 182
foreclosure abuse fines, 92, 101–102
Fortis, 6–7, 20, 23, 33, 38–39, 50, 63,
  110, 200–205, 434
  and ABN AMRO, 201–202,
    204–205
  and BNP Paribas, 203–205
  crisis handling grades, 205
  government ownership of,
    202–203, 204
  operative structure, 201
Fortis affair, 33
FPC (Financial Policy Committee), 61,
  75–76, 109, 111, 124, 137
FR (Financial Regulator), 171, 244
France
  bank capitalization, 27–28, 33, 35
  bank ring-fencing, 100–101,
    108, 116
  bonus payments, 46–47
  ratings, 490
  sovereign debt crisis, timeline, 442
  US model, 375–376
Freddie Mac, 8, 12, 15–17, 29, 31–32,
  39–40, 44–45, 61, 63, 66, 70,
  73, 83–84, 91–92, 109–110,
  114, 116–117, 121–125, 129,
  133–135, 137–140, 144–145,
  291, 308–309, 323–324, 335,
  338, 347–348, 366–368, 377,
  386, 403, 405
  capital support, xxix, 2

Freedom Bank, 29
Fremont Investment & Loan, 13
Friedman, Stephen, 372
FROB (Fund for Orderly Bank
    Restructuring), 85, 94
FROB (state bank resolution fund), 74,
    88, 100, 107, 129, 273–274, 276
FSA (Financial Security Assurance),
    31, 192–194
FSA (Financial Services Authority)
    (Denmark), 111–112
FSA (Financial Services Authority)
    (Iceland), 232–233
FSA (Financial Services Authority)
    (Ireland), 237–238
FSA (Financial Services Authority)
    (UK), 18–19, 53, 57, 61, 96,
    108–109, 155–158, 162–163, 326
FSB (Financial Stability Board), 51,
    86–89, 98, 107–108, 125–126,
    140–141, 359–360, 411–412,
    420–421, 481
FSCS (Financial Services
    Compensation Scheme), 153–154
FSOC (Financial Stability Oversight
    Council), xxxv, 65, 111–112,
    299–300, 359–360, 405–406,
    420–421, 424, 428
FTSE-100, 23–24, 155–156
FTT (Financial Transactions Tax)
    (Tobin tax), 84–85, 119, 124
Fuld, Dick, 316–317, 323–325
funds, recovery of, xxv
Futures and Trading Practices Act, 365

G-7 meeting (2008), 25
G-20 meetings (2008), 31
G-20 meetings (2009), 41, 46–47
G-20 meetings (2010), 58–59, 61–62
G-SIFIs (globally systemically
    important financial institutions),
    98, 139–140, 162–163, 199, 272,
    359–360, 428, 481, 487–488
GAAP (generally accepted accounting
    principles), 305–306, 308,
    358–359, 377, 434, 437–438
    see also IFRS
GAO (General Accountability
    Office), 416
GE Capital, 31, 111–112, 359–360

Geithner, Tim, 36, 40, 301–302, 336,
    349, 356, 372–374, 378–379, 381
Générale de Banque, 200
Generali, 274
Geniki Bank, 264
Gently, David, 251
Georges Quay, 5
German Bankers' Association, 181–182
Germany, 175–190
    bank borrowing guarantee, 25–27
    bank concentration ratio, 176
    bank debt, 75
    bank fragmentation, 175–176
    bank nationalization, 40, 48
    bank restructuring, 73
    bank ring-fencing, 103
    banking structure, 187–189
    banks pre-crisis, 175
    German depositor protection, 178
    government bank ownership, 187
    loan-to-value requirements, 175
    naked default swaps, 60
    ratings, 75
    see also Commerzbank; Hypo
        Real Estate; IKB Deutsche
        Industriebank AG;
        Landesbanken
Glass–Steagall Act, xv, 96, 115,
    303, 397
Glitnir Bank, 20–22, 24, 28, 93, 101,
    109–110, 135–136, 141,
    228–235, 237–238
global bank tax, 61–62
Global Synthetic Equities Trading
    Team, 84
GM (General Motors), 25–27, 33,
    52–53, 58, 71, 100–101, 124,
    126–127
GMAC (General Motors Acceptance
    Corporation), xxix, 34, 42, 50,
    52–54, 379
    see also Ally Financial
Golden Circle, 252–254
Golden West, 14–16, 354, 398, 409
Goldman Sachs, 4, 11–13, 19–20,
    25–27, 31, 42–45, 56–58, 63–65,
    71, 77, 83–84, 91–92, 94,
    105–106, 116, 118, 126,
    139–141, 178–179, 287, 293,
    303–304, 359–361, 364–366

Goodwin, Sir Fred, 25, 92, 109–110
Gordon, Jeffrey N., 476
Gorman, James, 54, 94
GOTA Bank, 121
Gramm–Leach–Bliley Act, 408–409
Granite SPV, 154–155
Great Britain *see* United Kingdom
Greece, 259–266
    austerity measures, 59, 260
    bank asset/GDP ration, xxix–xxx
    bank capital demand, 263
    bank recapitalization, 99–100, 112
    banking crisis, xxviii
    budget deficit, 259–260
    crisis handling grades, 264–266
    debt/GDP rate, 259–260
    financial/banking background,
        259–262
    government bonds, 93
    ratings, 59, 78, 99, 260–262, 441,
        489, 492
    sovereign debt collateral, 260
    sovereign debt crisis, xxviii,
        xxix–xxx
    timeline, 442
    support package (2010), 59
    support package (2012), 92, 260
    10-year bond yields, 260–262
    unemployment, 260
    see also Agricultural Bank; Emporiki
        Bank; Eurobank
Greenberg, Alan C., 307
Greene, Edward F., 405
Greenspan, Alan, 71, 362
Greenwich Capital Markets, 125
Gros, Daniel, 478
Group of 30, 94
Grübel, Oswald, 84
GSE (government-sponsored enterprises)
    see Fannie Mae; Freddie Mac
Gulliver, Stuart, 113

Haarde, Geir, 83, 94, 235
Hague international tribunal for
    complex financial transactions, 92
Haldane, Andrew, 98, 407, 488
Handelsbanken, 219–221
Hardibanki, 232–233
Hartford Financial Services, 31
Hassel, Gerald L., 83

HBOS (Halifax Bank of Scotland), 18,
    25–27, 49–50, 96, 143, 168–171
hedge funds, 64
Helaba *see* Hessen Thüringen
Hellenic Bank, 279–281
Hellenic Postbank, 263
Hellwig, Martin, 488
Heritable Bank, 24–25
Hessen Thüringen (Helaba) LB, 81, 95,
    188–190
HF Financial Co., 28–29
HFSF (Hellenic Financial Stability
    Fund), 112, 115–116, 134
HGAA (Hypo Group Alpe Adria),
    53, 55
High-Grade Structured Credit Master
    Fund, 3, 308–309
High-Grade Structured Credit
    Strategies Enhanced Leverage
    Fund, 3, 308–309
Hjaltason, Gudmundur, 101, 235
Hoenig, Thomas, 76, 405–406
Holder, Eric, 386
Home Loan Bank System, 339–340
home sovereign bonds, 129
Hong Kong Monetary Authority, 104
Honohan, Patrick, 248–249, 251
Hooley, Joseph, 55
Horta-Osório, António, 113
Housing and Economic Recovery
    Unit, 16
HRE (Hypo Real Estate), xxix, 6, 20–24,
    35, 40, 43, 48, 82, 118–119,
    181–183, 237–238, 244
    bail-outs, 254
    crisis handling grades, 183
    and Depfa, 181–182
    toxic assets, 182–183
HSBC (Hong Kong and Shanghai
    Banking Corporation), 2, 8, 12,
    14, 30, 67, 83–84, 86, 88, 99,
    108–109, 112–113, 126–127,
    358–359, 375
HSH Nordbank LB, 37, 39, 48,
    188–190
HSSL (High-Speed Swim Lane or
    "Hustle"), 137–138, 337–338
Hungary, loans to, 29
Huntington Bancshares, 28–29
Hurley, Cornelius K., 407–408

Hurley, John, 250–251
Hustle process *see* HSSL
Hypo Group Alpe Adria, 131–132,
    136, 139, 144–145, 190
Hypothekenbank Berlin AG, 192

IASB (International Accounting
    Standards Board), 44, 62
Ibercaja, 274
ICBC, 125–126
ICE Europe (InterContinental
    Exchange Europe), 56–57
Iceland, 227–236
    bank assets, 231–232
    bank assets/GDP ratio, xxix–xxx,
        238–239
    bank BIS ratios, 232
    bank capital, 28
    capital controls, 23–24
    commissioned studies on, 229–230
    comparison with Ireland, 238–239
    crisis cost percentage of GDP, 227
    crisis handling grades, 235–236
    current account as percentage of
        GDP, 229
    deposit guarantee fund, 131
    deposit-insurance liabilities, 48–49,
        233–234
    economic growth, 227–229
    economic improvements, 83
    EFTA Court of Justice ruling, 234
    financial support package, 31,
        233–235
    financial/banking background,
        227–230
    GDP growth rate, 228, 234–235
    government debt/GDP ratio, 229
    IMF loan, 28
    IMF requirements, 83
    ratings, 228–229
    repayments deal, 56
    see also Glitnir; Kaupthing;
        Landsbanki
Icelandic Chamber of Commerce
    economic study, 230
Icelandic Financial Supervisory
    Authority, 24–25
Icelandic Stock Market index, 234
Icesave, 23–24, 54, 56, 72, 78, 83, 102,
    231–233

IFRS (International Financial
    Reporting Standards), 305–306,
    358–359, 437–438
    see also GAAP
IKB Deutsche Industriebank AG, 4, 10,
    152, 178–181
    capital support, xxix
    crisis handling grades, 179–181
    losses, 5
    share prices, 177
    subsidiaries, 178–179
Iksil, Bruno, 95, 117–118
IL&P (Irish Life & Permanent),
    92, 244, 251
    bank data, 245
IMB HoldCo LLC, 340
IMF (International Monetary Fund),
    xxviii, 41, 45, 71–72,
    233–235, 256
INBS (Irish Nationwide Building
    Society), 56–57, 79–81, 246,
    251–252, 255–256
Independent Commission, on Banking,
    see Vickers Commission
Independent Commission,
    on Cyprus, 284
industry involvement, 149–151, 392
IndyMac, 14–15, 33–34, 37, 75,
    91–92, 99–100, 302, 334–342,
    366–368, 414–415
    crisis handling grades, 340–342
    infighting, 149
ING (Internationale Nederlanden
    Groep), 6, 24–25, 27, 49, 53, 97,
    138, 199, 205–206, 232–233
    crisis handling grade, 206
    share price (Amsterdam), 207
Institute of International Finance, 77
interbank money market rates/official
    rates, 327–329
international cooperation, 146, 391
Intesa San Paolo, 121, 375
Ireland, 237–258
    bank asset/GDP ratio, xxix–xxx,
        238–239
    bank capitalization, 254–255
    bank data, 245
    bank losses, 72
    bank nationalization, 246, 253
    bank profitability, 244–245

bank recapitalization, 33, 36, 43,
249–250, 256–257
bank stress testing, 77
banking crisis, xxviii
BIS requirements, 244–245
budget balance/GDP ratio, 241–242
budget deficit, 254
capital to risk-weighted assets,
244–245
capital–asset ratios, 244–245
comparison with Iceland, 238–239
crisis handling grades, 257–258
crisis response summary, 257–258
current account, 240
deposit guarantees, 247–249
deposit insurance, 19, 22
ELA (Emergency Liquidity
Assistance) to, 240
financial/banking background,
237–243
FR (Financial Regulator), 244
GDP growth rate, 239
GDP per capita, 239
government debt/GDP ratio,
241–242
IMF/EU support, 71–72
liabilities guarantees, 247–249
loan acquisitions, 254
loans to directors, 250–254
macroeconomic variables, 239–240
property price bubble, 240–242
public debt/GDP ratio, 254
ratings, 24–25, 41, 66–67, 72, 78,
81, 95, 104, 106, 130, 135, 249,
258, 490–491
sovereign debt crisis, xxviii
timeline, 442
state bank ownership, 55, 59–61,
68, 71–72, 79–80, 83, 92
stock market index, 242–243, 250
subordinated debt, 256, 258
support program exit, 126
10 year bond sale, 130
toxic assets, 47
toxic assets purchase, 56–57
see also AIB (Allied Irish Banks);
Anglo Irish Bank; Bank of
Ireland
Irish Bank Resolution Corporation, 81,
103, 255–256

Irish Financial Services Regulatory
Authority, 34
Irish National Pension Reserve
Fund, 256
Irish Stock Exchange, 250
IRR (interest rate risk) management, 54
IRS (Internal Revenue Service), 22, 356
ISDA (International Swaps and
Derivatives Association), 44, 93,
140, 260–262, 373, 490
Italy, 209–215
banking crisis, xxviii, 39
deposit guarantee, 25
domestic government bonds,
209–211
EU government bonds, 77
financial/banking background,
209–213
government bonds yields losses,
212–213
government debt/GDP ratio, 209–211
IMF concerns, 212–213
ratings, 490
sovereign debt crisis, xxviii
timeline, 442
Tremonti bonds, 214
see also MPS (Monte dei Paschi di
Siena)

J. C. Flowers, 34, 48, 119, 156–157,
173, 182, 340
Jóhannesson, Jón Asgeir, 135–136, 235
Johnson, James A., 335
Johnson, Simon, 408–409
Jones, David, 67
JP Nordiska Bank, 230–231
JPMorgan Chase, 12–13, 20, 25–27,
42–43, 47–48, 53, 56, 83–84, 89,
92, 94–95, 105–106, 116–119,
121–124, 126–127, 130, 136–
139, 208–215, 287, 303–304,
310–311, 313, 325, 344–348,
358–361, 386, 422–424, 434
JRC (Joint Research Center), 265–266
Jyske Bank, 80, 122, 132, 217–219

Kashkari, Neel, 349
Kaupthing Bank, 24–25, 28, 93,
109–110, 128, 135–136, 141,
230–235

Kaupthing Edge, 23–25, 230–232
KBC, 139–140, 195
KBL, 99–100, 195
KDB (Korea Development Bank),
    316, 323–324
Kelly, Robert, 25–27, 83, 378–379
Kempen & Co., 192–193
Kerviel, Jérome, 11
Key Corp, 28–29
KfW (Kreditanstalt für Wiederaufbau),
    152, 178–181
    see also IKB
Killinger, Kerry, 17, 89–91, 345–347
King, Sir Mervyn (later Lord King), 49,
    75–76, 114, 205, 362
Kohn, Donald, 312
Kolding, Eivind, 120–121
Kommunalkredit, 55, 193–194
Koon, Richard, 99
Kovacevich, Richard, 25–27, 54, 375,
    378–379
Kutxabank, 274

La Caixa, 272
Lacelles, David, 284
Laiki Bank see Popular Bank (Cyprus)
Landesbanken, 187–190
    see also individual banks
Landsbanki, 23–25, 54, 83, 109–110,
    135–136, 230–235
Landsbanki economic study,
    229–230
Landsbanki Icesave see Icesave
LaSalle Bank, 164, 381–382
Latvia, bank nationalization, 29–30
LBBW see Baden-Württemberg LB
LCH Clearnet, 56
LCR (Liquidity Coverage Ratio), xxxv,
    89, 101, 123, 165, 217, 479
legacy assets, 71–72
legal assessment, 149–151, 392
Lehman Brothers, 14, 17–18, 120,
    160, 193, 202, 246, 260, 304,
    316–317, 321–333, 361,
    366–368, 427–428
    crisis handling grades, 329–333
Lehman weekend, 366–368
Lenihan, Brian, 253, 256–257
leverage ratios, 58–59, 66, 482–484
Lew, Jack, 474

Lewis, Kenneth, 25–27, 36, 41, 48,
    54, 133–134, 314–319, 324–325,
    378–379, 381–385
liabilities guarantees, 145–146, 391
Liberbank, 107
LIBOR interest rates, 18, 95, 100–101,
    120, 123, 129, 368–369
Liikanen report, 1–2, 102, 130–131,
    479–480
liquidation, xxv
liquidity, 145–146, 391
liquidity support schemes, 94
living wills, 64
Lloyds Banking Group, xxviii, 11,
    25–27, 29, 49–52, 75–76, 85–86,
    88, 108–109, 111–113, 119–121,
    137, 143, 157, 160, 168–174
assets, 173
assets guarantee by government,
    171–172
capital shortfall, 173
capital support for, 172–173
crisis handling grade, 173–174
and HBOS, 168–171
and National Audit Committee,
    172–173
and Northern Rock, 153,
    156–158
and OFT (Office of Fair Trading),
    170–171
PRA ruling, 173
share prices, 172–173
Lloyds TSB, 18, 25–27, 38–39, 169
Lo, Andy, 1
Logue, Ronald, 25–27, 55, 378–379
London Scottish Bank, 33
London Whale affair, 121
Lone Star, 110, 132, 136, 179,
    182, 316
Long Beach, 3–4, 342–344
long-run viability, 146, 391
losses to taxpayers, xxv
LTCM (Long Term Capital
    Management), 316–317
LTRO (Longer-Term
    Refinancing Operation),
    5, 152–153, 454
LTV (loan-to-value), 398, 409
Luxembourg, EU Government
    bonds, 77

M-M (Modigliani–Miller) theorem,
 480–481
MAC (material adverse change),
 318–319
McAteer, Willie, 250–251
McCain, John, 115
McCarthy, Sir Callum, 326, 332–333
McGraw-Hill, 102–103
Mack, John, 25–27, 54, 318,
 378–379
McKillop, Sir Tom, 25–27
Macris, Achilles, 95
Madoff, Bernard, 130
Maiden Lane I, 12–13, 97, 311,
 422–424
Maiden Lane II, 370, 422–424
Maiden Lane III, 370, 422–424
Mairone, Rebecca, 137–138, 338
Maple 10 *see* Golden Circle
Marchall & Ilsley Corp, 28–29
Marsh, Tanya, 409
Martin-Artajo, Javier, 117–118
MBIA, 10–11, 14, 110, 337–338,
 364–366, 386
MBS (mortgage-backed securities),
 64, 101, 121–122, 125, 149–150,
 308–309, 337, 411
Meroni doctrine, 460–461
Merrill, Charlie, 314
Merrill Lynch, 6–7, 9–10, 12–15, 17,
 24–27, 34–36, 42, 52, 83–84,
 96–97, 119, 133–134, 160, 303,
 305, 314–321, 364–366, 381–382
crisis handling grades, 320–321
Messina, Carlo, 121
MetLife, 55–56, 93
MF Global, 86
micro prudential supervision, 52
Mihuzo bank, 10
Millennium bank, 264
Millennium BCP, 268
Miller, Alex, 22, 193
Mitsubishi UFJ, 19, 25–27
Mizuho bank, 316
MMIFF (Money Market Investor
 Funding Facility), 28
Moerland, Piet, 123
Monetary Policy Committee, 61
Monte dei Pasachi *see* MPS
Monti bonds, 104–105, 214

Moody's rating agency, 3–4, 6–7, 11,
 17, 19, 24–25, 43, 47, 63, 66,
 71–72, 75–78, 81, 85, 95, 104,
 118, 126, 130, 135, 194–195,
 228–229, 249, 258, 267,
 270–271, 273–274, 280, 310,
 341, 345, 360, 364, 489–492
moral hazards, 357, 404, 416,
 424–425
Morgan Stanley, 8–9, 19, 25–27, 43,
 45, 54, 65, 71, 94, 97, 105–106,
 116, 118, 126, 260, 287, 305,
 359–361
mortgage banks, 64
mortgage bonds, 42
mortgage credits, 77
mortgage delinquencies, 50
Mortgage Lenders Network, 2
Moynihan, Brian, 48, 54
Mozilo, Angelo, 10, 69, 335–337
MPS (Monte dei Paschi di Siena),
 xxviii, 6–7, 104–105, 126, 129,
 136–137, 140–141, 213–215
 Antonveneta purchase, 214
 crisis handling grade, 215
 derivative contracts, 208–215
 government bonds yields losses, 214
 Monti Bonds, 104–105, 214
Mudd, Daniel, 16
Murphy, Antoin E., 248
Mussari, Giuseppe, 141, 208–215

naked default swap, 365
NAMA (National Asset Management
 Agency), xxix, 47, 51, 56–57, 67,
 103, 135, 249–250, 253–258, 491
NASDAQ, 20–22, 288
National Association of Realtors, 10
National Audit Committee, 172–173
National Bank of Commerce, 35
National Bank of Greece, 81–82, 132,
 262–264
National Banking Supervisor, 298
National City Bank of Cleveland
 Ohio, 28
National Credit Union Administration,
 56, 296–298
National Debt Clock, 22
National Debt Office, 30, 41
Nationalbanken (Denmark), 218

Nationwide Building Society, 112–113
NatWest, 49, 121, 159–160, 166
NBI (Nyí Landsbanki), 28, 233
NCG (Nova Caixa Galicia) Banco, 76,
    85, 98–99, 104, 129, 273–275
Neary, Patrick, 34, 237–238, 244,
    250–251
Netbank, 6
Netherlands
    bank borrowing guarantee, 25–27
    bank capital injection, 50
    bank leverage ratio, 118
    bank nationalization, 102
    bank tax, 81
    financial/banking background,
        199–200
    and SNS Reaal Bank, 115, 206–208
New Century, 2, 91–92
New Hellenic Post Bank, 264
New Proton Bank, 115–116, 264
NIBS, 230–231
Nikkei, 23–24
Nin, Juan Maria, 272
Nomura, 17–18, 141, 208–215, 326
non-core assets, 135
non-core healthy assets, 149
Nonnenmacher, Jens, 48
Nordbanken, 121
Norddeutsche LB, 188
Nordea Bank Denmark, 41, 88–89,
    112, 121–122, 217–219
Nordea Bank Sweden, 139–140,
    219–221, 481
Nordic Bank data, 219–221
Northern Rock, 6, 9, 11, 52, 56–57,
    67, 88, 94, 117, 143, 151–159
    absence of bankruptcy regimes,
        157–158
    absence of resolution schemes,
        157–158
    attempted sales of, 153, 156–158
    Bank of England support, 153
    bank run, 151–153
    capital-adequacy regulation, 156
    cost to taxpayer, 158
    crisis handling grade, 157–159
    deposit insurance system, 157–158
    FSA supervision of, 155–156
    in FTSE-100 list, 155–156
    growth rate, 155–156

ineffective financial supervision,
    157–158
    interest rates, 155–156
    liabilities, 154–155
    liquidity, 153
    maturity-gap problem, 154–155
    mortgage securitization, 154–155
    nationalization of, 156
    sale to Virgin Money, 156–158
Northern Trust, 28–29, 43
Norway, capital requirements, 108
Nota Italia derivative contract,
    208–215
Nova Bank Fyn, 218–219
Novo Banco, 138
NPL (non-performing loans), 279–280
Nyberg report, 245–246, 248
Nyí Glitnir, 233
Nyja Kaupthing, 233
Nykredit Realkredit, 122
NYSE (New York Stock
    Exchange), 288

Obama, Barack, xxv, 36, 54, 56, 66,
    373–374, 381
OCC (Office of the Comptroller of
    the Currency), 2, 10, 43, 65, 99,
    114–115, 294, 296–298, 300–301,
    310, 359–360, 377
OECD Economic Department, 488
OFT (Office of Fair Trading), 170–171
OLA (Orderly Liquidation Authority),
    xvi, xxxiv–xxxv, 299, 327, 404,
    421–422, 426, 428, 476
Old National Bancorp, 42
OLF (Orderly Liquidation Fund),
    xxxvi, 429–432, 472
Omni National Bank of Georgia, 40
OMT (Outright Monetary
    Transactions), 96, 454
Onaran, Yalman, 381–382
O'Neal, Stanley, 6–7, 314–316
OneWest Bank, 93, 340
Open Bank Assistance, 427
option ARM, 343, 398, 409
ORA (Orderly Resolution
    Authority), 428
ORF (Orderly Resolution Fund),
    xxxvi, 433
Orion Bank, 95

Ormond Quay, 5
Ortseifen, Stefan, 178–179
Ospel, Marcus, 13
OTC derivatives, xv, 18, 40–41, 67–68,
     94, 106–107, 131, 361, 364–365,
     479–480
OTC regulator, 17–19
OTS (Office of Thrift Supervision),
     6, 20, 33, 37, 43, 56, 65, 233–234,
     295–298, 300–301, 329, 334,
     339–341, 344–346, 349–350

Pandit, Vikram, 25–27, 97, 356,
     378–379, 381–382
Parex Bank, 29–30, 144–145
Paulson & Co, 57–58
Paulson, Hank, 2, 19, 25–27, 34–35,
     316–319, 324–325, 332–333,
     348–349, 363, 378–379, 381–385
payback salaries/bonuses, 79–80
PBB (Deutsche Pfandbriefbank), 182
PCA (Prompt Corrective Action),
     305, 320, 434
   bank undercapitalization, 420
PDCF (Primary Dealer Credit Facility),
     13, 54–55, 311, 321
People's Bank of China, 24–25
Perry, Michael W., 15, 100, 340–342
Philipponnat, Thierry, 478
Pick-a-Pay, 354, 398, 409
PIIGS countries *see* Greece; Ireland;
     Italy; Portugal; Spain
Piraeus Bank, 96, 108, 132, 262–264
PNC Financial Services, 28–29, 93
Pohjola bank, 219–221
Ponzi scheme, 130
Popular Bank (Cyprus), 108, 264,
     279–281
Portes, Richard, 230
portfolio risks, internal models, 410
Portogon Financial Services, 189
Portugal, 267–269
   bank capital demands, 268
   bank capitalization, 78, 267
   banking crisis, xxviii
   budget deficit, 267
   crisis handling grades, 269
   financial/banking background,
        267–268
   government debt/GDP ratio, 267

IMF/ECB loan, 78
ratings, 59, 63, 77, 81, 106, 267
sovereign debt crisis, xxviii
timeline, 442
Pozen, Robert C., 372
PPIP (Public Private Investment
     Program), 40, 70
PRA (Prudential Regulatory
     Authority), 61, 109, 111–113,
     173, 461, 485–486
Prates, Marcelo Madureira, 401
Precision Capital, 99–100, 195
Price Waterhouse Coopers, 478
Prince, Charles, 8, 377
proactive supervision, 145–146, 390
Probank, 262
Proposal 1, 18
Proposal 2, 428–432
Proposal 3, 433–434
proprietary trading restrictions, 84
Proton Bank, 115–116, 264
Prudential, 55–56, 111–112, 359–360
Prudential Supervisory Authority, 116
public sector interventions, as
     percentage of GDP, xxxi

qualified financial contracts, 427
quantitative easing, 454
quantity-related remuneration/bonus
     structures, 412
Quinn, Sean, 245–246, 252

Rabobank, 75–76, 123, 127, 199
Raiffeisen Bank International,
     131, 136
Raines, Franklin, 335
Rato, Rodrigo, 94, 110–111, 273
RBS (Royal Bank of Scotland), 6–7, 9,
     11, 14, 24–27, 29, 35, 37–38, 49,
     52, 55–56, 81–82, 85, 92, 94, 97,
     103, 108–109, 111, 121, 124–127,
     132, 140, 143, 157, 159–168
   and ABN AMRO, 161–166
   Asset Protection Scheme, 166
   bank data, 161
   BIS ratio, 161–162
   capital position, 162–163
   capitalization, 161–162
   credit trading, 166
   crisis handling grades, 161, 166–168

RBS (Royal Bank of Scotland) (cont.)
    FSA report (2011), 162–163,
        165–168
    government (UKFI) ownership of,
        160, 166
    Irish lending, 240–241
    LCR (Liquidity Coverage
        Ratio), 165
    leverage ratio, 304
    losses (2008), 163
    size/assets, 159–160
    supervision failures, 167
    UKFI share value, 167
Regions Financial, 28–29
regulated holding companies, 100
regulatory arbitrage, 322, 369, 404
regulatory authorities, 412–413
    track record, 390
regulatory capture, 413
Reich, John, 35, 301–302
remuneration/bonus structures, 412
Repo 105/108, 322–325
Reserve Bank of Canada, 24–25
Reserve Primary Fund, 18
resolution
    bank recovery, xxvi, 115
    in banking union, xvii
    slow, 149
    UKAR, 157
Resolution Fund, xxxvi
resolution funds, xxxvi, 433
resolution schemes, Northern Rock,
    157–158
Rheinland-Pfalz LB, 15
Richard, Pierre, 22, 193
Richman, Richard Paul, 476
ring-fencing, 146, 391, 479–480
Ringe, Wolf-Georg, 476
risk weight classification, 86, 88
RMBS (residential mortgage-backed
    securities), 101–103, 343–344
Robeco Bank, 230–231
Rockefeller, John D., 363
Romero, Christy L., 124
Roskilde Bank, 25–27, 218
Rosner, Joshua, 403–405
Rotella, Steve, 89–91, 346–347
Royal Park Investments, 110, 204
RWA (risk-weighted assets), 88–89,
    111–112

Saar LB, 188
Sachsen LB, 189
Salgado, Ricardo, 137, 492
Sanderson state bank, 33
Santorini, 129
Santorini derivative contract, 208–215
SAREB, 100, 104, 274–276
Sarkozy, Nicolas, 25–27
Sberbank, 95
SCAP (Supervisory Capital Assessment
    Programs), 37
Schneider, David, 89–91, 346–347
Schumer, Charles, 14–15, 313,
    339–340
Schwarz, Anna Jacobson, 312
Scott, Kenneth E., 399
SD (selective default), 260–262
SEB Sweden, 219–221
SEC (Securities and Exchange
    Commission), 10, 15–16, 18–19,
    57–58, 64–65, 68–69, 75, 91–92,
    117–118, 125, 295–298, 303,
    310, 332, 340–342
Security Pacific Bank, 29–30
Sedlabanki, 230–232, 236
SEFs (swap execution facilities),
    68, 123
Semerci, Osman, 316
Senior Preferred Stock Purchase
    Agreement, 39
Serageldin, Kareem, 110
SFIL (Société de Financement
    Local), 198
Shabudin, Ebrahim, 117
shadow-banking, 411–412
Shellem, Kenneth, 99
Sherman Act, 362
Shiller, Robert J., 5
short-selling, 18–19
Sibert, Ann, 229–230
SIFIs, 107–108, 114–115, 122, 125–126,
    130–131, 139–140, 462
    see also G-SIFIs
SIGTARP (Special Inspector General
    for the Troubled Asset Relief
    Program), 292, 351–352
    see also TARP
Sigurdsson, Hreidar Mar, 128, 235
Silver State Bank, 17
Singer & Friedlander, 24–25, 230–233

Single Point of Entry, 434
SIV (structured investment vehicle), 32, 178–179
skin in the game, 411
Small Business Administration, 32
SNB *see* Swiss National Bank
SNCI (Société National de Crédit à l'Industrie), 200
SNS Reaal Bank, 102, 111, 206–208
and Dutch government, 206–208
Société Générale, 11, 31, 81–83, 108, 126–127, 375–376
SoFFin, 12, 25–27, 32–35, 40, 48, 116, 178–179, 181–182, 185–186, 189, 244
sovereign bond holdings, 81–83
sovereign crisis phase, 1–2
sovereign debt crisis, xxviii
timeline, 442
Sovereign Wealth Fund, 9
Spain, 270–277
bad loans, 274
bank borrowing guarantee, 25–27
bank consolidation data, 276–277
bank equity sales, 63
bank nationalization, 88, 273–274, 276
bank recapitalization, 95, 98–99
bank rescue fund, 43
banking crisis, xxviii
banking sector, 271–275
bond yields, 270
central bank, 40
crisis handling grades, 275–276
current account deficit, 270–271
DTA (deferred tax assets) reclassification, 120, 275
EU bank aid conditions, 275
financial/banking background, 270–271
FROB *see* FROB
government debt/GDP ratio, 270–271
internal devaluation, 270–271
property construction boom, 271
ratings, 76, 85, 95, 270–274
savings bank sector plans, 74, 273
savings to commercial bank conversions, 273

sovereign bonds, 270
sovereign debt crisis, xxviii
timeline, 442
support program exit, 126
ULC (unit labor costs), 270–271
Sparebank 1 group, 24, 232–233
Special Liquidity Scheme, 13
Special Resolution Unit, 461
Spector, Warren, 4
speed of intervention, 145–146, 390
SPV (special purpose vehicle), 61
SRB (Single Resolution Board), xvii, 128, 132–133, 458–461, 474–475
SRF (Single Resolution Fund), 127, 133, 457, 474–475
SRM (Single Resolution Mechanism), xvi, xxxiv–xxxv, 115, 128, 132–134, 451–453, 459–461, 474–477
SSFI (systemically significant failing financial institutions) program, xxix, 292, 382–383
see also G-SSFI
SSM (Single Supervisory Mechanism), xvii, 107, 120, 132–133, 455–456, 459–461, 474–477
Stabilization Fund, 41
Staley, Jes, 95
Standard Chartered, 112–113, 375
Standard & Poor's rating agency, 3–4, 6–7, 10–11, 14, 19, 23–24, 28, 41–42, 59, 66–67, 78, 81–83, 98–99, 102–104, 106, 129–130, 136, 139–140, 228–229, 258, 260–262, 270, 339–340, 343–344, 364, 441, 490
State Street Bank, 25–27, 43, 359–360
Steel, Robert K., 324–325, 332–333, 354
Stevens, Philip, 400–401
Stiglitz, Joseph, 373
stigmatization, 149–151, 392
Straumur-Burdaras, 39
stress testing, 48, 66, 76–78, 81–82, 85, 92, 123, 131–135, 140–142, 262–264, 379, 435, 439
Stumpf, John, 54, 94, 113
subordinated debt, xvi–xvii, 475
subprime crisis phase, 1–2

subprime mortgages, 343
Sullivan, Martin J., 11–12, 366
Summers, Larry, 381
Sun Trust, 28–29, 93
Sundal, 230–231
super fund consortium, 7
supervision, in banking union, xvii
Supreme Court of New York
   State, 118
Suskind, Ron, 381
Swedbank, 219–221
Sweden
   bank capital requirements, 135
   bank guarantees, 27, 81
   bank recapitalization, 36
   capital ratios, 88–89
   Deposit Insurance Fund, 484–485
   EU Government bonds, 77
   mortgages, 59
   resolution fund, 472
   SIFI rules, 122
   stabilization fund, 474
   state bank ownership, 112, 121
Swedish central bank, 20, 24–25
Swiss National Bank, 9, 18–22, 24–25,
   27, 43, 59, 113, 124–125
Switzerland
   countercyclical capital buffers, 104
   executive pay limits, 105
Sydbank, 122
Sydney Appeals Court, 135
Syron, Richard F., 16
systemic crises, 146, 391
systemic crisis phase, 1–2
Systemic Risk Board, xxxv, 52
systemic risk exception,
   355–357, 416

TAF (Term Auction Facility),
   9, 31, 54–55
TAGP (Transaction Account Guarantee
   Program), 27, 376
TALF (Term Asset-Backed Securities
   Loan Facility), 32, 46, 54–55
TARP (Troubled Assets Relief
   Program), xxix, 19–23, 25–37,
   40–47, 49–50, 52–54, 56, 64, 66,
   70, 74, 81, 94, 97, 99, 112, 127,
   237–238, 292–293, 303, 305,
   318–319, 321, 327, 341–342,

   369, 373–375, 378–380, 382–385,
   412, 418, 439
SIGTARP, 292, 351–352
TARP/CPP capital received/implicit
   subsidy, 384–385, 435
Tarullo, Daniel, 304–305, 362
taxpayer-funded bail-outs, xxv–xxxii,
   xxix–xxx
taxpayers' money refunds, 146, 393
Taylor, Bean & Whittaker, 81
TBTF (too-big-to-fail) institutions, xv,
   xxv, xxvii, xxxv, 18, 66, 76–77,
   86–88, 94, 98, 120–121, 126, 334,
   358–363, 374–375, 399–400,
   403, 405–407, 413, 421–422,
   426–432, 434, 454–456, 479–480
TBTF (G-SIFI), 428, 487–488
TCE (Tangible Common Equity), 84
TCE (True Core Equity), 47, 69, 72,
   79, 85, 114
Temasek Holdings, 9, 316
Thain, John, 14, 25–27, 35–36,
   316–317, 325, 331, 378–379
Thomas, Pierre-Henri, 196
Thompson, Kennedy, 14–16, 354
Thompson Reuters, 89
thrifts, 65, 295
TLAC (total loss absorbing capacity),
   141, 487–488
TLGP (Temporary Liquidity Guarantee
   Program), 27, 31, 321, 376, 416,
   435, 438
Tobin tax *see* FTT
Todd, Christopher, 313
Together loans, 155
top tax rate, Great Britain, 52–53
Tourre, Fabrice, 57–58, 63, 79, 117
toxic assets, xxxiv, 5, 11, 32, 34–35,
   40, 47–48, 50–51, 53, 56–57, 131,
   146, 157, 173–174, 182–183,
   187, 325–326, 376, 380,
   383–385, 387, 389, 391
toxic derivative products, 411
toxic securities, 12–13, 51–52
TPG Capital, 13, 344
trade repositories, 131
trading assets weighting, 410
Trading with the Enemy Act, 99
trading-book assets, 76
Tremonti bonds, 214

Trichet, Jean-Claude, 86
TSB (Trustee Savings Bank), 119, 137, 169, 173
TSLF (Term Securities Lending Facility), 12, 54–55, 321
Tucker, Paul, 124
Turner review, 44, 149–151

UBS, 3, 6–7, 9, 11, 13, 27, 32, 39, 43, 46, 69, 83–84, 116, 125–127, 304–306, 358–359, 375
UCBH Holdings Inc, 28–29
UK Treasury bills, 13
UKAR (UK Asset Resolution), 11, 117, 157–159
UKFI (UK Financial Investments), 11, 29, 88, 120–121, 133, 156–157, 166
Ukraine, IMF loan, 28
Ulster Bank, 240–241
Umpqua Holdings Corp, 28–29
Unicaja, 274
UniCredit, 81–82, 131–132, 375
uninterrupted service, 145–146, 149, 390
United Commercial Bank, 117, 353
United Kingdom
   bank BIS ratios, 150
   bank guarantee program, 33
   bank levy, 61–62, 70
   bank liabilities charges, 75
   bank nationalization, 156
   bank ring-fencing, 100–102
   bank share prices (2008), 163
   banks leverage, 150–151
   co-insurance, 153–154
   deposit insurance, 153–154
   financial crisis causes, 149–151
   household savings/income ratio, 151
   Iceland deposits, 231
   property prices, 149
   ratings, 42–43, 104
   see also Lloyds Banking Group; Northern Rock; RBS (Royal Bank of Scotland); UK
United States
   asset purchases, 289
   bank capital requirements, 304–305
   bank equity issues, 440
   bank failures, 287–288, 353, 434
   bank leverage ratios, 304
   bank profitability, 436, 440
   bank risk degrees, 303–304
   banking regulatory authorities, 294–298
   banks by assets, 383
   capital injections, 289
   capital requirements, 304–305, 482–484
   compared to European banking, 437–441
   deposits/GDP ratio, 287
   FDIC role in crisis, 293–302
   Federal Reserve role in crisis, 293–302
   financial regulation overhaul, 60
   financial support programs, 289–291
   financial/banking background, 287–293
   homeowners' negative equity, 78
   leverage ratios, 482–484
   output loss, 289
   ratings, 43, 71, 83
   regulatory authorities bureaucratic infighting, 300–301
   regulatory authorities summary, 296–298
   share prices, 288
   state Departments of Financial Institutions, 296–298
   state Insurance Departments, 296–298
   stimulus programs, 292
   Treasury role in crisis, 293–302
   types of banking institutions, 294
   unemployment, 288–289
   see also CPP; Dodd–Frank Act; FDIC; Federal Reserve; *individual banks/financial institutions*; TARP
Unnim, 85, 273–274
US Bancorp, 43, 93
USB, 100–101

Valley National Bancorp, 28–29
Van Dellen, Scott, 99
VaR model, 97
Verwilst, Herman, 202
viability, 146, 149, 391

Vickers Commission, 78, 84–85,
    102, 168
Victoria Mortgage Funding, 6
Vigni, Antonio, 141
Viniar, David, 31
Virgin Money, 11, 88, 94, 156–158
Vitter, David, 109
VIX volatility index, 28, 329–330
Volcker, Paul, 49, 312, 400
Volcker rule, 49, 54, 56, 64, 127,
    130–131, 404, 413
Votron, Jean-Paul, 202

Wachovia Bank, 2, 8, 14–16, 20–23,
    237–238, 288, 344, 348, 350,
    352–357, 416
Walker, George H. IV, 324–325
Wall Street Reform and
    Consumer Protection Act *see*
    Dodd–Frank Act
Wallison, Peter, 407
Walsh, Michael, 251–252
WaMu (Washington Mutual), 3–4, 9,
    13, 16–20, 33, 37, 77, 89–91, 119,
    122–124, 288, 301–302, 327,
    329, 334, 342–352, 354–355,
    414, 424
  crisis handling grades, 348–352

Warner, Mark, 114
Warren, Elizabeth, 115, 363,
    382–383
Washington Federal, 28–29
Weill, Sandi, 96
Welding, Lárus, 101, 135–136, 235
Wells Fargo, 2, 14, 20–23, 25–27, 42,
    47–48, 53–54, 92, 94, 105–106,
    113–116, 118, 121–122, 129,
    287, 293, 300–301, 304, 356,
    359–361, 379, 384–385, 416, 434
Wessel, David, 307
WestLB (Westdeutsche Landesbank),
    xxix, 50–51, 57, 75, 95,
    188–190
Westpac, 173
White, Mary Jo, 117
Williams & Glyn, 121, 166
Williams, Jerry, 95
Willumstad, Robert, 370
Winston-Salem, N. C., 409
Wuffli, Peter, 3
Wym, Oliver, 245–246

Zapatero, José Luis Rodriguez,
    25–27, 271
Zions Bancorp, 28–29, 133, 434
Zurich Insurance, 274

2455022